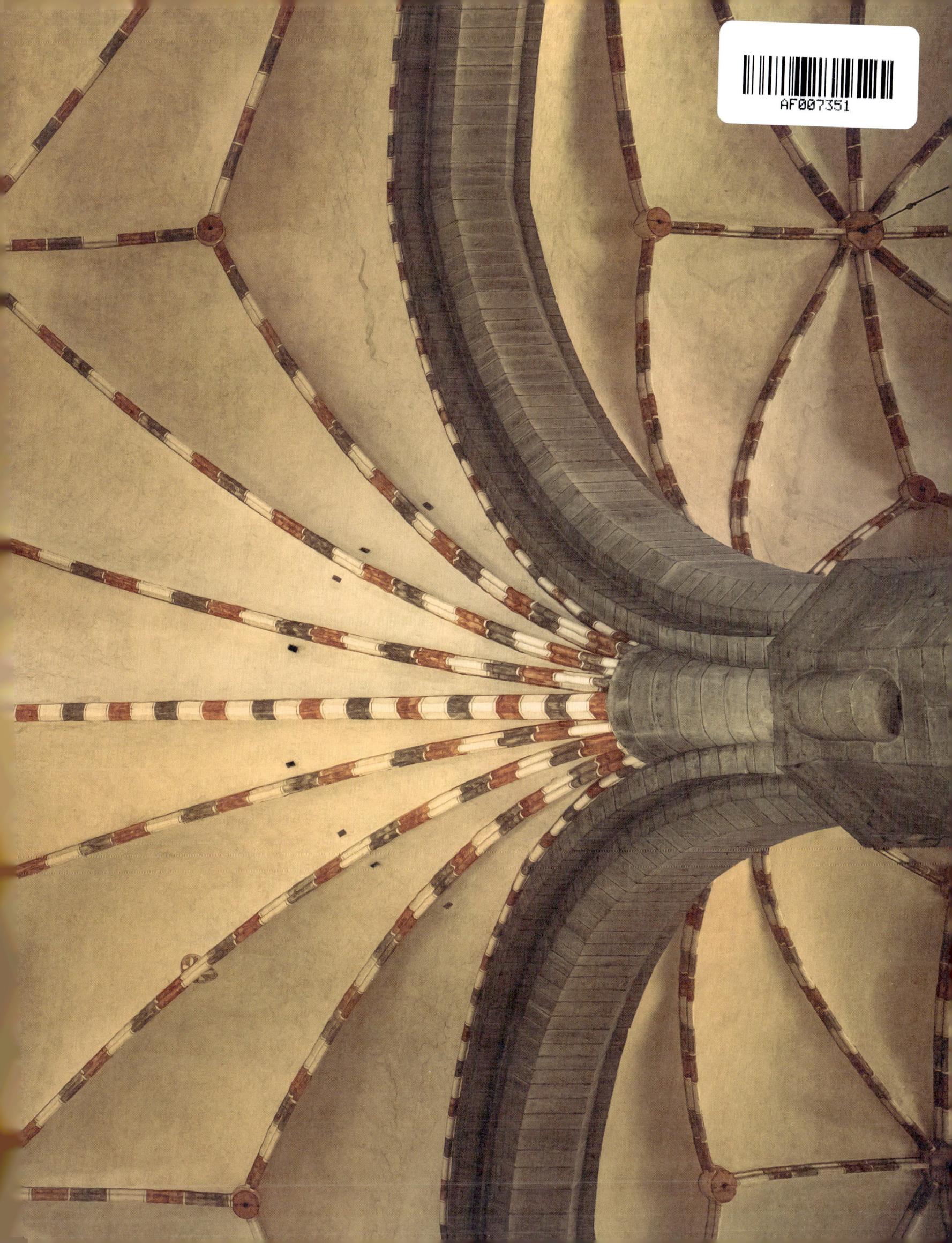

DERRY BRABBS

GREAT PILGRIMAGE SITES OF EUROPE

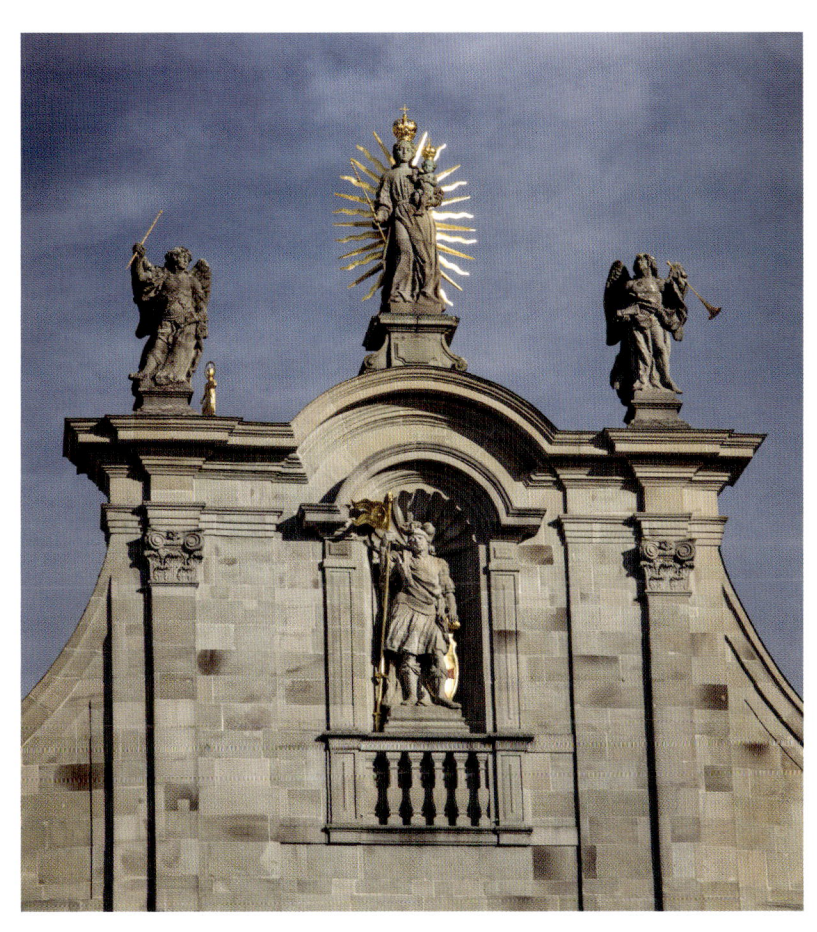

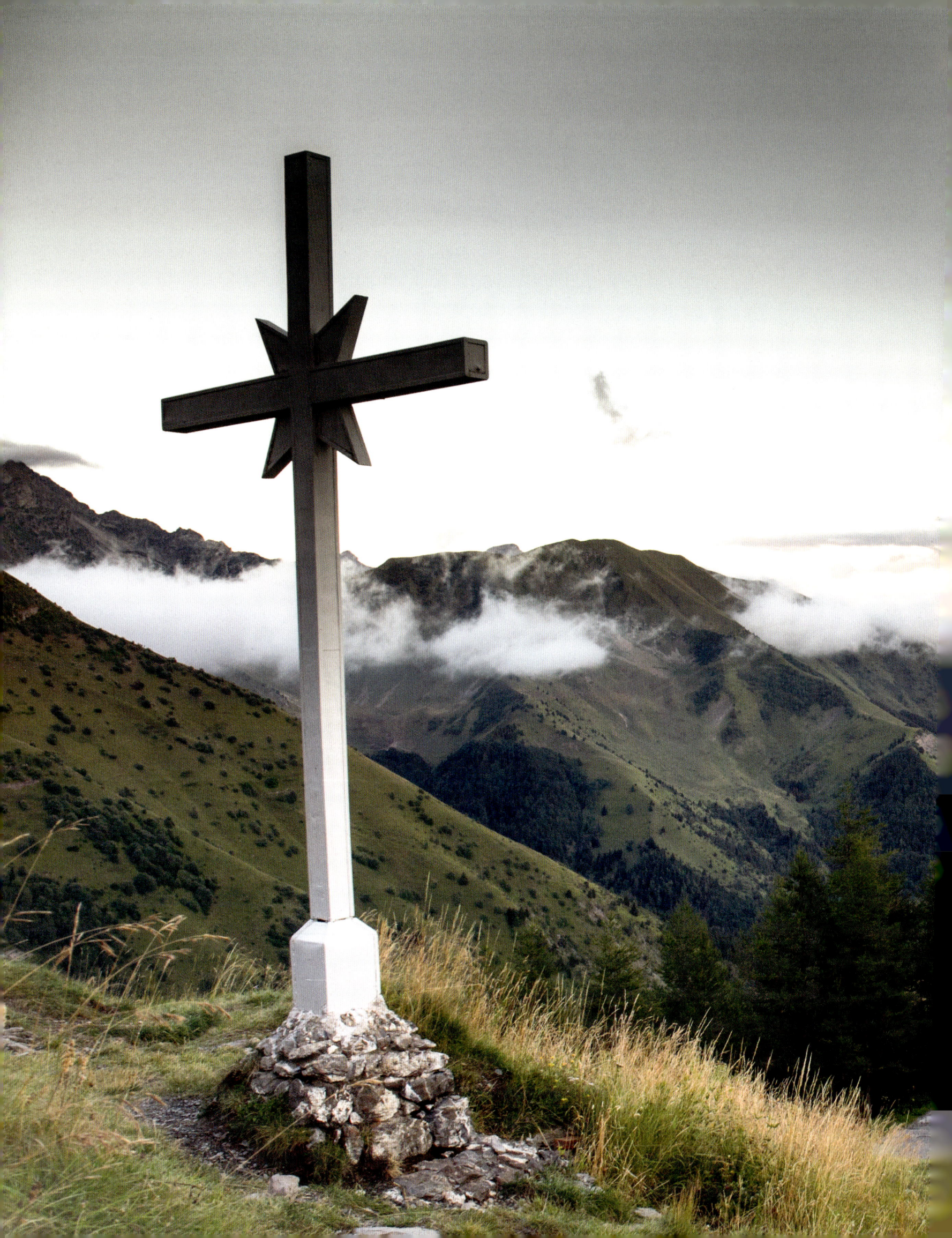

DERRY BRABBS

GREAT PILGRIMAGE SITES OF EUROPE

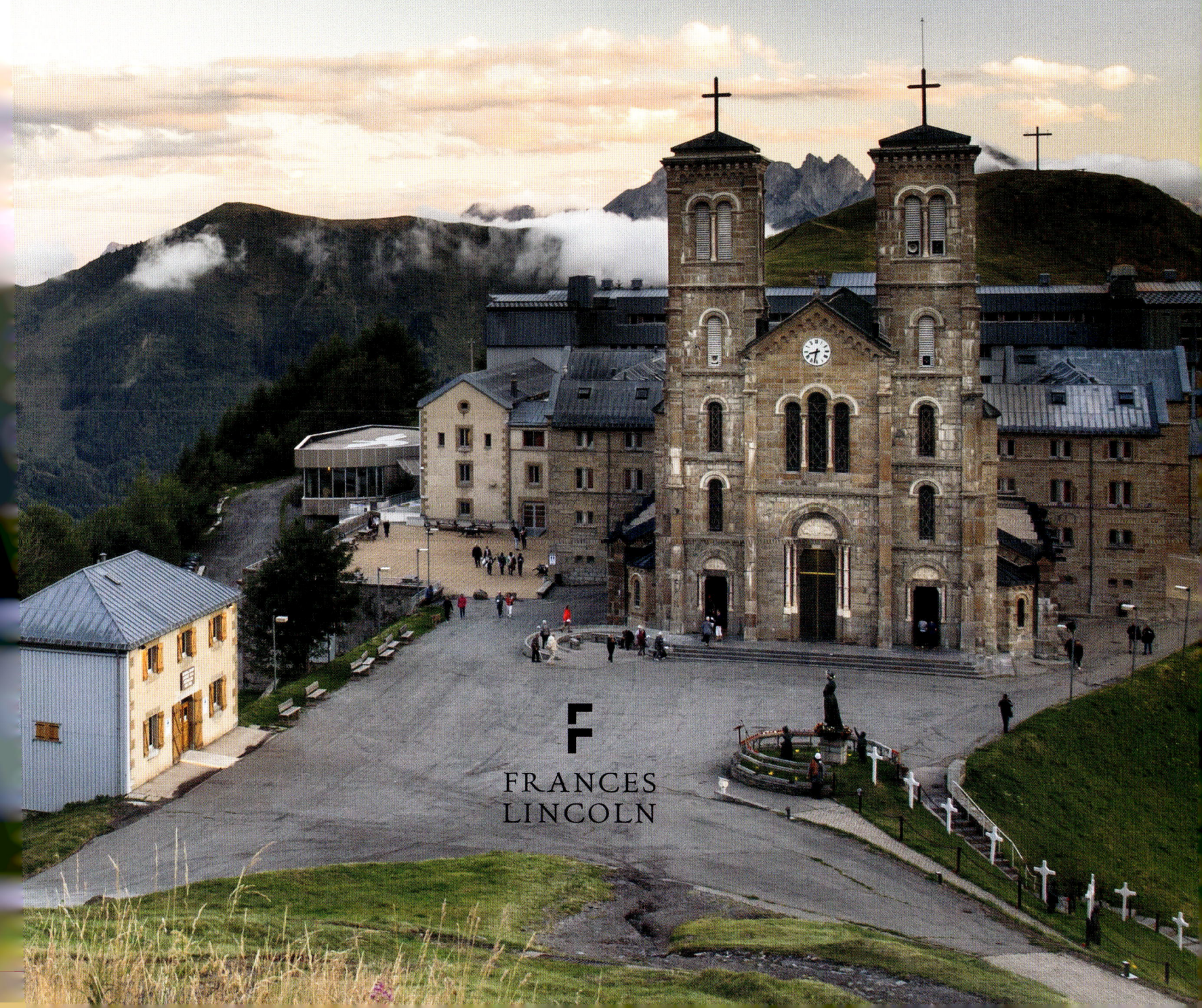

FRANCES LINCOLN

CONTENTS

INTRODUCTION   6
ENGLAND   12
   HOLY ISLAND   14
   ELY   20
   WALSINGHAM   26
   CANTERBURY   32
FRANCE   38
   LISIEUX   40
   CHARTRES   44
   LE PUY-EN-VELAY   52
   LA SALETTE   58
   LOURDES   68

DENMARK, NORWAY AND SWEDEN   76
   RIBE   78
   ODENSE   84
   FANEFJORD & ELMELUNDE   90
   TRONDHEIM   96
   RINGEBU   102
   VADSTENA   108
POLAND AND SLOVAKIA   114
   CZĘSTOCHOWA   116
   LICHEŃ STARY   124
   ŠAŠTÍN-STRÁŽE   130

(*half title*) Einsiedeln Abbey Church, Switzerland.
(*title page*) The Sanctuary of Our Lady of La Salette, France.
(*this page*) The Basilica of St Francis of Assisi.

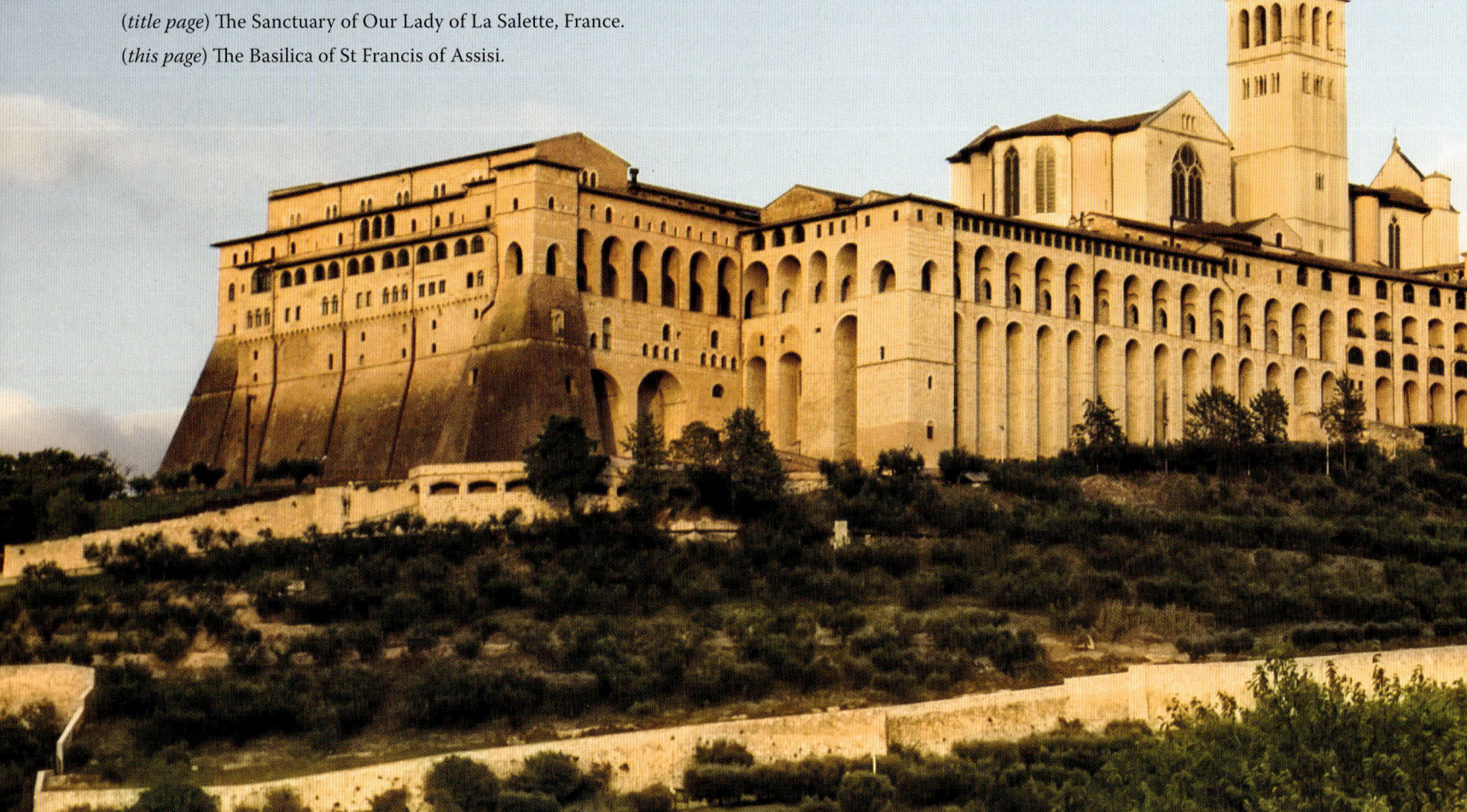

GERMANY, AUSTRIA		**SPAIN AND PORTUGAL**	**214**
AND SWITZERLAND	**136**	SANTIAGO DE COMPOSTELA	216
COLOGNE	138	COVADONGA	222
AACHEN	144	ZARAGOZA	228
ALTÖTTING	152	MONTSERRAT	236
MARIAZELL	158	EL ROCIO	242
EINSIEDELN	164	FÁTIMA	248
ITALY	**170**		
PADUA	172	INDEX	254
ASSISI	180	ACKNOWLEDGEMENTS	256
ROME	186		
LORETO	206		

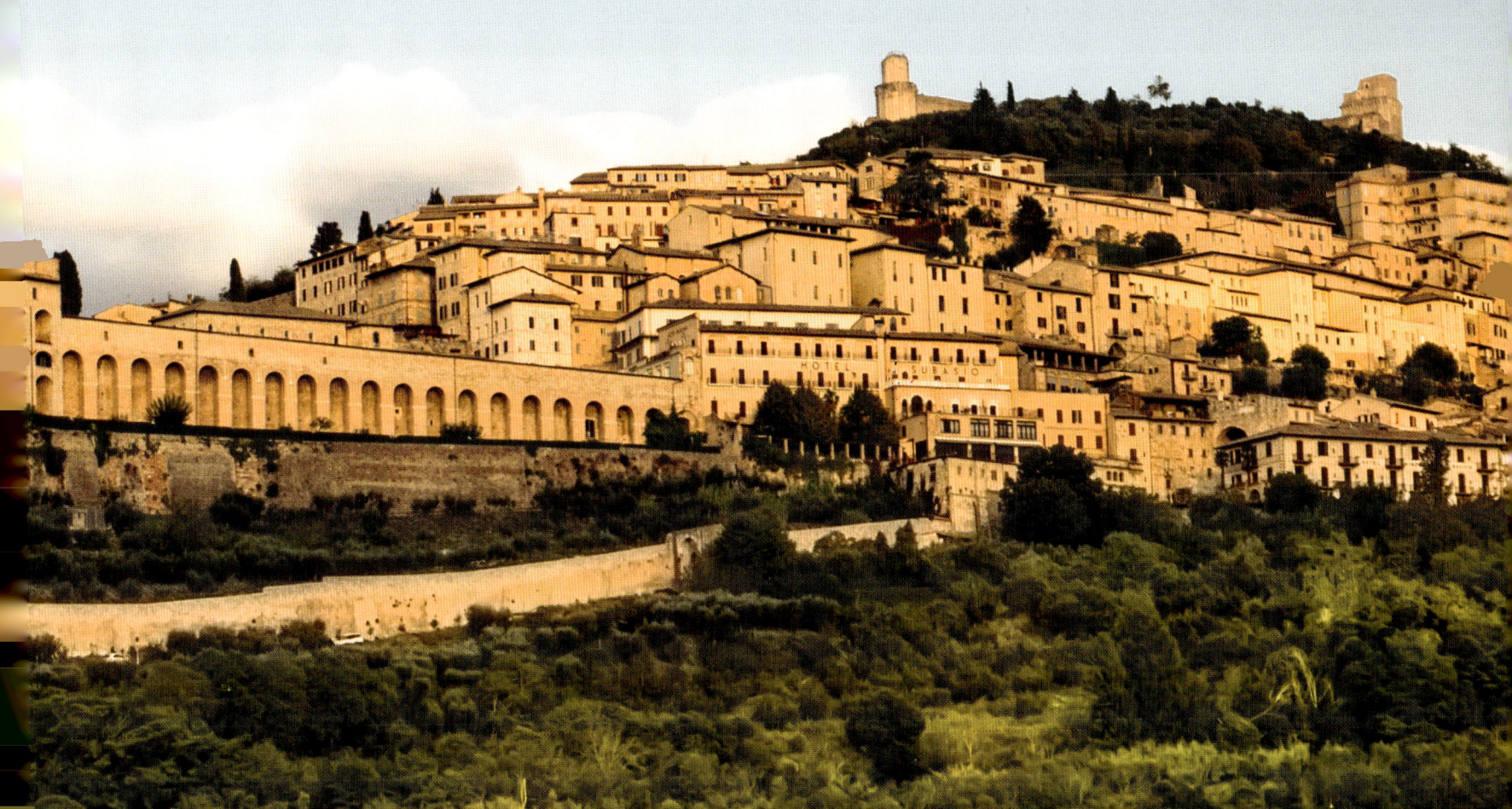

INTRODUCTION

By its very nature, a pilgrimage is a journey. And of course every journey has a destination. However, times have moved on and many of those undertaking a twenty-first-century pilgrimage will likely not be in the same mindset as their medieval counterparts. Only by standing in the nave of one of the great Romanesque or Gothic cathedrals associated with a pilgrimage to a once-venerated shrine can one appreciate the sheer power of the combination of faith, love and fear that was the basis of medieval Christianity. Such churches and cathedrals were the physical manifestation of those elements, but it was the deeper spiritual beliefs pertaining to the fate of a human soul when parted from its mortal body that created the cult of relics and the phenomenon of pilgrimage.

From the vantage point of the more rational, scientifically advanced and perhaps overtly cynical era in which we now live, it is all too easy to scorn what are frequently perceived as groundless and somewhat primitive ideologies. On the tympanum of almost every Romanesque church is a graphic portrayal of the two available options, with room for neither manoeuvre nor compromise. The human soul is depicted as being weighed by St Michael the Archangel, and those tipping the scales in the right direction are gently transported aloft in the company of angels. For those found wanting when called to account, the outcome was not a prospect to be countenanced! The populations of the Middle Ages had no choice but to believe that the most effective way of obtaining divine forgiveness and purification of the soul was by making contact with saints who could intercede on their behalf. If the saints were martyrs, so much the better, but if they were martyred apostles then better still, hence the popularity of pilgrimages to Rome and Santiago de Compostela. Paying homage at the shrines of St Peter and St Paul in Italy and of St James in Spain represented a worthwhile investment towards a comfortable eternity.

The sixteenth-century Europe-wide Reformation that fuelled the arrival of Protestantism resulted in the desecration, mutilation and obliteration of almost

The Sancta Sanctorum is set in front of the Archbasilica of St John Lateran in Rome. It hosts the Scala Sancta (Holy Stairs), the marble steps from Pilate's palace that were ascended by Jesus Christ during his Passion. This staircase is a parallel flight for public access to the chapel above.

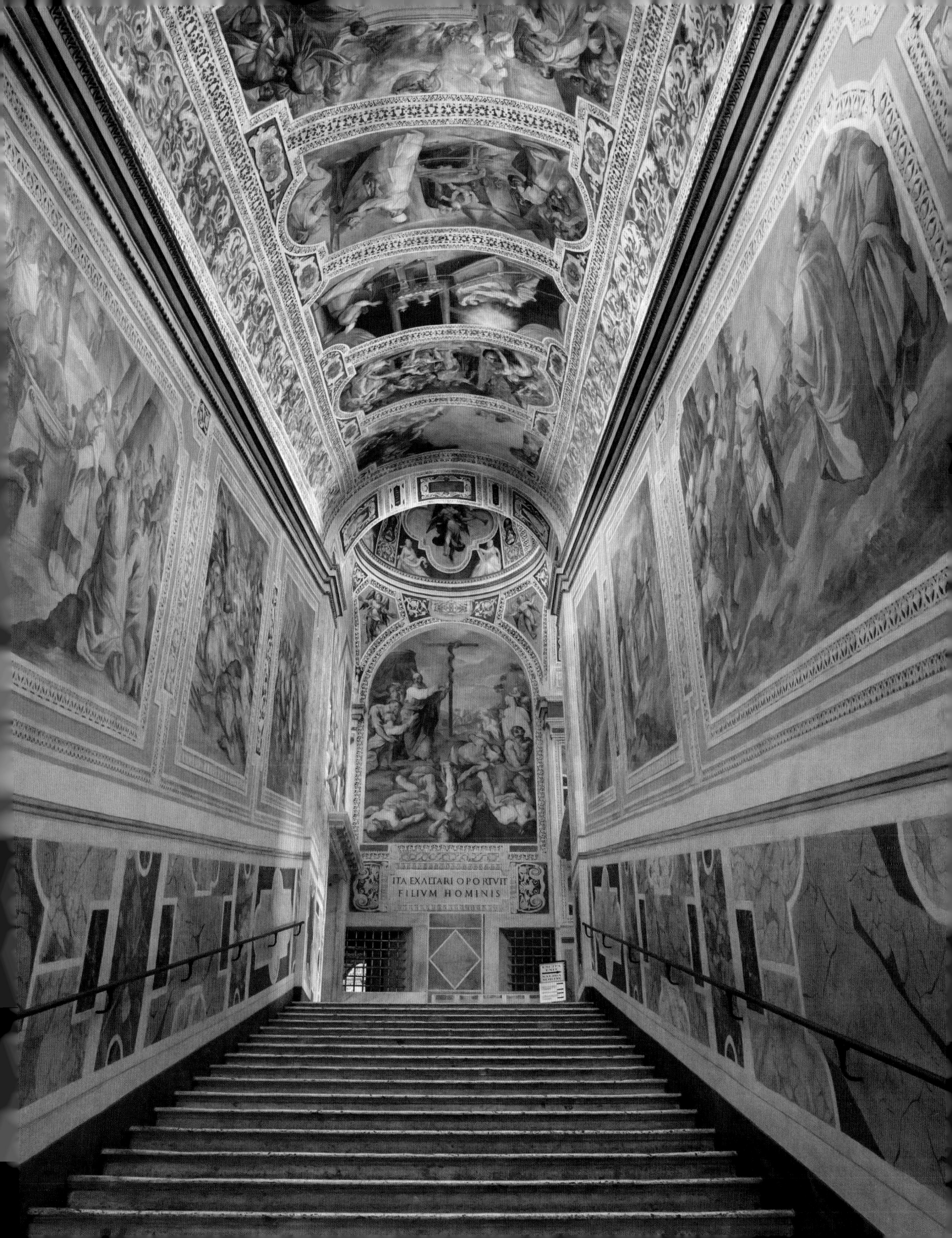

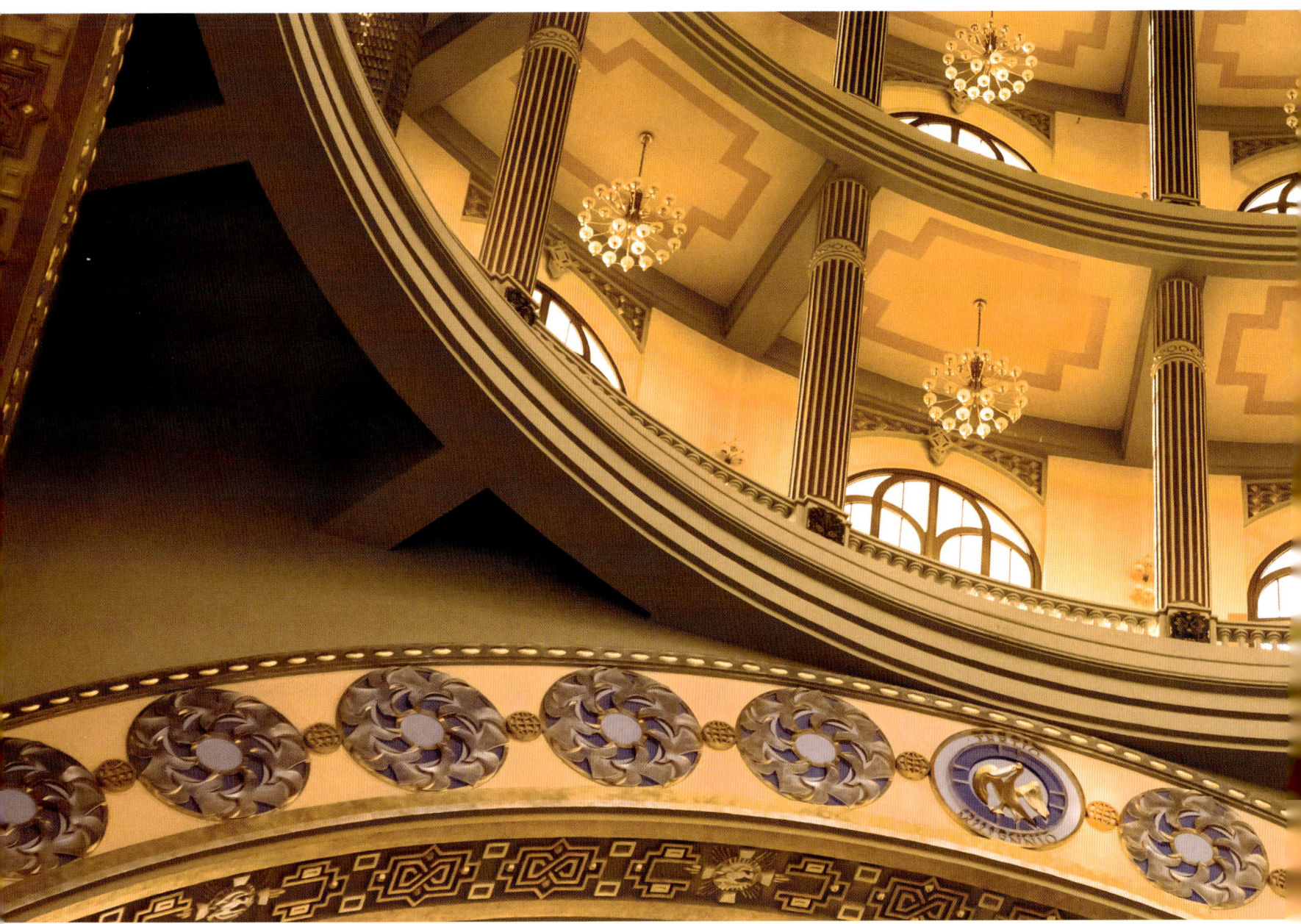

every trace of medieval iconography. The sweeping advance of that reforming movement across western Europe transformed once-colourful churches adorned with painted and sculpted artworks into bland whitewashed arenas, where the spoken word replaced the centuries-old visual narrative. The establishment of the Church of England in 1532 and the split with Rome amounted to Henry VIII's sixteenth-century version of Brexit. The ensuing Dissolution of the Monasteries in 1536 resulted in the loss of our own great medieval shrines, but in Germany there are two notable surviving examples of what stunning sights might have faced pilgrims at the culmination of their journey. Cologne Cathedral still has the elaborate Shrine of the Magi, and Aachen the stunning golden reliquary of Emperor Charlemagne (pages 143 and 151).

The rejuvenation of pilgrimage can be largely attributed to the foundation of the Council of Europe's Cultural Routes in 1987. The first project was the route to Santiago de Compostela, which reawakened people's awareness of the great journeys made centuries ago. As a result, the byways of Europe are once again

The Basilica of Our Lady of Licheń is set in the rural landscapes of Poland, and it is undoubtedly one of the great pilgrimage sites of Europe. It may have the attributes of a medieval cathedral, but work on this amazing building did not begin until 1994.

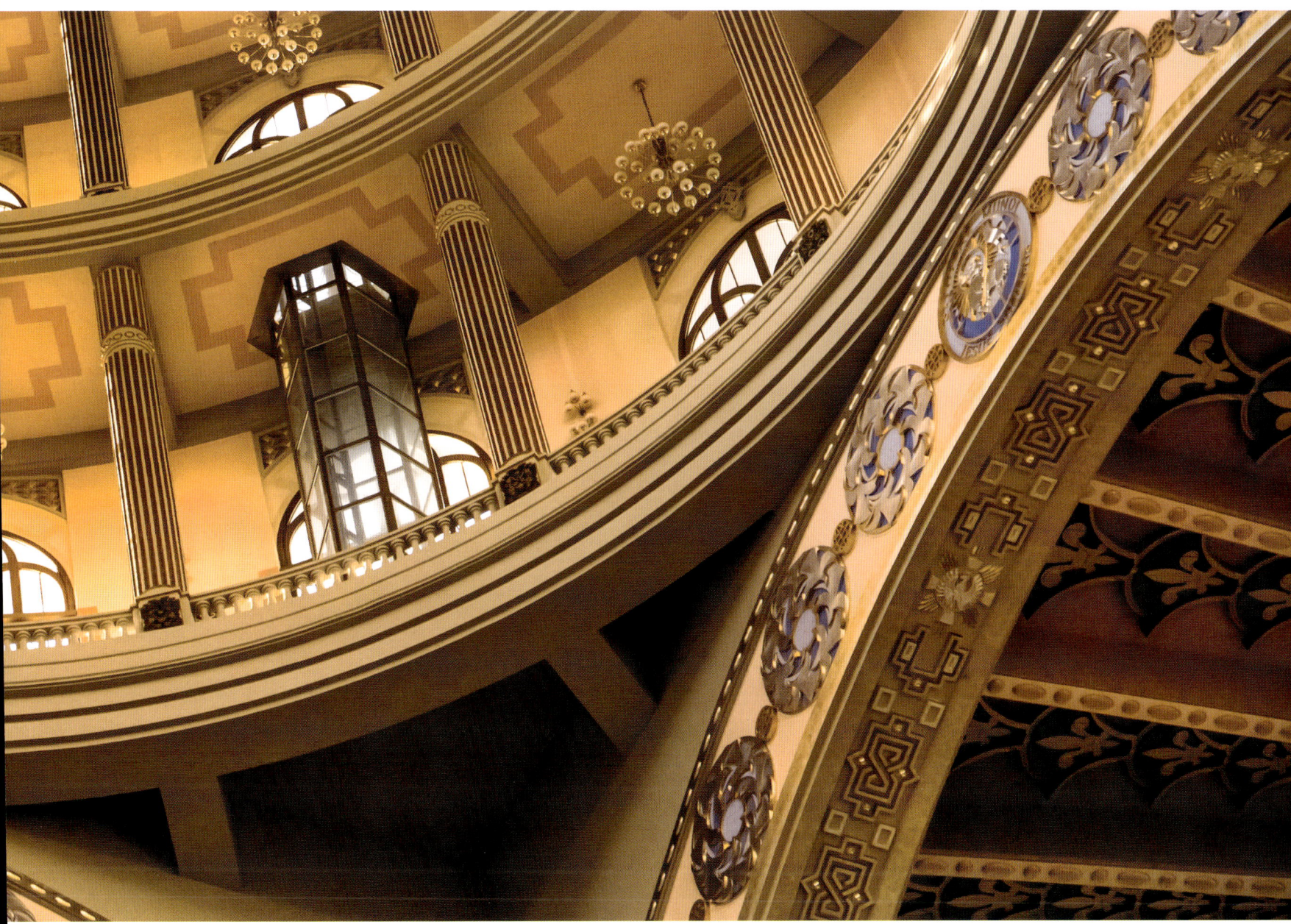

resounding to the sound of pilgrims' boots. Many of the people travelling along the pilgrim routes today seek the solitude of the open road to make the journey either as confirmation of an existing faith or as a temporary respite from an increasingly troubled world.

The most memorable event I attended was the Feast of the Assumption celebration at the shrine of Our Lady of Częstochowa in Poland (page 116), where groups of pilgrims marched joyfully through torrential rain to reach their destination. The devotion and reverence displayed at the shrine and the great outdoor mass made it a very humbling experience. Famous pilgrimage churches are also everyday places of worship, though, and I abhorred the lack of respect shown by many noisy, selfie-stick-wielding tourists towards those kneeling in prayer or sat in quiet contemplation before a shrine to the Virgin Mary. Thankfully, most cathedrals open very early in the morning and that is the best time to relish the absolute silence and timeless atmosphere of our great pilgrimage sites.

10 GREAT PILGRIMAGE SITES OF EUROPE

✝ GREAT PILGRIMAGE SITES OF EUROPE

ENGLAND
1. Holy Island
2. Ely
3. Walsingham
4. Canterbury

FRANCE
5. Lisieux
6. Chartres
7. Le Puy-en-Velay
8. La Salette
9. Lourdes

DENMARK
10. Ribe
11. Odense
12. Fanefjord & Elmelunde

NORWAY
13. Trondheim
14. Ringebu

SWEDEN
15. Vadstena

POLAND
16. Częstochowa
17. Licheń Stary

SLOVAKIA
18. Šaštín-Stráže

GERMANY
19. Cologne
20. Aachen
21. Altötting

AUSTRIA
22. Mariazell

SWITZERLAND
23. Einsiedeln

ITALY
24. Padua
25. Assisi
26. Rome
27. Loreto

SPAIN
28. Santiago de Compostela
29. Covadonga
30. Zaragoza
31. Montserrat
32. El Rocio

PORTUGAL
33. Fátima

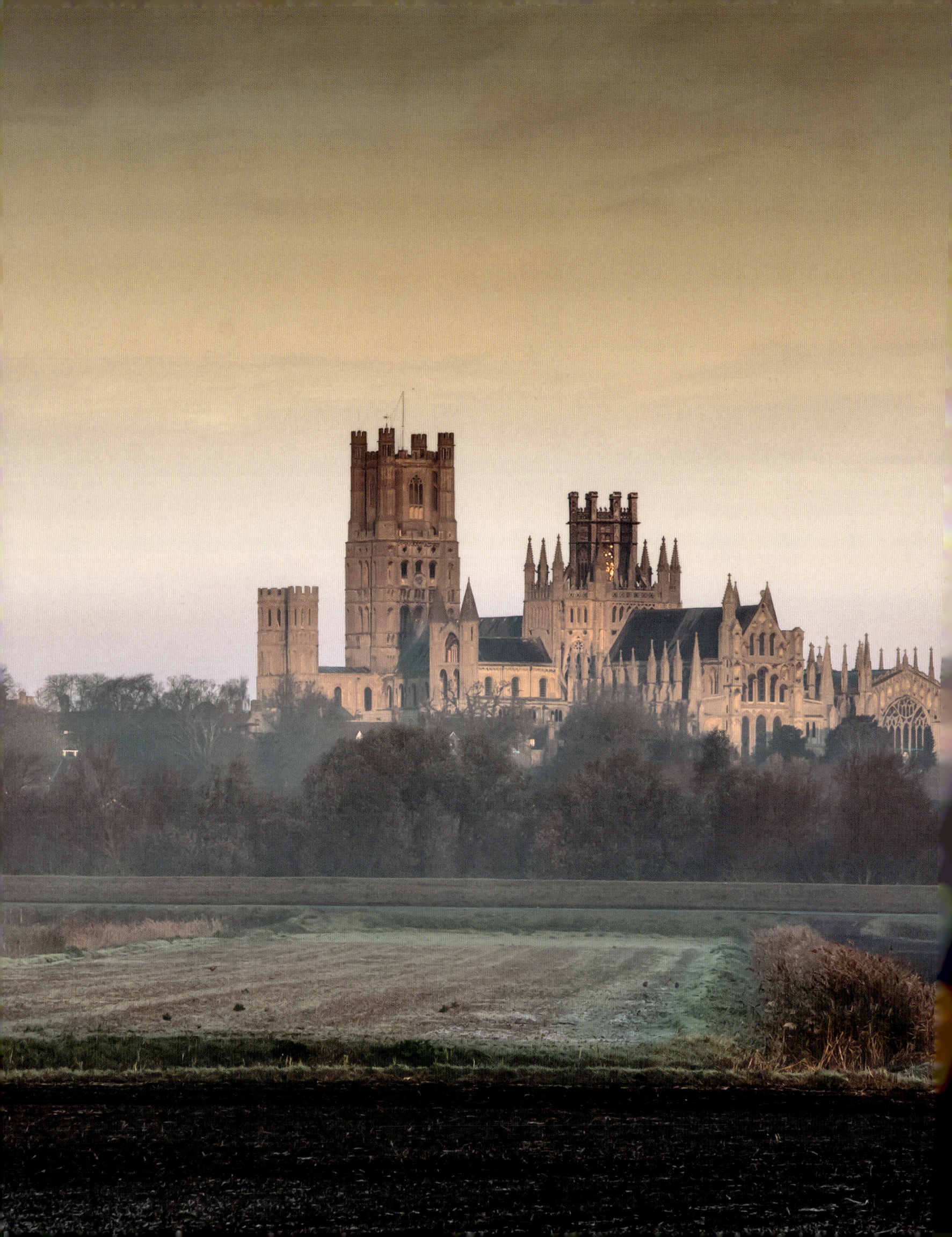

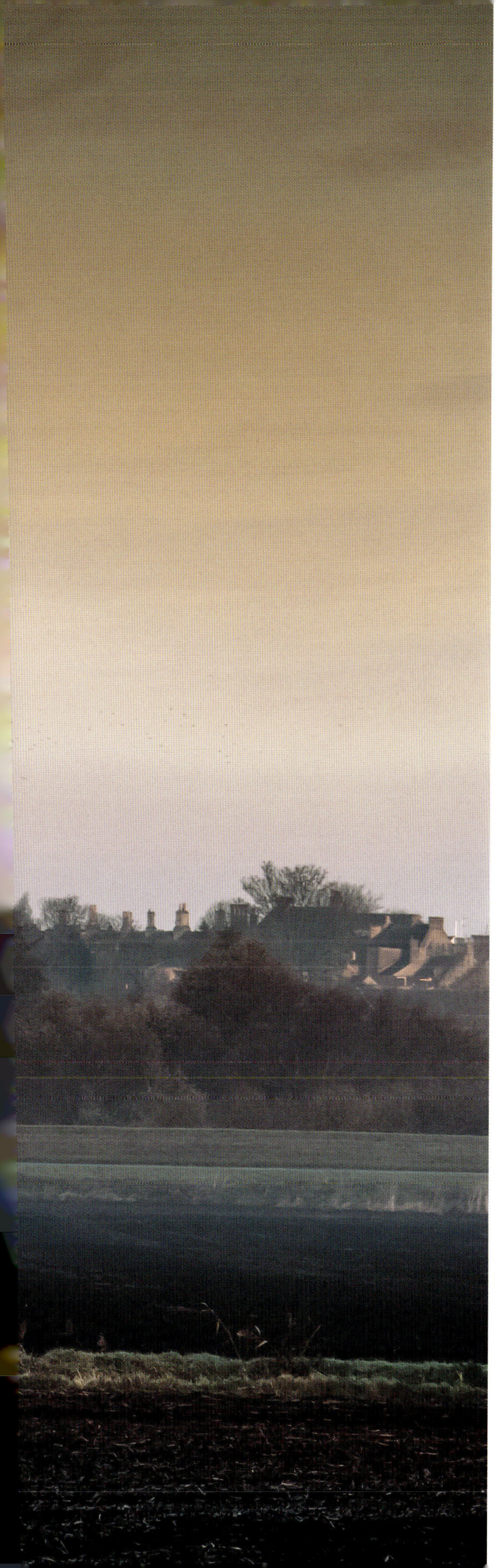

1

ENGLAND

LINDISFARNE PRIORY
Holy Island, Northumberland

Few places exhibit the spirit of early Christianity as much as Holy Island (also called Lindisfarne), and one somehow becomes immediately enveloped in the timeless atmosphere that pervades the island. The resident population is below 200 but the island annually receives more than 650,000 visitors and pilgrims. It is heartening to note that there is no new housing development and that caravanning and camping are forbidden, but there are ample bed spaces for pilgrims in local guest houses, hotels and hostels.

St Aidan was a Celtic monk from St Columba's monastery on the Scottish island of Iona and he was drawn to the peace and isolation of Lindisfarne when asked by King Oswald of Northumbria to bring Christianity to his kingdom. The first monastery was founded there in 635 and it would probably have followed the Irish tradition of a group of huts set around a simple timber church. However, although Aidan was responsible for the initial foundation of a religious community on the island, it was the legends and history surrounding the life and death of his successor, St Cuthbert, that elevated Lindisfarne to a much-revered place of pilgrimage.

Cuthbert was a significant contributor to the spread of Christianity during the seventh century, but his missionary zeal was interspersed with periods of solitude and reflection. He withdrew to a small island adjacent to Lindisfarne but actually preferred the even greater isolation of the Farne Islands farther out into the North Sea. It was there that he died in 687. Cuthbert was buried beneath the church on Lindisfarne. However, when disinterred for enshrinement more than a decade later, the monks discovered that his corpse exhibited no signs of decomposition. Cuthbert's body was reverentially installed in a new wooden coffin, which thereafter remained unburied next to the altar. News of this miracle spread to the mainland and Lindisfarne increasingly became known as Holy Island as pilgrims flocked across the causeway.

This miraculous event was probably the inspiration behind one of Celtic Christianity's greatest treasures, the Lindisfarne Gospels, a work instigated by Bishop Eadfrith around 700. Its 258 pages are beautifully inscribed and

(*previous pages*) Ely Cathedral.

(*right*) The beautiful red sandstone ruins of Lindisfarne Priory, now in the care of English Heritage, are sufficiently intact to provide an indication of the foundation's importance. Despite its isolated location, it remained a significant place of pilgrimage in honour of St Cuthbert during the medieval period.

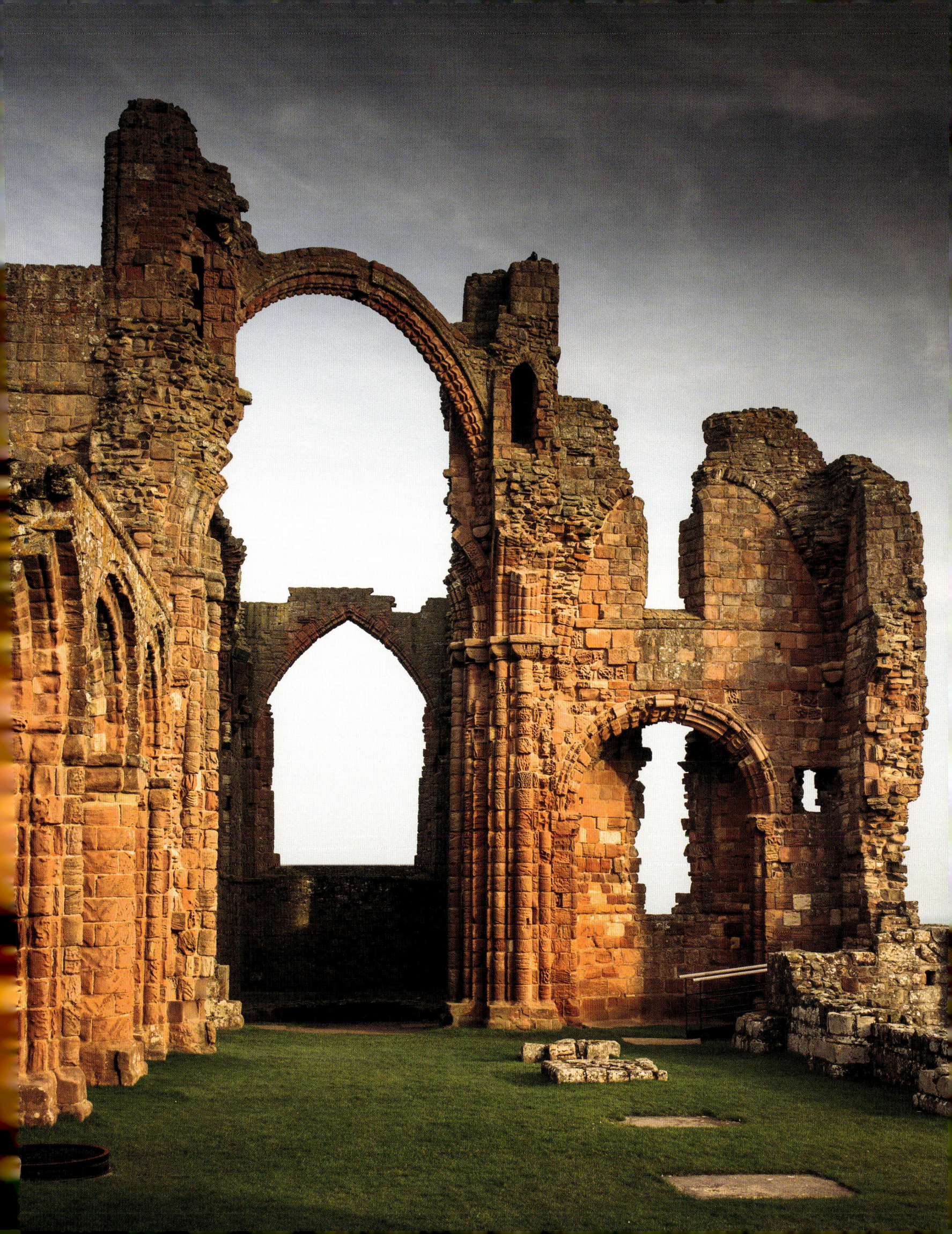

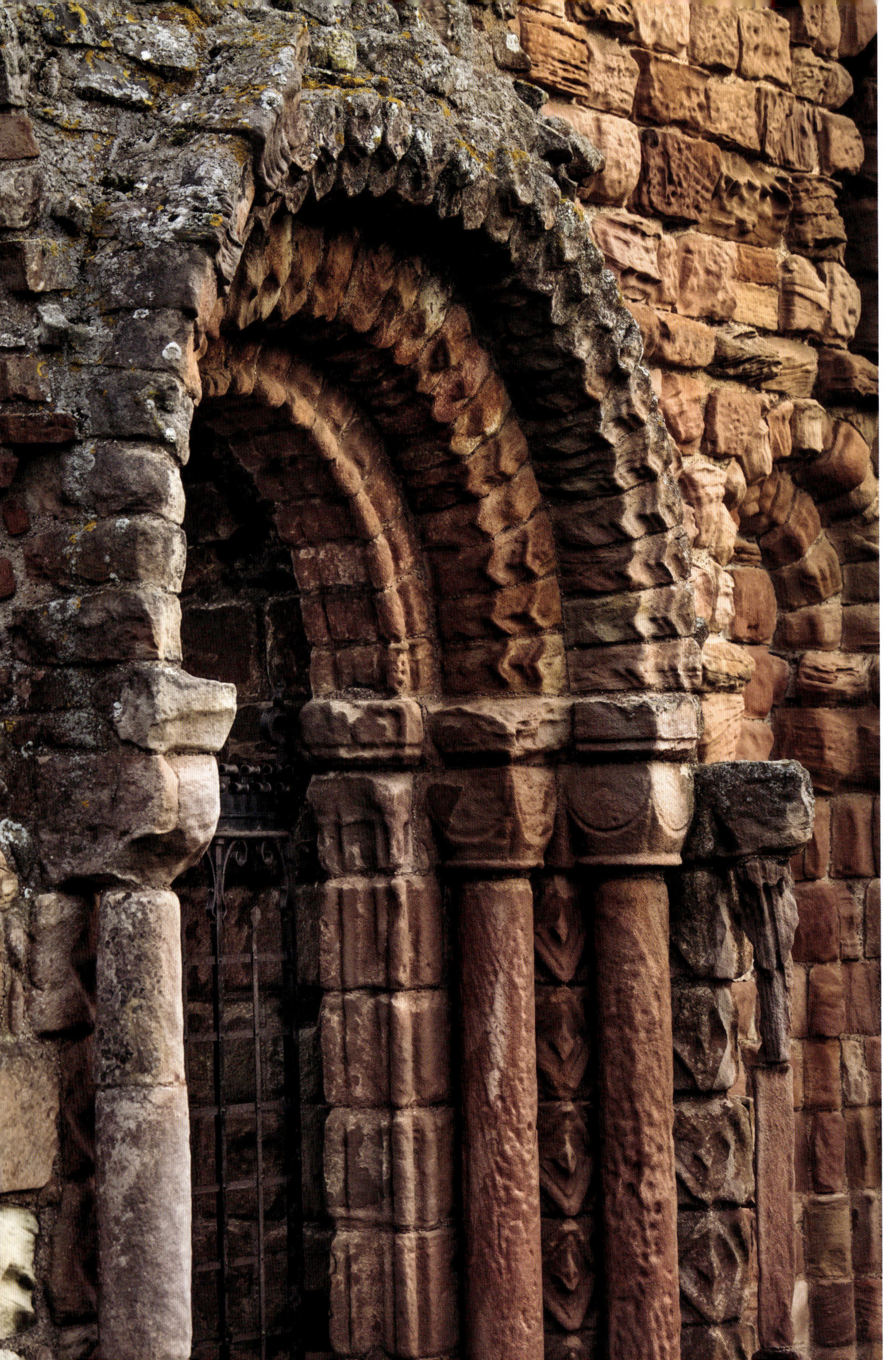

(*left*) The arch of the main portal into the priory church is decorated with the typical zigzag and dogtooth designs featured on many Romanesque churches. Unfortunately, both the capitals and supporting columns have succumbed to centuries of erosion and their intricate decoration has faded.

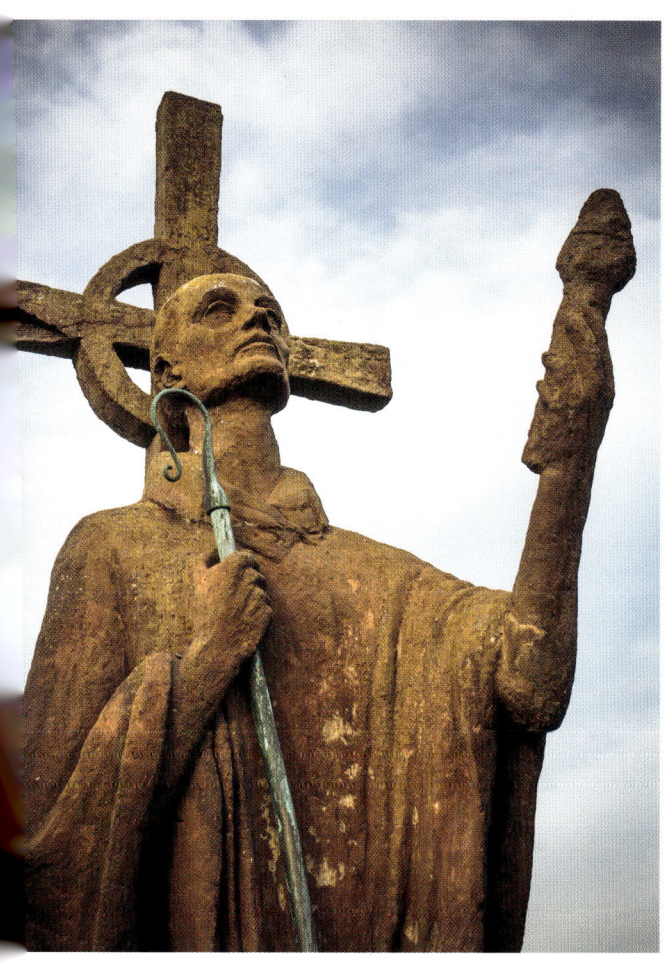

(*above*) The statue of St Aidan stands adjacent to both the priory ruins and the parish church of St Mary. His back is supported by the distinctive outline of a Celtic cross; in one hand he holds a bronze crook and the other bears a symbolic torch.

decorated, but the book's crowning glory is the introductory page to each Gospel, featuring intricate lettering and colour of indescribable intensity. This artistic masterpiece is now housed in the British Museum, London.

The legend of St Cuthbert did not actually end at the church altar, because in 793, the first of countless Viking raids on English shores took place on the island. Although the monks survived several further encounters with the Scandinavian raiders, they eventually decided that enough was enough and fled to the mainland, taking St Cuthbert's coffin and other precious relics with them. It was well in excess of a century before they settled in Durham and St Cuthbert was safely interred within a new church, one that would later be replaced in the late eleventh century by the magnificent cathedral that still hosts the saint's relics today.

The Benedictine monks of Durham were responsible for the building of the new priory on Lindisfarne, which survived until disbanded during Henry VIII's cruel Dissolution of the Monasteries (1536–41). The ruins of that solid Romanesque priory church are famous for the 'rainbow arch', the one surviving vault rib from the crossing. It is extraordinary how one fragment of stone can be so symbolic, signifying for many the enduring strength of Christianity.

There are two routes by which pilgrims and visitors can access Holy Island from the mainland, but whether making the traditional crossing over the sands or using the tarmac causeway, both can only be attempted at low tide. The pilgrim's crossing is marked by a long line of tall marker posts set into the sand. Even with a clearly identified route, it is still not recommended to attempt the crossing unless accompanied by someone with local knowledge. Regardless of whether one intends to journey to Holy Island on foot or by car, common sense and prudence are advised.

One of the great events that reflects the medieval era of pilgrimage is the Northern Cross ecumenical Easter pilgrimage to Holy Island. Groups of pilgrims start out from various northern locations to walk 110–190 kilometres/70–120 miles, and each group shares the burden of carrying a wooden cross. The participants rendezvous on the mainland shoreline and then traverse the sands together at low tide on Good Friday, to thereafter spend the weekend until Easter Sunday in prayer, contemplation and, ultimately, celebration.

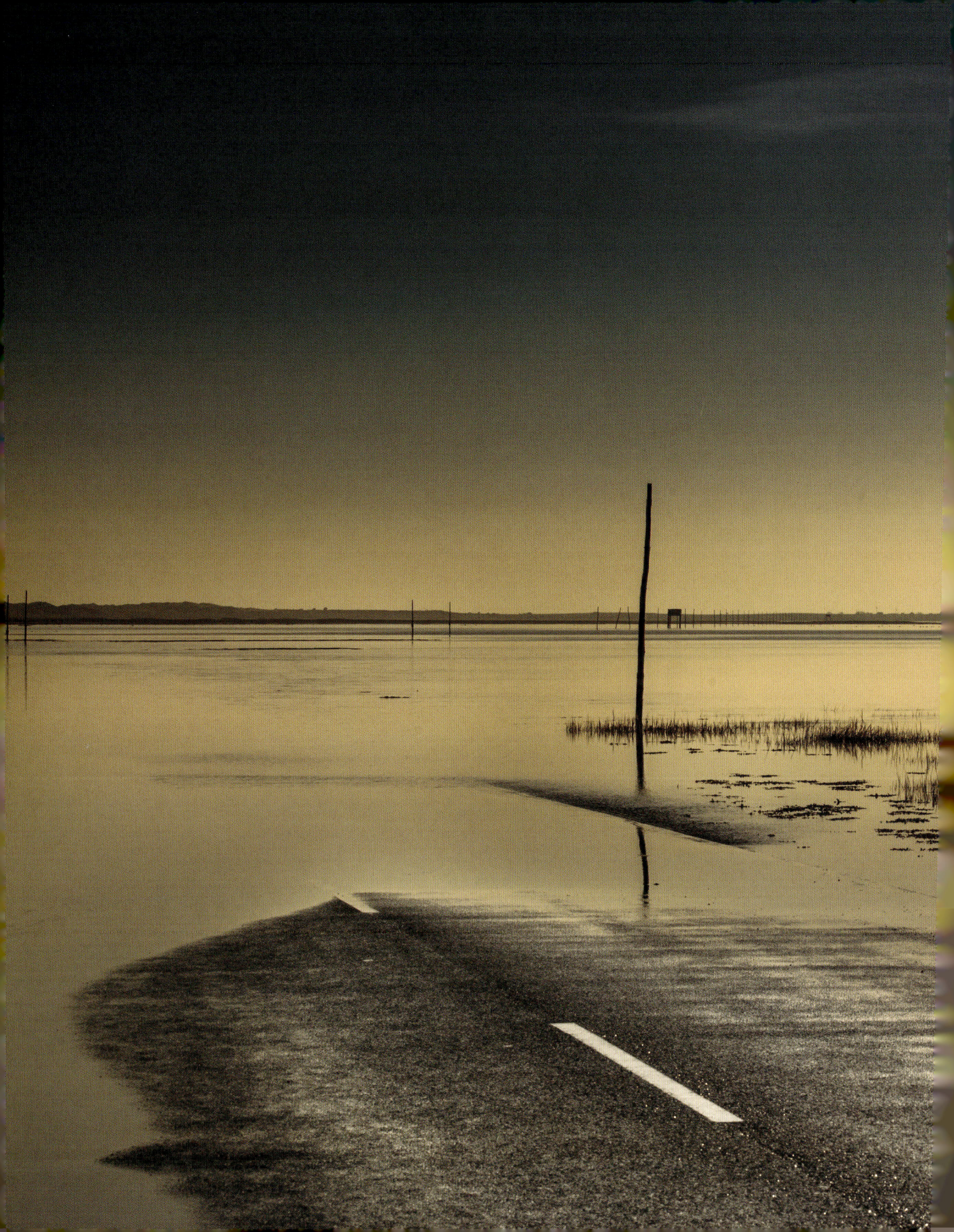

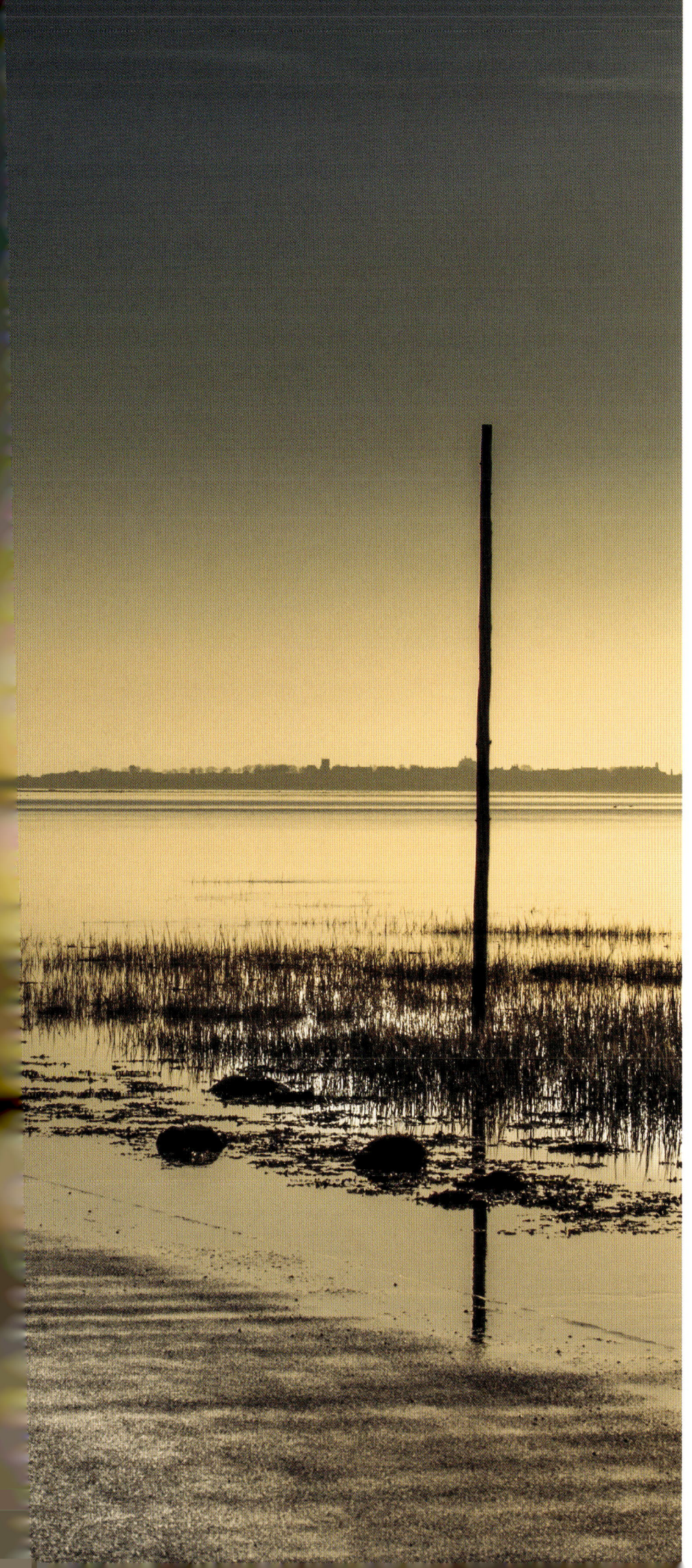

A view of the causeway leading from the Northumbrian mainland towards Holy Island at sunrise. As the tide slowly recedes to expose more and more tarmac, cars belonging to nonresident hotel and catering staff will impatiently wait until it is safe to cross the bay.

ELY CATHEDRAL
Ely, Cambridgeshire

The small town of Ely is set amid the rich agricultural expanses of the Fens, a low-lying coastal plain in eastern England, which, until drained in the seventeenth century, was alternately flooded by the sea or water from major local rivers. As might be deduced from its spelling, Ely is translated as 'isle of eels', a reference to the staple diet of the Saxons who inhabited this elevated ridge. The fact that such a mighty cathedral and monastery were built here was a remarkable achievement and lasting testimony to those who regarded such natural hazards as flooding simply as challenges to be overcome for the glory of God.

A religious house and church have existed in various guises at Ely since first founded in 673 by Etheldreda, a Saxon princess and daughter of the East Anglian king, Anna. Although the monastery flourished for more than 200 years, most of the buildings were then destroyed by Danish raiders. They were later restored and converted into a Benedictine monastery, at the behest of King Edgar of England, during the later decades of the tenth century following an inexplicable event concerning the abbey's original founder. Etheldreda died of a neck tumour, but when her remains were ceremonially exhumed and inspected some seventeen years later, both her body and the clothing in which she had been buried were totally untainted. It was also discovered that her tumour had posthumously healed itself, an extraordinary event immediately regarded as a miracle. For centuries thereafter, and until its dissolution in 1539, Ely became a sacred destination visited by huge numbers of medieval pilgrims, from monarchs right down the social scale to the humblest peasant.

After the conquest of England in 1066, William I (the Conqueror) appointed an elderly Norman abbot named Simeon to take charge of Ely and a rebuilding programme was subsequently instigated in 1080. Many magnificent elements from that original Romanesque period survive as integral parts of today's cathedral. However, the collapse of the central tower in 1322 fortuitously resulted in the creation of the octagon, one of the most astounding feats of medieval architectural design and construction.

The exterior view of Ely's octagon provides an initial indication of the structure's complexities. However, the parlous state of the cathedral's fabric remained long-hidden from view and only a protracted and expensive late-twentieth-century restoration programme saved the cathedral from terminal decline.

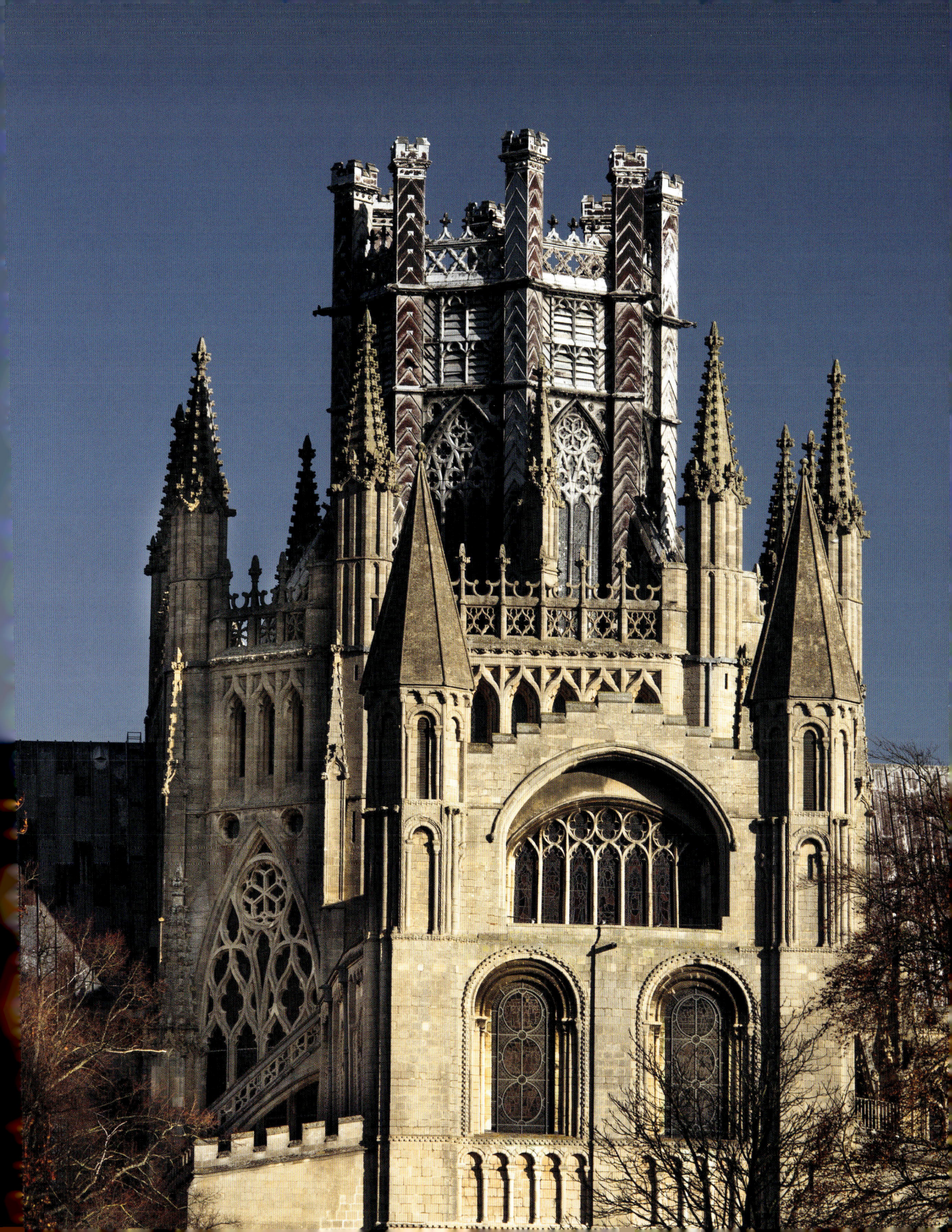

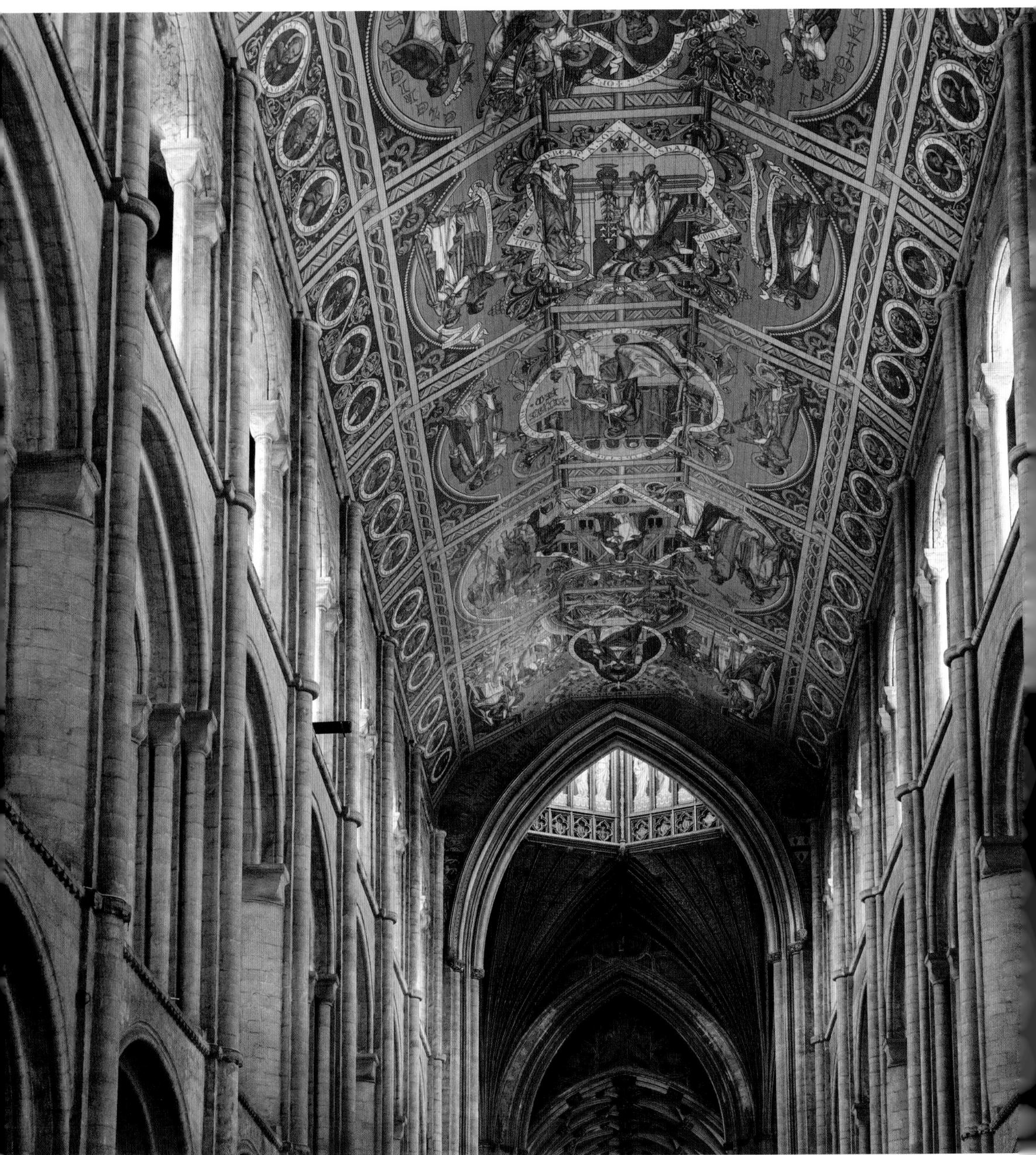

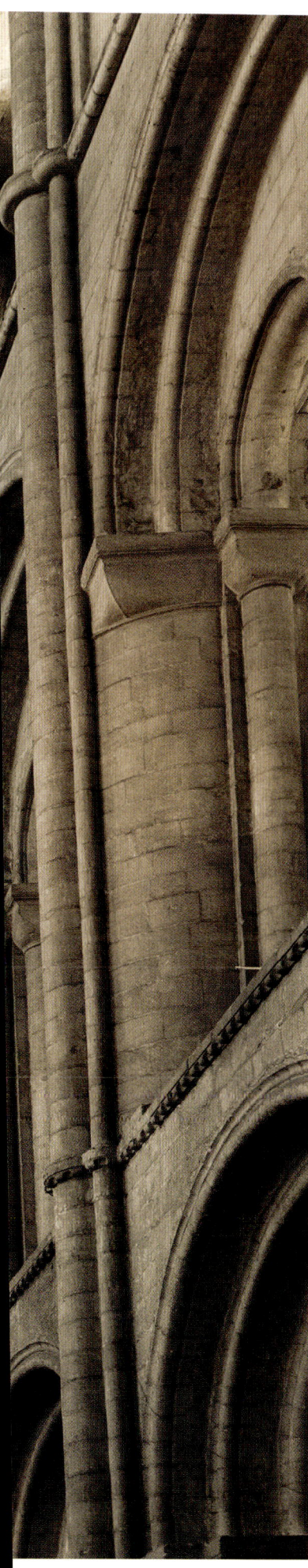

(*left*) The painted nave roof features familiar scenes from the Old Testament, but the Nativity and Christ in Glory appear as the panels progress towards the east end and high altar. Styleman Le Strange sadly died before completion and the remainder was executed by Thomas Gambier Parry.

(*overleaf*) Standing directly beneath the glazed and colourfully painted lantern of the octagon, it is impossible for any layman to fully grasp just how timber and lead weighing more than 363 tonnes/400 tons can seem so effortlessly suspended. Many twenty-first-century architects might wonder the same.

It is difficult to comprehend just how traumatic the tower's collapse would have been. But the cathedral's sacrist, Alan of Walsingham, who was in charge of all building projects during that period, somehow managed to conceive a revolutionary new feature that even today might challenge many architects. Extending up from the lower octagon, an inner lantern was created using eight long upright sections of oak (virtually the whole tree trunk), supported by a geometric network of wooden struts. The enormous weight was then transferred downwards and out towards the tower's walls and pillars.

Timber was used equally effectively in the nave roof. Although the majority of medieval cathedrals were built with stone vaulted roofs, timber was used occasionally, through necessity rather than aesthetic consideration, to prevent high-walled naves being subjected to an additional burden. Many East Anglian churches made a feature of their wooden hammerbeam roofs, but in Ely's case, it was decided to panel over the purely functional timbers during the cathedral's major nineteenth-century restoration. Obscuring the network of beams merely replaced one eyesore with another – a drab expanse of plain wood that sat uneasily between the majestic soaring piers and Romanesque arches of the twelfth-century nave. The painted decoration was conceived by a dedicated local amateur artist named Henry L'Estrange Styleman Le Strange, who first traced out the designs on huge sheets of paper before transferring their outlines on to the ceiling. It sounds simple, but imagine the complexities of fighting with swathes of heavy paper, potentially unstable scaffolding and gravity.

Etheldreda's incorrupt body had been reinterred in a Roman sarcophagus and was finally laid to rest in a magnificent shrine. It was visited by a constant flow of pilgrims, despite the fact that Ely was accessible only *via* a causeway across the Fenland landscape. As the cult of the Virgin Mary escalated, Ely created the Lady Chapel, a light and airy space adorned with delicate fan vaulting and painted statues. However, all these artistic treasures and Etheldreda's shrine were destroyed in 1541 during Henry VIII's Dissolution of the Monasteries.

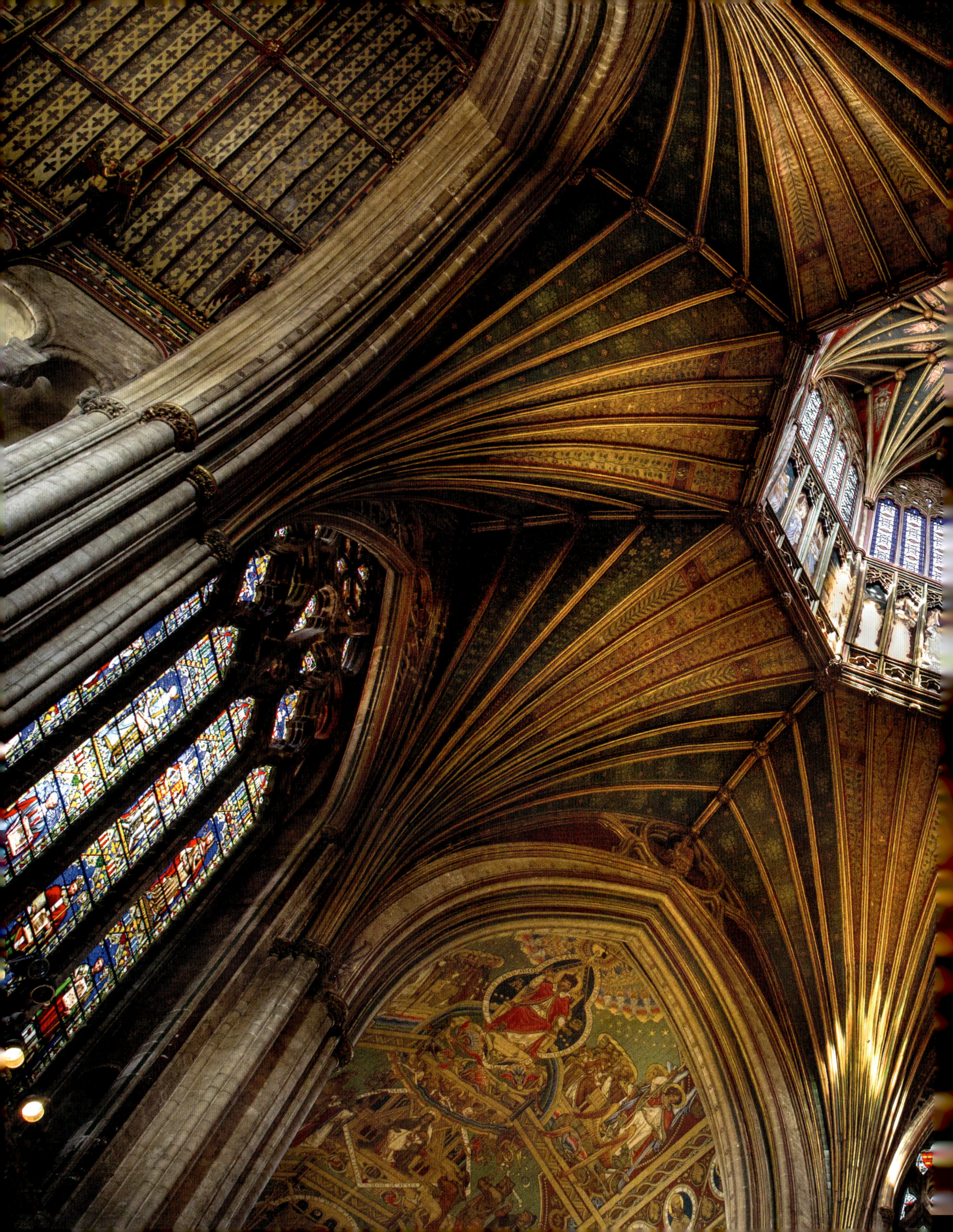

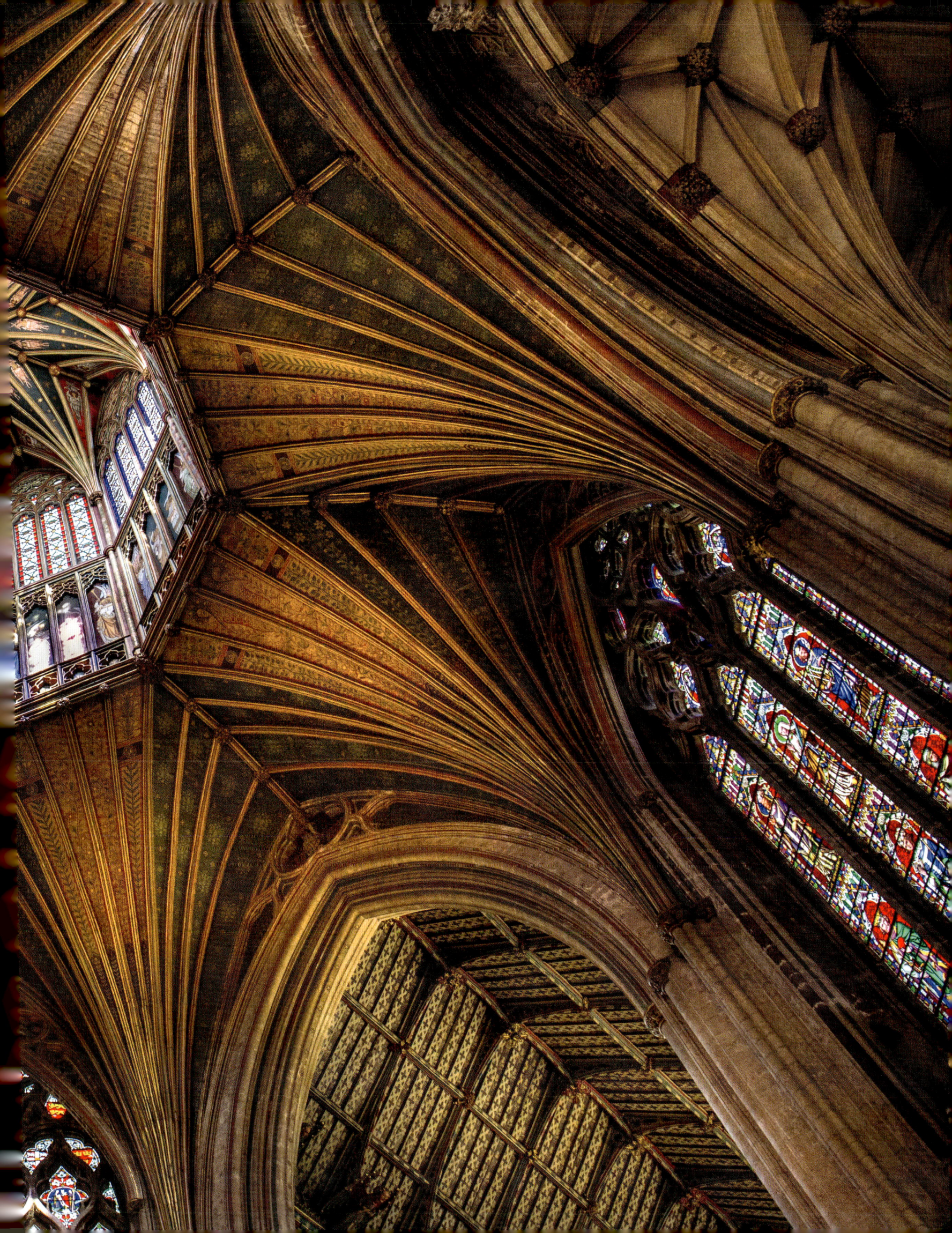

THE SHRINES OF OUR LADY OF WALSINGHAM
Walsingham, Norfolk

Britain is no longer associated with the ostentatious public displays of religious devotion predominantly seen in Catholic European countries, such as the Semana Santa (Holy Week) processions in Spain. However, in a remote corner of rural Norfolk in East Anglia lies Little Walsingham, a village that was originally the most important place of Marian pilgrimage in medieval England and that has witnessed a rebirth of pilgrimage and iconic veneration. There are actually two neighbouring Walsinghams, a 'Little' and a 'Great', but in general parlance size tends not to matter. What makes Walsingham unique within the context of modern-day English religion is the fact that there are now both Anglican and Catholic shrines to Our Lady of Walsingham in the same village. However, perhaps the most surprising element of this twenty-first-century ecumenical landscape is the fact that the Orthodox Church is actually doubly represented. The former Victorian Methodist Chapel in Great Walsingham was internally redesigned and converted into the Church of the Transfiguration in 1988 and the now-defunct railway station was transformed into the Chapel of St Seraphim. The brightly painted icons associated with Orthodoxy create a refreshing contrast with the more traditional forms of religious art and St Seraphim's now houses both a museum and school of iconography. The pomp, ceremony and joyous celebration of pilgrimage combine in the Anglican National Pilgrimage held on each May Bank Holiday, when it is strange to witness a statue of the Virgin Mary being borne aloft in a howdah amid a long processional line of bishops and clergy in their gleaming 'Sunday best' apparel.

The Bank Holiday pilgrimage is not the longest in Europe and the distance from the Anglican shrine church that is home to Our Lady of Walsingham to journey's end in the grounds of Walsingham Abbey is actually little more than 200 metres/656 feet. However, the act of pilgrimage is not solely about pounding along dusty roads, and the Walsingham event is preceded by a night vigil. Along with other community events and church services, the whole weekend is one of prayer, contemplation and rejoicing. There could not be a finer backdrop for the post-processional service held before the sole surviving arch of the Augustinian priory church.

The mighty east end of the Augustinian priory church soars above the assembled congregation of pilgrims as the clergy bearing the statue of Our Lady of Walsingham arrive for the celebration mass, joyfully singing the special hymn dedicated to the object of their veneration.

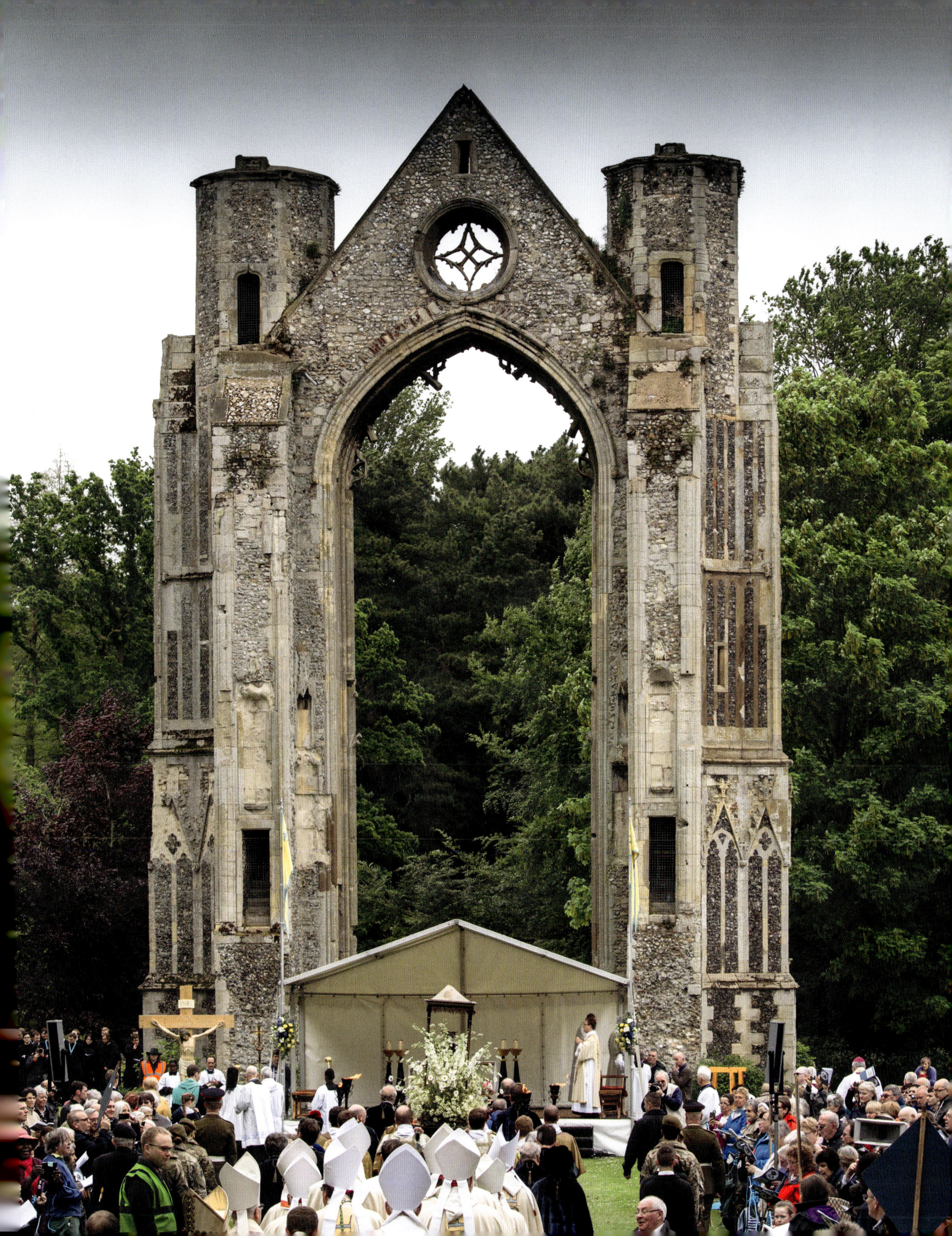

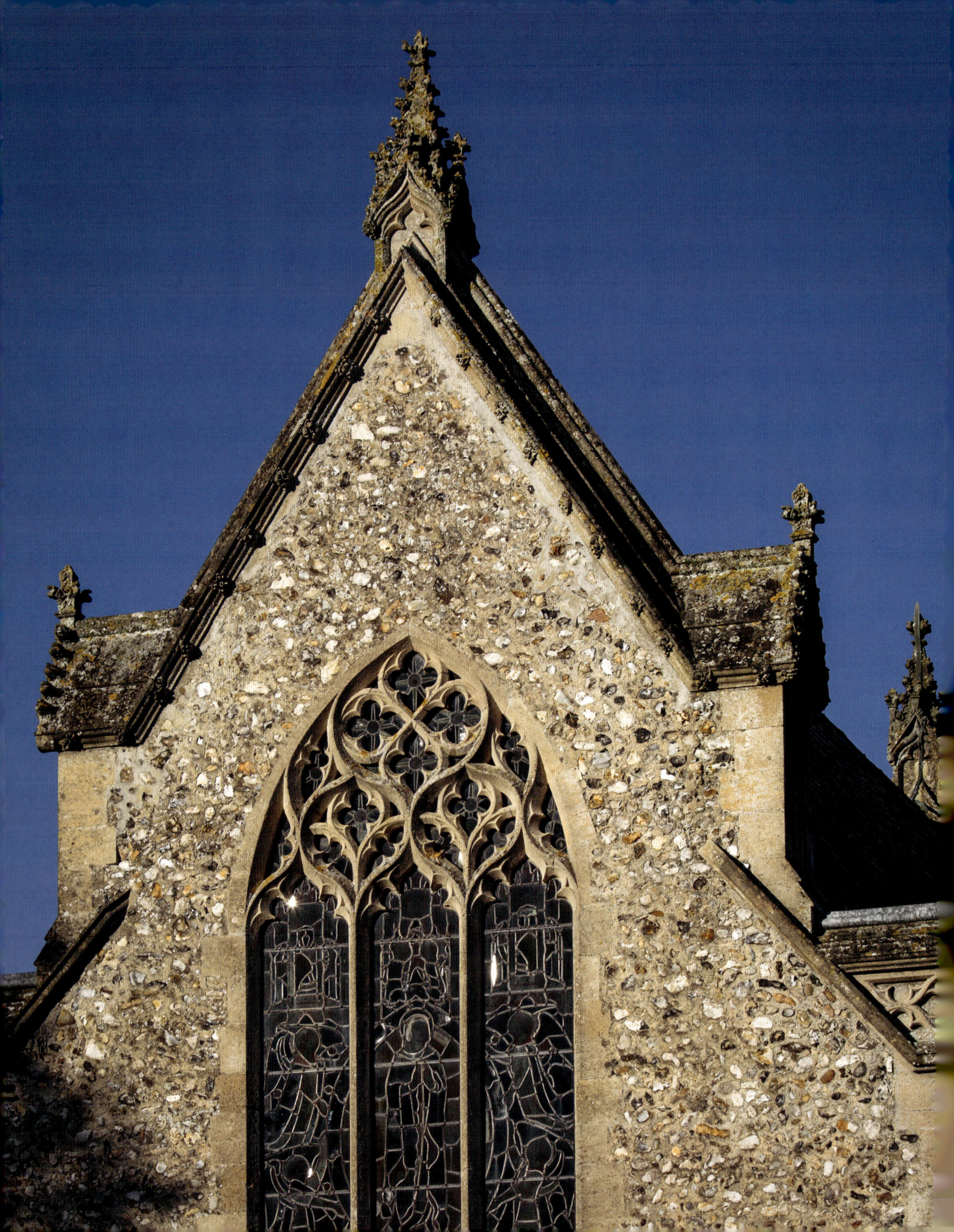

(*left*) The Slipper Chapel is now restored to its former glory, having spent centuries as a cow shed, food store and farm utility building. The chapel had originally been dedicated to the martyred fourth-century Egyptian St Catherine of Alexandria, who was tortured on the wheel. It is thought that the spinning fireworks known as Catherine wheels derived their name from this event.

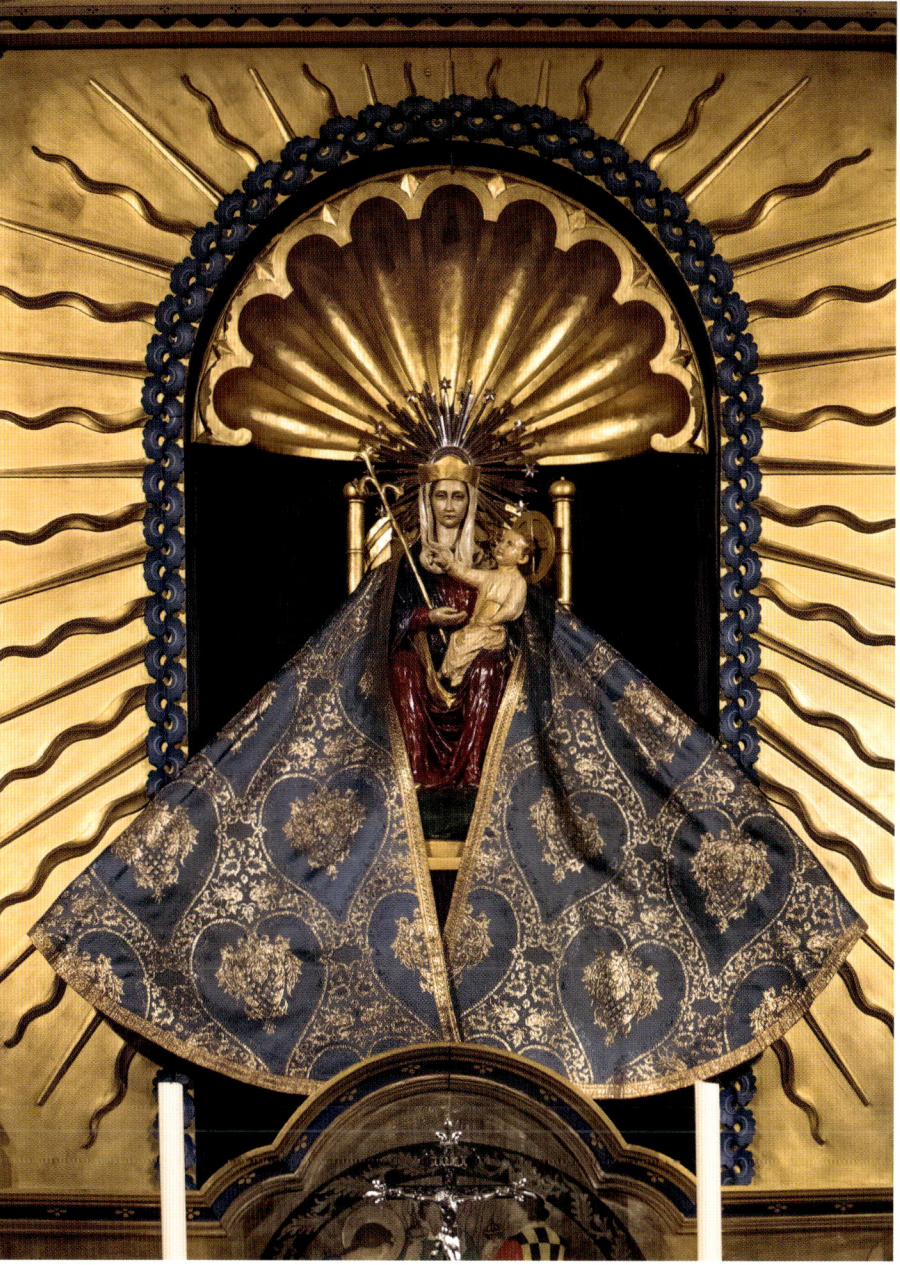

(*above*) The statue of Our Lady of Walsingham was carved in 1922 based upon the seal originally used by the Augustinian Canons Regular. Their priory was built close to the original model of the Holy House of Nazareth, commissioned by Richeldis de Faverches at the behest of the Virgin Mary. The shrine itself is beautifully constructed, creating an intimate sanctuary within the main church.

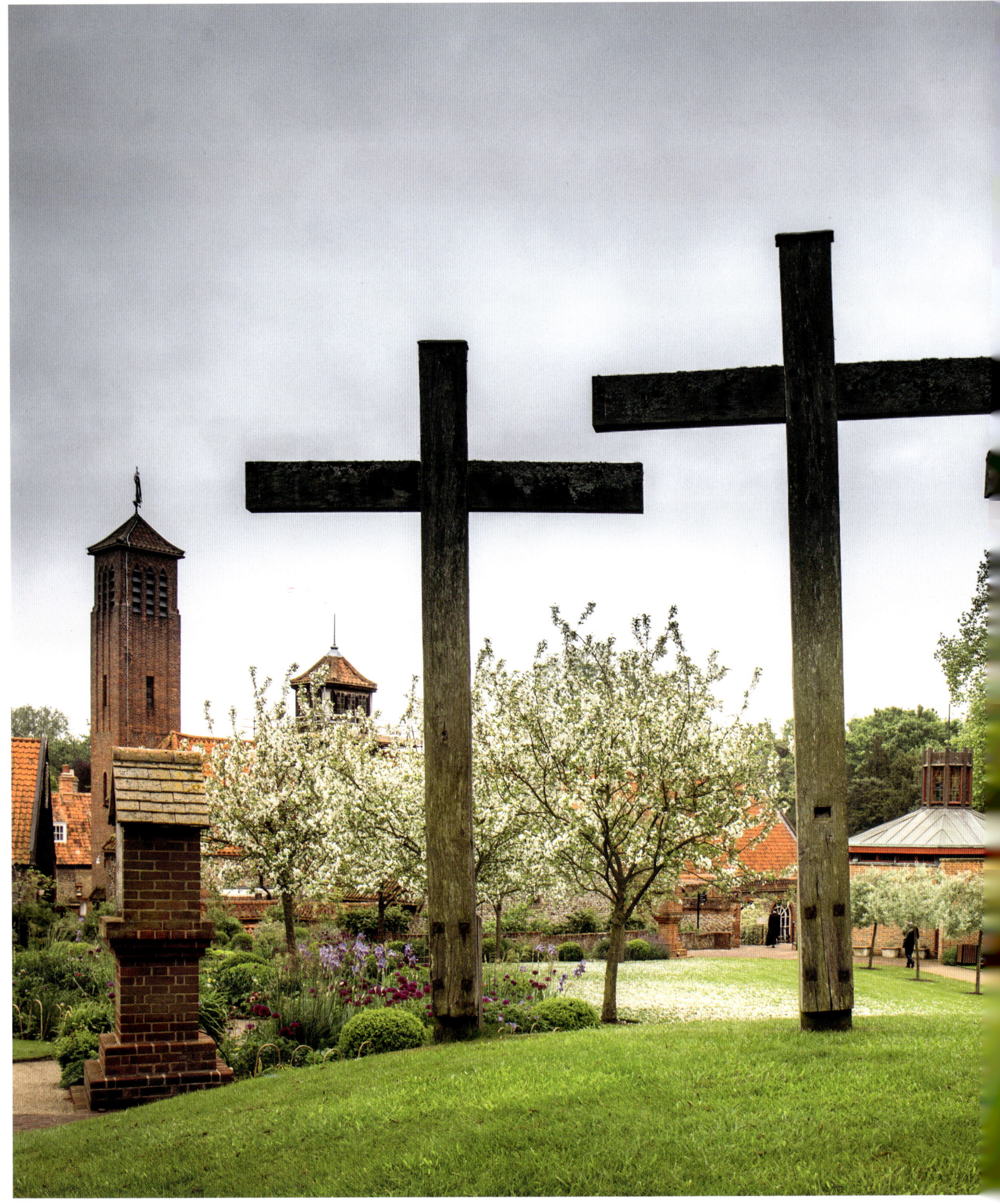

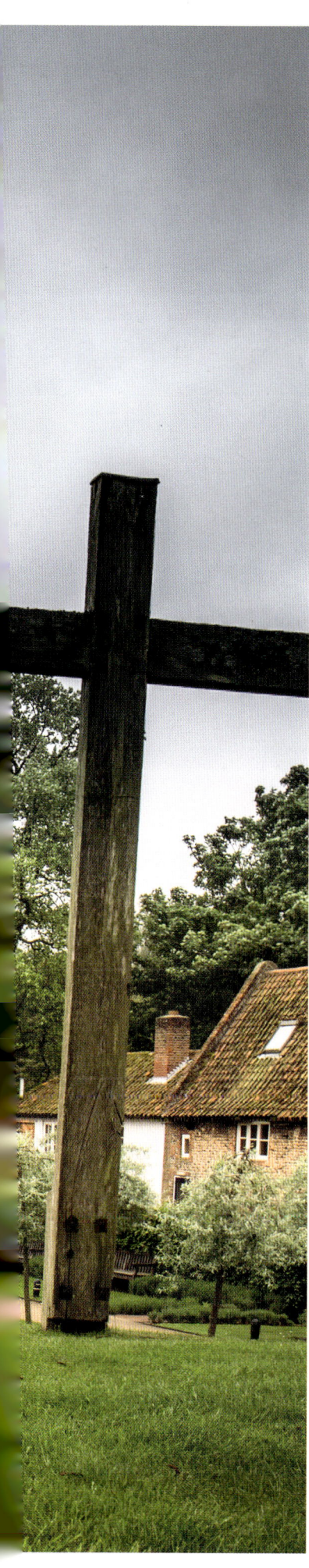

In common with many other pilgrimage sites throughout Europe, the Anglican shrine found itself being overwhelmed by pilgrim numbers, and a new church and accommodation had to be built. The beautiful gardens set within the walls of the shrine provide ample space for private contemplation.

The history of the Walsingham pilgrimage dates back to 1061 when the lady of the manor, Richeldis de Faverches, had a vision in which she was transported to the Holy Land by the Virgin Mary, who exhorted her to build a replica of the Holy House of Nazareth where the Annunciation had taken place. During the twelfth century, an Augustinian priory was established over the shrine and as the act of religious pilgrimage was escalating rapidly throughout Christian Europe, Walsingham became the most visited shrine in Britain. Because the shrines of Ely and Walsingham were separated by the comparatively short distance of 80 kilometres/50 miles, the perceived spiritual rewards on offer to pilgrims were deemed well worth the extra journey, even though the Ely leg might have been an uncomfortable slog through Fenland mud. The Shrine of Our Lady boasted an impressive 'guest list' of nobility and monarchs, the most supportive of whom was Henry III, who made the first of many visits in 1226 and later made substantial endowments to the Augustinian Canons. It seems ironic that the last pre-Reformation royal pilgrimage was by Henry VIII, whose 1536 Act of Dissolution resulted in the destruction of the Holy House. The Virgin Mary's statue was taken back to London and burnt.

The rebirth of the Walsingham pilgrimage did not occur until the twentieth century, when both Anglican and Catholic shrines were established. It was in the early 1920s that the Anglican pilgrimage was revived and a statue of the Virgin Mary was created based on the image borne by the Augustinian priory's original seal. The Holy House was recreated in a new shrine church during 1931 and it has been subsequently extended and modernized to cater for the increasing numbers of Anglican pilgrims visiting Walsingham. The Catholic National Shrine of Our Lady is located 1.6 kilometres/1 mile from Walsingham in the village of Houghton Saint Giles and centred around the fourteenth-century 'Slipper Chapel'. It is here that the Catholic Church's own shrine and statue of the Virgin and Child is located. The Slipper Chapel's name was derived from the accepted tradition that pilgrims should remove their footwear and walk the final mile in bare feet.

CANTERBURY CATHEDRAL
Canterbury, Kent

Canterbury Cathedral's 76-metre-/250-foot-high central tower dominates the medieval core of the city originally named Durovernum by the Romans. It was at Canterbury in 597 that St Augustine began his crusade at the behest of Pope Gregory to bring Christianity back to England, and his first cathedral thereby made Canterbury the cradle of English Christianity and subsequently mother church of the Anglican faith. As a consequence of Danish raids on the south-east of the country, the cathedral was all but destroyed by fire in 1067, just one year after the Norman Conquest. William I installed Lanfranc as archbishop to restore the cathedral, although his work was almost obliterated by another serious fire in 1174, an event that could have had dire consequences for Canterbury's future.

Just four year earlier, in 1170, the then-Archbishop of Canterbury, Thomas Becket, was murdered in his cathedral by four of Henry II's knights, in response to their king's exasperated, but probably rhetorical question 'Will no one rid me of this turbulent priest?' Becket had been Henry's chancellor and the pair had been good friends for many years, but when given the archbishopric, Becket became overly pious and fought the church's corner rather than unquestioningly supporting his monarch. Henry II paid a heavy personal price for his ill-judged words, because in July 1174 the King of England was obliged to walk barefoot through the streets of Canterbury in penance, being whipped by monks along the route.

Experiencing Canterbury as a twenty-first-century tourist is perhaps not too dissimilar to its medieval heyday, when bands of travellers (such as those depicted in Geoffrey Chaucer's *The Canterbury Tales*) would arrive after completing the prescribed pilgrim routes or country tracks, many of which still exist and are used for their original purpose.

The narrow medieval streets leading up to the cathedral remain awash with visitors today, although the medieval pilgrims' visits would have been painstakingly organized by monks rather than umbrella-waving tour guides. Pilgrims would have been escorted through the cathedral, pausing at the murder spot and high altar before finally being allowed to savour a few blessed moments of prayer, thanksgiving or supplication before the shrine.

This elevated view of Canterbury Cathedral accentuates its stature in relation to the huddled dwellings lining the city's narrow medieval streets. Medieval cathedrals in England are starting to seriously feel their age and scaffolding is becoming a semi-permanent fixture on their walls, spires and towers.

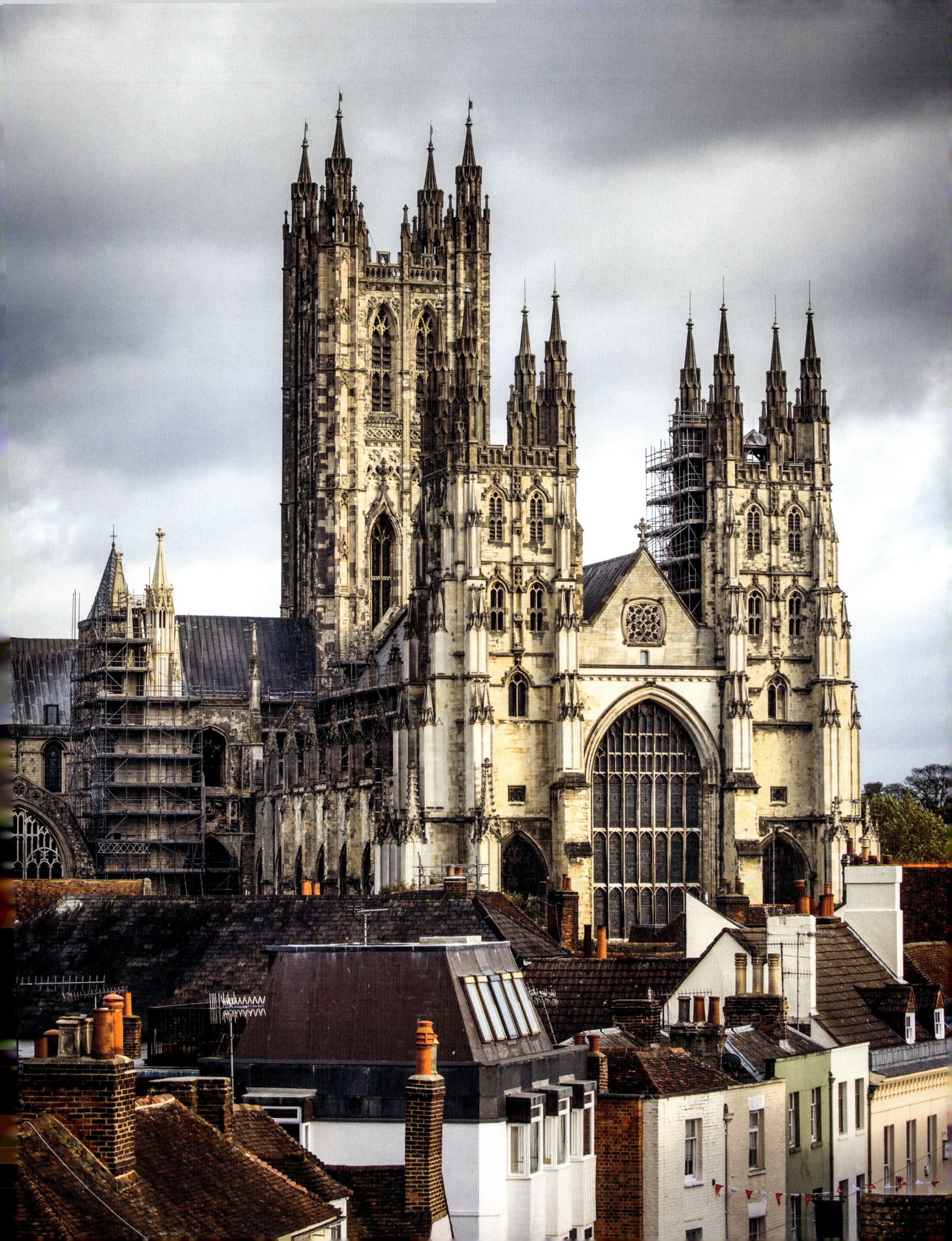

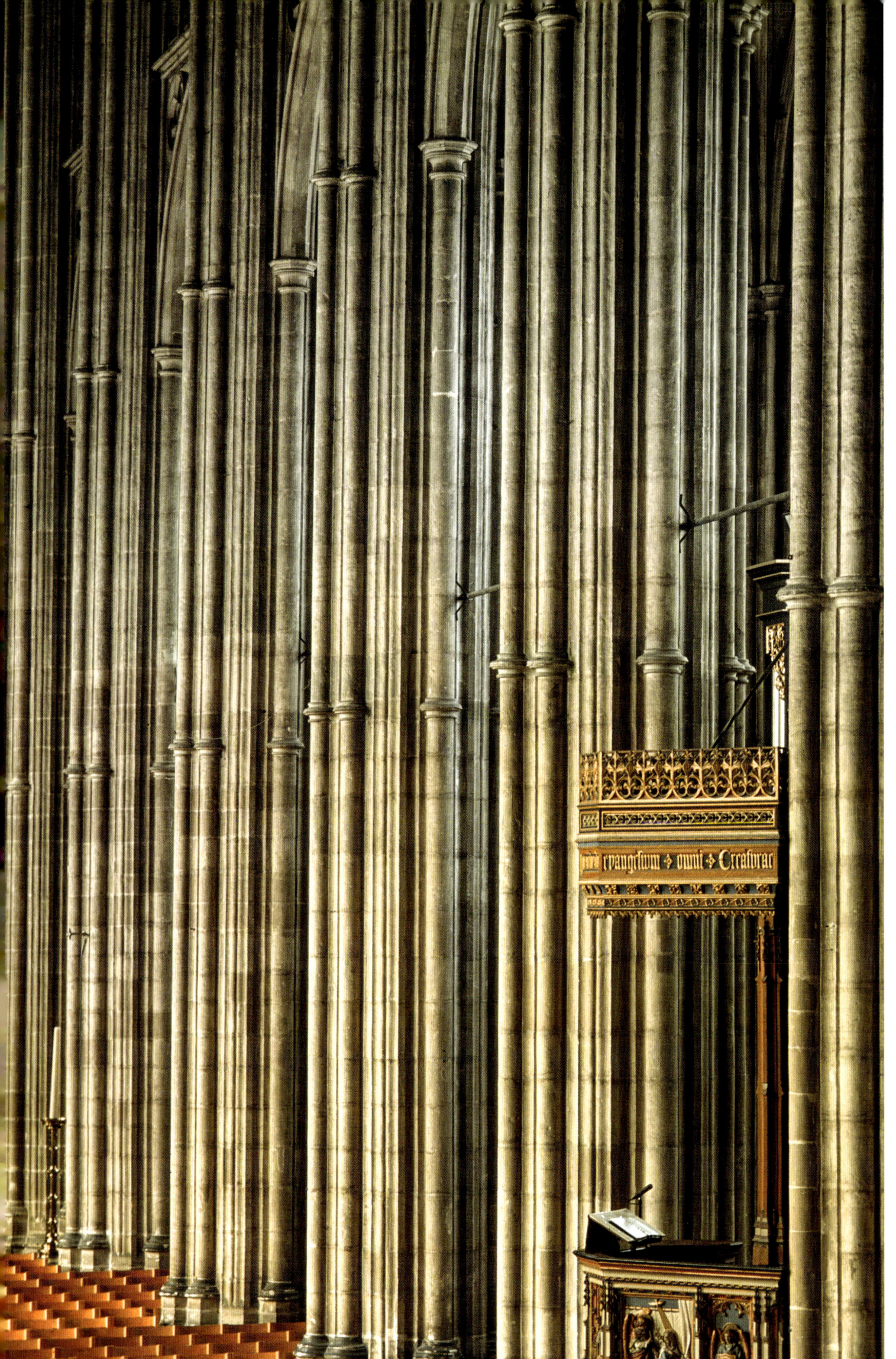

(*left*) The soaring pillars of the cathedral's nave must have presented a daunting sight to many first-time visitors on a pilgrimage. A brief glimpse of the seating in the bottom left corner of the photograph accentuates the sense of power exercised by the Church.

(*below*) The elaborate tomb of Edward, Prince of Wales, the 'Black Prince', is attributed to Henry Yevele. The prince was the eldest son of King Edward III of England and he was renowned for his military prowess at the Battle of Poitiers in 1356 during the Hundred Years' War.

Becket's martyrdom, canonization and subsequent enshrinement led to Canterbury eventually vying with Walsingham to be the greatest pilgrimage destination in the country. Had it not been for the fact that Becket's tomb was lodged down in the magnificent crypt, the means by which Canterbury Cathedral could secure its future could have literally gone up in smoke after the fire in 1174.

Reconstruction of the interior was undertaken in two phases of development, separated by 200 years. The nave was the work of Henry Yevele, a builder of outstanding talent who served two successive monarchs, Edward III and Richard II. For such a huge enclosed area, the nave seems particularly well lit, an effect contrived by introducing higher arcades backed by large windows. One can scarcely imagine the awe felt by pilgrims as they progressed eastwards, with cleverly placed flights of steps through the nave and choir creating a sensation of triumphant ascension towards the high altar and Becket's golden, jewel-encrusted shrine in the Trinity Chapel beyond. To gain an impression of Canterbury's true atmosphere, there is no better way than to attend choral evensong on a winter's afternoon. All the main lights are extinguished, save for those in the choir, and the choristers' spine-tingling anthems reverberate out into the nave's dark, cavernous void.

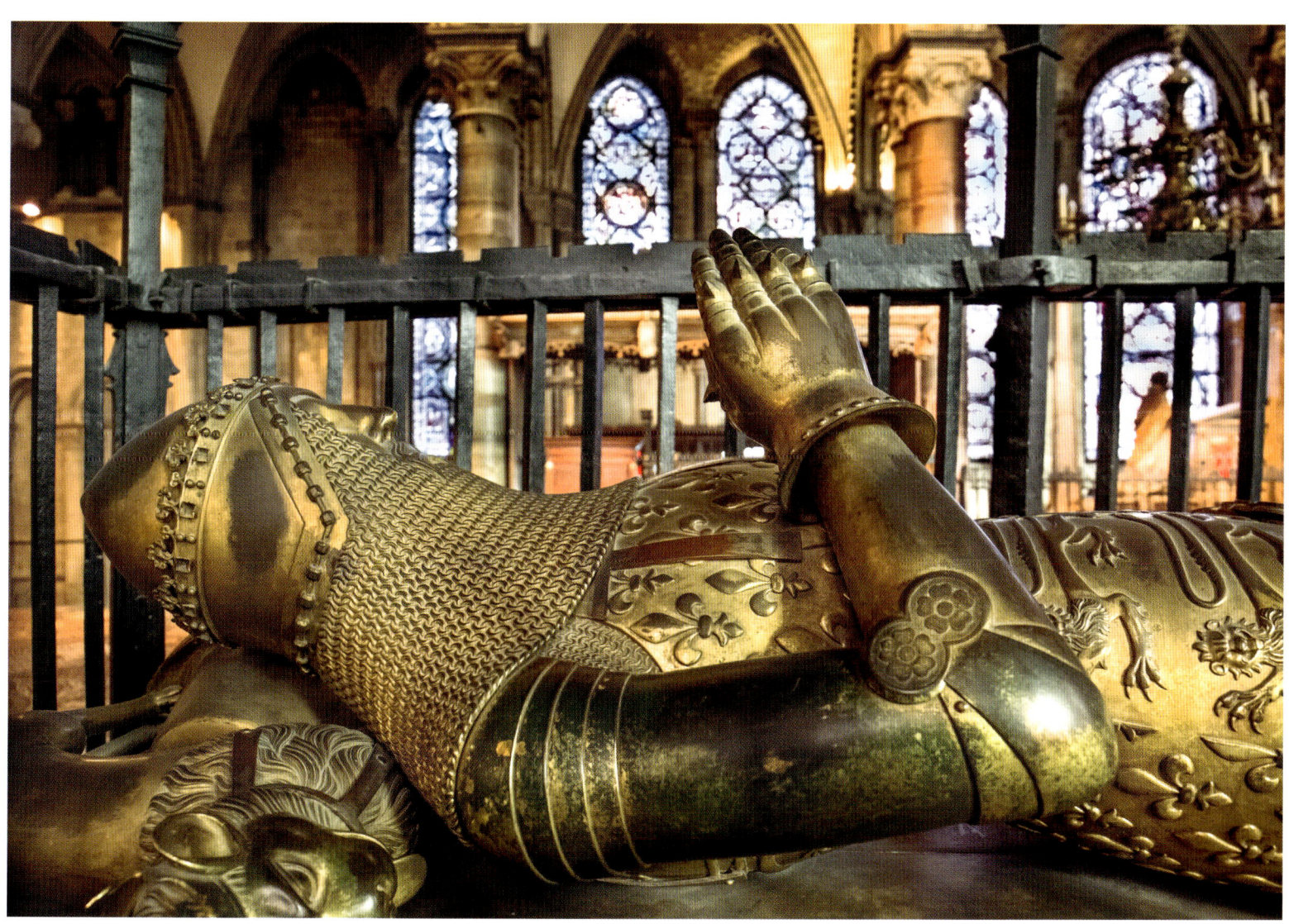

(*right*) Canterbury Cathedral possesses an astounding collection of early medieval stained glass. In this magnificent portrait of Thomas Becket, one wonders whether he is scowling across at Henry II, and if so, should it perhaps have been his middle digit raised in the air?

(*below*) The Trinity Chapel was stripped of Becket's shrine by Henry VIII, but despite the fact that the allocated space is now lit by a solitary candle, the view back down through the choir to the nave's west end is still mesmerizing.

Despite increasing clamour for greater access to the relics of Thomas Becket, his shrine was not set in place until the Trinity Chapel's completion in 1220. A mid-thirteenth-century pilgrim reportedly described his impressions of the shrine by saying 'The shrine surpasses all belief, covered over with plates of pure gold, but the gold is hardly visible for the variety of precious stones with which it is studded.' The more pilgrims that visited the shrine, the farther afield the word spread regarding this miraculous place. As more pilgrims travelled to Canterbury, the cathedral coffers became even fuller, enabling further building works to take place. The final piece of this remarkable architectural jigsaw was inserted in 1500, and it is well worth the inevitable neck ache to stare up into the tower and marvel at the exquisitely delicate fan vaulting.

Travelling the roads of medieval England always carried a degree of risk, which is why people banded together for safety in numbers. One of the most diverse and eternally famous groups making their way from London to Canterbury featured in Chaucer's greatest work, *The Canterbury Tales*, a fictional account, with serious documentary undertones, about a mixed bag of pilgrims from the top, bottom and middle rungs of medieval society. Chaucer was the first writer to be interred in the Poets' Corner of Westminster Abbey, although he might just have preferred Canterbury Cathedral.

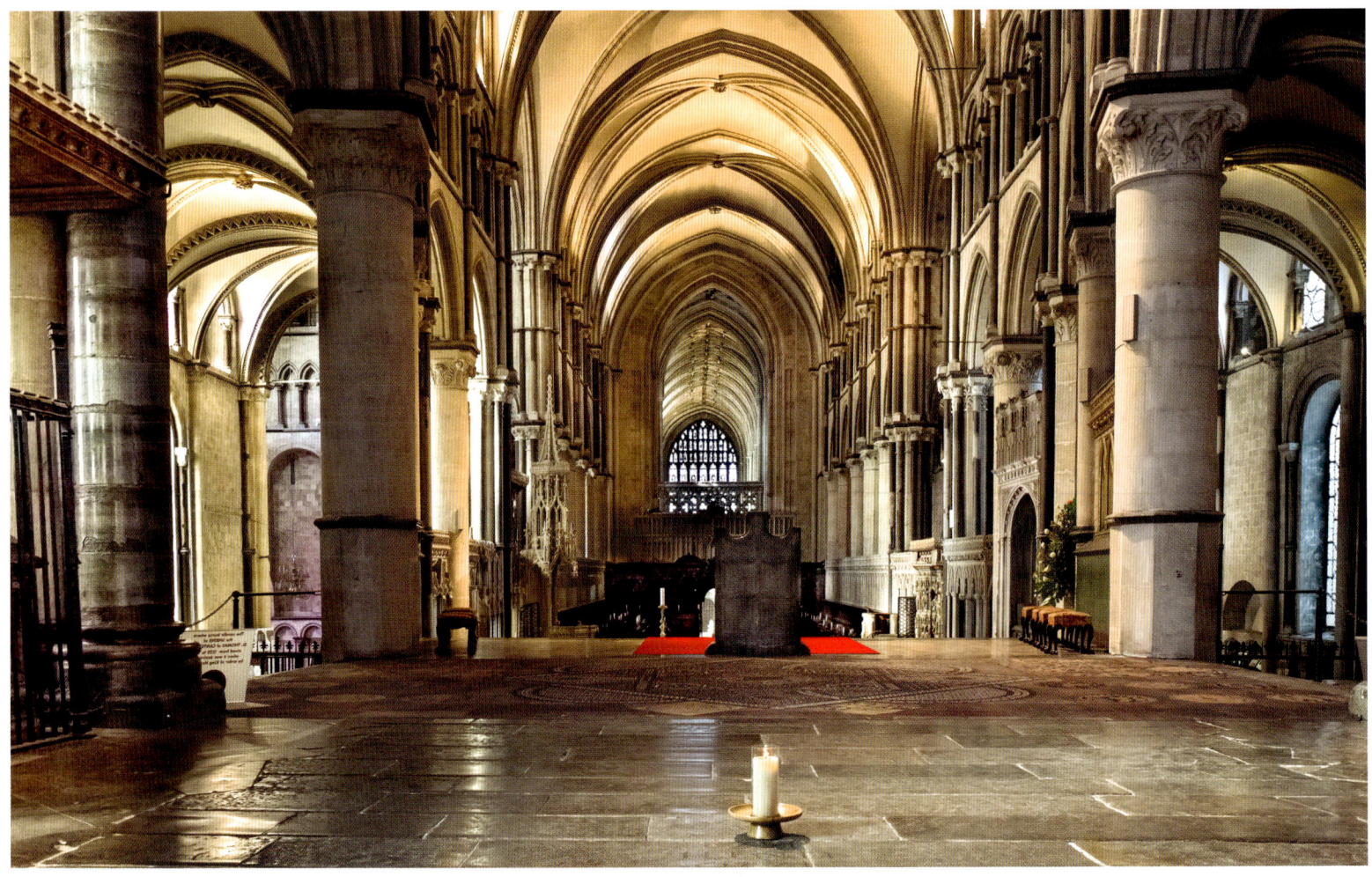

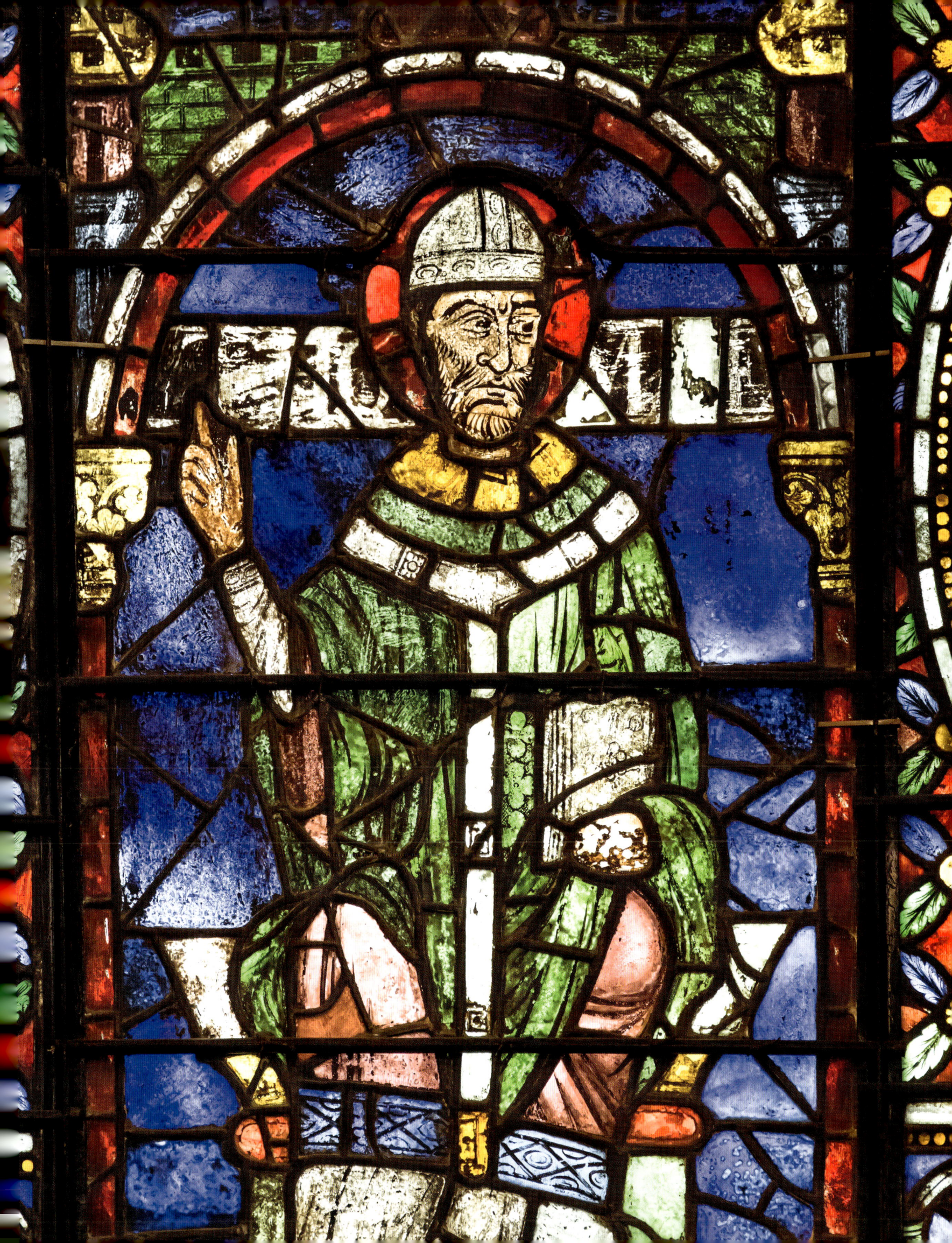

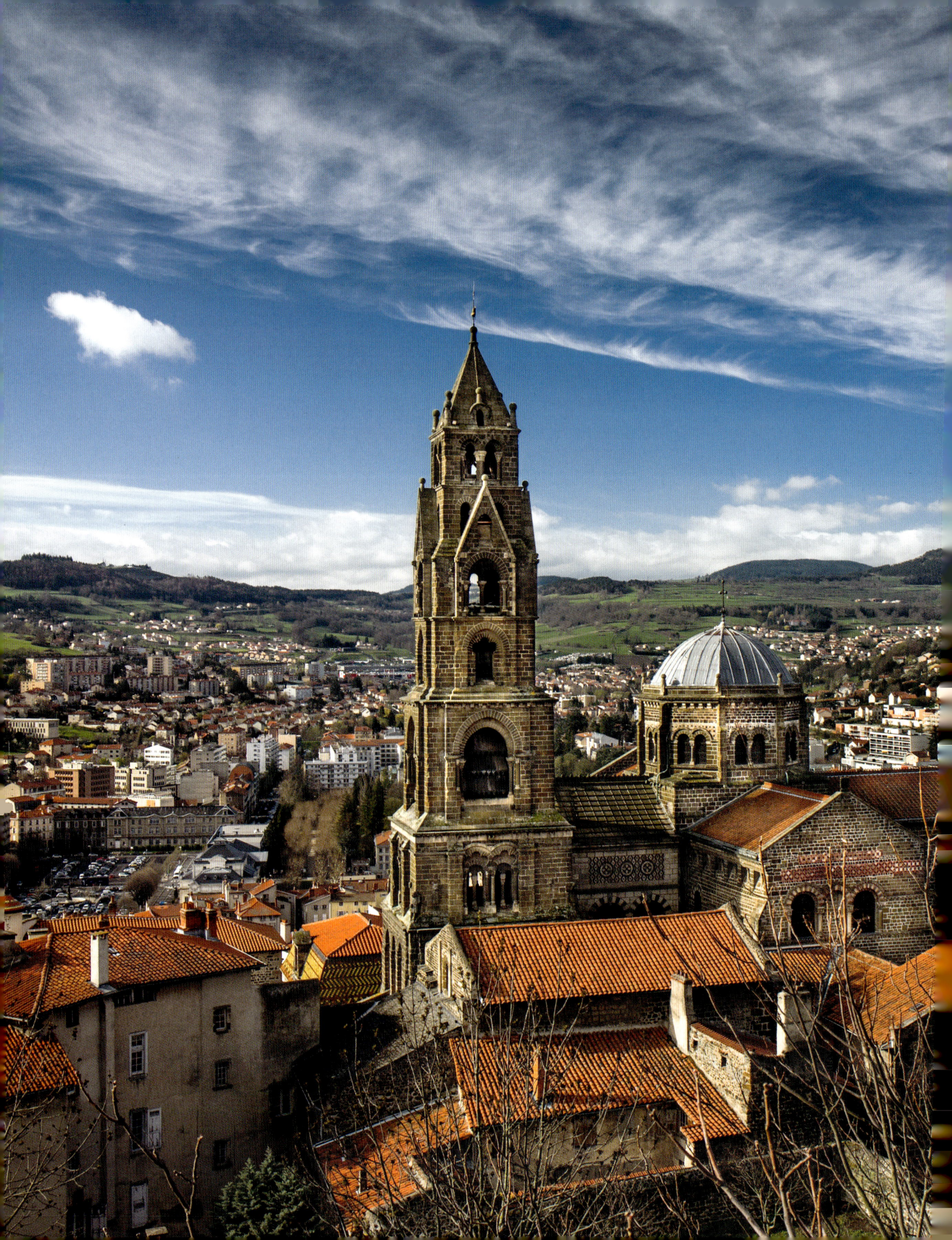

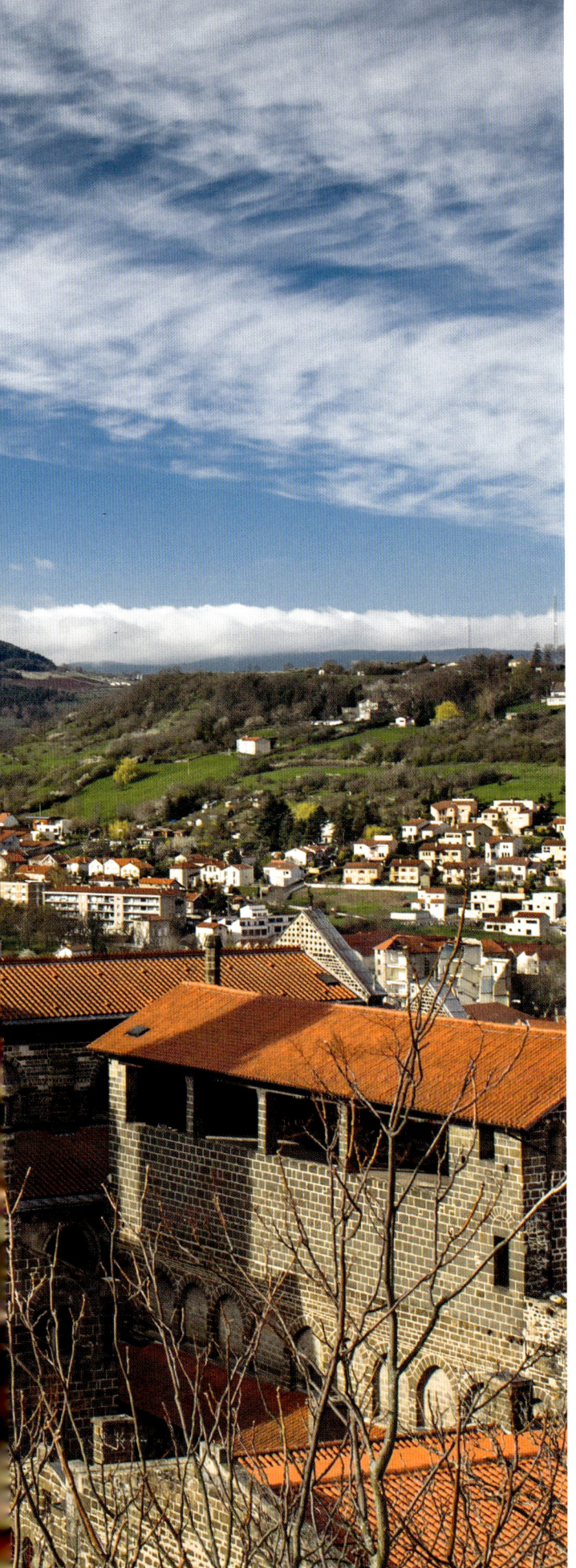

2

FRANCE

BASILICA OF ST THÉRÈSE
Lisieux, Normandy

The history of Lisieux extends back to Roman times and although this Normandy town is endowed with the Gothic cathedral of St Pierre, that is not the focus of the hundreds of thousands of pilgrims who have made Lisieux France's second most visited shrine after Lourdes. Their destination is the gleaming neo-Byzantine basilica set high upon a hillside overlooking the town, and the object of their veneration is one of the nation's nine patron saints, Thérèse of Lisieux. It could be regarded as unusual in the panoply of Catholic saints that such a relatively young person, who had no connection with either miracles of healing or Marian visitation, should be so highly revered in the late nineteenth century. Thérèse Martin came from a pious family and because all four of her elder sisters were nuns, she too developed a deep interest in spirituality at a young age and entered the Carmelite convent in Lisieux when only fifteen years old.

Thérèse lived a relatively simple life within the sisterhood, although illness severely blighted her young life and she died from tuberculosis at the age of twenty-four. She was largely anonymous in life, but it was the collection of her posthumously published writings on a simple but honest approach to life, religion and spirituality that brought her to public attention. These works were collected, edited and published as an autobiography titled *L'Histoire d'une âme* (The Story of a Soul, 1898). The book's humble, common-sense piety touched many people throughout France, especially with observations such as, 'One word or a pleasing smile is often enough to raise up a saddened and wounded soul.'

So great was her popularity that all customary timeframes for posthumous honour within the Church were suspended, and Thérèse was beatified by Pope Pius XI in 1923 and canonized just two years later. However, the ultimate and rare accolade was awarded in 1997 when Pope John Paul II declared her the 33rd Doctor of the Church, one of only four women to have been similarly honoured. The doctorate is an award granted to saints deemed to have made a significant contribution to theology through their writings, and St Thérèse certainly fulfilled that criterion.

(*previous pages*) Cathedral of Our Lady of Le Puy.

(*right*) The kneeling bronze figure of St Thérèse of Lisieux faces the mighty twentieth-century neo-Byzantine basilica built in her name, the plans for which were first mooted in 1925, the year of her canonization. The large numbers of pilgrims travelling to Lisieux had no designated church at which to pay homage, and so with the encouragement of Pope Pius XI an appeal for funds was launched and the first stone was laid in 1929. Inevitable delay caused by the Second World War meant that the basilica was not consecrated until 1954.

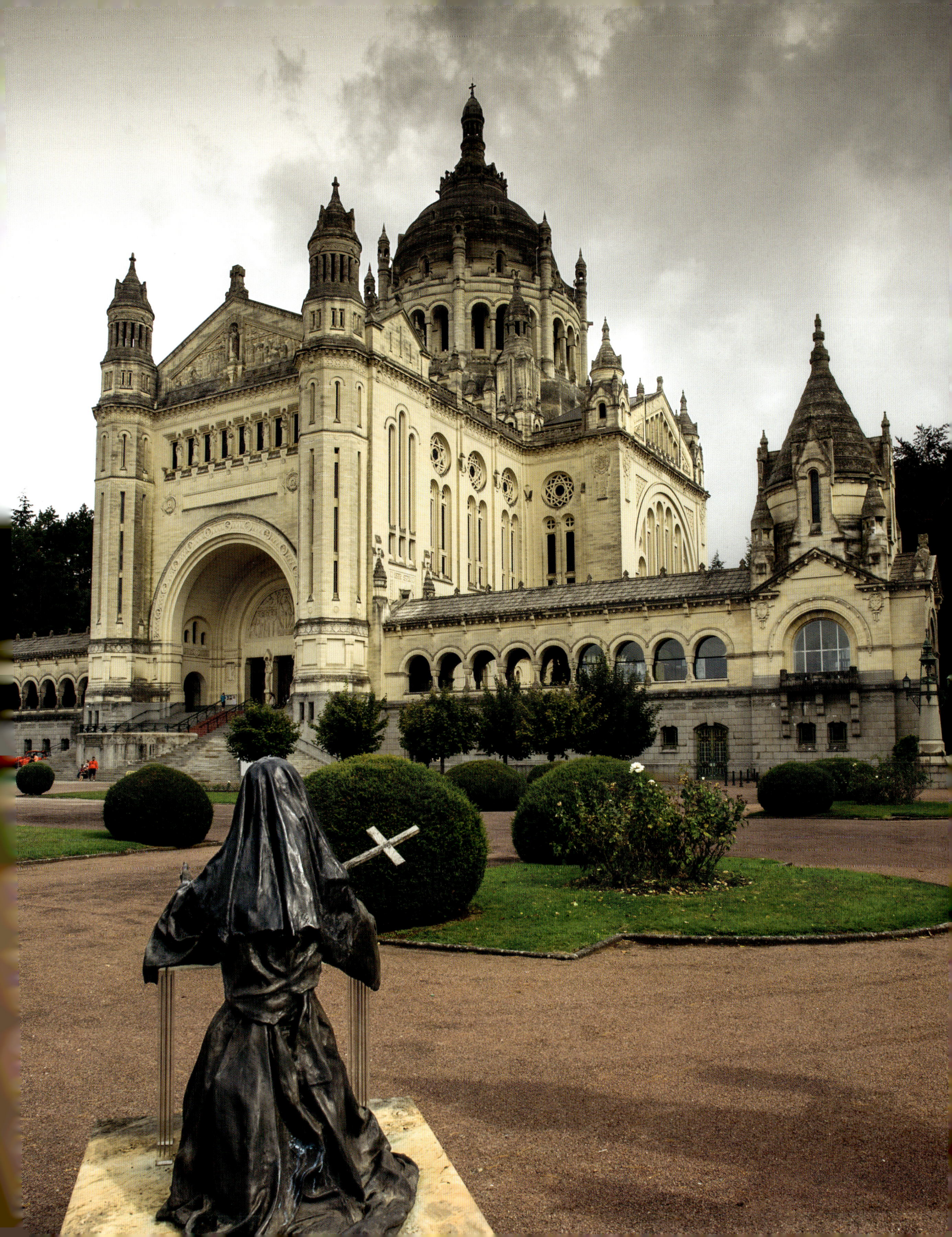

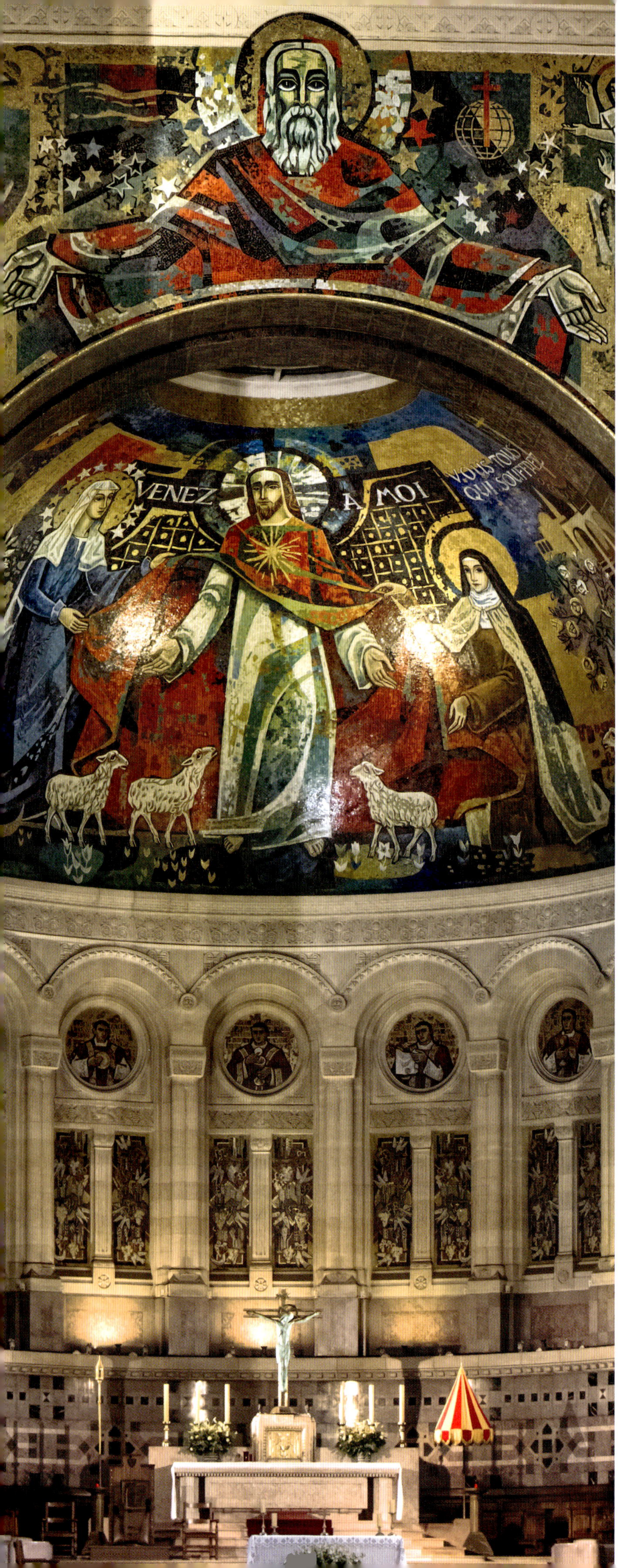

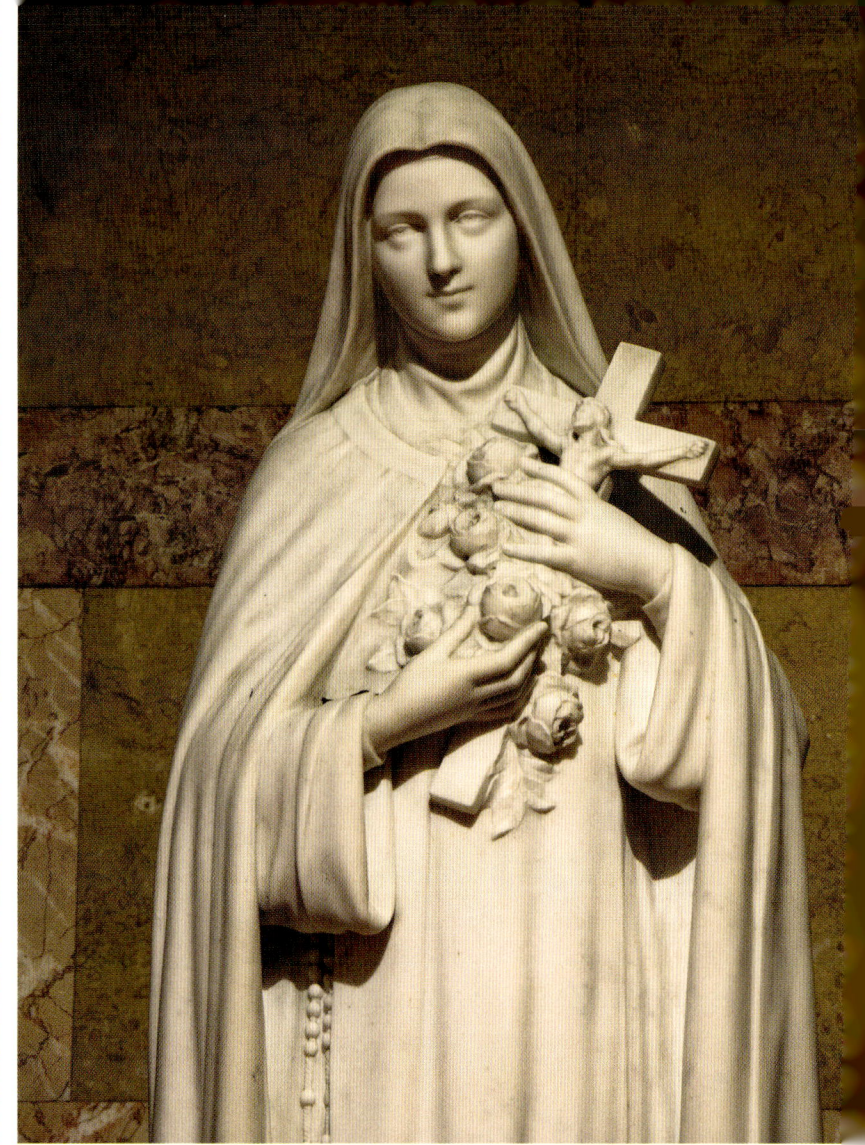
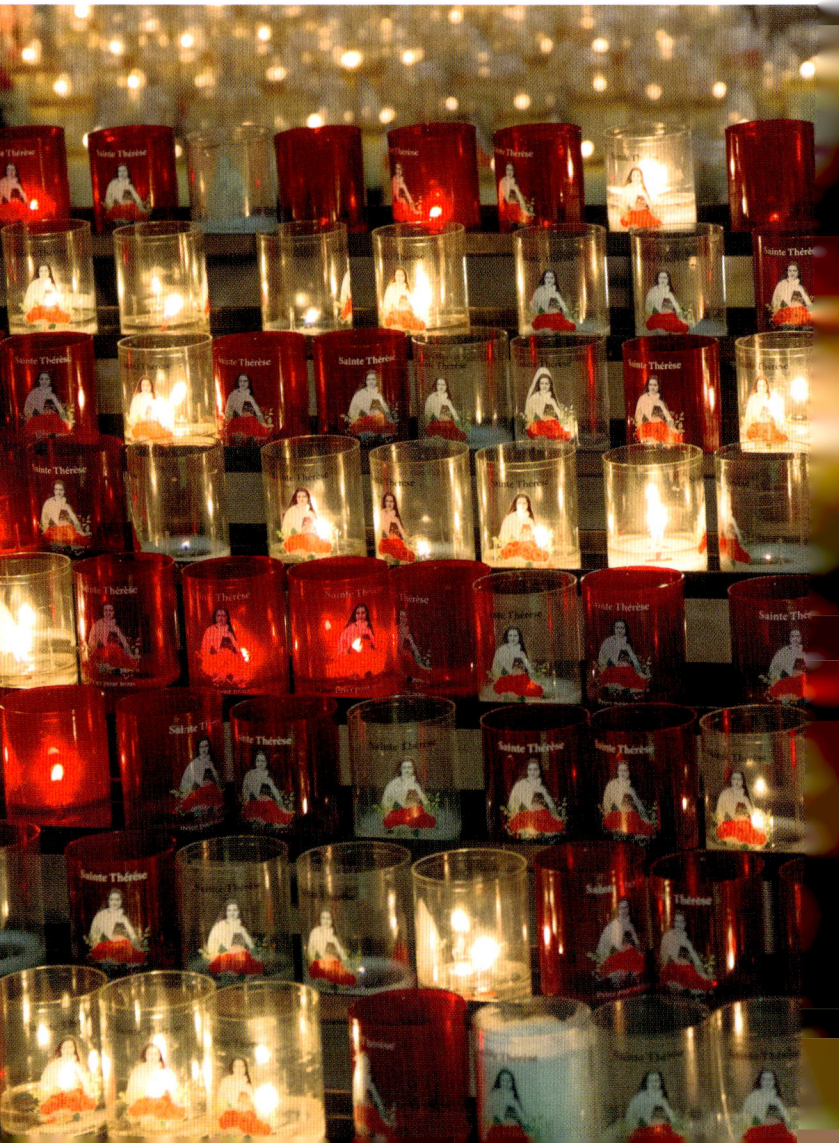

(*below*) The distinctive mosaics and glass of the basilica are the work of French artist Pierre Gaudin, whose ideal was to introduce a modern style of art into churches. The dome overlooks the nave, which is capable of seating 3,000 worshippers.

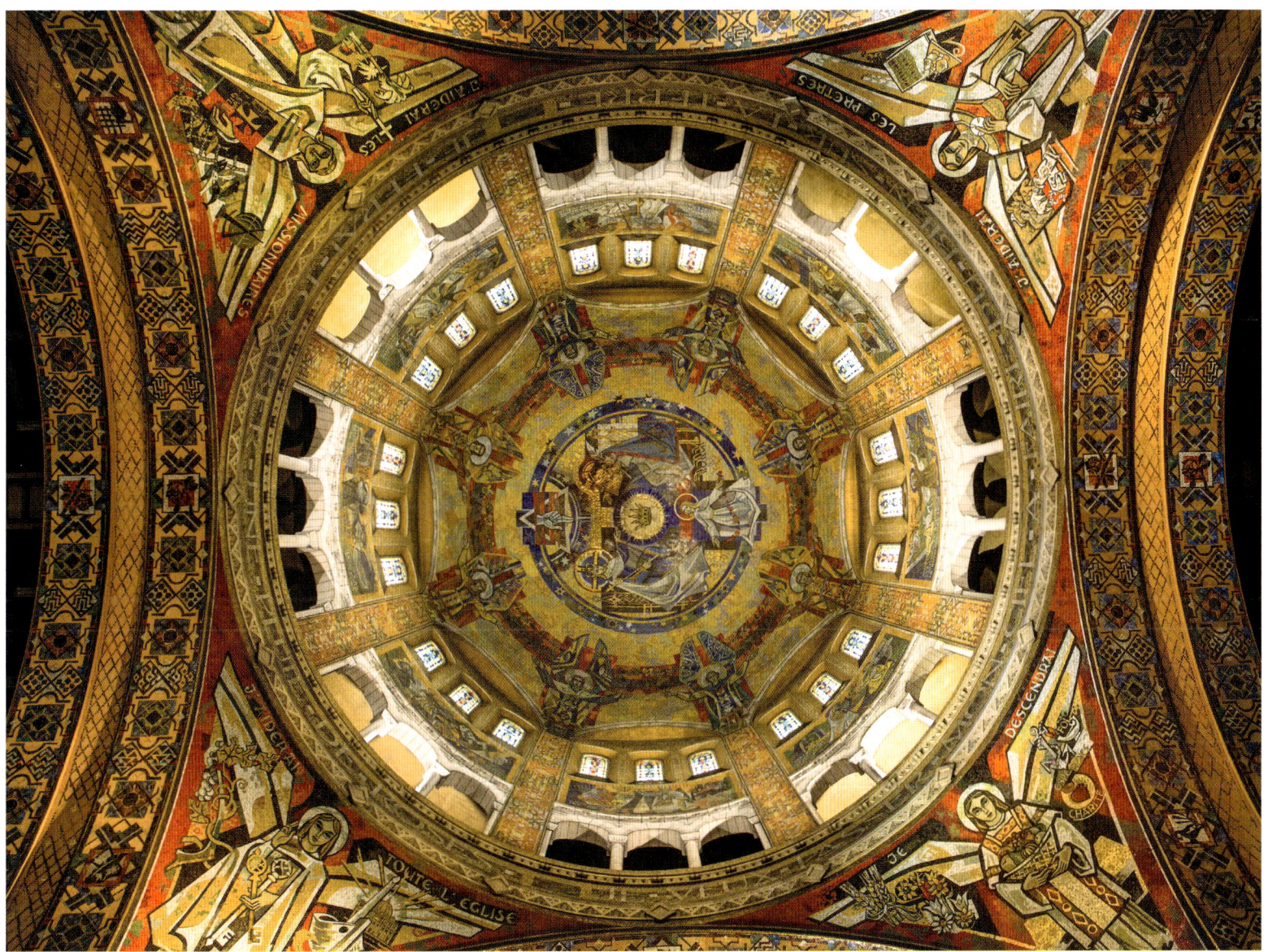

(*far left*) The basilica's high altar and apse are adorned by Gaudin's unique interpretation of medieval religious art. (*left above*) The elegantly simple marble statue of St Thérèse. (*left below*) The vast array of colourful votive candles in the Chapel of the Crucifixion.

OUR LADY OF CHARTRES CATHEDRAL
Chartres, Centre-Val de Loire

Visible for miles across the fertile plain of La Beauce, some 90 kilometres/56 miles south-west of Paris, this most celebrated of French cathedrals towers above the rooftops of Chartres and was listed as a World Heritage Site by UNESCO in 1979. Since its mid-thirteenth-century consecration, the cathedral has miraculously escaped the worst ravages of both time and man, but there has inevitably been some damage over the centuries, including the loss of several stained glass windows. However, when one considers that two World Wars were fought on its doorstep, those who believe in the grace and power of the Virgin Mary will suggest that the preceding centuries of pilgrimage reaped a bountiful harvest.

A church existed in Chartres as far back as the fourth century and documents referring to the life of sixth-century bishop St Béthaire mention 'a holy man kneeling before an altar of the Blessed Virgin Mary'. The cathedral's greatest treasure is the Sancta Camisia, the tunic or veil of the Virgin Mary still displayed in the treasury. This most precious relic was donated by Charles II the Bald, emperor of the Carolingian Empire, in 876, due to the renown of Chartres as a place of Marian pilgrimage, and it is extraordinary to contemplate what power such relics possessed in the medieval era.

The veil's greatest achievement was surviving the disastrous fire of 1194, which burnt much of the town and also a vast proportion of the cathedral, which had only recently been completed after the damage inflicted by another fire sixty years earlier. The relic was discovered unscathed amid the piles of smouldering embers, and at once the gloom and doubt of the devastated population was dispelled. Every member of French society vowed to raise an even better cathedral than its charred predecessor. The wealthy gave money and the poor gave their time and labour, such was the desire to reinstate the great pilgrimage church of Chartres. Countless legends of healing miracles spurred people on and, with the exception of the spires, it is thought that much of the work was accomplished within twenty-five years, although the cathedral was not formally reconsecrated until 1260.

Chartres Cathedral is renowned for its magnificent medieval stained glass and sculpture. It is rightly regarded as one of the high points of French Gothic art and architecture. The current building arose from the ashes of a disastrous fire in 1194.

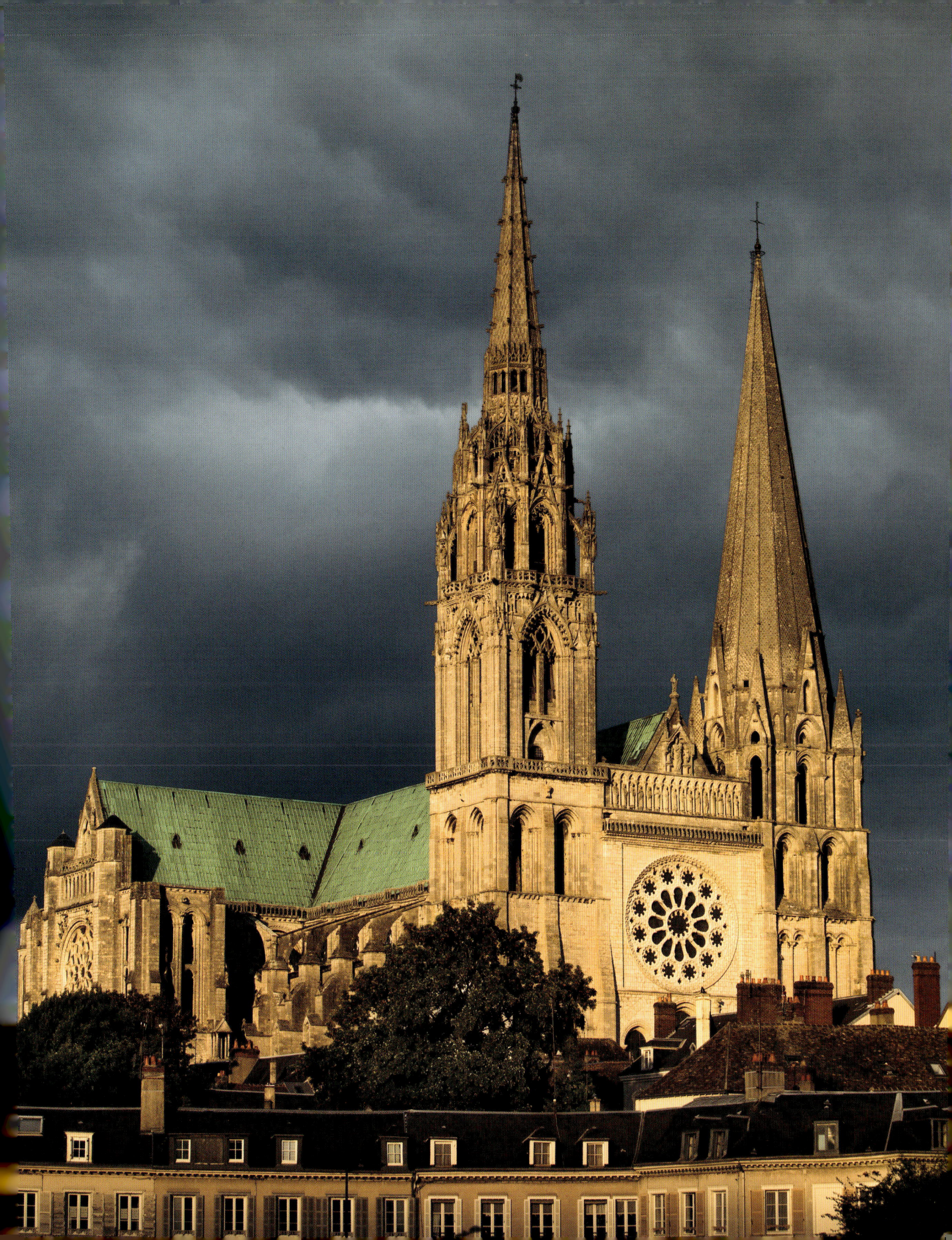

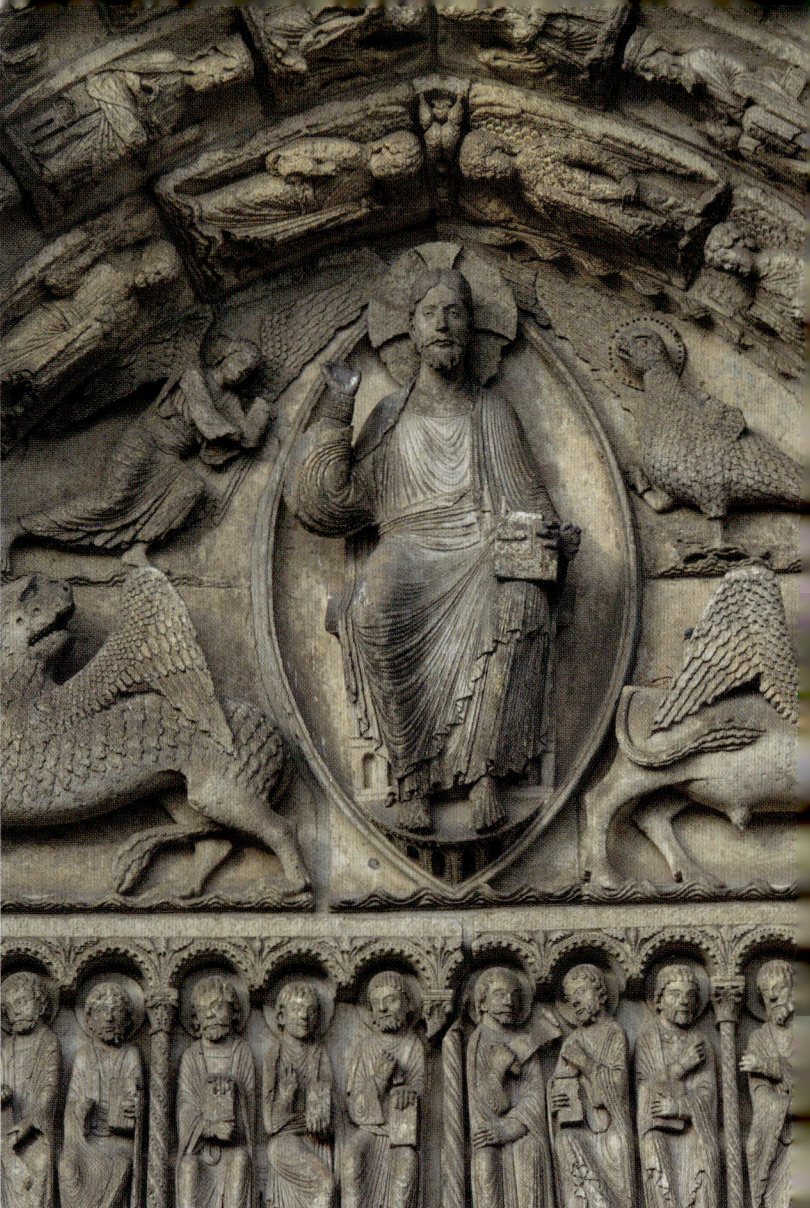
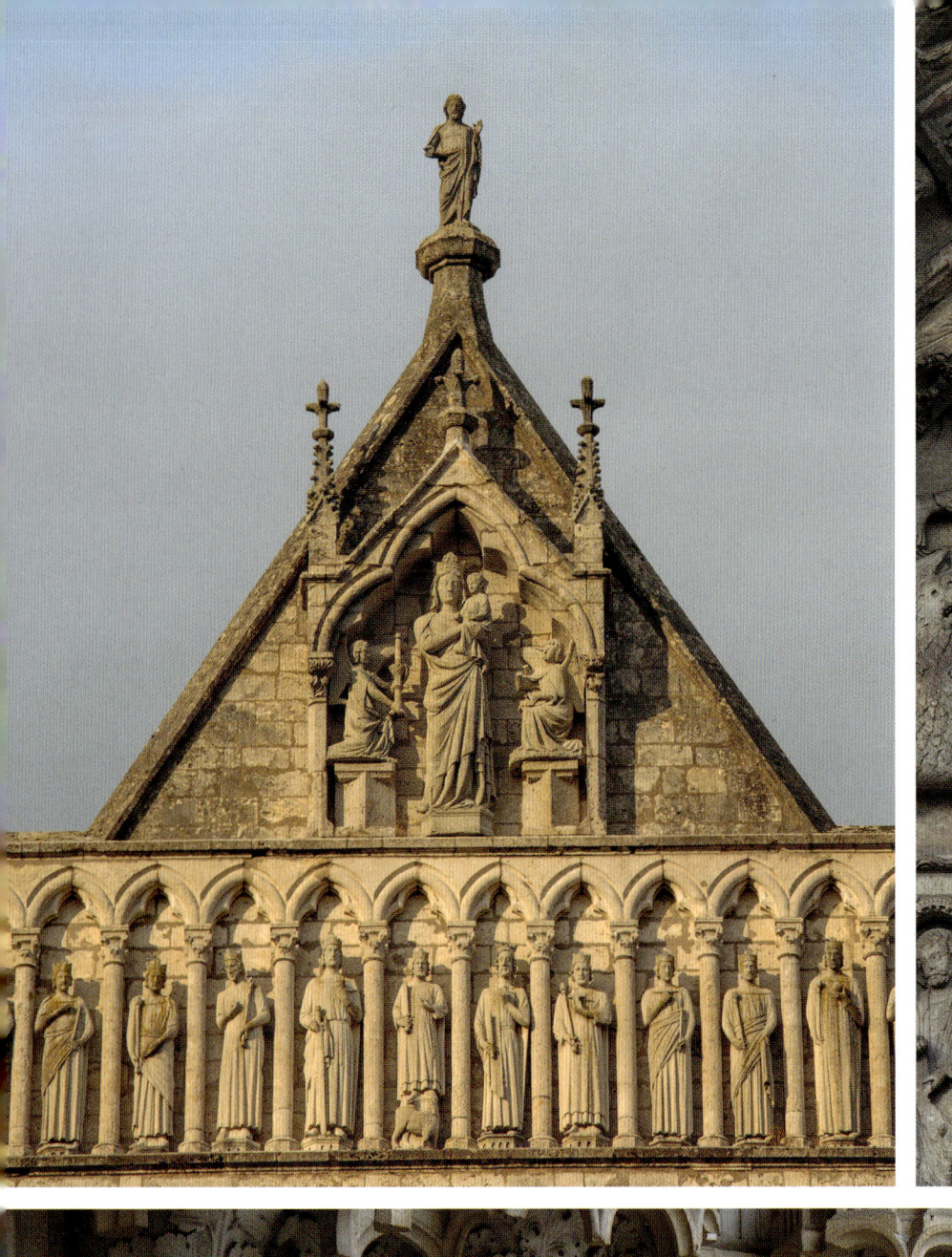

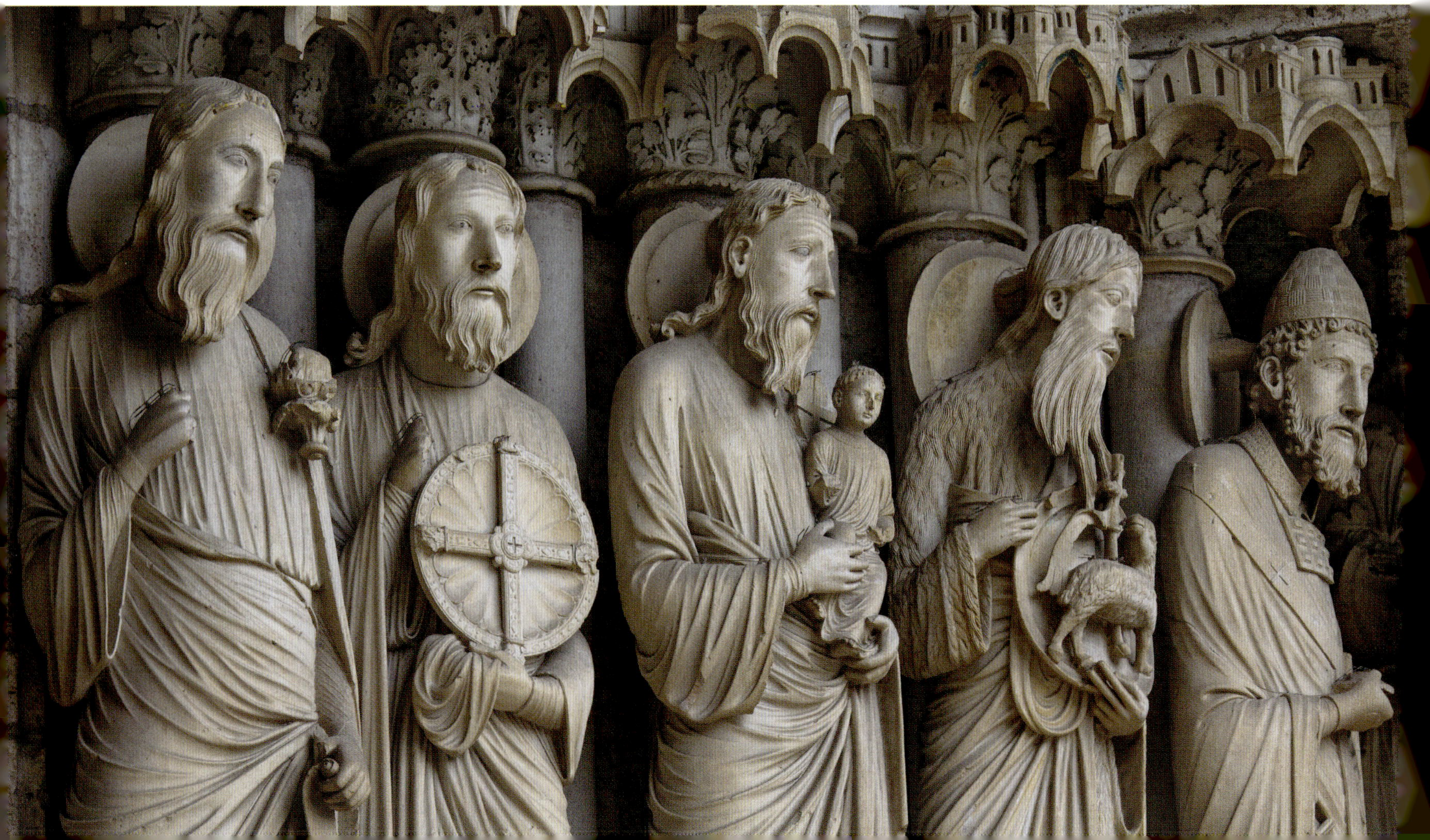

(*top left*) The gable of Chartres Cathedral is set above the west front's rose window and features a gallery of kings and the Virgin and Child with Christ above. (*top right*) The Royal Portal's twelfth-century tympanum is crowned by Christ set within a mandorla. (*bottom*) The north transept porch features three bays of outstanding medieval sculpture, completed around 1230. This image shows portraits of the Prophet Isaiah, Jeremiah, Simeon with the infant Jesus, John the Baptist and St Peter. The figures were substantially enhanced by restorations in 2001.

Chartres Cathedral marks the high point of Gothic art and architecture and it was used as a template by the architects of other superb examples of the genre, such as those at Reims and Amiens. The remarkable thing about Chartres is that in its rise from the ashes of 1194, it featured most of the structural and design elements that subsequently became the hallmark of the Gothic era, not just in tentative incremental stages but all together. The cathedral is renowned worldwide for its stained glass, but every aperture in a building's fabric inevitably creates a weak point. The pointed arches replacing the solid rounded style of the preceding Romanesque period were less able to play a role in weight distribution. Chartres was, therefore, pushing the established boundaries of the height-versus-weight equation towards a potential Icarus conclusion. However, the collapse of walls weakened by so many window piercings and compressed by a massive roof was averted by the employment of flying buttresses. They became a common external feature of Gothic cathedrals, and architects who shunned their load-bearing capacities in favour of visually untainted external walls risked a legacy of rubble.

Both before and after the two great twelfth-century fires, Chartres' reputation as a place of healing and miracles drew pilgrims from far and wide to worship before the icons of the Virgin Mary. For many people, the physical act of undertaking a pilgrimage was not always attainable, and yet to not make such a journey was deemed a short cut to spiritual disaster. However, in Chartres there existed a viable alternative. Chartres is one of the few remaining pilgrimage destinations still in possession of a labyrinth, and the one inlaid into the nave's west end is by far the finest survivor, giving an authentic link to medieval piety. In terms of one's spiritual salvation, it was the combined mental and physical act of pilgrimage, rather than the distance travelled, that really mattered and the 262-metre-/860-foot-long maze was either walked or negotiated on one's knees. The labyrinth is now frequently obscured by congregational chairs, but on designated days the seating is removed and this complex maze can still be used by twenty-first-century pilgrims.

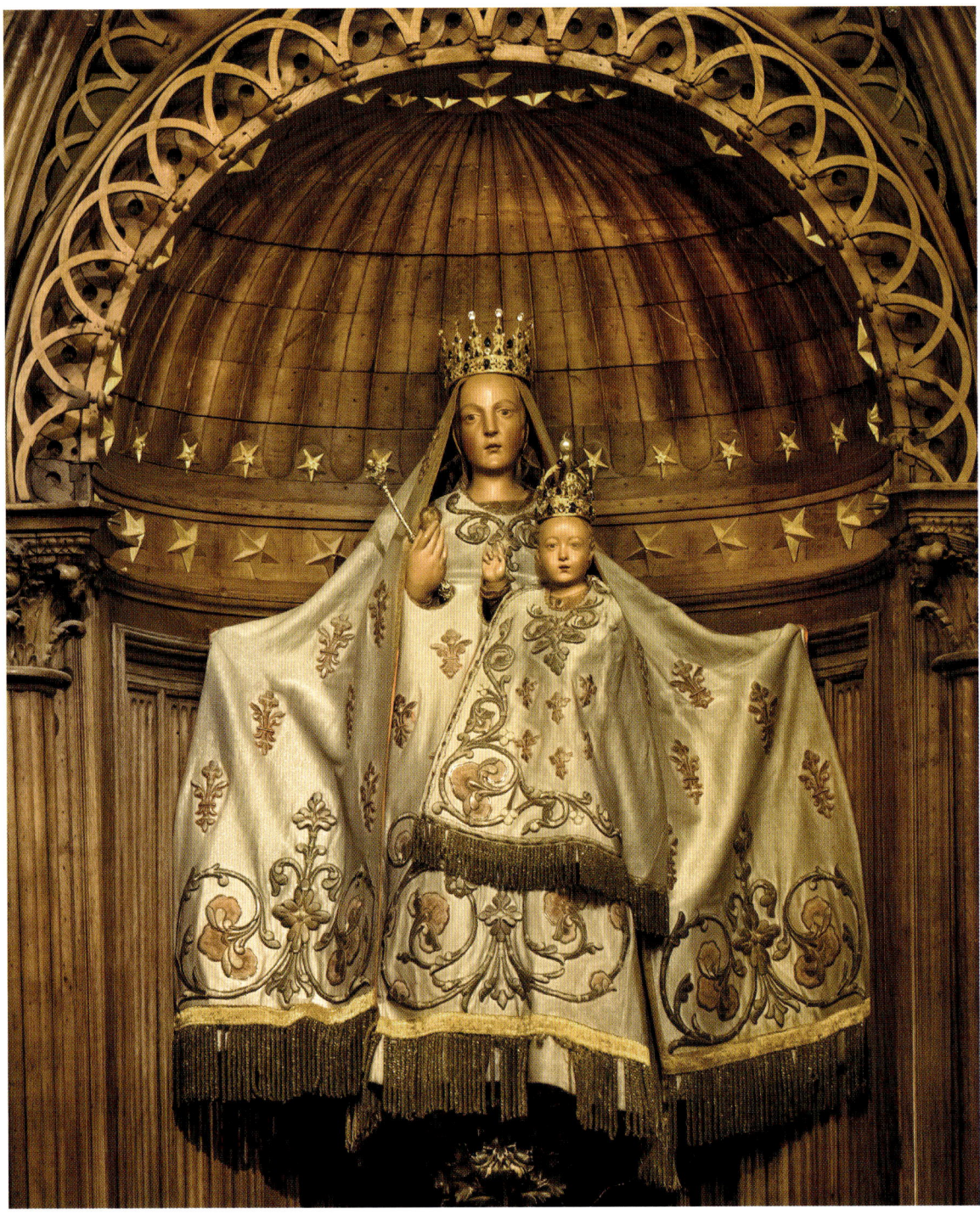

(*above*) The long restoration programme at Chartres Cathedral produced many positive results. Removing the grime and pollution from the stained glass and stone not only ensures continued preservation but also shows visitors what it would have looked like centuries ago. Most of the work has received the highest accolades, but there have been rumblings of discontent that the Black Virgin of the Pillar has been transformed into a somewhat bland sculpture of Mary and the baby Jesus, now sadly devoid of all its original character.

(*right*) Between April and October, Chartres Cathedral and other historic buildings in the city are spectacularly illuminated and either live or recorded music is synchronized with the light show. The artistry and technology involved in this now world-famous event are truly astounding.

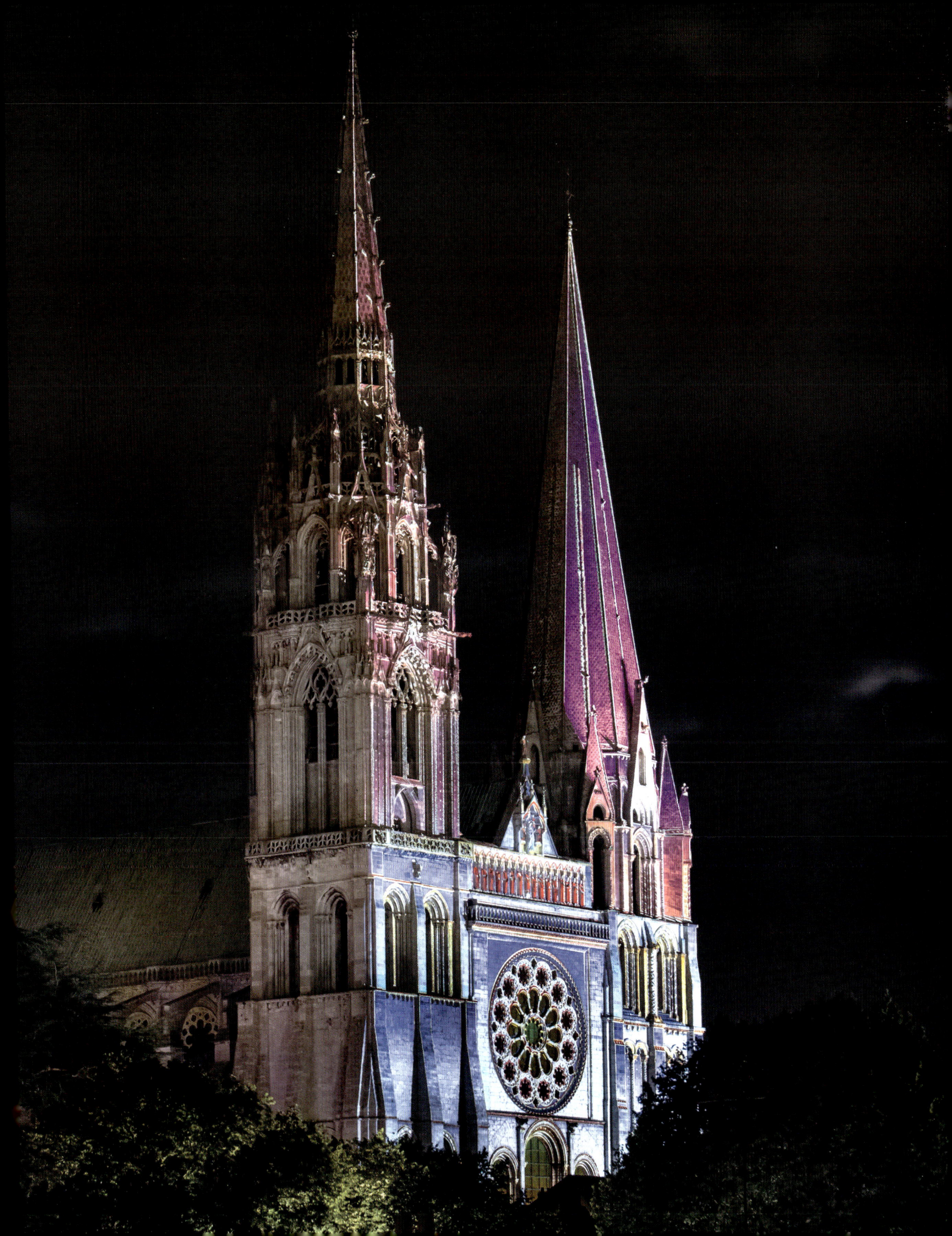

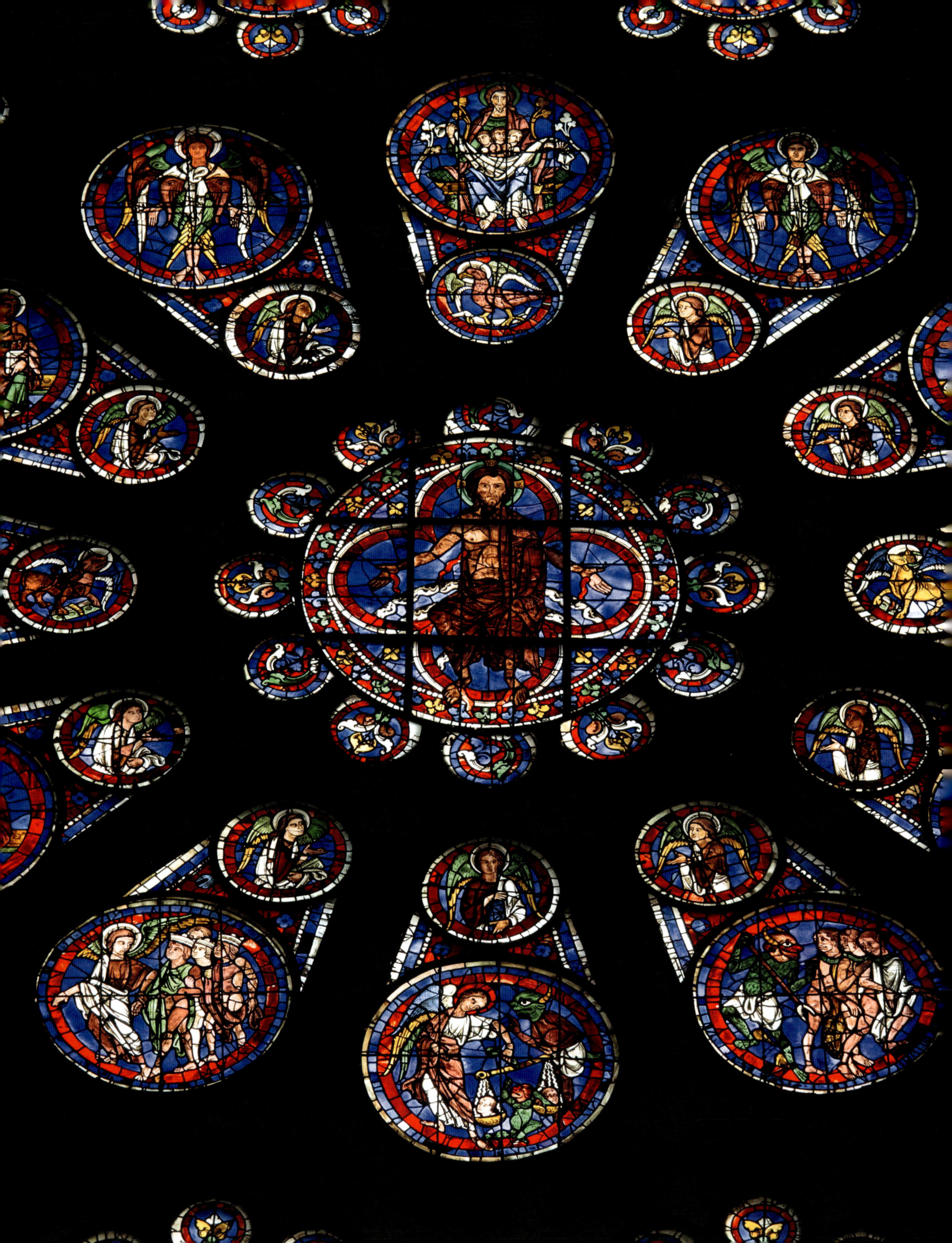

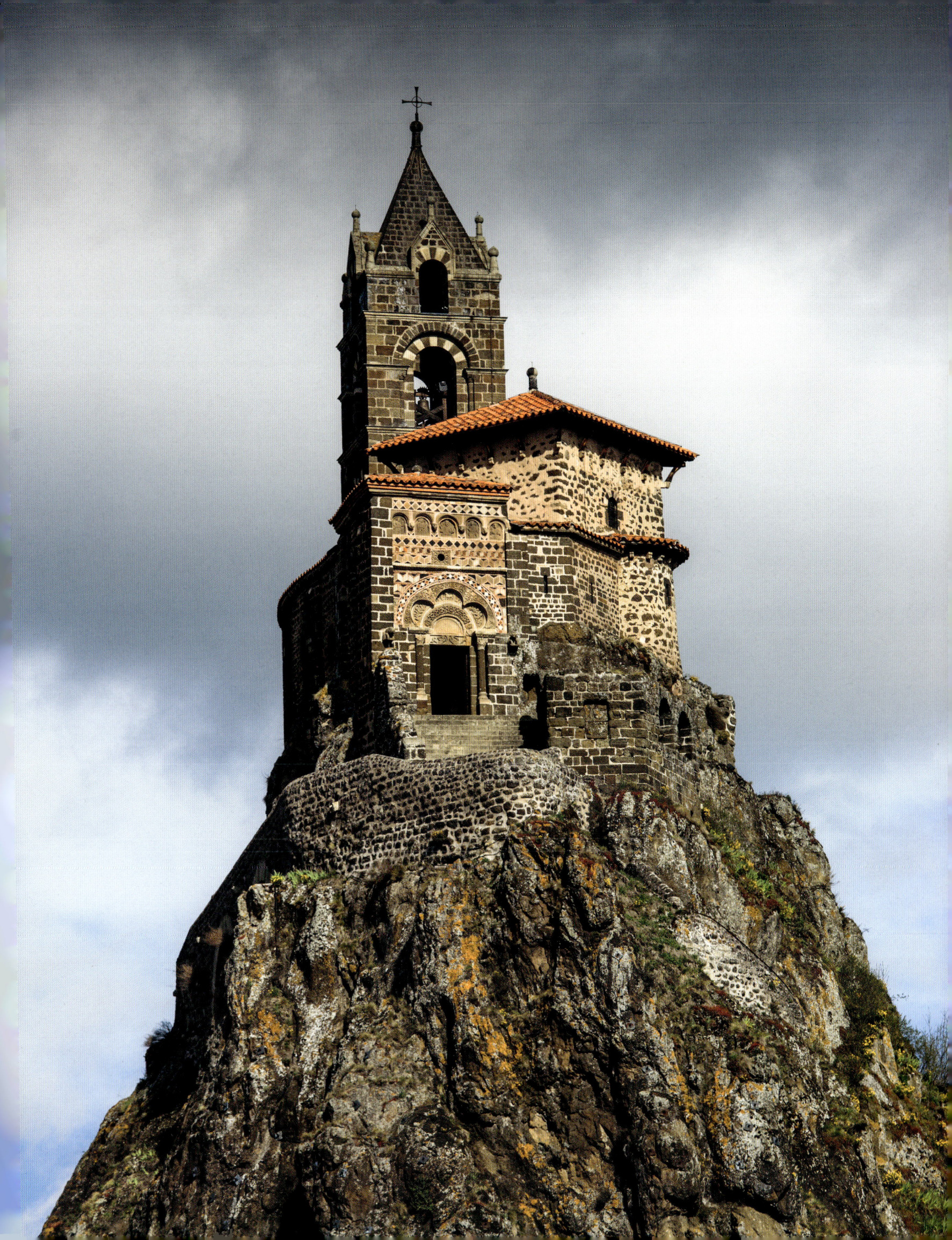

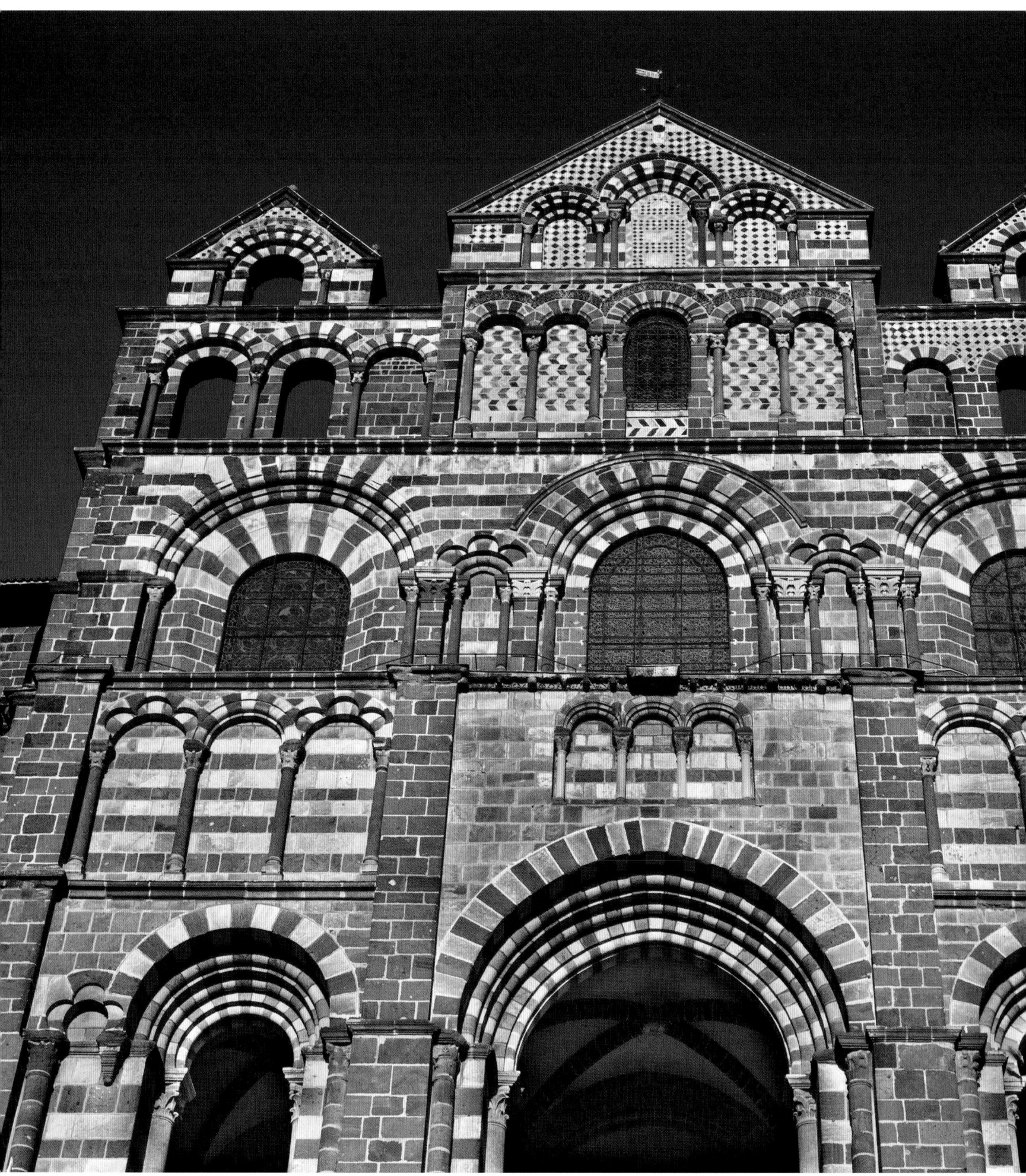

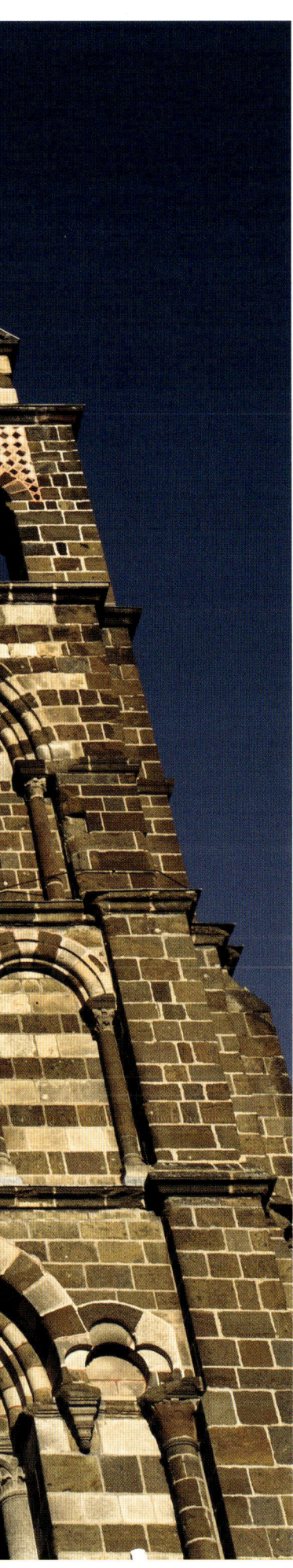

Le Puy is one of France's most distinctive cathedrals. The cathedral's polychromatic Romanesque façade is reminiscent of the style employed in the grand mosque of Cordoba, an architectural cross-pollination that substantiates the well-established cultural links between southern France and the Moorish Empire.

Le Puy's most immediately noticeable landmarks may be set upon volcanic pinnacles but the town's glorious cathedral was also built upon volcanic rock. The base of the Corneille Rock was the platform upon which the Romanesque cathedral of Notre-Dame was built, a site that had existed for centuries as a significant place of Marian pilgrimage. The legend of Le Puy's veneration of the Virgin Mary extends back to the fifth century, when a terminally ill local woman laid upon a dolmen stone to pray for help. She was visited and cured by the Virgin, who in return requested that a church be built in her name. The sanctuary was built upon the site now occupied by the cathedral, and the dolmen, renamed the 'fever stone', still rests inside the cathedral.

Le Puy became a renowned place of pilgrimage and the wealth accrued from donations and endowments enabled the building of a cathedral, one whose fame escalated significantly when St Louis (King Louis IX of France) presented the famous 'Black Virgin' statue upon his return from the Seventh Crusade in 1254. The ebony statue was taken away and burnt during the French Revolution in 1794, but a replacement was created soon after and it is that replica that is still venerated today.

Although not such an arduous journey as visiting St Michel d'Aiguilhe, accessing the cathedral does still necessitate the ascent of a long flight of steps climbing steeply up from the square below. The steps do not simply stop upon arrival at the main portal, but continue upwards into the church, emerging into the heart of the nave. Although possibly perceived as a unique design feature, they were actually created out of sheer necessity because the cathedral builders did not have sufficient rock platform upon which to add the nave's final two bays later in the twelfth century. Consequently, they had to compensate for the steep slope by combining strong piles with the massive arcading that dominates the base of the façade. The blind Romanesque arches and creative use of polychrome granite and black basalt stonework give a strong feeling of Byzantine and Islamic architectural design, the latter influence having spread eastwards from Moorish occupied Spain to be eventually incorporated into some Christian architecture.

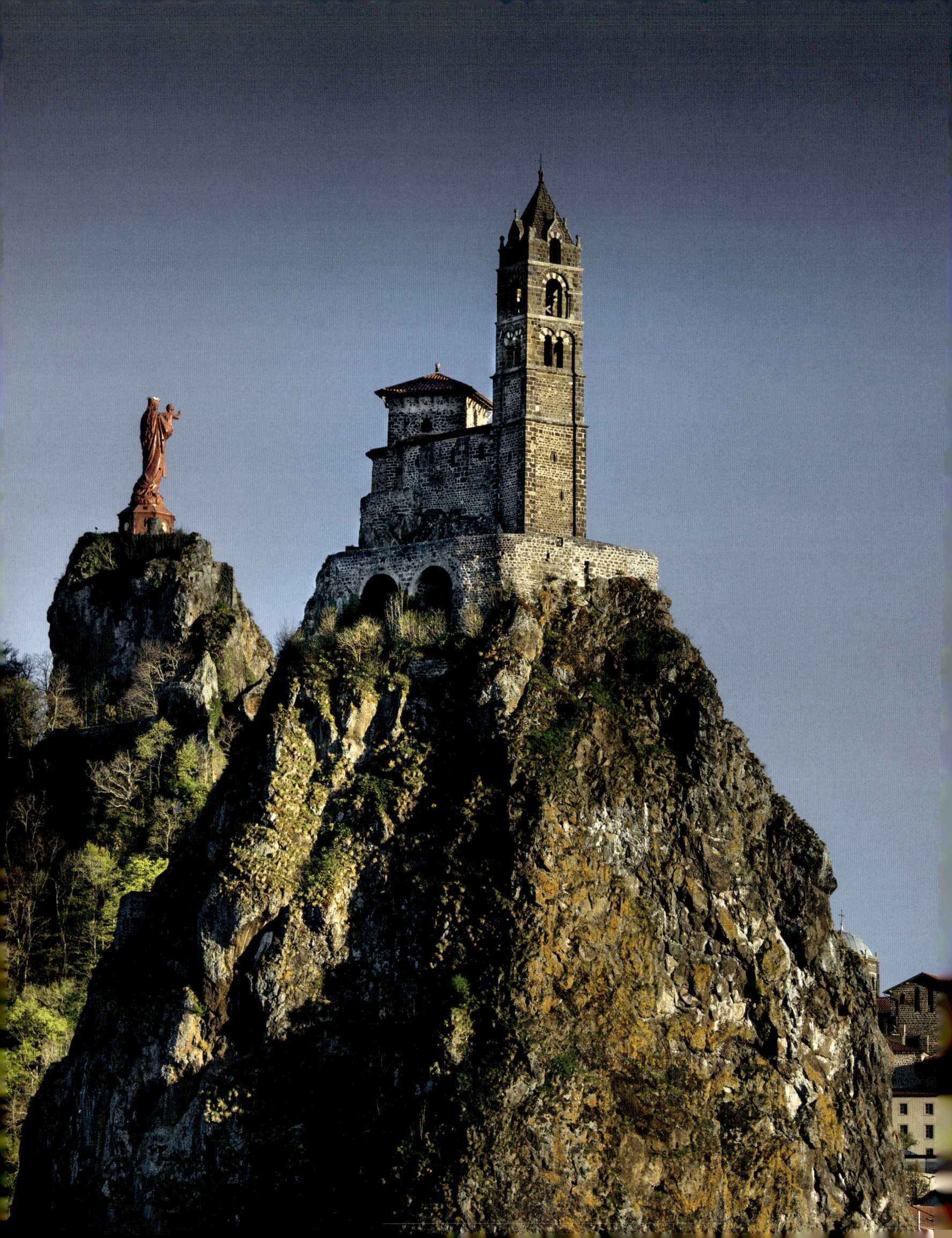

(*left*) The trio of St Michel d'Aiguilhe, Notre-Dame de France and a cathedral also dedicated to the Virgin Mary creates a unique visual composition and there could not be a more uplifting starting point for a pilgrimage to the Pyrenees and across Spain to Santiago de Compostela.

(*below*) Notre-Dame de France was cast from the metal of 213 Russian cannons captured during the Crimean War and gifted to the town by Emperor Napoleon III. The kneeling figure is Archbishop Auguste de Morlhon, who blessed the statue on 12 September 1860.

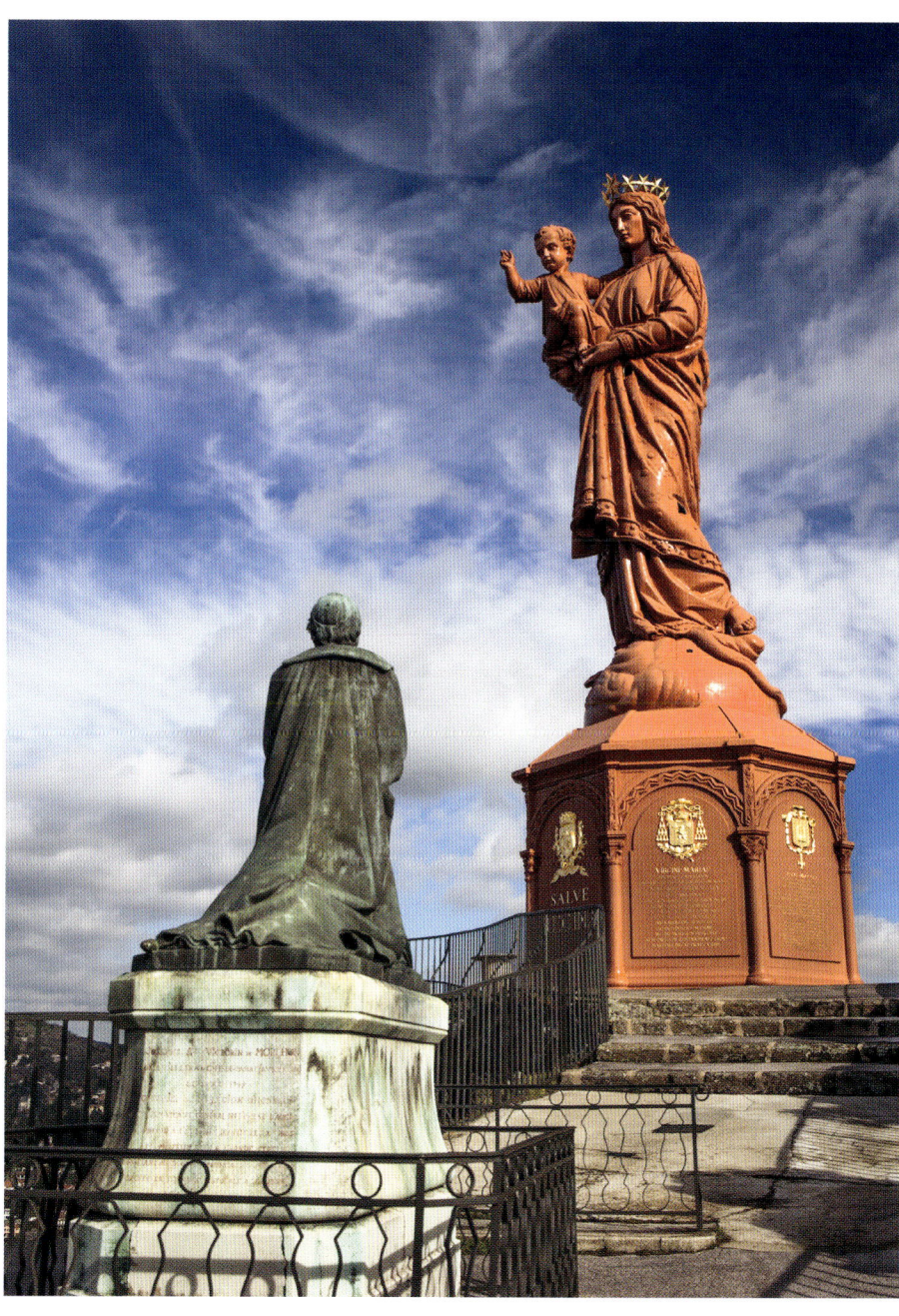

THE SANCTUARY OF OUR LADY OF LA SALETTE
La Salette, Auverne-Rhône-Alpes

The N85 road from Grenoble to the French Riviera is known as the 'Route Napoleon', because it was the one taken back to Paris by the exiled emperor following his escape from the island of Elba in 1815. As the road traverses glorious Alpine scenery on the western fringes of the Écrins National Park between La Mure and Gap, it passes through the village of Corps and it is from here that a 14-kilometre-/8½-mile-long narrow road ascends to the sanctuary of Our Lady of La Salette. Located at 1,800 metres/5,900 feet above sea level, La Salette was the collective name of a scattered group of farming settlements subsequently made famous by the Marian apparition of 1846. The site of that apparition is now occupied by a magnificent basilica and monastery, which is arguably the most atmospheric of all the Marian apparition shrines in Europe. La Salette has no dedicated airport, no vast coach park, no streets crammed with shops selling cheap trinkets; instead, the heavily forested slopes give way to mountain pastures, bare rock and ancient footpaths, where even the most sceptical visitor will surely be moved by such a monumental manifestation of faith.

During the evening of Saturday 19 September 1846, two young farm children, Maximin Giraud (aged eleven) and Mélanie Calvat (aged fourteen), were minding their grazing animals on the mountain plateau when they saw a dazzling light, which gradually dissipated to reveal a 'beautiful lady' clad in white robes, wearing a headdress and slippers both adorned with roses. Her shoulders bore a heavy chain, and the crossbeam of the golden crucifix hanging around her neck bore a hammer and nails at one end and a pair of pincers at the other. The lady sat upon a rock with her head bowed and wept copiously while she addressed the startled children.

The message imparted by the vision of the Virgin Mary centred upon the lamentable disintegration of the Church in the decades following the French Revolution and how she was finding it increasingly difficult to restrain her Son from wreaking havoc upon the people who had seemingly abandoned their faith. She told them that church attendance on the Sabbath had plummeted and working on Sundays had become the norm; as the tears continued to flow, she also cited the fact that cart drivers, labourers and other workers openly blasphemed her Son's name when cursing and swearing.

The sanctuary of Our Lady of La Salette lies within the Écrins National Park to the south of Grenoble. Although it is surrounded by spectacular scenery, the most significant feature is the distant jagged outline of the Dévoluy massif and the dominant peak of Mount Obiou.

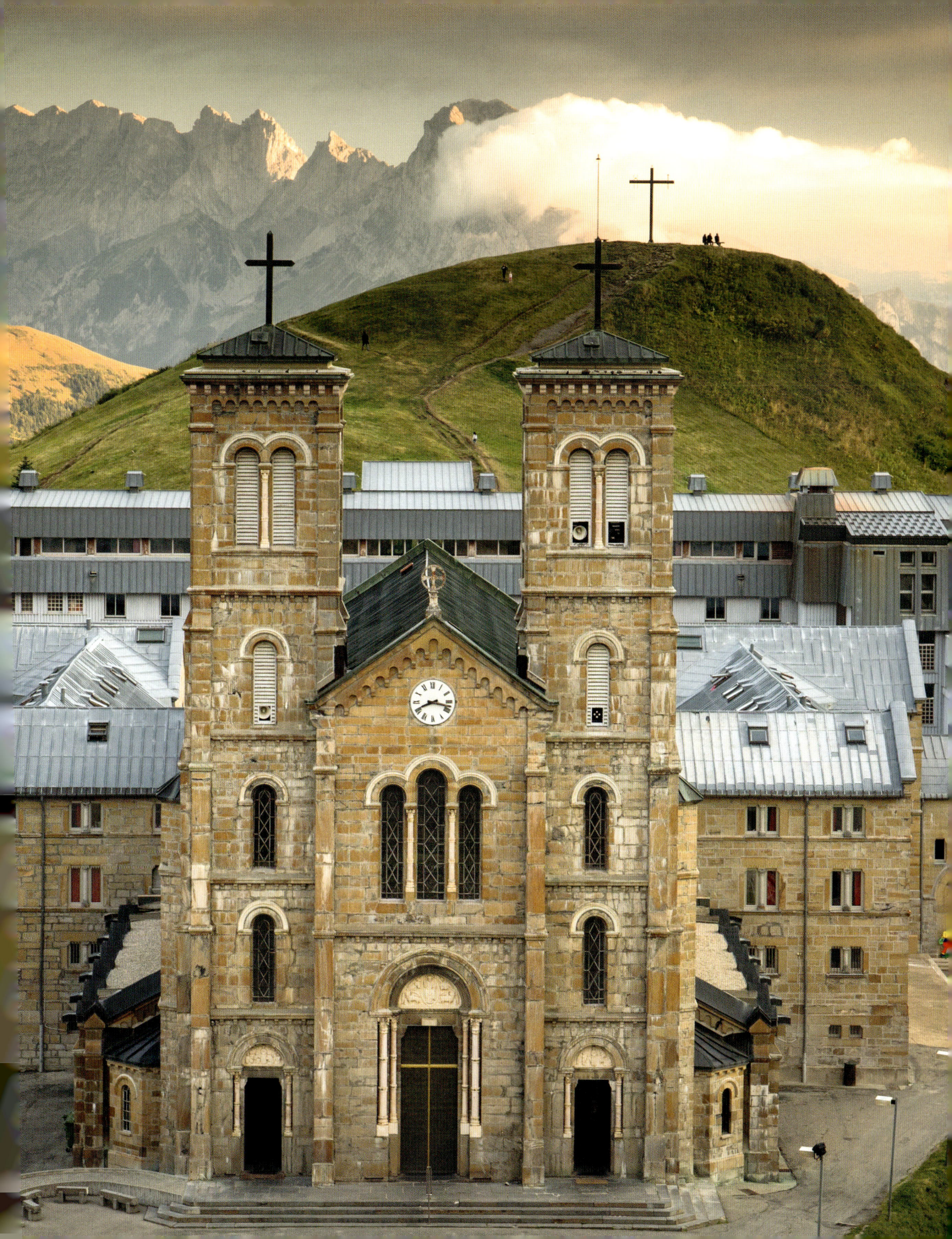

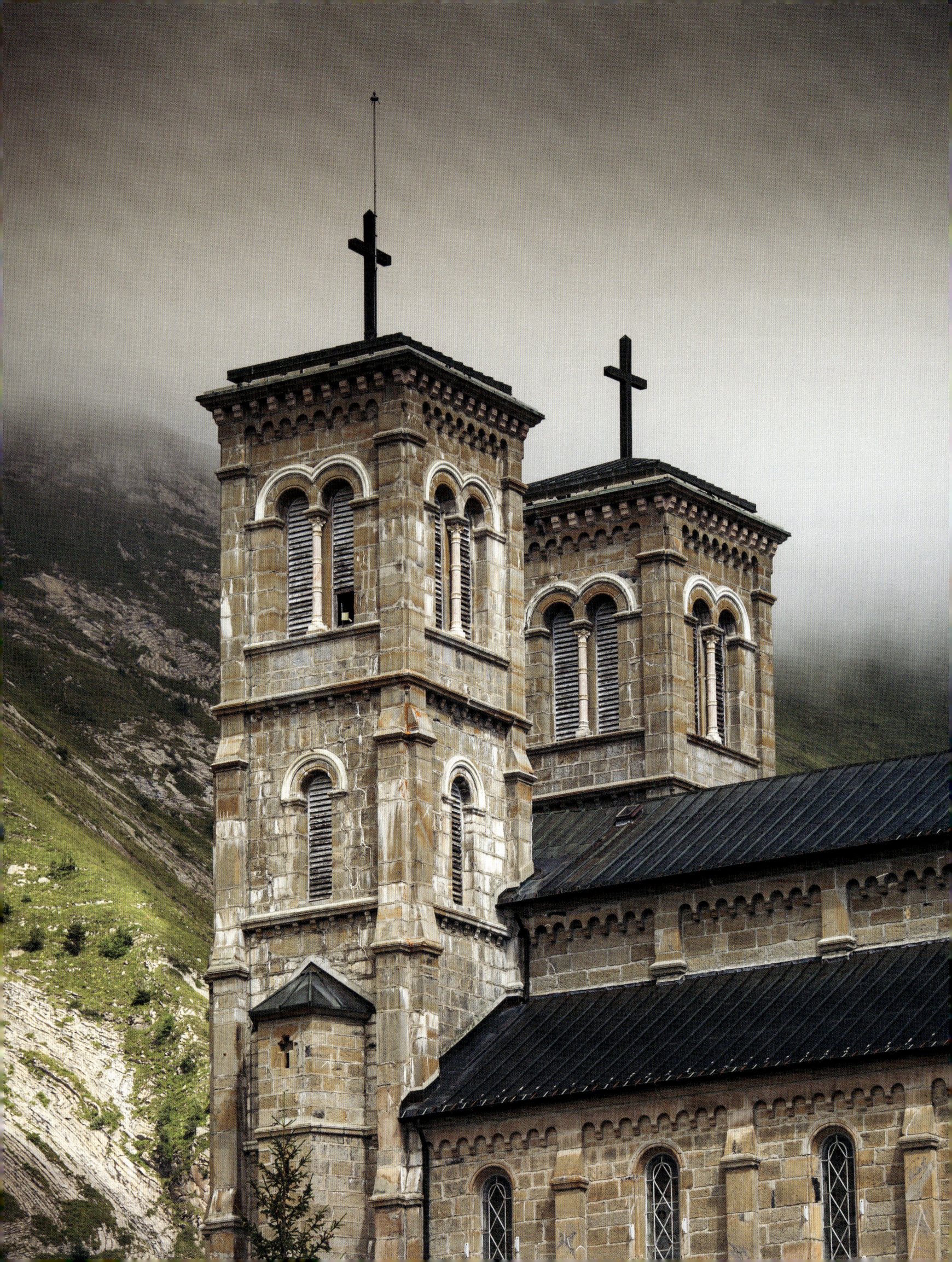

(*left*) The basilica's majestic twin towers serve as a welcoming landmark to pilgrims travelling to La Salette on foot. The site is frequently shrouded in low cloud and mountain mist, but when poor visibility conceals the cross-country routes, the deep, sonorous church bells guide travellers safely to their destination. The robust design and construction of the towers are at one with the rugged Alpine landscape, and the plain neo-Romanesque arches are aesthetically better suited to the setting than the more delicate, pointed style of the Gothic period.

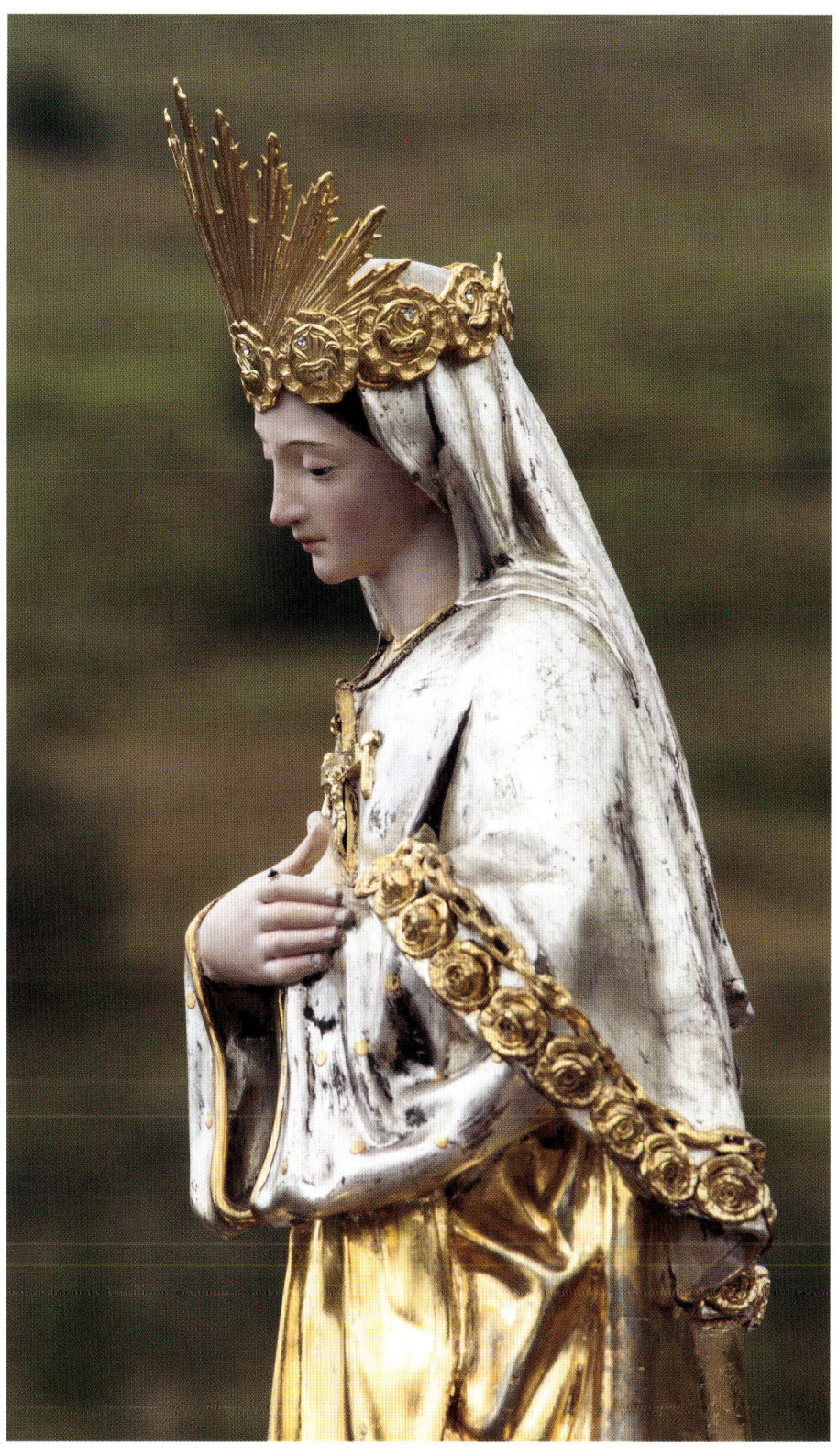

(*above*) The statue of Our Lady of La Salette is always carried from the basilica to lead a symbolic pilgrimage to the Valley of the Apparition after each feast day mass. She is depicted wearing the golden crown described by the children at the apparition.

Although spectacularly glorious on a clear day, the mountain weather can be extremely fickle, and even in the height of summer the pilgrim's outdoor mass can be held amid a thick swirling shroud of cloud and mist, rendering the church and congregation virtually invisible.

The threat of crop failure and famine, if the population did not mend its ways, was the message given to the children. Even though Maximin and Mélanie were barely literate, they were informed that the rediscovery of daily prayers, even in their most basic form, was the only route to salvation. In both France and Ireland, in particular, the mid-1840s were indeed a time of extreme hardship and famine, with potato blight and crop failures making it an era nicknamed the 'hungry forties'. The winter of 1846–7 was particularly bad. When the apparition of the Virgin Mary vanished from view in a searing pool of light, Maximin and Mélanie recounted the experience to their parents in such an earnest and heartfelt manner that the village priest was informed and he began his own investigations. Even when the children were questioned individually, their accounts never wavered nor varied, and despite hostile reaction from some quarters, the priest ultimately had no option but to report the matter to his 'line manager' Philibert de Bruillard, the Bishop of Grenoble. The priest's hand had also been forced by other unexplained events, such as when one of the local investigators broke off a piece of the rock upon which the apparition had been seated and a spring of water gushed from the fissure. A terminally ill woman who then rapidly recovered had apparently drunk the water for nine consecutive days, and there were several other alleged miracles connected to the spring's healing powers. That same source still flows today and it is located next to the shrine, marking the exact location of the encounter.

The most tangible miracle was of a more spiritual nature, namely that the local population had once again begun to attend mass and go to confession, Sunday working became the exception rather than the perceived norm and pilgrimages to the site of the encounter became more and more frequent. France had always been at the forefront of the veneration of the Mother of God and vast numbers of its churches and cathedrals were dedicated to the Virgin Mary, not least during the twelfth century when cathedral building proliferated to an extraordinary degree. Although less than half a century had elapsed since the desecration inflicted upon both the ethos and fabric of religion by the Revolution, embedded love and devotion drove the bishop onwards in his quest to have the encounter officially recognized as a genuine apparition.

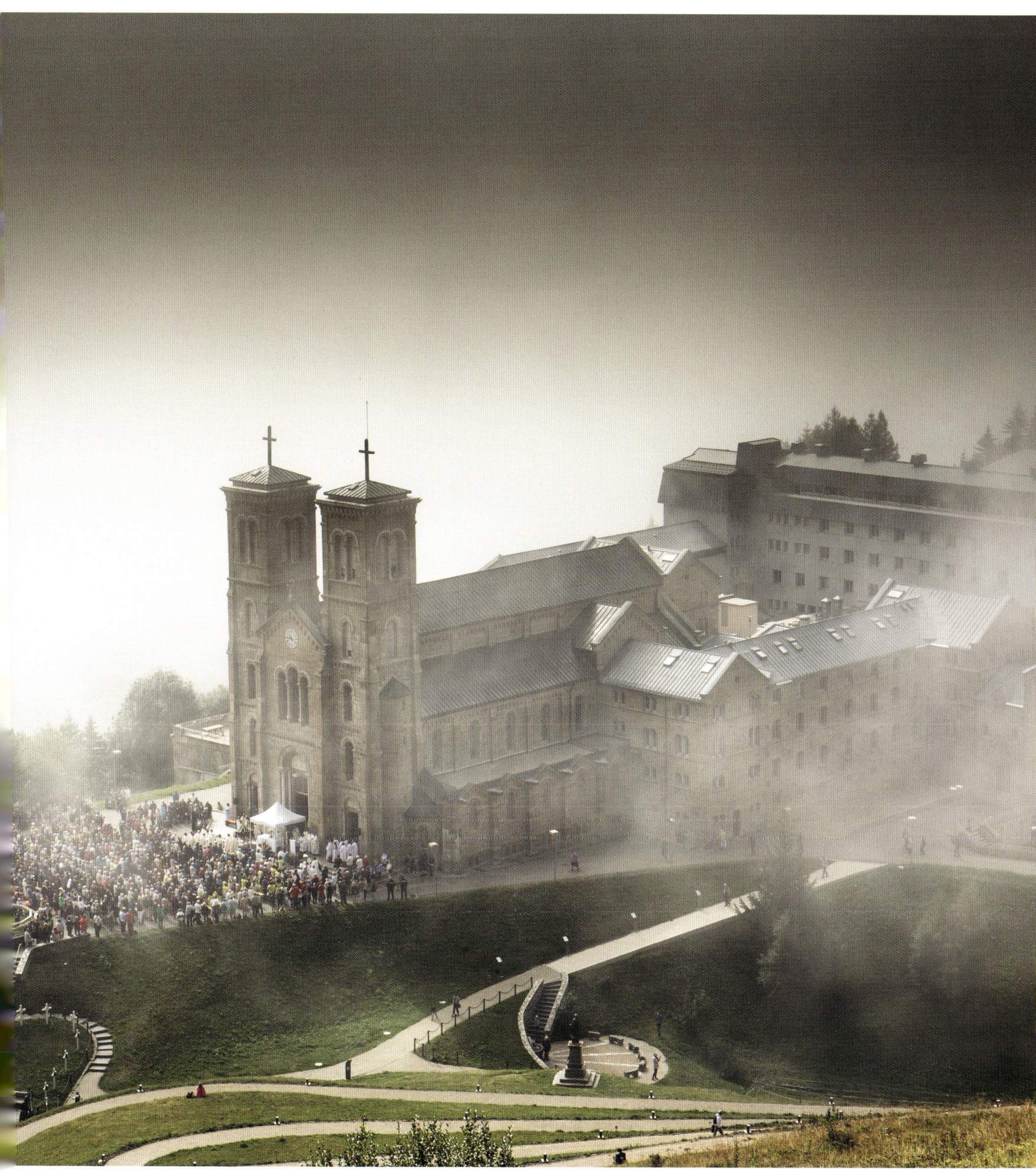

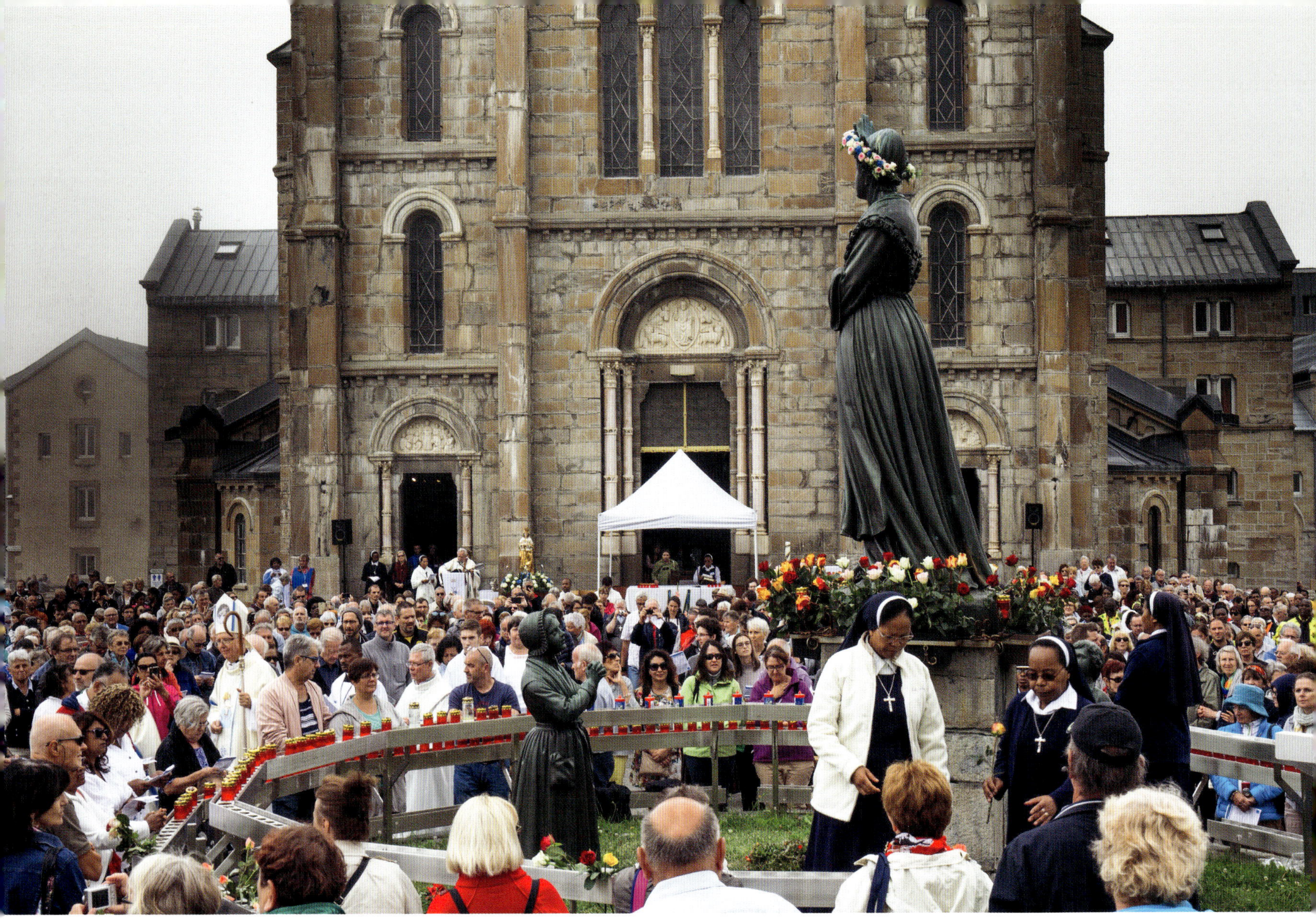

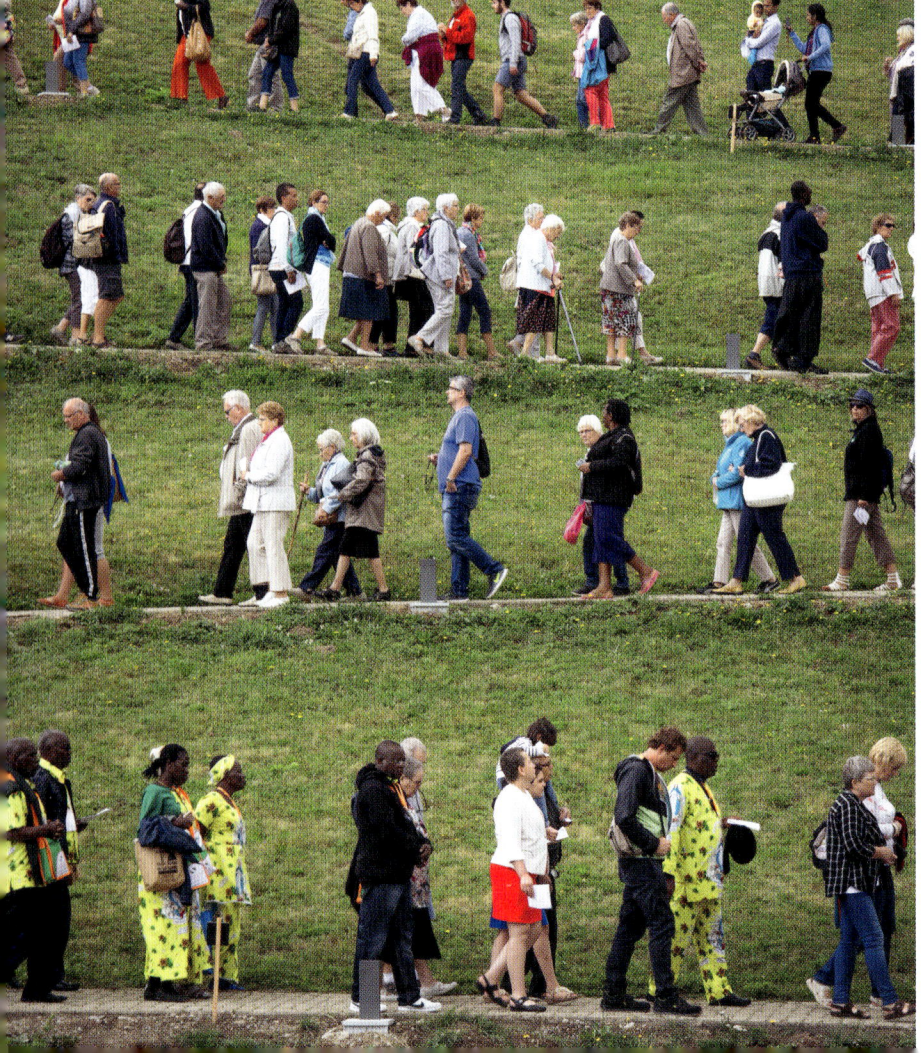
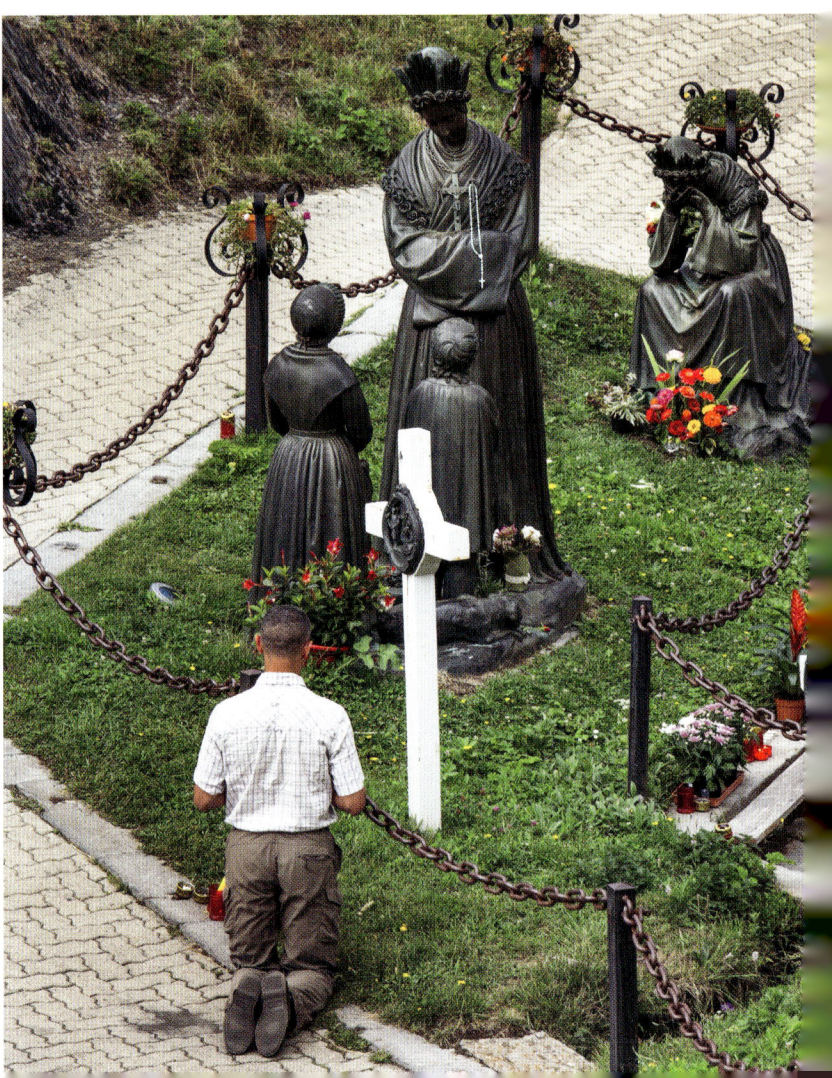

(*top*) The votive shrine of Our Lady of La Salette stands near the basilica's main portal and it is a focal point for pilgrims attending outdoor masses. It is especially atmospheric at night when the statue is bathed in soft candlelight. (*bottom left*) An important part of the feast day ritual at La Salette is the walk of contemplation around the Valley of the Apparition. (*bottom right*) The shrine marks the location of the apparition. (*overleaf*) The night-time candlelit procession from the basilica is said to be a very moving experience.

After five years of investigation, and with both the children and their bishop having faced much hostility and threats of physical violence and imprisonment, the matter came to a conclusion in November 1851, when Bishop Bruillard made an official pronouncement that the apparition was perfectly valid. One year later, the cornerstone of the mighty church was laid.

Our Lady of La Salette was completed in 1862 and subsequently elevated to the status of a basilica in 1879. The austerity of the church's exterior appropriately reflects the harshness of its mountain environment, but the interior is significantly more welcoming and its builders have creatively drawn upon different architectural styles, including Romanesque vaulted ceilings supported by Byzantine columns. Even on days when the wind howls ferociously through the mountain pass outside, the interior of Notre-Dame manages to sustain a calm aura of welcoming and reflective tranquillity.

Directly adjacent to the basilica is the Valley of the Apparition, where a pilgrimage path snakes down the hillside in tight serpentine loops to the actual site of the children's encounter with the Virgin. There, a shrine adorned by a group of bronze statues was erected in 1864 to mark the event. There are many festivals and special services held throughout the year, but the two most important are the Feast of the Assumption of the Virgin Mary held in mid-August and the celebration of the apparition itself on 18 and 19 September. For both events, there are outdoor pilgrim masses, and the highlight of each day's series of prayer vigils or masses is a candlelit procession. Pilgrims follow behind a litter borne by several priests, who transport the basilica's magnificent statue of Our Lady of La Salette around the illuminated Valley of the Apparition.

Our Lady of La Salette offers hostel facilities to individual travellers, families or groups of pilgrims, and regardless of one's personal religious beliefs, for those who stay the night, either 'on retreat' or as a base for walking the many cross-country trails, the experience of being amid the silence and special atmosphere of this unique Alpine sanctuary will live long in the memory.

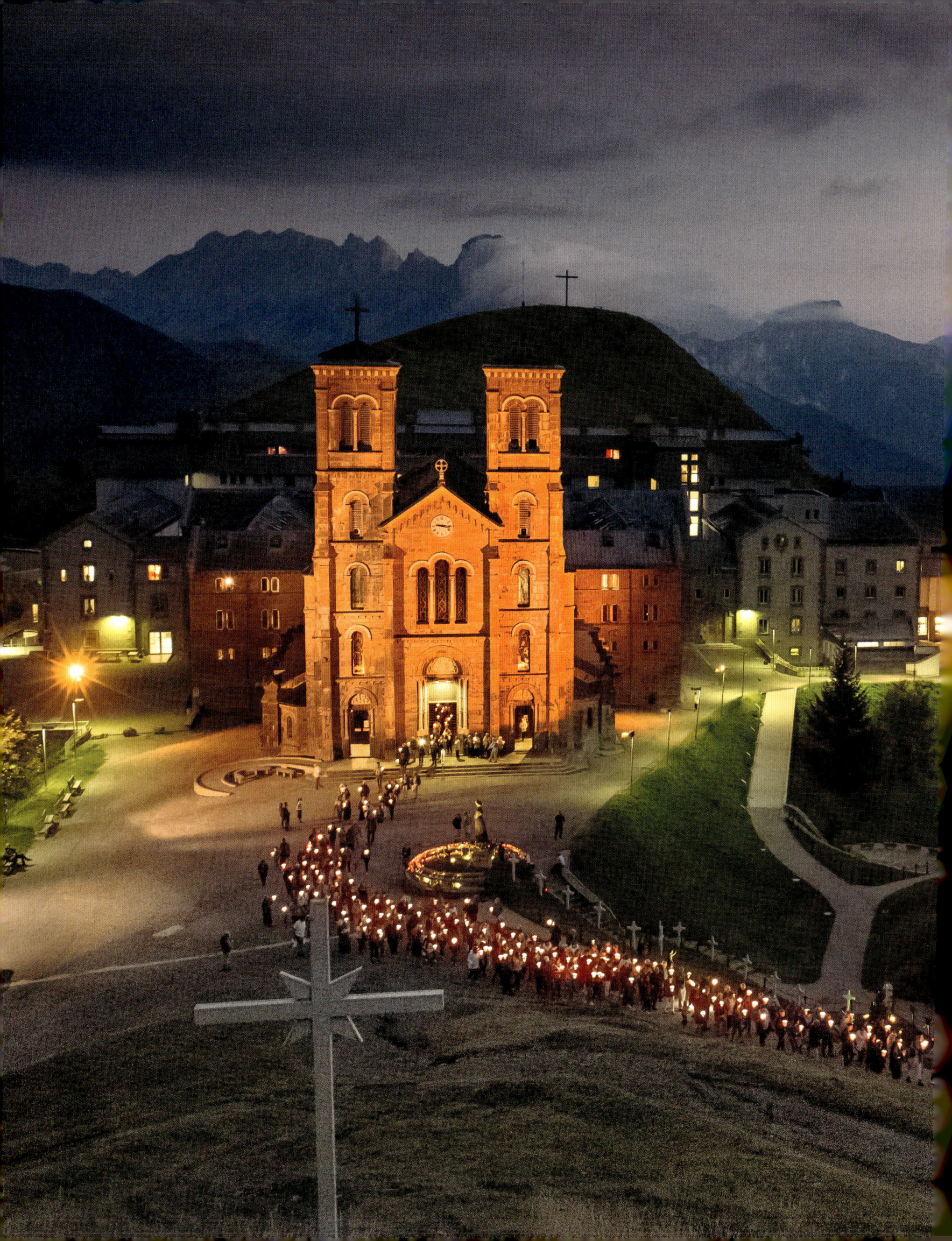

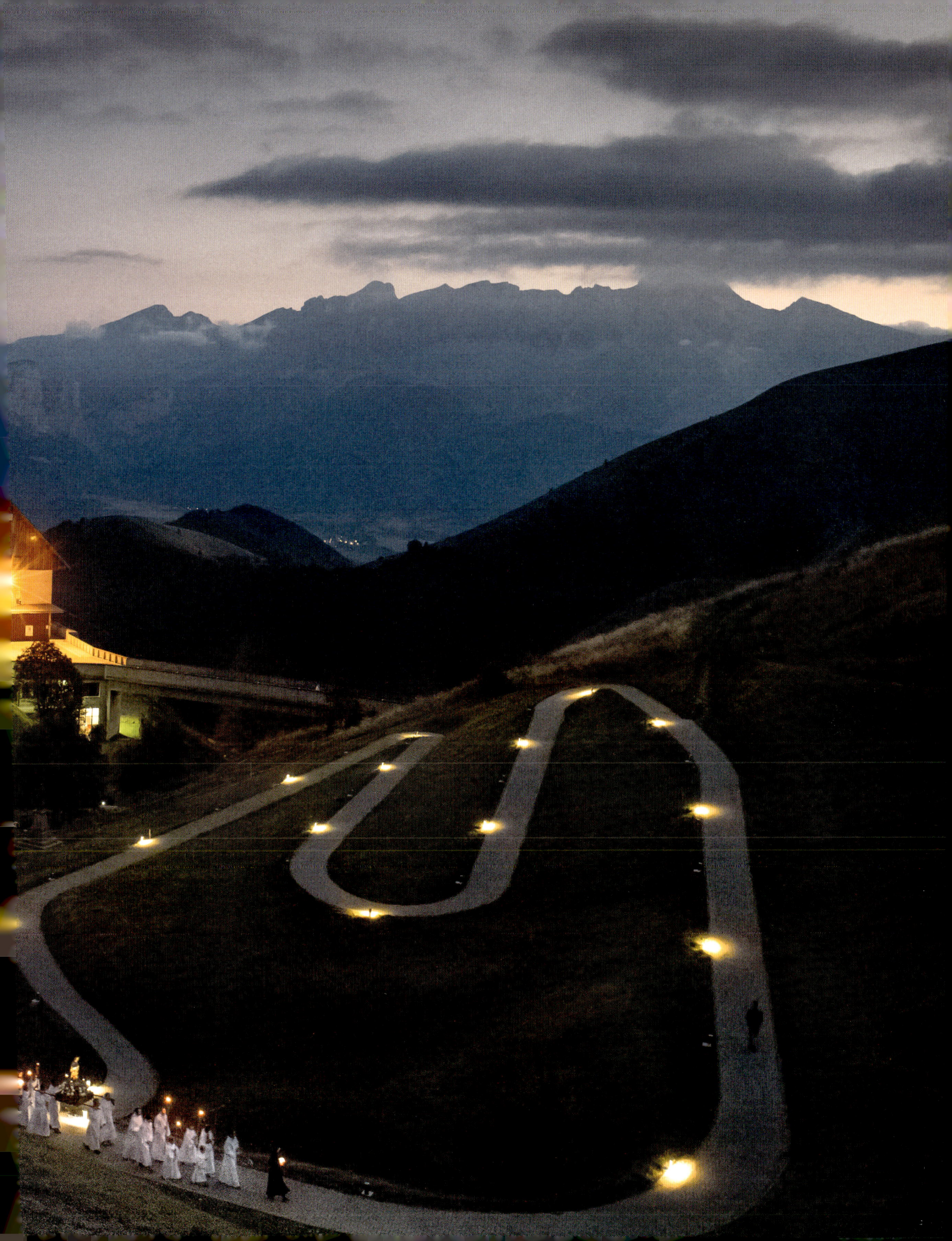

THE SANCTUARY OF OUR LADY OF LOURDES
Lourdes, Hautes-Pyrénées

Prior to the mid-nineteenth century, Lourdes was a small country mill town in the Pyrenean foothills of south-west France. However, on 11 February 1858, the first of seventeen Marian apparitions appeared to a young local girl, thus fuelling the town's rapid elevation to a significant pilgrimage destination. Bernadette Soubirous was the largely illiterate fourteen-year-old chosen to receive the visitations, but she met with much hostility from both Church and State before her accounts were reluctantly accepted as genuine and worthy of official recognition. The Soubirous family had sadly fallen on hard times due to industrial advances in the milling industry, which had rendered her father's water mill superfluous. As a result of financial hardship, they were evicted from their home in 1854. The family soon descended into extreme poverty and they were forced to live in derelict mill buildings and other uninhabitable dwellings until they finally ended up in Le Cachot, a damp, one-room dwelling previously used as a prison cell. This dire environmental situation made Bernadette's ill health worse, as she suffered from bronchitis and severe bouts of asthma.

On the first day of the apparitions, she was collecting firewood in the vicinity of Massabielle, a large rocky outcrop with a cave at its base set alongside the fast-flowing Gave de Pau river. As her friends waded across to the river's far bank, Bernadette was somehow drawn towards the grotto, which was where the first event happened. It manifested in the form of a gushing wind and a faint glow of light emanating from a rock fissure, from which a smiling girl dressed in white briefly emerged before disappearing. At a later encounter, Bernadette was instructed to drink from what was merely a patch of mud, but, although unwilling to disobey, she found it impossible to fulfil the request until a stream of water suddenly gushed out of the ground from a hitherto unknown spring.

Her companions and other townsfolk who had started to accompany Bernadette to the grotto were becoming increasingly bemused by the visits because only Bernadette could see and communicate with the smiling girl. However, they not only witnessed the new source of water, but more significantly noticed a marked change in Bernadette's health and behaviour. Her asthma abated and she seemed permanently endowed with an uncharacteristically serene demeanour, a trait that increased with every new visitation.

When viewed from Lourdes' imposing hilltop castle, the majority of the sanctuary's vast estate is obscured by trees, leaving the slender, neo-Gothic towers of the upper basilica as the most dominant feature. The church is built directly over the grotto of the apparitions.

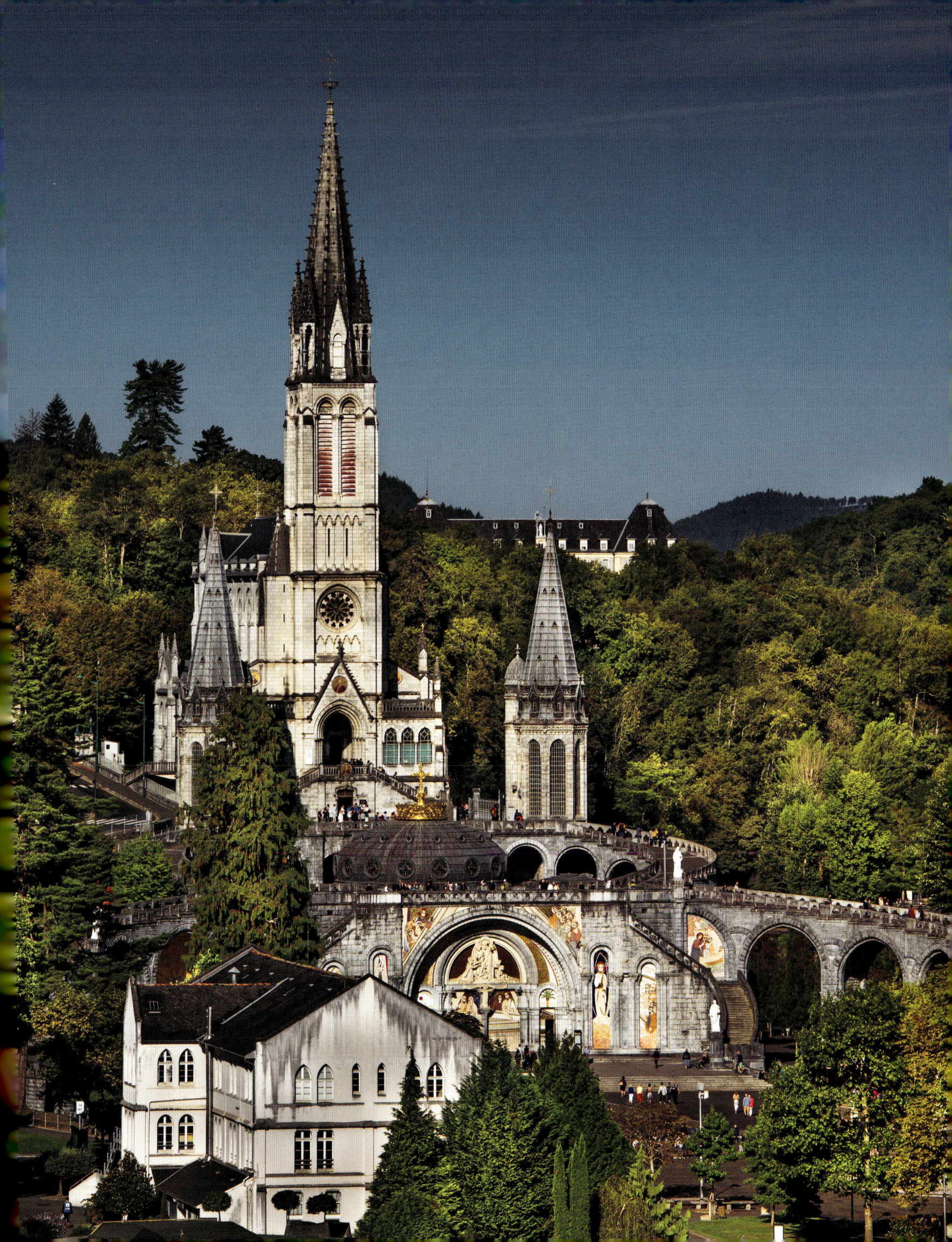

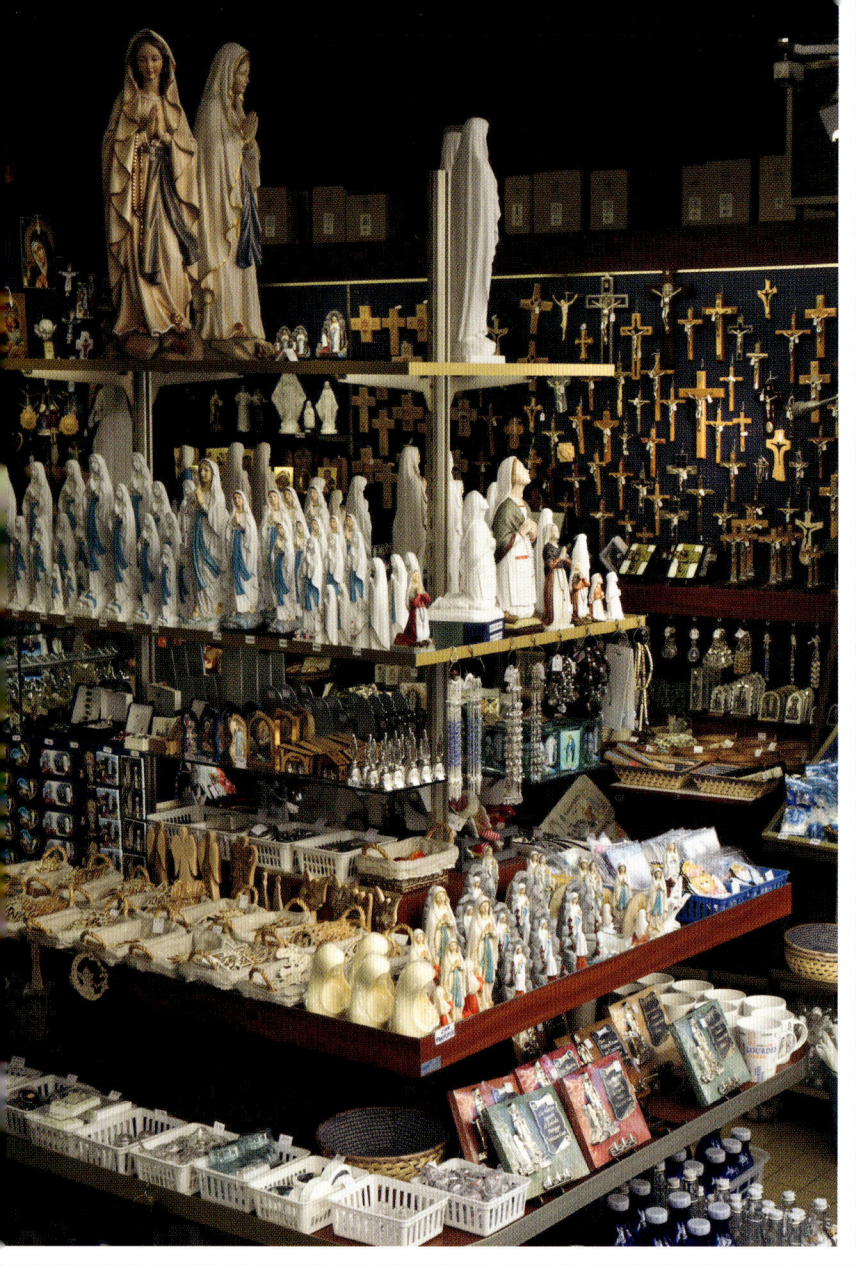
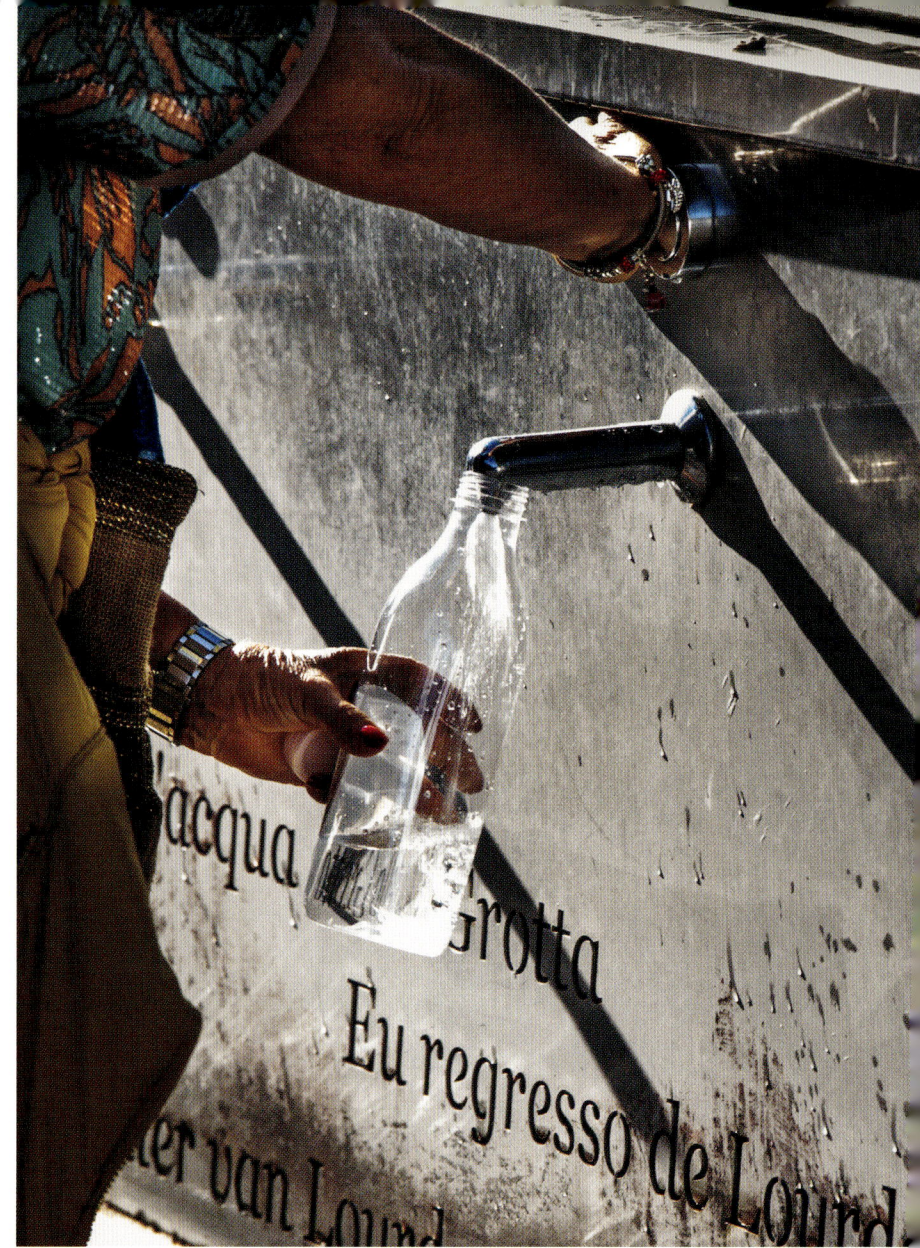

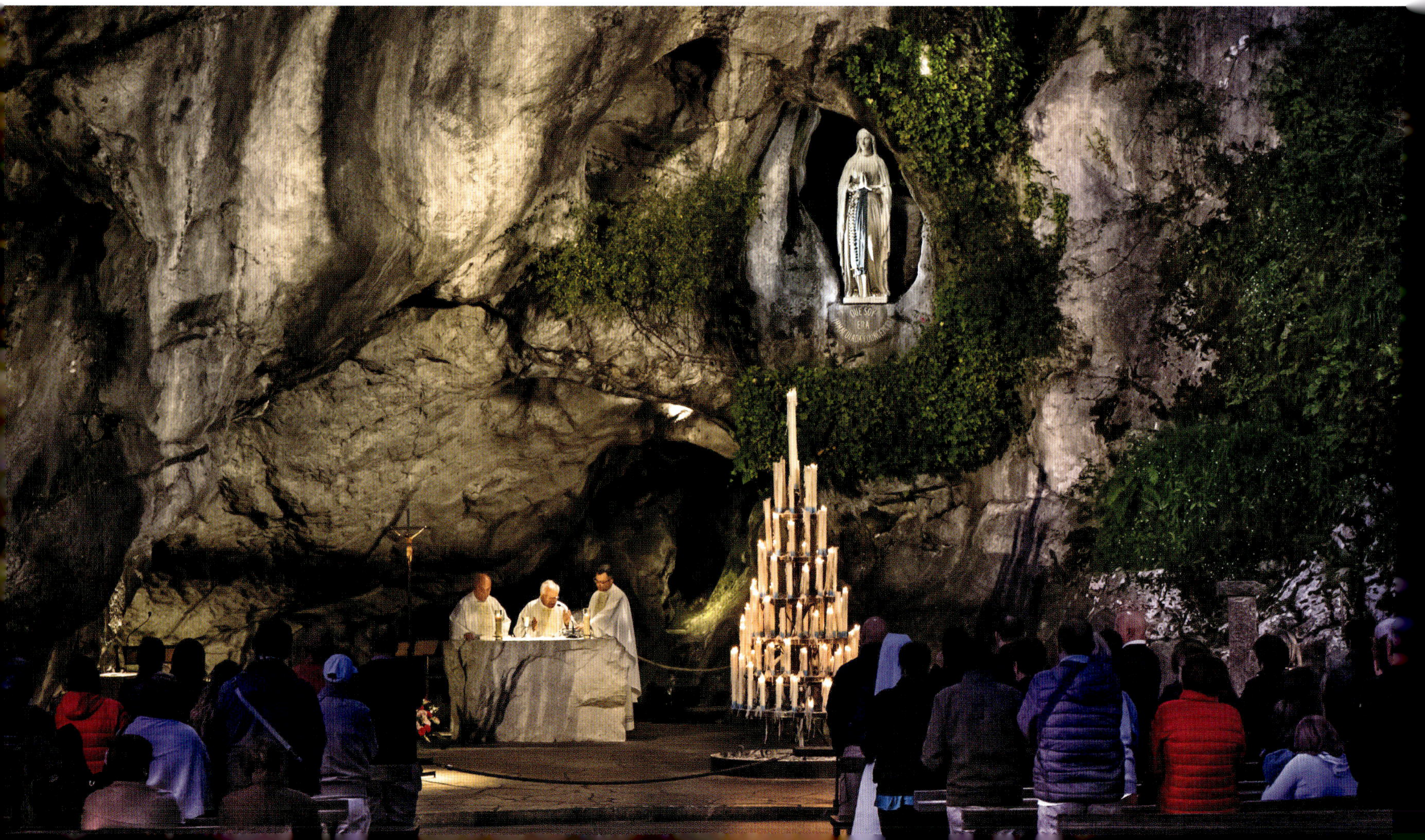

(*top left*) Pilgrimage and tourism are irrevocably entwined in Lourdes and every possible kind of memento is available from a plethora of gift shops. Plastic bottles emblazoned with pertinent images are hugely popular for collecting water from the miraculous spring. (*top right*) Visitors draw water from the sanctuary's array of taps linked directly to the 'holy spring'. Scientific tests have revealed that it is 'just water', but there remains unfettered belief in its healing properties. (*bottom*) Night-time masses held in the grotto have a memorable atmosphere.

At one of the later encounters, Bernadette was instructed to tell the clergy that they should build a chapel by the grotto. However, when she passed on this message to the local priest, Father Peyremale, he responded angrily by suggesting that this alleged holy vision should identify herself if she was to have any credence. That is precisely what happened next, because on 25 March, the day of the Annunciation, Bernadette repeatedly asked the young girl in white who she was and was rewarded with a simple answer: 'I am the Immaculate Conception.'

The priest was astounded by this response because there was no way a simple peasant girl could have any knowledge of that phrase or its meaning, especially as it was only four years earlier, in 1854, that Pope Leo IX had officially pronounced the Catholic Church's acceptance that Jesus Christ had been conceived without original sin. Consequently, his attitude changed to such an extent that when Bernadette was later hounded and persecuted Father Peyremale became her staunchest defender. Soon, the new spring was being credited with possessing healing properties, as locals with physical ailments and deformities were cured after drinking the water. Officialdom started to get anxious, though, and Bernadette was harassed and examined by government officials, psychologists and Church hierarchy. She was pronounced to be mentally and emotionally sound by eminent doctors, but the authorities became increasingly worried about this uncontrollable phenomenon for which they had neither comprehension nor a rulebook to guide them. The inevitable first response was to close access to the grotto, but the word of miracles associated with Lourdes was rapidly spreading and nothing could stop the increasing tide of pilgrims. The bishop was forced to accept the validity of the apparitions and formally approved the shrine in 1862, just four years after the initial encounter between Bernadette and the Virgin Mary.

Despite having appeared to be in better health, Bernadette never really managed to shrug off her lifelong ailments, sadly made worse by the constant pressure of being perceived as either a conduit to the Mother of God or nothing but a troublemaker. The railway arrived in 1866, and more and more pilgrims flooded into Lourdes. Bernadette decided that enough was enough and she joined the Sisters of Charity at their convent in Nevers that same year. She remained there until her death from tuberculosis in 1879.

72 GREAT PILGRIMAGE SITES OF EUROPE

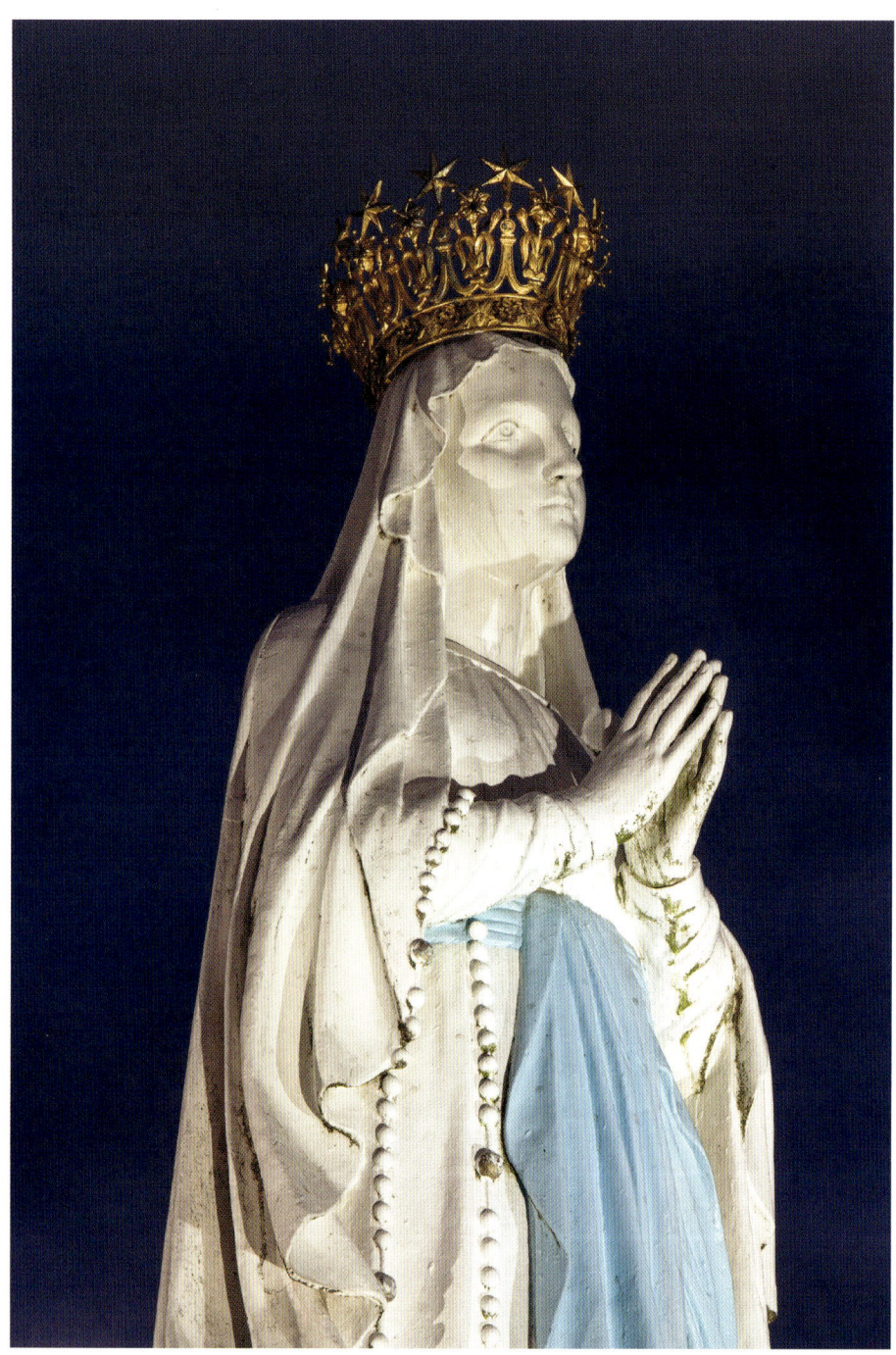

(*above*) The statue of the Virgin Mary was erected in front of the basilica in 1864, but Bernadette did not approve, deeming it 'far too big and too old'. Experts had apparently decided that at the time of the Annunciation, Mary would have been around seventeen years old. Bernadette, though, was insistent that the girl she had seen was no older than twelve.

(*overleaf*) The basilica and statue of the Virgin Mary photographed in the final moments of a dramatic sunset and immediately prior to the hugely popular candlelit procession.

(*right*) The Rosary Basilica is one of the three churches built above and adjacent to the grotto of the apparitions. The large dome surmounting the Byzantine-influenced nave is adorned with a gilded golden crown and cross, donated by the Catholic fraternity of Ireland in 1924.

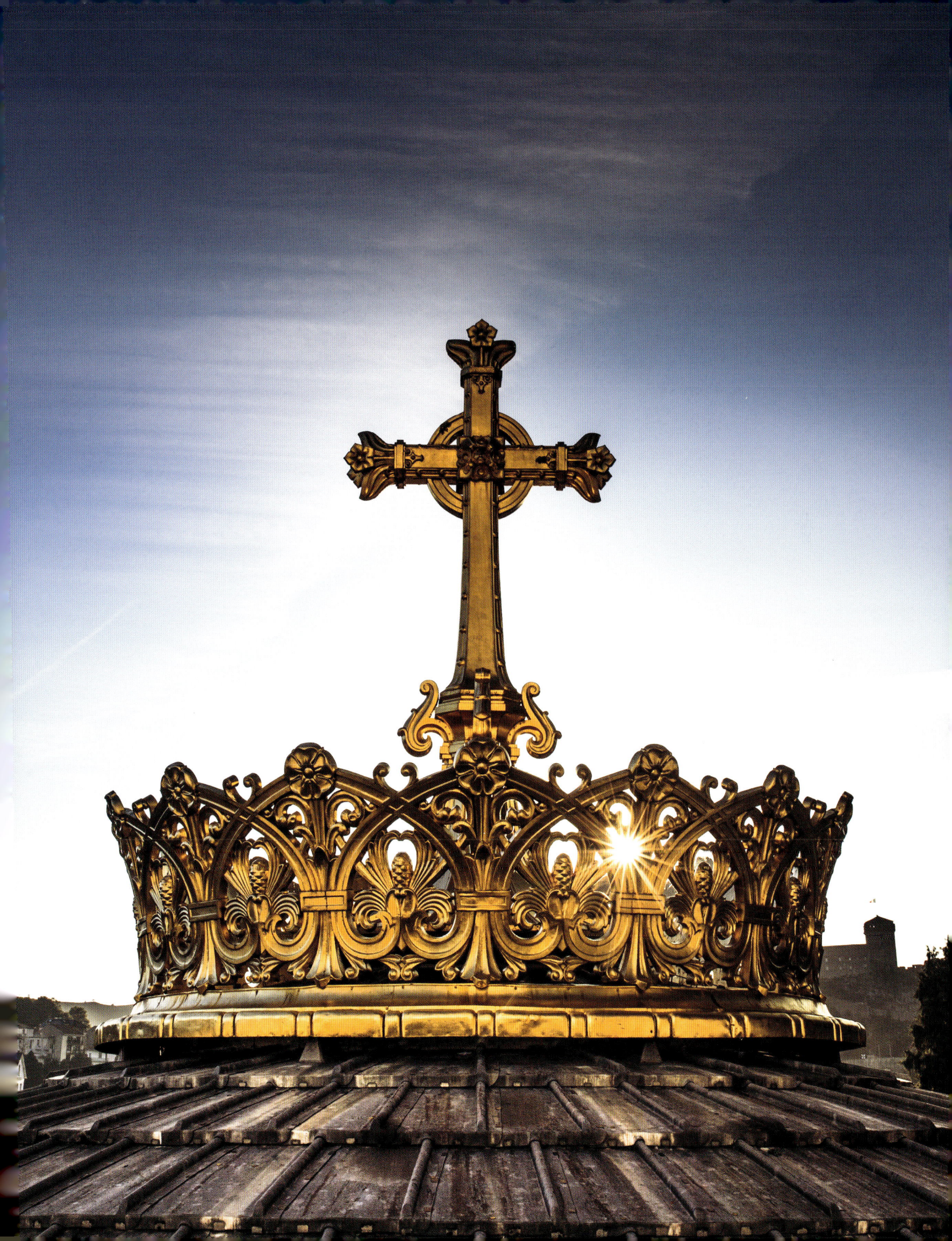

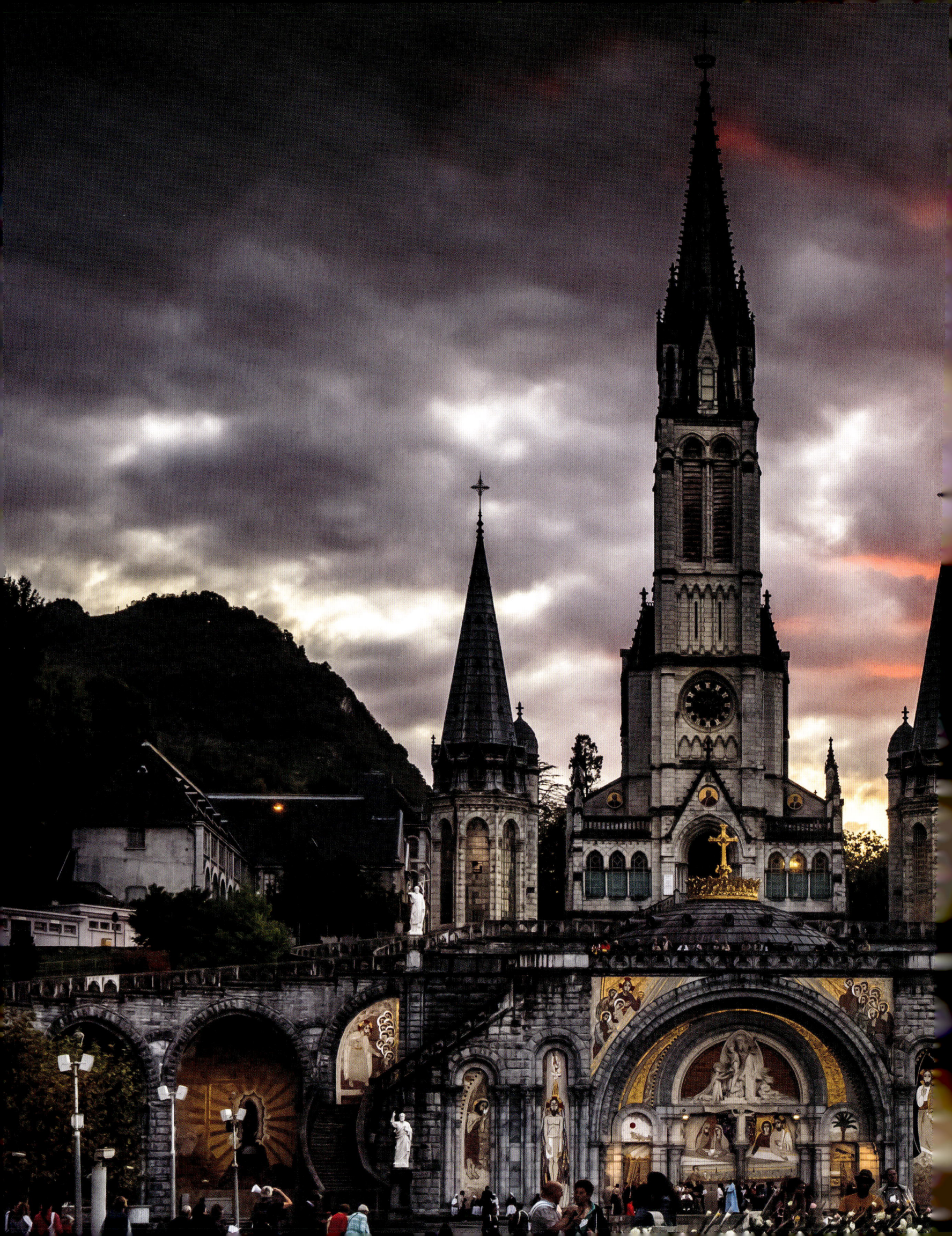

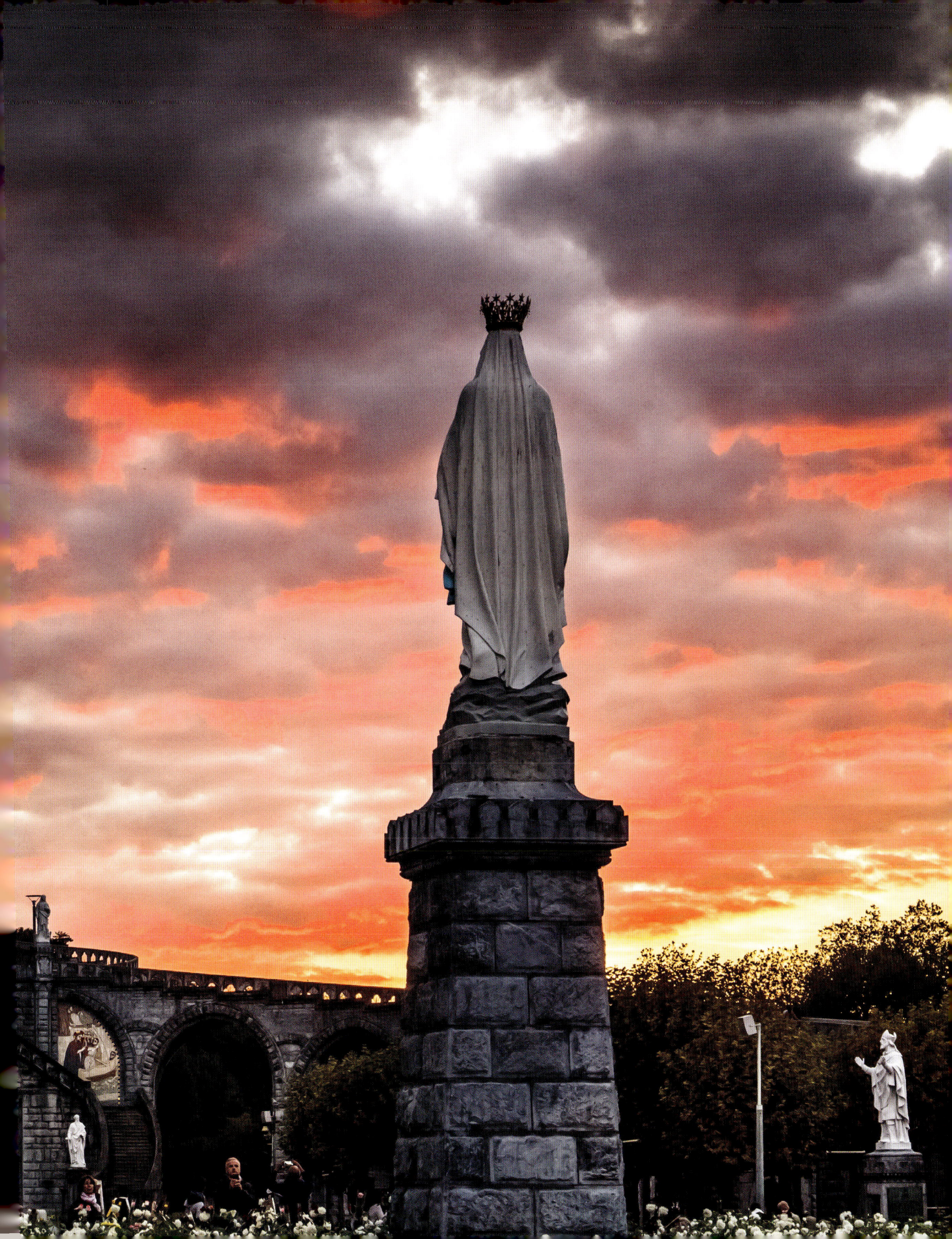

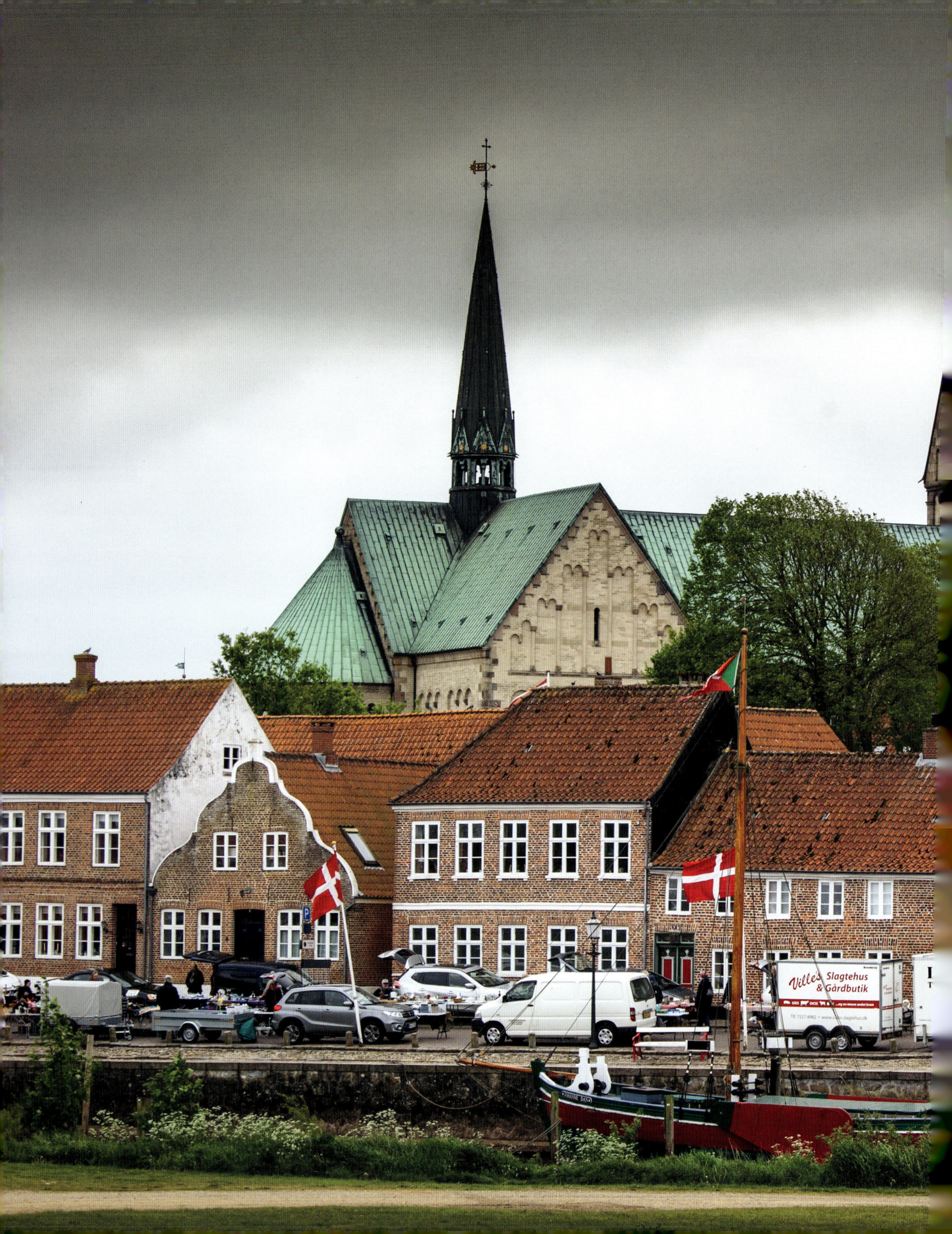

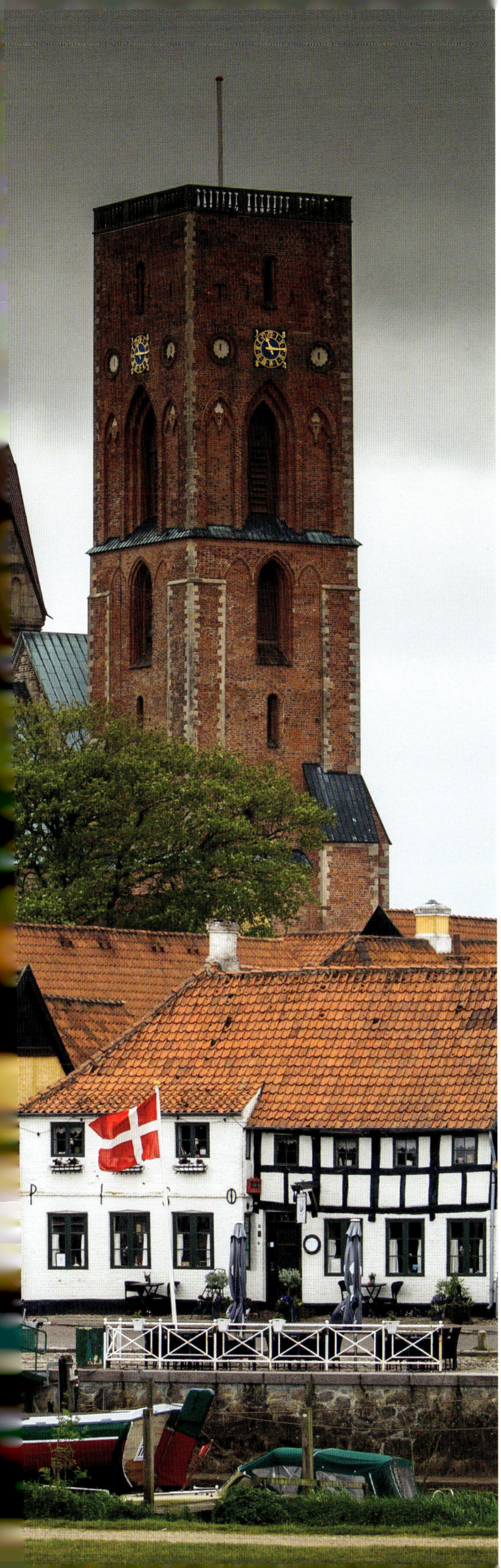

3

DENMARK, NORWAY AND SWEDEN

DENMARK

RIBE CATHEDRAL (THE CHURCH OF OUR LADY)
Ribe, Jutland

Ribe is Denmark's oldest town and it is located on the south-west coast of Jutland, the peninsula protruding from the German mainland. The town is linked to the sea by a tidal river and this direct access to northern Europe shaped Ribe's religious and architectural history. Vessels line the quayside and the atmospheric medieval town centre is dominated by the cathedral's 52-metre-/170-foot-high Commoner's Tower. The heart of Ribe has been designated a conservation zone and it comprises a network of narrow cobbled streets lined with a variety of architectural styles, including sixteenth-century half-timbered houses. Although Ribe faces the distant expanses of the North Sea, the inland waters immediately off the coast form part of the Wadden Sea, the world's largest unbroken network of intertidal sand and mudflats designated a World Heritage Site by UNESCO in 2008.

Religion first arrived when the great ninth-century missionary St Ansgar, Archbishop of Hamburg, was granted permission in the 850s to erect a church in Ribe. Ansgar was called the 'Apostle of the North' due to his dogged determination to convert pagan Scandinavia. That first religious foothold was actually short lived and it was not until the consecration of Bishop Leofdag in 948 that the Catholic Church became firmly established in Ribe. The bishop was tragically murdered after only a year and, although never officially canonized, he was revered locally as both a saint and a martyr. His remains were later interred within the cathedral.

Christianity first sailed into Ribe from Germany and it was from the same source that most of the building material was imported when work on the Romanesque cathedral dedicated to the Virgin Mary began in 1150. As there was no suitable stone in the region, durable volcanic tufa was imported by sea from Cologne. Architectural and artistic inspiration was also drawn from Germany and the Netherlands, with construction continuing until the mid-thirteenth century. The cathedral's slender pointed tower is an exact replica of many Rhineland churches, but it was eventually dwarfed by the brick-built Commoner's Tower. Such structures were common in the Low Countries, serving as watchtowers equipped with a bell to warn of floods or fire.

(*previous pages*) Ribe Cathedral.

(*right*) Ribe's medieval streets are lined with beautiful houses. They create a perfect foreground for the cathedral, with its contrasting square brick watchtower and elegant Rhineland tower to the rear. It is an architectural ensemble that perfectly complements Ribe's stature as Denmark's oldest town and cathedral.

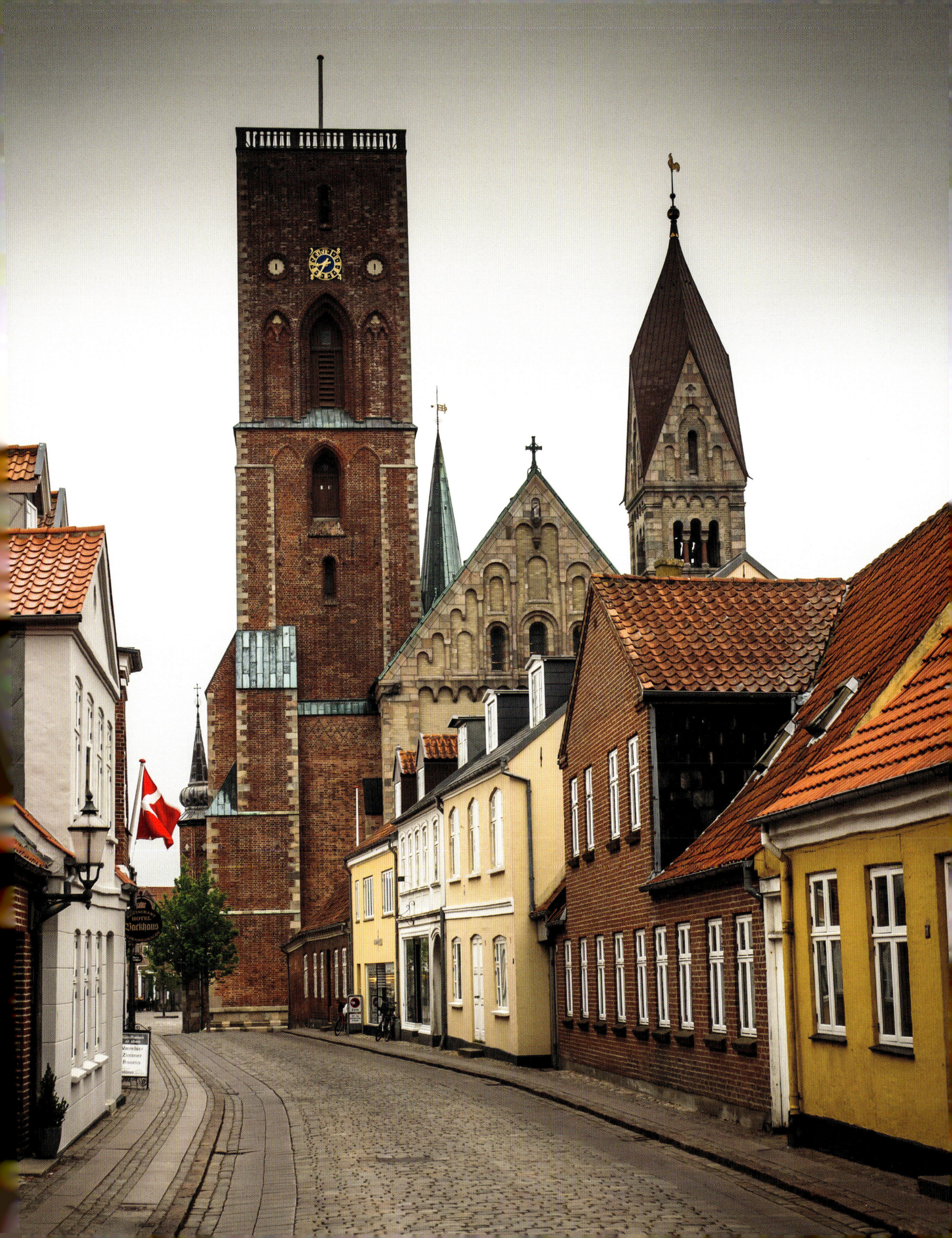

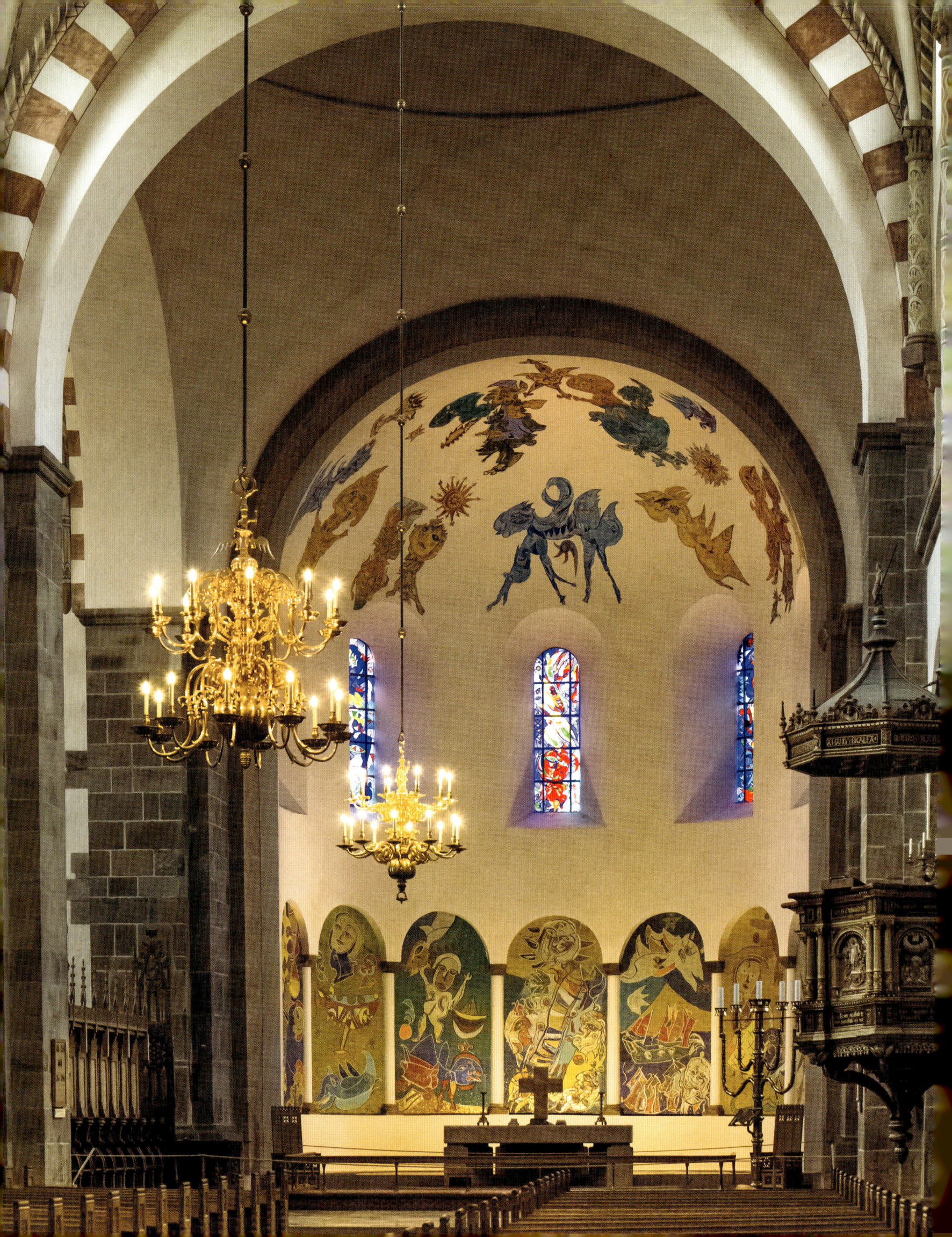

The fabric of Ribe's ancient cathedral has been rescued and restored from serious decline. Although the chandeliers, pulpit and vaulting are little changed, the high altar and apse received a 'facelift' in the form of twentieth-century mosaics and frescoes by Carl-Henning Pedersen.

The cathedral was originally designed to comprise a nave, transepts and two aisles, but in common with many similar churches, the arrival of Gothic architecture resulted in amendments. The most significant was the replacement of flat wooden ceilings in the central nave and transepts with 'modern' ribbed vaulting.

The oldest surviving royal tombstone in Scandinavia is that of Christopher I, who was originally buried by the cathedral's high altar. The grave's black Belgian marble memorial stone was later removed from the monarch's tomb in 1987 and put on display. With the exception of the red-brick Commoner's Tower, much of the cathedral's layout and design follows the customary design progression of medieval churches, through the Romanesque, Gothic and later phases – until, that is, one arrives at the altar and apse.

Architectural and artistic styles change with the passage of time and we readily accept the fact that some churches will combine work from the earliest Romanesque period and then perhaps incorporate elements of the Baroque from 500 years later. Having had to undertake a massive renovation programme during the early twentieth century in order to save the building's fabric, the church authorities in Ribe also leap-frogged several centuries. They commissioned Danish artist Carl-Henning Pedersen to submit a collection of designs and subsequently held a public ballot to determine whether the cathedral's ancient apse should become a vehicle for modern abstract art. It was somehow inevitable that the opinion of the 10,000 who viewed the designs would be so evenly divided that the ultimate decision rested on the church council's shoulders. They gave the green light and the three separates genres were executed between 1982 and 1987. Mosaics form the lower line behind the altar, new stained glass was created for the windows and the dome of the apse was filled with frescoes. While readily accepting that the creator was an artist of international renown, and although I did try very hard to equate the title of each work with its actual content, I nevertheless left the church thinking of another famous creative Dane, Hans Christian Andersen, and one of his wonderful short stories, *The Emperor's New Clothes*!

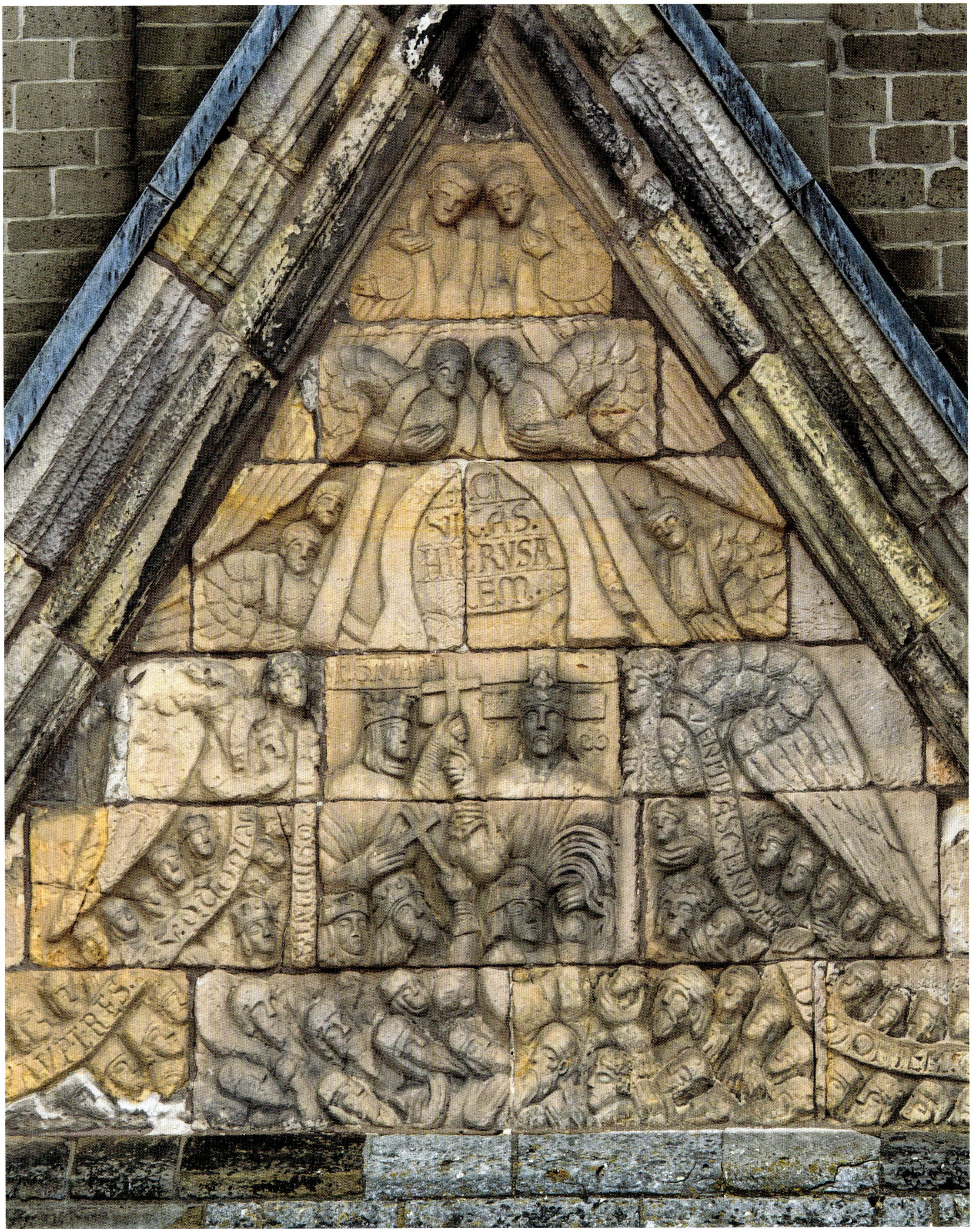

82   GREAT PILGRIMAGE SITES OF EUROPE

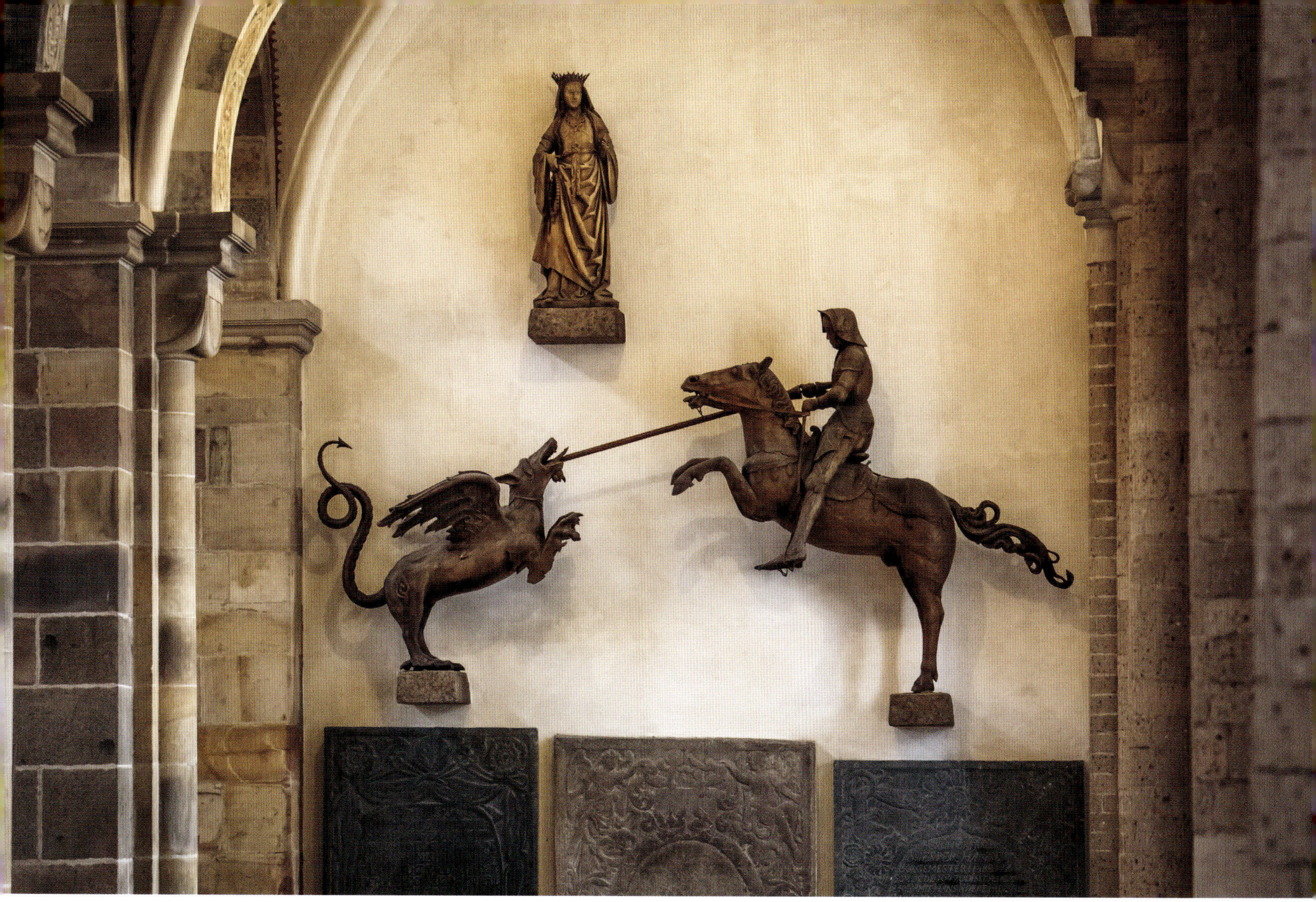

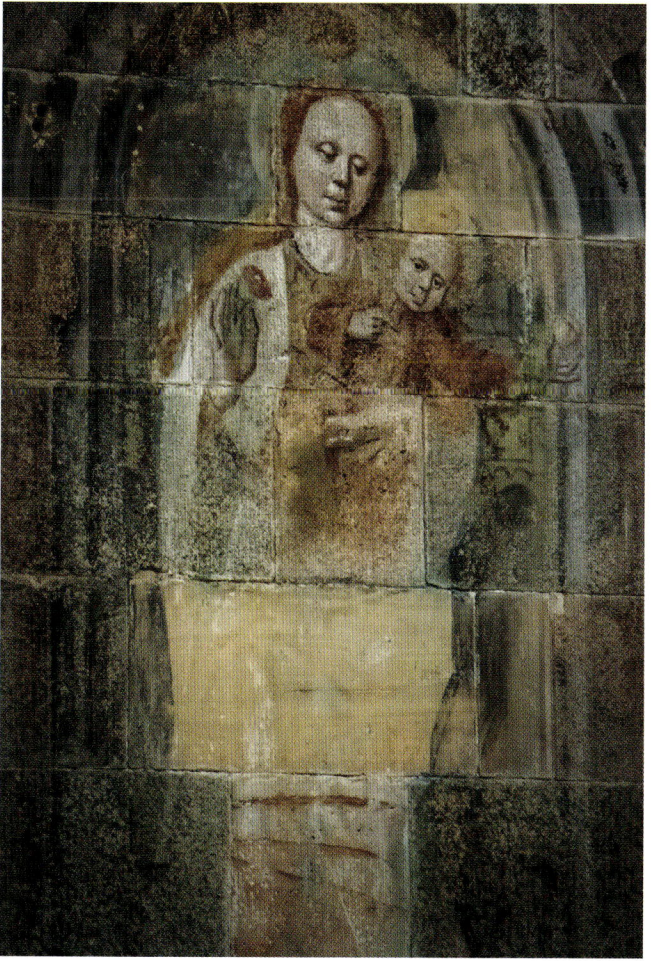

(*above*) This sculpture from 1475 depicts St George and the Dragon, with a representation of the Virgin on the wall above. St George was a Christian martyr killed by Roman Emperor Diocletian in 303. The dragon was thought to be a symbolic thirteenth-century embellishment.

(*far left*) The triangular pediment is set above the famous twelfth-century 'cat's head portal'. It is thought that the door was so named due to either a pair of lions supporting the flanking columns or a lion's head door-knocker. The tympanum bears a graphic Romanesque depiction of Jesus being lowered from the cross and the pediment is a complex relief of the Heavenly Jerusalem from the early thirteenth century.

(*left*) A rescued early sixteenth-century fresco of the Virgin and Child on a central nave pillar.

DENMARK
ST CANUTE'S CATHEDRAL
Odense, Funen

Funen is Denmark's third largest island and its main centre of population is the city of Odense. The cathedral is dedicated to Canute IV of Denmark, who was slain in 1086 at the altar of St Alban's church while seeking sanctuary after attempting to quell a peasant's revolt. The king's brother, Benedict, and seventeen retainers were also murdered, and it was not long before a cult grew up in support of the martyred monarch, with miracles allegedly taking place at his grave. Canute was succeeded by his brother, Olaf I, who made representations to Rome for canonization. He was not successful, though, and also suffered at the hand of fate when a disastrous crop failure was viewed as divine retribution for the mass murder. Under the later reign of Eric I, Danish envoys to Rome once again pleaded Canute's case, and in 1101 Pope Paschal II awarded him the posthumous honour of being Denmark's first saint. The Danish monarchy around that time seemed to have been a strange family affair, because Canute and the four brothers who either preceded or succeeded him may have all shared the same father, Sweyn II, but not the same mother, and records show that Sweyn had up to twenty offspring out of wedlock.

The site of the present cathedral and its immediate surroundings have produced a quantity of archaeological evidence supporting the existence of one or more buildings, although there has been some confusion over which piece of limestone wall belonged to which church. It is known that a group of Benedictine monks arrived from England and settled in the monastery and adjoining church built by King Eric to perpetuate the legend of St Canute the Holy. A martyred and subsequently canonized monarch was a priceless asset and the monks worked diligently and honourably to ensure the future well-being of the city's religious standing and economy through the well-established conduit of pilgrimage. The former church was partially destroyed by fire in 1247, but it was not until the latter years of the thirteenth century that Bishop Gisico of Odense began the reconstruction process that eventually resulted in the Gothic brick masterpiece standing today.

St Canute's Cathedral is dedicated to the eleventh-century king of Denmark, who was murdered in 1086. Older churches originally occupied the site and the Gothic brick cathedral was built between 1300 and 1500. The tower was added during a full restoration in 1580.

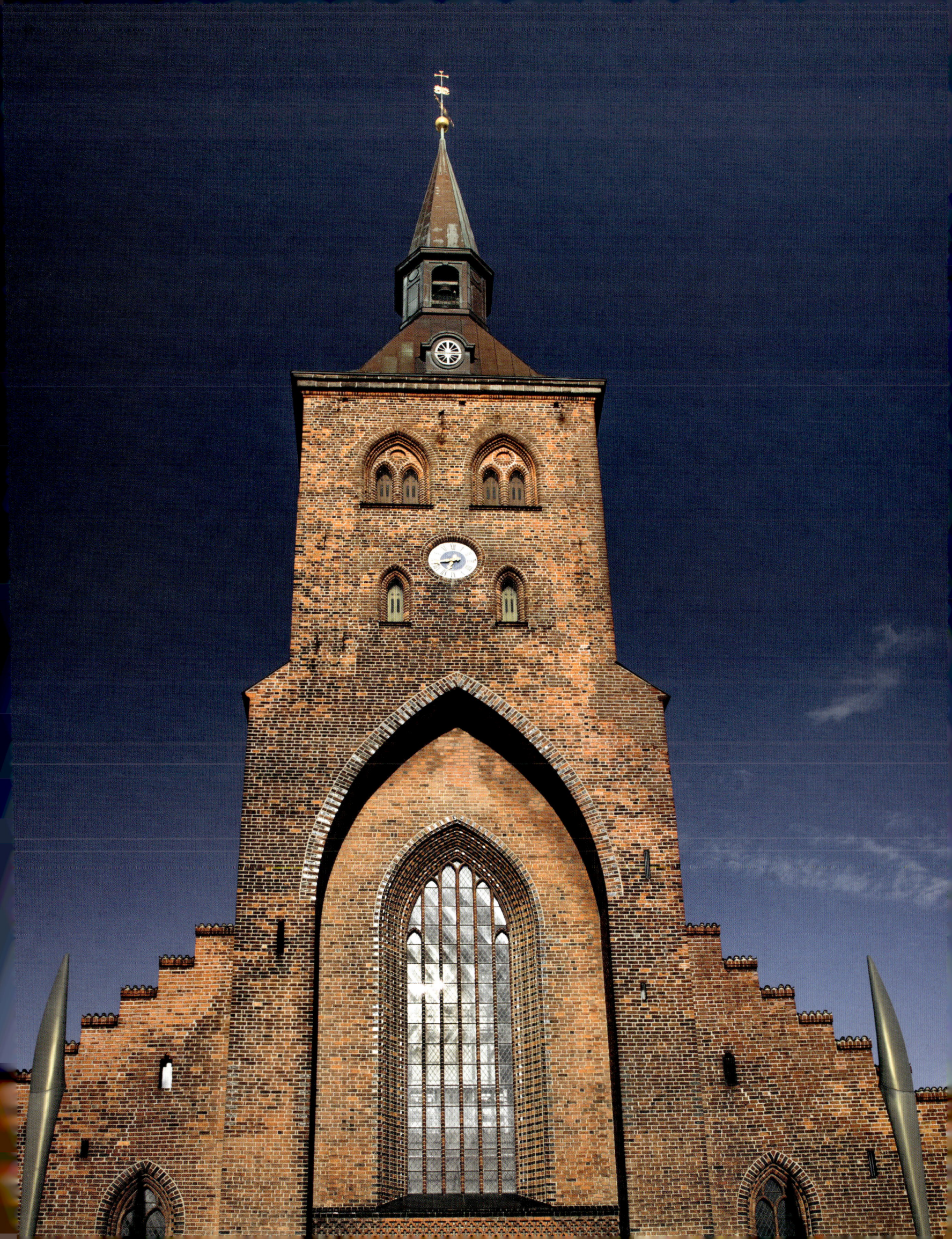

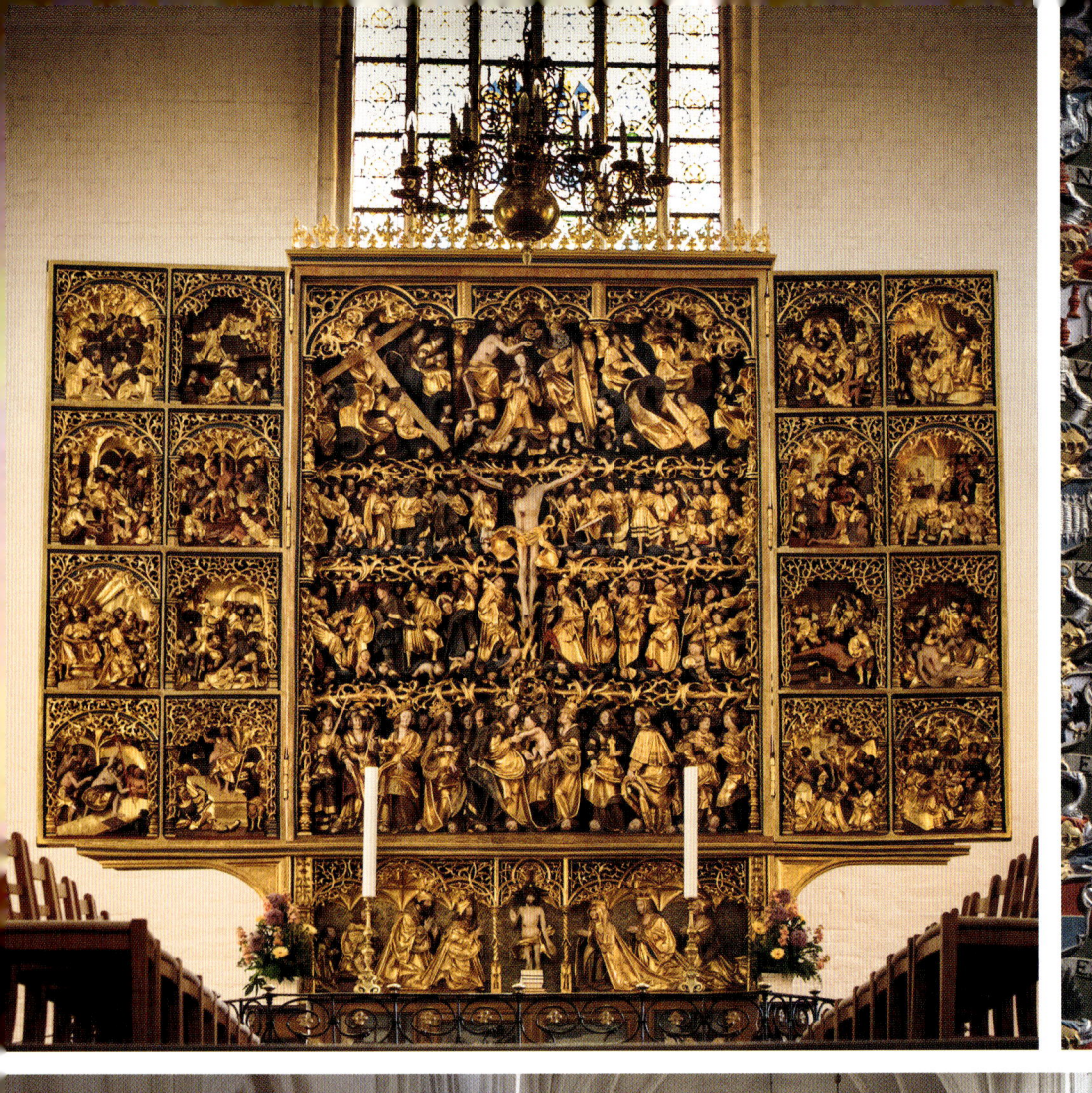
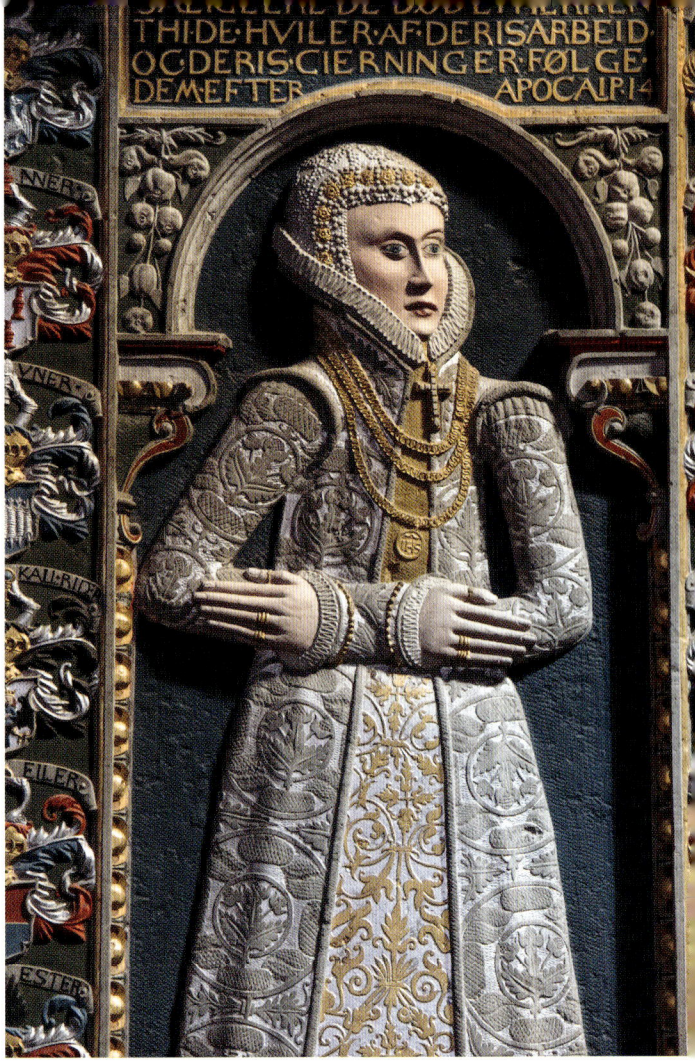

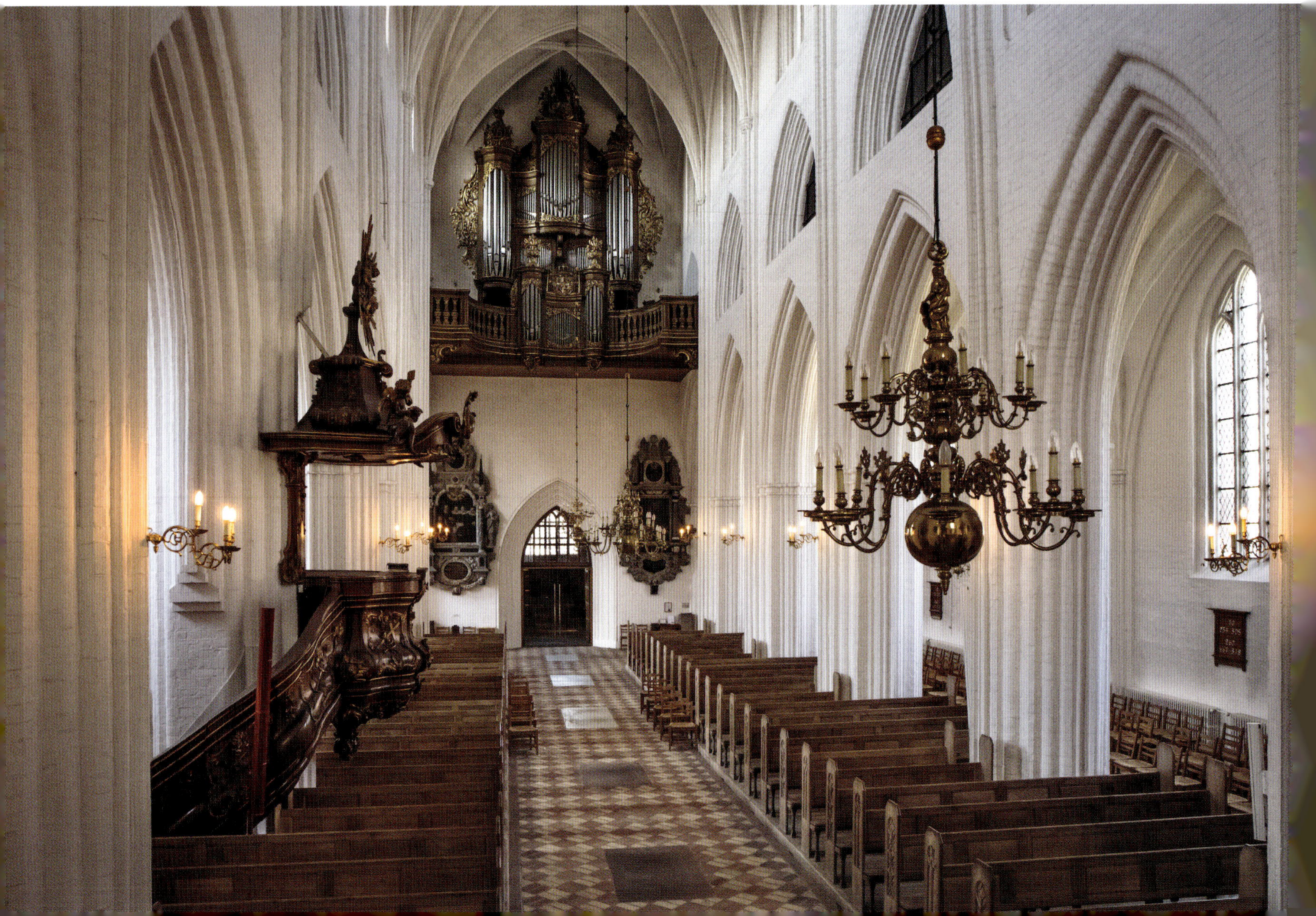

(*top left*) The magnificent altar screen was executed during the early sixteenth century and it is a complex and intricate work, with many of the figures swathed in gleaming sheets of 23-carat gold leaf. (*top right*) This elaborate memorial is dedicated to Queen Margaret of Denmark, Norway and Sweden (although she largely ruled solely as Regent in Denmark and Norway). (*bottom*) The elegant, bright interior of the Gothic cathedral is a refreshing change from the darkness of many dimly lit stone churches from the same period.

(*overleaf left*) A detail from the altarpiece has the Crucifixion as its central point of focus. One of the most endearing features is that the figures are portrayed as sixteenth-century characters. (*overleaf right*) The awesome Gothic brickwork and windows of the main portal.

The red-brick exterior of St Canute's Cathedral may have suffered areas of discolouration over time, but the unadorned white painted interior is light and airy, due to the large windows devoid of coloured glass. Of course, one can say that stained glass windows played a significant role in the medieval Church because they instructed, enlightened and entertained congregations who had a high percentage of illiteracy. This particular church does not need to paint graphic pictures, though, because a short walk along the nave and down a flight of stairs into the crypt is all one needs to comprehend this particular slice of history. The crypt is a beautiful space with a very low vaulted roof, reminiscent of those found in Romanesque churches. It actually belonged to the old church and was only rediscovered during late nineteenth-century restorations of the cathedral. It was renovated and redecorated in preparation for receiving its two most honoured guests. Two identical oblong glass cases enclose the oak and ash coffins bearing the neatly laid out skeletons of Canute and Benedict, with the king's skull resting upon a pillow of ninth-century yellow silk adorned with bird motifs. The relics are presented in full view to pilgrims and visitors, and it feels quite strange looking at the basic ingredients of a human being and realizing that we are actually all more or less the same on the inside.

Although the reliquaries lying in the crypt are a memorable and thought-provoking link to the past, the cathedral's greatest religious art treasure is accessed *via* a flight of steps leading up to the high altar. The triptych altar screen was executed between 1513 and 1523 by the wood carver, sculptor and painter Claus Berg. It is a remarkably complex piece of work based mainly around the Passion and the Crucifixion, with other pertinent figures and events slotted in between the main narrative. The work was originally commissioned by Queen Christina as part of an elaborate royal sepulchral chapel to be established in the now long-demolished Greyfriars Church in Odense. The cathedral may be comparatively plain in terms of interior decor but it has atmosphere aplenty to captivate twenty-first-century pilgrims.

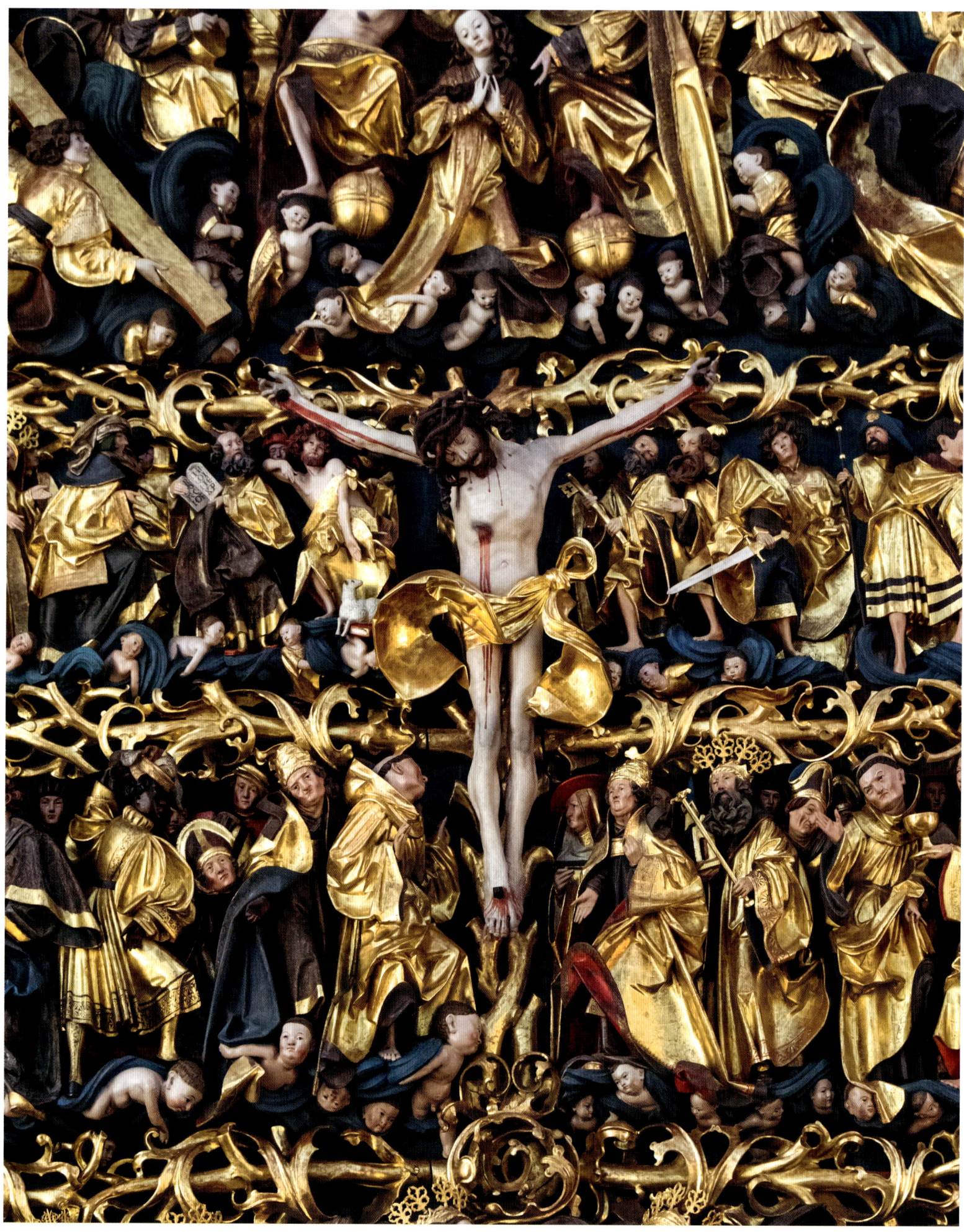

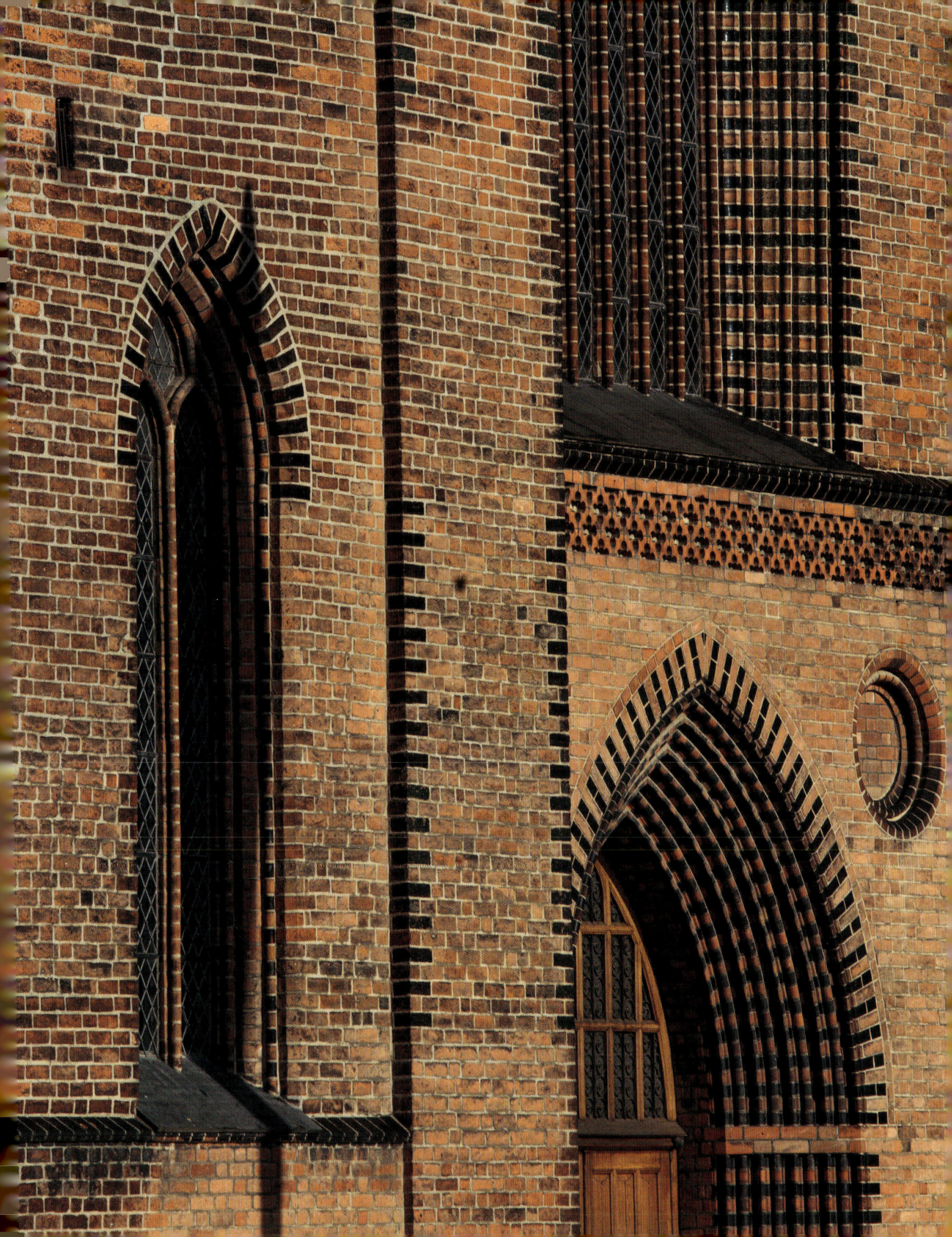

DENMARK
MØN
Fanefjord & Elmelunde

The small Danish island of Møn is renowned for its dramatic band of chalk and limestone cliffs, recently declared by UNESCO to be one of the world's most important collections of ancient fossils. The searing white cliffs on the island's south-east coast have gradually revealed their prehistoric contents through millennia of pounding by the Baltic Sea. Møn's hidden treasures are not confined solely to the natural world, though, because some of its rural churches host a spectacular gallery of religious frescoes, which were themselves hidden by limestone. However, in the case of Fanefjord and Elmelunde, the limestone was applied by brushes in liquid form during the sixteenth-century Reformation, a period of religious turmoil when most iconography was either concealed or destroyed. Because the majority of these frescoes were created around 1500, they were comparatively new and less likely to disintegrate beneath the limestone coating. We should also be grateful to those whose patience and skill were combined so effectively with technological advances during the restoration. Many of the paintings and frescoes that once adorned the walls of European churches and cathedrals have been irrevocably lost due to the over-enthusiasm of well-meaning but unqualified nineteenth-century restorers. Luckily, the frescoes in both Elmelund and Fanefjord have been sensitively restored and enhanced by art experts from the National Museum in Copenhagen, having been initially uncovered in the 1880s and 1930s respectively.

Elmelunde is the oldest church on the island, dating back to 1085, and although some traces of Romanesque art have been discovered, it was deemed impossible to proceed further due to a combination of technical and financial constraints. These sorts of equations are becoming an inevitable part of twenty-first-century conservation issues throughout the world. Yes, we need to conserve the past for the education and enlightenment of future generations, but priorities have to be carefully weighed up. As a result, the attempted restoration of faded twelfth-century religious art segments in a remote corner of Denmark would probably not be very high up the agenda. Fortunately, the identically themed late-fifteenth-century frescoes of Elmelunde and Fanefjord have been given five-star treatment and are an absolute joy to behold.

Fanefjord church dates from the thirteenth century and occupies a prominent position overlooking an inlet of the Baltic Sea. Its tower served as a reassuring landmark for mariners and ministered to both the rural community and crews from ships plying their trade around Denmark's coastal waters.

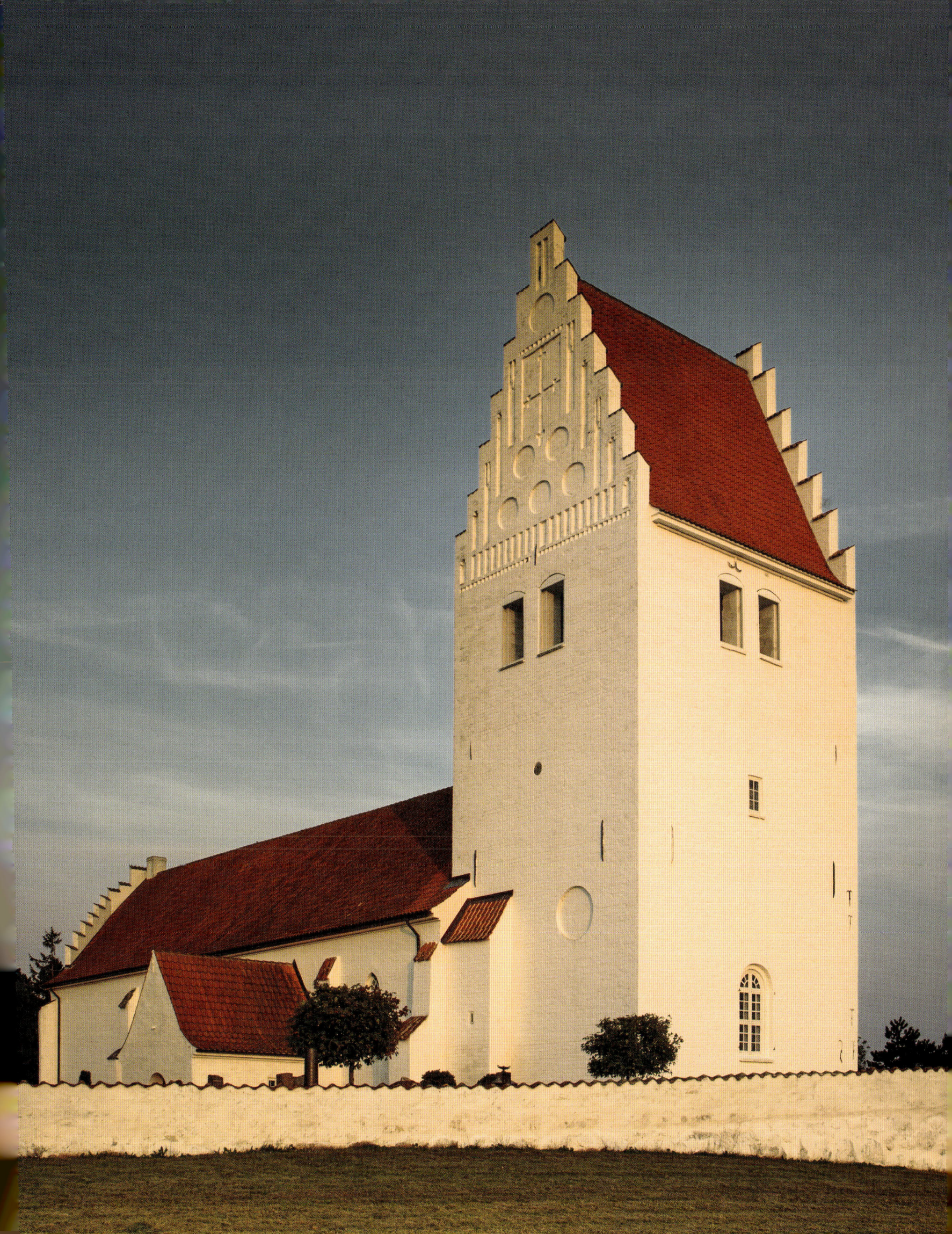

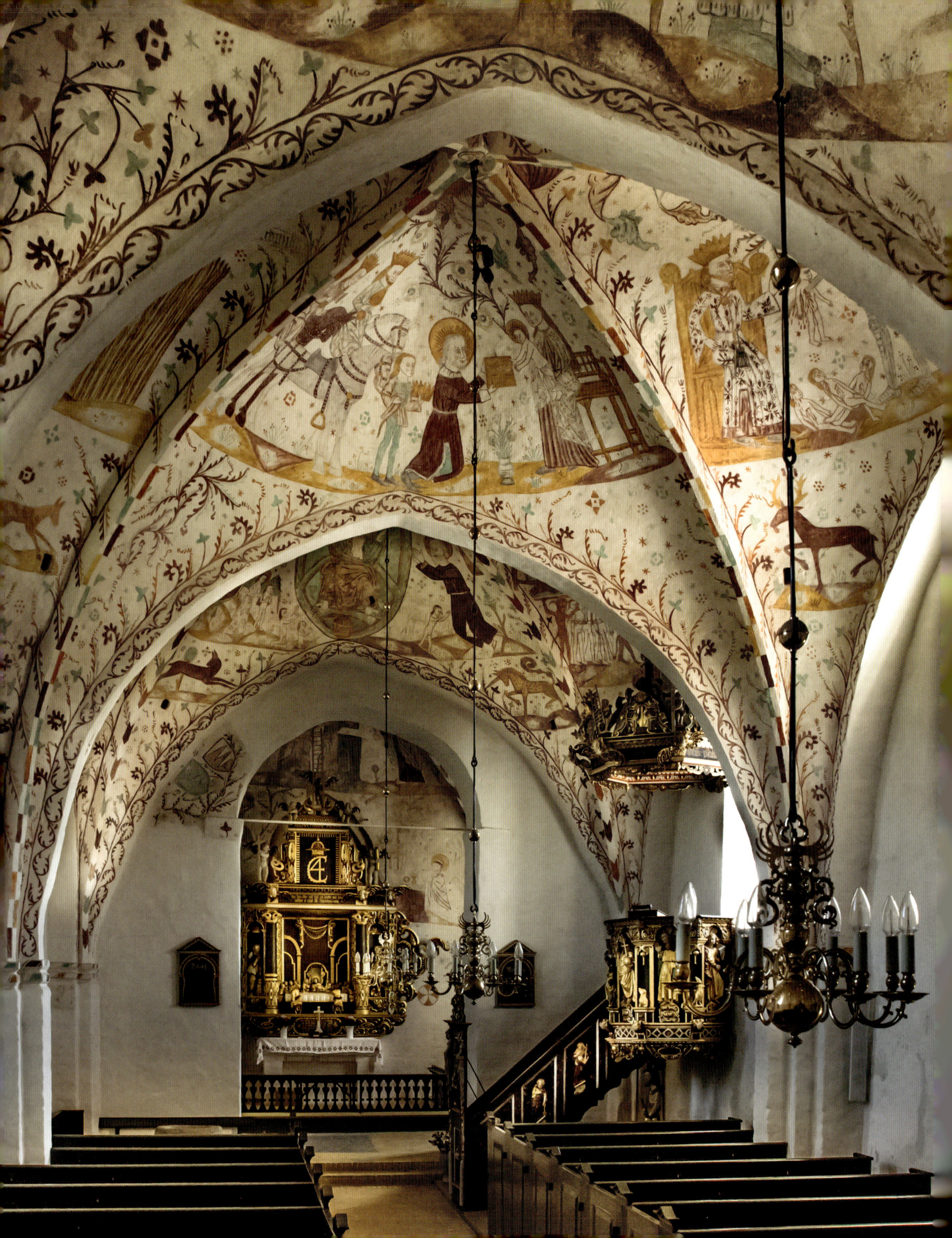

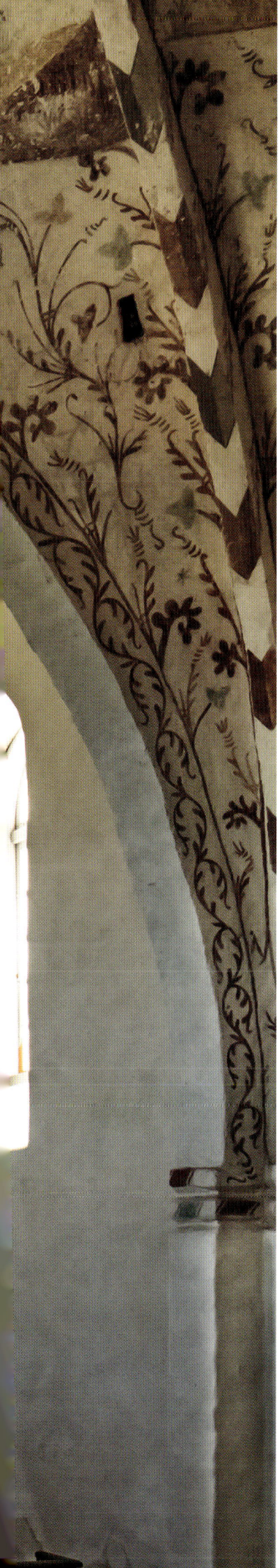

The decorated nave of Elmelunde church features the rich brown, gold and green tones of the Elmelunde Master's work. Both the altar and pulpit are from the 1640s and they were presented to the church by the family of Christian IV, King of Denmark and Norway.

Despite being separated by almost the width of the island, both churches (and one other in the village of Keldby) were the work of the same artist. For whatever reason, his name has never been recorded and consequently the frescoes are always referred to as being executed by the 'Elmelunde Master'. Because the interiors of both churches were similarly constructed using deep vaulting, the four segments of each became the equivalent of individual pages in a book, and both locations feature almost identical themes based on key elements from the Old and New Testaments. The content includes most of religion's key players, such as a wonderful representation of the Garden of Eden, in which Adam is cleverly portrayed as still bearing the scar from where a rib was removed to create his partner Eve. The artist's choice of topics charts a predictable course from Eden through to the Last Judgment, but with an interesting mix of creative diversions in between the main events. The biblical scenes are interspersed with illustrations of contemporary rural life, so there are occasional panels featuring the ploughing of fields, hunting and harvesting crops. The canvases are embellished with twisting vines, stars and other motifs to break up the starkness of a plain white background. The principle behind the work was the same as a publication from the later medieval period known as the *Biblia Pauperum*, the Pauper's Bible. The first manuscripts were created in Bavaria during the fourteenth century and the work became more widely distributed when a basic block-book version was produced in the Netherlands a century later.

Medieval wall paintings, frescoes and stained glass were partly educational tools to enable a largely illiterate population to understand the messages of the Bible and the likely outcomes of either a devout or sinful life. In a way, the *Biblia Pauperum* was the equivalent of a religious comic strip, comprising graphic illustrations with basic captions. Creating any kind of illustrated manuscript was too expensive for most pockets, but the basic block versions were produced in greater numbers and so it became sufficiently affordable for a parish priest to acquire one to serve and educate his congregation, in a fifteenth-century version of the traditional Sunday School.

Are these churches true pilgrimage sites? Confession forms an integral part of the pilgrimage ritual, so I now have to make my own: no medieval saints lie buried within either Fanefjord or Elmelunde churches. But the Elmelunde Master is someone whose work is certainly worth making a journey to view.

94 GREAT PILGRIMAGE SITES OF EUROPE

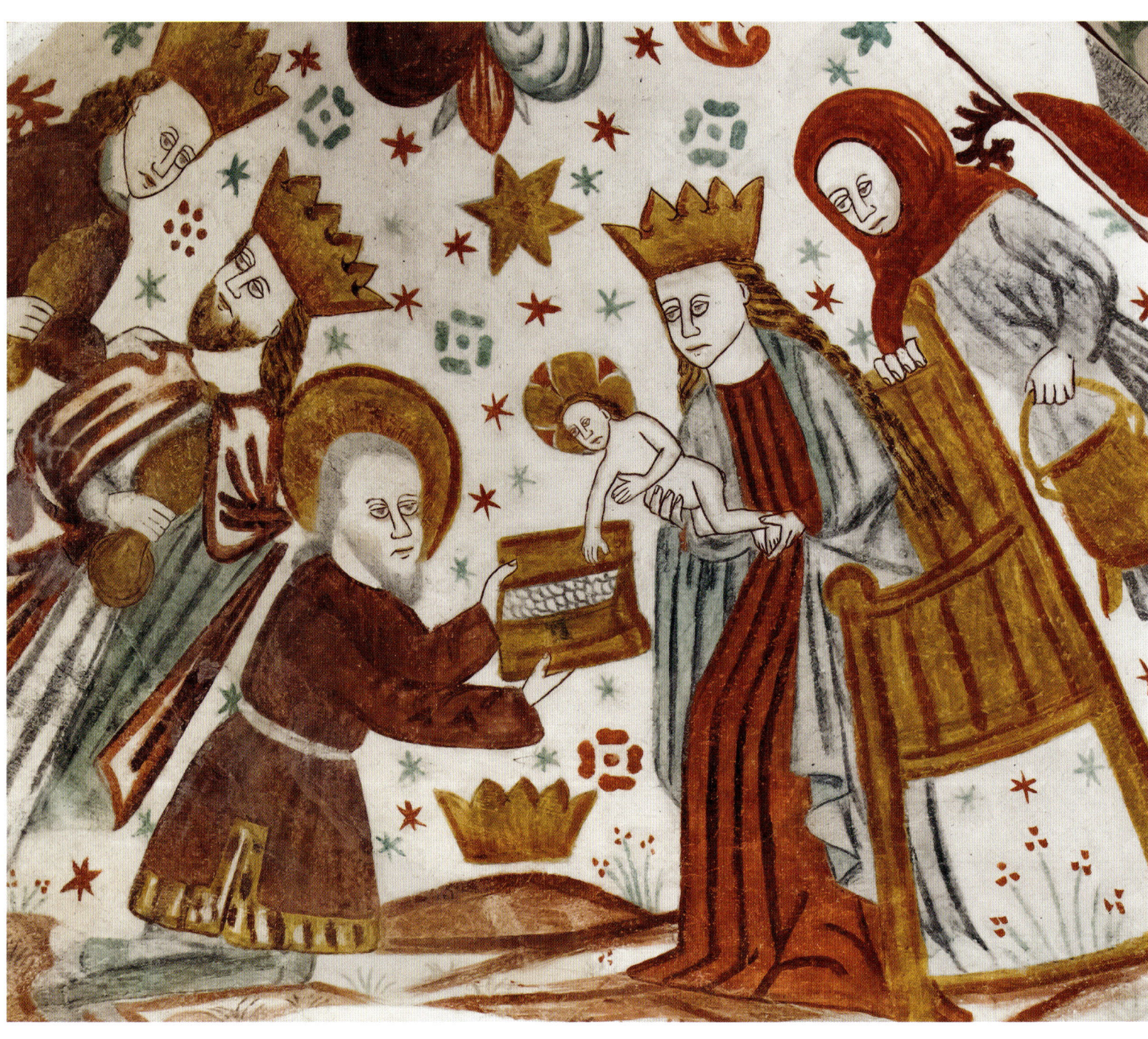

(*above*) This is the Fanefjord version of the Epiphany depicting the arrival of the Magi in Bethlehem. It is interesting to compare this one with the Elmelunde representation, which, although almost identical, shuffled the Wise Men around and gave Mary a new wardrobe.

(*right*) One side of the nave in Fanefjord features yet another version of St George and the Dragon set on the chancel wall. The Epiphany is on one of the centre vaults, and in the upper segment of this picture there is a rather graphic version of the Slaughter of the Innocents.

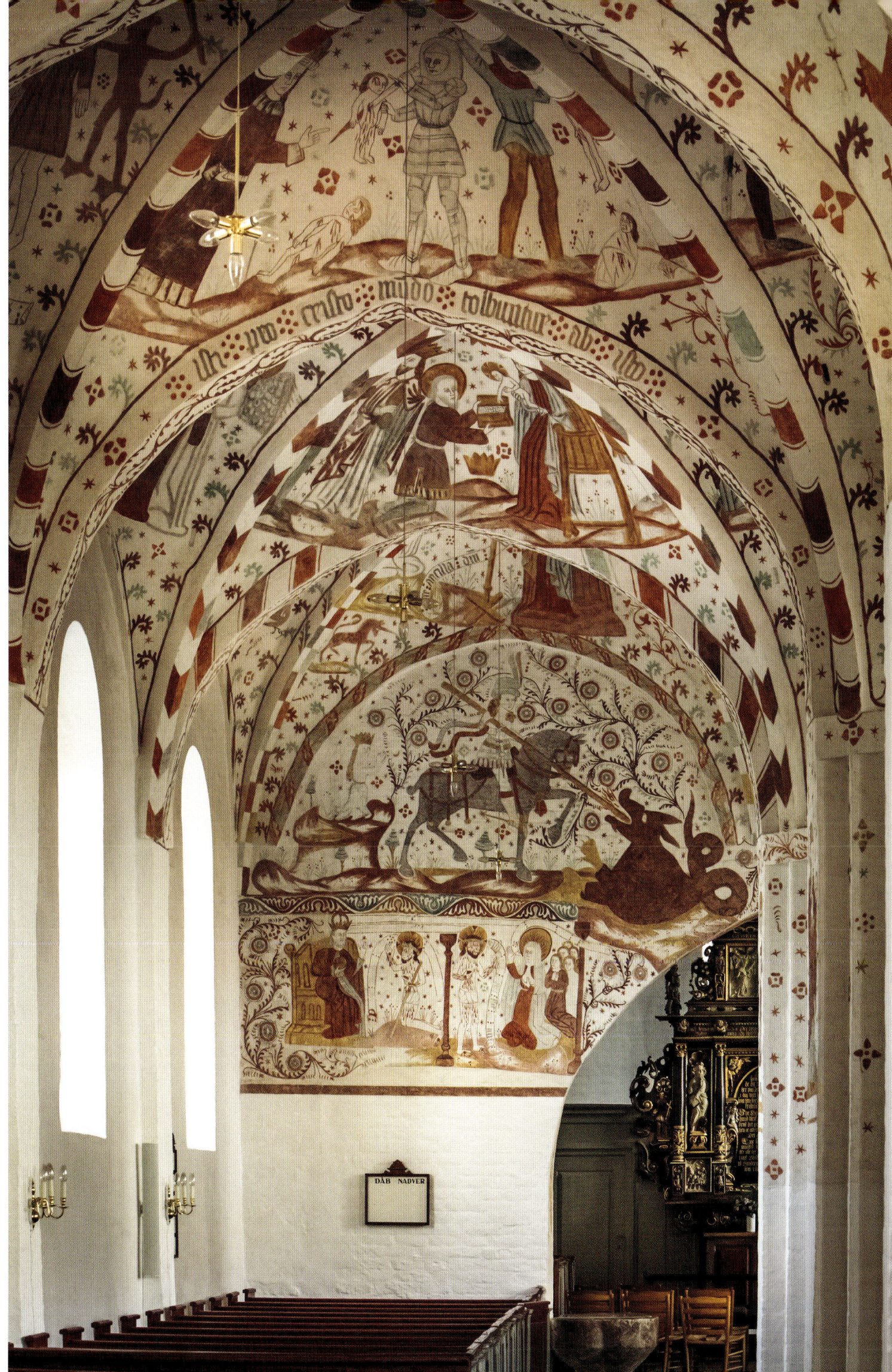

NORWAY
NIDAROS CATHEDRAL
Trondheim, Trøndelag

Nidaros was the ancient name for Trondheim and its cathedral is not only Norway's national shrine but also that of its patron saint, Olaf II Haraldsson. Olaf was a genuine Viking and was campaigning around Denmark at the age of twelve. Four years later, he sailed with a combined force of Norwegians and Danes to plunder England. Sometime during that period, Olaf travelled to France and discovered that Normandy was already inhabited by permanently settled Vikings. It was there that he embraced Christianity, noting that the ruling dukes of Normandy had complete control over both State and Church. Olaf returned home and began a campaign to assert himself as king of all Norway. He was deeply committed to two dreams, whereby the country would be unified as an independent kingdom with Christianity as the state religion. Dreams turned to nightmares when he was defeated in battle by Canute of Denmark and England. However, after Canute's return to England and the death of his Regent in Norway, Olaf sensed the door of power had been left slightly ajar. His return was not universally welcomed, though, and Olaf was opposed by a peasant army of his own countrymen at the Battle of Stiklestad in July 1030. The battle tactics went awry and Olaf was killed, allegedly having thrown down his weapon so that he could die a defenseless martyr. His corpse was placed in a shed, where a blind man seeking shelter for the night experienced a miracle. As he was groping around Olaf's body in the dark, he got blood on his hands and then wiped his eyes. Miraculously, he could see again. This was the first of many further recorded miracles associated with Olaf's tomb: only a year after the king had been buried, his coffin was opened and was found to smell of roses rather than decomposition. Furthermore, his hair and fingernails had continued to grow. He was instantly canonized by the bishop and there began the cult of St Olaf. Olaf's shrine was placed in a wooden church built specifically to accommodate the martyred king and in 1070 the wooden structure was replaced by a stone one, which, over time, evolved into the majestic cathedral that is now enjoying a resurgence as a place of pilgrimage.

Nidaros Cathedral is the national shrine of Norway. It was also a pilgrimage destination for those wishing to pay homage at the shrine of St Olaf, the nation's patron saint. During the Catholic Middle Ages, its dedication was to Christ rather than to St Olaf.

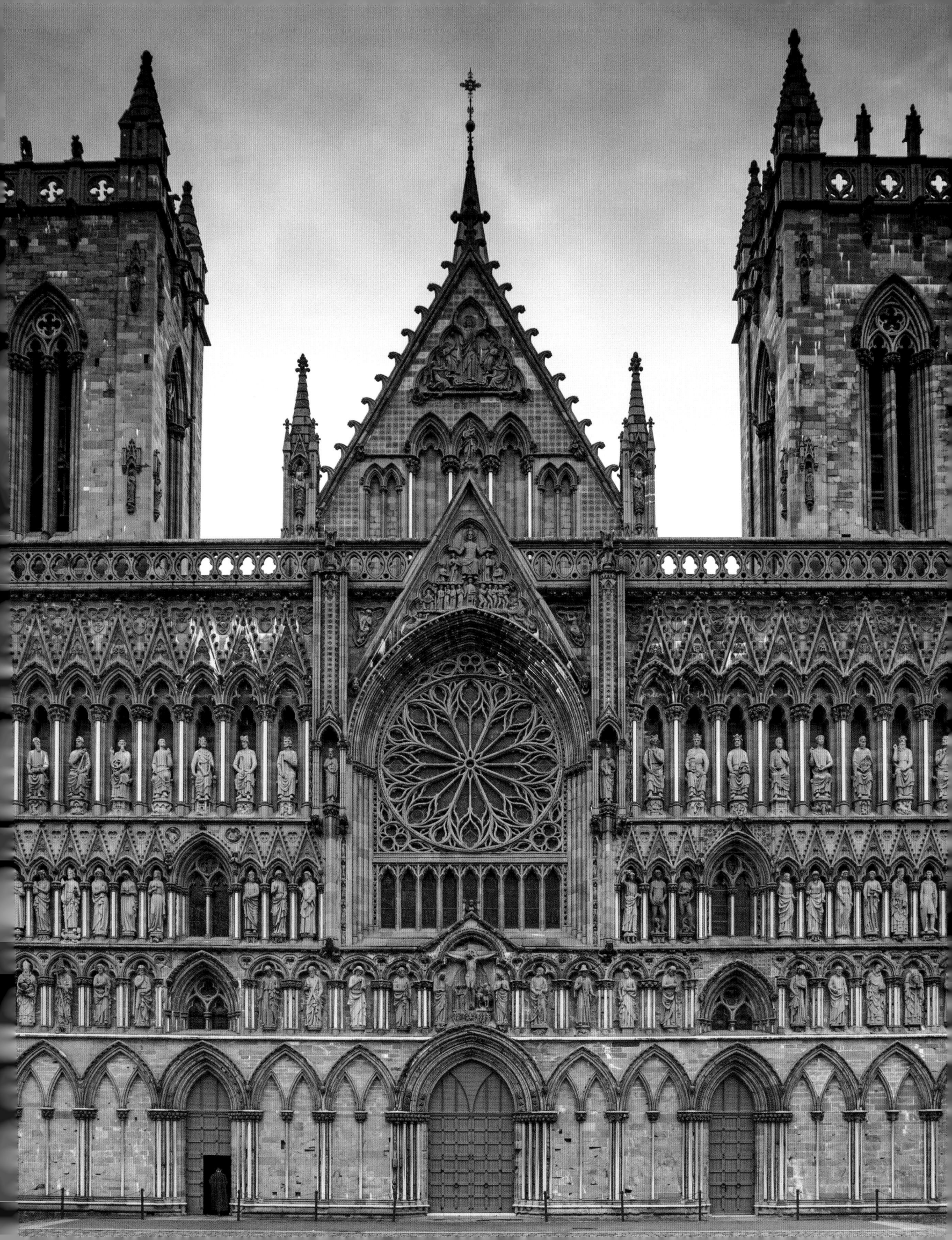

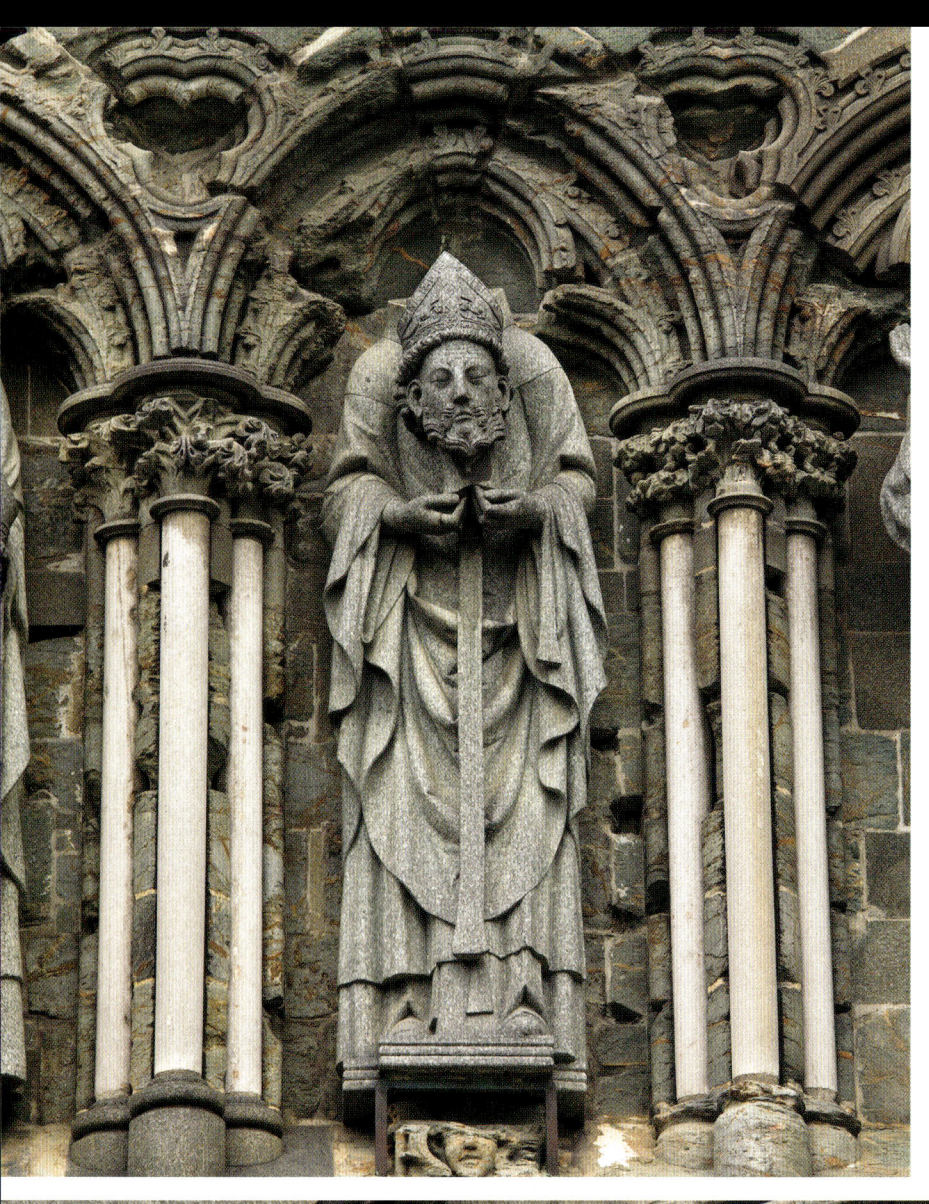
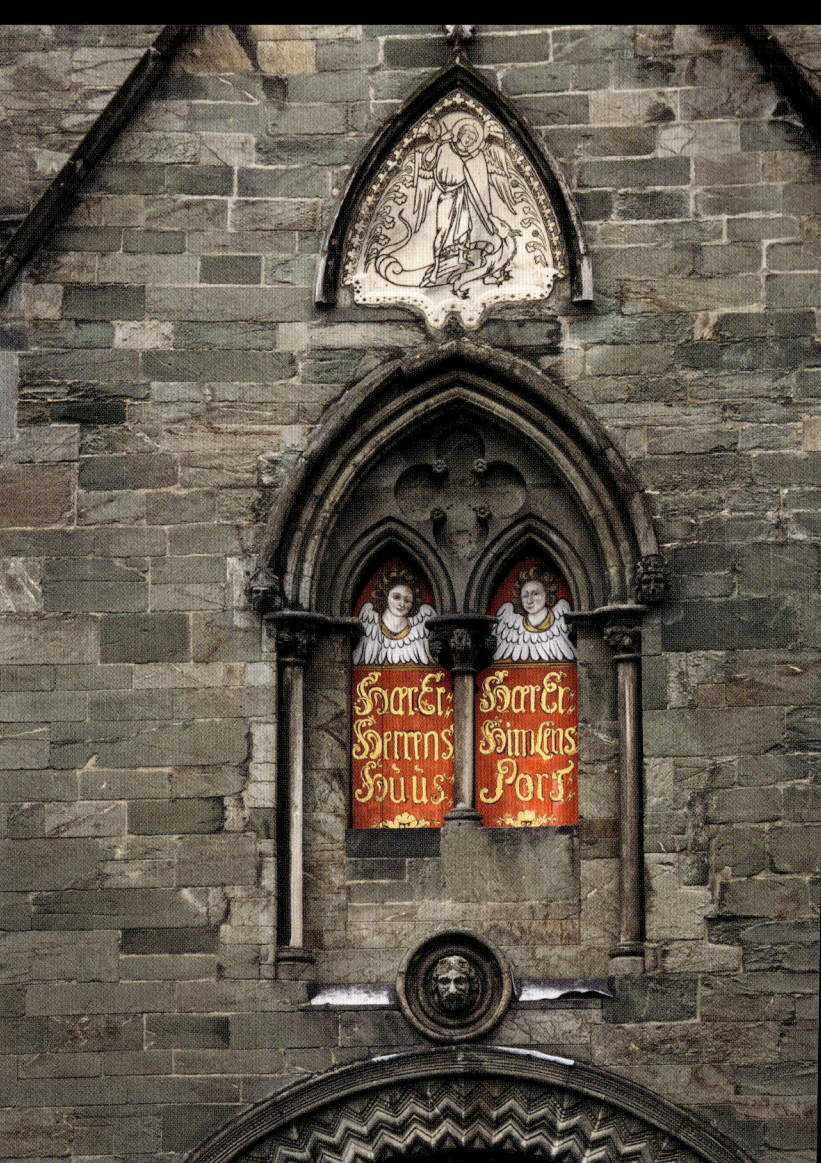

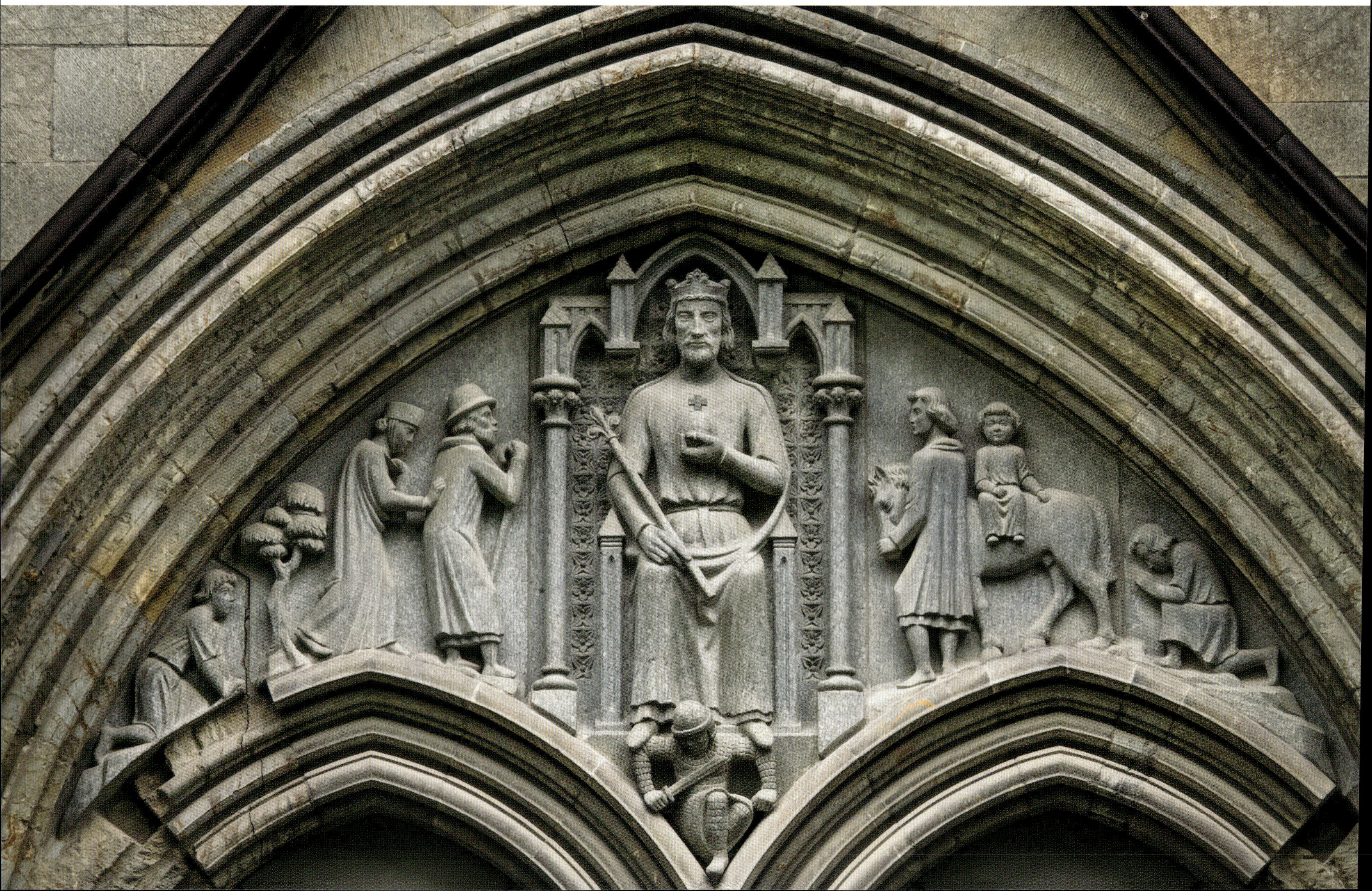

(*top left*) One of the statues on the west front gallery is of St Denis, the third-century martyr who is patron saint of France. This form of sculpture is known as a *cephalophore*, taken from the Greek for 'head carrier' and it customarily depicts a saint martyred by beheading. (*top right*) The south transept portal shows the transition from Romanesque to Gothic through the differing arches: the rounded arch with zigzag decoration is Romanesque and the pointed arch is the progression into the Gothic era. (*bottom*) One of the cathedral's many gloriously sculpted portals.

(*overleaf*) Only five of the west front's original sculptures survived the cathedral's massive deterioration and they are now housed in the museum. Every figure visible today was the result of an extensive restoration programme, involving Norway's finest sculptors, that lasted from 1905 to 1983.

Work started on the future cathedral in 1070 and it took more than two centuries to complete the project, but from 1300, the magnificent Nidaros Cathedral became northern Europe's greatest pilgrimage destination. The majority of pilgrims came from Scandinavian countries but increasing numbers travelled from farther afield, bearing testimony to the magnetic spiritual power exercised by martyrs and miracles.

The archbishopric was created in 1153 and one of the early incumbents was Eysteinn Erlendsson, who had been educated in Paris. Having made the obligatory journey to Rome to receive the pallium (ecclesiastical vestment) from Pope Alexander III in 1161, he later travelled to England in 1183 and visited both Lincoln Cathedral and Westminster Abbey, where the new Gothic style of architecture was being employed as a replacement for the heavier Romanesque version. The archbishop was inspired by the more delicate designs and upon his return to Norway he began the process of harmoniously blending Romanesque and Gothic in Nidaros. A particularly fine example of that transitional style is portrayed in the Chapter House, the small 'church within a church' with its own choir, transept and nave. It became a revered corner of the cathedral because it hosted the gold ring bearing a drop of Christ's blood acquired by Archbishop Erlendsson during his trip to Rome.

The curse of medieval cathedrals was fire and Nidaros suffered the first of three major outbreaks in 1328, followed by another in 1432 and the most destructive of all in 1531. This last blaze caused horrendous damage, including an almost totally ruined and roofless nave. However, the wheel of fortune eventually creaked into action and the cathedral became the nation's coronation church when Charles III John was crowned there in 1818. An illustration from 1661 had apparently portrayed the cathedral as a pathetic crumbled ruin, but time, money and colossal effort have ensured the ravages of time no longer gain a foothold in the cathedral's fabric. The fact that the cathedral is now restored to its medieval glory can be attributed largely to the Restoration Workshop, first established in 1869 and still in operation today after 150 years of dedicated work by specialist stonemasons, carpenters, glass craftsmen, metalworkers and art experts.

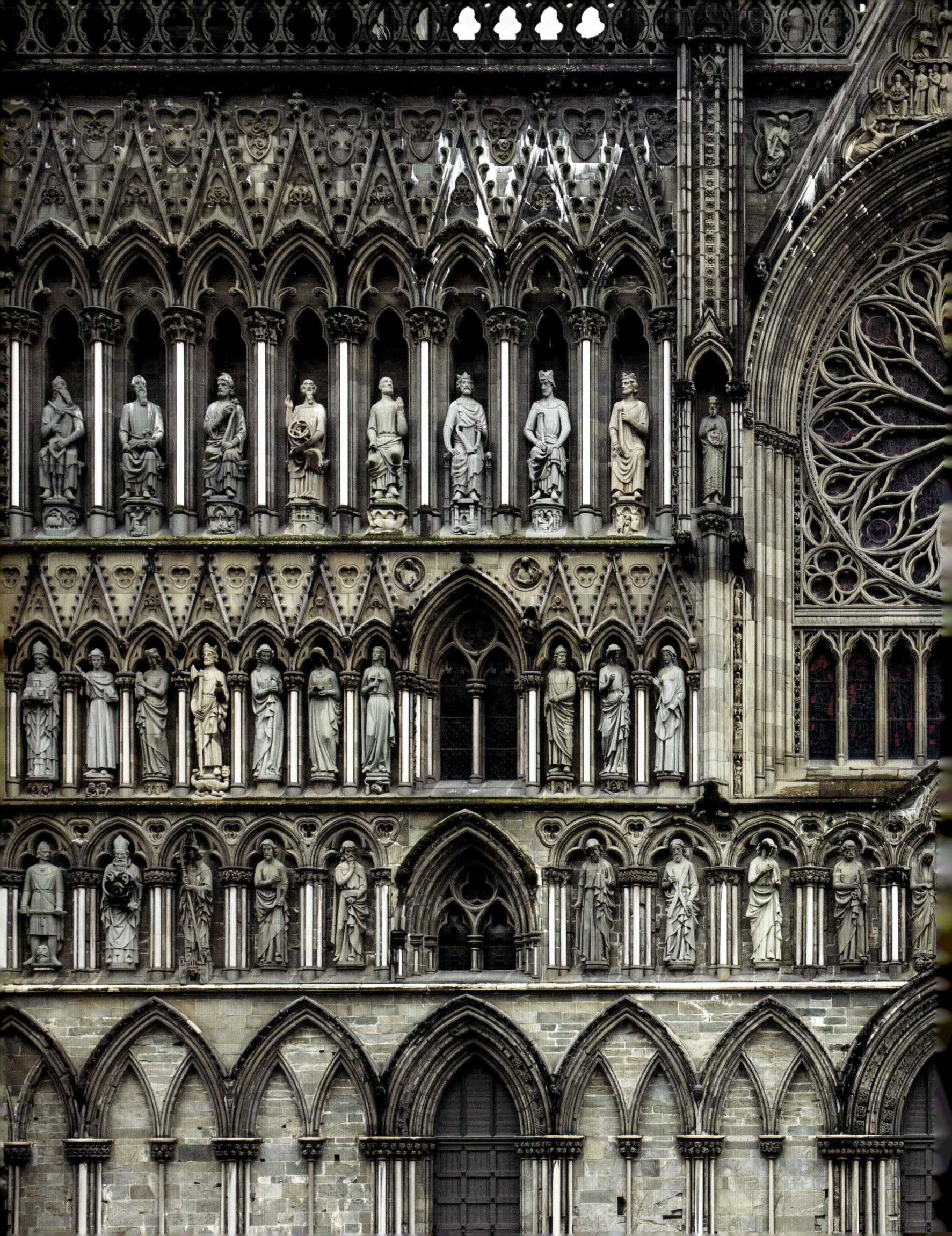

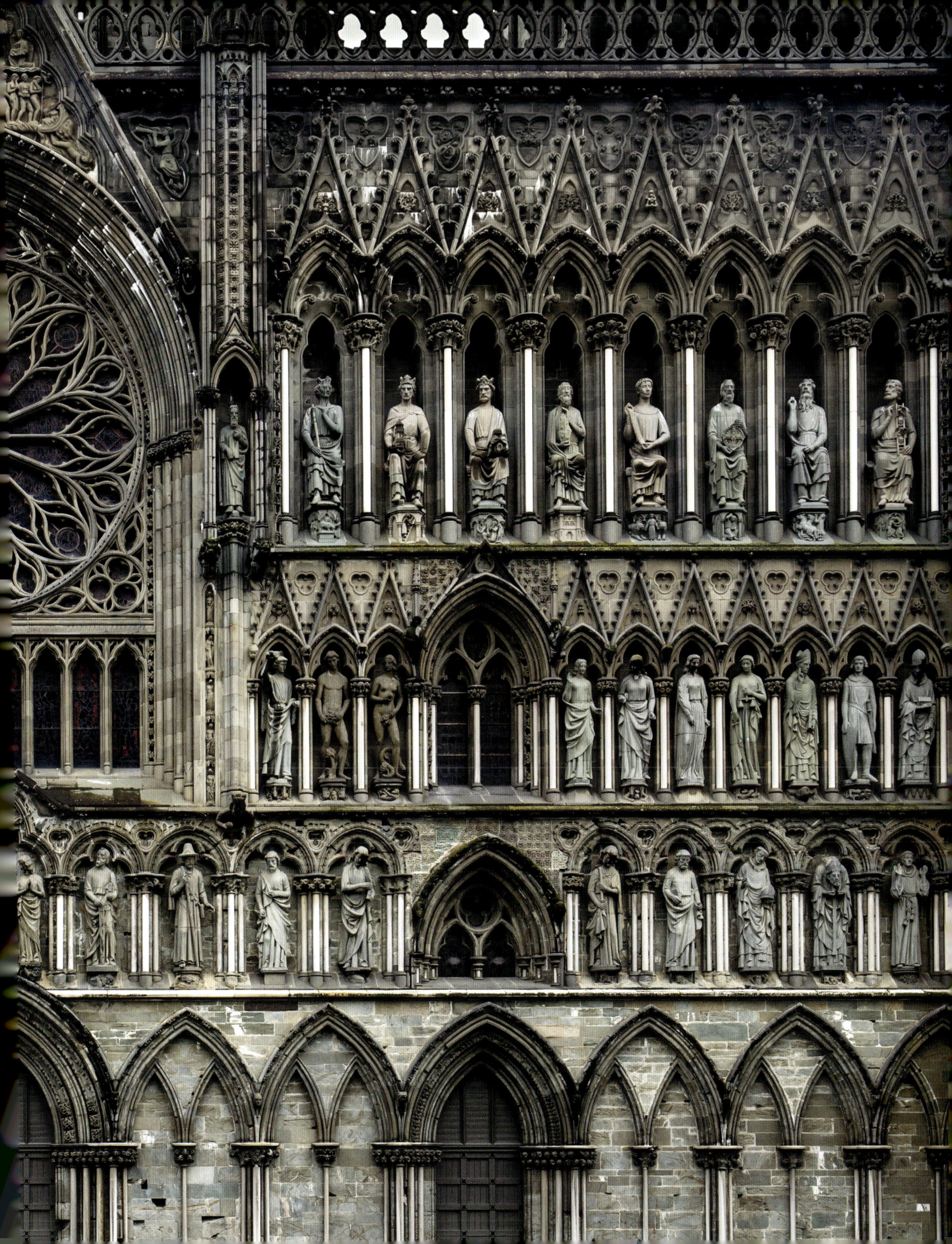

NORWAY
RINGEBU STAVE CHURCH
Ringebu, Innlandet

Christianity was slow to reach Norway. Although missionaries had made numerous attempts to persuade the hitherto pagan country that there were many benefits to be derived from being in the 'family', scepticism prevailed over Catholicism and religion did not really gain a serious foothold until around the end of the tenth century. From that time until the mid-sixteenth-century Reformation, approximately 1,000 stave churches were built, of which only twenty-eight now remain. Ringebu dates from 1220 and although it has been significantly altered over time the nave of the original church survives. In 1717, the interior was partially painted, but it was later totally covered in white, an aesthetic travesty not corrected until major restoration works in 1921.

Ringebu is one of the more important resting places on the marathon pilgrim route from Oslo to the shrine of St Olaf in Nidaros Cathedral in Trondheim. Although the walking can be extremely taxing, the rewards of solitude and being at one with nature are to be treasured – if the prospect of 643 kilometres/400 miles is not too daunting. The original name of the medieval route taken by pilgrims making their way to the shrine of St Olaf from the late eleventh century until the Reformation is once again in use, although for a non-Norwegian-speaking pilgrim, *Gudbrandsdalsleden* is a bit harder to pronounce than St Olaf's Way. The route was afforded the status of being declared a Cultural Route of the Council of Europe in 2010, an accolade that helped considerably with practicalities and funding for publicity and safety. The latter is particularly important because to the north of Ringebu lies a significant section of bleak terrain that can be snow-covered well into June. By the time the initial version of the Ringebu stave church was completed, the pilgrimage to Nidaros had been in existence for more than a century. For medieval Catholic pilgrims, a physical break prior to facing the Dovre mountain region was obviously important, but even more significant was the opportunity to put one's spiritual affairs in order. Ringebu was perfectly placed for that purpose and must have provided solace and consolation to countless pilgrims over the ages.

Ringebu stave church occupies an elevated position some 2 kilometres/1¼ miles from the village centre. The early thirteenth-century church was built over the site of an earlier one and archaeological evidence suggests that pagan worship was also conducted in the vicinity before Christianity arrived.

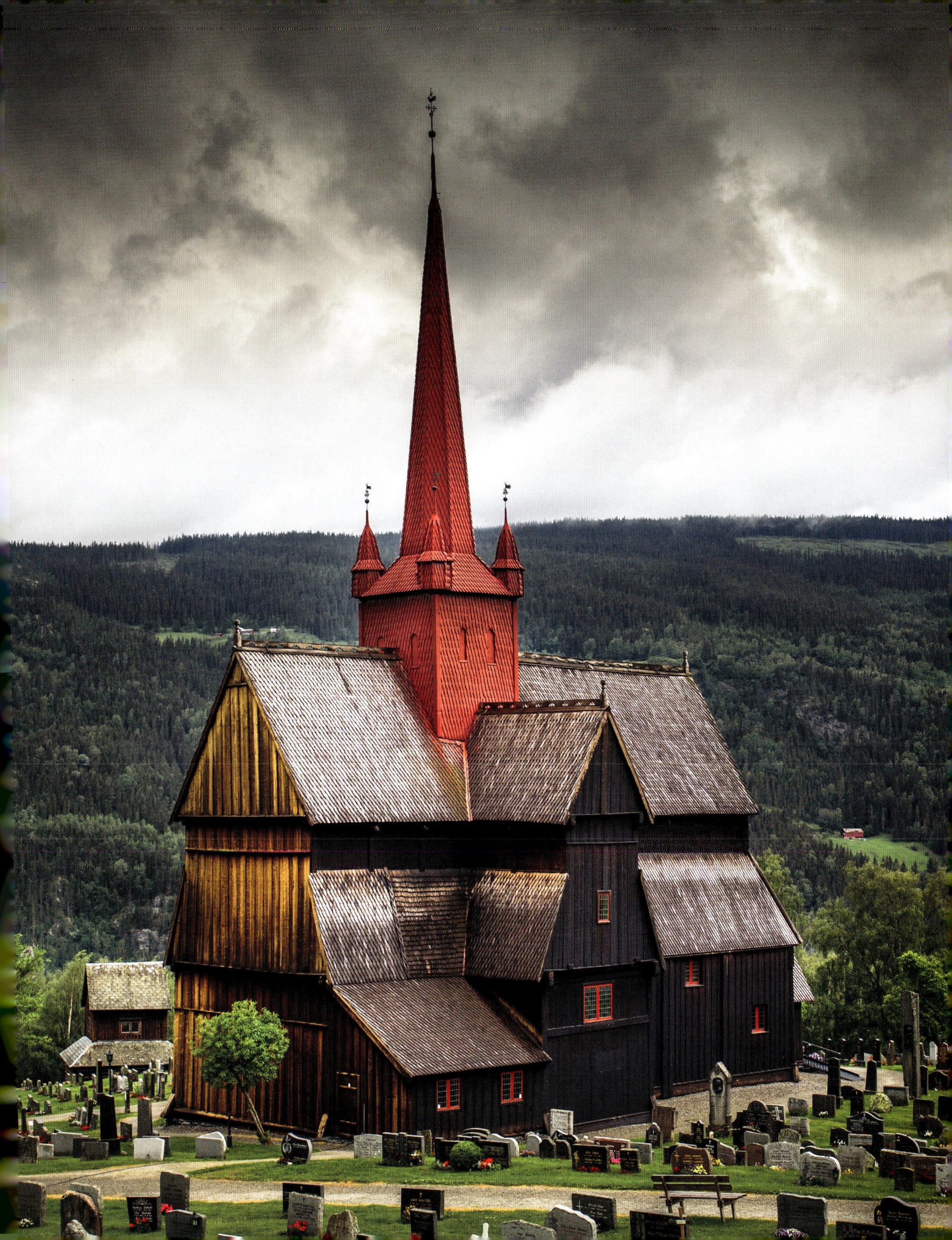

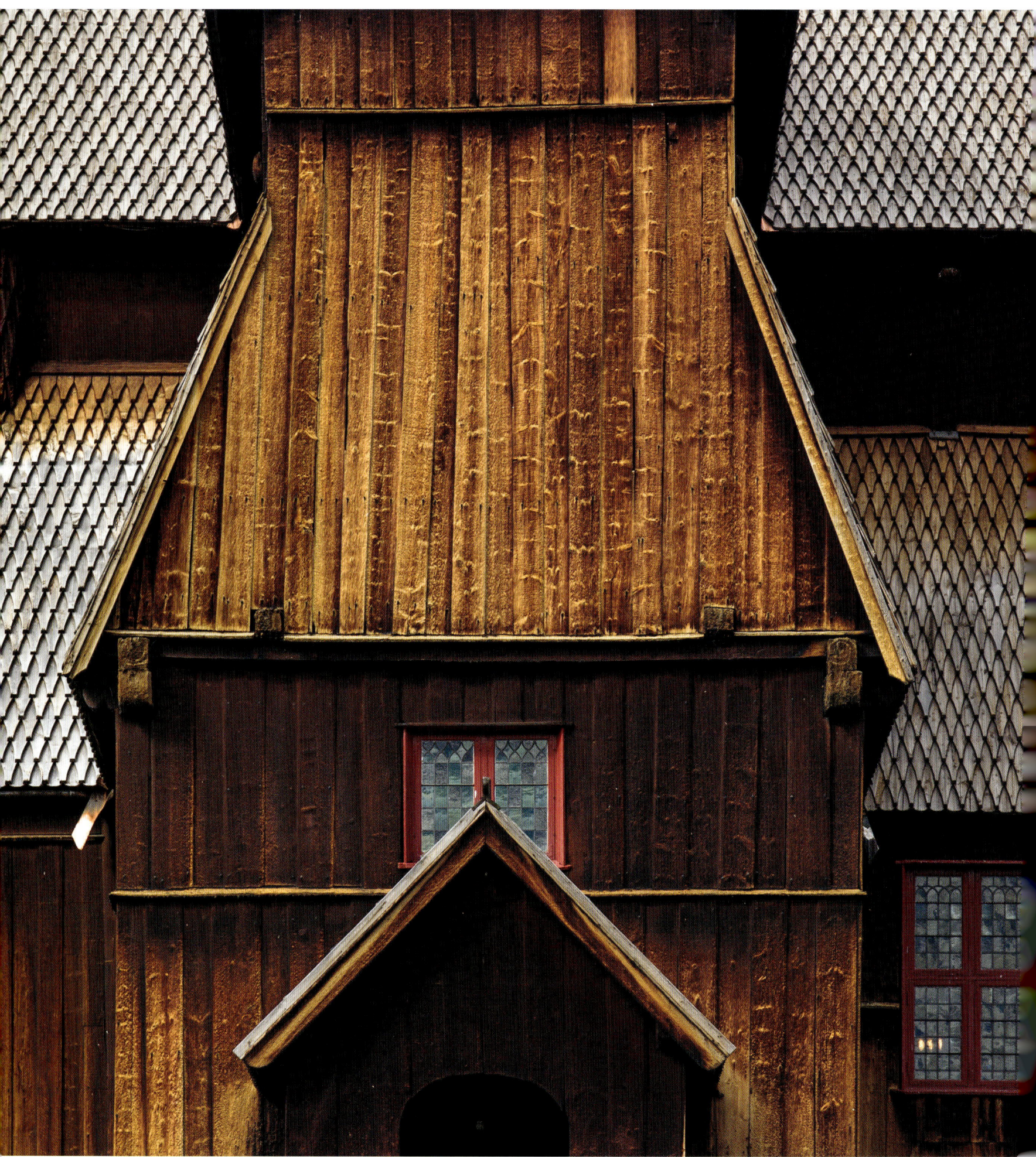

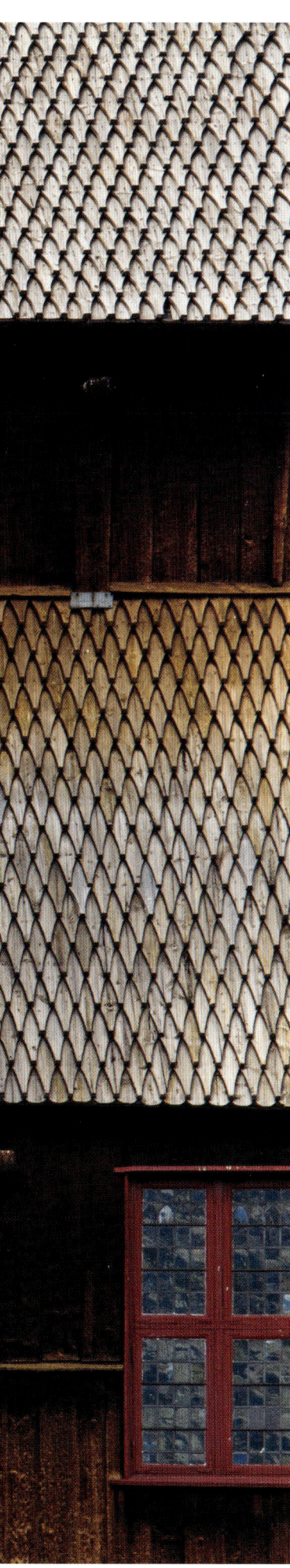

Stave church construction was a complex matter and although some features appear as embellishments, almost every piece of wood has a role to play in the building's stability. The exception is the carved dragon heads above the main portal, designed to ward off evil spirits.

Advances in building technology and machinery enabled archaeologists to safely investigate the ground directly underneath the church. Almost 1,000 coins from different periods were recovered, but there was a predominance originating from the thirteenth century and the reign of Håkon Håkonsson. The coins were either offerings or had been accidentally dropped, and most were discovered on what would have been the male side of the church. The other fascinating find was a series of holes belonging to a previous pole church. The supports for a pole church were planted directly into the ground and consequently had a limited life span of about one hundred years before they simply rotted away. Although stave churches were once familiar sights in both Denmark and Sweden, the only surviving examples are scattered throughout the Norwegian countryside. The most remarkable construction detail is that they were constructed without recourse to nails or other metal fixing, and all joints were dovetailed. The building was also effectively free-standing because it comprised vertical posts with horizontal wall planks resting upon ground sills. Doing a 'hands and knees' exploration is a fascinating and enlightening insight into the simplicity of stave church design, but it is also thought provoking in terms of how the sheer weight of individual beams was managed. When a church is being built from stone, each block is obviously heavy, but the weight of massive timber beams must have been even more of a challenge in terms of their excessive length.

When medieval pilgrims on their way to St Olaf's shrine rested at Ringebu, they would have gathered together in a significantly different style of building. During most of the pre-Reformation Catholic era, the church would have comprised external galleries and an apse, and it would have been a dark and gloomy space due to the almost complete absence of windows. The only light creeping into the nave would have been from small portholes set high up the walls. There was, therefore, little chance of ventilation and the enclosed space might not have been the most fragrant. Ringebu's characteristic red tower was added during the post Reformation building process, which created a church that still welcomes pilgrims *en route* to Nidaros Cathedral.

(*right*) Despite the fact that timber is not as heavy as stone, the same construction principles of load bearing and weight distribution apply to these complex structures. The wood shingles cascade down the steep roof like the glistening silver scales of a freshly caught salmon.

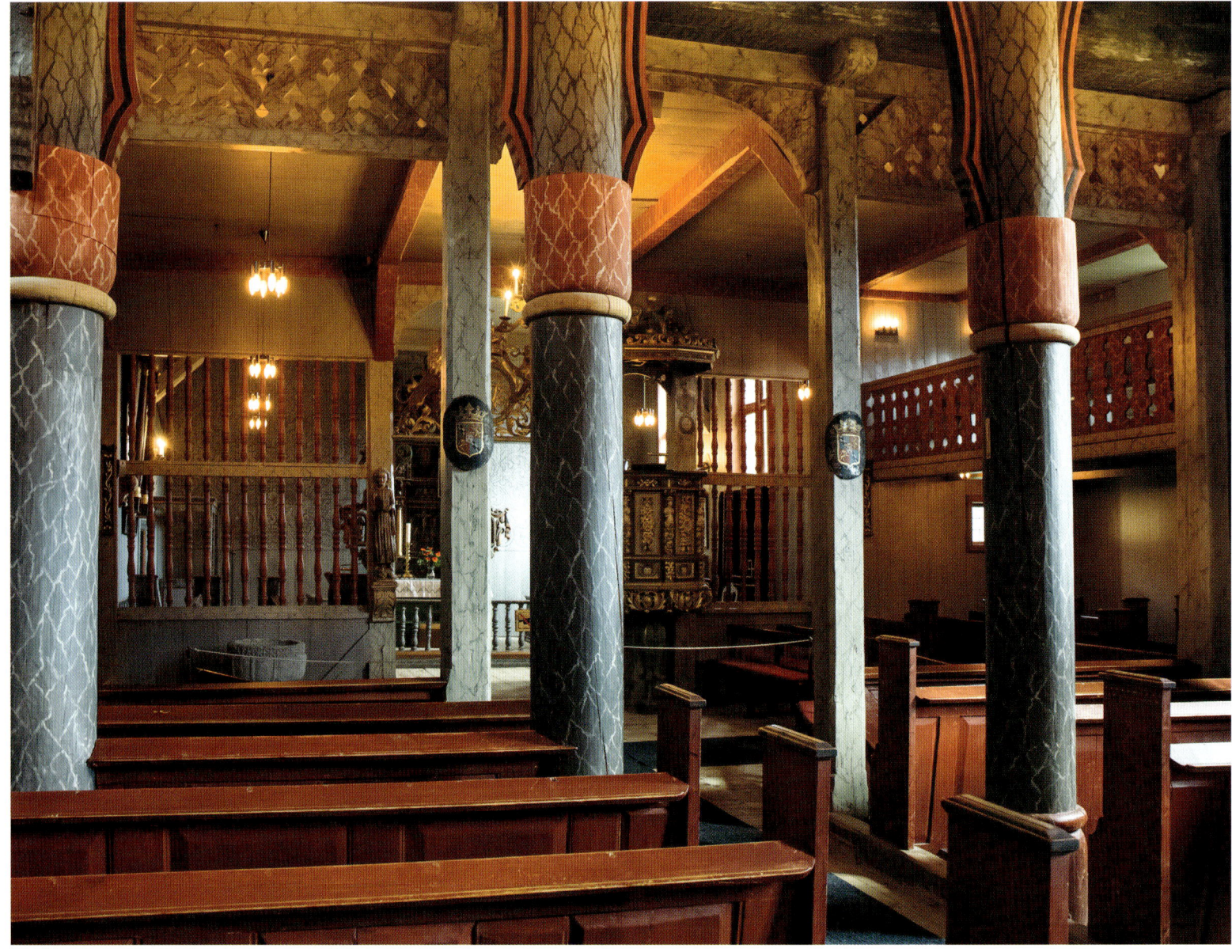

(*above*) The nave pews did not exist in the medieval church and although benches lined the walls for the elderly the congregation was expected to stand. The soapstone font is a survivor from the earlier pole church, the altar piece an elaborate seventeenth-century contribution.

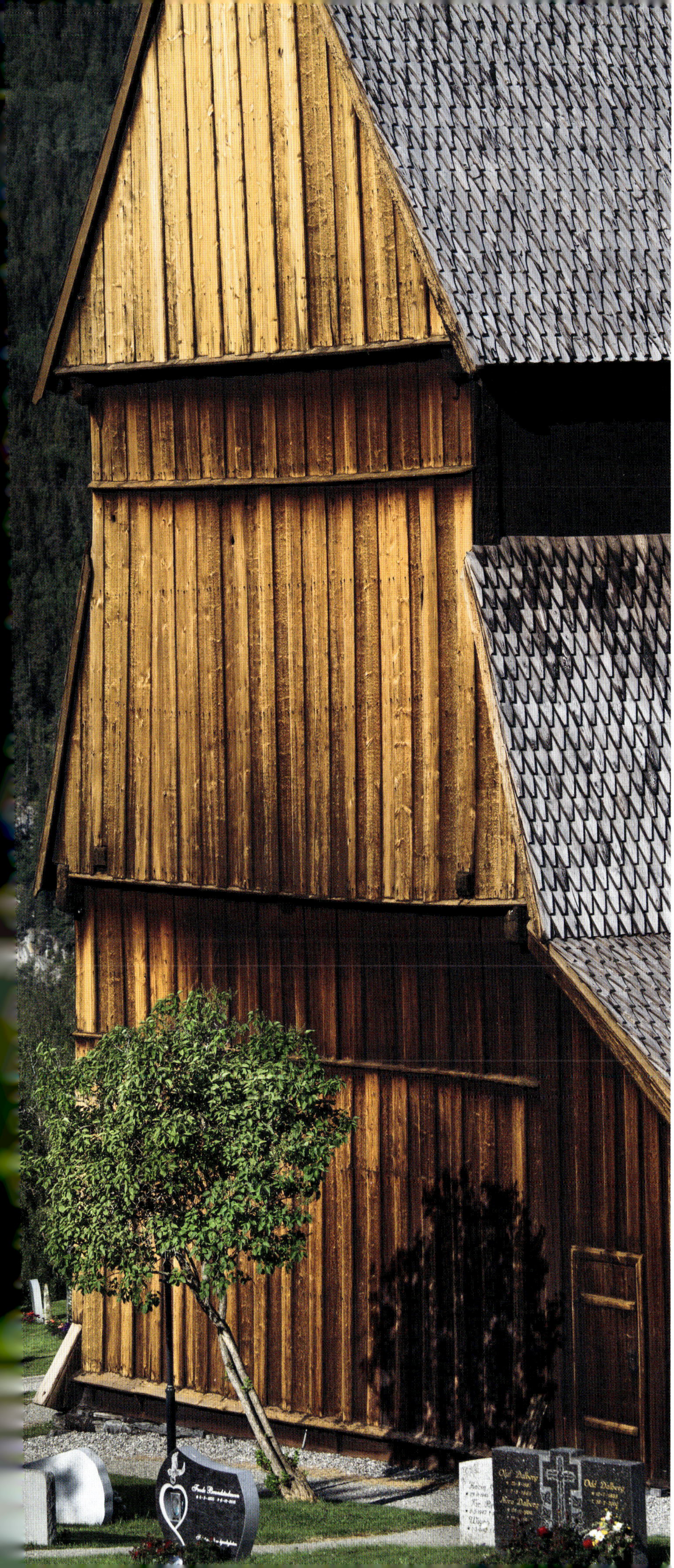

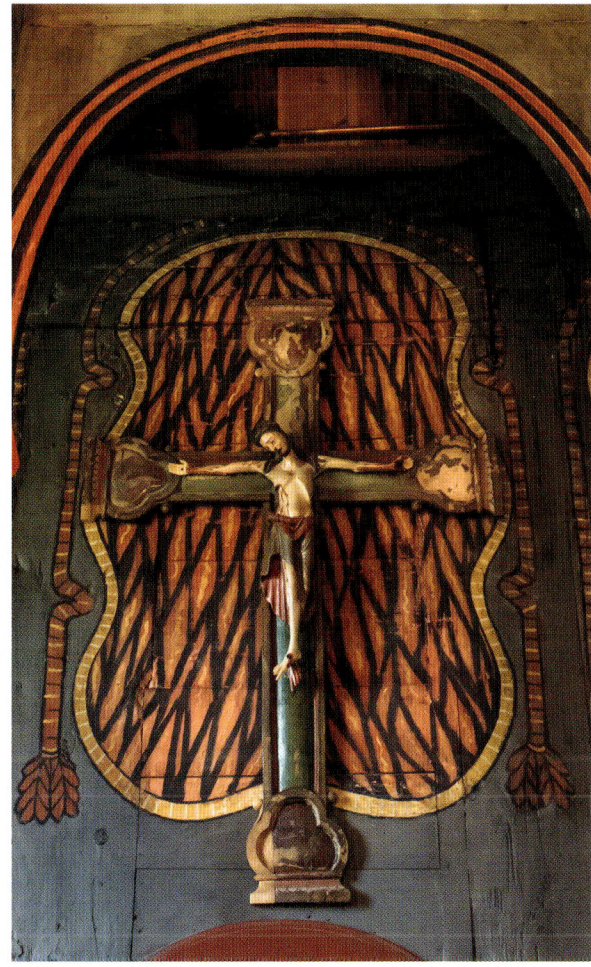

(*above*) Two ancient crucifixes are still displayed in the nave and the one above the west door is typical of early-fourteenth-century sculptures. This particular one is a doubly moving example due to the inclined head of the dead Christ set against the patchily flaked paintwork.

SWEDEN
THE ABBEY CHURCH OF VADSTENA
Vadstena, Östergötland

Vadstena lies within a sheltered bay on the north-eastern shore of Vättern, Sweden's second largest lake. At either end of the shoreline lie Vadstena's two most prominent and historically important buildings: a sixteenth-century moated castle and the even older Abbey Church of Vadstena, whose origins date back to the fourteenth century. This was the mother church of the Order of the Most Holy Saviour, more commonly known as the Bridgettine Order. This monastic order for both monks and nuns was founded by St Bridget, who is Sweden's patron saint. She was also declared one of the six co-patron saints of Europe by Pope John Paul II in 1999. St Bridget was born into the upper echelons of Swedish society, as her mother was connected to the extended royal family. She married at the surprisingly tender age of thirteen and ultimately bore eight children, six of whom survived past infancy into adulthood. Bridget served as a lady-in-waiting at the royal court of King Magnus Eriksson and Queen Blanche. It was during her time at the palace that Bridget experienced a divine revelation that she should create an abbey from the palace building. Fortunately, she was able to secure assurances from the king and queen that they would bequeath a substantial portion of the palace for conversion into an abbey and monastery.

Seven years prior to the Bridgettine Order's foundation in 1346, Bridget and her husband Ulf undertook the first of two pilgrimages: to the shrine of St Olaf in Trondheim, followed in 1341 by the monumental undertaking of a journey to Santiago de Compostela and the shrine of St James the Apostle. Her husband unfortunately died upon their return in 1344 and Bridget stayed at the monastery until she left for Rome five years later. Although she spent more than two decades in Rome doing charitable work in churches and hospitals, she was mainly striving to seek papal ratification for the rules governing her monastic order. This was not an easy task during the period of the Avignon papacy, but she eventually secured the blessing of Pope Urban V in 1370 towards the end of his three-year spell back in Rome.

Vadstena Abbey at sunrise. The abbey became a popular place of pilgrimage visited by thousands each year during the late Middle Ages. Many of those paying homage to St Bridget would subsequently make the arduous cross-country journey to St Olaf's shrine in Trondheim, Norway.

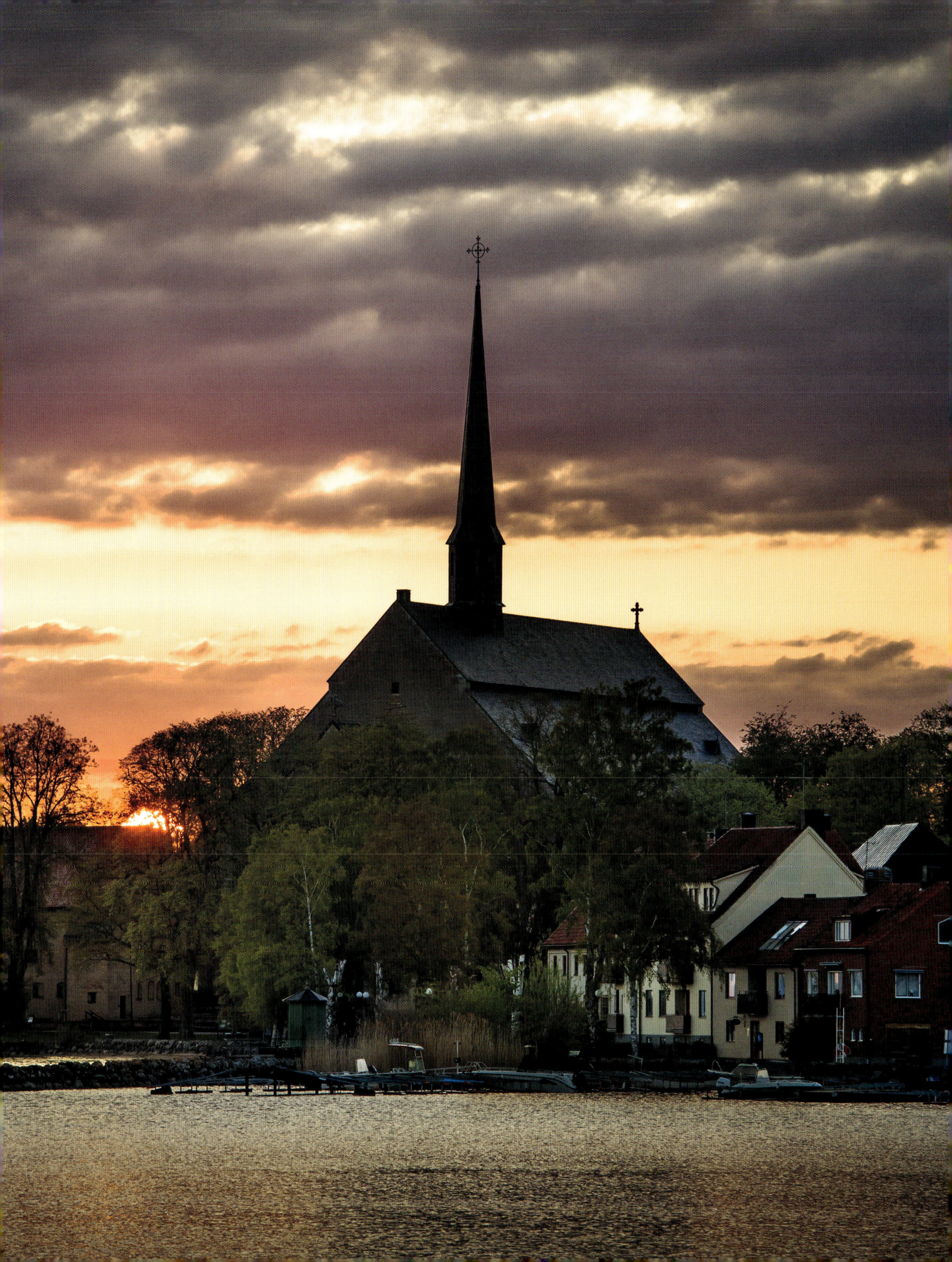

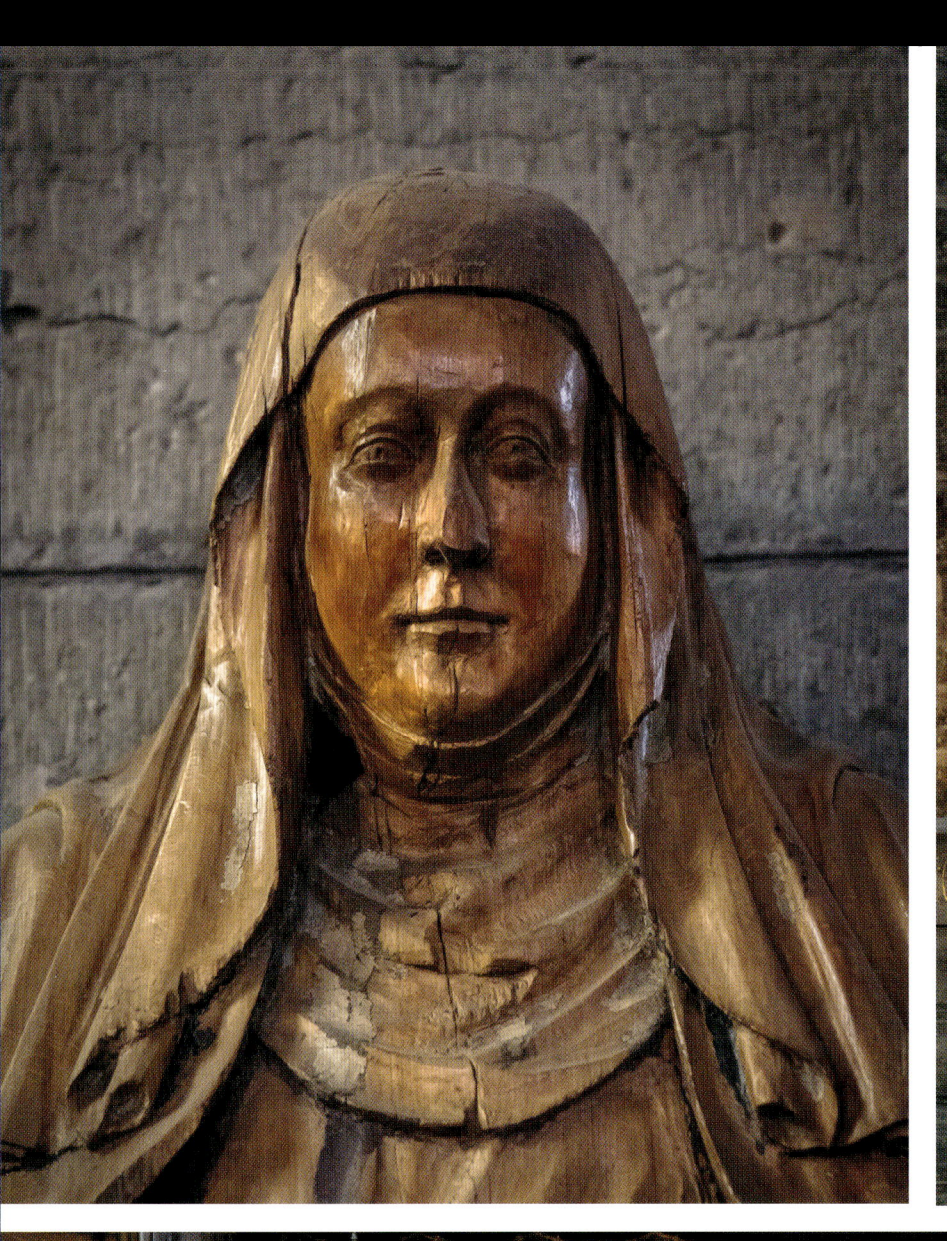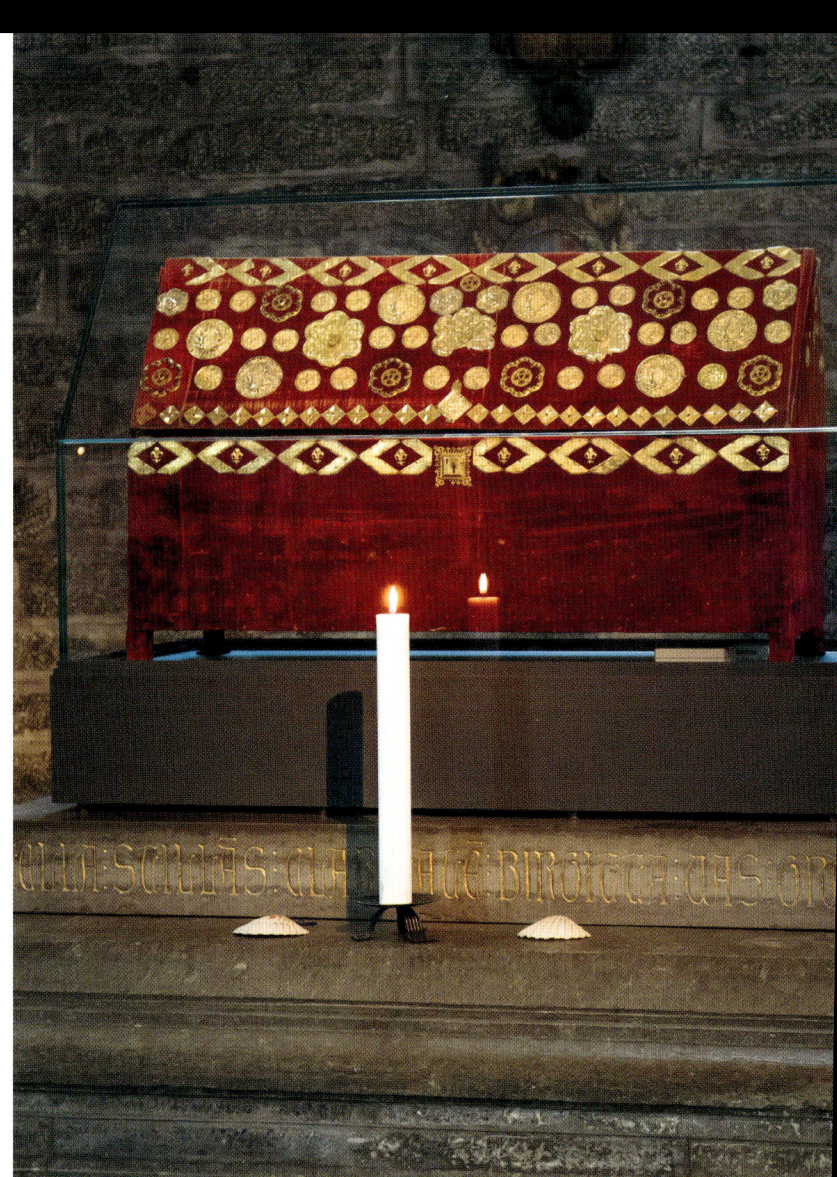

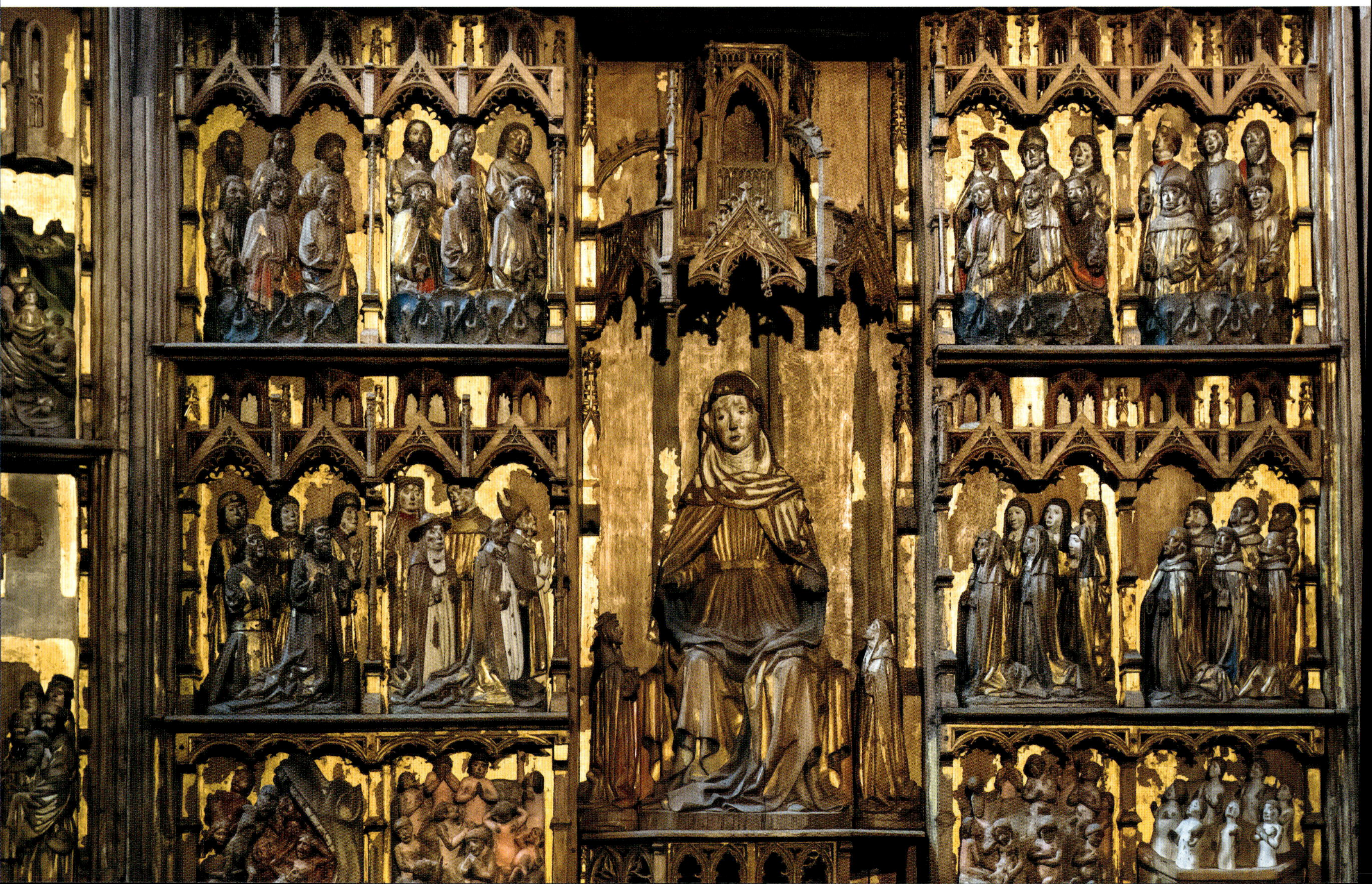

(*top left*) The oldest known sculpture of St Bridget was carved in the fourteenth century and it was originally intended as part of her dedicated altar. (*top right*) The velvet-clad shrine of St Bridget was originally deemed too simple, and a 90-kilogram/200-pound silver shrine was crafted in Stockholm. It was almost immediately melted down by Johan III. (*bottom*) This painted and gilded triptych was crafted in northern Germany in about 1460. St Bridget is seated in the centre, flanked on the upper level by apostles, saints and other characters.

Bridget was relieved to have finally achieved official recognition of her order and despite her advancing years decided that it was appropriate to make the most important Christian pilgrimage of all. Accompanied by her children, she set off for Jerusalem. Most of Bridget's life had been governed by divine spiritual visions, but shortly after her departure from Rome she received an unwelcome message that one of her offspring would not return from the Holy Land. That subconscious revelation unfortunately became reality when her son, Carl, fell ill and died before they got past Naples. Despite her grief, Bridget continued in the hopes of finding solace and comfort in Jerusalem. The demands of such mental and physical strain took their toll and Bridget died shortly after her arrival back in Rome, on 23 July 1373, the exact date that had been predicted to her in a vision received five days earlier. Bridget's daughter, Catherine, organized the return of her mother's coffin to Vadstena and the partially constructed abbey. Catherine thereafter returned to Rome, where she not only campaigned hard for Bridget's canonization but also secured ten papal decrees protecting the abbey, including the stipulation that Vadstena Abbey should be recognized as the mother church of the Bridgettine Order. Bridget was eventually canonized by Pope Boniface IX on 7 October 1391 and Catherine was beatified a century later, thereby enabling her veneration in all Bridgettine abbeys and churches.

Bridget's reliquary in the abbey is a glass-encased wooden shrine, clad in a sumptuous red velvet drape adorned with gilded medals. Forensic tests carried out on the bones and skulls lodged within the casket confirm that some do indeed belong to Bridget, others to her daughter. Some relics remain unidentified. The abbey church is a wonderfully tranquil place and although there is free-standing statuary of the most important religious figures, such as the Virgin Mary, St John the Baptist, St James the Apostle and Bridget herself, the space is not cluttered nor the walls over-decorated with stone carvings. The unadorned approach to both interior and exterior adheres to Bridget's instruction that its construction should be 'of plain work, humble and strong'.

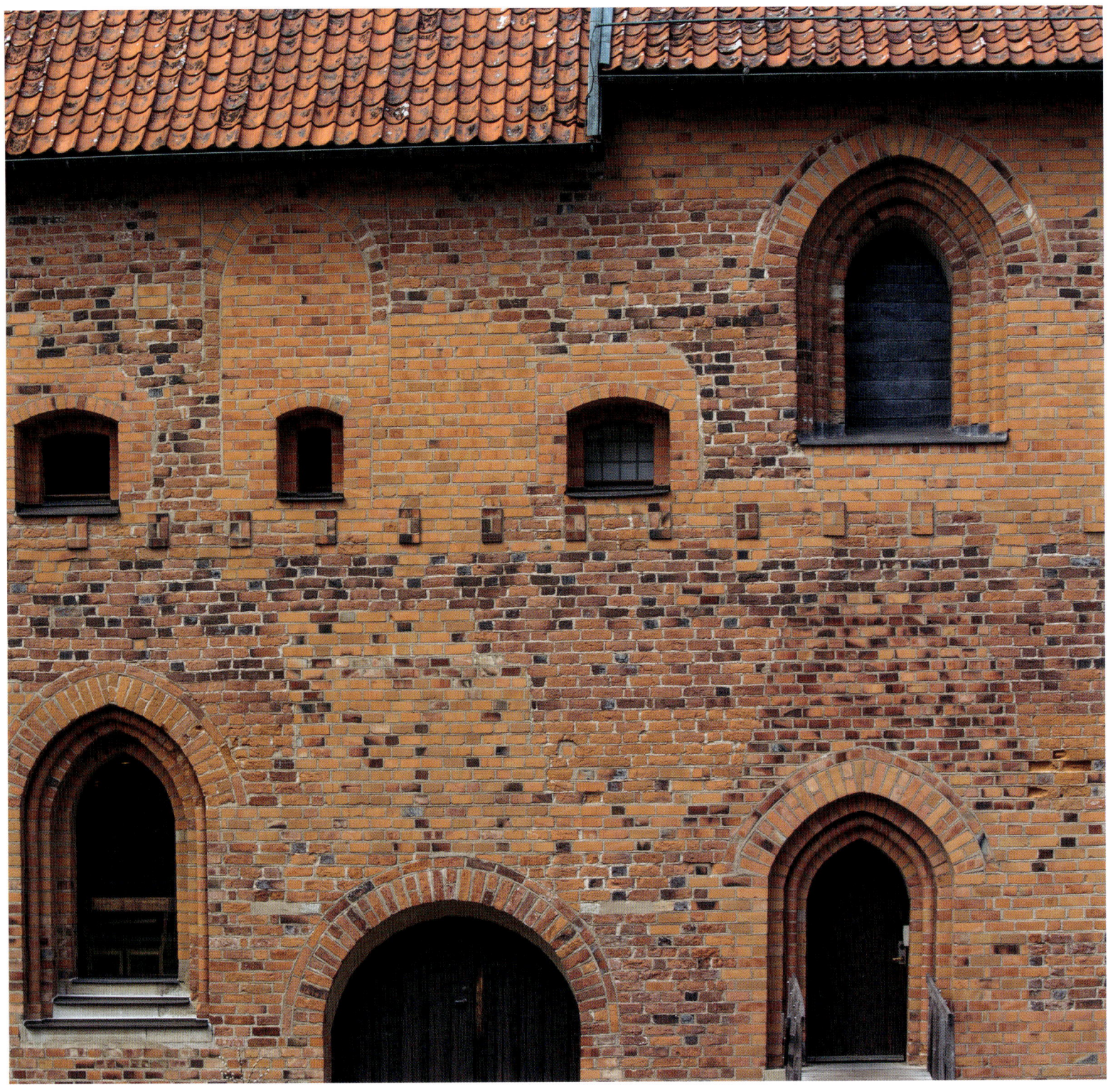

(*above*) The brick building to the north of the church is just one part of the former convent, which had originally been the thirteenth-century royal palace. It now serves as the breakfast room of a hotel created from another part of the monastery.

(*right*) The three equal-sized naves are adorned with geometric vaulting and glowing chandeliers to enhance the tranquil atmosphere of this former abbey church. There once were separate doors leading into the church for the monks and nuns of the Bridgettine Order.

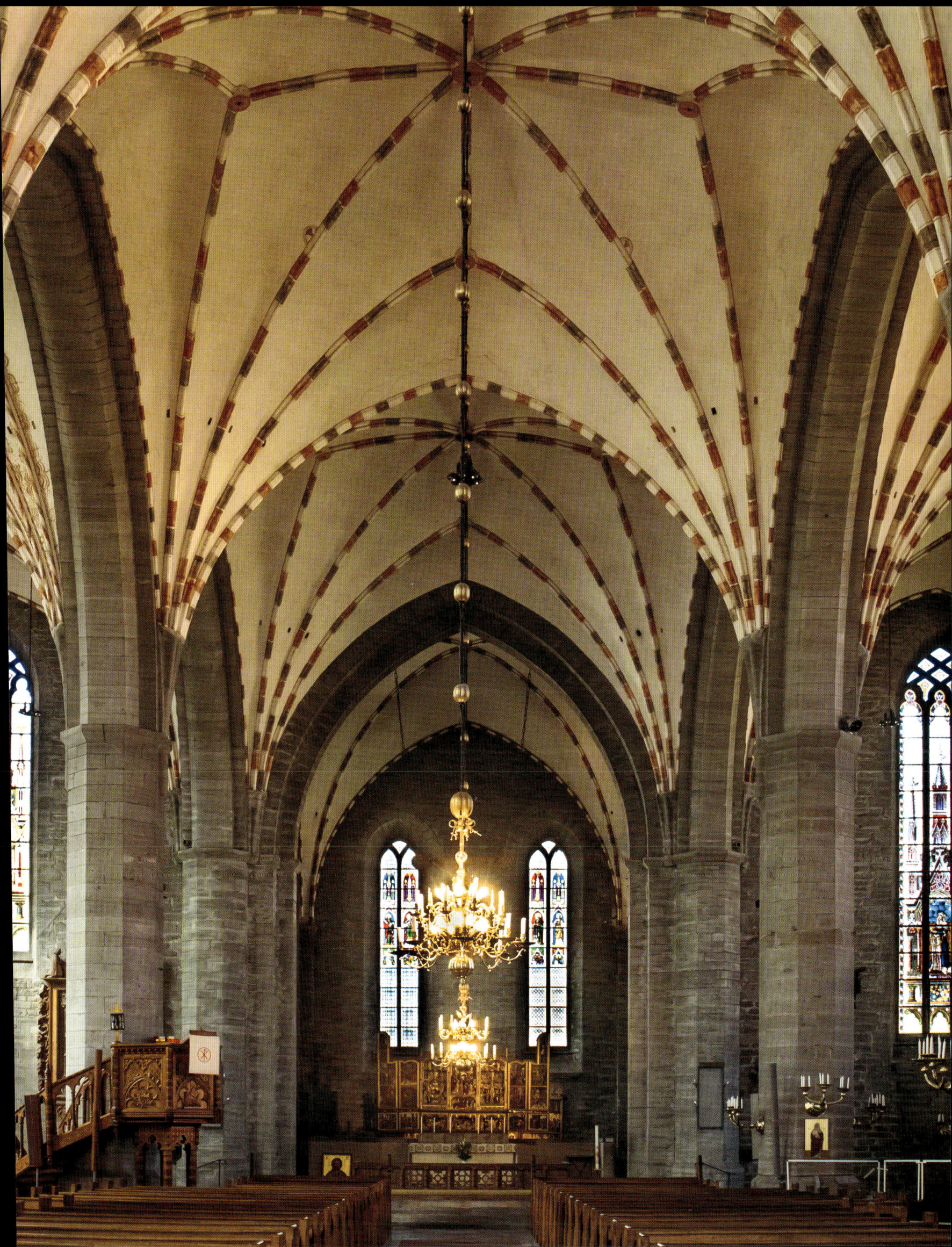

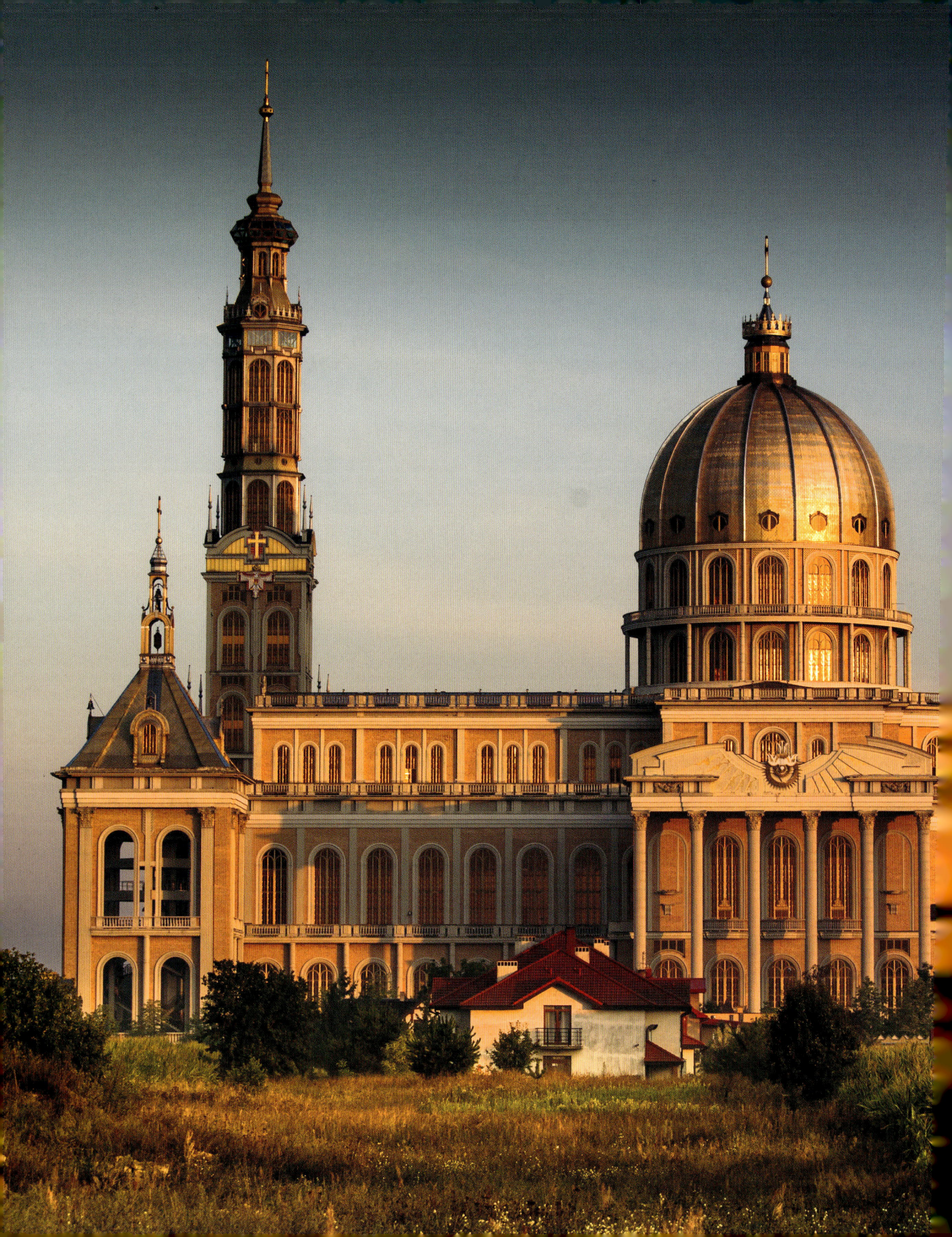

4

POLAND AND SLOVAKIA

POLAND

THE SHRINE OF OUR LADY OF CZĘSTOCHOWA
Jasna Góra

One of the most significant feast days in the Catholic Church is the Assumption of the Virgin Mary, universally celebrated on 15 August. Most of the predominantly Catholic countries of Europe hold significant celebrations to mark this date and none more so than Poland. The monastery of Jasna Góra in Częstochowa is renowned for its painting of the Virgin and Child, and the chapel in which it is housed is now honoured as the Polish national shrine. In common with other paintings and statuary of the Virgin Mary that have become discoloured after centuries spent in small, candle smoke-filled rooms, this icon is referred to as the Black Madonna of either Jasna Góra or Częstochowa.

The tradition of organized pilgrimages to Jasna Góra can be traced back to the early eighteenth century, and for those walking from the farthest parts of Poland, the journey can take up to twenty-one days. Most pilgrims arrive the day before the celebration and take part in ceremonial outdoor masses and community events, all conducted from a specially designed presbytery and altar set high up on the monastery walls and protruding outwards towards the congregation like the prow of a ship.

There are always legends as to how and when ancient icons appeared and the same applies to this portrait of Our Lady. The definite Byzantine influence and style of the painting are comparable to the *Salus Populi Romani* painting of the Virgin and Child in Rome's Basilica of Santa Maria Maggiore. Both were deemed to have been contemporary portraits by St Luke the Evangelist, but modern forensic evidence points more towards the thirteenth century. No such doubts exist about the monastery itself, as Jasna Góra (bright mountain) was first established in 1382 by a group of Pauline monks from the Roman Catholic monastic order founded a century earlier in Hungary. The Pauline brothers had travelled to Poland at the behest of Vladislaus II of Opole, Count palatine of Hungary, who had been gifted the Madonna and sought to create an appropriately respectful and safe refuge for the sacred painting.

(*previous pages*) Basilica of Our Lady of Licheń.

(*right*) Although many individuals undertake the Feast of Assumption pilgrimage, the majority of those travelling to the shrine do so in church and community groups. The sense of joy and achievement emanating from those arriving at the monastery's fortified exterior is an incredibly moving sight.

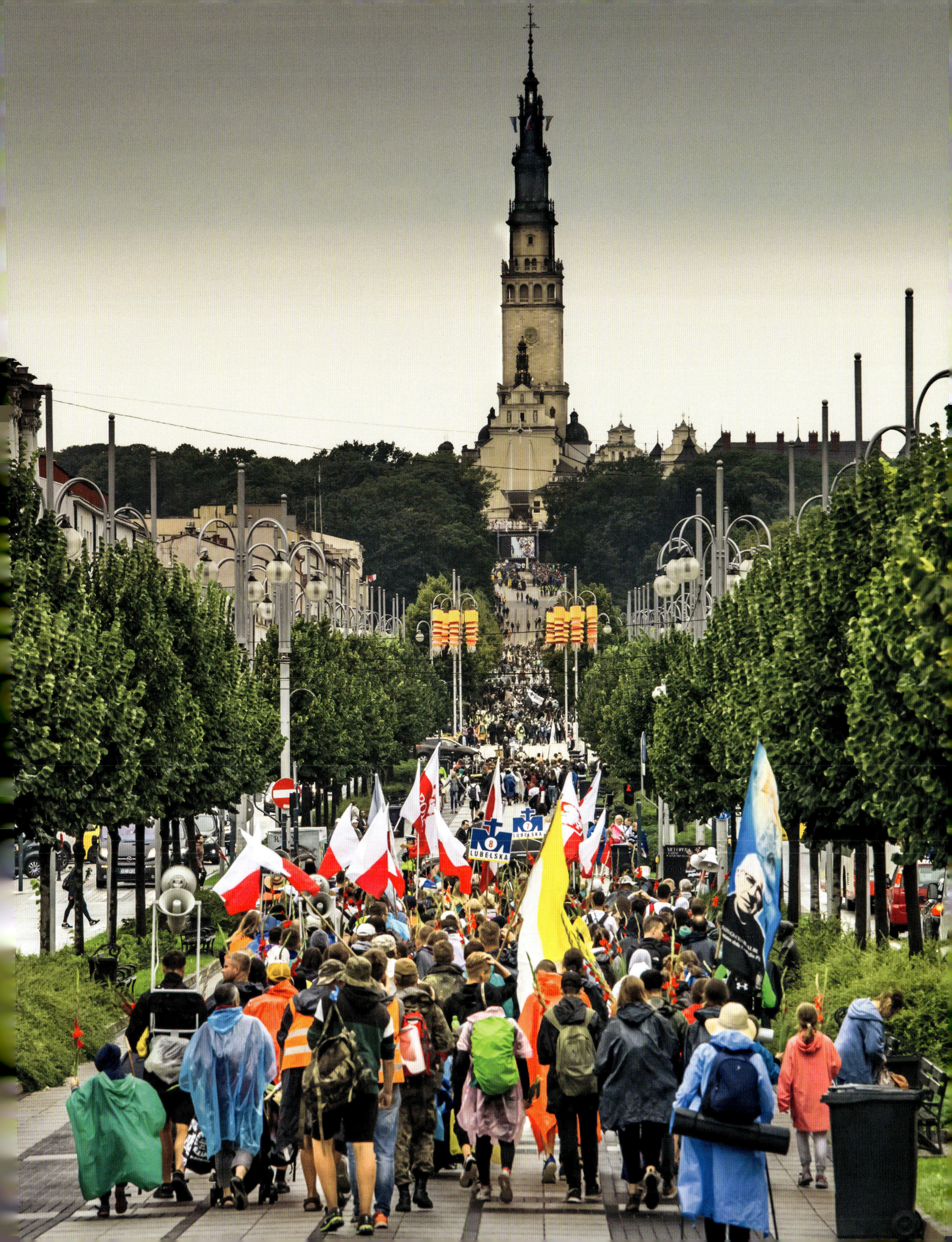

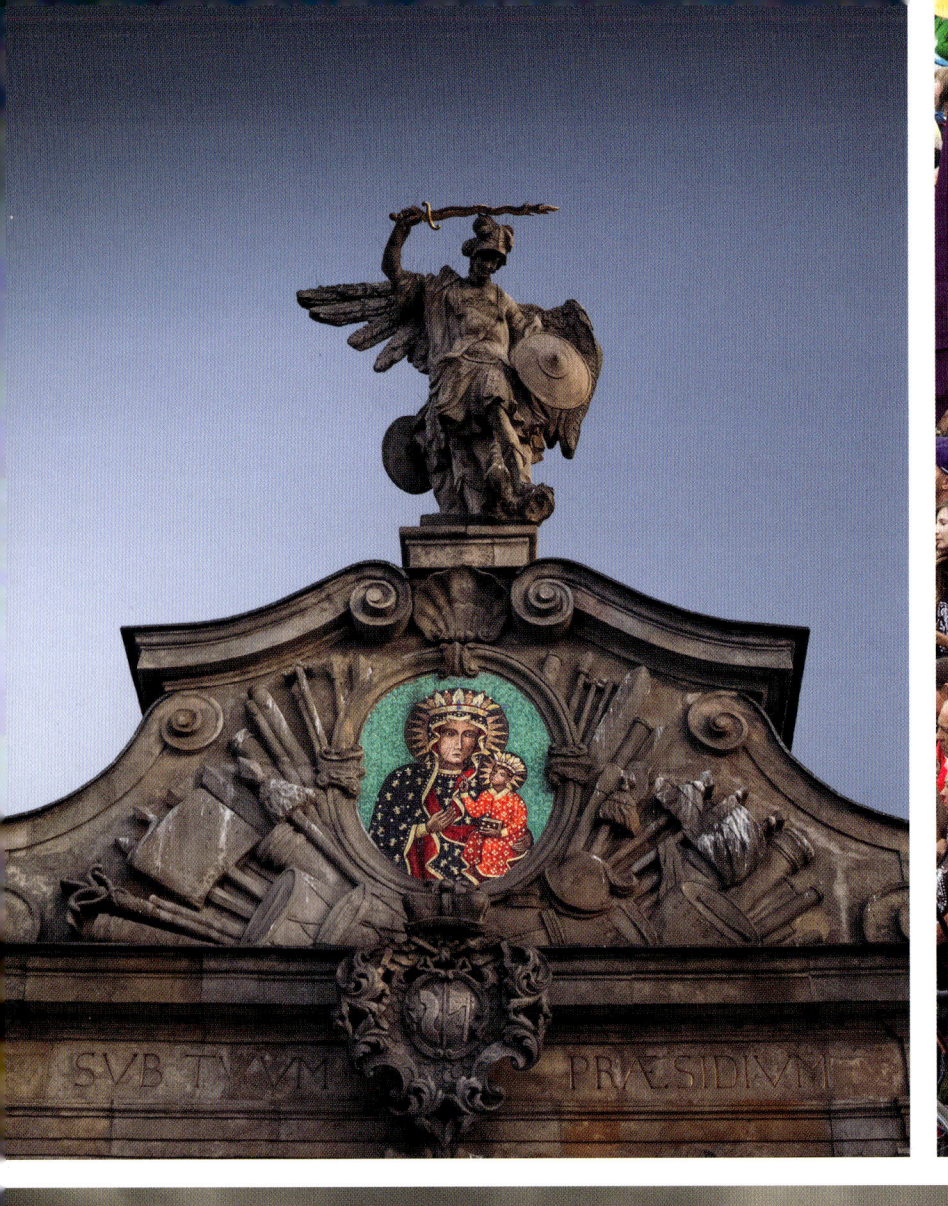
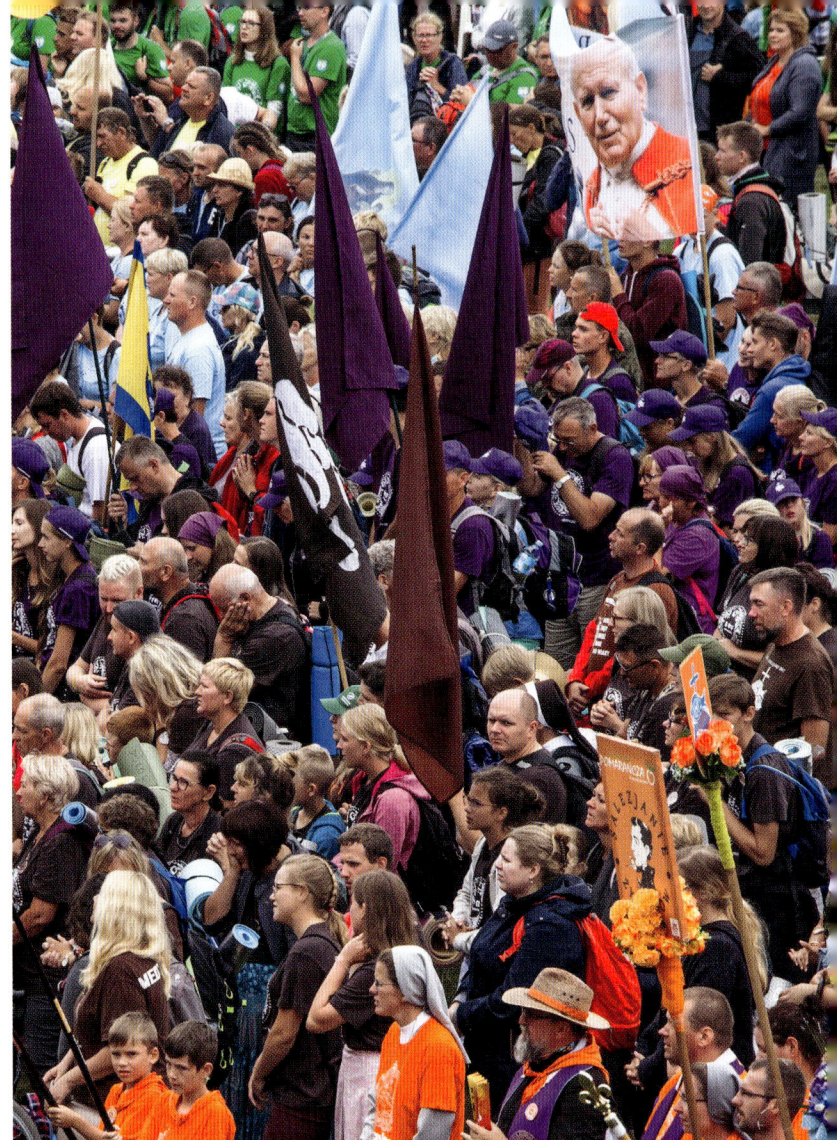

SVB TVVM PRAESIDIVM

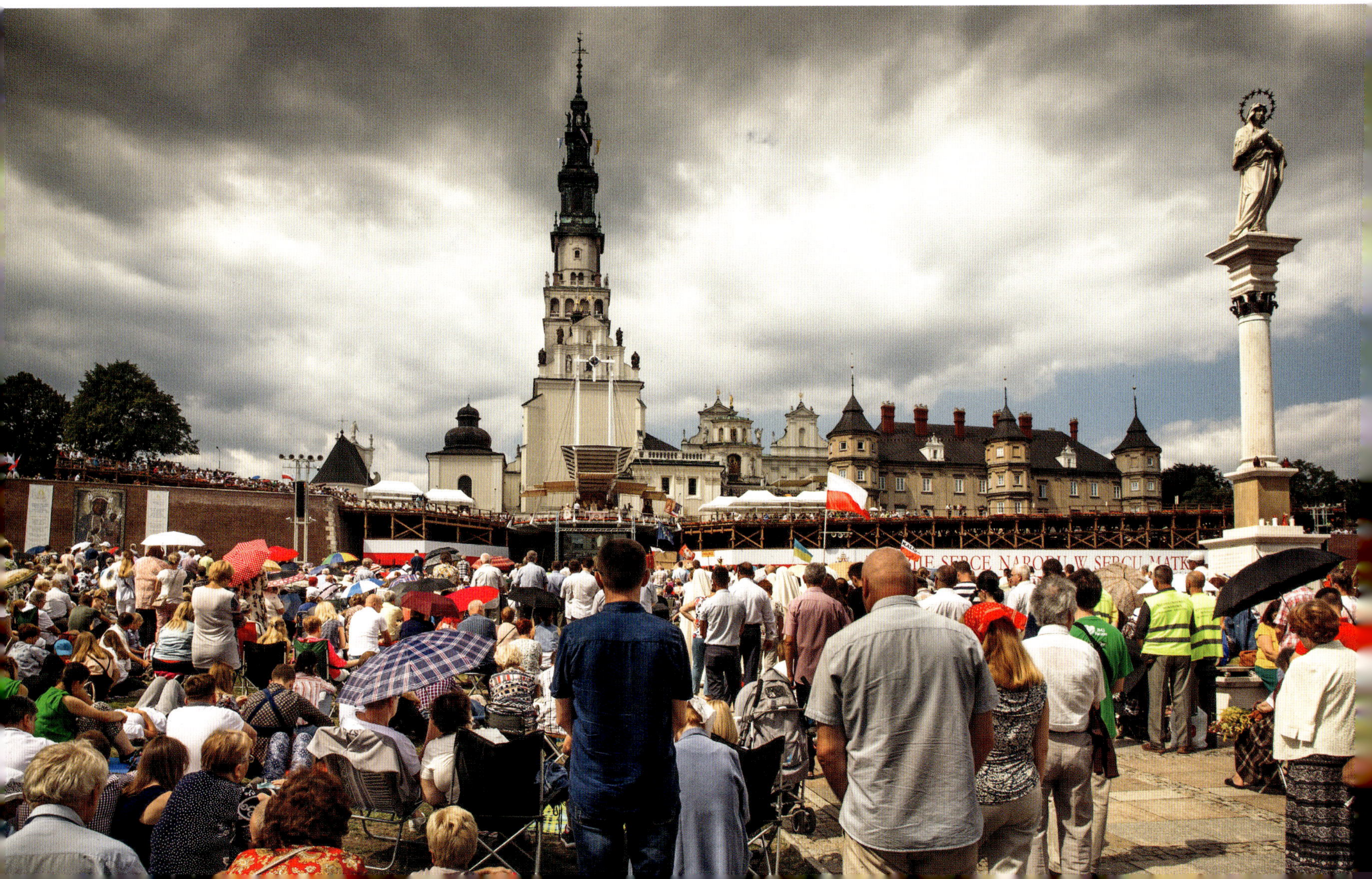

(*top left*) The gates into the monastery of Jasna Góra not only lead into the nation's most sacred shrine but also reflect the fact that this is a stoutly fortified place, designed to protect the nation's iconic shrine. (*top right*) Church and youth groups assemble before the walls of Jasna Góra for special services on the eve of the Assumption. (*bottom*) The tightly encircling monastic walls simply cannot accommodate the numbers of pilgrims who gather for major celebrations and so outdoor masses are the norm, especially for the Feast of the Assumption.

(*overleaf*) The church nave is a joyous interpretation of the Baroque style and the high altar is dominated by one of the most outstandingly dramatic renderings of the Assumption of the Virgin. The sparkling chandeliers create an ambiance eminently suitable for such an iconic church.

The initial churches on the site were of timber construction, but significant pilgrim contributions and royal endowments soon facilitated the stone and brick buildings, forming the core of the complex, that occupy Bright Hill today. However, it was not until the seventeenth century that the fortified basilica and monastery really started to take shape, due largely to the Thirty Years' War, which began in 1618 and devastated large parts of central Europe. Jasna Góra just happened to be strategically situated, and so it was decided to not only fortify the monastery as part of the national defensive network but also to maintain the icon's security during times of conflict. Probably the most significant event was in 1655, when the monastery was attacked and besieged by invading Swedish forces but remained resilient in the face of overwhelming odds. As word of this triumph spread, public opinion concluded that the iconic Madonna was undoubtedly the nation's saviour. Thereafter, the number of pilgrimages to the shrine increased markedly, but even though the Swedes had been frustrated in their repeated attempts to destroy the monastery, nothing could prevent the colossal damage caused by a large fire in 1690.

Fortunately, the painting survived the catastrophe and rebuilding began almost immediately. As a result of the intense, but nevertheless protracted, programme of reconstruction, most of the basilica and associated buildings welcoming pilgrims today date from the eighteenth century onwards. The restored and restyled nave of the church is a portfolio of the finest Baroque architectural style and decoration, and although the chancel of the chapel hosting the altar of the Virgin is a darker, more intimate space, its adjoining nave mirrors the exuberance of the main church. The walls of the shrine are laden with votive offerings, but the most significant historical collection is now housed in the dedicated Votive Treasury of the Blessed Virgin Mary, comprising gifts from royalty and nobility as well as many papal offerings. One of the most dedicated and frequent visitors from the Vatican was Pope John Paul II, a native of Poland who was adored by the nation's Catholic population. There may be countries where secularism is nibbling away at organized religion, but certainly not in Poland, where many thousands of pilgrims journey to the Shrine of Our Lady of Częstochowa.

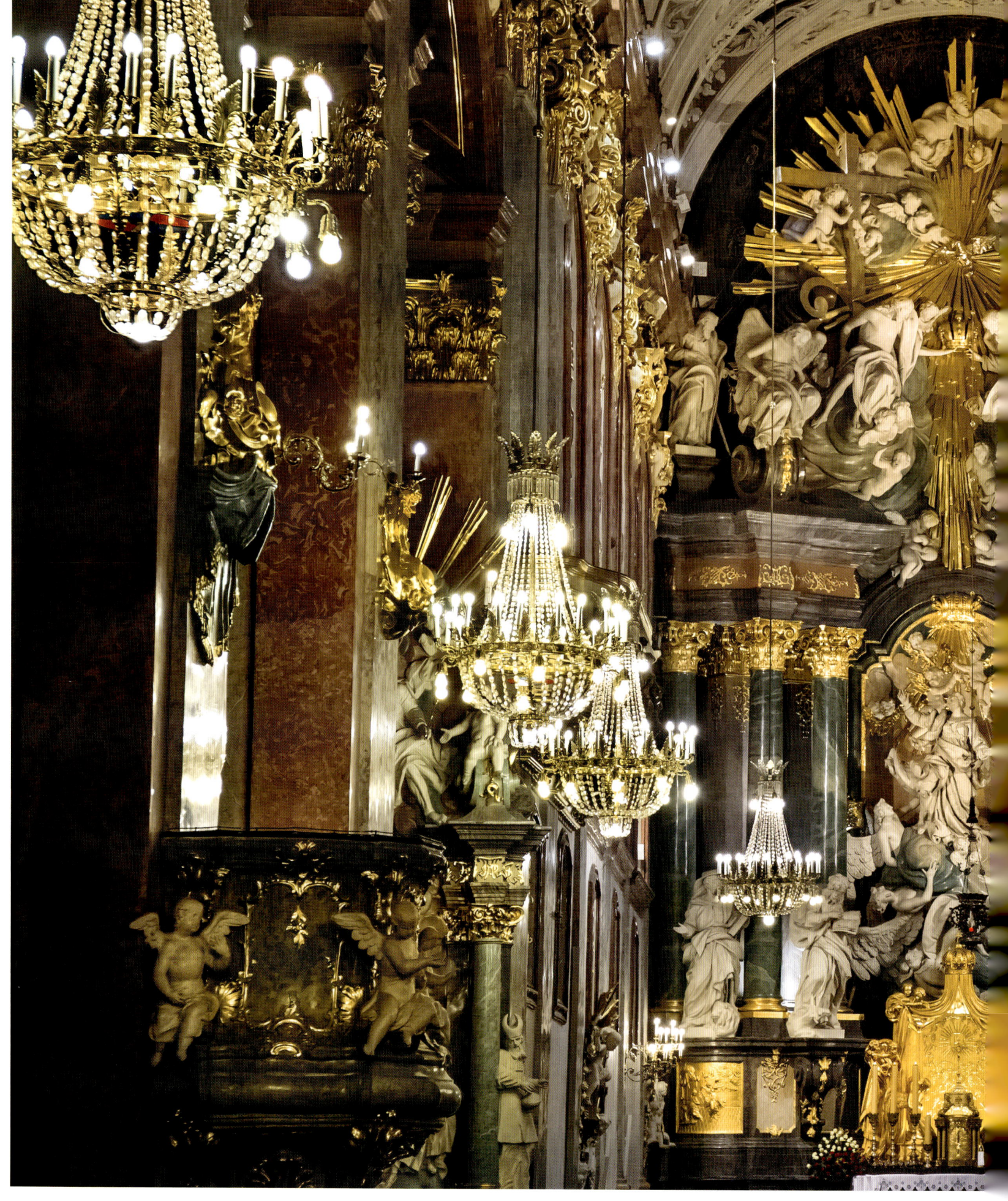

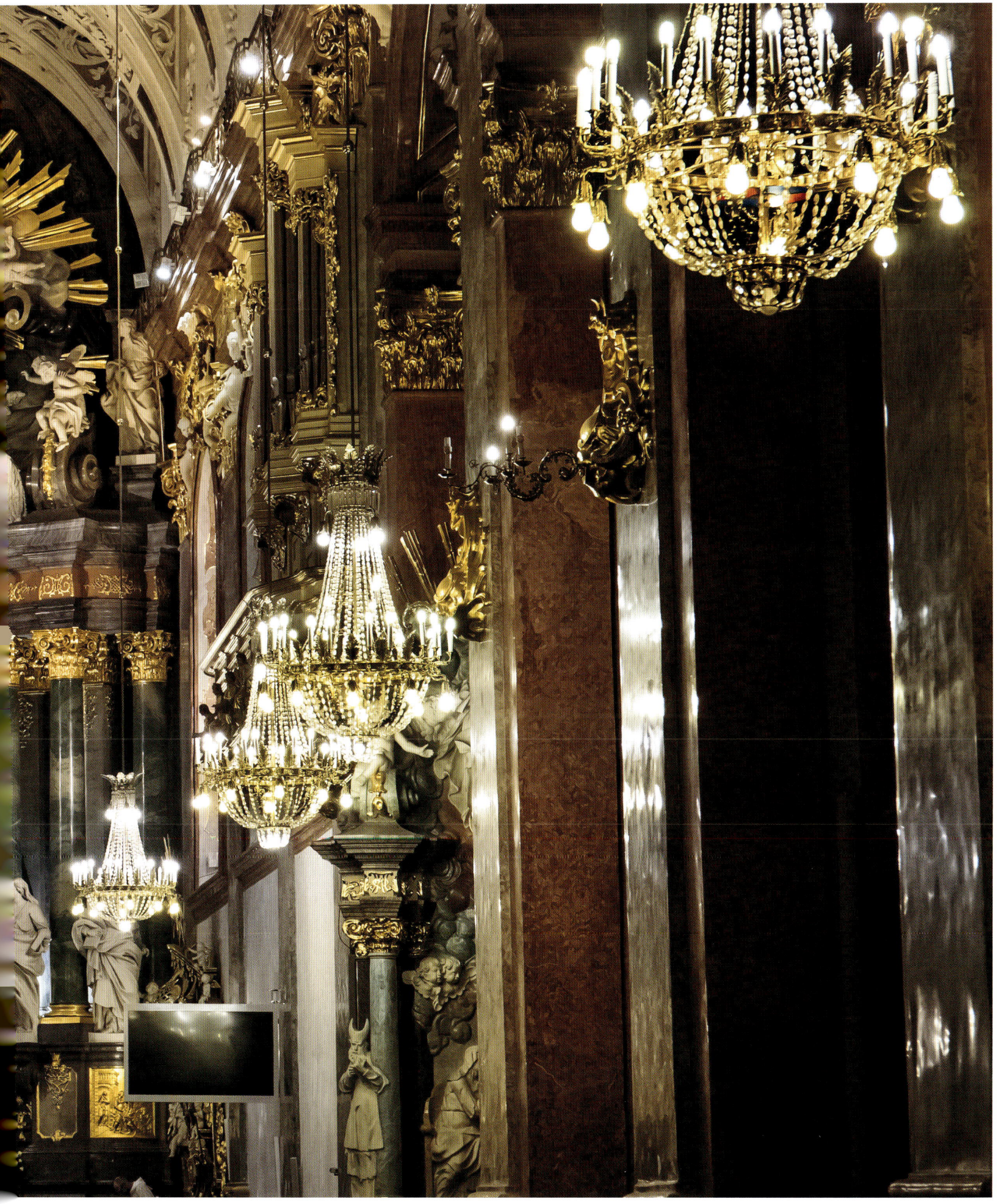

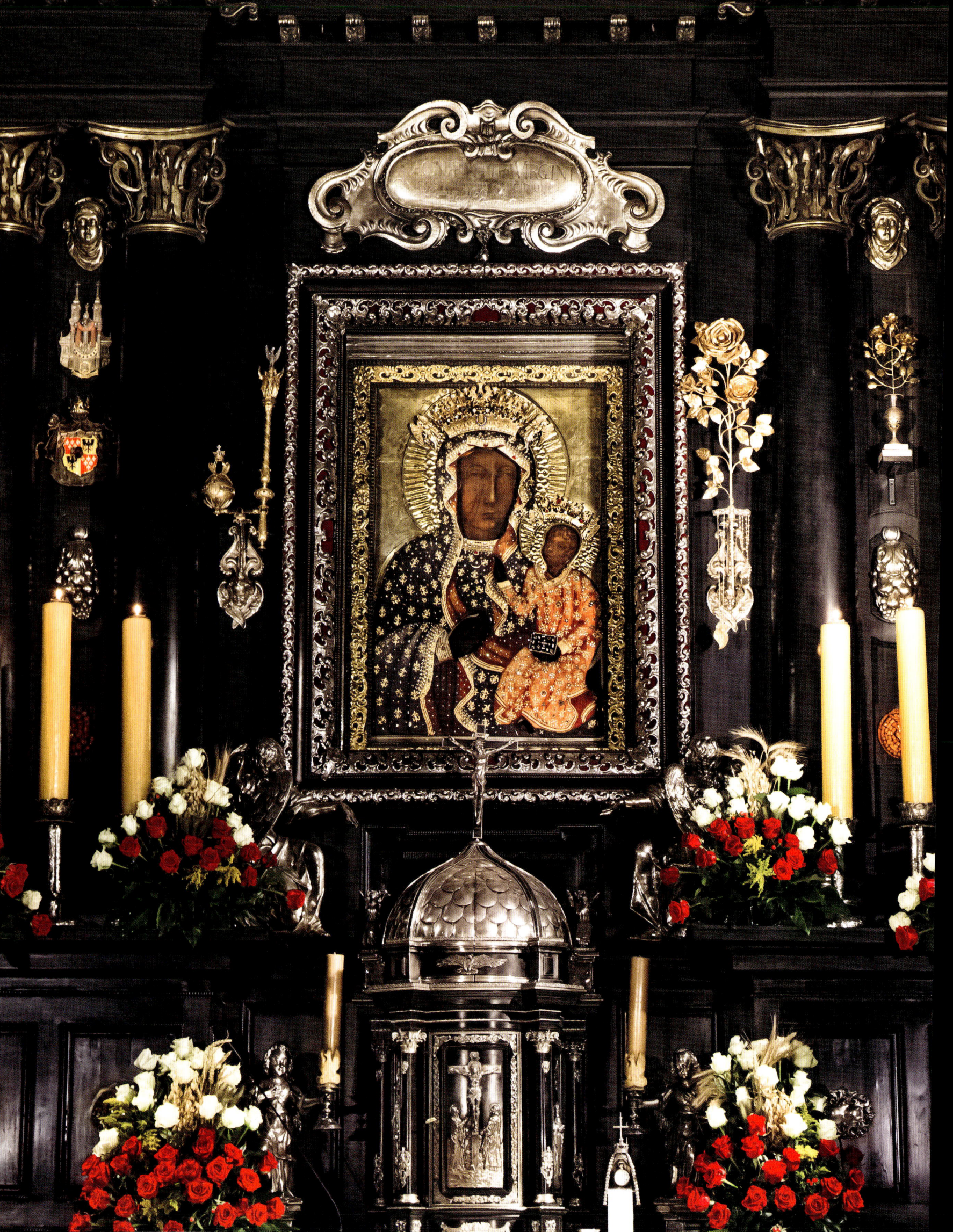

POLAND AND SLOVAKIA 123

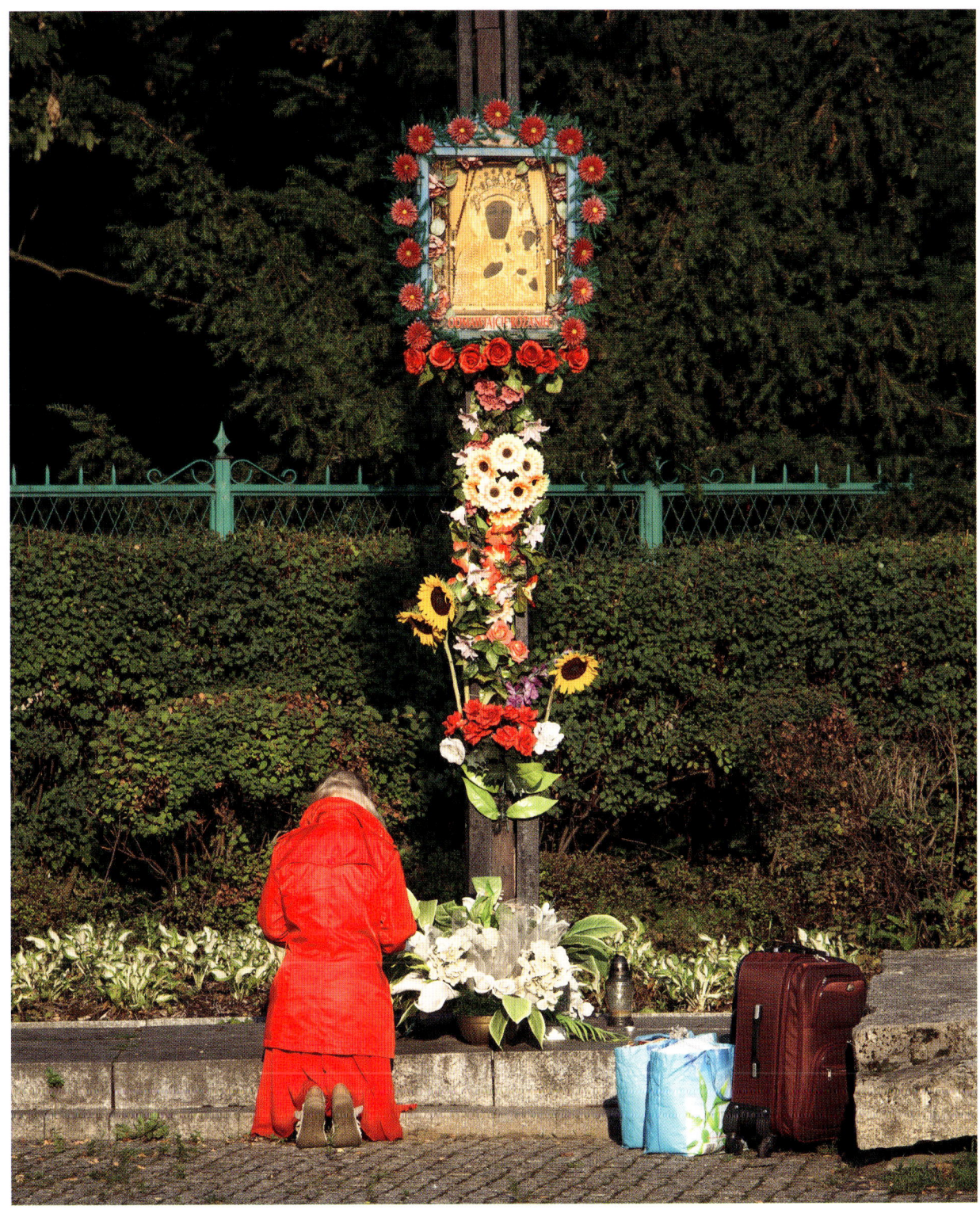

(*left*) The altar bearing the image of Our Lady of Częstochowa is dramatically set in front of dark wood panels, which act as a perfect foil for the elaborate frame containing the icon and the many silver votive offerings, floral tributes and permanently lit candles.

(*above*) A solitary replica shrine of Our Lady is set at the foot of the final approach to the monastery. Even on the great feast day of the Assumption, not everyone wants to be engulfed in the mass celebrations taking place nearby.

POLAND

BASILICA OF OUR LADY OF LICHEŃ
Licheń Stary

Set amid vast swathes of agricultural land, forests and lakes, the village of Licheń Stary may only have a population of about 1,500 people but history, legend and deep-seated faith have combined to make it the location of Poland's largest church, and currently also the eighth largest in Europe. We tend to associate religious shrines with centuries-old medieval churches and cathedrals, but in the case of Licheń Stary, the basilica's gleaming golden dome and adjacent towers only appeared as dominant features of the landscape in 2004. In a curious juxtaposition of scale, the vastness of the basilica contrasts sharply with the diminutive size of the Virgin, as reflected in the 15.5 × 9.5-centimetre/ 6 × 4-inch dimensions of the Miraculous Image for which the shrine was built.

The origins of the legend of the Miraculous Image, whose full title has evolved into 'Our Lady of Licheń, the Sorrowful Queen of Poland', are traced back to a Polish soldier named Tomasz Kłossowski. While fighting with anti-French coalition forces in their victory against Napoleon's army at the Battle of Leipzig in 1813, Tomasz was seriously wounded. He was praying for help when he was approached by a beautiful woman whom he recognized as the Virgin Mary. In exchange for his life, the soldier was instructed to find an image bearing her likeness and place it within an appropriate place of veneration in Poland.

It took more than two decades of searching before he encountered the tiny portrait in a roadside chapel, but he opted to take the picture home rather than make it public as instructed. Some eight years later, during a serious illness, he was visited again and reminded of his obligation and so hung the portrait on a tree just 3 kilometres/2 miles from Licheń. The soldier later died, and a local herdsman who had frequently prayed before the image was also visited by the apparition of the Virgin. He was told that people had to lead more respectful lives, abandon alcohol and embrace the Church – or trouble would ensue. The authorities shunned his accounts as pure fantasy, until a serious cholera outbreak jogged their memories and the tiny shrine was overwhelmed with penitents.

Our Lady of Licheń is a stunning combination of architectural innovation and creative design. The golden dome's roof was made using anodized aluminium, and although the tower is renowned for its record height, it is also the carefully crafted detail that catches the eye.

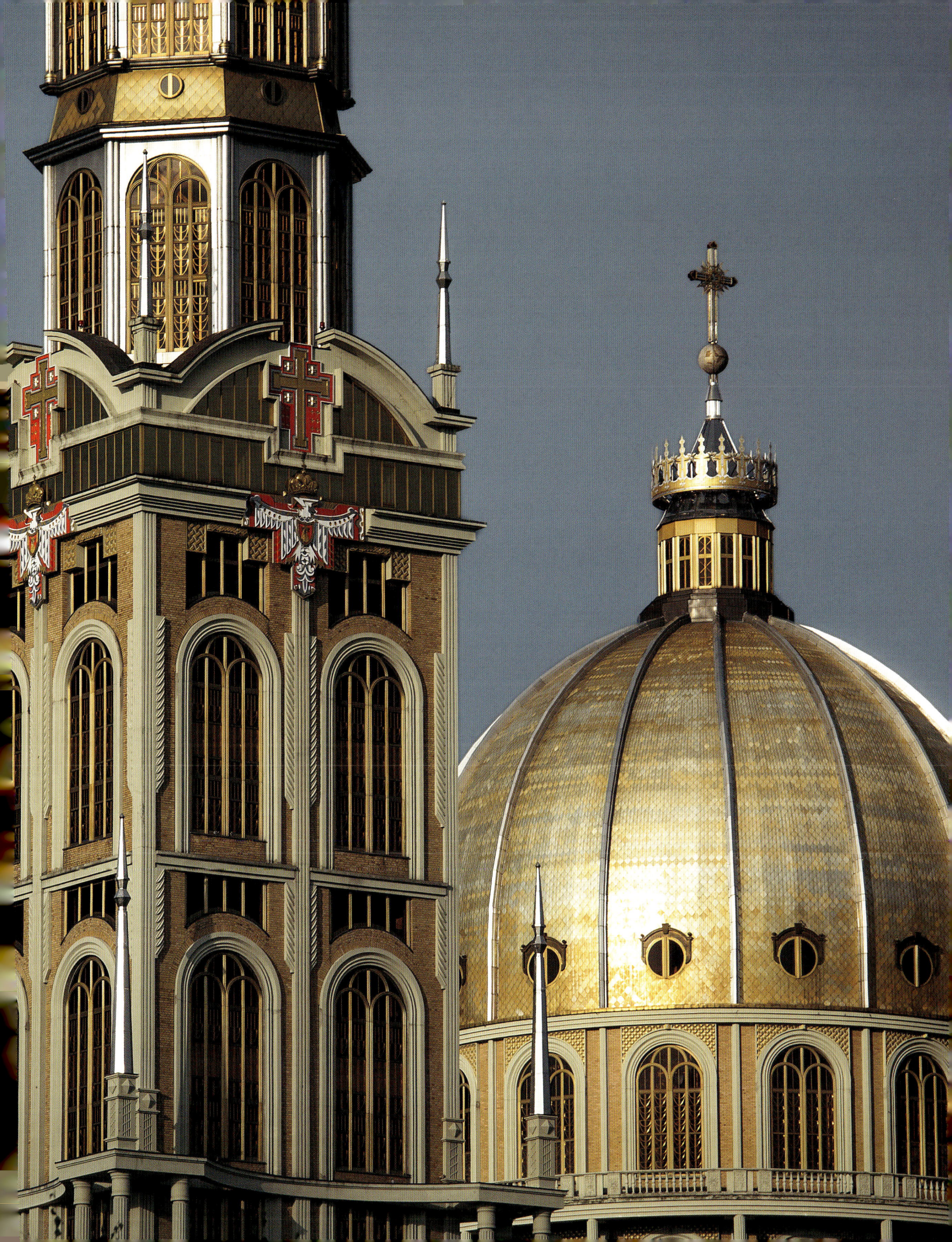

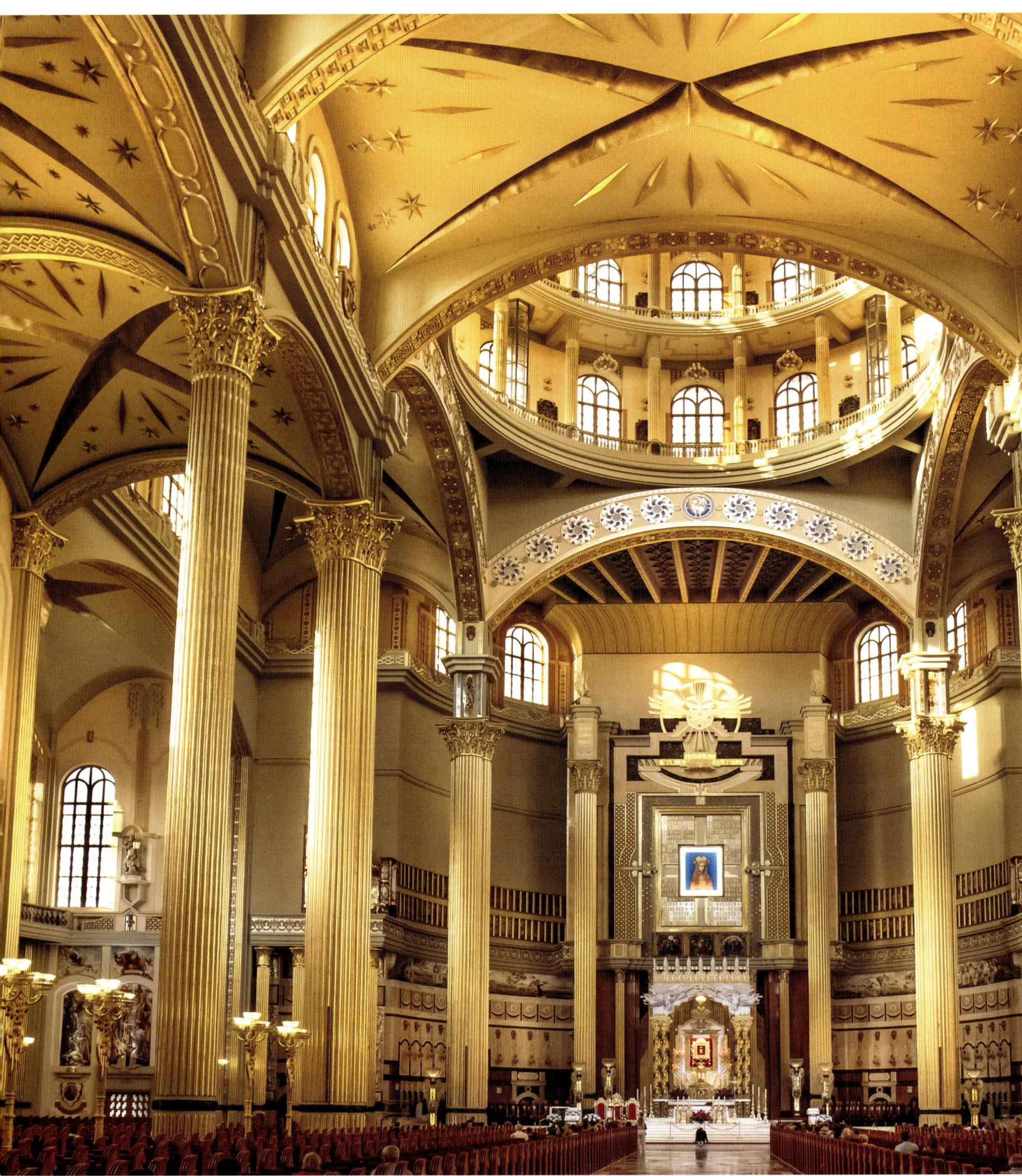

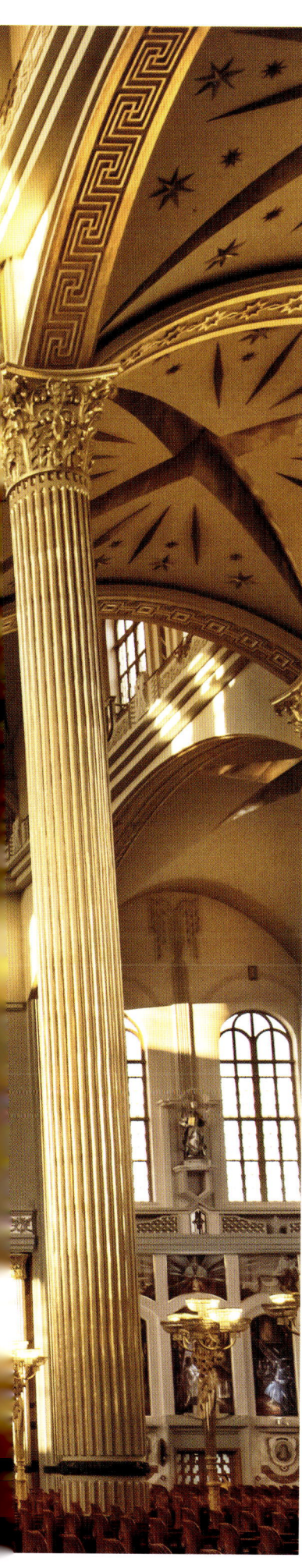

The colour scheme of gold and yellow throughout the basilica is designed to create a mellow feeling of warmth. There can be no grey days because every one of the 365 windows (one for each day of the year) is tinted so that sunshine always prevails.

When the cholera outbreak receded, it was perceived as a miracle and the image was first relocated to a small graveyard chapel in Licheń and subsequently to the parish church of St Dorothy, which, by the mid-nineteenth century, had become established as a significant pilgrimage destination.

The Miraculous Image's popularity showed no sign of diminishing over the next one hundred years. As a result of constant overcrowding, the shrine's custodian, the Reverend Eugeniusz Makulski, suggested that a new church should be built to honour the Virgin's image. However, this proposal was not only about creating a slightly bigger building, because, with the millennium approaching, it could also be perceived as a votive offering from the Polish nation to celebrate 2,000 years of Christianity. This concept was universally well received, and so both national and international appeals generated the funds needed to build a magnificent new temple.

Our Lady of Licheń is an innovative and bold piece of architecture: the width of the basilica's façade is an incredible 162 metres/532 feet, the height of the tower is 141.5 metres/464 feet and the golden dome is 103.5 metres/340 feet high. The building has all the traditional elements one would expect from a shrine church but it also incorporates design features from more recent eras, rather than simply trying to replicate Gothic, Baroque or Renaissance.

Initial work on the site began in 1994, and a year later the project truly got under way when a stone taken from the tomb of St Peter in Rome, and blessed by Pope John Paul II, was formally laid. It is quite remarkable that the work took just ten years to complete. In 2006, the Miraculous Image of Our Lady of Licheń was ceremonially transferred from St Dorothy's to its new home. There may well be traditionalists who baulk at the artistic concept and execution of Our Lady of Licheń, but, in the grand scheme of things, it matters little whether or not the church matches one's individual aesthetic tastes. What does matter is that it houses a much-revered iconic image of the Virgin, it is a significant place of pilgrimage and, like countless other pilgrimage destinations over the centuries, it owes its existence to donations made in faith, hope and devotion.

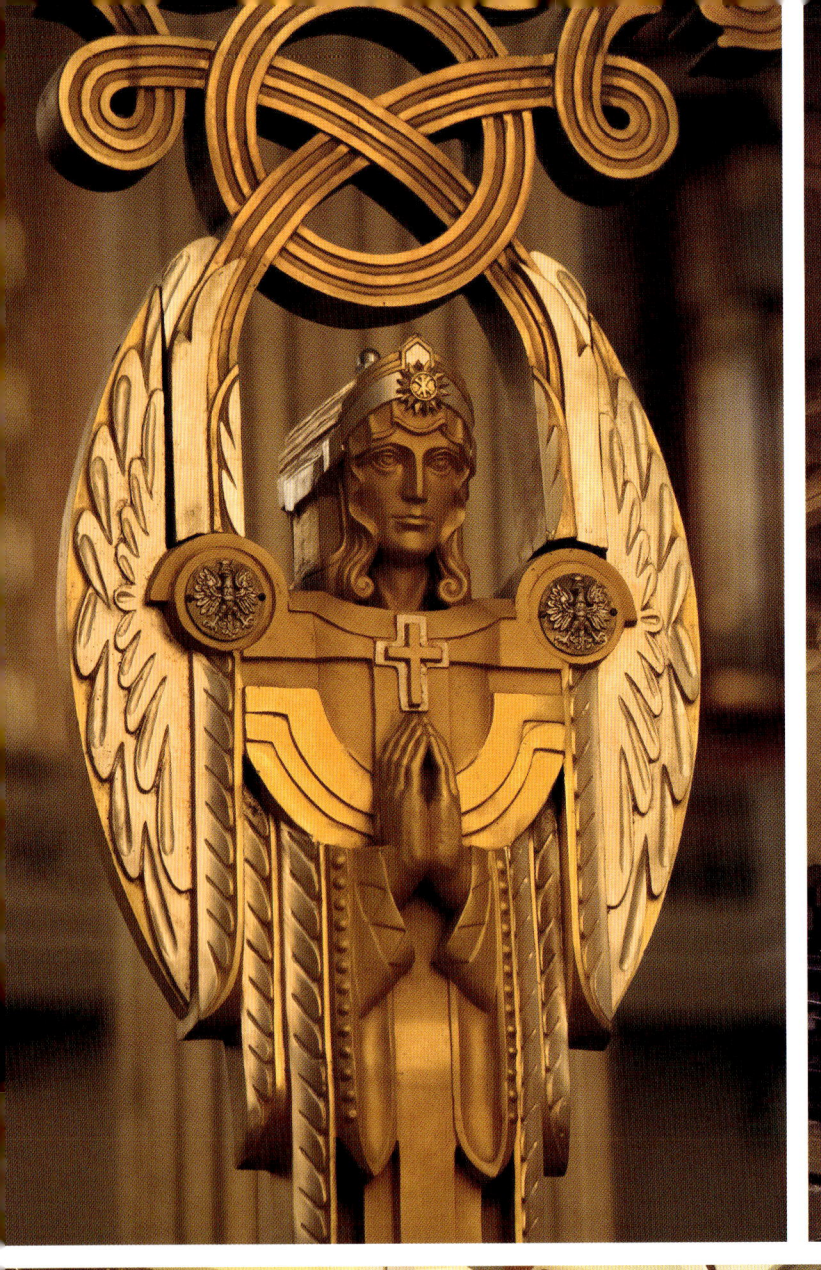
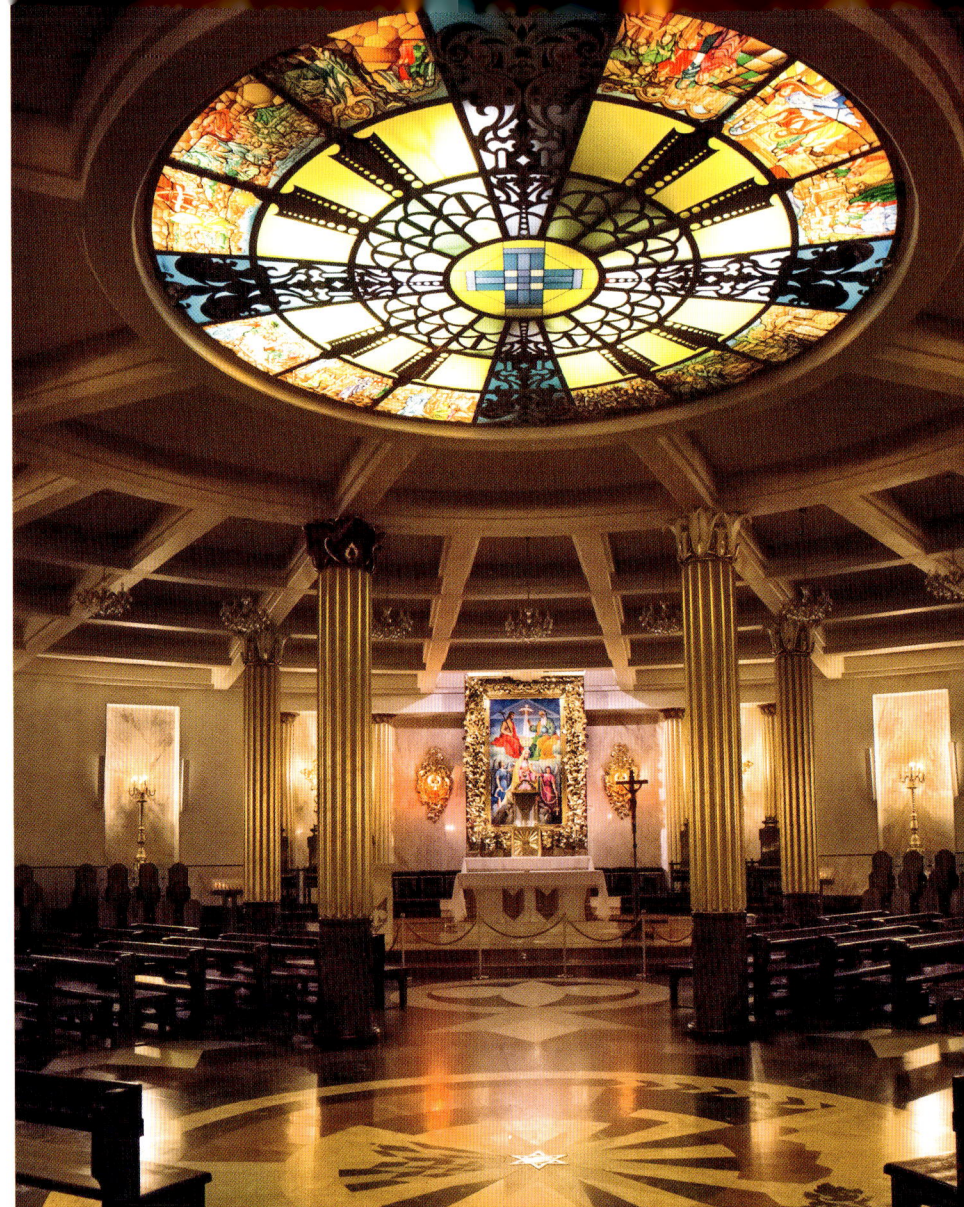

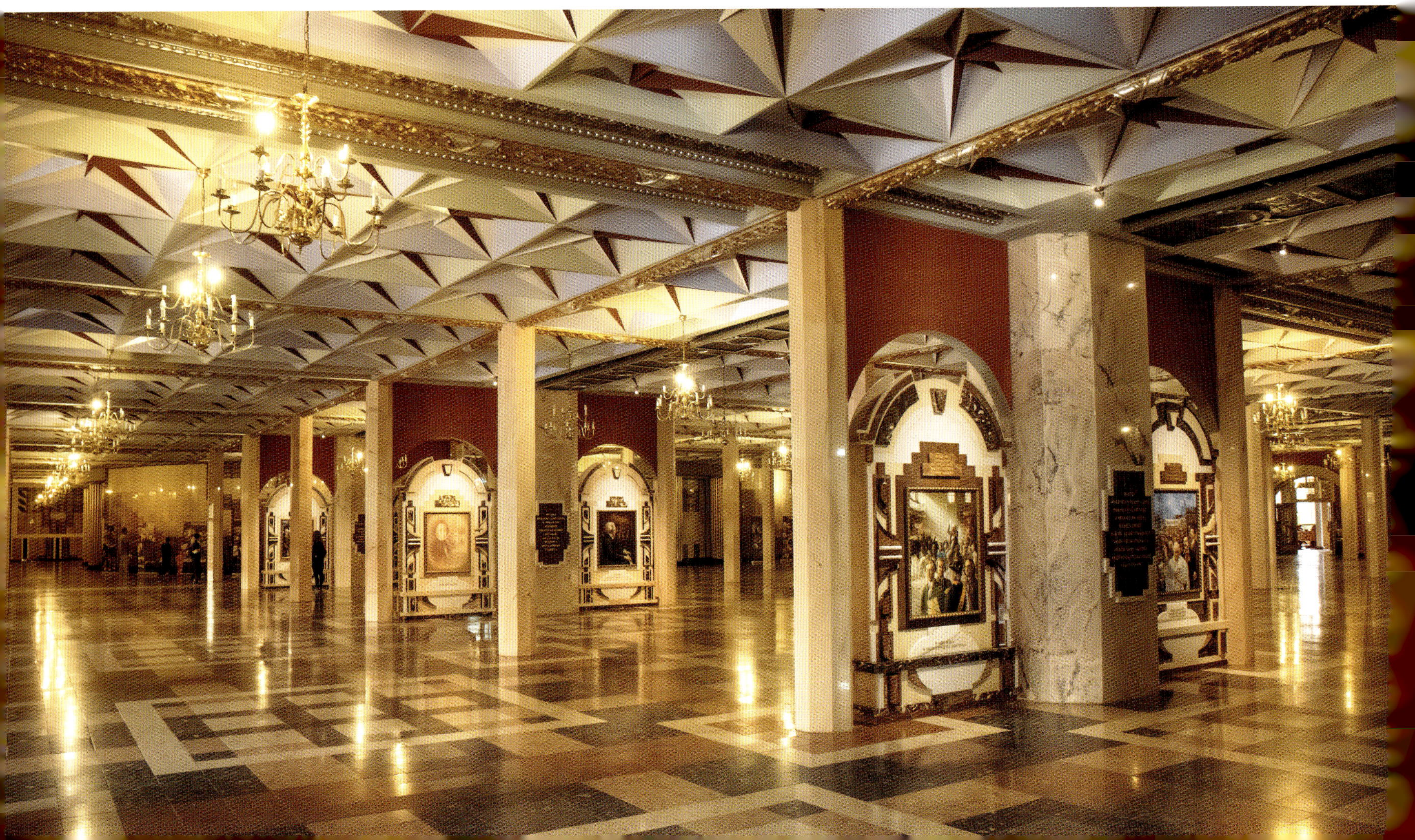

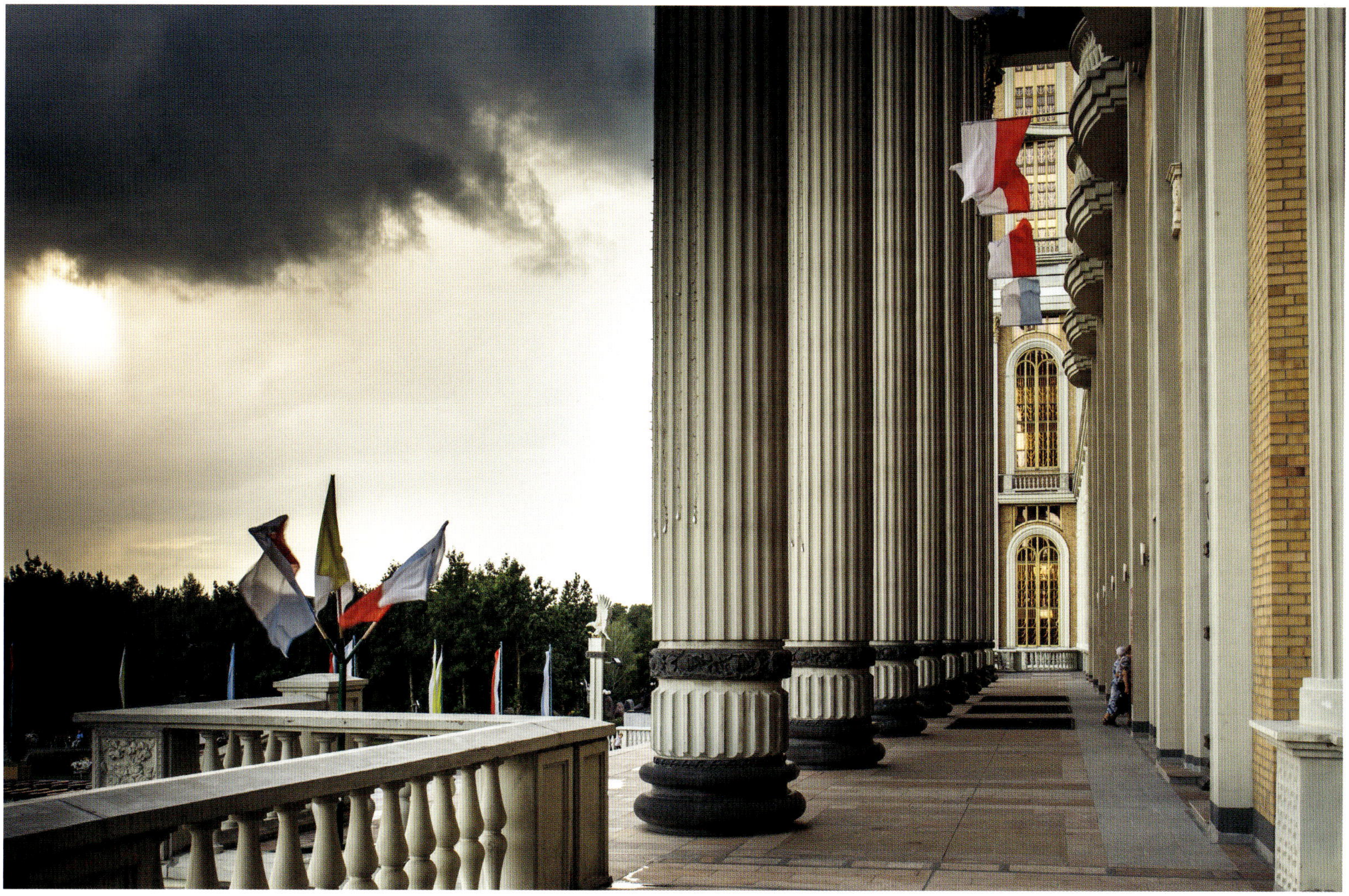

(*above*) The basilica is built on two levels, with the main body of the church accessed via a flight of steps leading up to the imposing portico.

(*right*) At the head of the vast nave is an altar bearing the portrait of Our Lady of Licheń.

(*opposite, top left*) The Art Nouveau-style angels adorning the nave pillars are significantly different from the more traditionally sculpted versions encountered in churches and cathedrals. (*top right*) The Chapel of the Holy Trinity is just one of the many small chapels located in the basilica's ground floor area. It is used when a more intimate scale of service is appropriate. (*bottom*) A view of the ground floor's network of chapels reveals that they are interspersed with pieces of highly distinctive artwork that veer away from more traditional interpretations of religious themes.

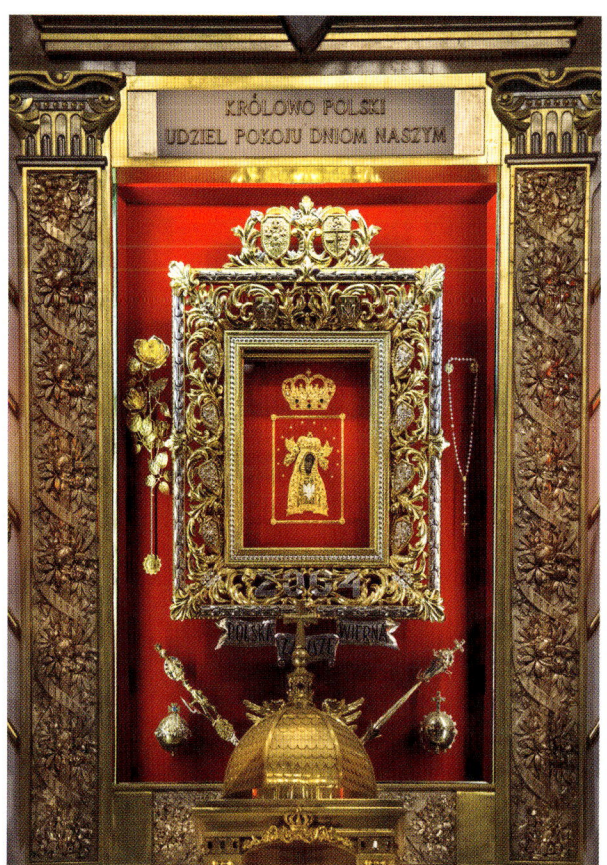

SLOVAKIA

BASILICA OF OUR LADY OF SEVEN SORROWS
Šaštín-Stráže, Trnava

The pietà of the Virgin Mary recognized by the epithet Our Lady of Sorrows is the patron saint of Slovakia, and the Basilica of Our Lady of Seven Sorrows in Šaštín-Stráže is the country's national shrine. The word 'Seven' is frequently omitted but the meanings are identical. Within the Catholic faith, the seven traumas endured by the Virgin Mary as Mother of God have great resonance and they form the basis for some of the most moving examples of religious art. The legend associated with Our Lady of Seven Sorrows and Šaštín-Stráže dates back to the sixteenth century and it is an interesting variant on the more common visitations or miracles of healing. Count Imrich Czobor was owner of the ancient Šaštín estate and had a reputation for disrespecting and harshly treating his wife, Angelika Bakičová. Matters came to a head during a coach ride through the village, when a heated argument boiled over and Angelika was pushed out of the carriage on to the road. While lying bruised and disheveled, she made a vow that if her husband were to relinquish his appalling behaviour she would create a statue of the Virgin. Within a matter of hours, and throughout the following days, the count became a kind, considerate and devoted husband, and so the statue was duly carved and deposited on the roadside where the incident had occurred.

The statue was later housed in a small triangular chapel erected on the site and over time it was deemed responsible for countless miracles of healing and spiritual restoration.

From the medieval era onwards, the area was strategically located on the intersection of important trade routes and thus a defensive fortress was located close to the villages. It was into the castle's chapel that the statue was taken for safe-keeping between 1654 and 1710, during the Turkish Wars. Upon restoration of peace, the statue was returned to the public domain and miracles continued to be recorded. However, it was decided that an official investigation was imperative to verify the hundreds of claims that had accrued over time. On 25 August 1732, the statue was relocated to the Loreto Chapel of the Šaštín parish church and a commission of enquiry was held.

The Basilica of Our Lady of Seven Sorrows is Slovakia's national shrine and the representation of the Virgin Mary cradling her crucified Son is the country's patron saint. The distinctive 'squashed onion' domes of the monastery church are reminiscent of the style used in many Austrian churches.

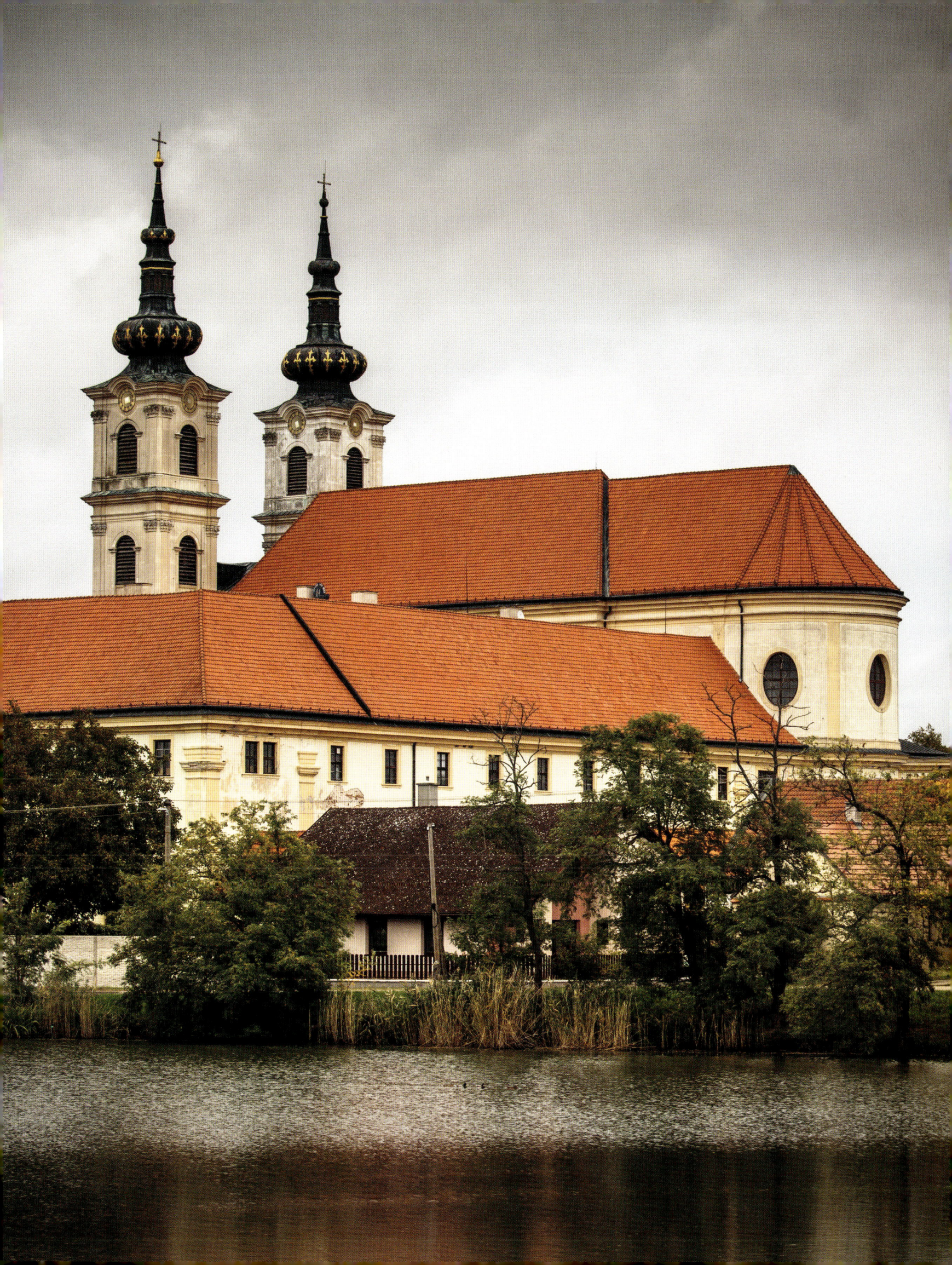

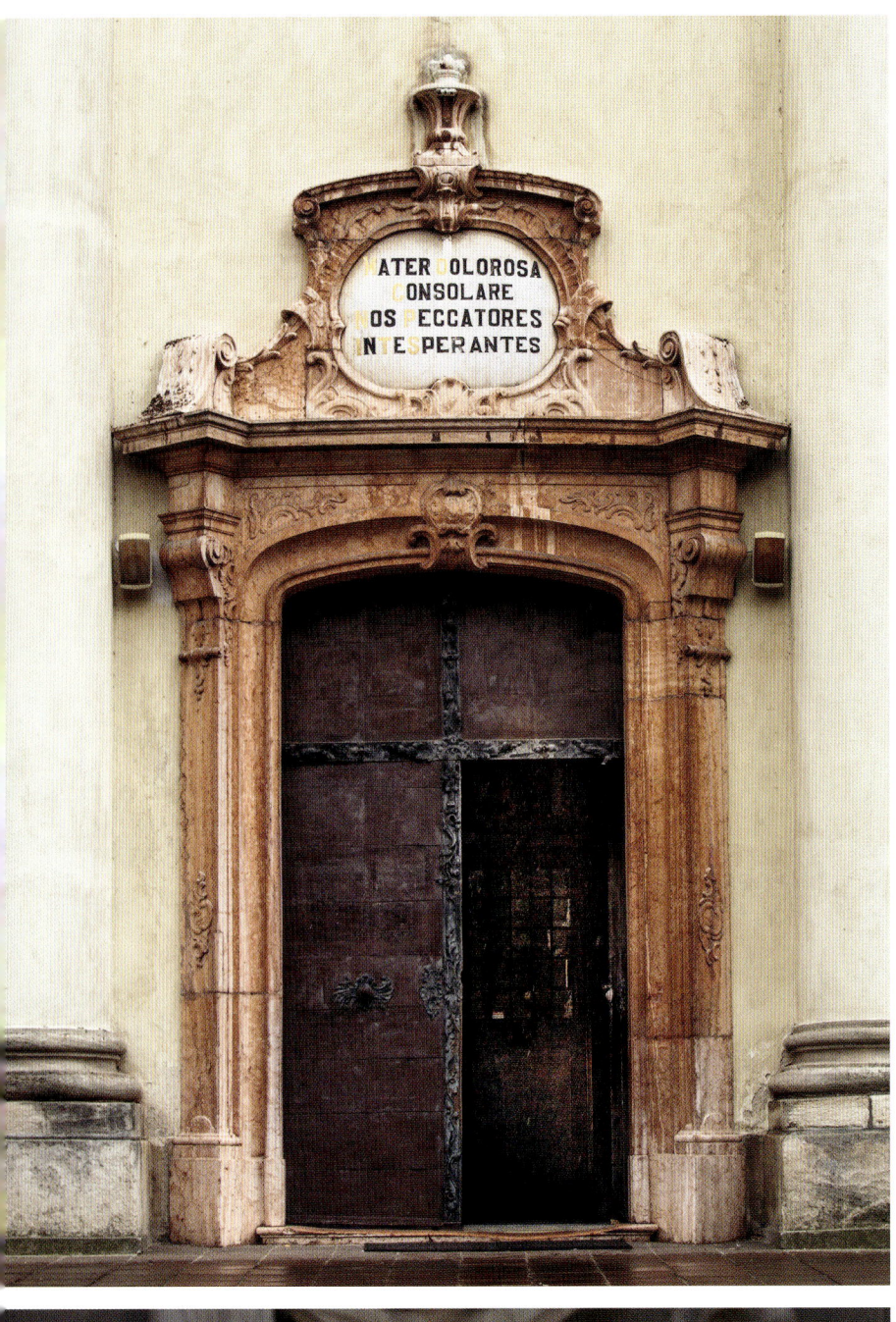
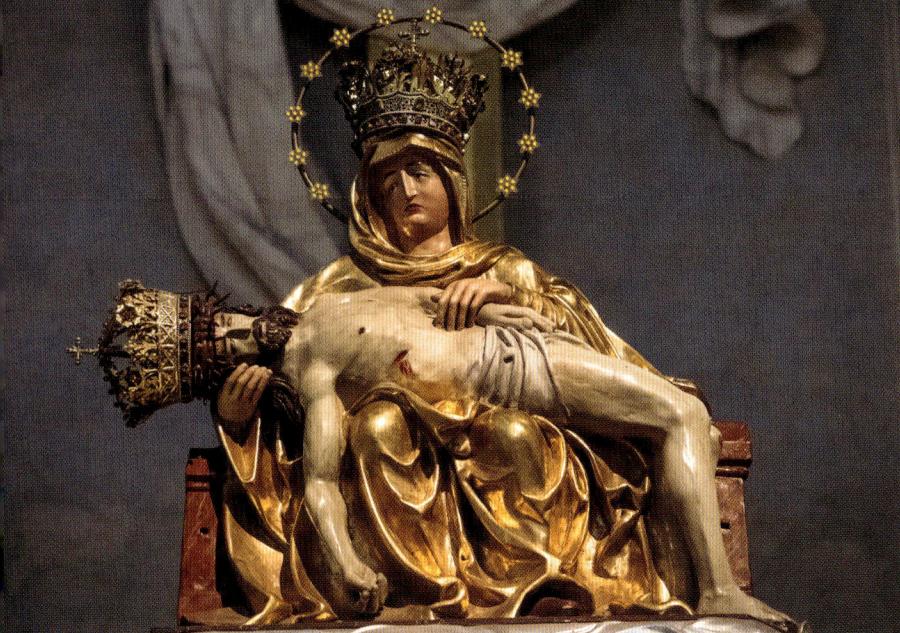

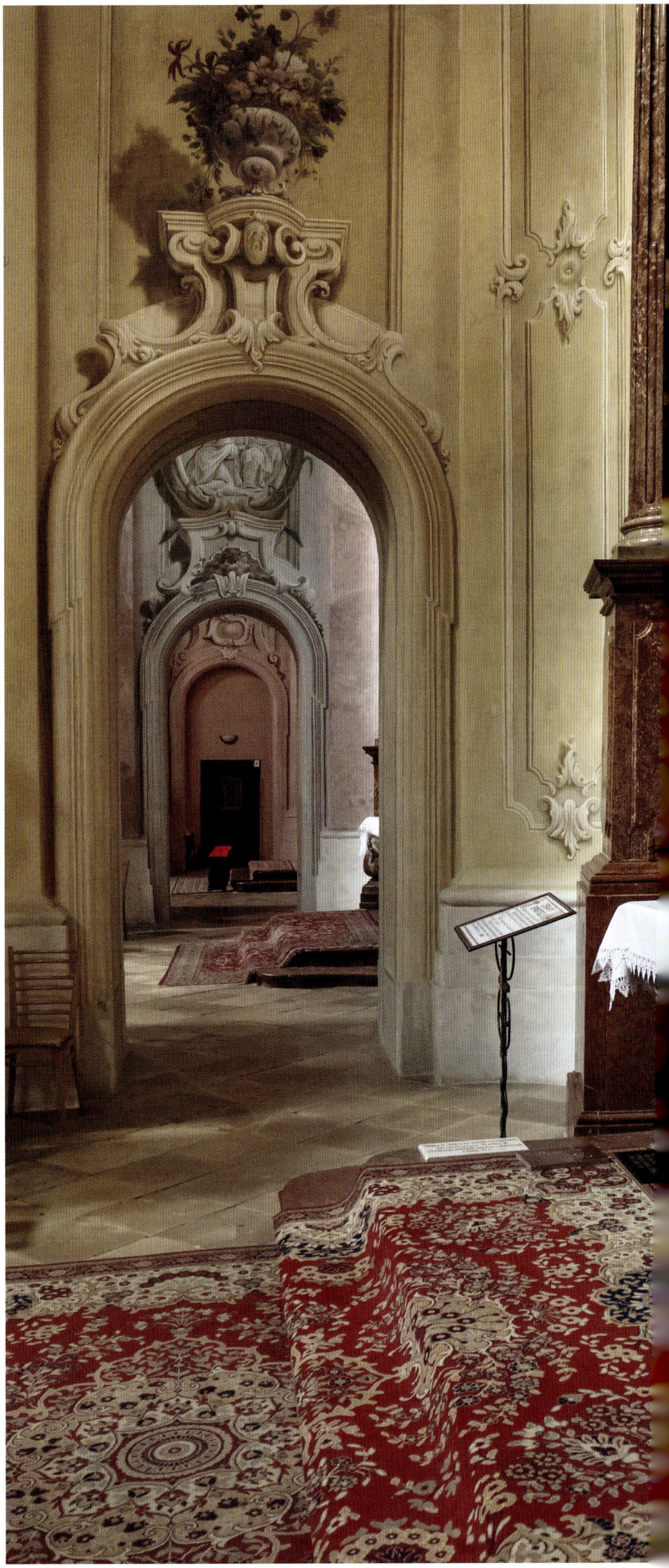

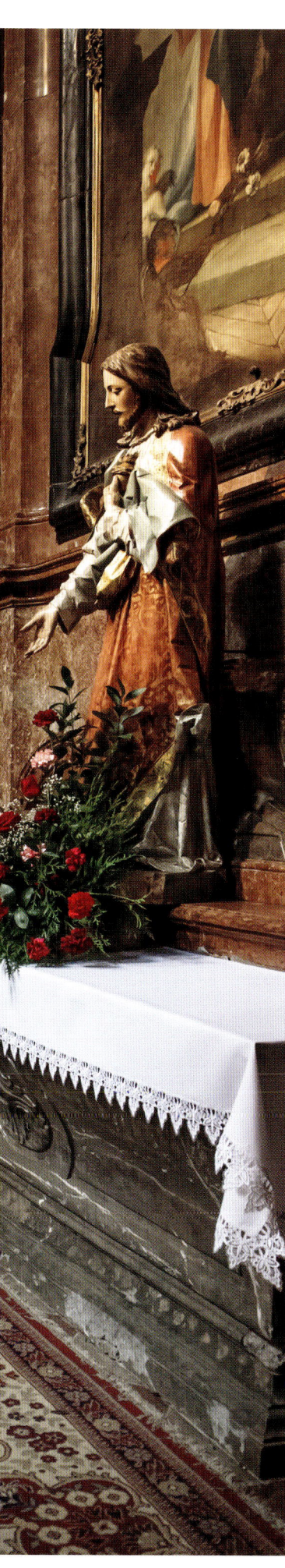

(*far left, above*) The basilica's entrance is a simple door, framed by sculpted surrounds and a Latin inscription. (*far left, below*) The sanctified golden crowns were placed on the Virgin and Jesus at the shrine's 300th anniversary celebrations in 1864. (*left*) Three interconnecting chapels line each side of the basilica's nave, and all are thoughtfully equipped with oriental carpets to both minimize excess noise and protect knees.

(*overleaf*) The faded elegance and muted colours of the basilica's nave are pierced by the sharp golden light of the shrine.

Over a period of three months, the hearing interviewed countless clergy and a vast number of pilgrims. After much deliberation, it solemnly proclaimed the statue to be miraculous. Although the statue returned to its home in the triangular chapel, a fraternity of monks from the Pauline Order arrived to take control of the precious carving and began building a church and monastery. The construction and decoration of the church interior continued for a further three decades, culminating in a consecration ceremony held on 12 August 1762. Three days later, on the Feast of the Assumption, the statue of Our Lady of Seven Sorrows was ceremonially transferred to the main altar of the new church.

Throughout the ensuing centuries, the church underwent renovations, restorations and restyling, but was spared any major calamitous structural failures. The 300th anniversary celebrations in 1864 were attended by some 300 clergy and more than 100,000 pilgrims, culminating in a ceremony at which the statue of the Virgin and her Son was adorned with golden crowns sanctified by Pope Pius IX. To celebrate Šaštín's next centenary, in 1964, Pope Paul VI decreed that the church be elevated to the status of a minor basilica.

The church and monastic buildings present a beautiful sight from the adjacent small lake and, aside from any purely aesthetic aspects, the joy of the basilica is that on ordinary weekdays it is a quiet country church, albeit one that hosts a much-revered and worshipped icon of the Catholic Church. On special feast days and other celebratory events, the village and environs of the basilica are flooded with pilgrims and worshippers, but on any other day there are no coaches, no tour guides waving flags or umbrellas and, joy of joys, not a selfie stick to be seen. I witnessed just a few parishioners paying their respects and, most touchingly, several young couples patently in advance of marriage who seemed to be making affirmations to each other in the presence of Our Lady of Seven Sorrows. The communities of Šaštín and Stráže will always be divided by the physical barrier of the Myjava river, but they were officially joined and duly hyphenated when awarded city status by the Slovakian government in 2001.

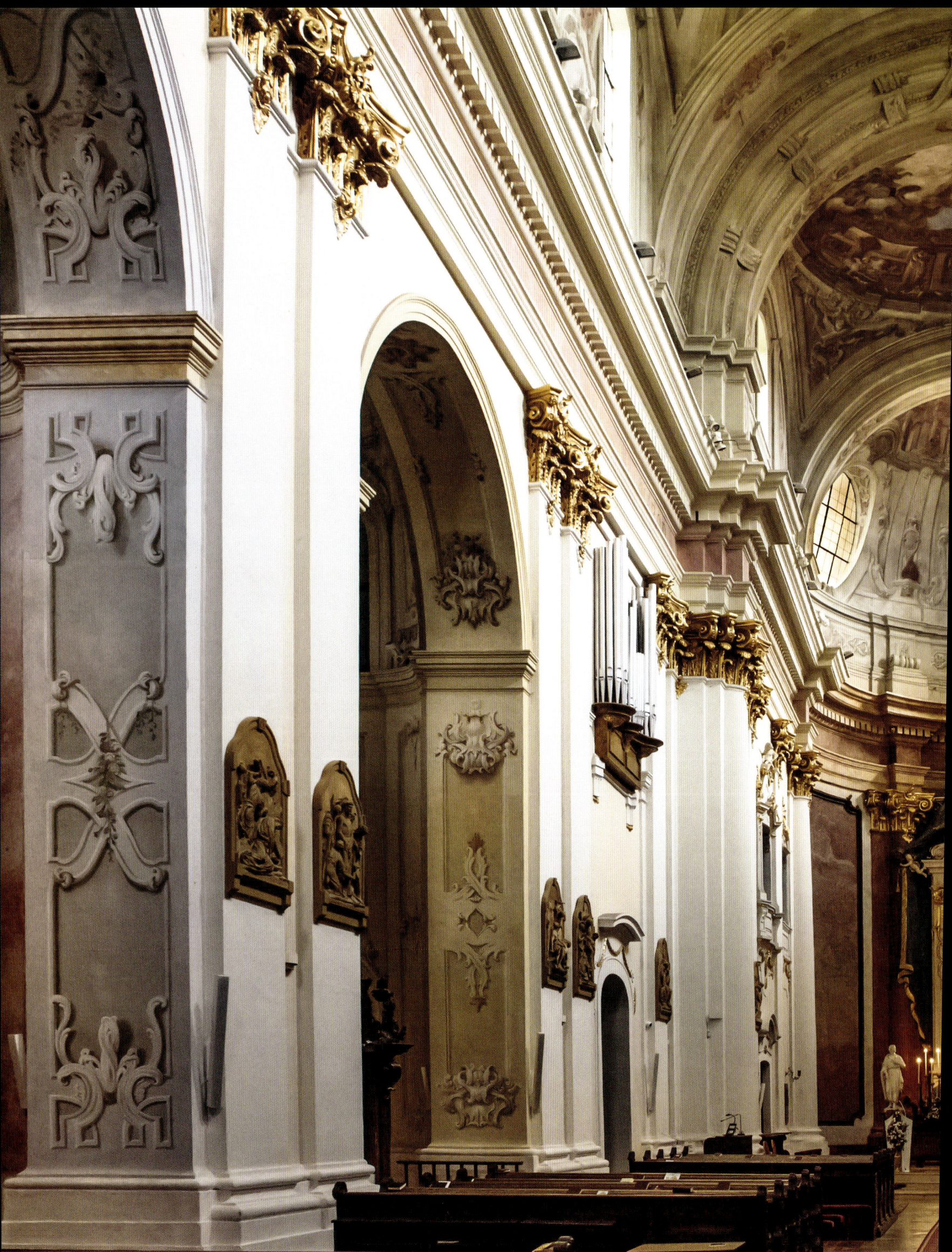

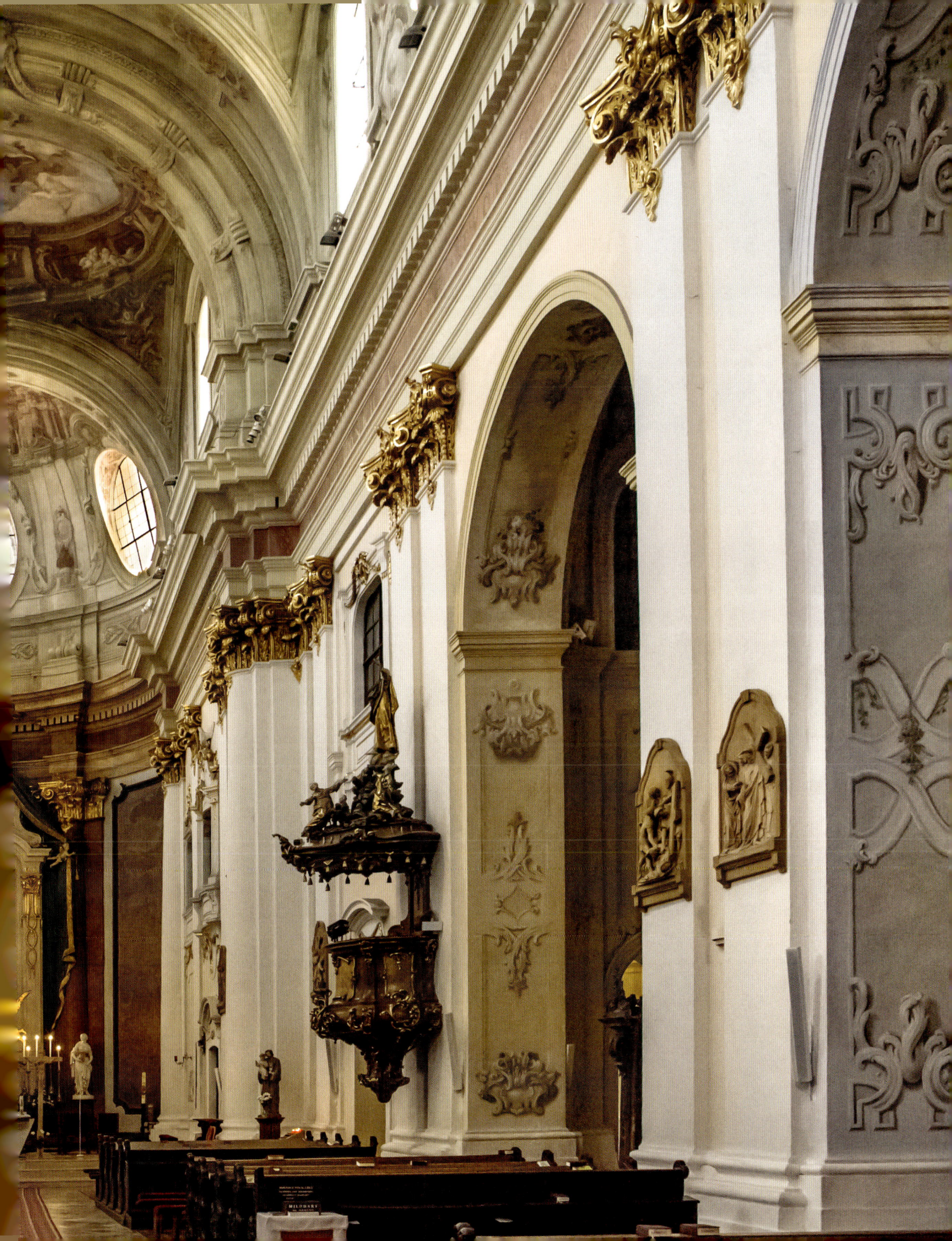

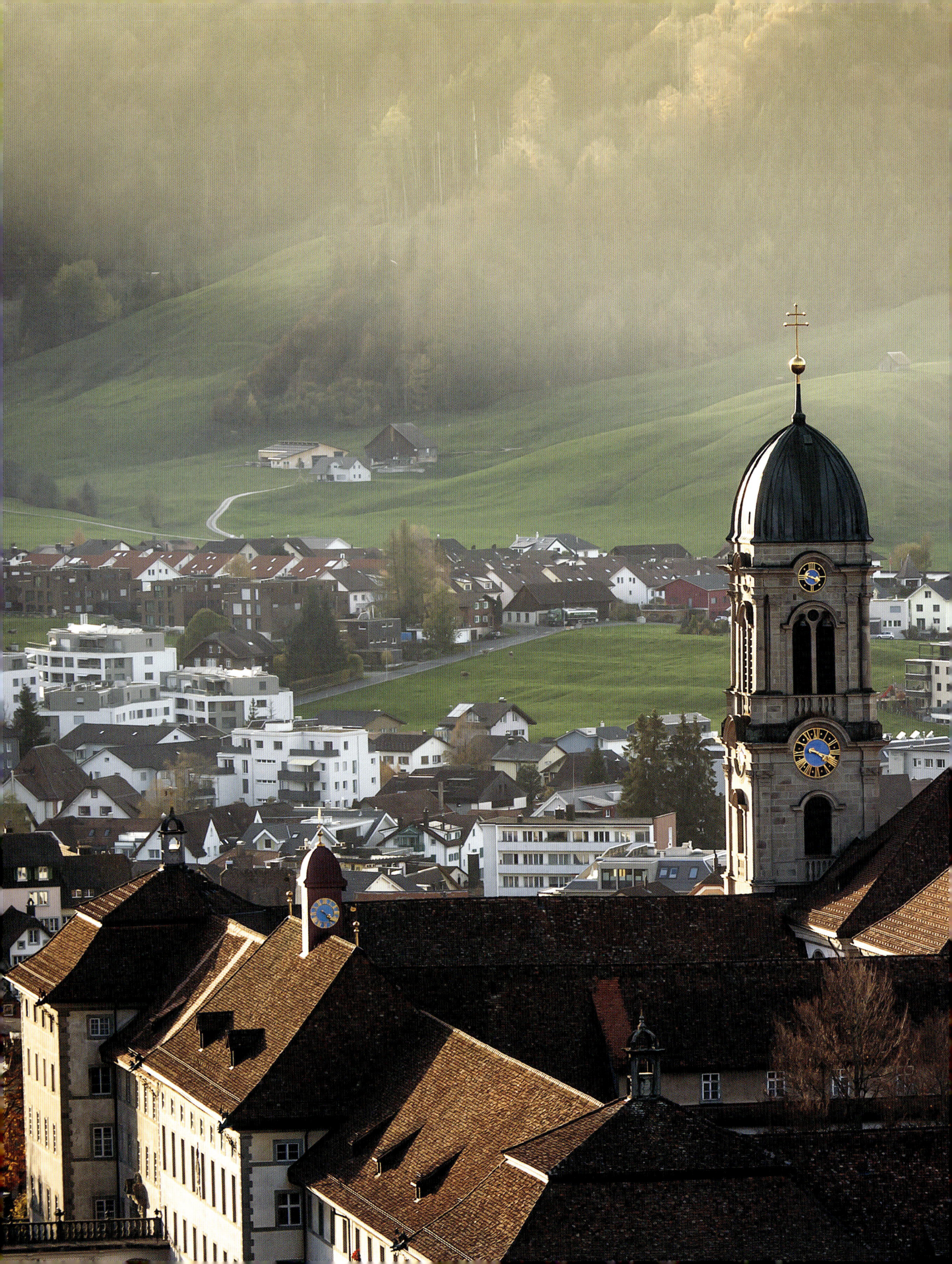

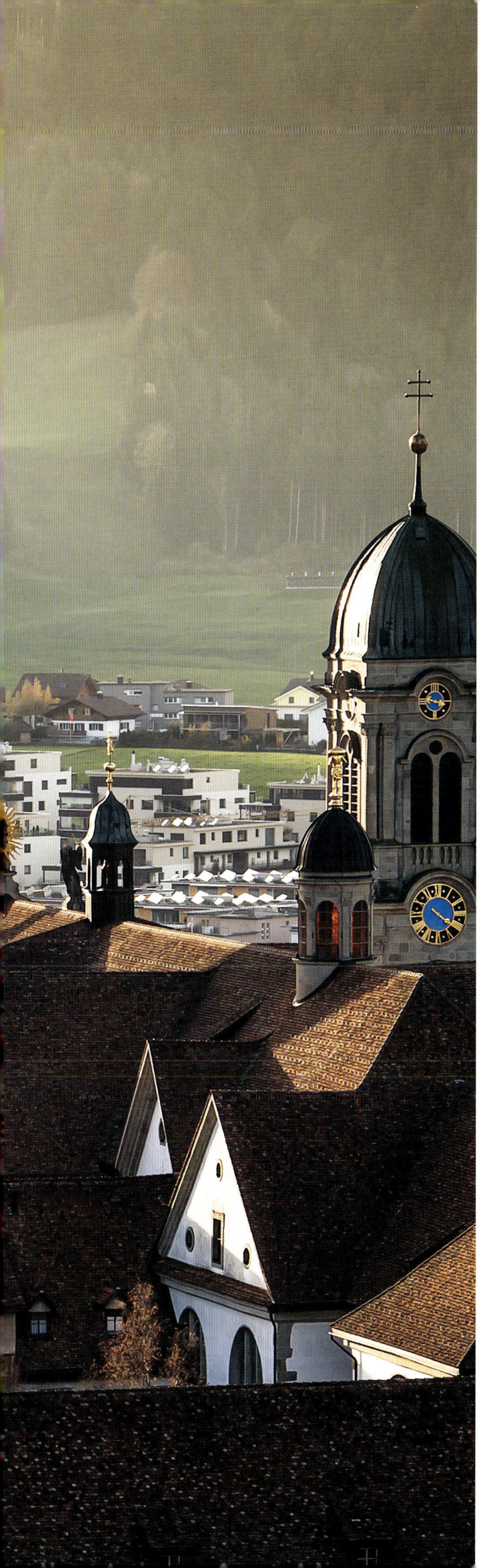

5

GERMANY, AUSTRIA AND SWITZERLAND

GERMANY
COLOGNE CATHEDRAL
Cologne, North Rhine-Westphalia

The twin spires of Cologne's cathedral soaring above the banks of the river Rhine create one of Europe's most iconic and unforgettable architectural landscapes. A substantial Carolingian cathedral, consecrated in about 870, was already in existence, but the catalyst for building this ambitious Gothic replacement was the arrival in Cologne of the most precious relics of the Three Magi. This religious treasure was a gift made in 1164 by Holy Roman Emperor Frederick I to Archbishop Rainald of Dassel, in return for his invaluable help in the recapture of Milan two years earlier. Some time around 1190, the celebrated goldsmith and enamellist Nicholas of Verdun was commissioned to create the inspirational gold-plated and semiprecious stone-encrusted reliquary that still graces the cathedral today.

Upon the shrine's completion some two decades later, plans were drawn up for a new cathedral that would, in effect, serve as a vast stone reliquary destined to become one of the premier pilgrimage sites in Europe. The foundation stone was laid in 1248 by Archbishop Konrad von Hochstaden on what has always been the most significant date in the Catholic calendar: 15 August, the Feast of the Assumption of the Virgin. Thus began construction of the first Gothic church in the Rhineland. Its design was inspired by some of the great cathedrals being erected in northern France, such as Amiens and Reims. By 1322, the cathedral's choir had been consecrated and, upon completion of that first phase, the Shrine of the Three Kings was temporarily placed in a chapel adjacent to the choir, thereby enabling the wide ambulatory to fulfil its role as a pilgrim's path.

However, surviving records from the later Middle Ages indicate that the speed and progress of subsequent building work fluctuated considerably until finally coming to a complete halt in 1528. This dramatic reversal in fortunes was attributed to a chronic lack of funds, combined with a dwindling enthusiasm for the Gothic architectural style. Even so, the cathedral continued to function adequately in its partially completed state. The usable sections at the time of cessation comprised the choir, the ground floor of the nave, parts of the transept and, although not really part of the active church, the two lower storeys of the south steeple. Unfortunately, the cathedral experienced

(*previous pages*) Eisiendeln Abbey.

(*right*) The twin spires of Cologne's Roman Catholic cathedral are one of Europe's most iconic landmarks and, for a decade following their completion in 1880, they were the continent's tallest building. Years of atmospheric pollution from Germany's industrial heartland have gradually blackened the sandstone and conservationists work tirelessly to arrest further erosion.

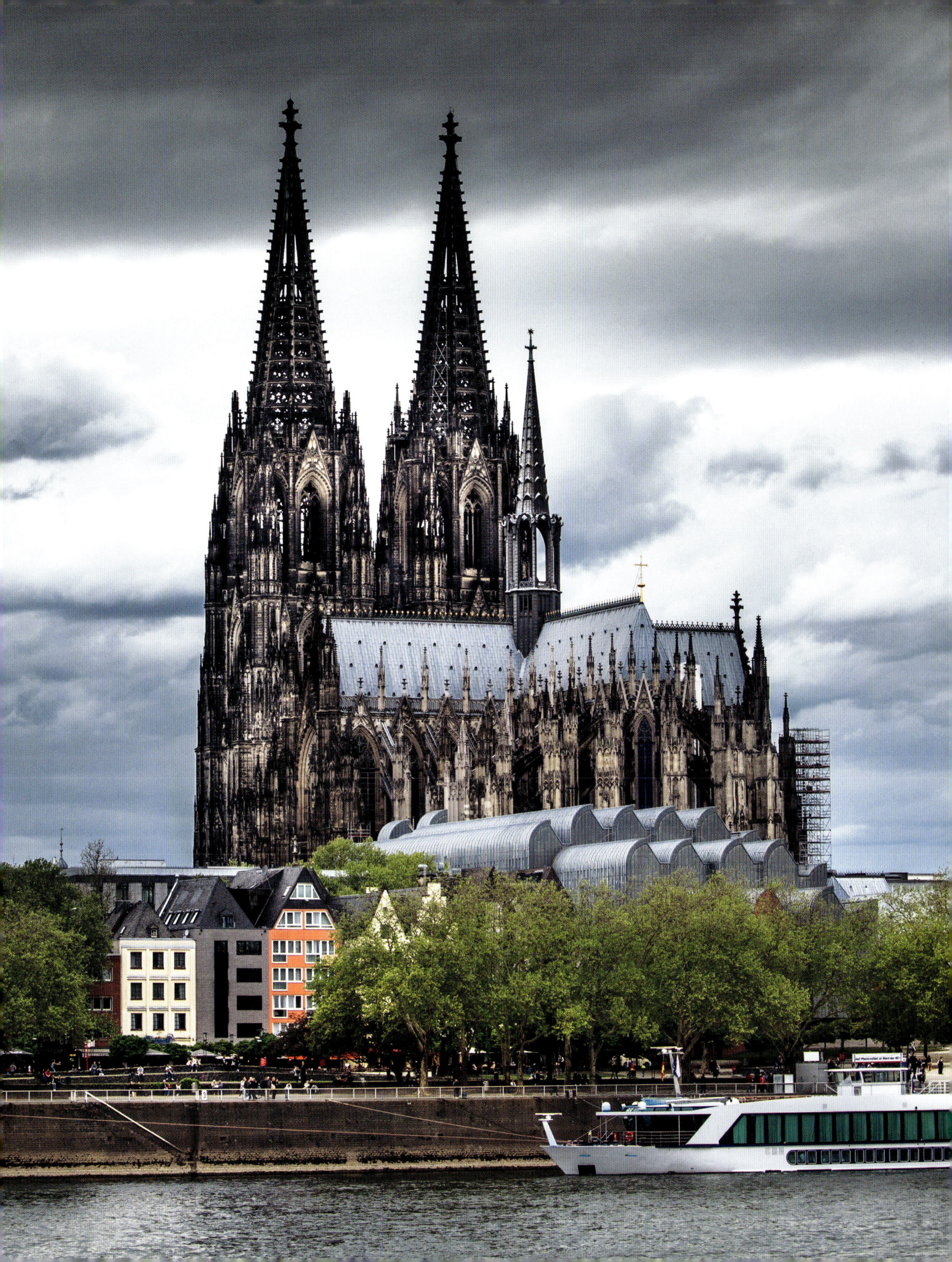

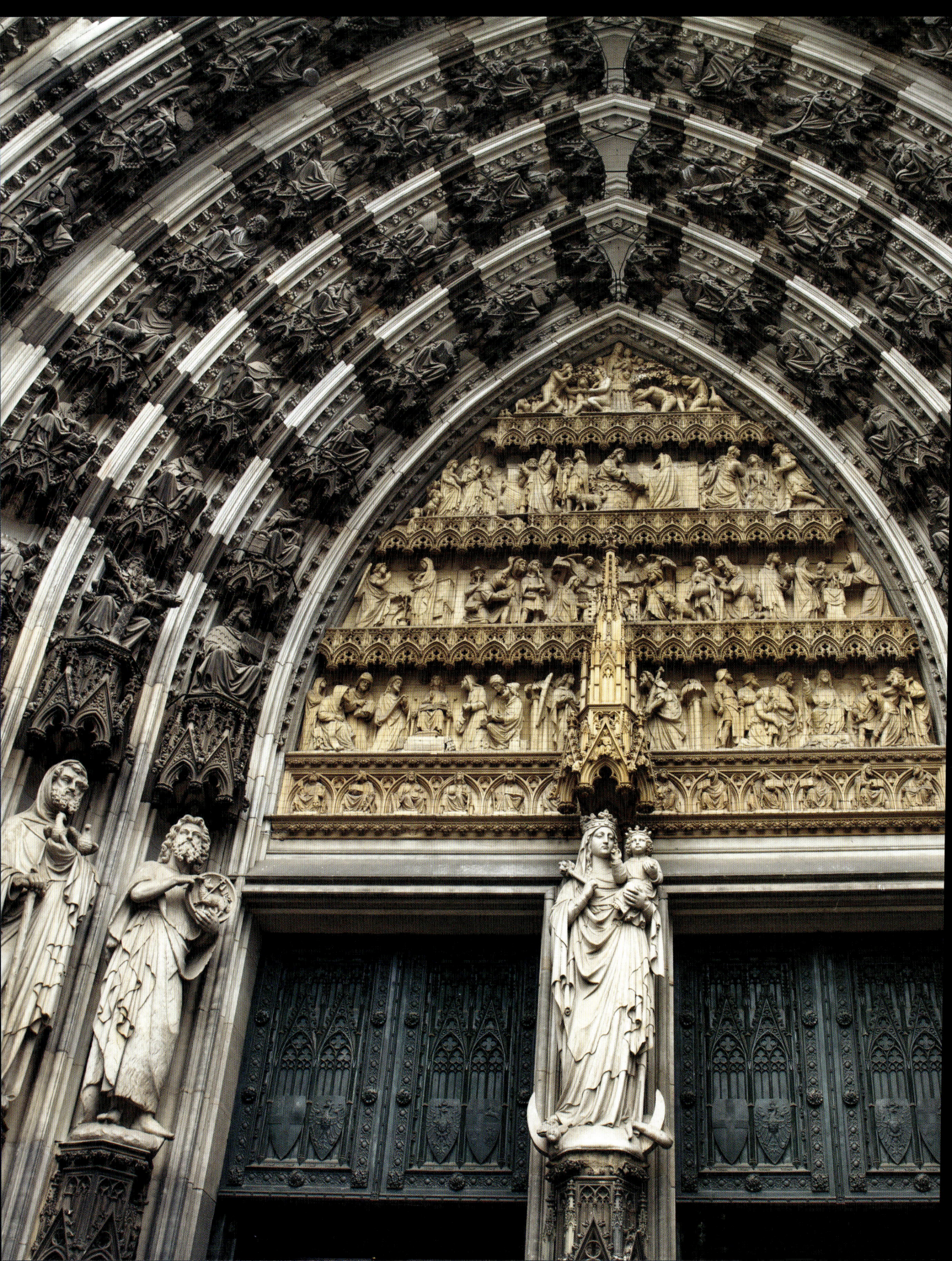

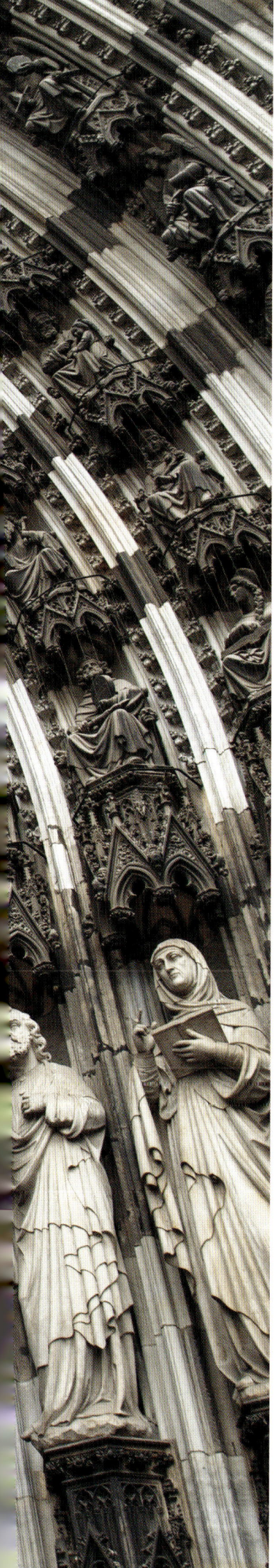

The main portal is dominated by a sculpture of the Virgin Mary and Jesus. The jambs on either side comprise figures from the Bible and the tympanum presents a biblical storyboard, including Noah's Ark, Moses and the Tablets, the Annunciation and Nativity, and the Sermon on the Mount.

further decline when Cologne was seriously affected by the first of two major international conflicts it would have to endure. In 1794, it was occupied by troops of the French Revolution, the archdiocese was dissolved and the cathedral was reduced to being little more than a place for fodder storage and a rather grandiose holding cell for prisoners.

Fate smiled more kindly on the cathedral during the early decades of the nineteenth century, when a renewed wave of public optimism fuelled a desire to achieve completion of the forlorn church. The first of two key events that moved this process forward happened in 1815, when Cologne became part of Prussia. In less than a decade, the State assumed responsibility for the cathedral's restoration. That process was given an almost seismic boost of good fortune when the original fourteenth-century drawings for the mighty twin-steepled main façade were rediscovered. They were neither idealistic nor tentative sketches but sheets of parchment that when joined together revealed a 4-metre-/13-foot-high detailed plan. The assembled parchment jigsaw covered every intricate detail of the embellished gables, slender buttresses and tapering spires, whose finished height was 157 metres/515 feet.

The cathedral's ascendancy towards the magnificent church that currently receives up to 6 million pilgrims and tourists each year finally began in 1842. Thirty-eight years later, the final stone was ceremonially inserted into the finial of the south steeple – a mere 632 years after the first foundation was laid. The trials and tribulations of the damage caused during the French Revolution pale into insignificance if one considers the bomb damage inflicted upon Cologne during the Second World War. Contemporary black and white photographs taken in the aftermath of the most devastating attack of 1942 reveal a city virtually reduced to rubble in many places, but one nevertheless still dominated by the soaring twin spires of its cathedral. The cathedral was badly hit, but the spires miraculously survived intact. One cannot begin to imagine what an emblematic source of hope and inspiration that sight must have been.

The building's colossal interior proportions are best appreciated from the nave entrance. Despite the cathedral's stunning length and width of 145 metres/475 feet and 45 metres/147 feet, there is nevertheless a surprising aura of intimacy within its massive stone walls and magnificent coloured glass windows. The Shrine of the Magi is now located behind the high altar and if one is fortunate enough to be able to walk around the wide ambulatory during a quiet period, the timeless atmosphere that settles around the choir feels very much imbued with the awe and respect experienced by centuries of pilgrims.

142 GREAT PILGRIMAGE SITES OF EUROPE

(*right*) The magnificent Shrine of the Three Kings was such a precious religious relic that it was deemed worthy of having its own cathedral. The early thirteenth-century work is more than 2 metres/7 feet long and exhibits a moving and detailed portrayal of the most significant figures in Christianity.

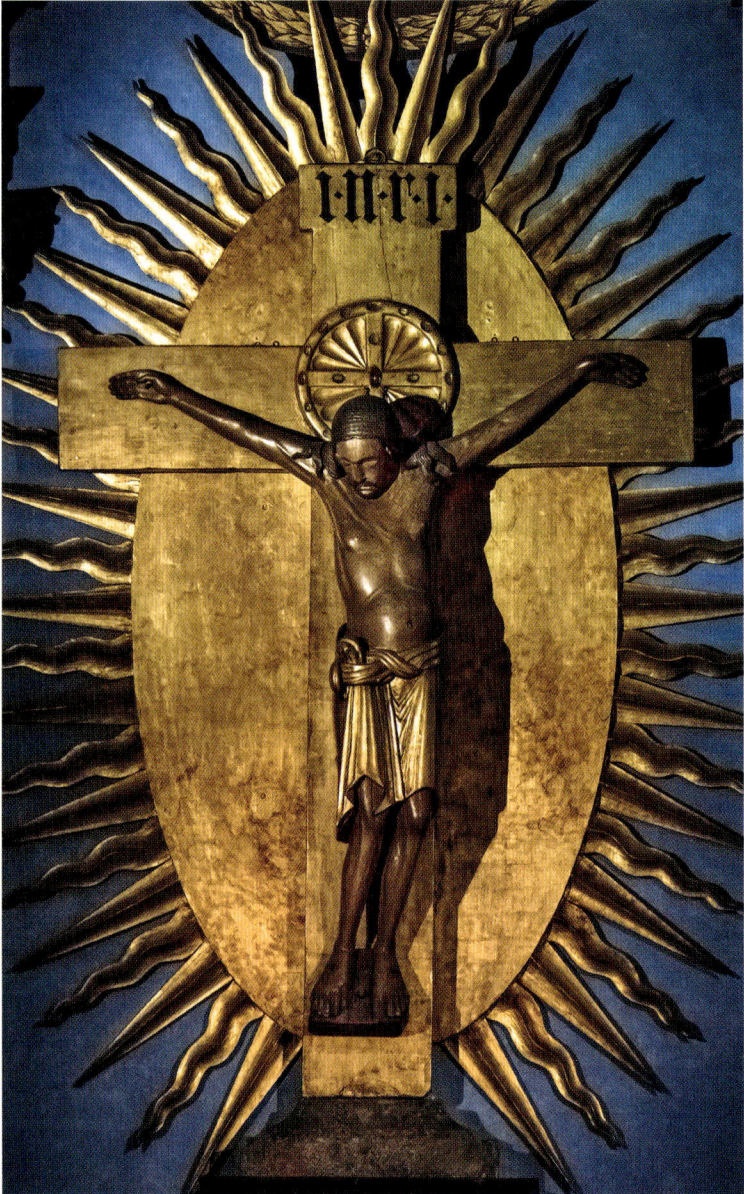

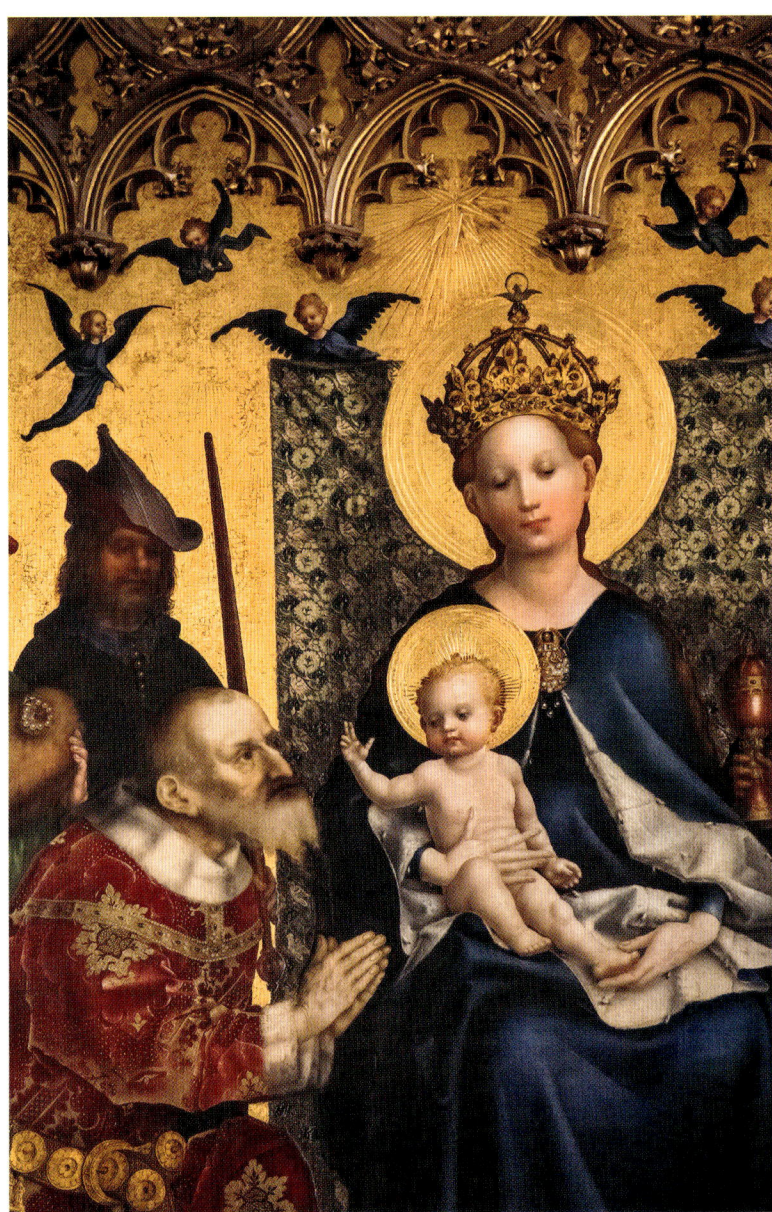

(*above*) The tenth-century depiction of the Crucifixion was presented by Archbishop Gero and the larger-than-life-sized sculpture is named after its donor. The Gero Cross sought to portray Christ at the exact moment of his death and consequently the redemption of mankind.

(*above*) The Adoration of the Magi features in the centre panel of the *Altarpiece of the City's Patron Saints*, a thirteenth-century triptych now displayed in the cathedral's Lady Chapel. It was originally created for the City Hall's chapel of Our Lady in Jerusalem.

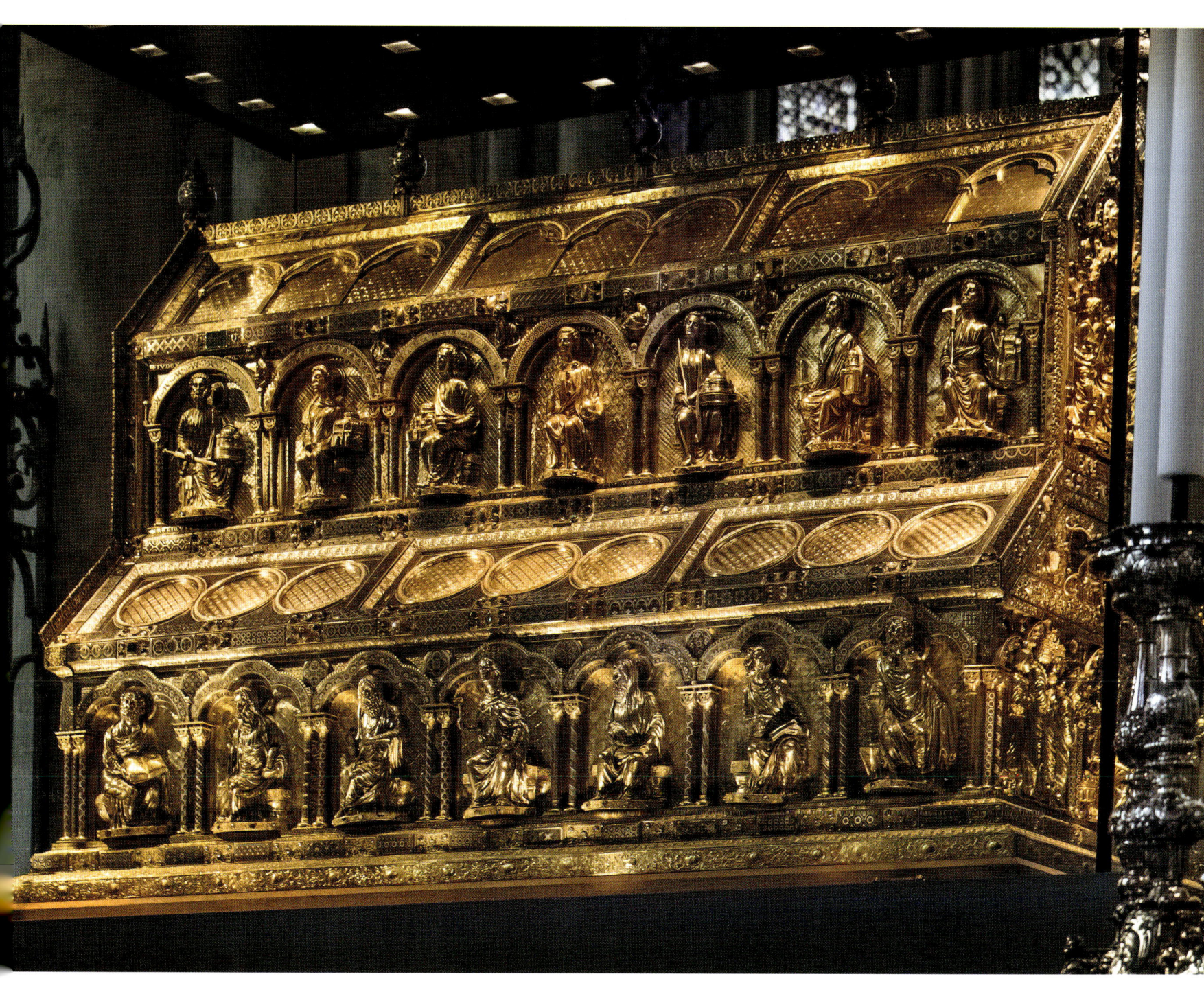

GERMANY
AACHEN CATHEDRAL
Aachen, North Rhine-Westphalia

Aachen Cathedral was the first German site to be included on the UNESCO World Heritage Site list, and this jewel of Carolingian architecture and art will undoubtedly surpass the expectations of all those who visit its ninth-century Palatine Chapel of Charlemagne, which forms the central part of the cathedral. Charlemagne became the deeply committed Christian ruler of vast swathes of western and central Europe through a combination of inheritance and protracted military campaigns. The establishment of that vast empire received both religious and political recognition when he was crowned Emperor of the Romans by Pope Leo III on Christmas Day 800.

The original chapel is now accessed *via* a Baroque entrance pavilion leading to the main door, where a lintel bears a Latin inscription requesting that visitors should 'Remember to enter this shrine to the Virgin Mary reverently'. Charlemagne's dedication of his church to the Virgin Mary was unusual for that period in history, because the European Catholic Church's tradition of venerating the Mother of God's Son did not become widespread until more than two centuries later.

Inspiration for the magnificent two-storey octagonal chapel, with its elegant, gold, mosaic-adorned cupola, was drawn from the Early Christian Byzantine sixth-century church of San Vitale in Ravenna, Italy. Each level of the octagon is encompassed by an ambulatory, the upper of which houses one of Aachen's most important historical artefacts, Charlemagne's throne. This ostensibly modest structure, comprising plain marble slabs, was nevertheless used for more than thirty coronations of German kings and queens up until 1531. Frederick I was crowned there in 1152 and his gift to the cathedral, the Barbarossa chandelier, remains one of its most striking visual features. Geometrically configured with eight faces to perfectly match the octagonal chapel, the enormous chandelier endows the church with a sublime atmosphere when all its candles are lit on special feast days.

The church evolved into the most important place of pilgrimage north of the Alps during the Middle Ages because of its greatest treasure, the Virgin Mary's shrine. This spectacular gold and silver gilded wood structure was fashioned into the shape of a single nave basilica with transepts, and it contains four of

Aachen Cathedral's exterior presents a contrasting array of architectural styles that have evolved over 1,200 years. The most eye-catching part of the complex is the Carolingian octagon that formed Charlemagne's original ninth-century Church of St Mary, crowned by the earliest post-classical cupola to be built north of the Alps.

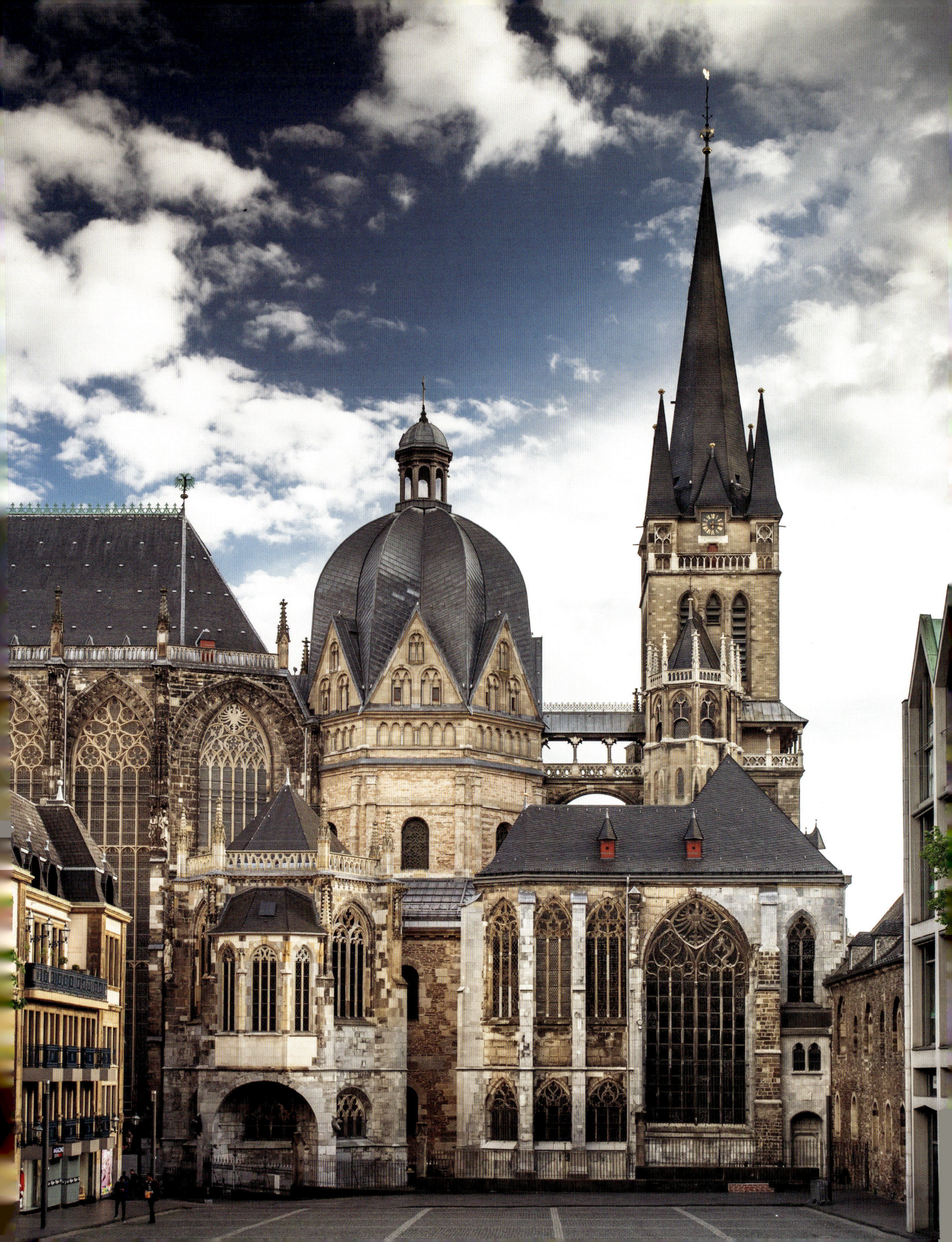

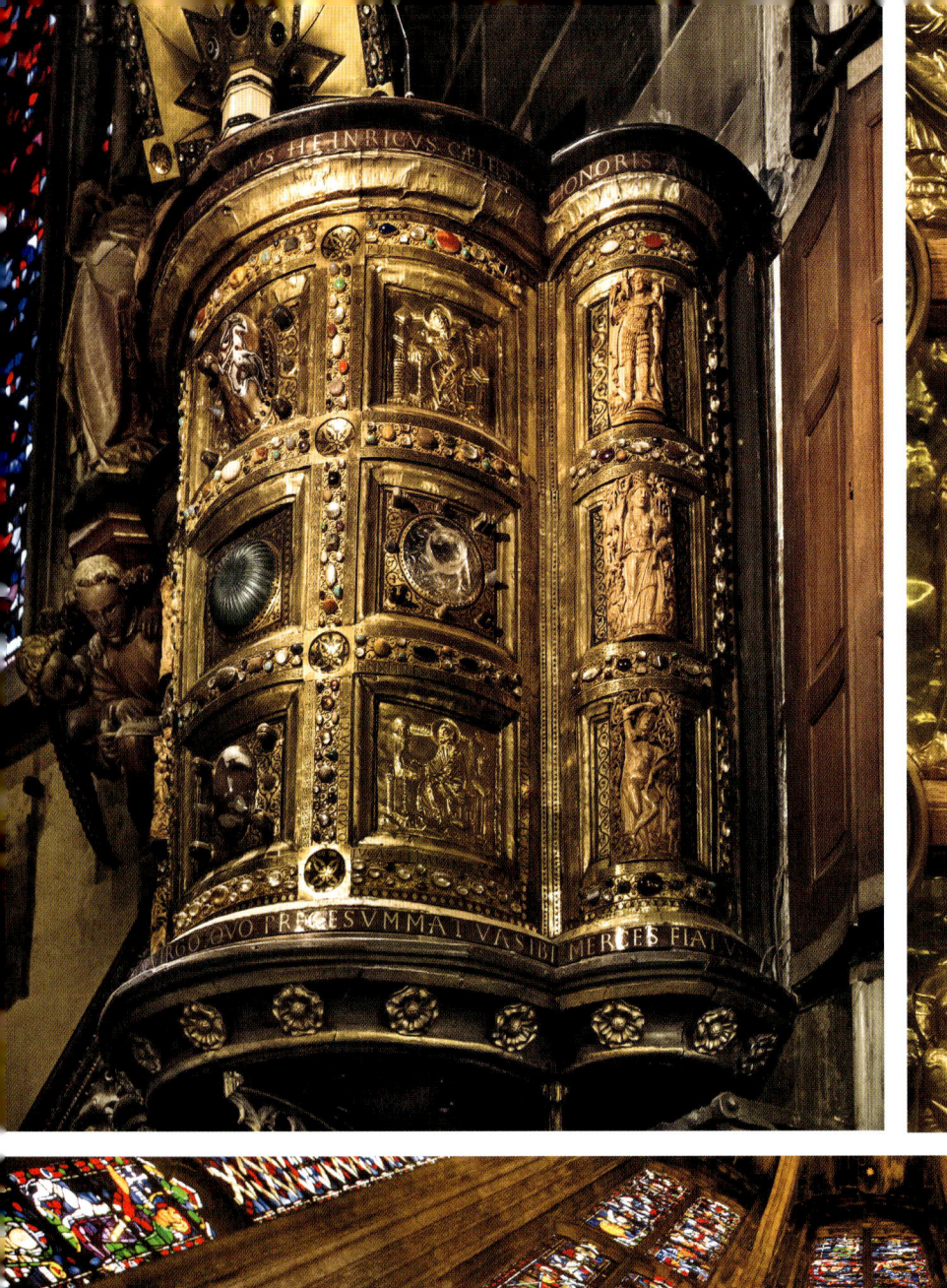
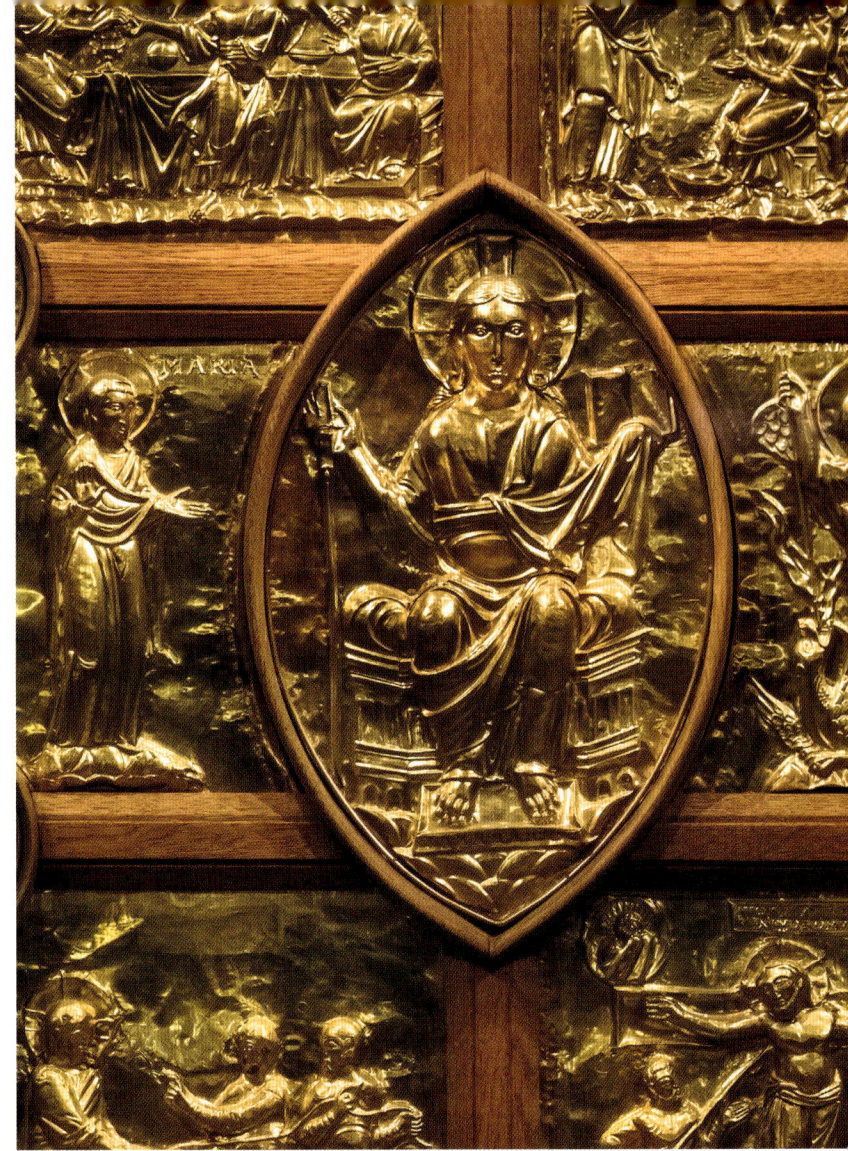
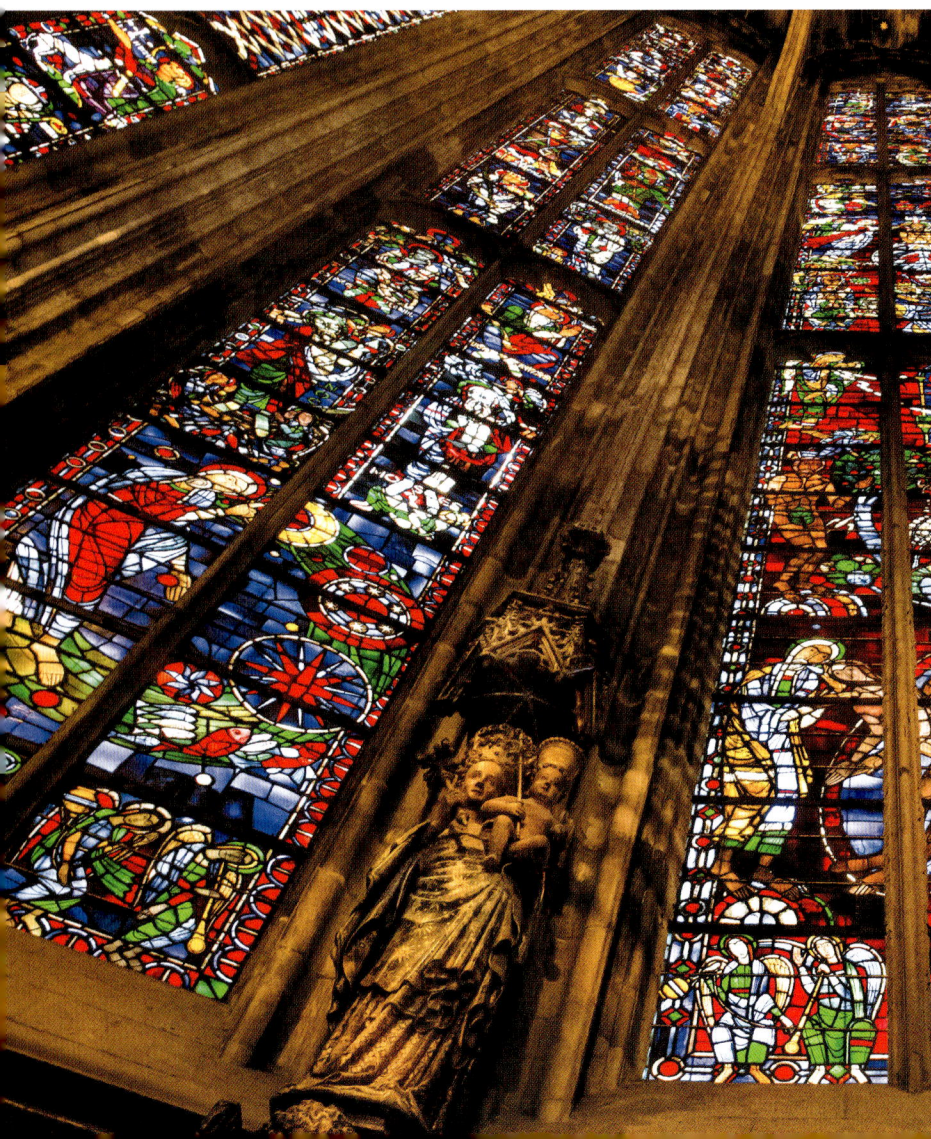

(*top left*) Set high into the wall overlooking the altar is the early eleventh-century ambo (pulpit) decorated with precious stones, ancient glass bowls and a complex jigsaw of ivory carvings and other figures. (*top right*) The Pala d'Oro is a gold altarpiece comprising several gold panels set in a wooden frame, with the central mandorla portraying the risen Christ as ruler of the world. Other panels depict scenes from the Passion and on either side of the mandorla are the Virgin Mary and St Michael the Archangel slaying a dragon.

(*bottom*) The Gothic chancel was built to accommodate more pilgrims, but the designers also wanted to put Aachen 'on the map' and so created 1,000 square metres/10,765 square feet of glass windows, surpassing even the magnificent Sainte-Chapelle in Paris, which had been their inspiration.

the most precious items imaginable: the robe of the Virgin Mary, the swaddling bands of baby Jesus, the loincloth Jesus wore at his Crucifixion and the cloth upon which John the Baptist's head was placed after his beheading.

Pilgrim numbers were becoming so consistently overwhelming that it was decided to extend the octagon eastwards. The perfectly harmonious outcome, consecrated in 1414, was the Gothic chancel, dominated at its eastern end by an arc of thirteen slender glass windows, 27 metres/89 feet high. Further capacity was created from the fifteenth century onwards by the addition of several side chapels radiating out from the octagon, and they still provide the opportunity for solitude and private prayer away from the inevitable tourist hubbub.

The view from the nave towards the chancel now comprises an extraordinary array of treasures, one of which is the fourteenth-century statue of Our Lady of Aachen set against one of the mighty pillars of the octagon. The high altar stands just inside the chancel, and its main façade is entirely covered by a gold-panelled frontispiece dating from around 1000, known as the Pala d'Oro. The much-venerated early thirteenth-century shrine of the Virgin Mary is now set immediately behind the high altar; almost directly beneath the soaring wall of coloured glass lies the equally impressive golden tomb of Charlemagne, consecrated some two decades earlier than the Virgin's in around 1215. Charlemagne's shrine combines intricate carved portraits of the sixteen rulers in power between his own reign and that of Frederick II, with representations of key events in the Holy Roman Emperor's life.

Although individual pilgrimages are still very much part of Aachen Cathedral's ethos, international tourism generates most of the visitor numbers, except for a very special ten-day mass pilgrimage event that has been held every seven years since 1349. Since that date, the four relics from the *Marienschrein* (Mary's Shrine) have been put on display for the adoration of pilgrims from both Europe and the wider world, and the next scheduled pilgrimage, known as the *Heiligtumsfahrt*, will be in June 2021.

148 GREAT PILGRIMAGE SITES OF EUROPE

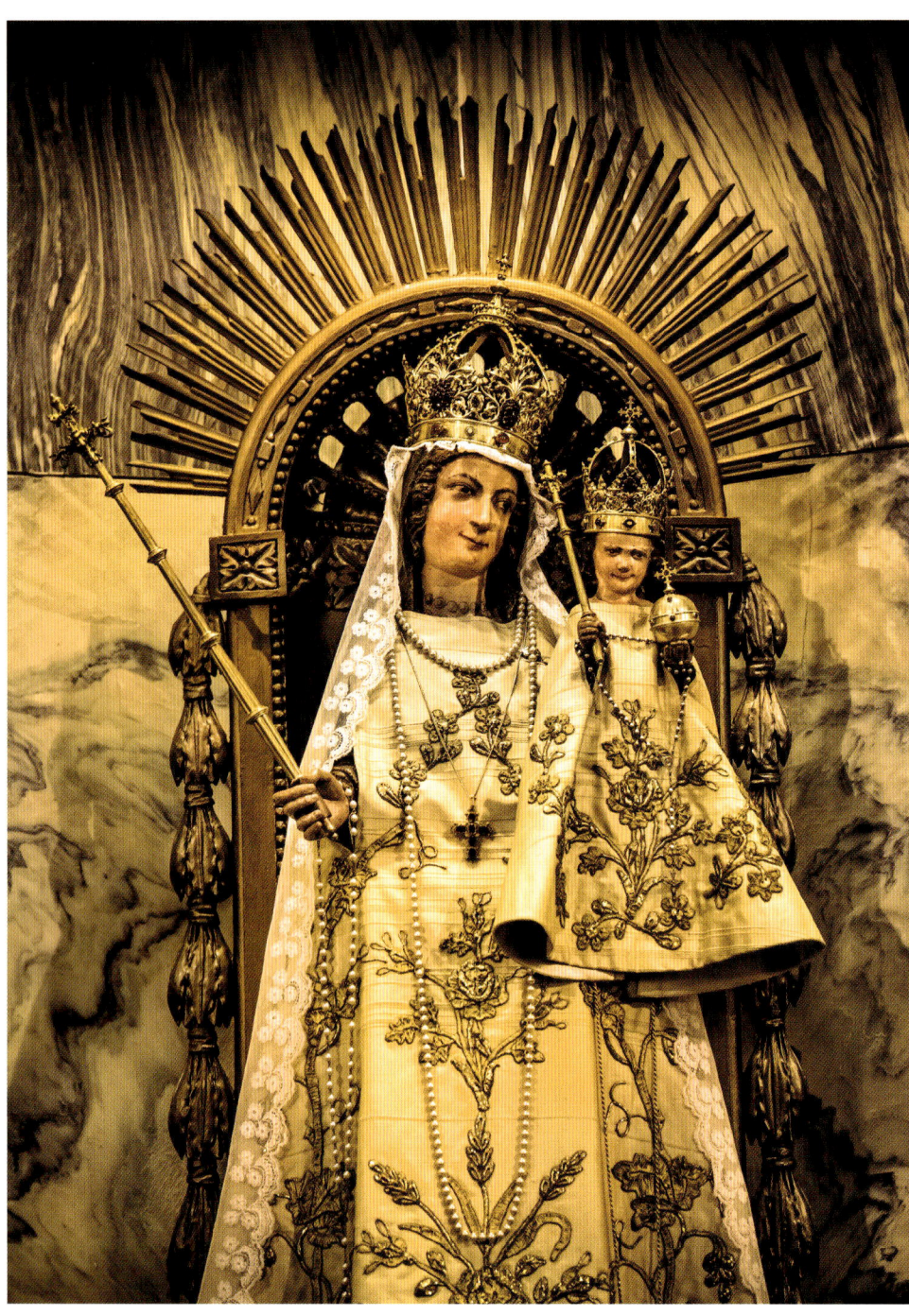

(*above*) Our Lady of Aachen is a fourteenth-century statue of the Virgin Mary and Jesus thought by many to possess miraculous powers. It was all but destroyed by fire, and only heads and hands survived. The remains were cleverly restored and incorporated into a new figure.

(*right*) The unique interior of Charlemagne's octagon, with the Barbarossa chandelier, is one of the great church interiors of Europe. Although much of the decoration dates from the late nineteenth and early twentieth centuries, due to damage and decay, the spirit of the original church is omnipresent.

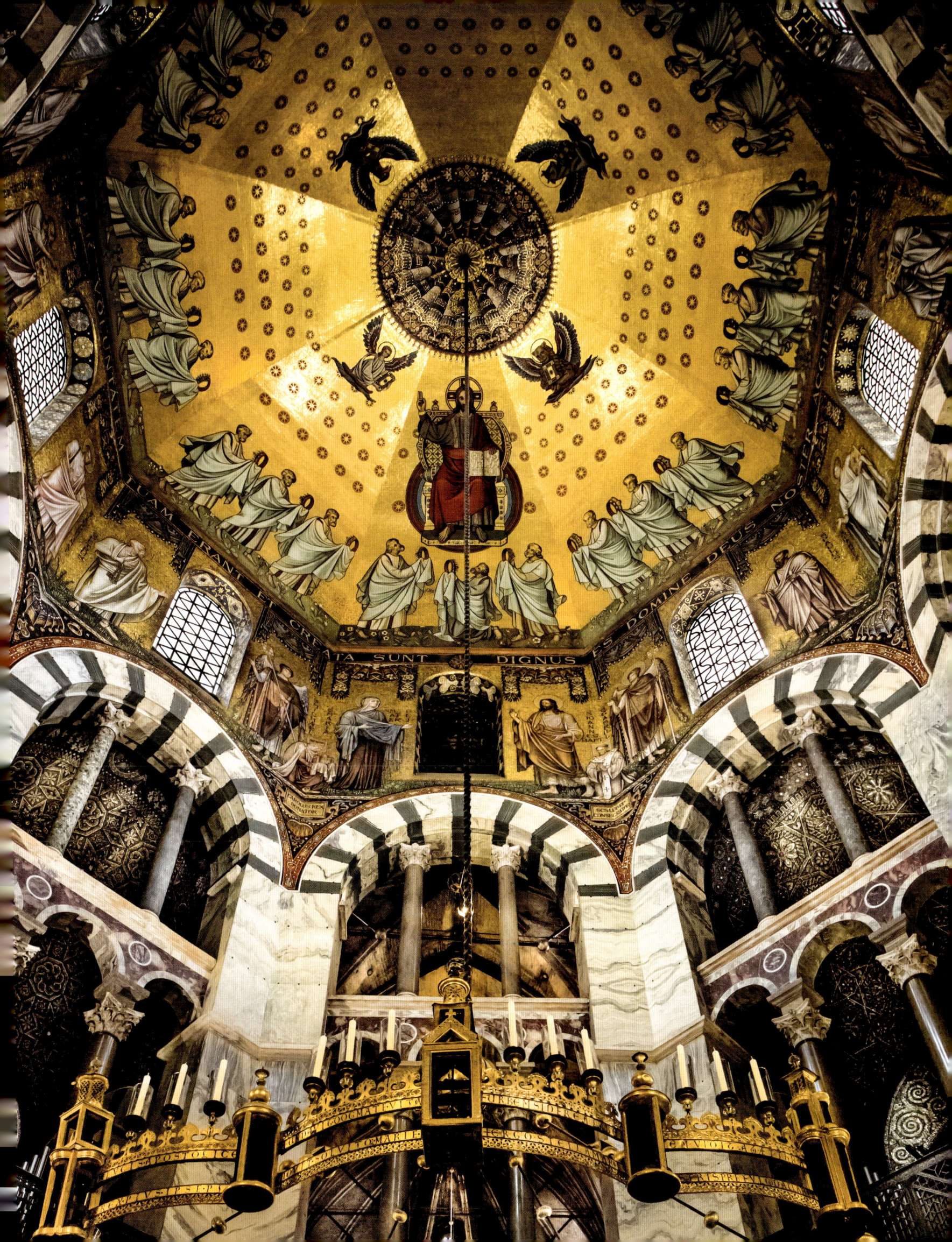

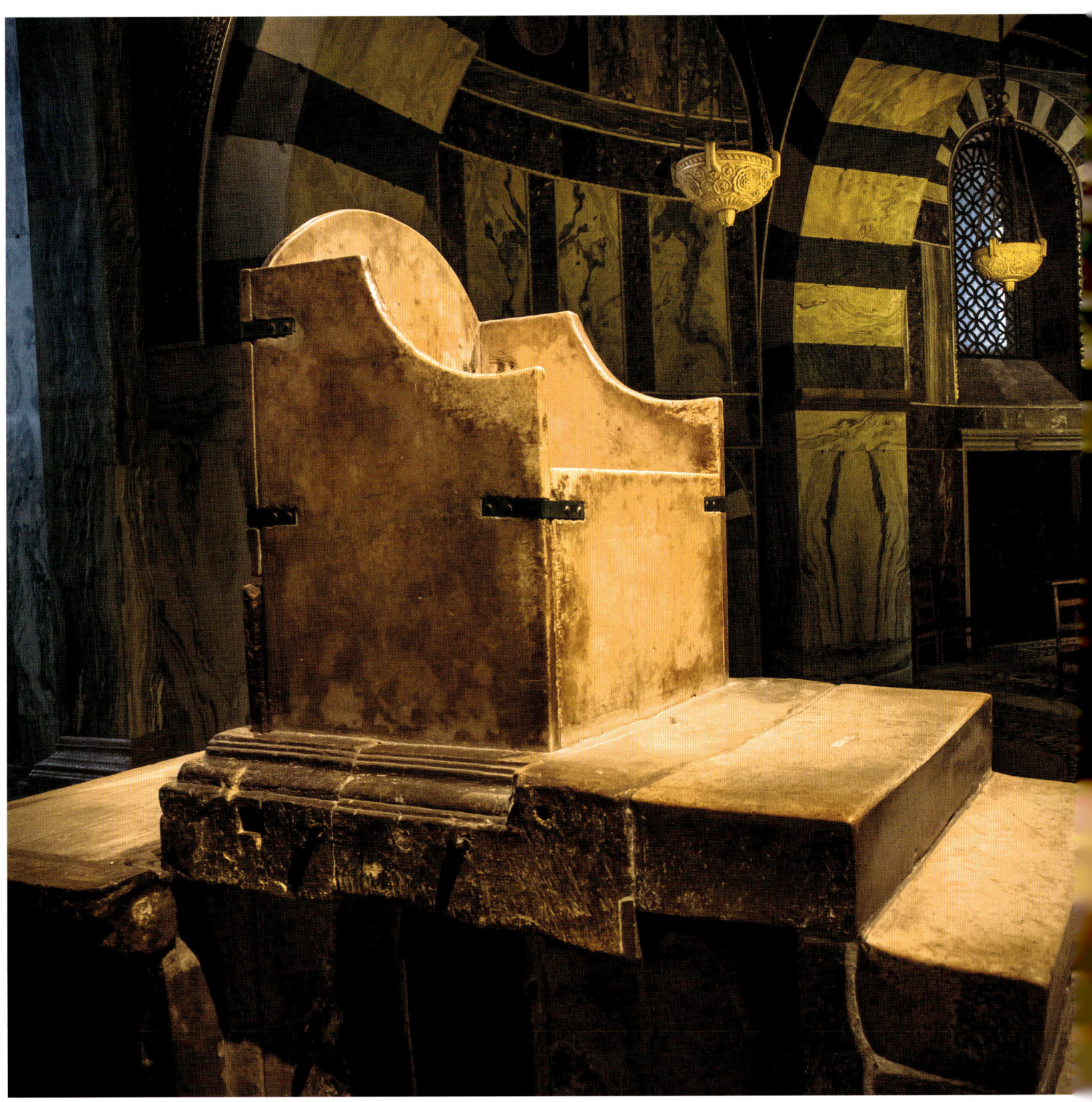

(*above*) Charlemagne's throne is a surprisingly simple structure, comprising recycled ancient marble slabs joined by bronze clips and accessed by six steps, as was King Solomon's. From Otto I's coronation in 936, the throne was used for coronations over a period of 600 years.

(*opposite*) The magnificent shrine containing the relics of Charlemagne is a masterpiece of gold craftsmanship. The end facing into the chancel and the high altar portrays Charlemagne flanked by Pope Leo III and Archbishop Turpin of Reims, with Christ above giving a blessing.

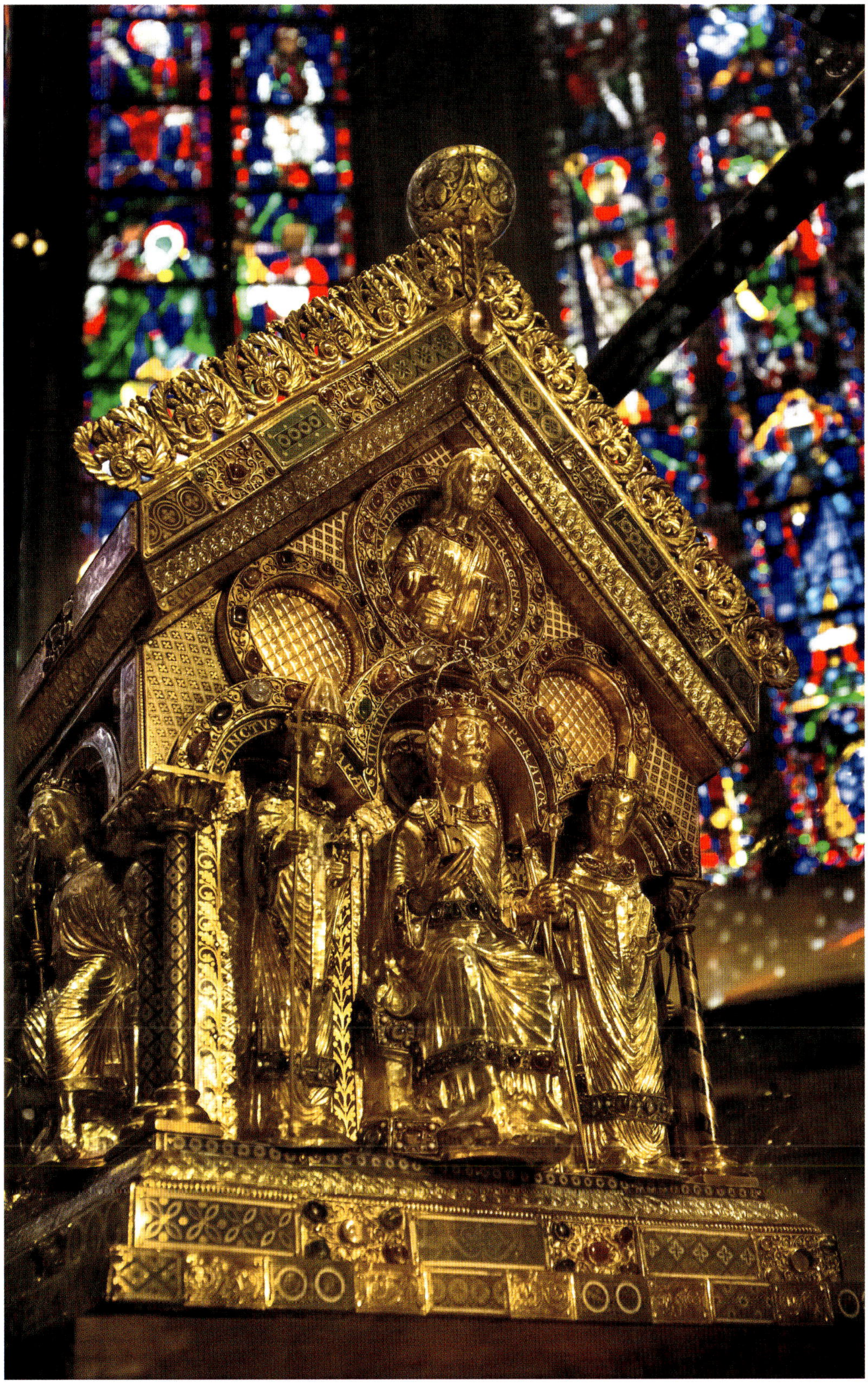

GERMANY, AUSTRIA AND SWITZERLAND 151

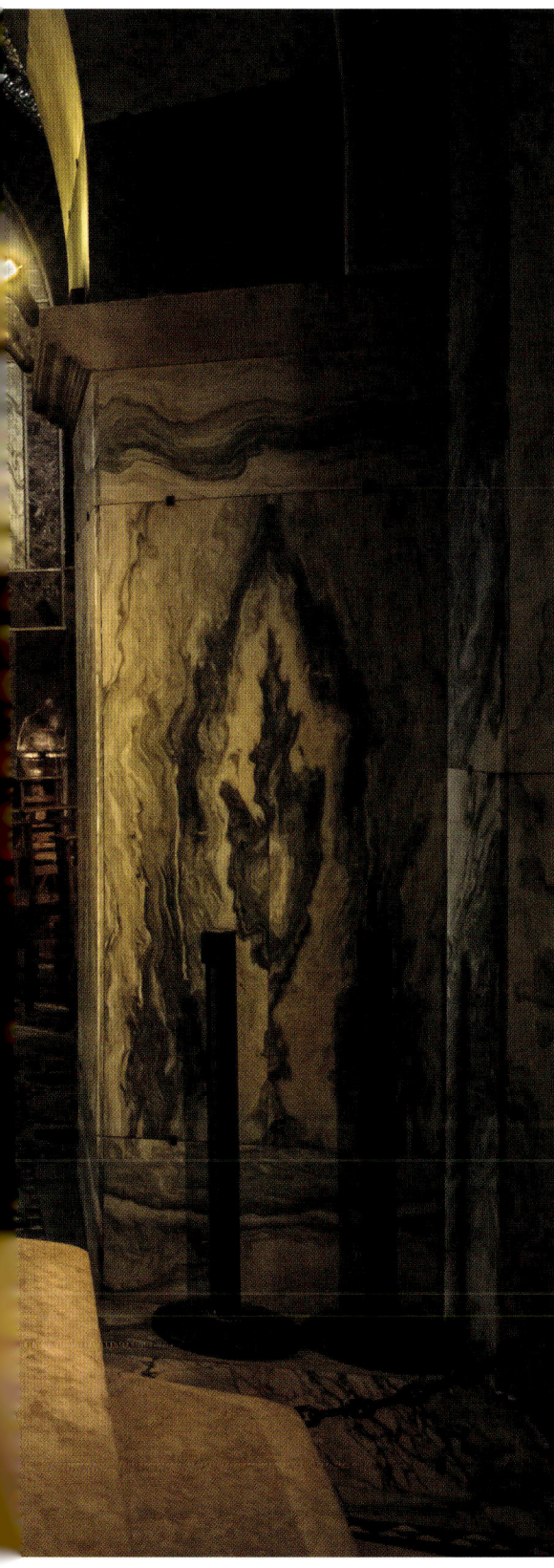

GERMANY
CHAPEL OF GRACE
Altötting, Bavaria

The Chapel of Grace stands alone in the centre of Altötting's Chapel Square, a vast space combining paved pedestrian paths with immaculately tended areas of grass. Neighbouring churches, the town hall and other buildings are set around the square's outer perimeter, affording the chapel the respect it rightly deserves as Germany's most visited Marian shrine. It currently attracts more than a million pilgrims each year.

The octagon is the oldest part of the chapel and in that confined space the shrine of Our Lady has been created to honour a statue of the Virgin Mary holding the infant Jesus. It is set in a niche above the altar, surrounded by candles whose shimmering light dances around the silver statues, gold and silver votive plaques and small silver urns containing the hearts of six kings, two queens, two electors and a field marshal, all set in wall compartments facing the statue. The atmosphere within the tiny Chapel of Grace is unique among the Marian shrines I have visited, and the candle-smoke-darkened, windowless and womblike space creates a moving aura of sanctuary, peace and reassurance.

Although the chapel's precise date of origin and purpose remain partially shrouded in the historical mists of uncertainty, there is documentary evidence indicating that the octagon was used by Bishop Rupert of Salzburg to baptize Theodore, Duke of Bavaria, into the Church in 700. In terms of the town's historical association with pilgrimage, a notable date was 865, when Charlemagne's great-grandson, Carloman (king of Bavaria and Italy), moved his royal court to Altötting and founded a monastery and also a church dedicated to the Virgin Mary. Carloman had acquired a large collection of religious artefacts, which he then donated to the new church, the most significant of which was a reliquary of Philip the Apostle's arm. As a consequence of this and other treasures, the town became a popular pilgrimage destination, particularly once the cult of relics began to play an increasingly meaningful role in people's religious ethos.

The distinctive octagon of the Chapel of Grace is the most revered Marian shrine in Germany. It is intrinsically linked to the ruling Wittelsbach dynasties of Bavaria, and female members of the family had a tradition of providing the crowns and elaborate garments adorning the Virgin and Child statue.

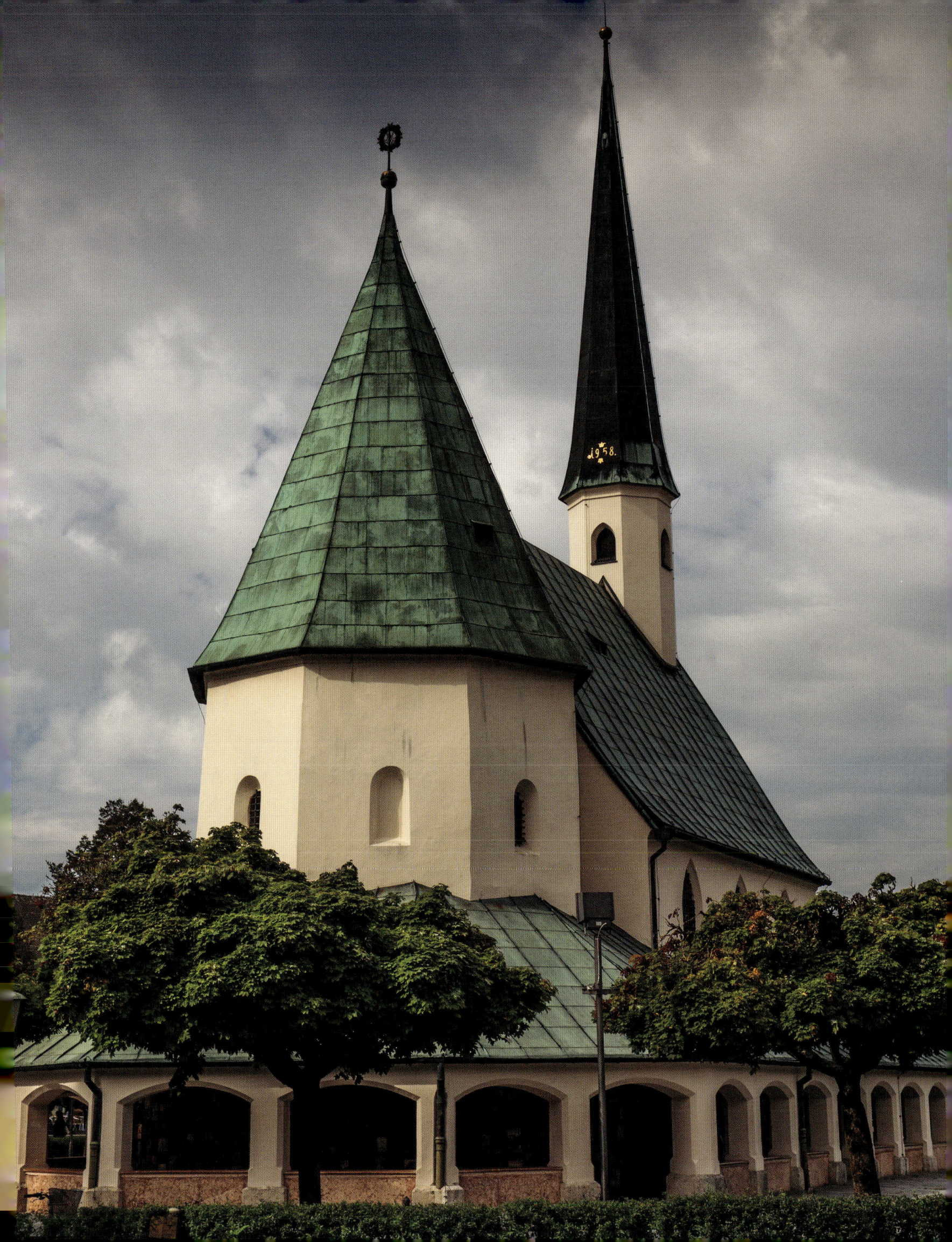

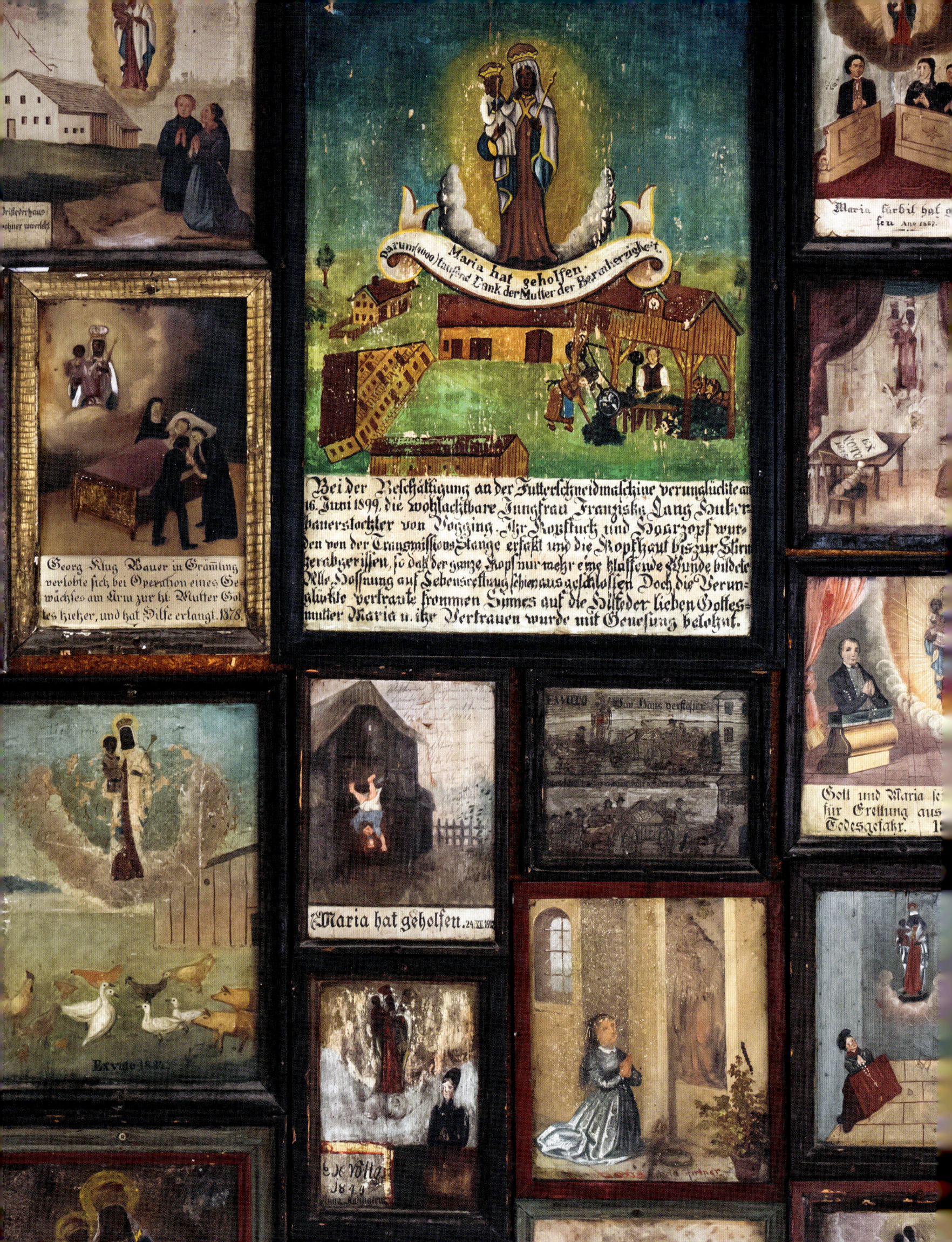

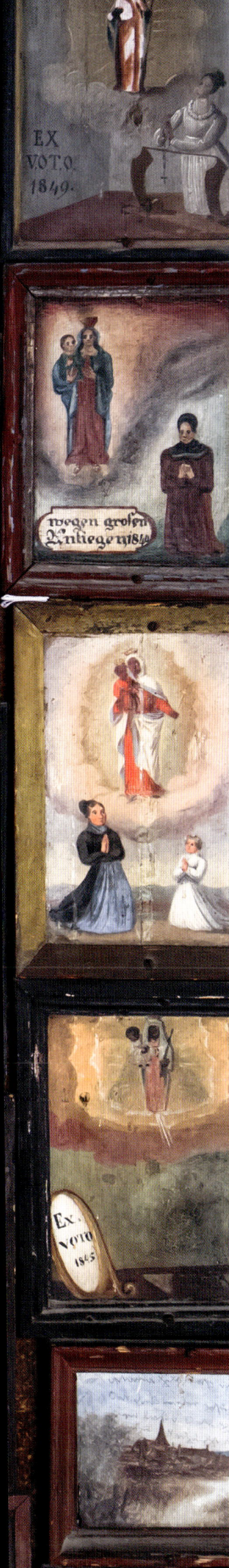

The covered walkway or ambulatory around the chapel's exterior contains a moving and utterly fascinating gallery of votive painted artwork dating back centuries. There is also a stack of symbolic wooden crosses to enable worshippers to partake in a multicircuit pilgrimage around the ambulatory.

The lime wood statue in the Chapel of Grace, now universally known as the Black Madonna (a title acquired through centuries of exposure to candle smoke rather than heritage), was thought to have originated in Lorraine or Burgundy and been brought to Altötting in 1330. Although the 66-centimetre-/26-inch-tall representation of the Virgin had been revered and worshipped since its introduction into the octagon, it was not until 1489 and two miraculous events attributed to the Virgin's miraculous powers that pilgrimage to the town was rejuvenated after a gradual decline. A three-year-old child fell into the local stream and was immersed for more than thirty minutes before his lifeless body was rescued. In sheer desperation, the mother laid her son on the Virgin's altar, where he was instantly revived. There was also a horrific crushing incident involving a young child, a horse and a cart; that, too, had a miraculous outcome.

Pilgrim numbers escalated rapidly and as the travellers could not be readily accommodated in or around the tiny chapel, it was decided to add the nave, a small tower with a distinctive needle-sharp spire and an outdoor covered ambulatory – all of which survive unaltered to the present day. The ambulatory is quite an extraordinary place, because its inner roof and walls are adorned with votive paintings and artwork dating back centuries. Every framed picture portrays events or situations in which the distinctive image of the Virgin and Child has patently been deemed as the saviour or comforter of very many families.

The Marian shrine of Altötting has received significant papal support. When Pope John Paul II visited the shrine in November 1980, he was accompanied by Cardinal Joseph Ratzinger (a native of the area). When the latter was elected to the papacy as Pope Benedict XVI in 2005, he made a return pilgrimage a year later to pay homage at the shrine. He donated the episcopal ring he wore as Bishop of Munich and that gift now adorns the Virgin's sceptre. From Easter onwards, through the summer months, the Chapel Square of Altötting comes alive with the arrival of mass pilgrimage groups, celebrations of religious feast days and festivals, and there is now even a thanksgiving mass for motorcyclists held towards the end of September.

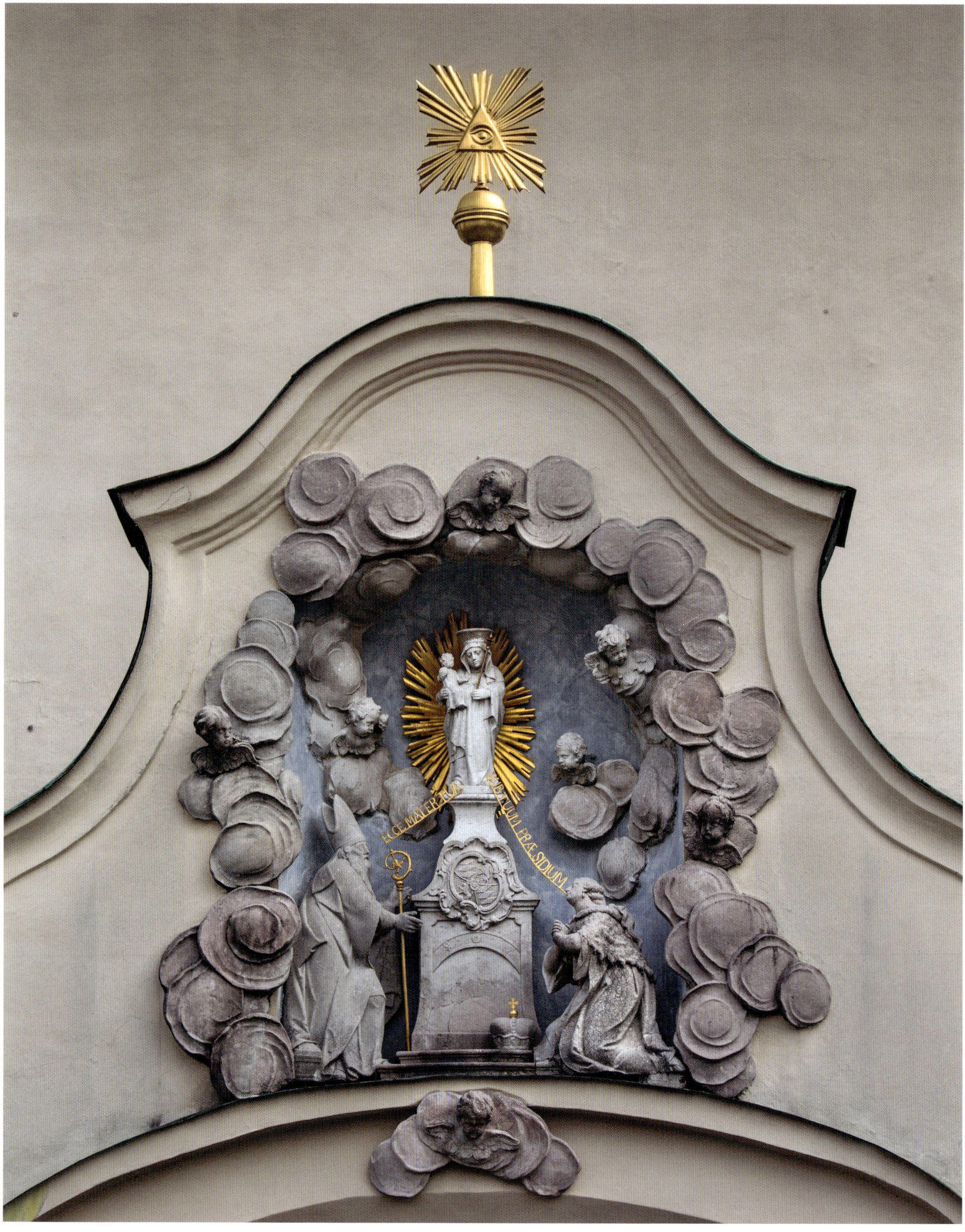

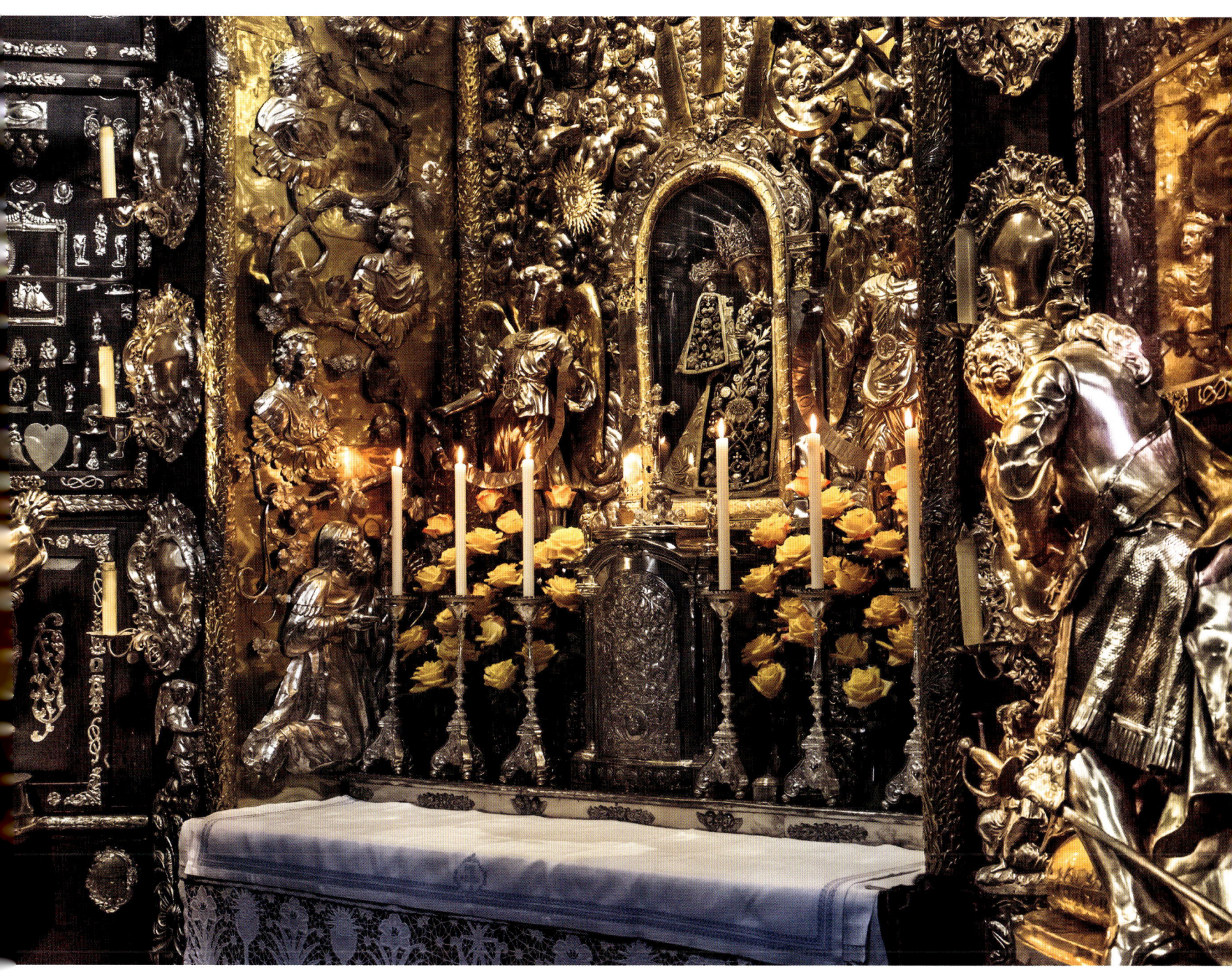

(*left*) The elegantly styled pediment above the entrance to the Chapel of Grace is topped by a gilded gold representation of an ancient Christian symbol, the Eye of Providence. God's all-seeing and protective eye is set within a triangle denoting the Holy Trinity: God, Jesus Christ and the Holy Spirit. The sculpted representation of the Black Madonna is flanked by Latin text from a devotional prayer to the Virgin Mary.

(*above*) The Chapel's Gothic shrine and altar were redesigned in Baroque style during the seventeenth century. Flanking the niche containing the Black Madonna is a life-size silverwork figure of a ten-year-old Prince Maximilian III Joseph of Bavaria kneeling in homage and gratitude for his life. The work was commissioned by his father, Charles Albert, elector of Bavaria (also later Holy Roman Emperor Charles VII), in celebration of his son's recovery from a life-threatening illness.

AUSTRIA
MARIAZELL BASILICA
Mariazell, Styria

Mariazell is a small town set amid the Alpine scenery of Austria's Styria region. There, a Romanesque statue of the Virgin, housed in the basilica and honored by the title *Magna Mater Austriae* 'Great Mother of Austria', attracts up to a million visitors each year. Although many individual and group pilgrimages originate within Austria itself, considerable devotion emanates from surrounding central and eastern European countries. Austria's Habsburg monarchy adopted the statue of the Virgin in Mariazell as its national shrine, and because each ruling archduke from 1440 until 1806 was also elected Holy Roman Emperor, that devotion to the *Magna Mater* was carried beyond the Austrian borders as the Habsburg dynasty expanded its territories. In more recent times, the collapse of the Berlin Wall in 1989 and the subsequent political independence of the Warsaw Pact countries closest to Austria enabled total freedom of movement for Catholics who previously had been denied the privilege of making a pilgrimage to Mariazell.

Mariazell's name evolved from the original description 'Mary in the cell', a reference to the humble chapel (cell) and monastic foundation established on the site of a miracle attributed to the Virgin Mary. In 1157, Magnus, a Benedictine monk from the important monastery of St Lambrecht, was dispatched to the area by his abbot to sustain the spiritual well-being of the population. But on 21 December, the monk's route was completely blocked by a huge boulder. Perhaps in hope rather than expectation, he sought comfort and guidance from the statue of the Virgin that he carried in his pack. His faith was almost immediately rewarded because the giant rock fell apart. Upon arrival at his destination, Magnus placed the statue on a tree stump and on that very site built the chapel whose original location remains unchanged to this day. It is now the Chapel of Mercy set within the basilica.

A carved date of 1200 set into the main entrance portal relates to the Romanesque stone chapel built to replace the humble wooden edifice. It was built as a token of extreme gratitude by Margrave Vladislaus Henry of Moravia (a margrave was a military commander of the Holy Roman Empire)

The fifteenth-century Gothic tympanum's complex carved lower segment is framed above and below by explanatory Latin text, in which the Virgin is referred to as the 'Madonna of the protecting cloak'. On her right is Louis I, King of Hungary, offering up a framed depiction of the Madonna he donated as a votive offering.

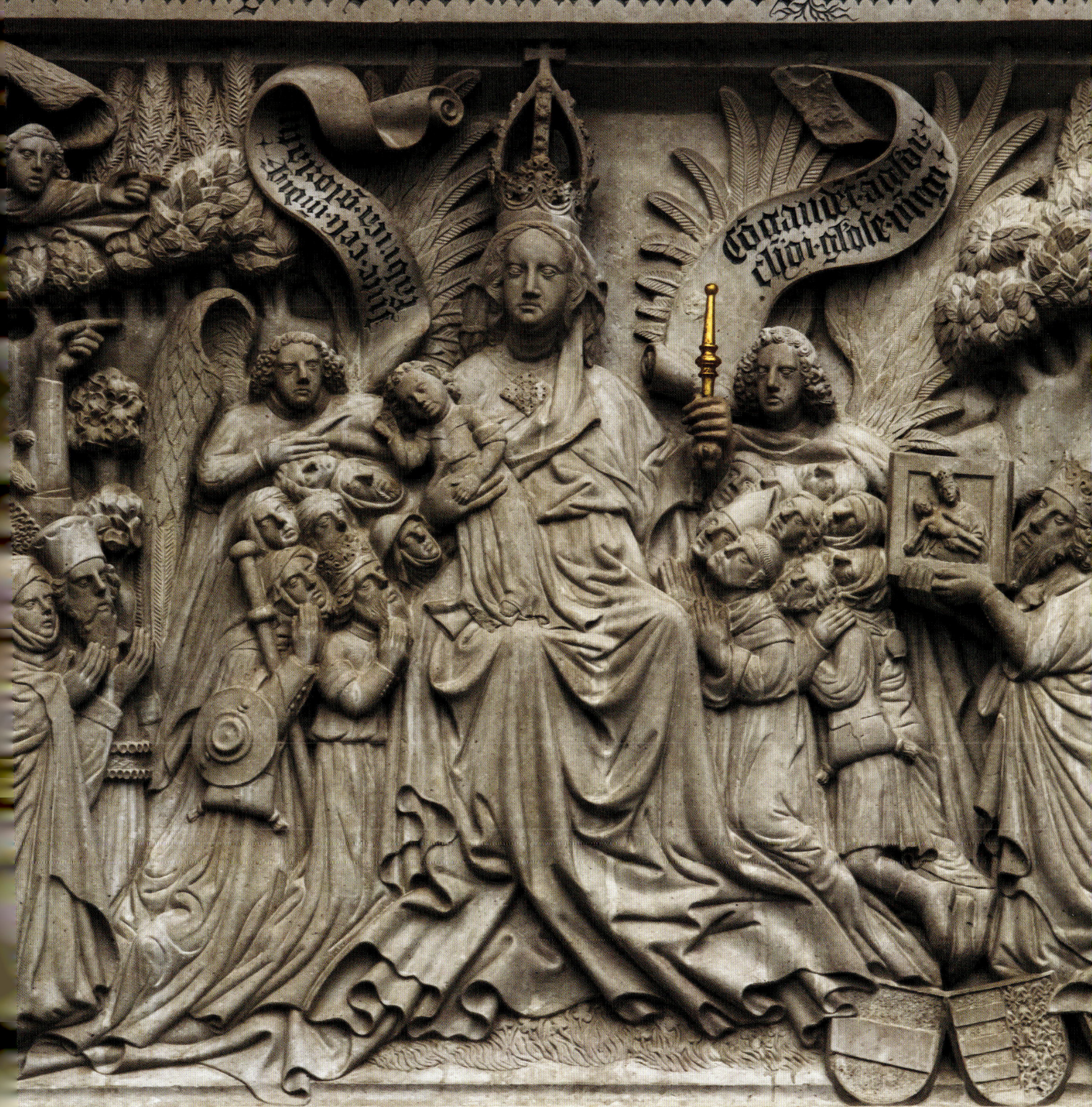

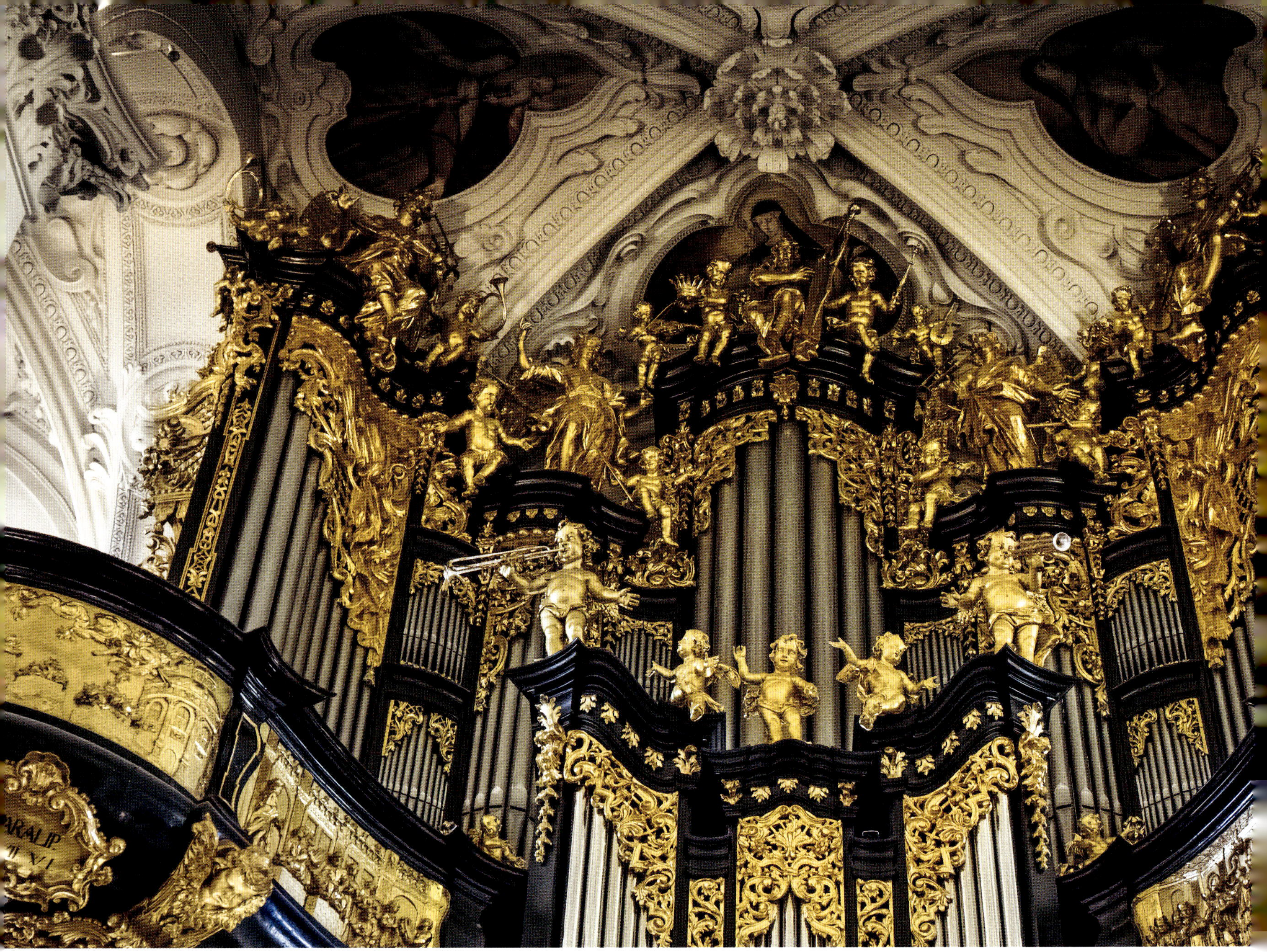

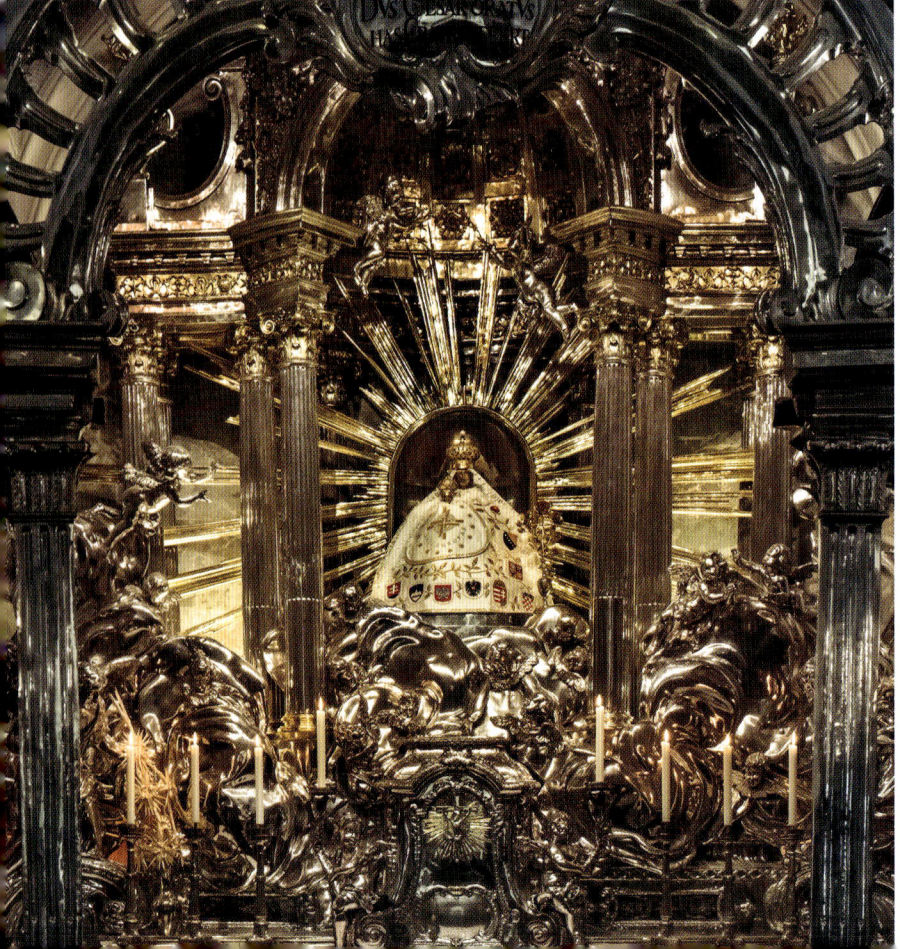
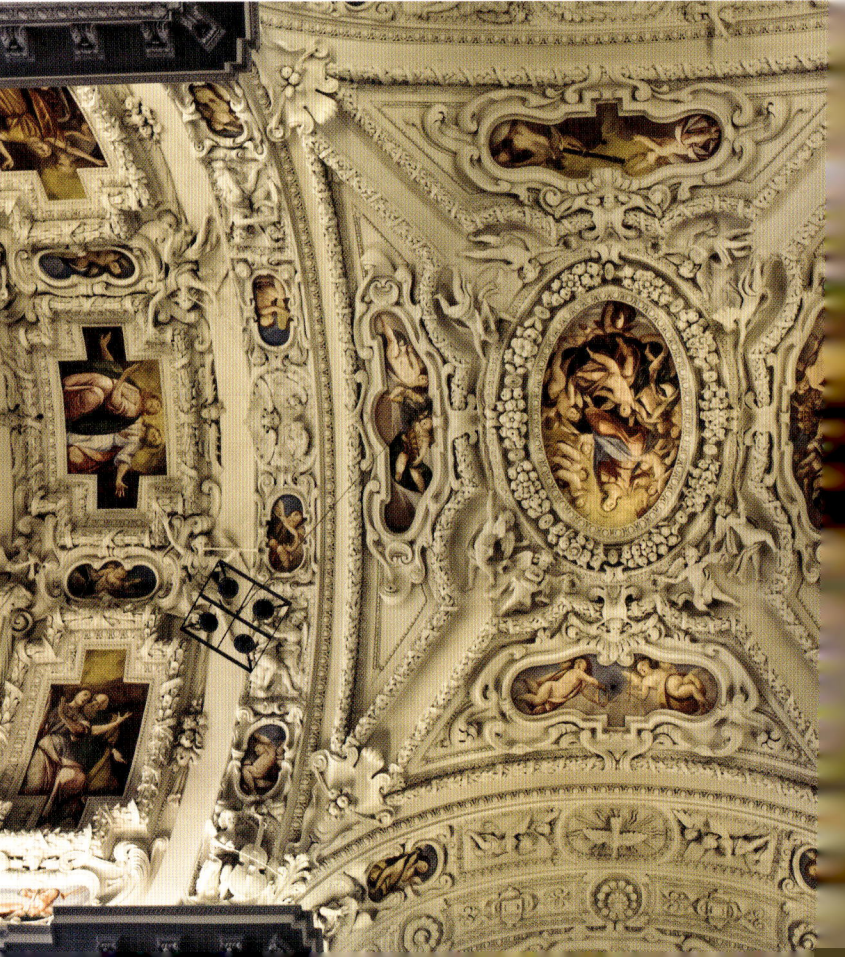

(*top left*) The basilica's lavishly ornamented organ.
(*top right*) The elaborate silver grille of the Chapel of Grace was donated by Emperor Francis I in 1756.
(*bottom*) Frescoes and stucco work of the Baroque interior.

(*overleaf*) Mariazell's basilica in its Alpine setting at sunset.

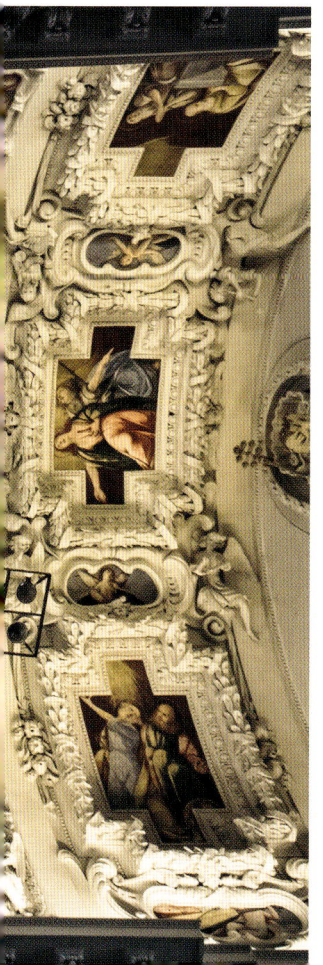

who attributed his recovery from serious illness to the Virgin Mary. The next architectural progression into the Gothic style was endowed by Louis I of Hungary, following successful military campaigns in which his troops marched into battle against the Turks bearing banners and portraits of the Virgin.

The popularity of Mariazell as a pilgrimage destination meant that despite its increased size and grandeur, the Gothic church was deemed patently inadequate to deal with escalating numbers, and so the building extant today is largely unchanged from the Baroque-style alterations and extensions added during the mid-seventeenth century. The Swiss master builder Domenico Sciassia extended and widened the existing nave and his sympathetic approach to the project resulted in the retention of the dramatic Gothic central tower and spire, accompanied by the equally distinctive main portal from that same period.

Numerous chapels now line each side of the nave. Running directly above them on the upper floor are elegant galleries filled with paintings, votive artwork and a wonderful collection of religious treasures, artefacts and relics displayed in both the north and south aisles. The Chapel of Mercy hosting the Virgin's statue occupies an appropriately prominent position in the heart of the nave, marking the point between the Gothic and Baroque segments of the basilica. It has been embellished and adorned with much silverwork commissioned during the eighteenth century, which, although visually impressive, could perhaps seem a trifle over-exuberant.

The statue of the Virgin and Child remains covered in the customary robes and crowns associated with the majority of Marian shrines throughout Europe, but the true artistry of the Romanesque carving may be viewed on just two special feast days when the garments are removed: the Birth of the Virgin on 8 September and the foundation of Mariazell on 21 December. The latter date is firmly established as one of the town's premier annual events and is doubly colourful because when Austria's largest traditional Advent Market is held here, the environs of the basilica are surrounded by stalls selling food and gifts from small replica Alpine huts festooned with Christmas lights.

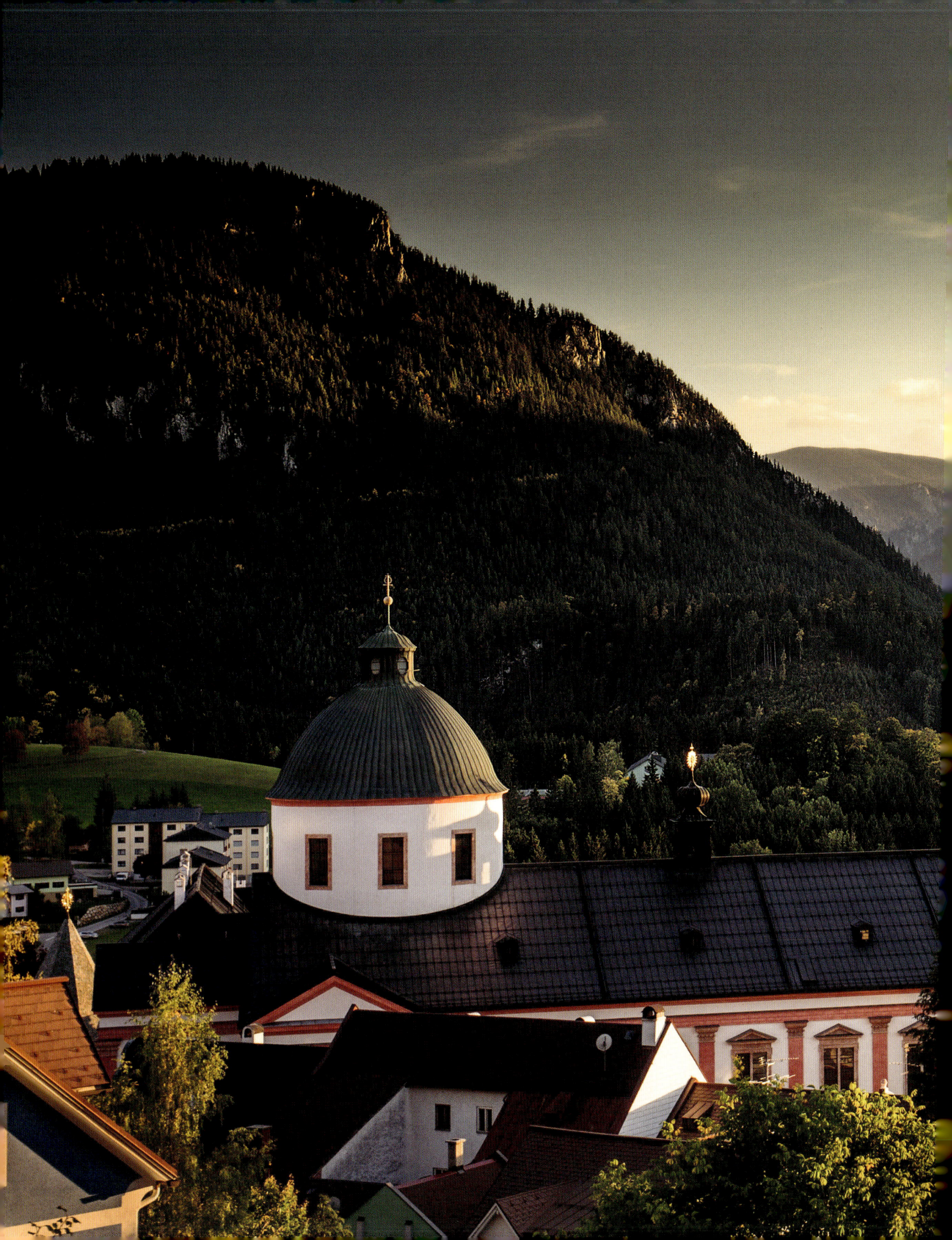

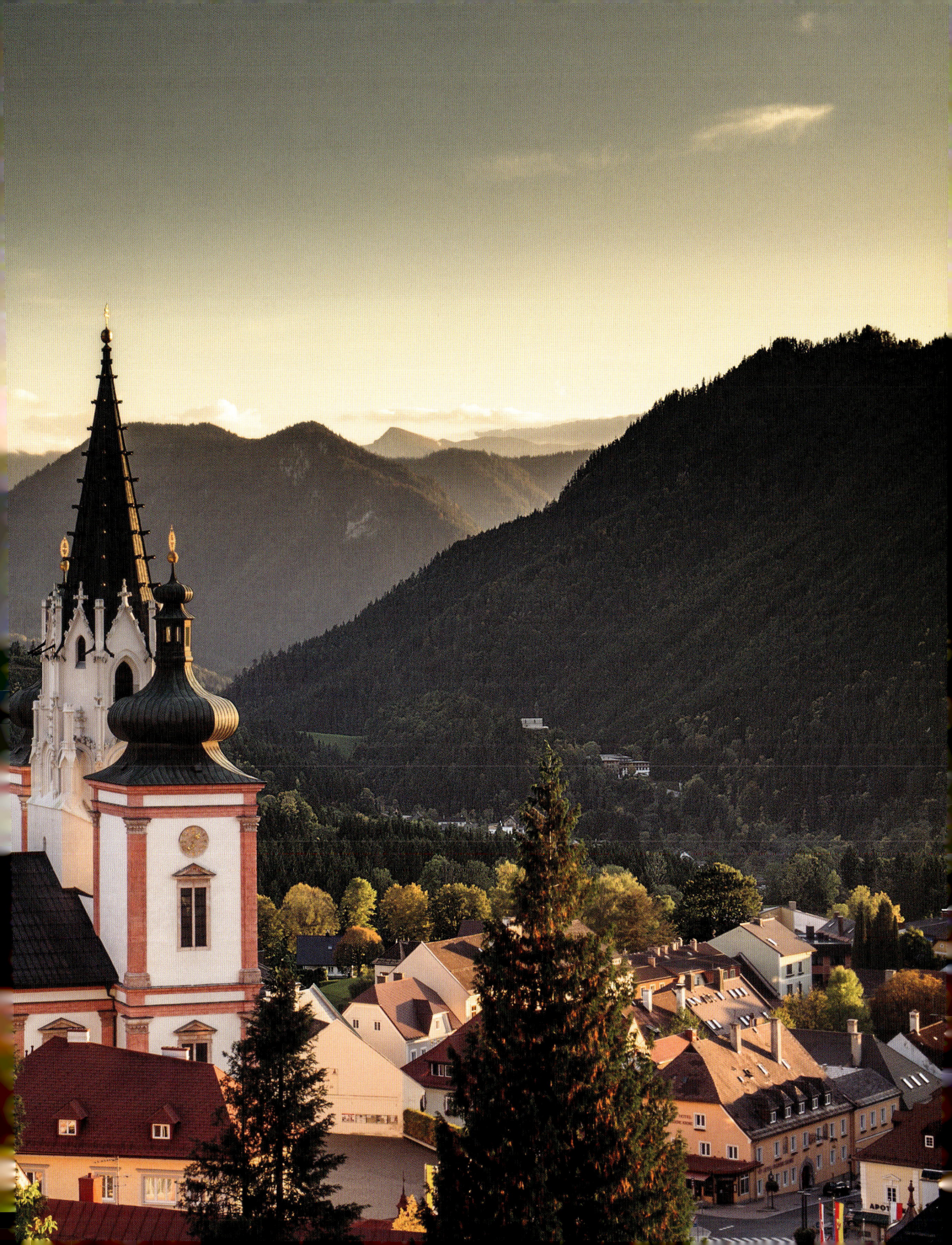

SWITZERLAND
EINSIEDELN ABBEY

Standing in front of the majestic plaza leading up to the abbey church and monastery of Einsiedeln, it is difficult to equate one of Europe's most impressive Baroque buildings with a remote hermit's cell. However, a monk named Meinrad from a nearby priory on the shores of Lake Zurich lived and prayed there in complete isolation until being brutally murdered by robbers in 861. To honour both his ethos and his memory, a small monastic community established itself on the site of his hermitage, and by 934 it had formally adopted the Rule of St Benedict and built a small church. Fourteen years later, the monks were about to be led by the Bishop of Konstanz in the sacred ceremony of consecration when a loud voice rang out three times to proclaim that the church had already been consecrated by Jesus Christ in the name of his Mother, Mary. There also exists a slight variant on that story, which insists that Christ himself and the four Evangelists appeared at the altar. However, regardless of which version was presented to Pope Leo VIII, the miracle was investigated and subsequently ratified not only by him but also by many of his successors, through to Pope Pius VI in the late eighteenth century.

The status of the monastery was significantly increased by news of this miracle and thereafter evolved into a popular pilgrimage destination, due partly to the miracle of the consecration and partly to the ancient statue of the Virgin. The abbey was also granted imperial status by Holy Roman Emperor Otto I and this elevated stature attracted support and generous gifts from the nobility and subsequent Holy Roman emperors. Unfortunately, such attention and rapidly accrued wealth affected how the monastery was run, and by the thirteenth century it had adopted the aura of an elite establishment, accepting only sons from the upper echelons of society. This lax approach and blatant disregard for the strict monastic rules of St Benedict resulted in a gradual decline of fortunes, and by the time of the Reformation during the mid-sixteenth century there were but a handful of monks remaining.

Set amid the hills and valleys of the northern Schwyz region of Switzerland, the Benedictine monastery of Einsiedeln comprises a majestic Baroque abbey church adorned with domes and cupolas. Twelve bells hang in the church towers, and on special feast days their sound is truly phenomenal.

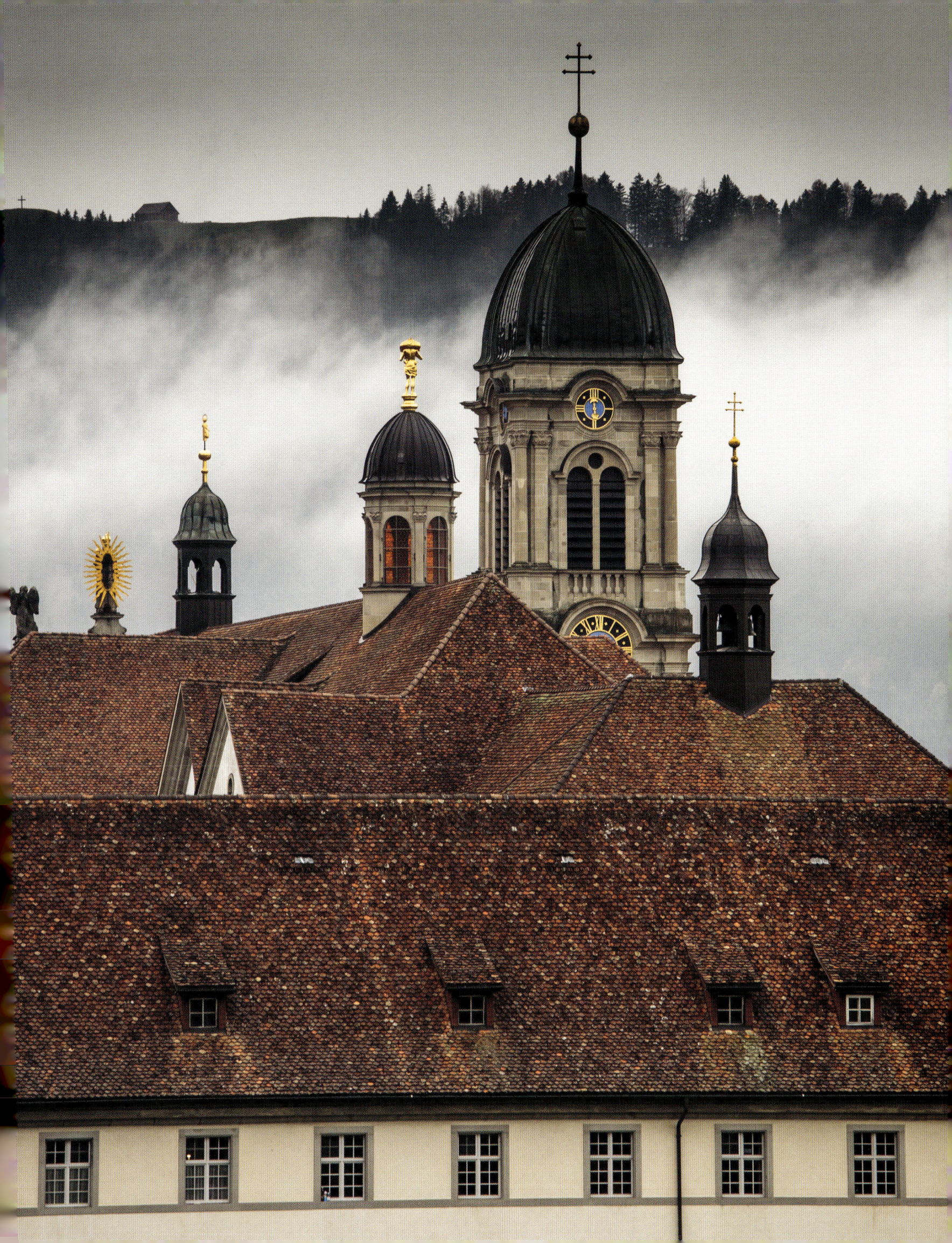

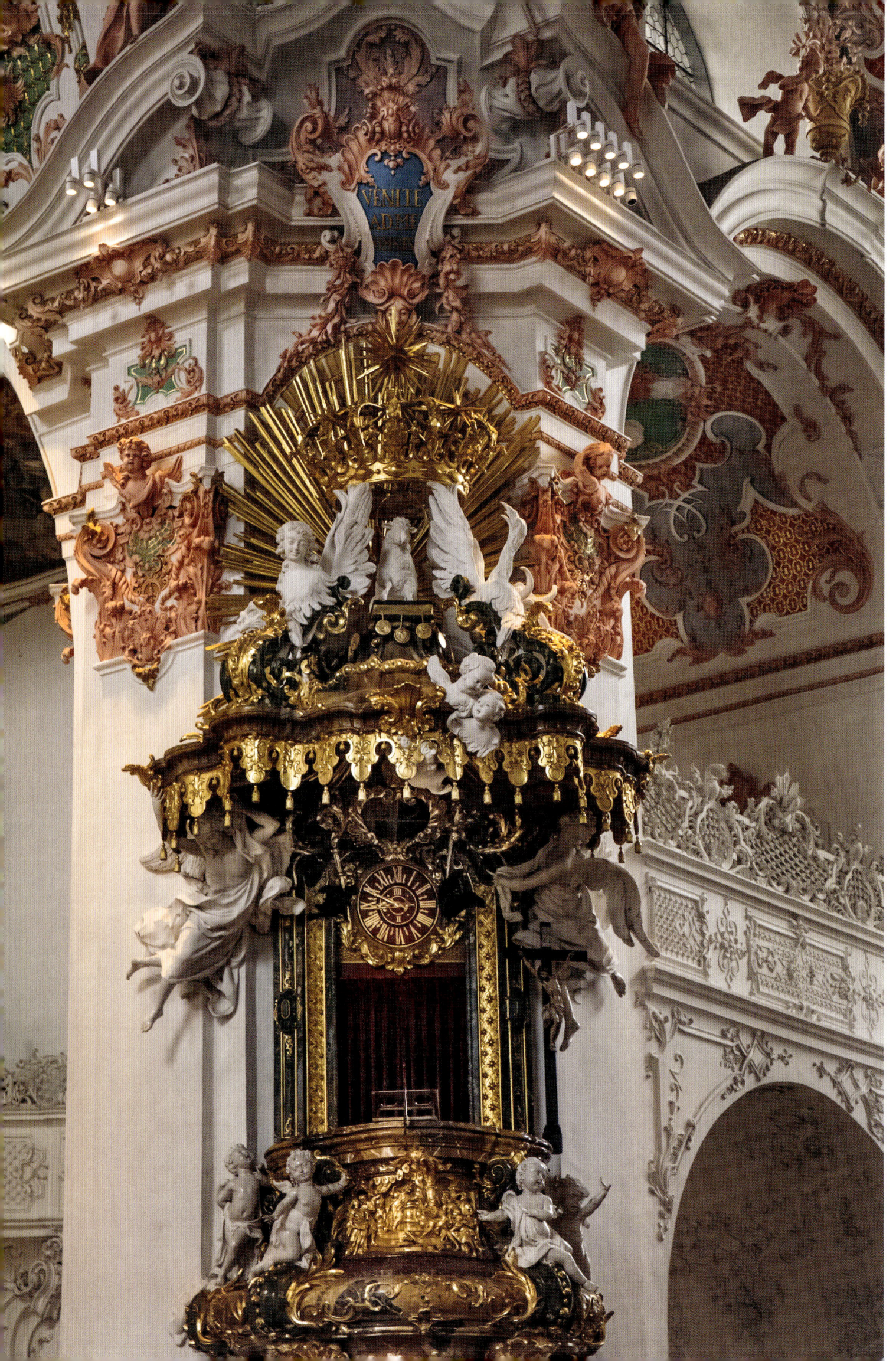

(*left*) Two of the more significant contributors to the sumptuous Baroque interior of the abbey church were the Asam brothers from Munich. They were renowned for working in perfect artistic harmony, with Cosmas Asam specializing in frescoes and his brother Egid a master of stucco work.

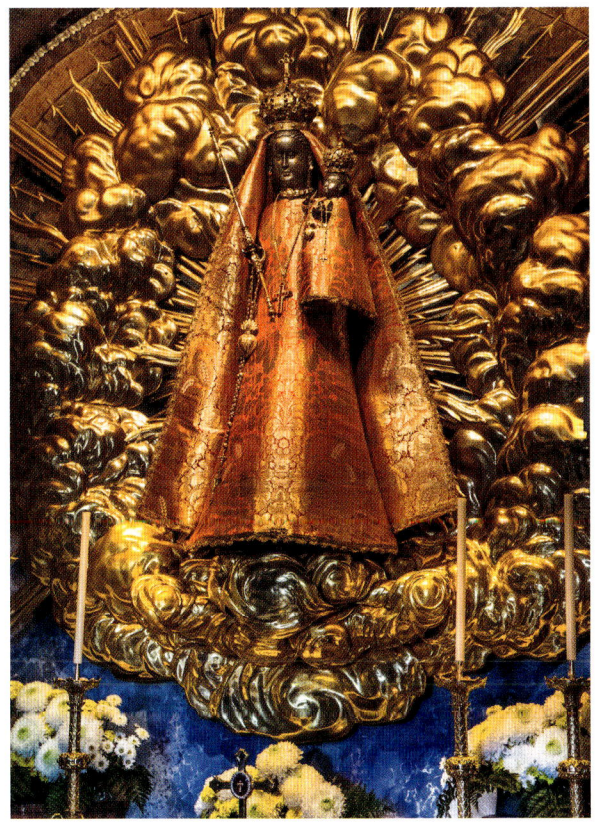

(*above*) The Black Madonna of Einsiedeln floats majestically on golden clouds in the Chapel of Grace.

(*overleaf*) The view down on to the monastery and abbey church of Einsiedeln from St Benedict's statue on the hillside above clearly portrays the impressive scale and pure symmetry of the buildings.

In a curious juxtaposition of fate and fortune, Einsiedeln's monastic decline coincided with its rise in popularity as a pilgrimage destination, once it became firmly established as an essential devotional detour for pilgrims crossing Europe *en route* to the shrine of St James in Santiago de Compostela.

Einsiedeln could easily have joined the many other monastic institutions throughout Europe that simply ceased to exist in the post-Reformation era, but the appointment of a new abbot created a fervent desire for survival. Because so much structural damage had been caused through fire and neglect over the centuries, and also because it was too small to accommodate the revitalized community, it was decided to completely rebuild the monastery buildings and church. The foundation stones were laid in 1704 and 1721, respectively.

Two tall towers flank the main entrance portal of the church, and as one enters the church, the elegant but comparatively plain exterior is replaced by a joyous celebration of ornate Baroque decoration and artwork. It must have been heartbreaking for the monastic community to be faced with the potentially disastrous consequences of the invasion of Switzerland during the French Revolutionary Wars. The monastery was ransacked for several days in 1798, but fortunately the monks had already fled to safety and the precious Black Madonna had been taken secretly to a secure location in Austria. Previously, the original statue had been destroyed by fire in 1465 and the Gothic replacement acquired a year later is the one standing in the Neoclassical-style Chapel of Grace today. The chapel is located just within the main entrance doors. The perfect conclusion to an Einsiedeln pilgrimage is to attend late afternoon Vespers there and hear the 'Salve Regina' sung by the unaccompanied Benedictine monk's choir. The resonance of the voices combined with sublime harmonies creates a deeply moving experience.

A large bronze statue of St Benedict stands on a steep hill overlooking the monastic complex. If his spirit still lingers amid the Alpine scenery, it is no doubt pleased to witness an almost perfect replica of the medieval foundations he inspired. There is an Einsiedeln abbey school, a renowned horse-breeding operation and other monastic-related businesses providing care and employment for the local community.

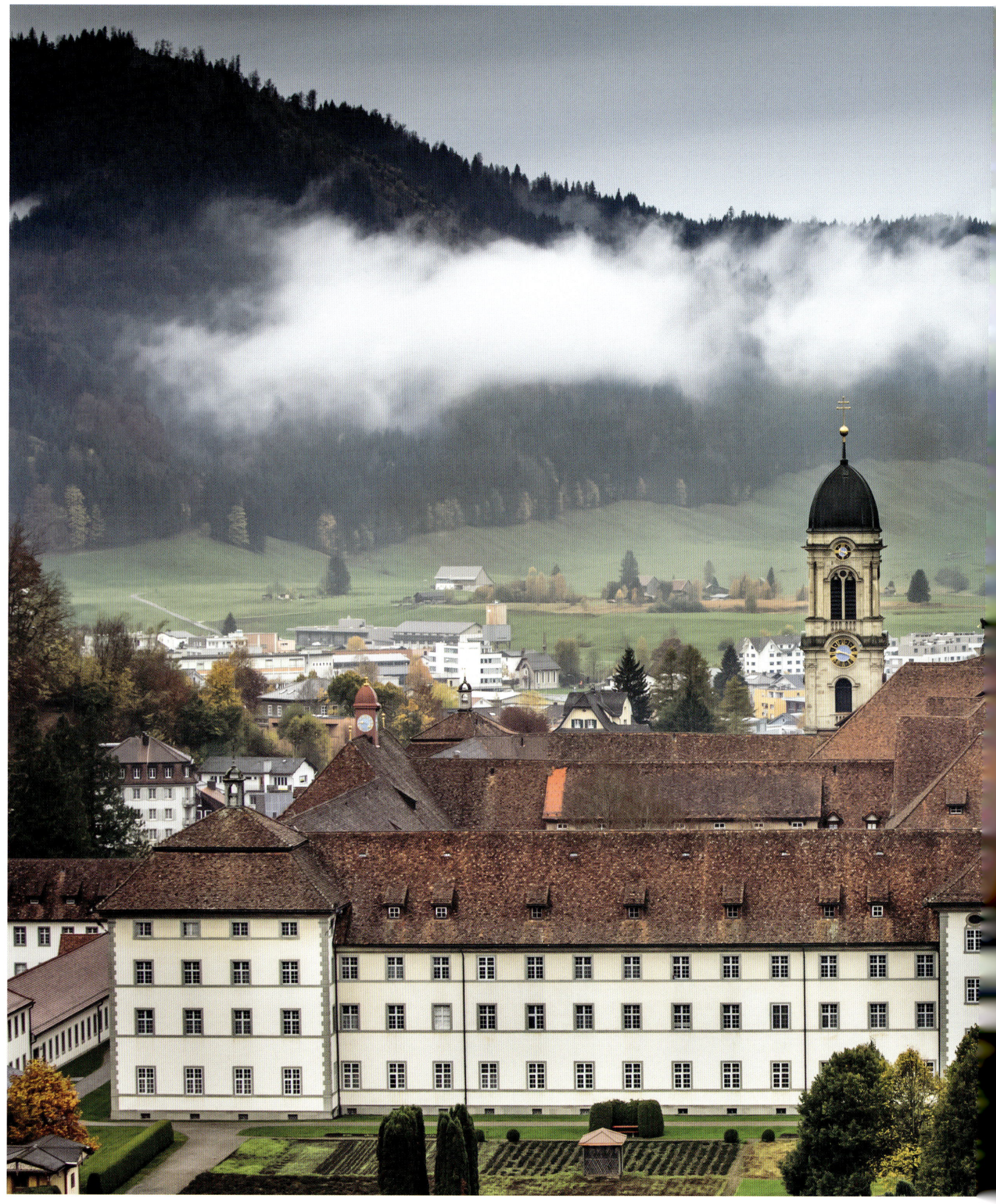

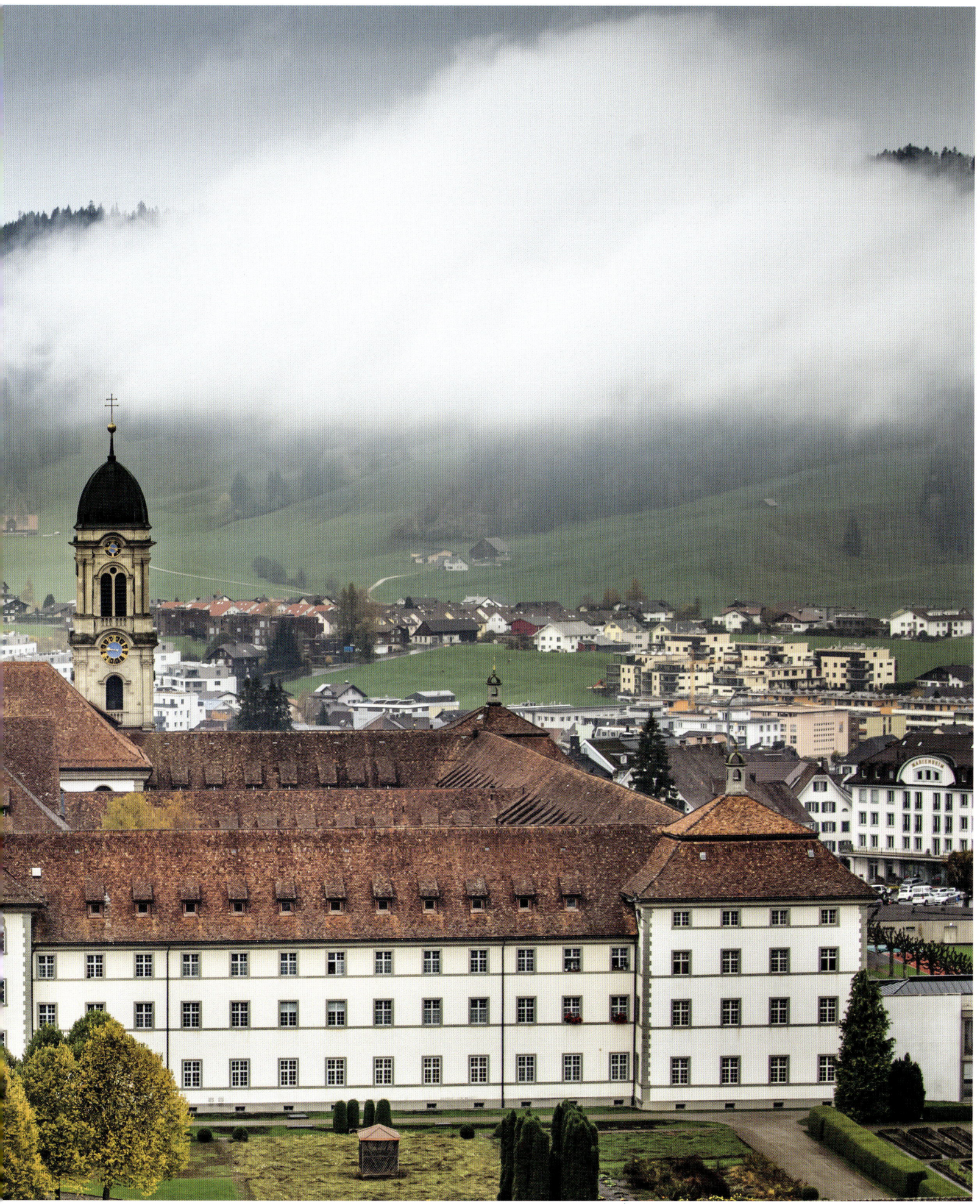

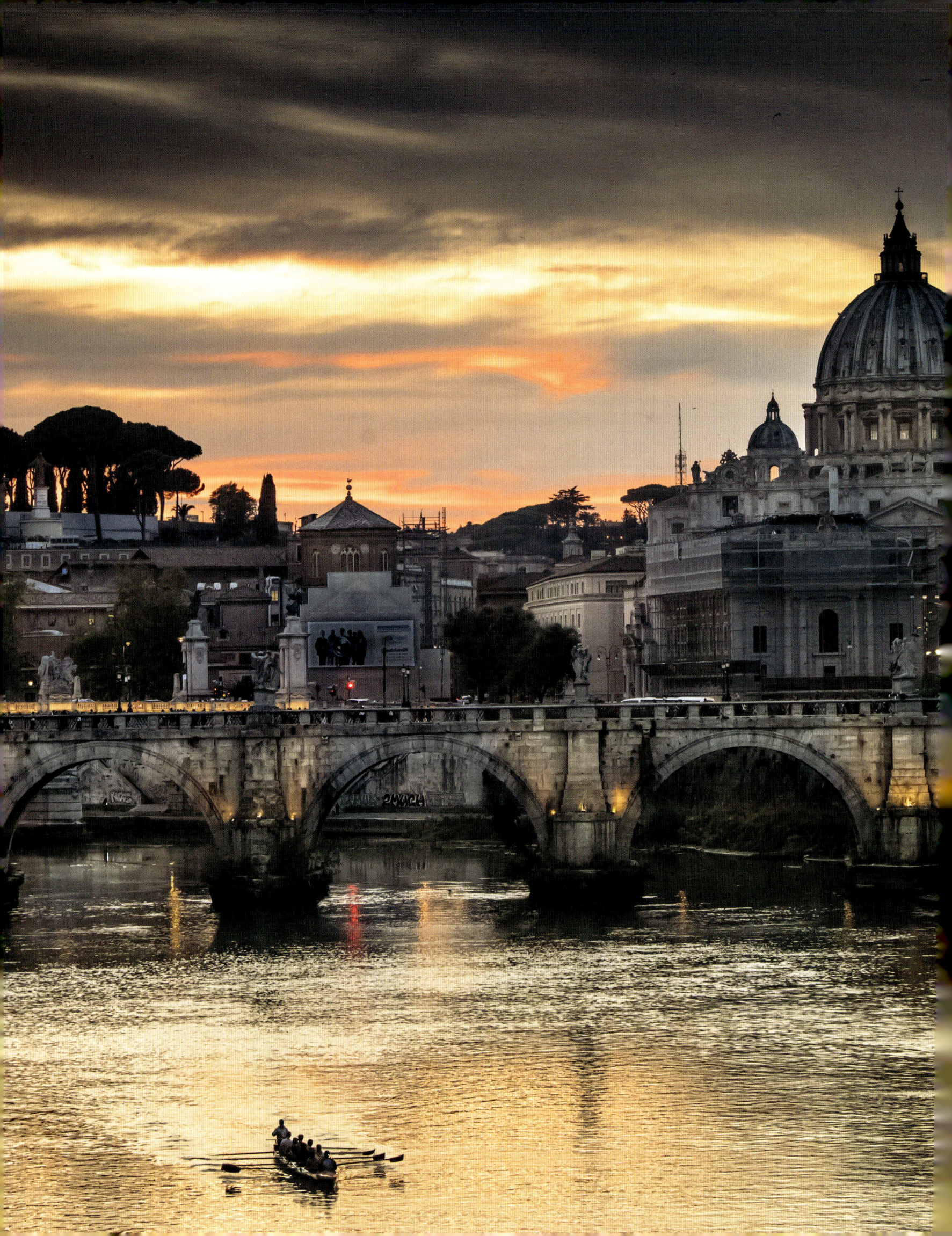

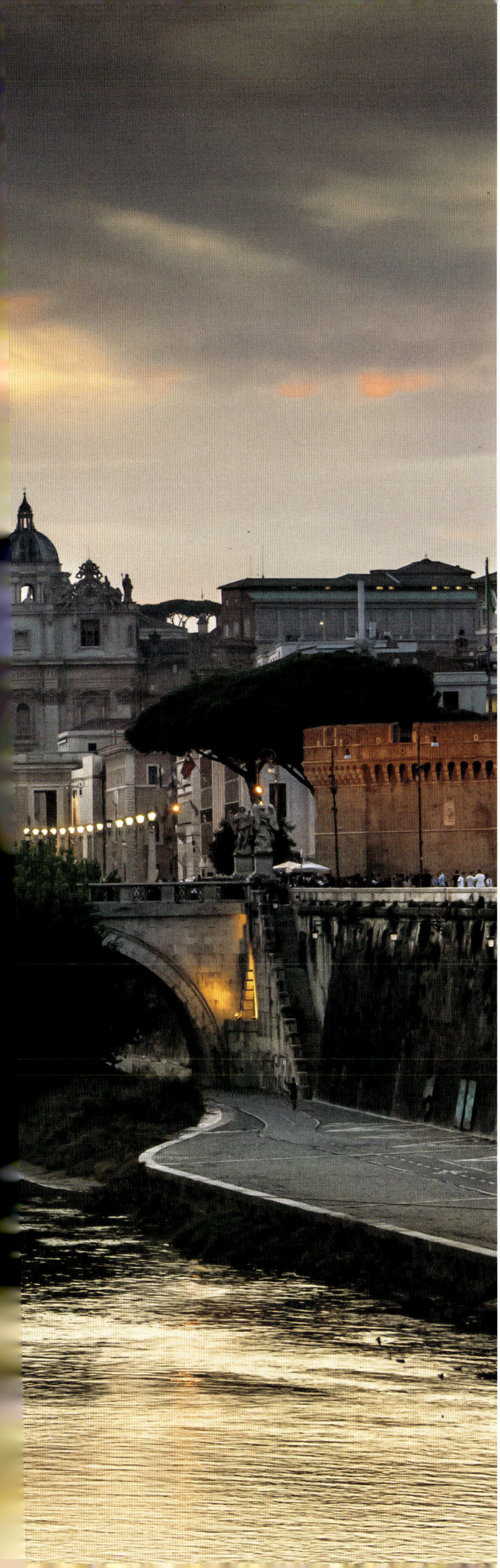

6

ITALY

THE BASILICA OF ST ANTHONY OF PADUA
Padua, Veneto

St Anthony of Padua was born in Lisbon, Portugal, but died at a comparatively young age in Padua. He was born Fernando Martins de Bulhões and was the eldest son of a wealthy family, who sent him to be educated at the local cathedral school. Despite being only fifteen years of age, he left school to join the Augustinian community at the Abbey of St Vincent near Lisbon. There are close similarities between the lives of St Anthony of Padua and St Francis of Assisi, as both came from affluent backgrounds but subsequently turned their backs on the prospect of a comfortable life in favour of spirituality, piety and poverty. Fernando was ordained as a priest at the age of twenty-five, and shortly thereafter, having spent some time with a group of Franciscans, he immersed himself in the teachings of St Francis. He also decided that he should take a new name and called himself Anthony, after the fourth-century Egyptian hermit St Anthony, seen by many as the father of monasticism.

Anthony's first intended expedition was to preach the Gospel in Muslim Morocco, but he fell seriously ill and was forced to sail back home. Unfortunately, a storm blew the ship so far off course that it landed in Sicily. Finding himself in Italy, he opted to travel up to Assisi and spend time with the Franciscan friars. Anthony so impressed all those who met him that he was asked to look after the spiritual well-being of a small mountain community. He was then sent farther afield, through areas of northern Italy and southern France viewed as hotbeds of heresy, and during that time two of the greatest legends associated with St Anthony occurred.

While trying to preach in the coastal town of Rimini, he was met by a wall of apathy and so turned to the sea and invited the fish to hear the word of God. Sure enough, row upon regimented row of fish poked their heads above the surface and listened with rapt attention. His other animal-related triumph occurred when a hardened heretic said he would only believe Christ was present

(*previous pages*) St Peter's Basilica, Rome.

(*right*) The exterior of St Anthony's basilica exhibits obvious Byzantine similarities to the domes of its close neighbour, St Mark's in Venice. Although Padua's hitherto anonymous architect may conceivably have drawn inspiration from the Venetian masterpiece, there are no published links between the two.

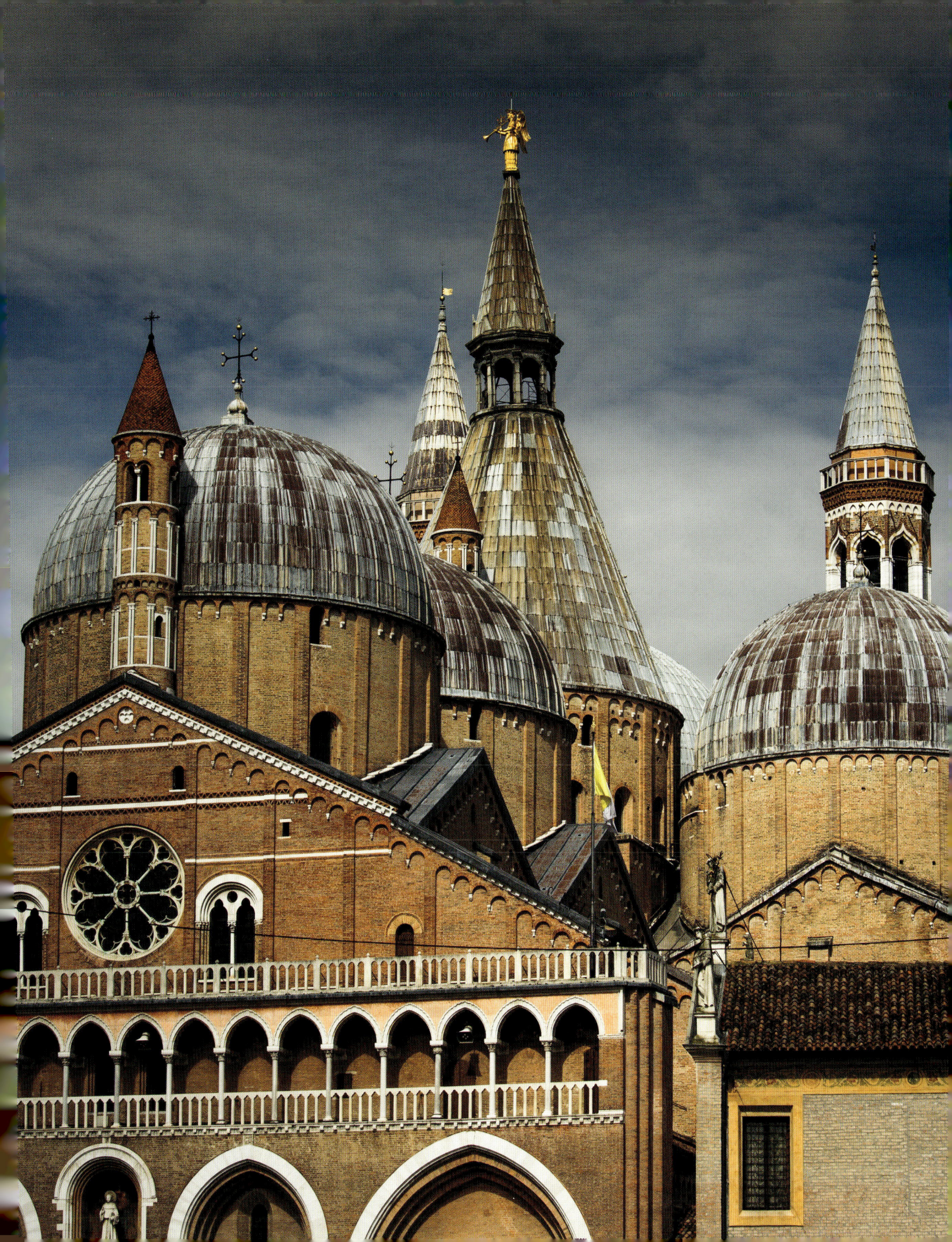

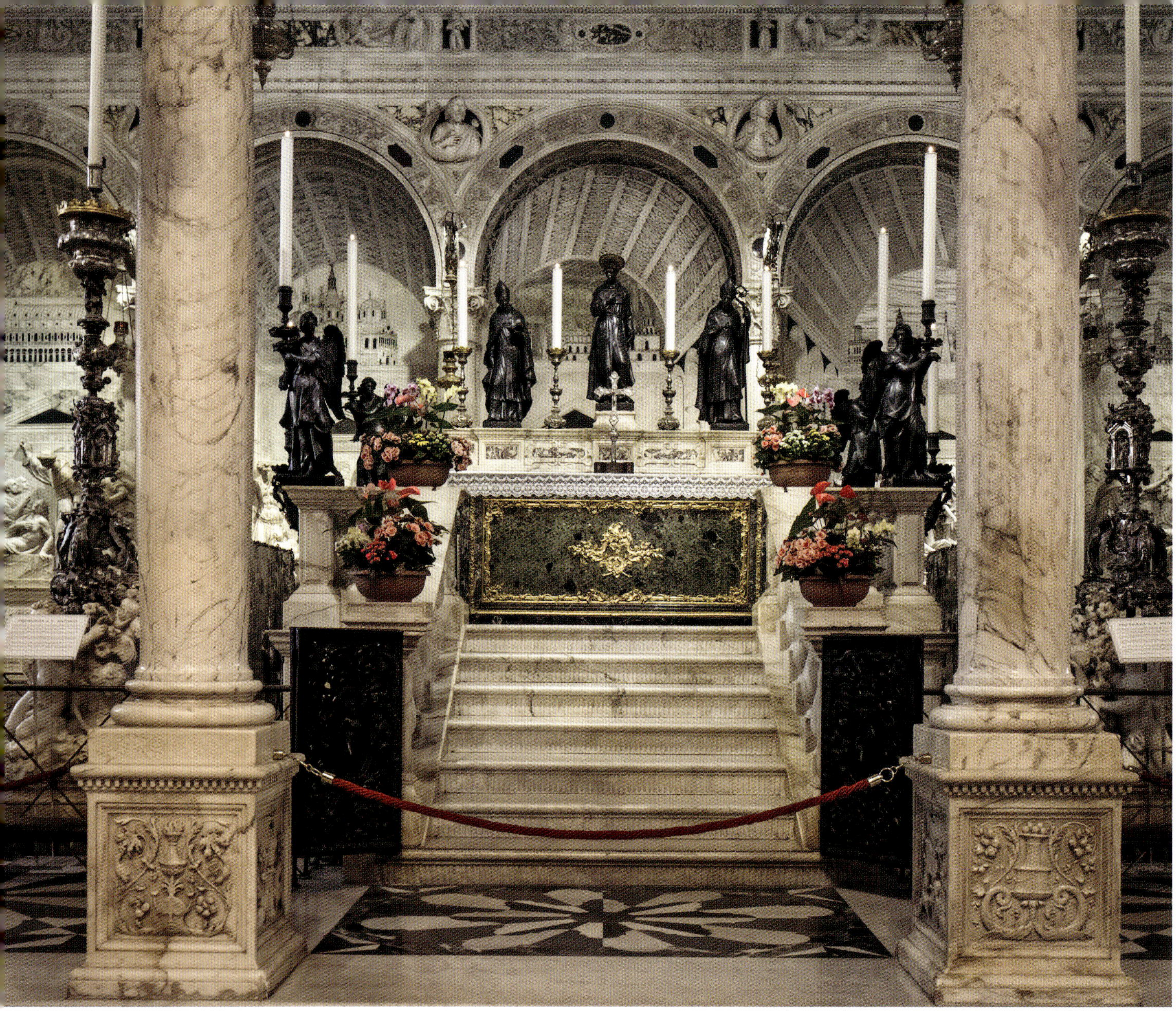

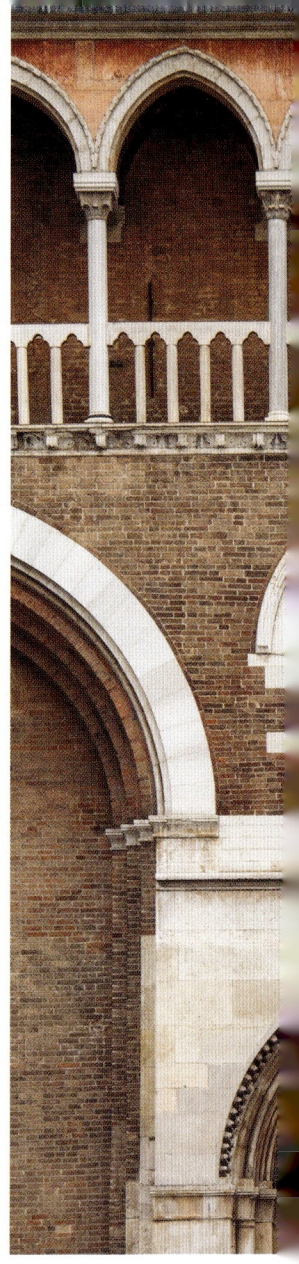
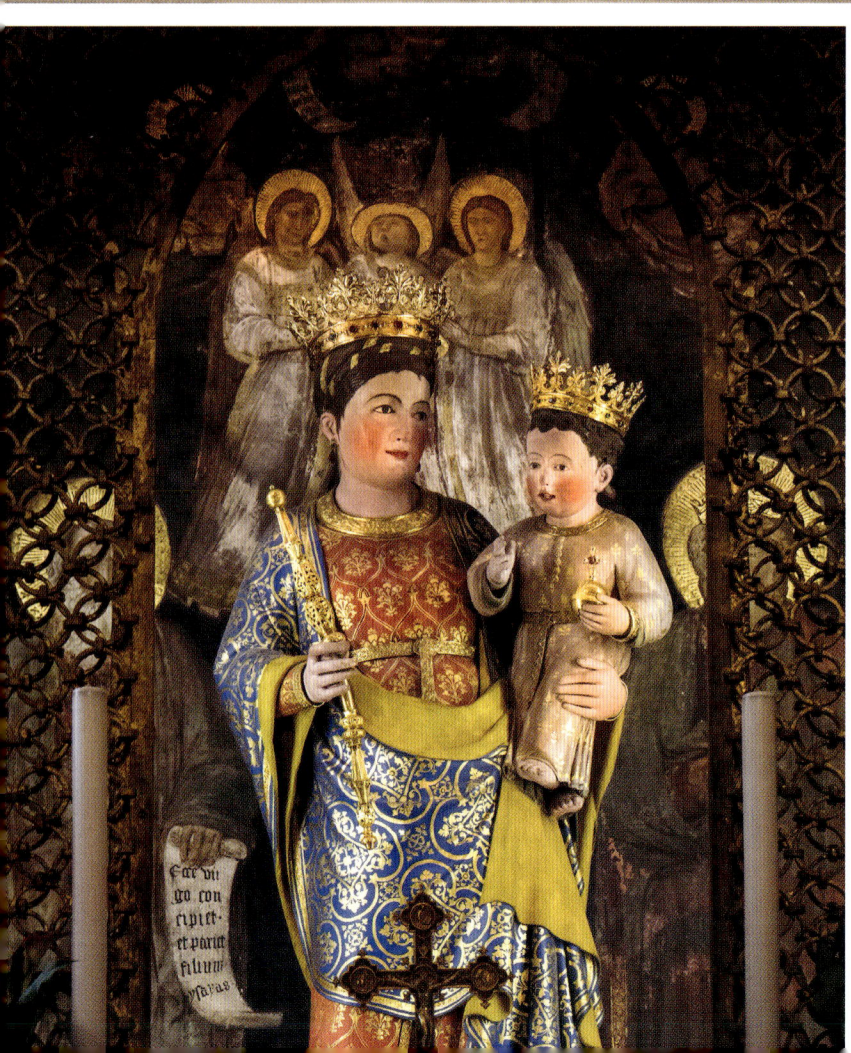
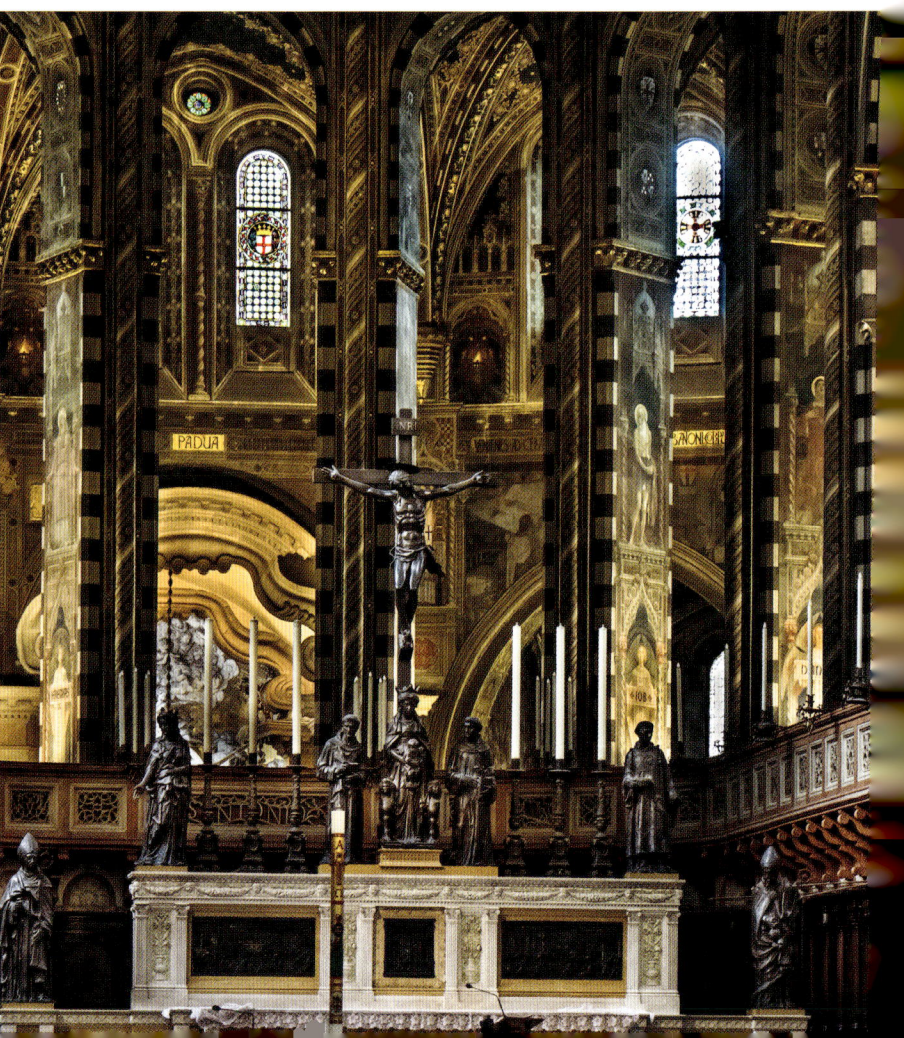

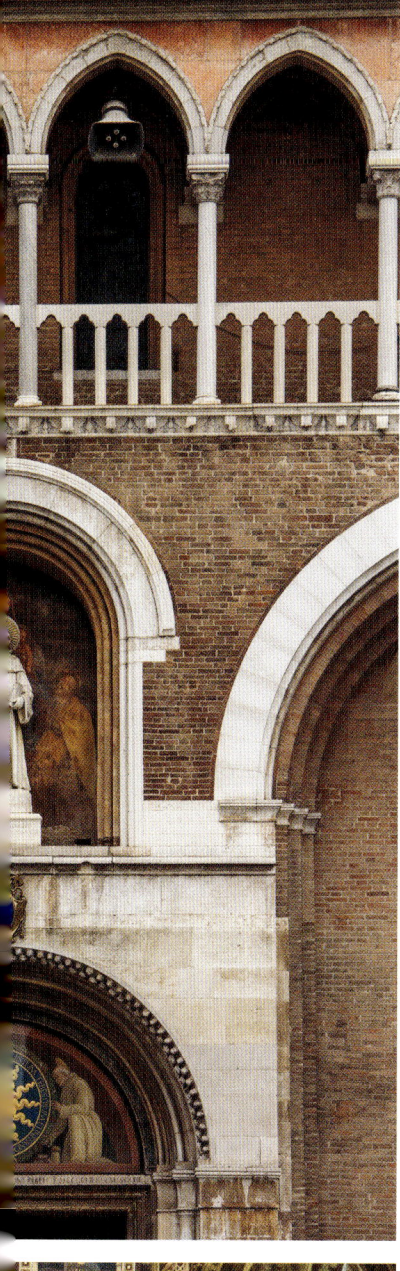
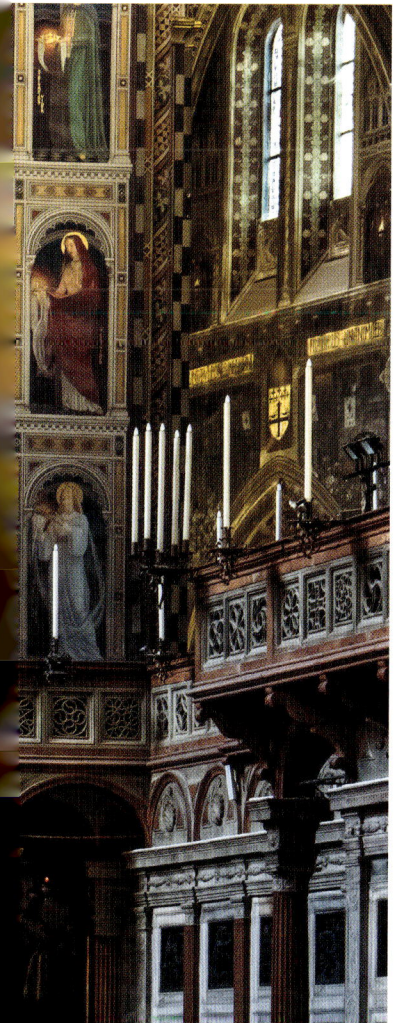

(*top left*) The marble-clad Chapel of St Anthony pays true homage to the saint through its monumental scale and sheer artistry. Lines of pilgrims patiently wait their turn to touch the altar tomb of the saint. (*top right*) Elegant arcading on the basilica's façade frames a statue of the saint. (*bottom left*) The Black Madonna was created in 1396 and stands in a chapel adjacent to St Anthony's. (*bottom right*) Frescoed pillars and Gothic arches frame the high altar and its outstanding bronze crucifix cast by Donatello in 1446.

in the Eucharist if his donkey bowed down to it. After three days of starvation, the ravenous mule was presented with the choice of his owner holding a large clump of grass or St Anthony with the consecrated host in his hand. The donkey went down on bended knees in front of the Blessed Sacrament and another doubter was duly converted.

Anthony's reputation and achievements were so great that he was canonized less than a year after his death in 1232, by Pope Gregory IX, and in that same year, work began on the magnificent basilica built in his name. The church is architecturally impressive and visually sublime, being crowned by no fewer than eight domes, two bell towers and two minor minarets. Although the Byzantine domes are a distinguishing feature, the imposing exterior structure is largely Romanesque and the majority of the basilica's interior is designed in the purest Gothic style. However, there were some later Renaissance and Baroque additions, most notably the spectacular Chapel of St Anthony, which houses the saint's tomb.

One of the basilica's other most visited treasures is the late seventeenth-century Baroque-style Chapel of Relics. In an almost theatrical setting, the niches of gold, silver and bejewelled reliquaries present an interesting array of items representing the glory of St Anthony. On display are the incorrupt tongue of the saint, his equally non-decayed vocal chords and jawbone, as well as skin from his head plus a finger. This may all sound a bit gruesome, but the relics are presented amid such lavish ornamentation that the treasures can be viewed with respect rather than squeamishness.

The Basilica of St Anthony is an imposing architectural masterpiece filled with outstanding works of art, but it is not the only religious building worthy of attention for pilgrims travelling to Padua. The interior of the tiny Scrovegni Chapel is completely covered with stunning frescoes by Giotto. This artistic masterpiece has to be seen, along with the cathedral dedicated to the Virgin Mary.

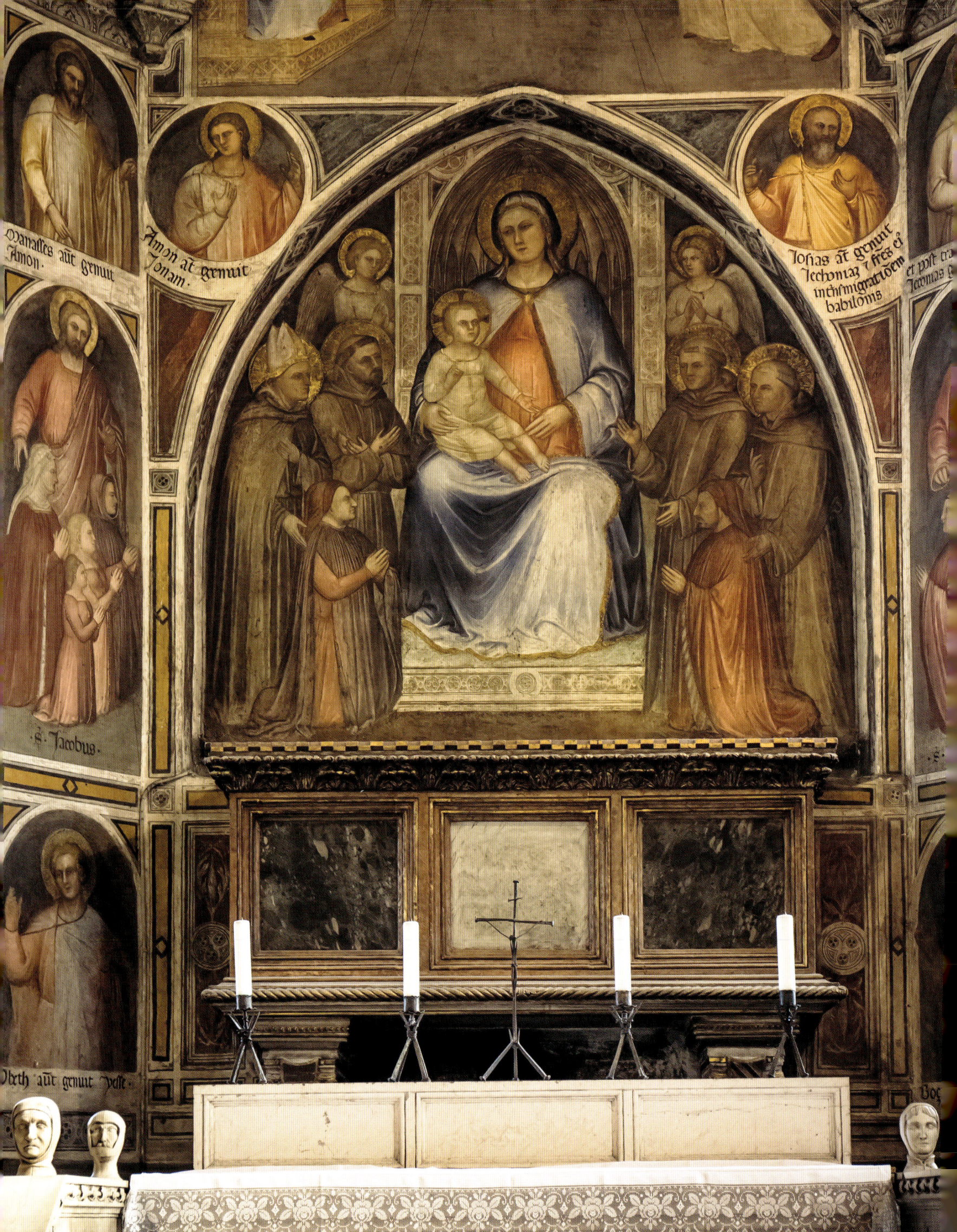

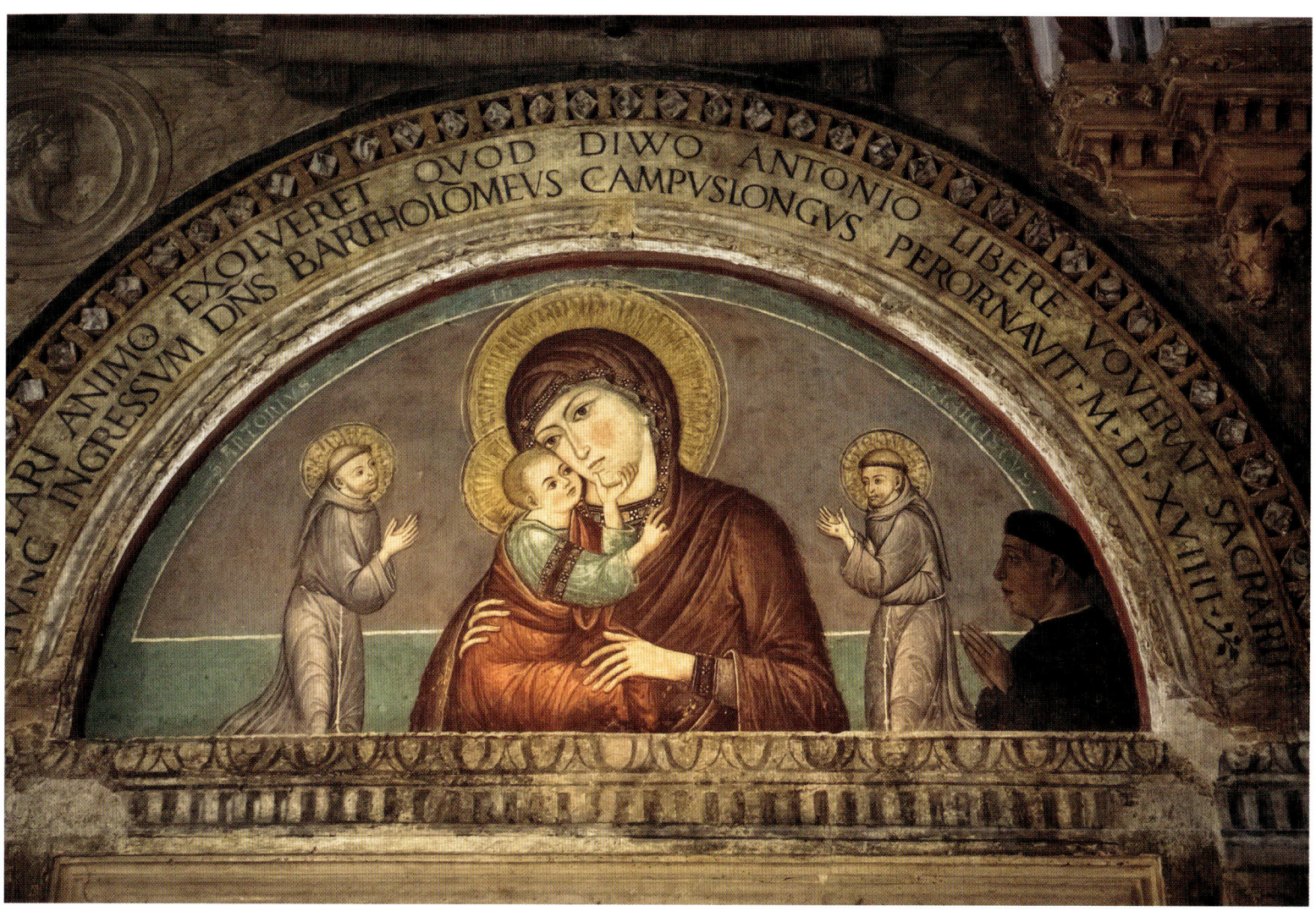

(*left*) The fourteenth-century Chapel of the Blessed Luke is dedicated to the close friend and disciple of St Anthony. It is lavishly adorned with a cycle of frescoes predominantly created by Giusto de' Menabuoi in 1382. Directly above the altar is an intimate portrait of the Virgin and Child titled *Our Lady Enthroned Among Franciscan Saints*.

(*above*) Set above a door into the sacristy is a thirteenth-century fresco titled *The Mother of God with the Child*. It is probably the oldest representation of the Virgin within the basilica and it features the kneeling figures of St Francis and St Anthony.

(*overleaf*) The ambulatory is adorned with an array of symmetrically perfect Gothic vaulting, which combines with the art and architecture of the radial chapels to create an aura of perfect visual harmony.

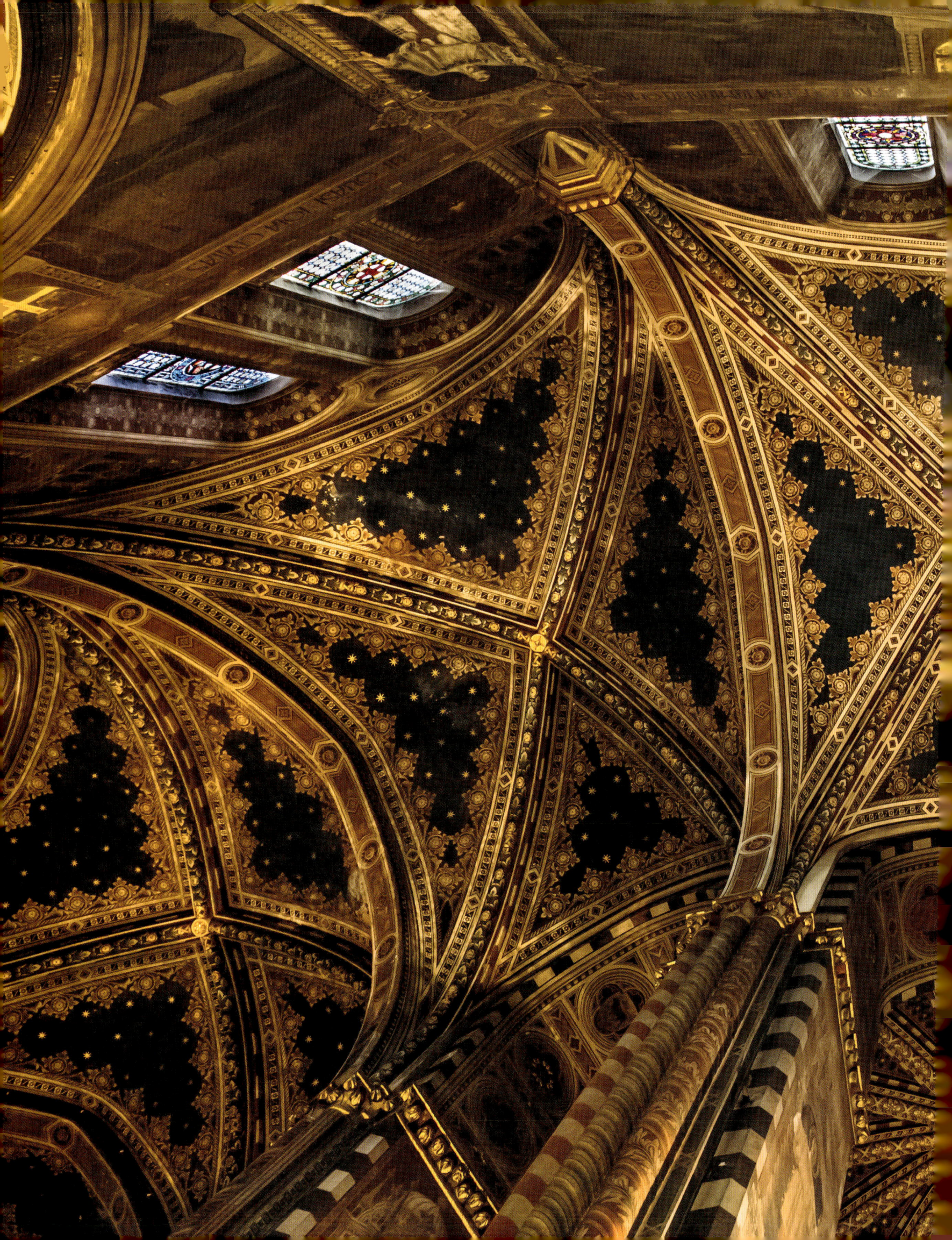

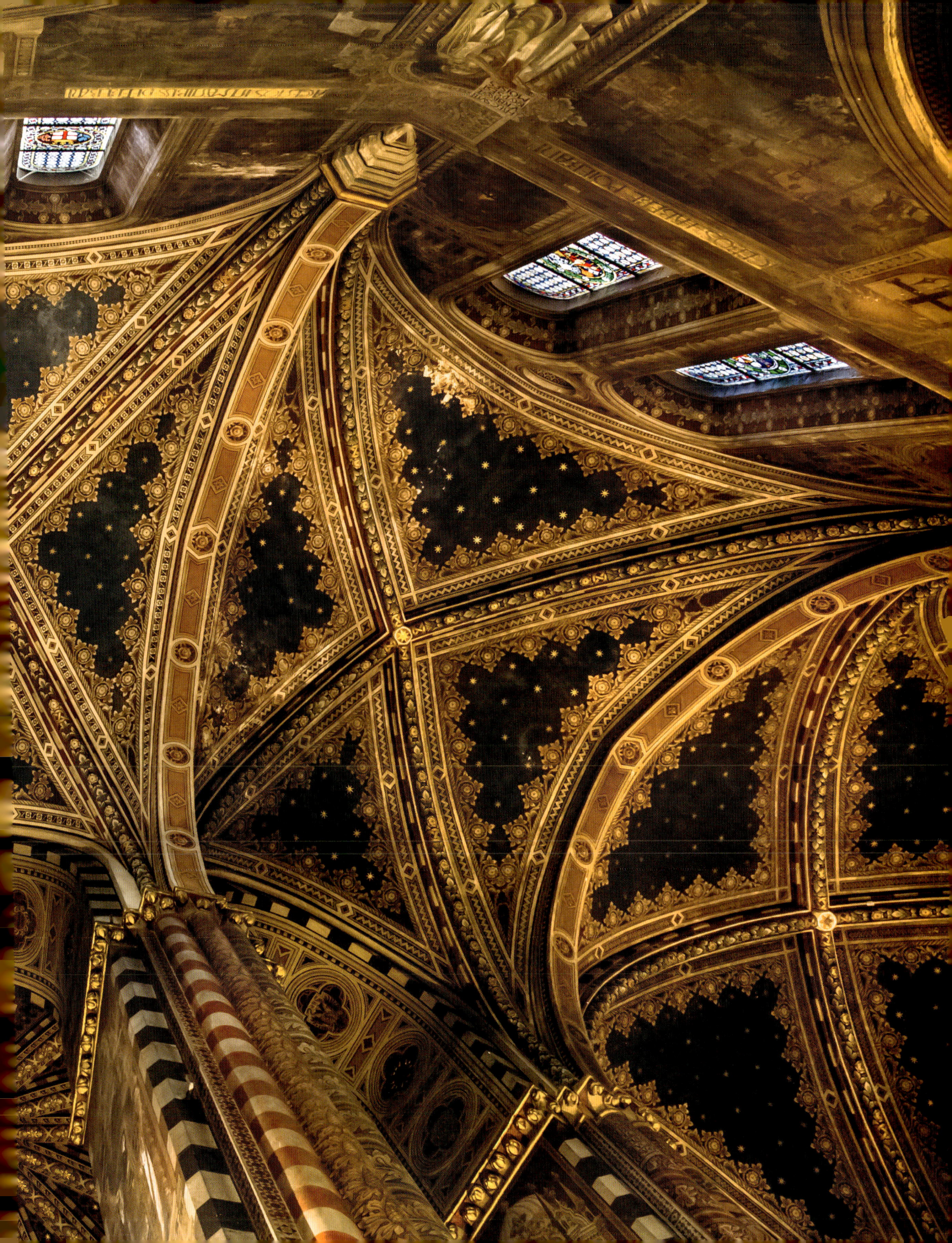

THE BASILICA OF ST FRANCIS OF ASSISI
Assisi, Umbria

Regardless of which mode of transport one uses to reach a pilgrimage destination, there is nothing more satisfying than having that ultimate goal in full view during the final few kilometres. For those travelling on foot, that final stage in our twenty-first-century world may involve trudging through urban sprawl and diesel fumes to reach journey's end in a city's medieval core. Rest assured, Assisi is pilgrimage perfect!

Assisi flows down the western slopes of Mount Subasio, whose pink-tinged limestone was quarried for most of the buildings in the town. The absence of any heavy industry within a wide radius has ensured that none has been discoloured over time by atmospheric pollution, and if one approaches from the wide plain opening out from the flanks of the mountain, the buildings are perfectly etched against its darker slopes. The most readily identifiable are the Basilica of St Clare, the Cathedral of St Rufinus, Santa Maria Maggiore and the unmistakable outline of the town's final, and most significant buildings, the iconic basilica and convent of St Francis of Assisi.

St Francis was born in Assisi in 1182 and died there at the age of forty-four. In that comparatively short life span, he became one of the most significant and influential contributors to the Church of the Middle Ages. Having renounced a potentially comfortable life as the son of a wealthy cloth merchant, Francis instead opted for a life of poverty, prayer and penance. A nomadic life as a ragged beggar intent on preaching the Gospels was an ethos invariably rejected by many but readily embraced by St Francis and his growing band of followers as a source of spiritual joy. In 1209, St Francis obtained approval from Pope Innocent III for his simple rule devoted to apostolic poverty, and his group adopted the title of 'Friars Minor' (Lesser Brothers), which later became universally known as the Franciscans. Just three years later, an all-female branch of the Franciscans, the Poor Clares, was created by St Francis and his friend St Clare of Assisi, and it is testament to the values espoused by the Franciscan movement that both orders are still active and performing invaluable work worldwide.

A view looking down the Upper Basilica's nave towards the transepts and altar. The bottom left fresco panel depicts the Liberation of the Repentant Heretic, one of the scenes from the life of St Francis. It completely covers the lower section of the nave walls.

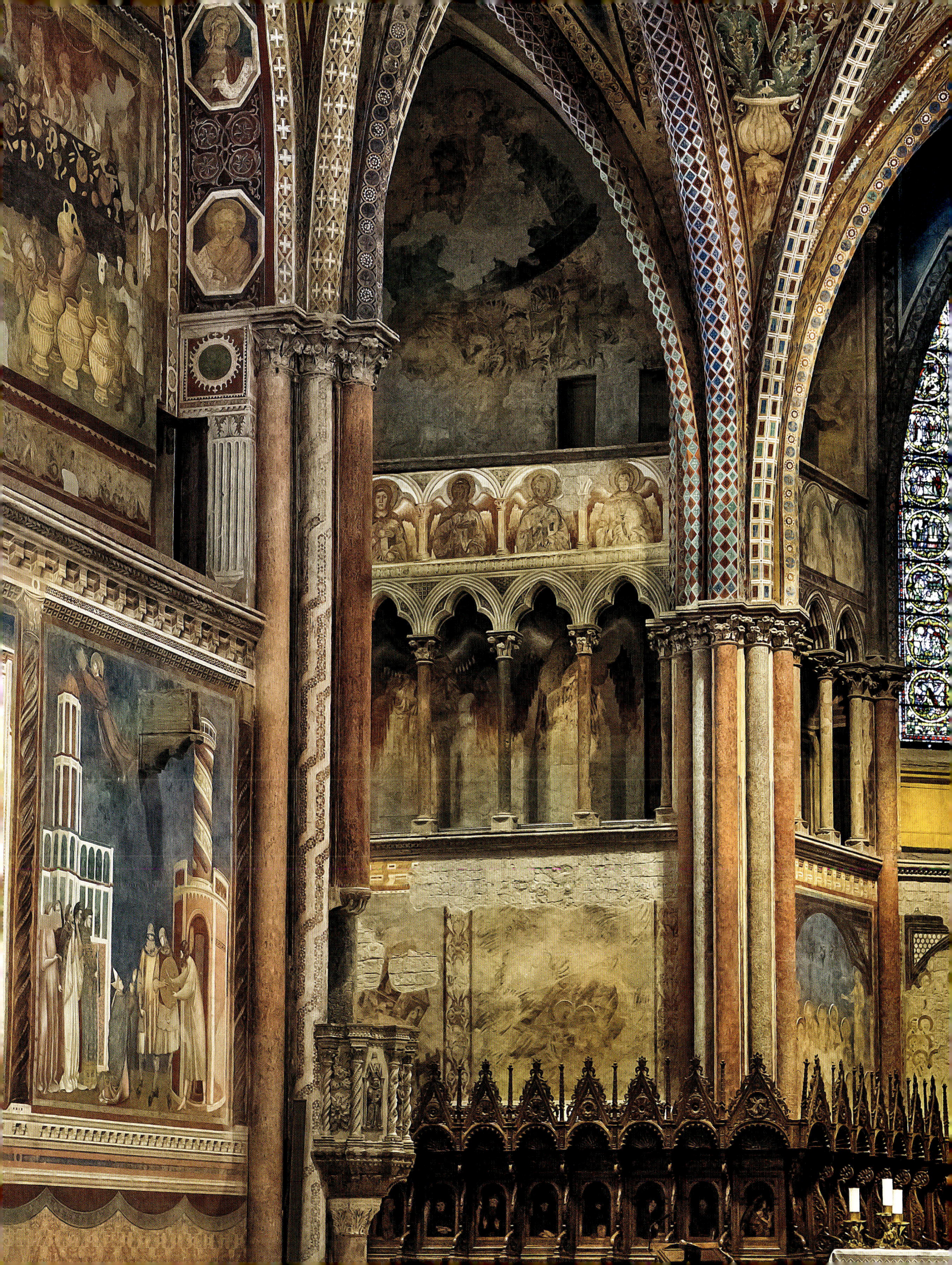

182 GREAT PILGRIMAGE SITES OF EUROPE

The Basilica of St Francis actually comprises two churches built on top of each other, and the one referred to as the Lower Basilica, which houses the saint's tomb, was begun immediately after his canonization in 1228. The architecture of the surprisingly low, heavily arched interior is mainly Romanesque, and the total coverage of the walls and vaults with a complex narrative of frescoes creates a most moving atmosphere. Interpreting many of the fresco panels requires a sharp eye because although several images might appear as random topics, scenes from the life of Christ are paralleled by equal numbers representing the life and poverty of St Francis. The hand of legendary Italian painter Giotto is present in both the lower and upper churches, not least in the four 'sails' directly over the high altar dedicated entirely to St Francis.

Flights of steps lead from the nave down into the crypt, which now houses the tomb and shrine of St Francis. In keeping with his humble lifestyle, it is a plain, unadorned but very intensely moving piece of architecture. Steps are also utilized to take visitors directly from the Lower Basilica into the upper church,

(*below*) One of the most significant frescoes in the Upper Basilica's life cycle of St Francis, painted largely by Giotto, portrays the saint and his first eleven followers presenting proposals for a new religious order to Pope Innocent III in 1209.

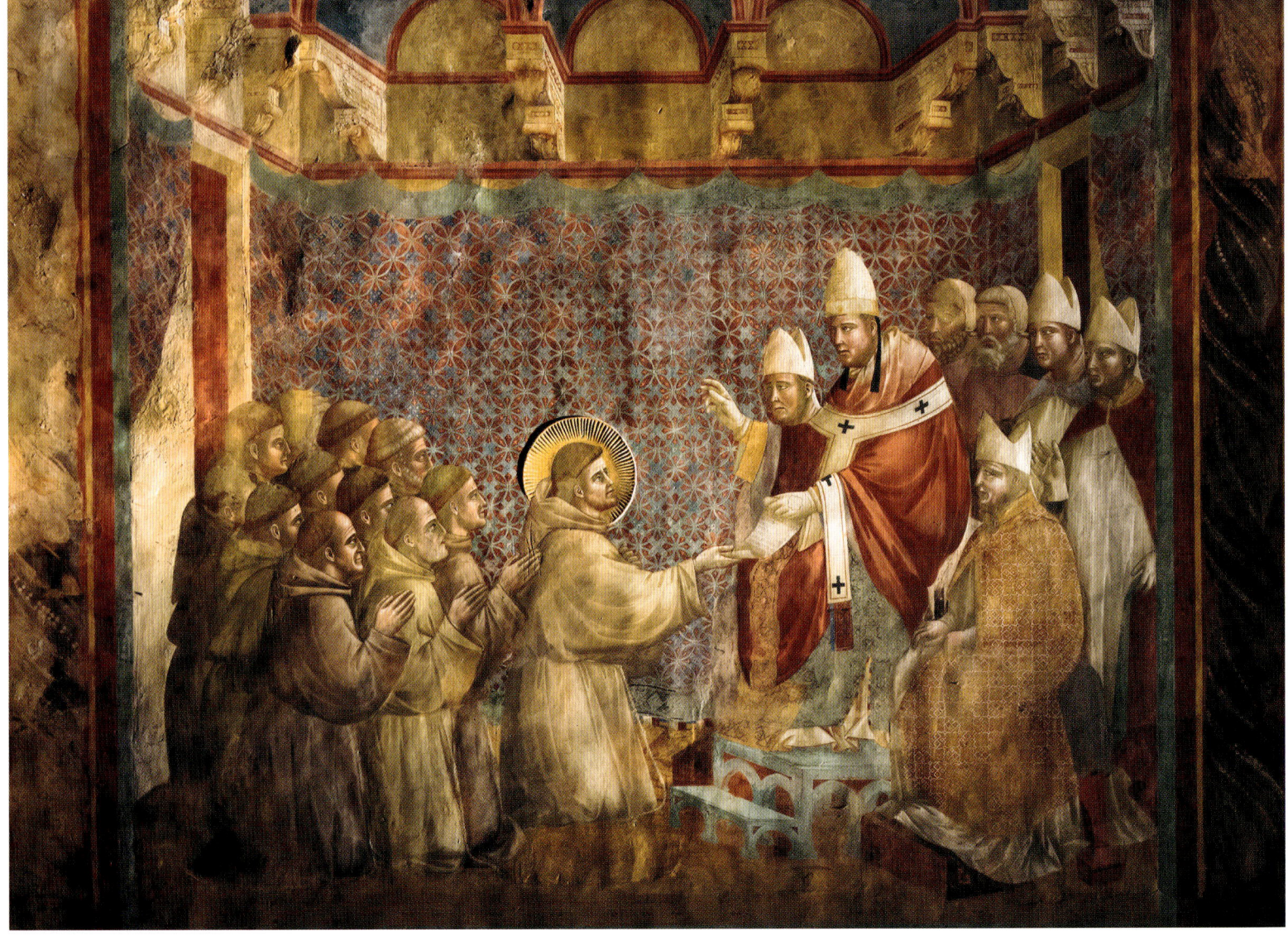

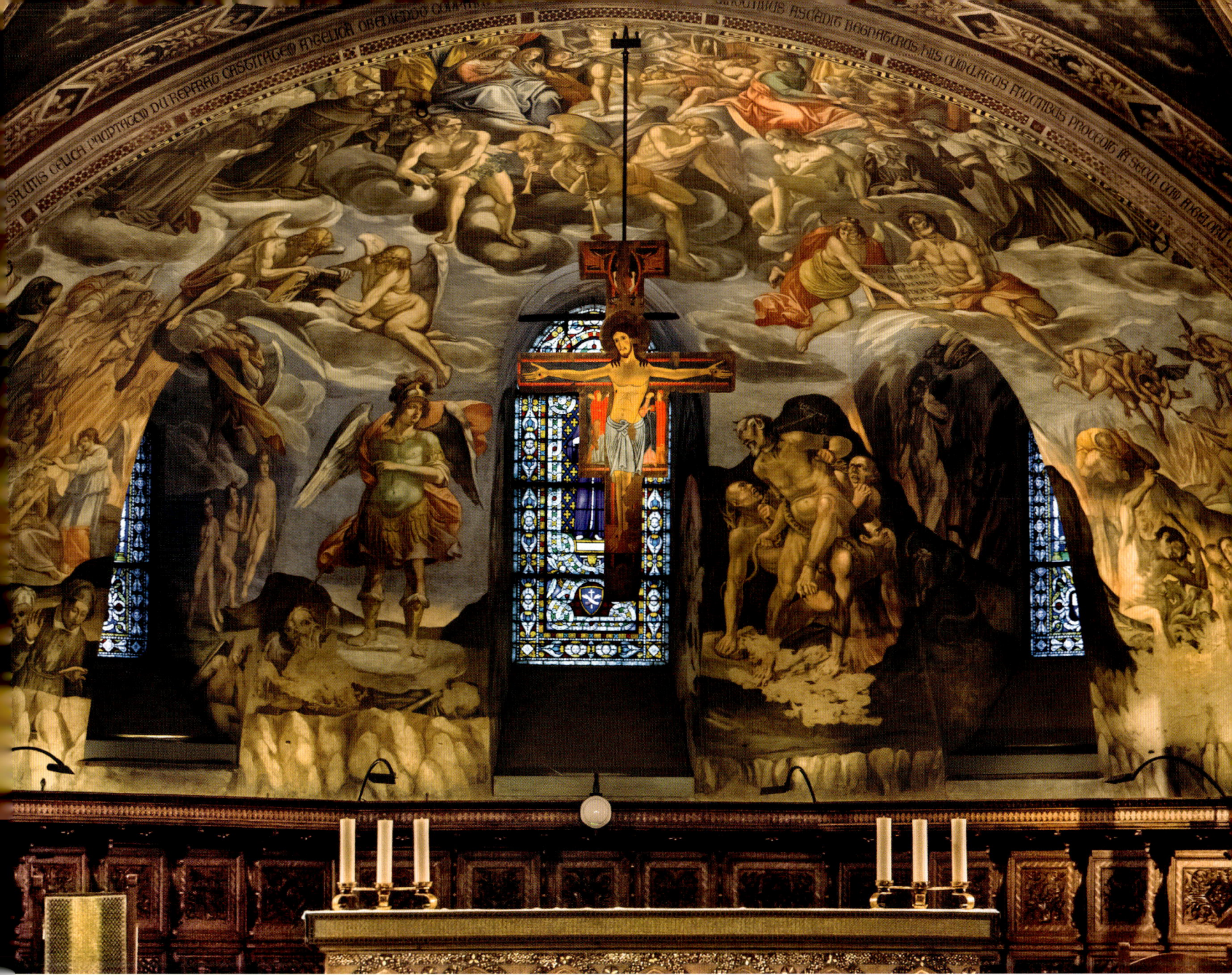

(*above*) The stunningly dramatic and complex portrayal of the Last Judgment entirely covers the Lower Basilica's apse behind the high altar. It was created by the artist Cesare Sermei in 1623.

(*overleaf*) A view of Assisi with the Basilica of St Francis on the left.

whose height and distinctive Gothic style is more airy, bright and delicate. There are still no unadorned areas of wall, roof or vaulting here, but the larger panels gave the artists freer rein and the lower walls are an illuminating documentary sequence conveying the key moments in the life of St Francis.

A dreadful earthquake in 1997 tragically caused deaths and major damage to the Upper Basilica and renovations took two years to complete. The basilica today is a testament to the skill and dedication of the architects, stonemasons, craftsmen and artists who seamlessly recreated and represented the work of their predecessors. Assisi has been a much-revered place of pilgrimage for centuries and, despite the heavy numbers of tourists in the height of summer, when the car and coach parks empty at the end of each day, the true atmosphere and tranquillity of Assisi once again envelopes this remarkable place.

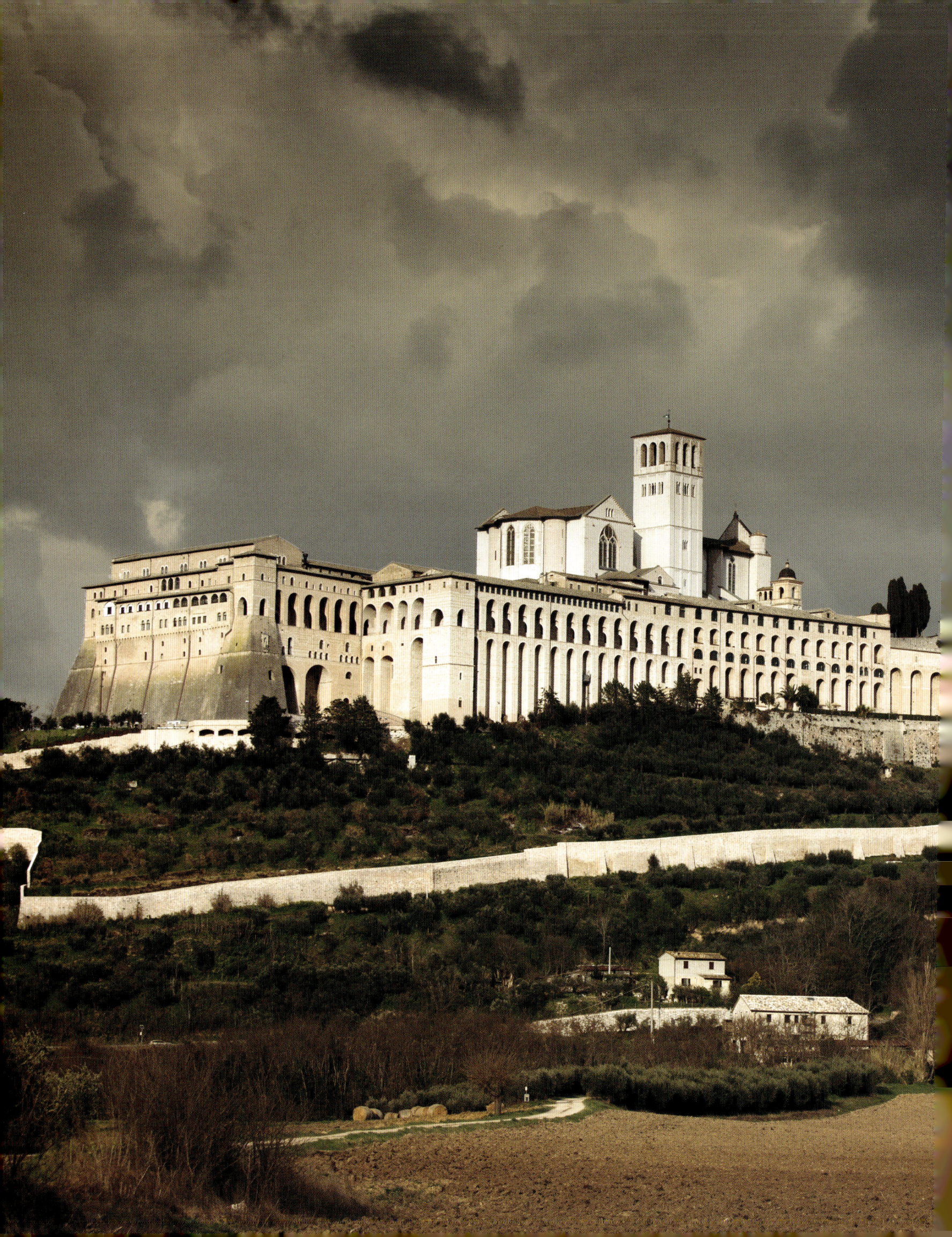

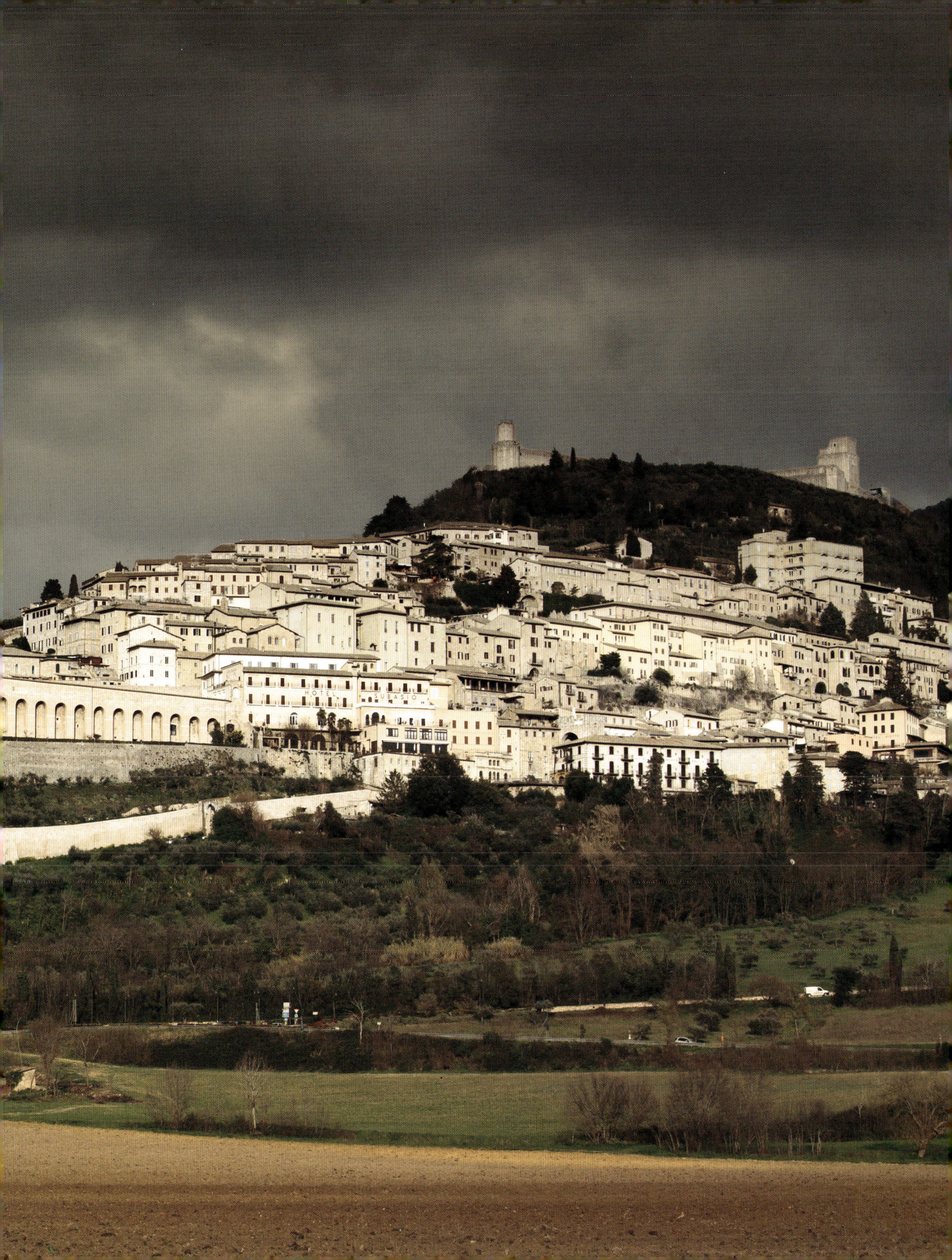

ROME

It is extraordinary to reflect upon the fact that by stepping into St Peter's Square one leaves Italy and enters Vatican City, officially listed as the world's smallest country. Diminutive though the independent state might be, the beating heart of the Roman Catholic Church extends its influence to just about every corner of the world. The mighty dome of St Peter's Basilica serves as a stunning visual reminder of the immense achievements of those who designed and built our monumental past. It is best appreciated from farther back along the wide expanse of the Via della Conciliazione before it reaches St Peter's Square. As one draws closer and becomes enveloped within the gently curving colonnades surrounding the piazza, the visual perspective alters and the dramatic façade of the basilica takes centre stage. Gian Lorenzo Bernini was the architect responsible for the inspirational layout and design of the external elements of St Peter's and his work also plays a significant role in the basilica's interior.

The history of Christian pilgrimage to Rome extends back to the fourth century, following Emperor Constantine's acceptance and support of the Christian faith. The veneration of saints, apostles and martyrs could finally be conducted in public by Christians, rather than at furtive private gatherings. The four papal basilicas were all either built or under construction by the fifth century and pilgrim numbers from across Europe quickly increased, especially once Rome began to play a significant role in the well-established tradition of pilgrimages to the Holy Land. Many travellers bound for Jerusalem had previously opted for the overland route, *via* Macedonia and Turkey, but they began to embrace Rome and its two martyred apostles as an essential spiritual stopover. One of the best documented accounts of a journey to Rome was produced by Sigeric, Archbishop of Canterbury, in 990, who went to collect the official pallium (ecclesiastical vestment) from Pope John XV. After the ceremonial business, Sigeric visited more than twenty churches prior to his return. His epic trip through France and across the Alps to Italy is recreated in an increasingly popular pilgrimage route known as the Via Francigena.

Rome now seems perpetually overcrowded due to the increase of mass tourism, but there is still one magical time to visit: around daybreak when the street lamps are still lit and the dawn sky casts a soft pink glow over St Peter's, with not a coach in sight.

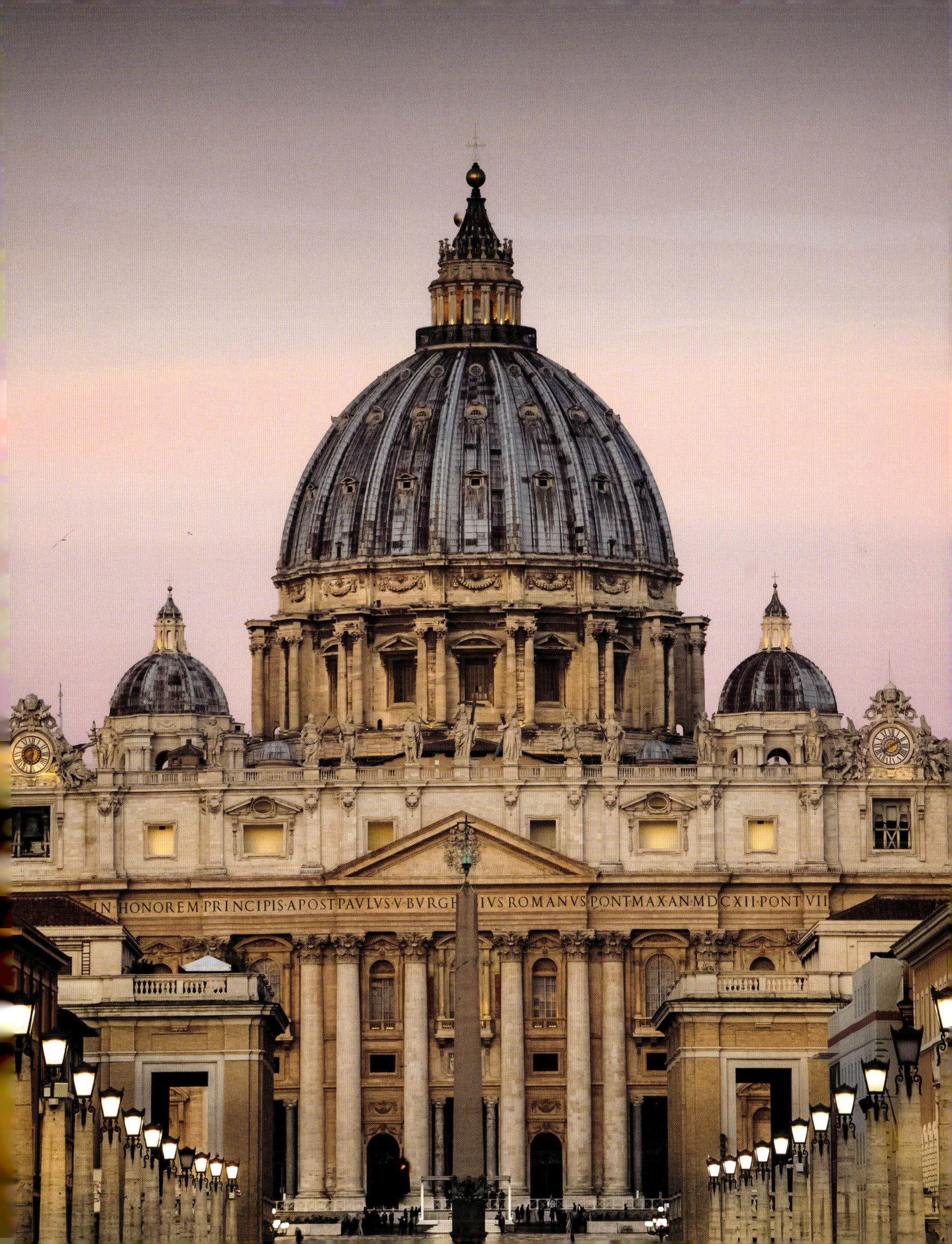

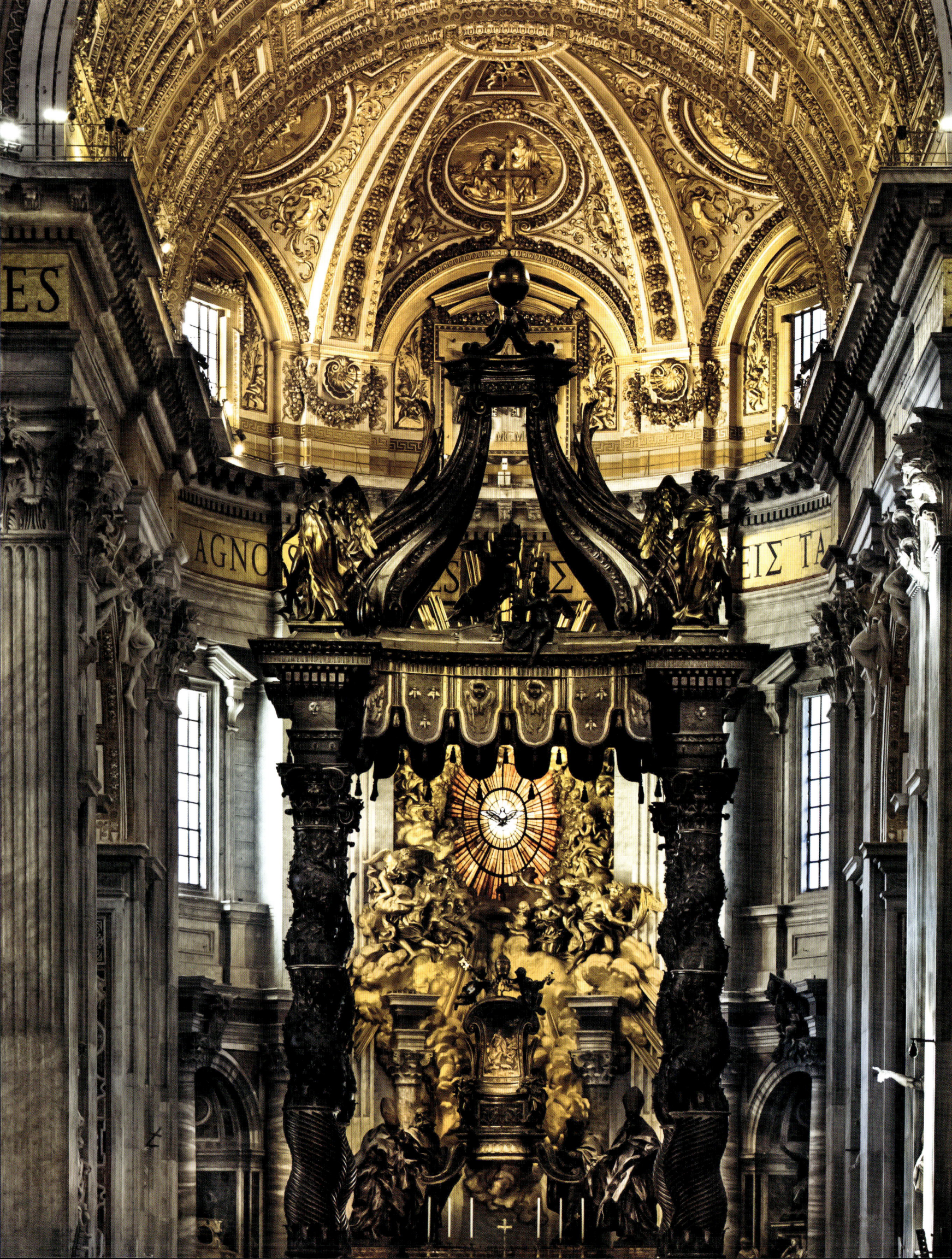

The dramatic focal point in the heart of St Peter's Basilica is Bernini's majestic baldachin rising high above the papal altar. Begun in 1624, it was unveiled by Pope Urban VIII nine years later and it is set in the crossing directly below the vast dome. In most important churches, the high altar is located in the chancel, but the break from tradition in St Peter's was due entirely to the fact that the tomb of the martyred apostle lies in the confessio set beneath the papal altar.

ST PETER'S BASILICA

Emperor Constantine's first and most important church was the basilica erected over the tomb of the martyred apostle St Peter, consecrated by Pope Sylvester I in 326.

The original building comprised a nave, four aisles and a narrow transept, and it was entered through an atrium graced by a fountain and a façade of glittering mosaics. The basilica's fortunes during the following centuries fluctuated between the rituals of religious ceremonies and imperial coronations and the damage inflicted by regular raids from Barbarians and Saracens. After almost 1,000 years of repairs and restoration, the fabric could take no more, and in 1452 Nicholas V was the first pope in office brave enough to proclaim that the matter of a new church needed to be addressed. Unfortunately, he died three years later and his successors returned to the 'patch up and pray' policy for another fifty years, until architect Donato Bramante submitted a radical plan to rebuild the basilica in the Greek cruciform layout, with a central dome above the crossing similar to the Pantheon. Unfortunately, the scheme's supporter, Pope Julius II, died in 1513 and the uncertainty continued until 1547, when Pope Paul III uttered the magic word, 'Michelangelo'! The seventy-two-year-old genius was already in post as chief architect to the Vatican and he was quoted as saying, 'To deviate from Bramante's design is to deviate from the truth.' However, Michelangelo did simplify some of the plan and, most significantly, he chose to create the present high dome rather than adhere to Bramante's shallower Pantheon style.

At the time of Michelangelo's death in 1564, the apse and transepts were complete and the dome had risen as far as the drum, but in terms of the floor plan, it was decided that the nave had to be extended into the Latin cross format to create space for liturgical processions and ceremonies. The final touches of architectural magic were the basilica's Baroque façade and the colonnades of St Peter's Square, added by Bernini in the seventeenth century. The collective genius of all the architects, stonemasons and artists continues to flourish in the Papal Basilica of St Peter's.

190 GREAT PILGRIMAGE SITES OF EUROPE

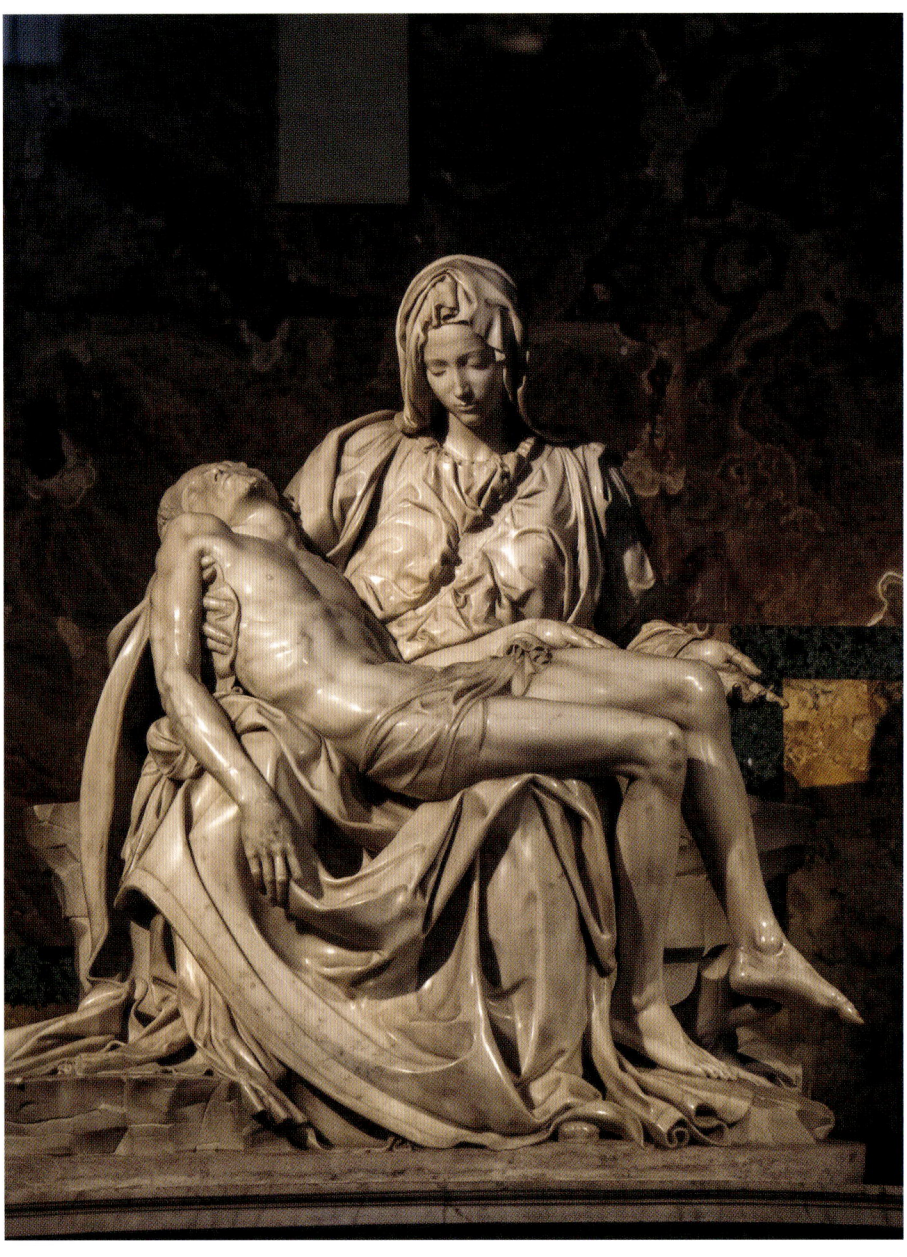

(*above*) Michelangelo's *Pietà* is arguably the world's most expressive and moving piece of religious sculpture. The work was carved between 1498 and 1500 from a single block of Carrara marble by an artist not yet twenty-five years old. Michelangelo actually engraved his signature on Mary's dress to dispel scepticism from those who doubted it could be the work of one so young. There are no tears of grief on the Virgin's face but simply an aura of questioning resignation, perfectly represented by the fingers of her outstretched hand.

(*right*) The dome of St Sebastian's Chapel overlooks the altar, beneath which are the remains of Pope John Paul II, the second longest serving pope from 1978 to 2005. Upon his arrival in St Sebastian's, the previous incumbent, Innocent XI, was relocated to another altar.

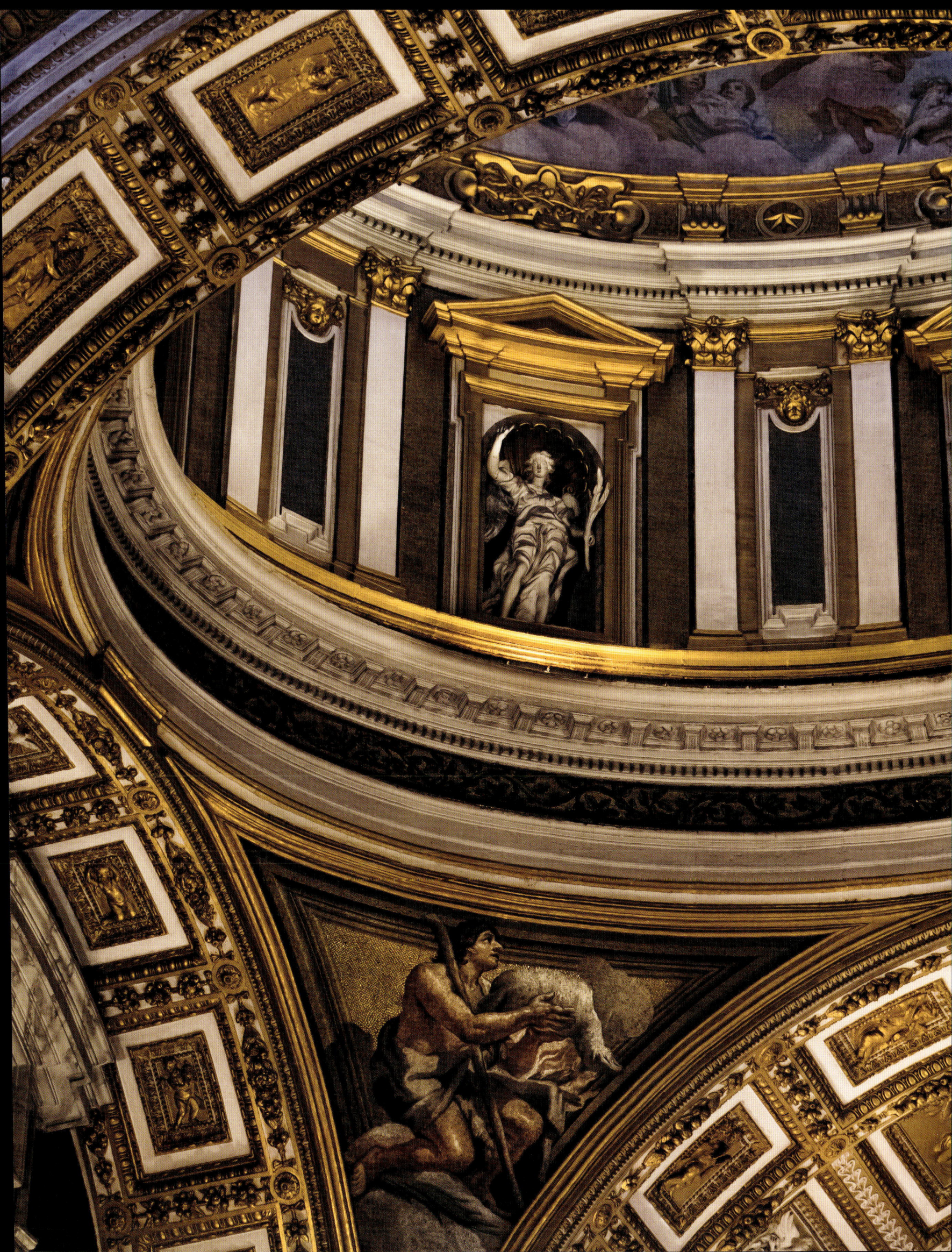

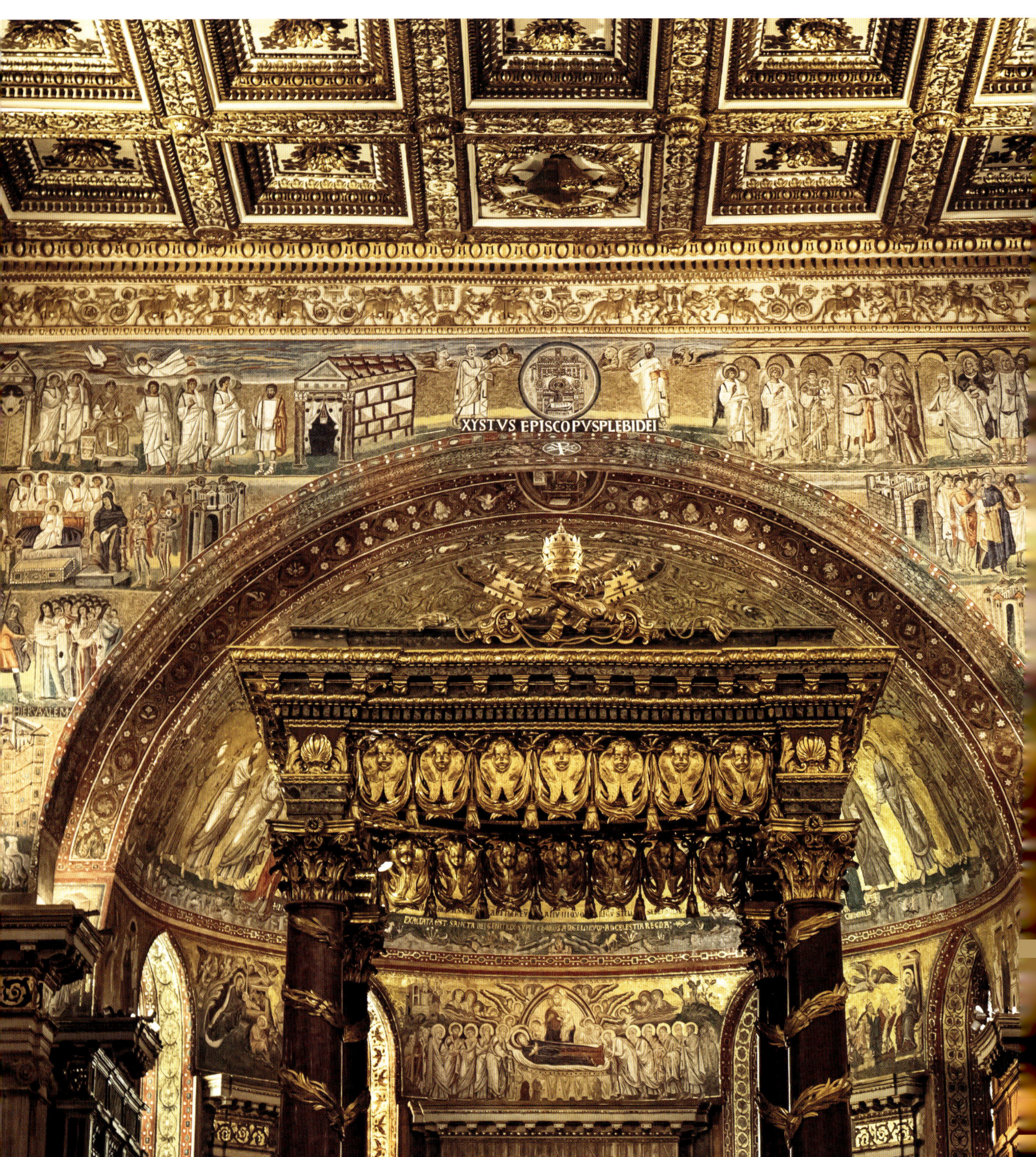

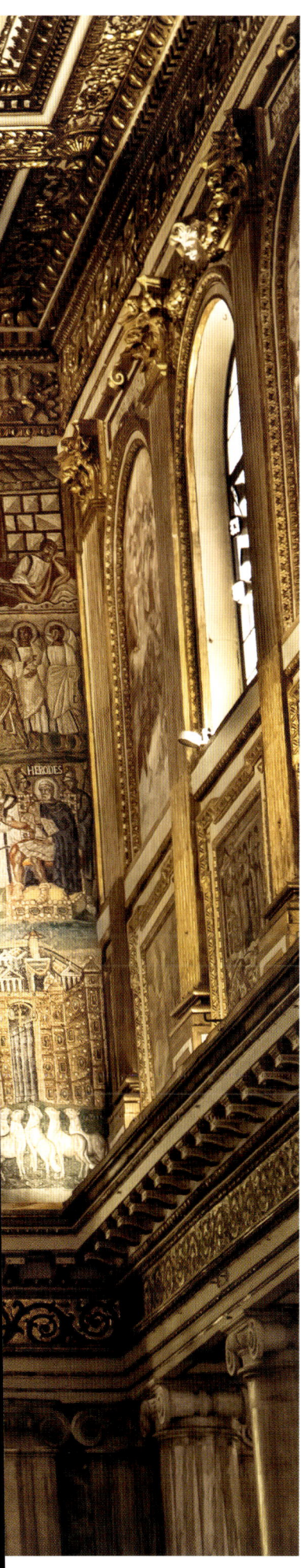

The fifth-century mosaics of the triumphal arch predominantly focus on the Virgin Mary and the early life of Jesus. The top left scene portrays the Annunciation and immediately below is the Epiphany, with Jesus sat on a throne rather than lying in a crib.

SANTA MARIA MAGGIORE

The Archbasilica of Saint Mary Major is one of the city's oldest and most significant churches, being the first and largest dedicated to the Virgin Mary. Santa Maria was built on the Esquiline Hill, the highest of the seven hills upon which ancient Rome was founded. According to legend, the location was seemingly chosen by the Virgin Mary herself. Appearing in a dream to Pope Liberius and also in a vision to a Roman Patrician named Giovanni, the Virgin said she would indicate where the church in her honour should be built. On the morning of 5 August 358, a geometrically perfect snowfall covered part of the Esquiline Hill. The miracle of the snow is solemnly celebrated on that same date every year, when a cascade of white petals replicating snowflakes tumbles down on the congregation.

The basilica has numerous important artworks, but one of Santa Maria's most precious and treasured legacies is the collection of mosaics adorning the nave, the triumphal arch and the dome of the apse. The nave carries the oldest examples dating back to the fifth century, created as a series of panels set above the entablature and largely comprising scenes from the Old Testament, featuring key episodes in the lives of Abraham, Jacob, Moses and Joshua. Despite the awesome beauty of the mosaics, the most venerated single piece of art is a Byzantine-influenced portrait of the Virgin and Child named *Salus Populi Romani* (Salvation of the Roman People), set above the altar in the sumptuously decorated Pauline Chapel. Locals have always revered the chapel as a place for prayer and reflection, to provide an enclave of comfort and hope in times of individual or collective anxiety and sorrow. A lengthy restoration was carried out on the painting in 2018 and tests by the Vatican's art experts revealed that it probably originated some time between the eleventh and thirteenth centuries. The results would have been determined by the most advanced technology available, but there will still be those who retain belief in the original legend: that it is a contemporary portrait by St Luke the Evangelist.

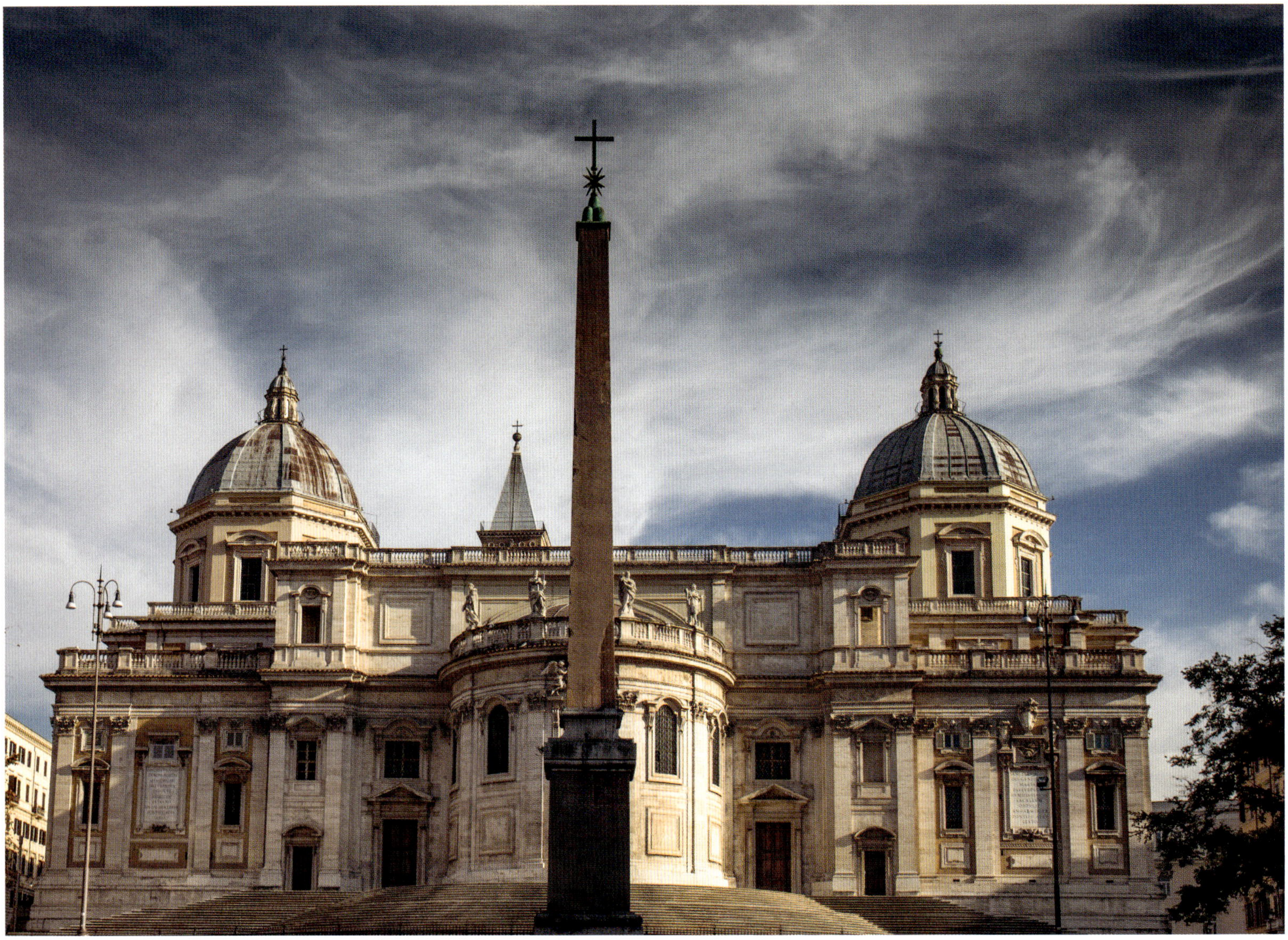

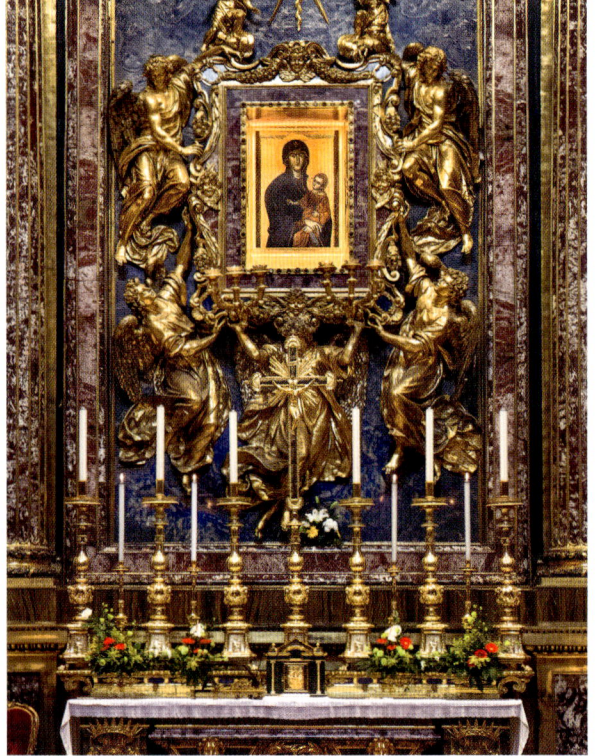

(*above*) The main façade of Santa Maria is impressive, but one nevertheless gets a historically more informative view from the foot of Piazza dell'Esquilino. The slope upwards to the basilica is surprisingly steep, but it would still have been below the snow line, especially in August.

(*left*) The *Salus Populi Romani* portrait of the Virgin and Child is set above the lavishly decorated altar in the Pauline (or Borghese) Chapel. The alternative title refers to the family name of Pope Paul V, who commissioned the chapel in 1611.

(*right*) The stunning imagery of the apse mosaic was created by the Francisan artist Jacopo Torriti at the end of the thirteenth century. The central medallion depicts the crowning of the Virgin flanked by surviving segments from the original fifth-century mosaic.

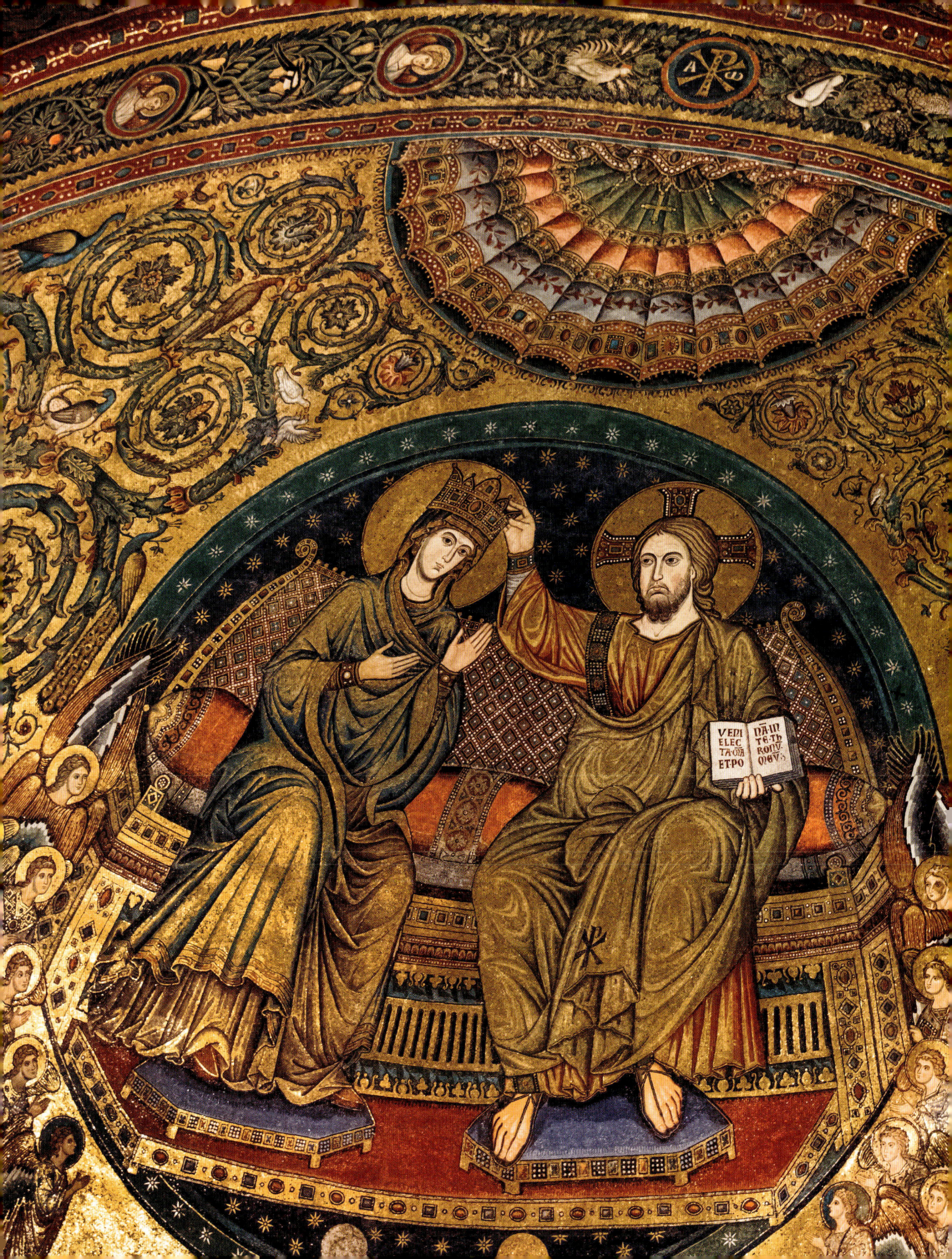

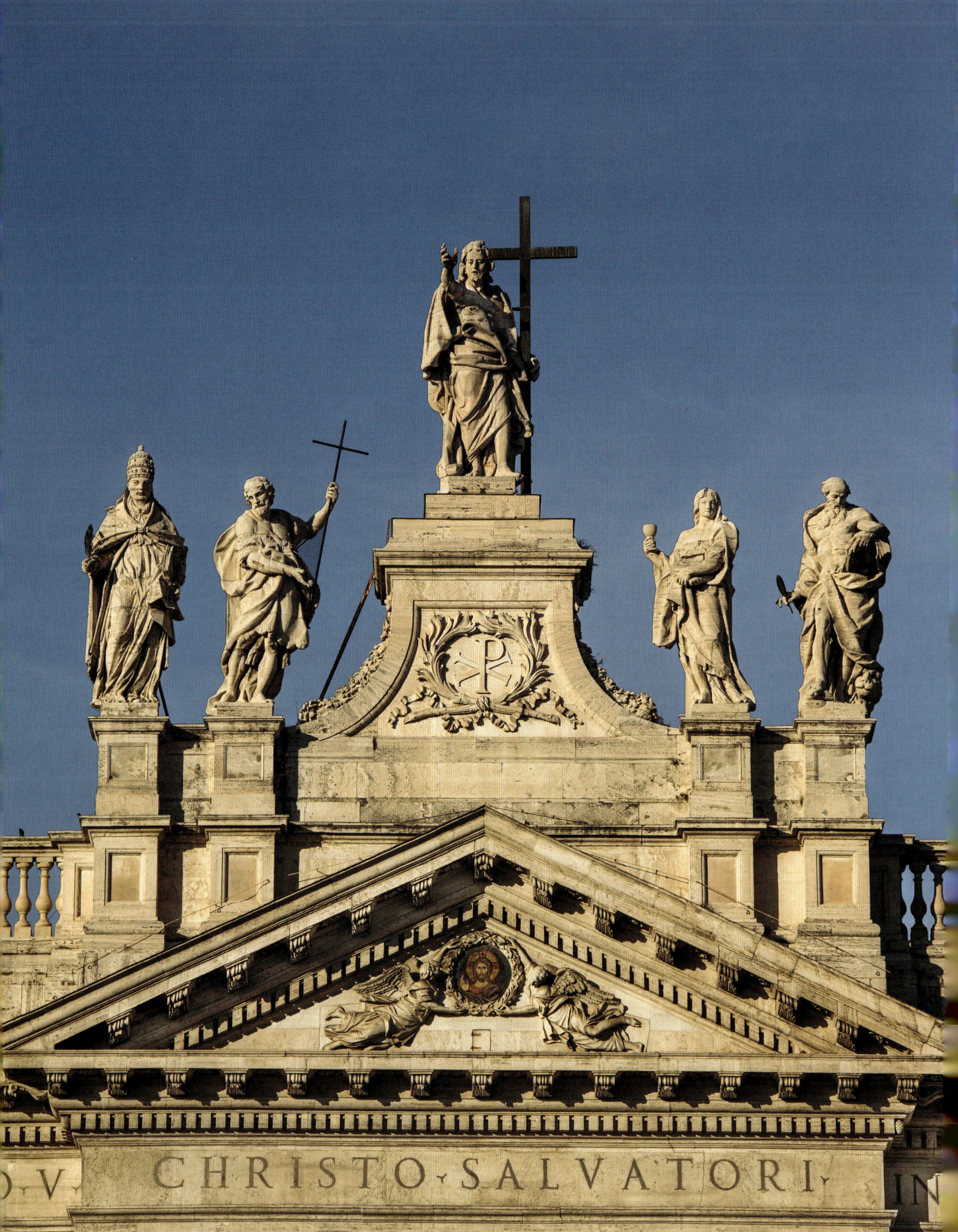

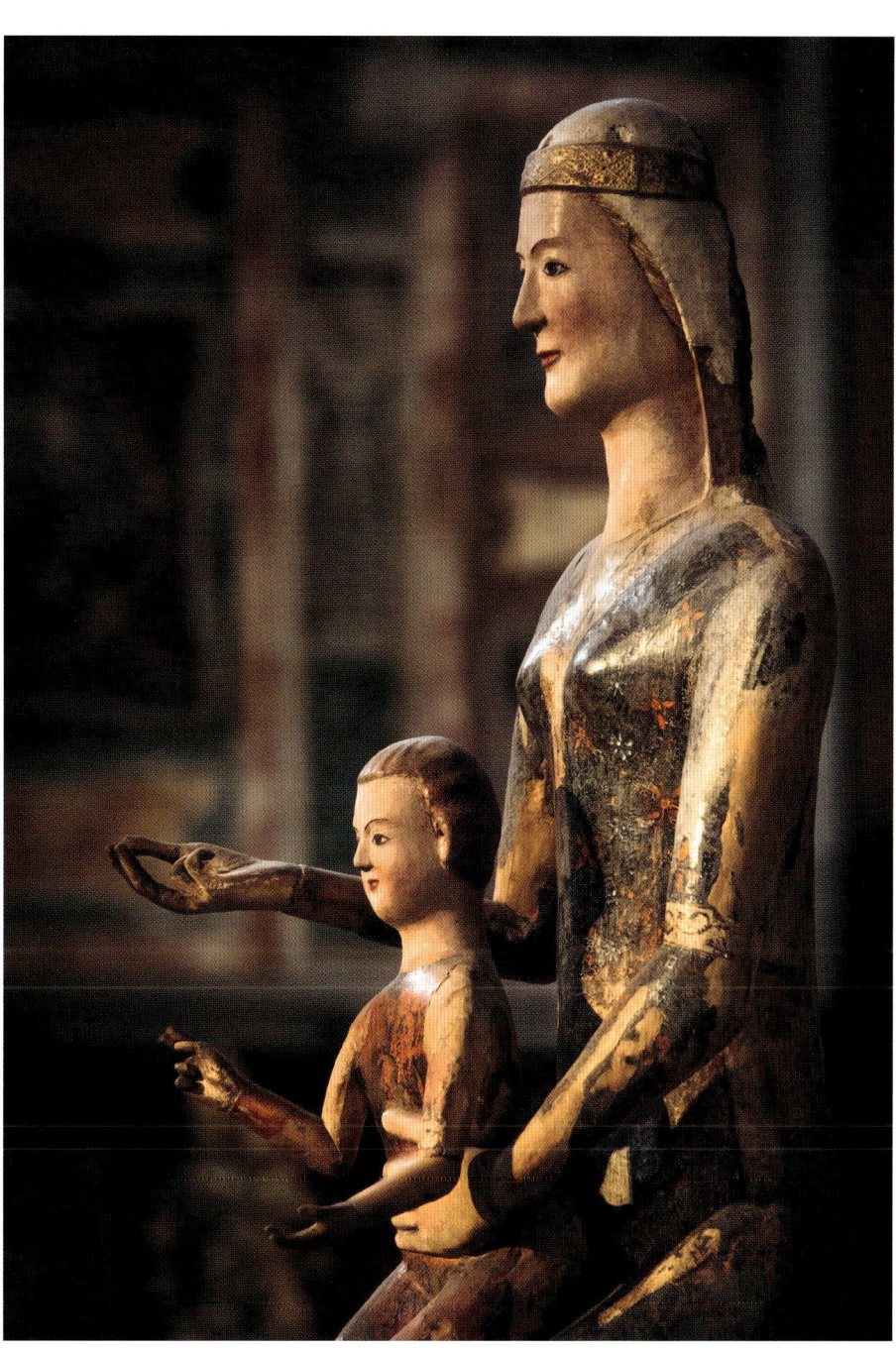

ST JOHN LATERAN

(*left*) The Archbasilica of St John Lateran is Rome's pontifical cathedral and, as the pope's seat, technically outranks the Basilica of St Peter in the Vatican. Huge statues of Christ flanked by St John the Baptist and St John the Evangelist adorn the pediment.

(*above*) The fourteenth-century hand-painted wooden sculpture of the Virgin and Child in the transept, provides a contrast to the larger than life stone statues of the apostles lining the nave.

(*overleaf*) The stunningly beautiful coffered nave ceiling was crafted by French cabinetmaker Flaminio Boulanger between 1562 and 1567. The project was initiated by Pope Pius IV.

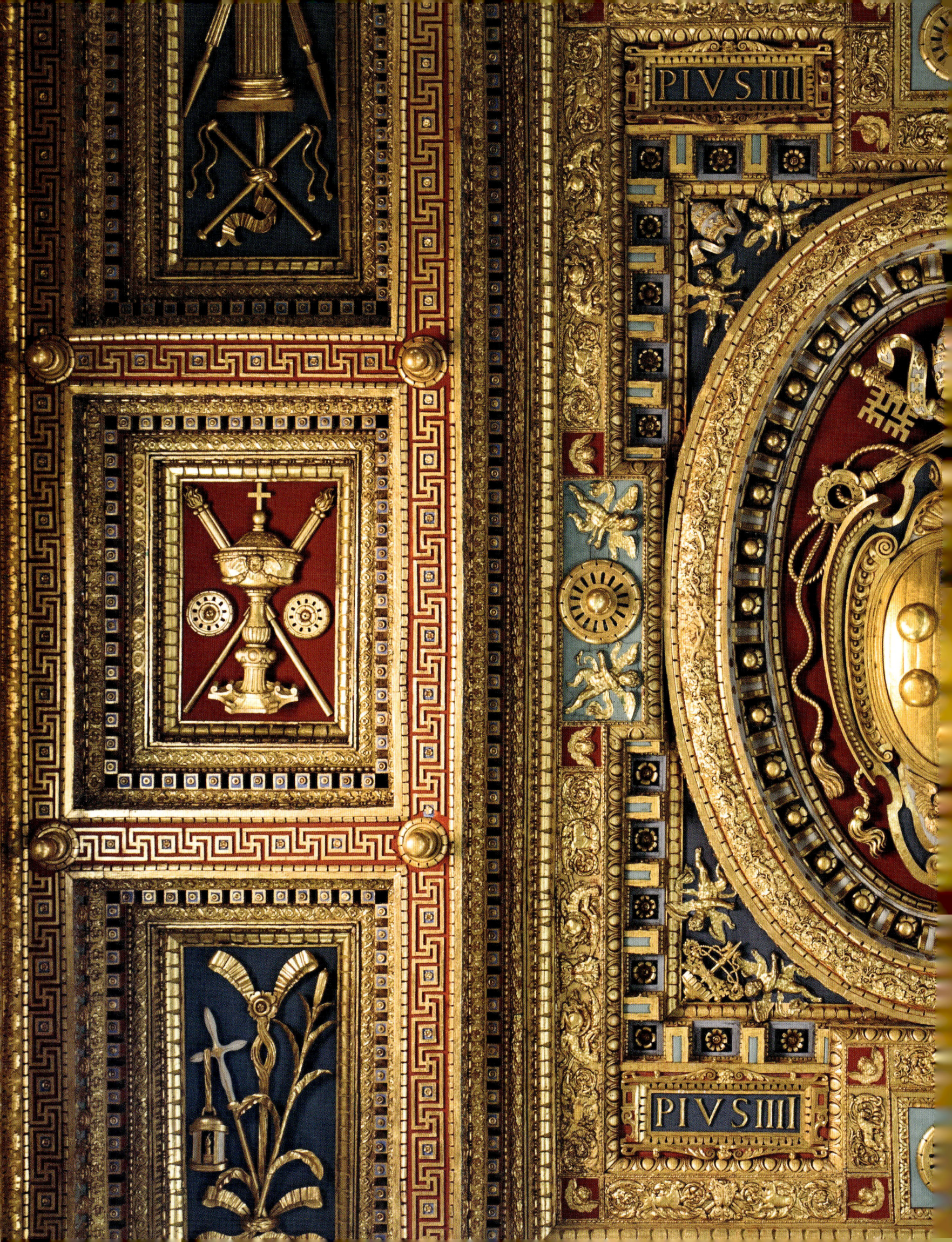

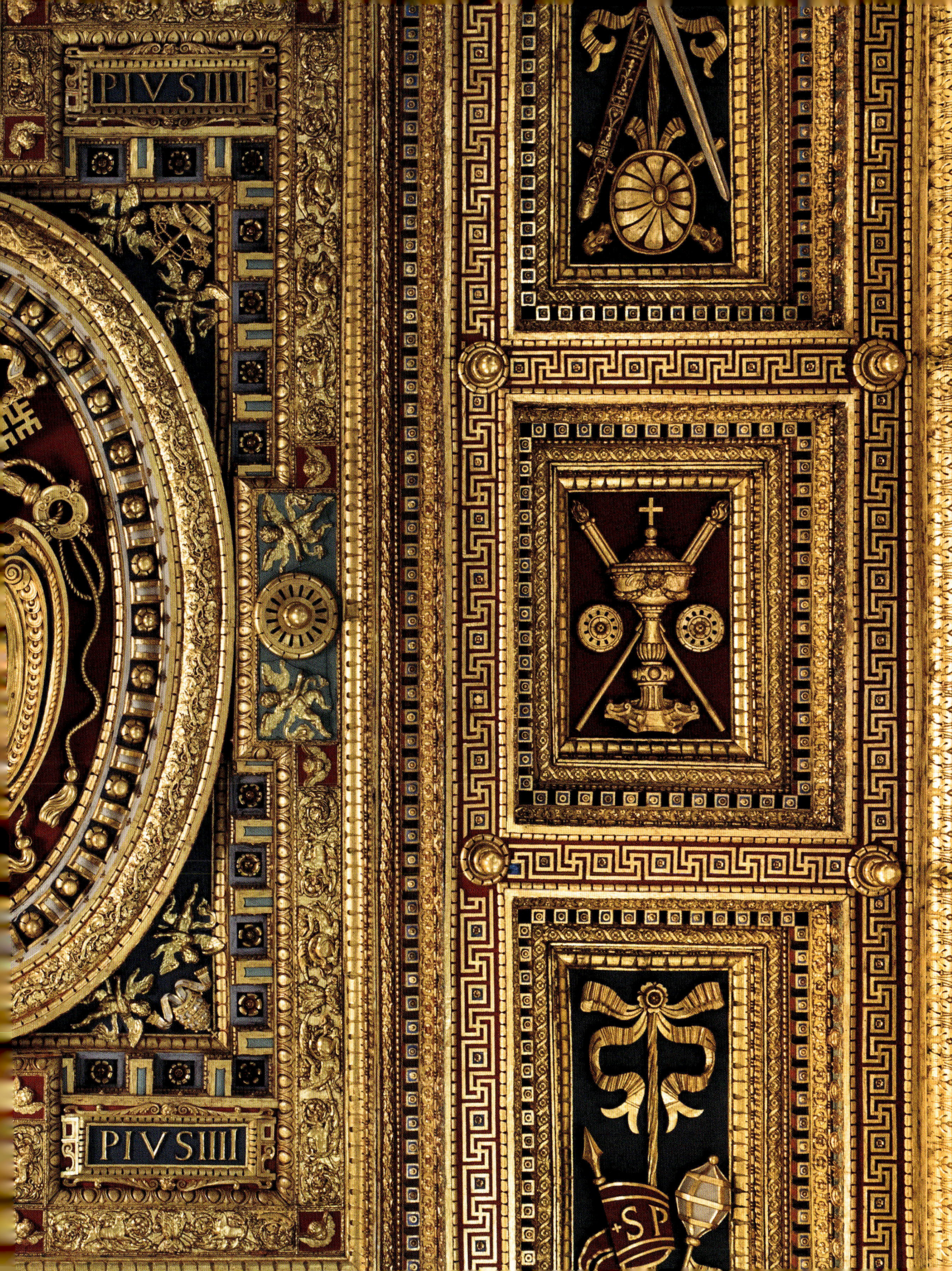

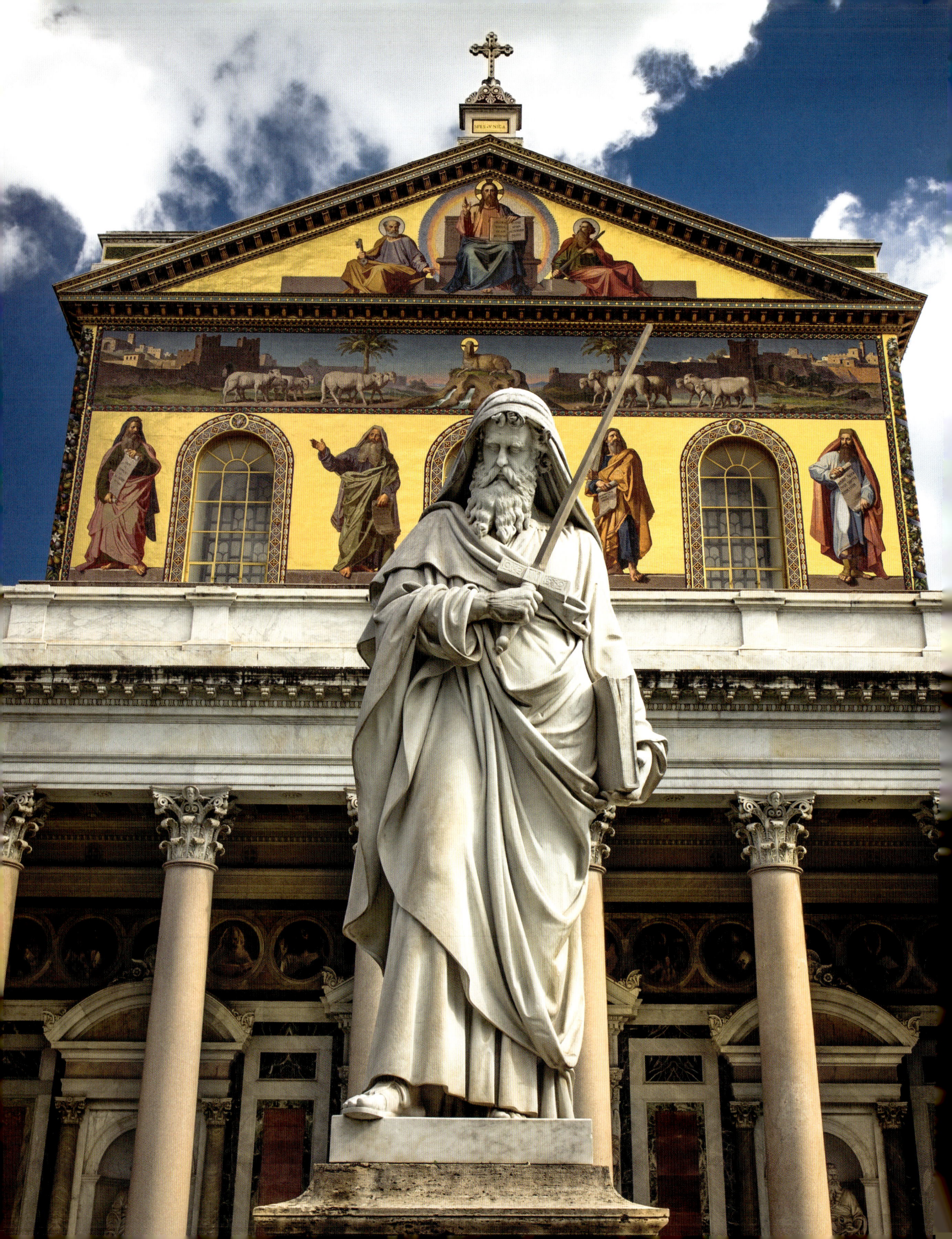

Almost everything about the basilica is imposing, not least the statue of St Paul by Giuseppe Obici. The mosaics depict Christ with St Peter and St Paul, the Mystic Lamb surrounded by four rivers symbolizing the four Gospels, plus twelve more lambs representing the apostles.

SAN PAOLO FUORI LE MURA

The Basilica of St Paul Outside the Walls stands on the site where the apostle was buried after his martyrdom some time between AD 65 and 67. There were many burial sites and necropolises set alongside the main roads radiating out from Rome's Aurelian Walls, and St Paul's final resting place, following his beheading at the hands of Emperor Nero, was some 2 kilometres/1¼ miles south, on the Via Ostiensis. It is assumed that St Paul and many other Christians (including St Peter) were somehow deemed responsible for the catastrophic fire that destroyed a significant percentage of the city in AD 64 and they were caught up in Emperor Nero's vindictive wave of persecution. A discreet Christian memorial originally marked St Paul's grave, but the Edict of Milan in 313 established freedom of worship and thereby ended the persecution of Christians and the need for secretive gatherings in private. Consequently, Emperor Constantine erected a simple rectangular hall church on the site of St Paul's tomb, which was consecrated a decade later by Pope Sylvester in 324. Just one year later, at the Council of Nicaea, the Christian faith was adopted as the official religion of the Roman Empire.

A great wave of church building ensued, and despite being located some distance from the heart of Rome, Constantine's Basilica of St Paul Outside the Walls was far from forgotten. By 386, it had become such a popular place of pilgrimage that three emperors, Valentinian II, Theodosius I and his son, Arcadius, decided to enlarge the existing building. However, the topographical constraints of its immediate surroundings, combined with the fact that the saint's tomb could not be moved, meant that the basilica's orientation was reversed, thereby placing the apse on the Via Ostiensis and the façade facing the river Tiber. This remarkable new building was consecrated in 395 by Pope Siricius. In its revised Byzantine format, it was, for many centuries, the largest church in Rome, until the sixteenth-century rebuilding of St Peter's in the Vatican.

From that point onwards, successive popes confirmed the Church's love for the basilica, because it was constantly being added to and embellished with mosaics, frescoes, paintings and chapels. Unfortunately, the basilica's isolated location outside the protection of the Roman Walls rendered it vulnerable (*top*) The great apse mosaic measuring 24 × 12 metres/ 78 × 39 feet was commissioned by Pope Honorius III. Although some segments survived the fire of 1823, many needed to be reworked. The restoration funds were raised after Pope Leo XII appealed to the Catholic world.

(*bottom left*) The nave and its four flanking aisles present an imposing sight. They are divided by eighty granite monoliths and the aisles are so large that the basilica could almost be deemed to have five naves. (*bottom right*) The adjoining cloister survived the fire. As a result, the twisted and encrusted marble columns by the renowned Vassalletto family are as created in the thirteenth century.

(*overleaf*) The majestic gold-coffered ceiling of the central nave bears the arms of Pope Pius IX, who consecrated the new basilica in December 1854.

to attack and it was sacked by the Lombards during the eighth century and by the Saracens during the ninth. Pope John VIII was extremely proactive in attempting to fortify and protect Rome from the increasing threat posed by the Saracens' advance northwards, and he walled both the basilica and the immediate monastic community. This newly created 'independent state' was endearingly referred to as 'Johannipolis'.

History shows that the basilica's well-being fluctuated thereafter. It survived a twelfth-century fire and the serious flooding of the Tiber in 1700, and just about kept going until 1823, when it was almost completely destroyed by a huge fire. Fortunately, some frescoes, mosaics and paintings were saved, but the rebuilding of the basilica was virtually a blank canvas. Luigi Poletti, a specialist in Neoclassical architecture, vowed to reconstruct an exact replica of the original. He kept his promise and Pope Pius IX consecrated the new basilica in December 1854.

Although many pilgrims will probably have witnessed the monumental scale associated with the buildings of ancient Rome and its churches, nothing can prepare one for the sight of the 135-metre-/443-foot-long nave with double flanking aisles, each separated by four rows of twenty granite columns leading up to a richly decorated gold coffered ceiling. However, from the perspective of the basilica as a place of pilgrimage, the greatest treasure of St Paul's was discovered during archaeological work carried out at the beginning of the twenty-first century beneath the papal altar.

The sarcophagus of the apostle was revealed in the exact place where Emperor Constantine had had the first altar built, and sitting just above the tomb of unpolished marble, a Latin inscription reads *PAULO APOSTOLO MART* (Paul Apostle Martyr). The ancient apse of the original basilica containing the tomb was also uncovered and a section is now visible beneath a sheet of reinforced glass.

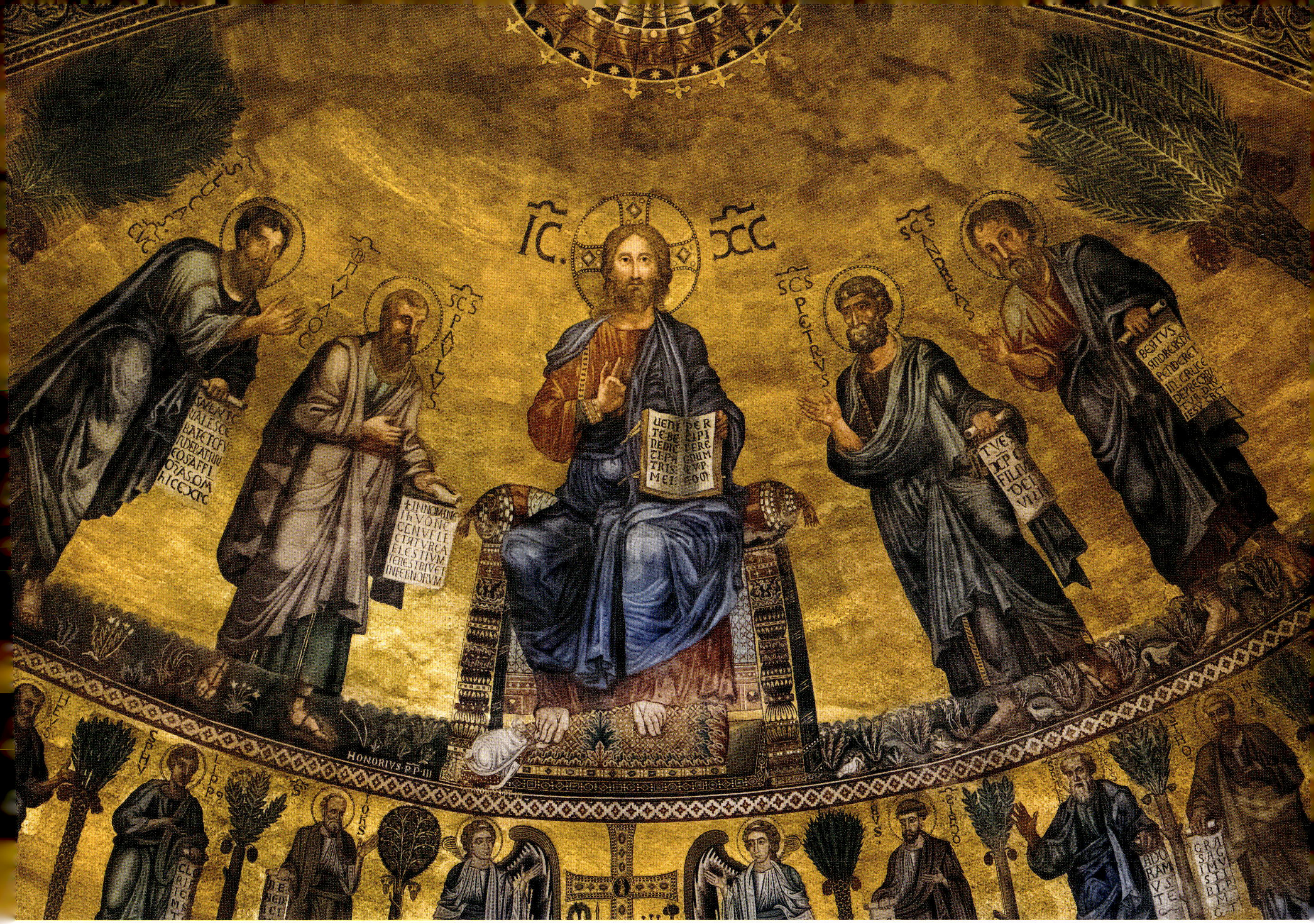

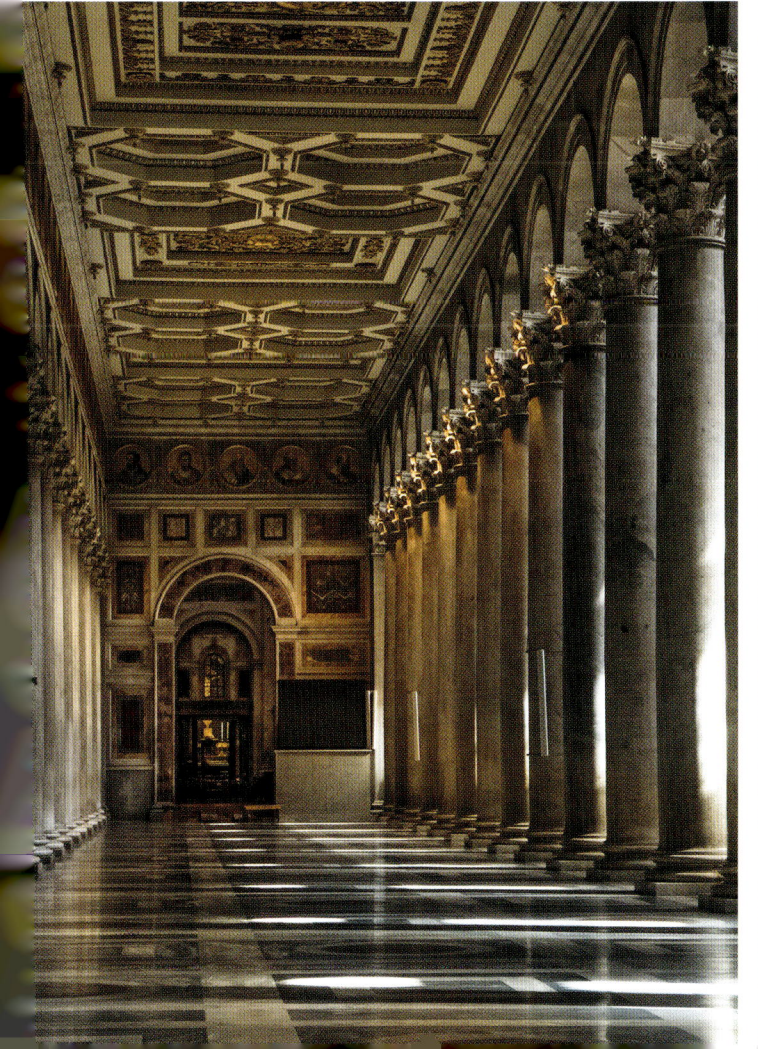
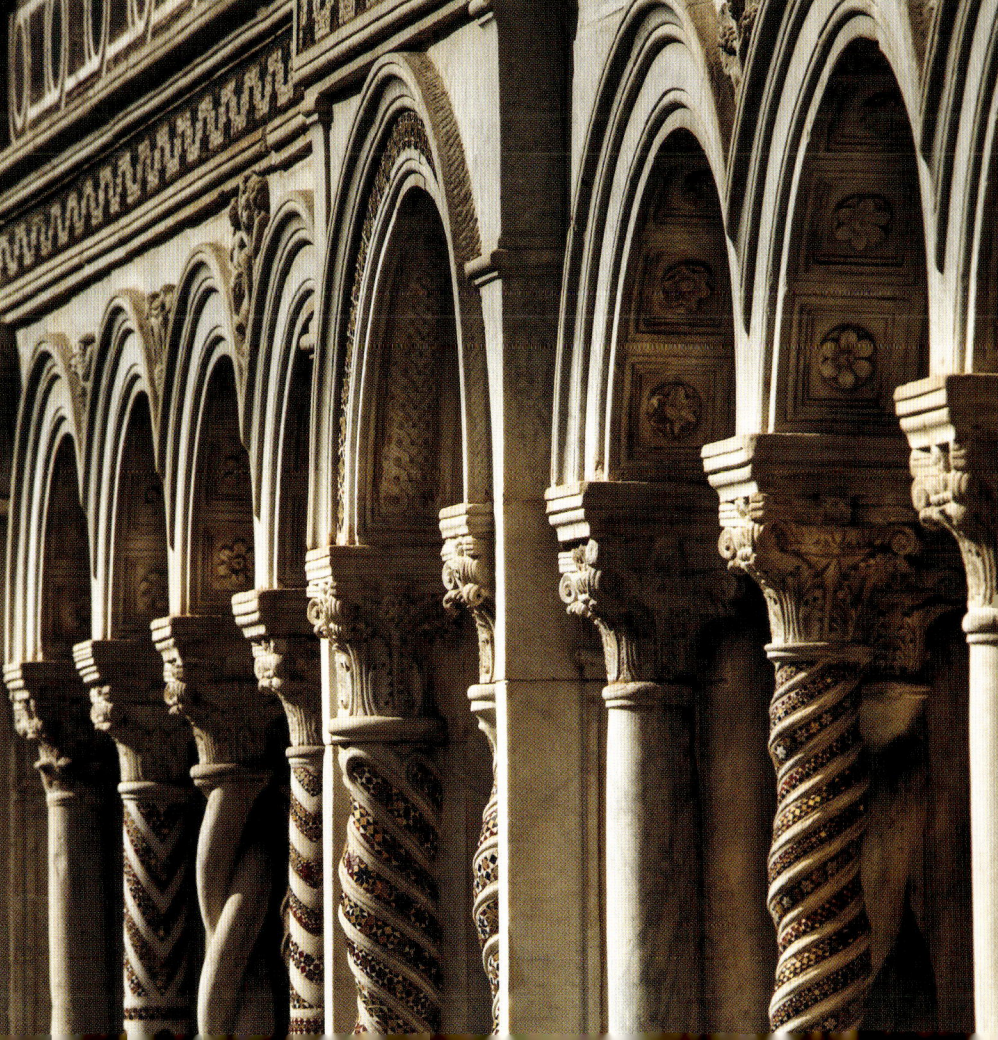

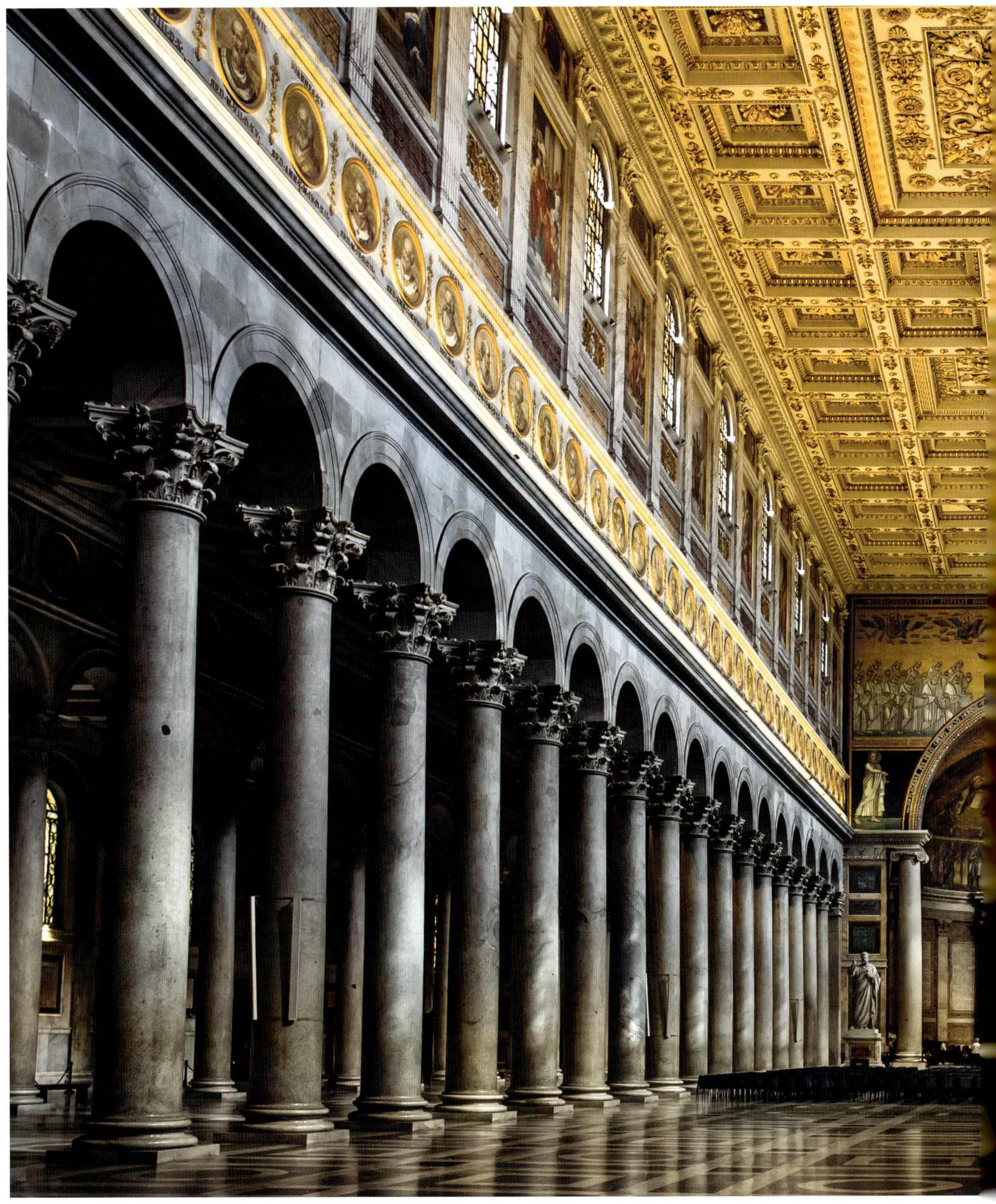

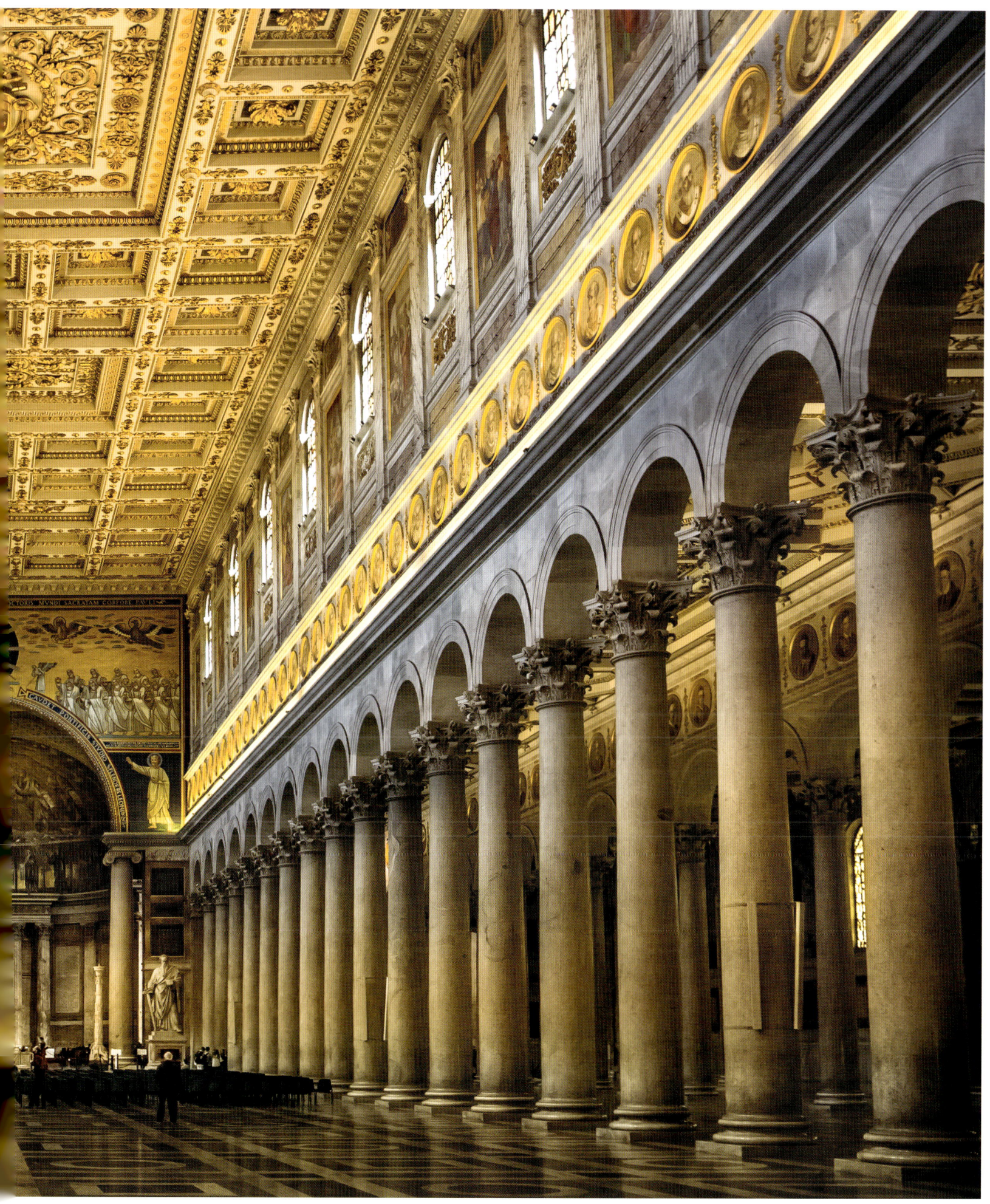

THE BASILICA OF THE HOLY HOUSE
Loreto, Marche

When viewed from afar, the hill town of Loreto in Italy's Marche region is dominated by the mighty dome of its basilica, rising above what appears to be an impregnable set of defensive walls. When viewed from within Loreto's protective shield, the sheer height and strength of the church's apsidal east end leaves one in no doubt that this is one of Italy's few fortified churches. A narrow cobbled path heads up to the rectangular Square of the Madonna, safely cocooned within its defensive perimeter, and the main entry portal of the basilica leads into one of Italy's most visited and holiest Marian shrines. Because Loreto lies just 3 kilometres/2 miles inland from the Adriatic coast, to the south of Ancona, the fortifications were deemed necessary to protect the basilica and its precious contents from the threat posed by marauding Turks and opportunist pirates from other countries bordering the Adriatic.

Essentially, the shrine within the basilica contains the Nazareth house of the Virgin Mary, where she lived with her husband, Joseph, and, perhaps more significantly for the Christian faith, where the Annunciation took place. This was, therefore, where Jesus spent his childhood and some of his adult life until the Crucifixion. This same humble dwelling was also believed to have been where his Mother lived after his death and resurrection.

It would not be unreasonable to ask, 'How did a brick-built dwelling get from the Holy Land to Italy *via* Croatia in 1294?' The answer unquestioningly accepted by the Catholic faith from the late thirteenth century and for many centuries thereafter was that it was flown there by a band of angels. The saving of the alleged Holy House seemingly took place in the final death throes of the Crusades, when the Muslim forces were completely dominant and the Christian armies were forced to withdraw. It has been the subject of consideration and investigation in more recent times by historians, archaeologists and forensic experts, and the consensus seems to be that claims regarding the structure have validity in terms of the brickwork's origin. Historical research into its mode of transportation has produced a potentially more viable (albeit less miraculous) alternative to the angelic couriers.

The exterior view of the transepts and apse make the basilica resemble a fortress with stylish windows rather than a church, but it actually served as both. The basilica was located just 3 kilometres/2 miles from the coast and so threats from seaborne attack were very real.

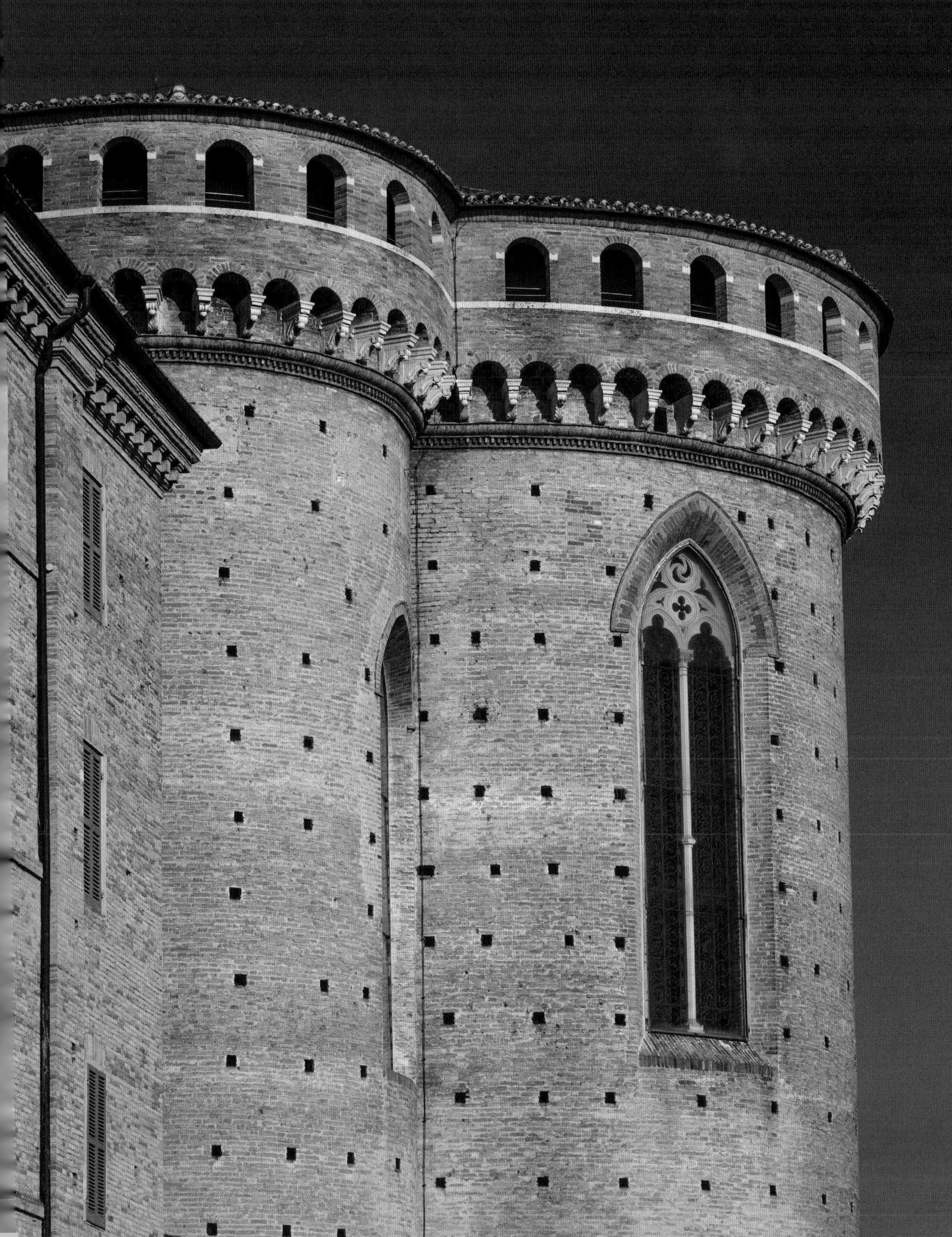

The rustic dwelling set within Bramante's lavishly sculpted marble casing was believed to be where Jesus Christ grew from infancy through childhood and on into adult life. Only the lower courses of stone are the originals from Nazareth and local Italian bricks complete the structure.

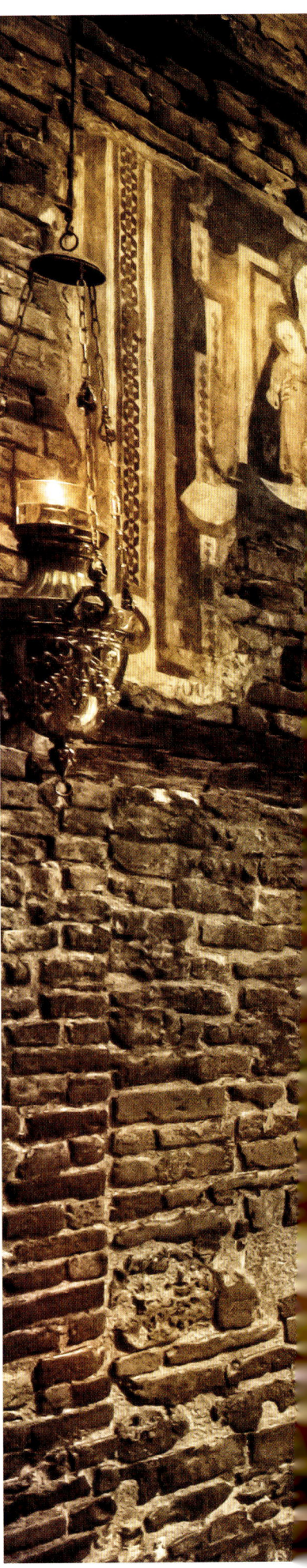

There are documents from the period of the Crusades suggesting that immediately prior to Nazareth being overrun and all vestiges of the Virgin's house being destroyed, a wealthy Christian family with the surname Angeli, or possibly Angelus, arranged for the building to be transported piecemeal overland and then shipped across the Mediterranean. However, at the end of the day, it all becomes somewhat irrelevant because the unwavering belief in the legend of the Holy House that prevailed for centuries will remain irrevocably lodged in the hearts and souls of all the Catholics from around the world who visit Loreto. Every Marian shrine has its own history, but each and every one possesses a statue of the Virgin, and it is that tangible presence, the opportunity for intense personal interaction with a physical representation of one's religious *raison d'être*, that really matters.

The original pilgrimage church containing the Holy House had a more basic Gothic structure and the long process of rebuilding the basilica was begun in 1468. One of the most influential architects involved in key elements of the design was Donato Bramante, who was commissioned by Pope Julius II in 1509 to design the elaborate marble shell encasing the Holy House. It was a complex project that was executed over several decades by most of the major sixteenth-century Italian sculptors, including Sansovino, Sangallo and Nerucci. Bramante also designed the twelve apsidal and circular chapels surrounding the crossing and transepts where the Holy House is located. The paintings and frescoes now adorning those chapels combine in a symphony of exquisite art to create the perfect foil for Bramante's marble masterpiece.

Bramante was also responsible for designing the remaining three sides of the Square of the Madonna, the most impressive elements being the long, imposing double-arched building extending away from the basilica's façade and the richly decorated mid-eighteenth-century campanile. Originally commissioned to be the Apostolic Palace by Pope Julius II, the upper gallery is now transformed into a museum displaying a great number of artworks, sculptures and other treasures donated to the sanctuary over past centuries.

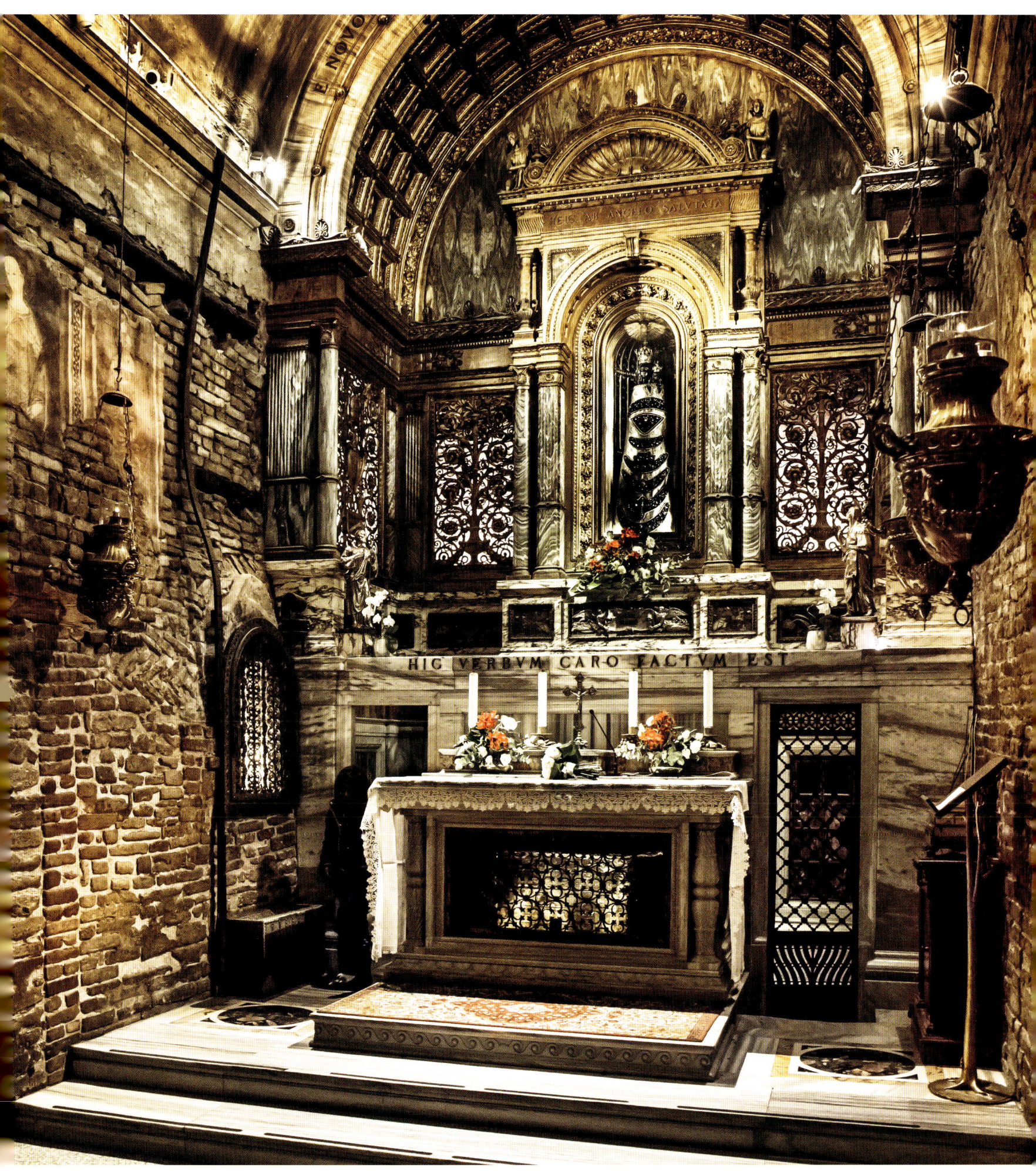

210 GREAT PILGRIMAGE SITES OF EUROPE

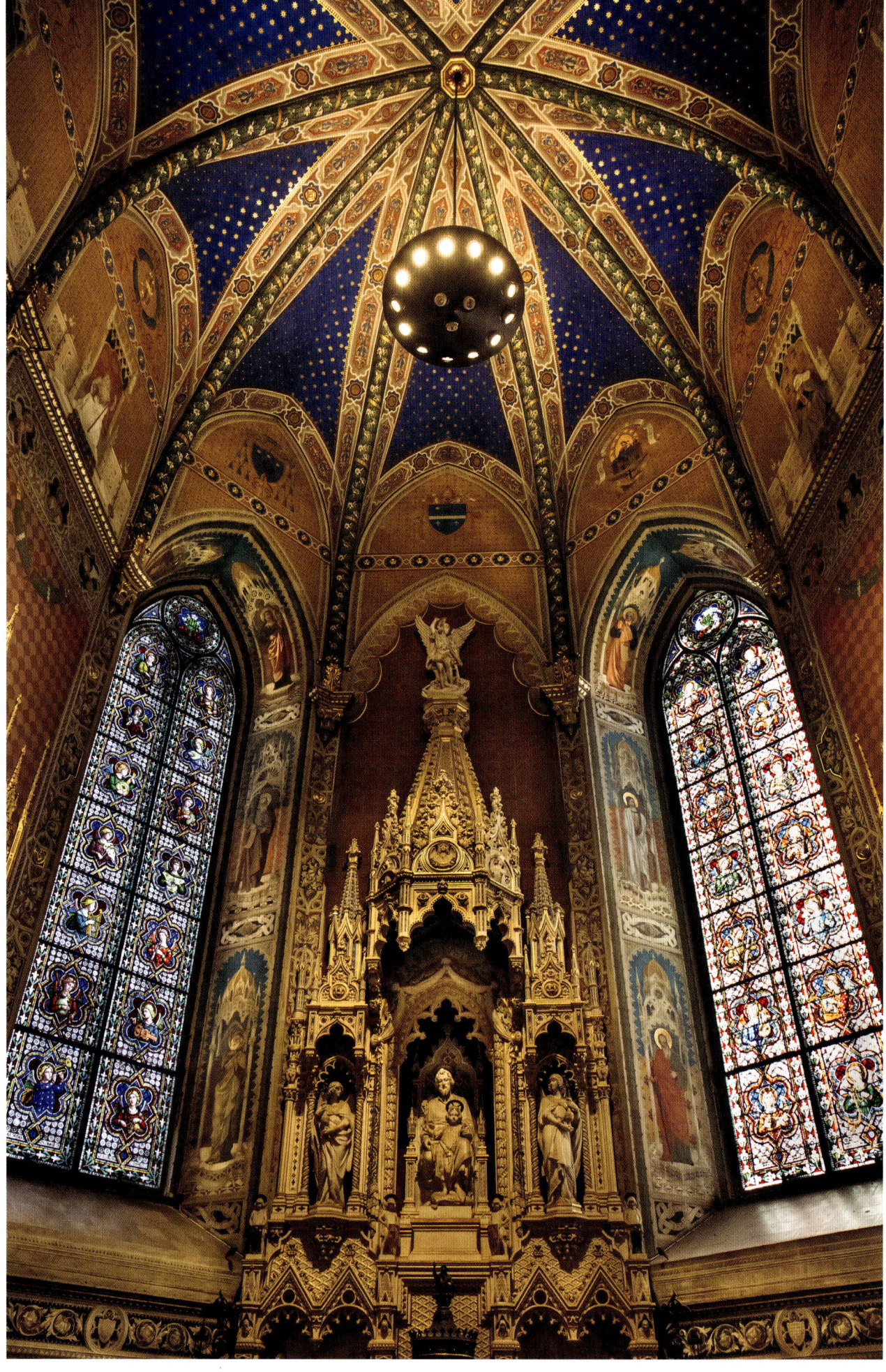

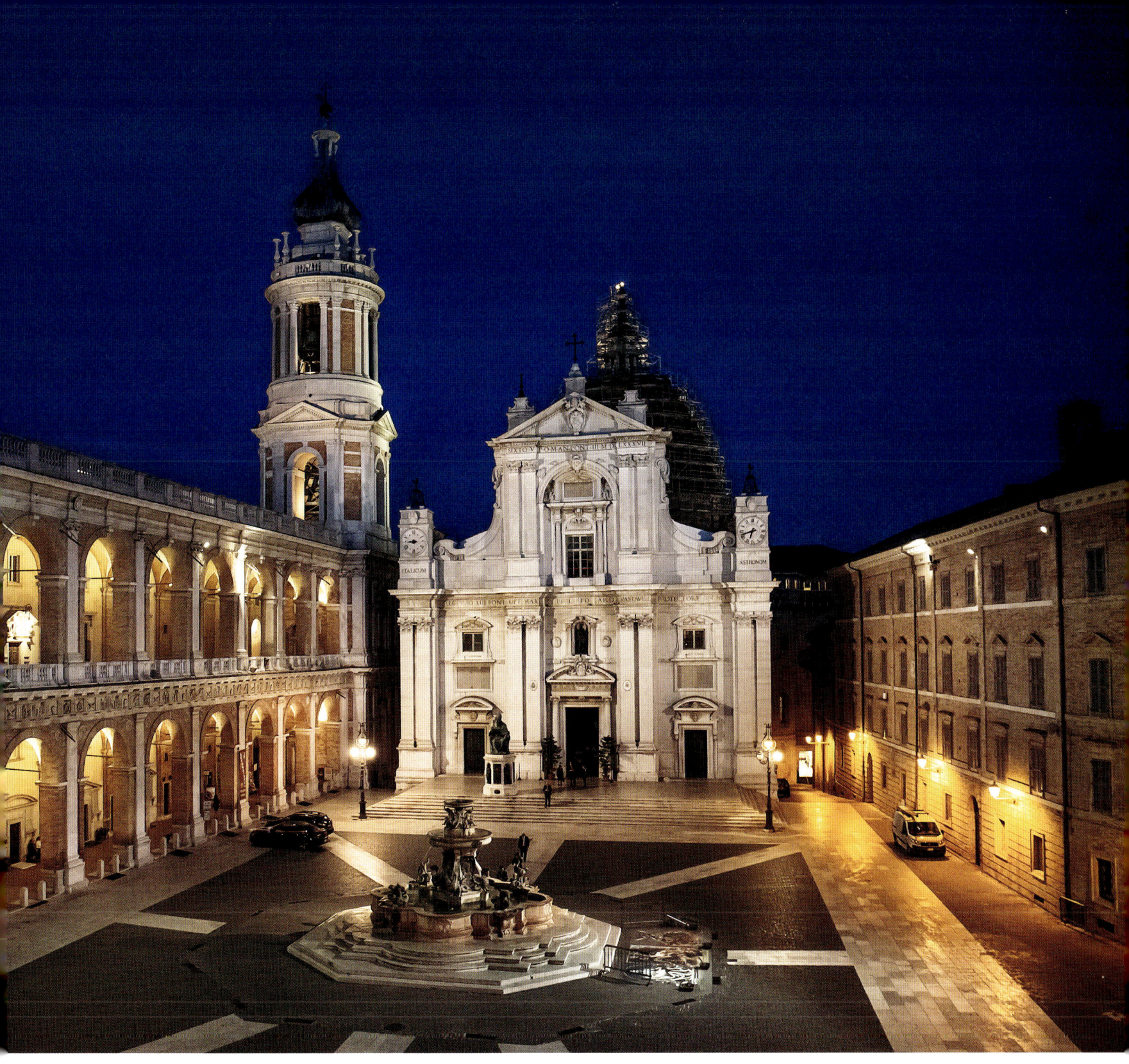

(*left*) The Spanish Chapel was one of several apsidal chapels needing restoration during the nineteenth century. Necessary funds for such work were raised in different nations, and chapels were appropriately renamed in gratitude. Consequently, the Chapel of St Joseph now has an alternative title.

(*above*) The Square of the Madonna, with its seventeenth-century fountain, is delightfully atmospheric at night.

(*overleaf*) The sacristy of St Mark's dome was created by Melozzo da Forlì, a master of perspective painting. The remarkable 3D effects were created using painted shadows.

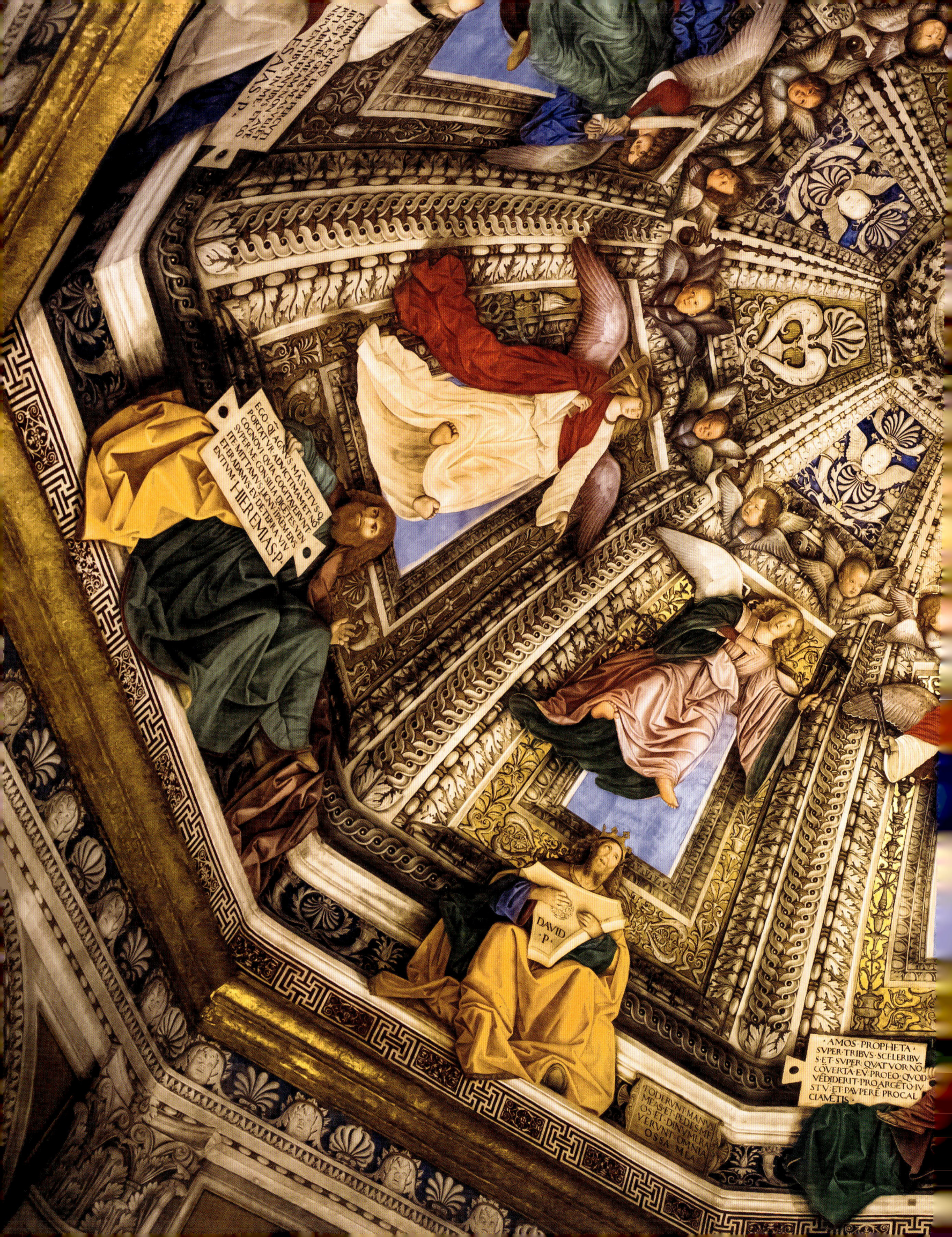

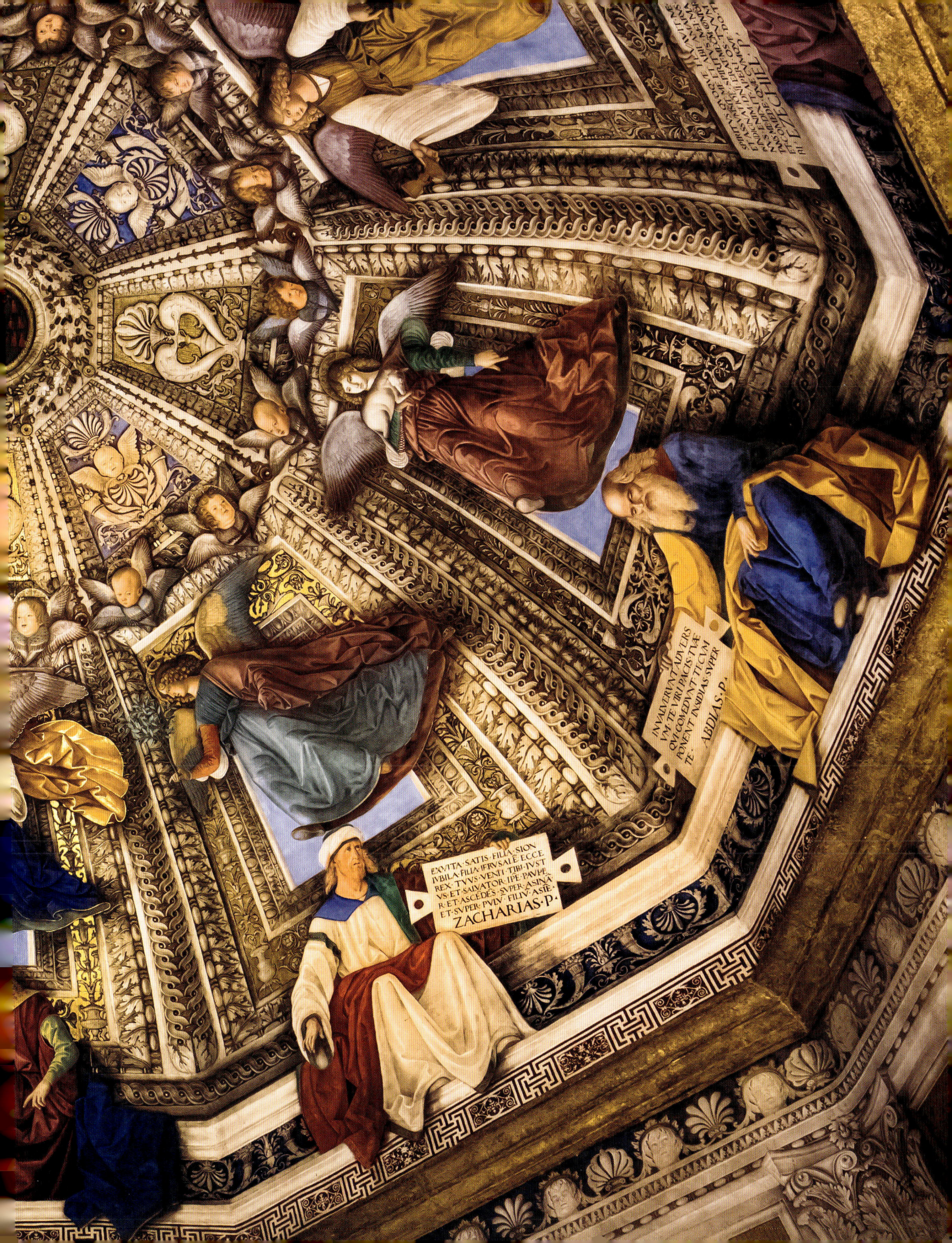

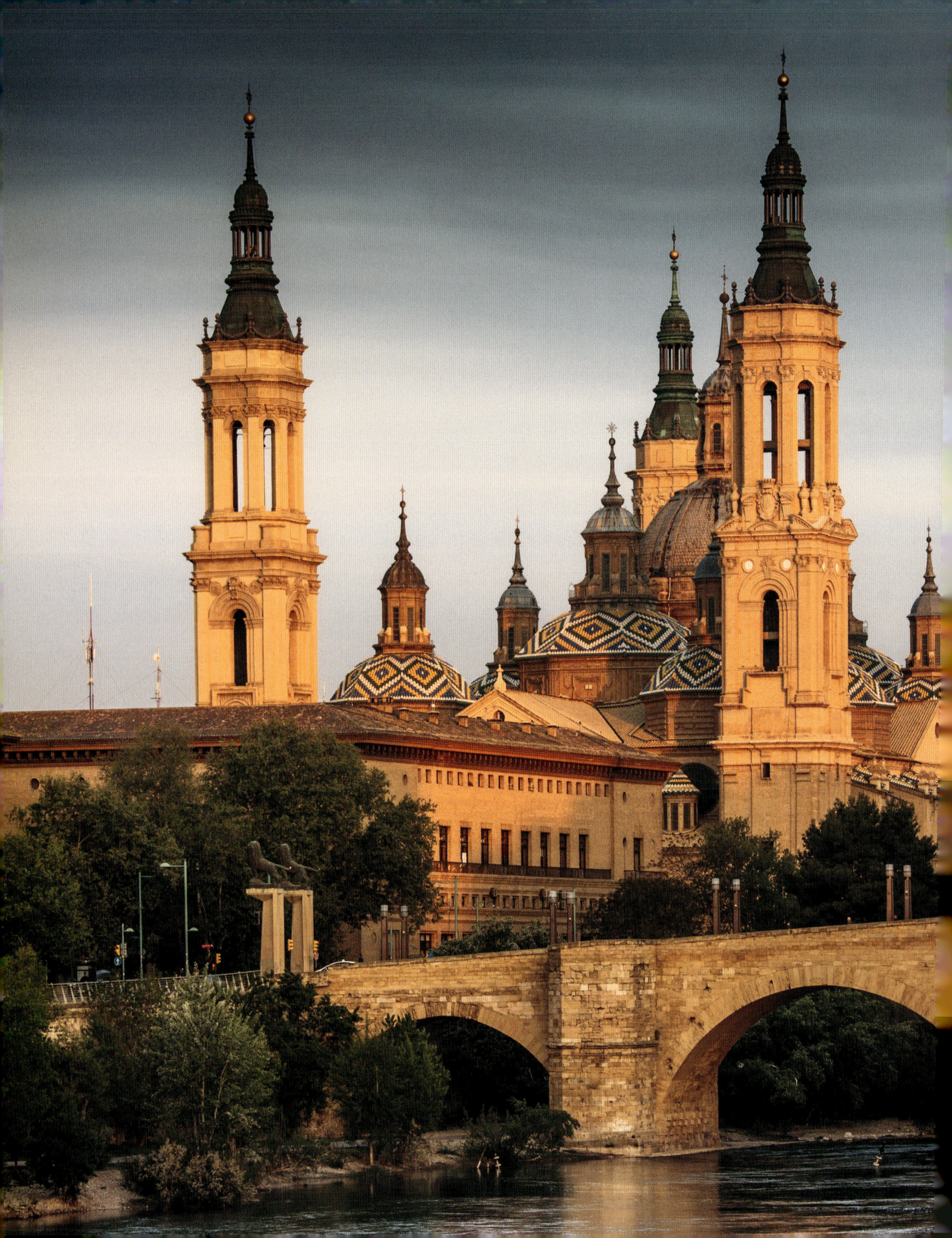

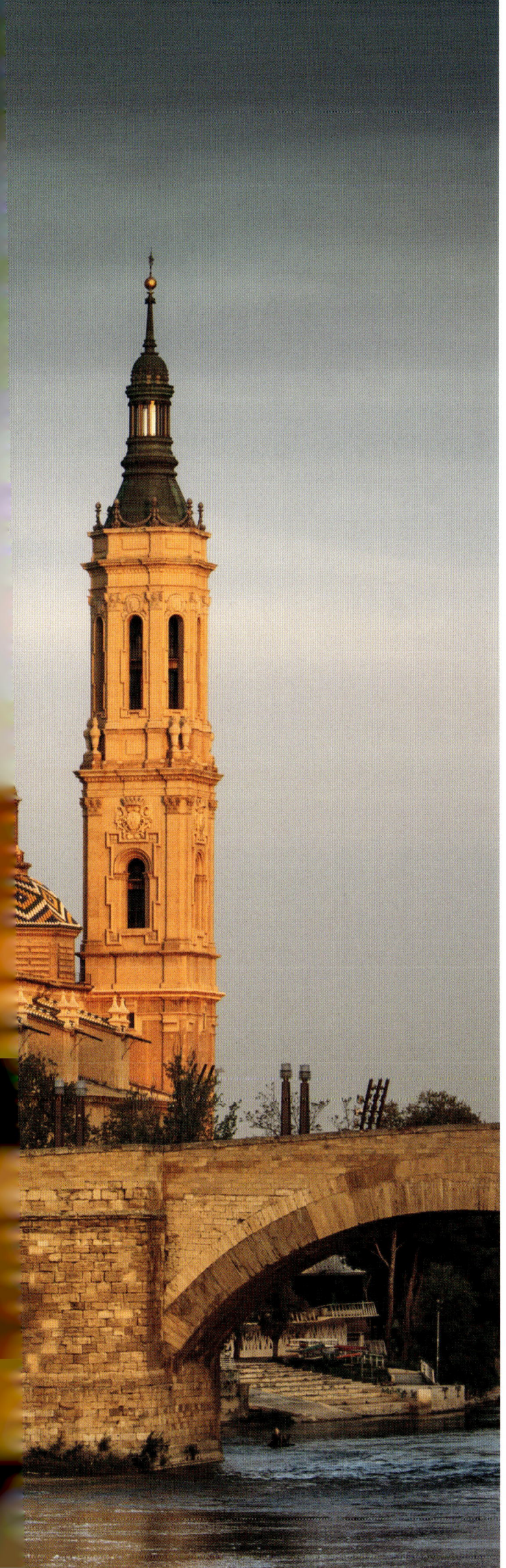

7

SPAIN AND PORTUGAL

SPAIN
SANTIAGO DE COMPOSTELA
Galicia

Photographing this book has been an enjoyable challenge but one nevertheless requiring a huge slice of good luck. Unfortunately, my time in Santiago de Compostela coincided with a long-term restoration programme on the cathedral, due for completion by the Holy Year of 2021. The feast day of St James is 25 July and a Holy Year is declared whenever it falls on a Sunday. The concept of a Holy Year was originated by Pope Callixtus II in 1122 and it was subsequently granted perpetuity through a papal bull issued by Pope Alexander III in 1179. Holy Years within the Catholic faith enable the granting of special graces and indulgences to those able to fulfil the necessary 'terms and conditions', comprising a combination of pilgrimage, prayer and charitable gifts and deeds.

Despite the majestic façade being free of scaffolding after some six years of work, most of the interior was closed so my photographic opportunities were disappointingly limited. However, when the restored sections are directly compared with those parts of the cathedral's fabric yet to be renovated, it serves as a salutary reminder of just how much we take the well-being of our medieval architectural heritage for granted. Perhaps the most frustrating thing was not being able to photograph one of the cathedral's greatest treasures, the Pórtico de la Gloria. This was the original entrance and the monumental twelfth-century work by the sculptor and architect Master Mateo is rightly considered the apogee of Spanish Romanesque religious sculpture. The theme of the Last Judgment is one that will have been encountered numerous times by pilgrims on the road and it is entirely appropriate that the best example should be presented on the portico's tympanum.

The cathedral's spectacular main façade, comprising various elements of Romanesque, Gothic and Renaissance architecture, was creatively and seamlessly harmonized by the eighteenth-century architect Fernando de Casas Novoa. His masterpiece of the Baroque was completed in 1750 after twelve years' work. It is hard to believe that the same site was once occupied by a humble ninth-century chapel erected over the place where the bones of St James were discovered.

(*previous pages*) Our Lady of the Pillar, Zaragoza.

(*right*) The soaring twin towers of the cathedral have long been a city landmark visible from miles away, and the warm coloured stone now positively glows following recent restoration. The dirt and lichen accumulated over time have been removed to reveal every subtle detail of the façade.

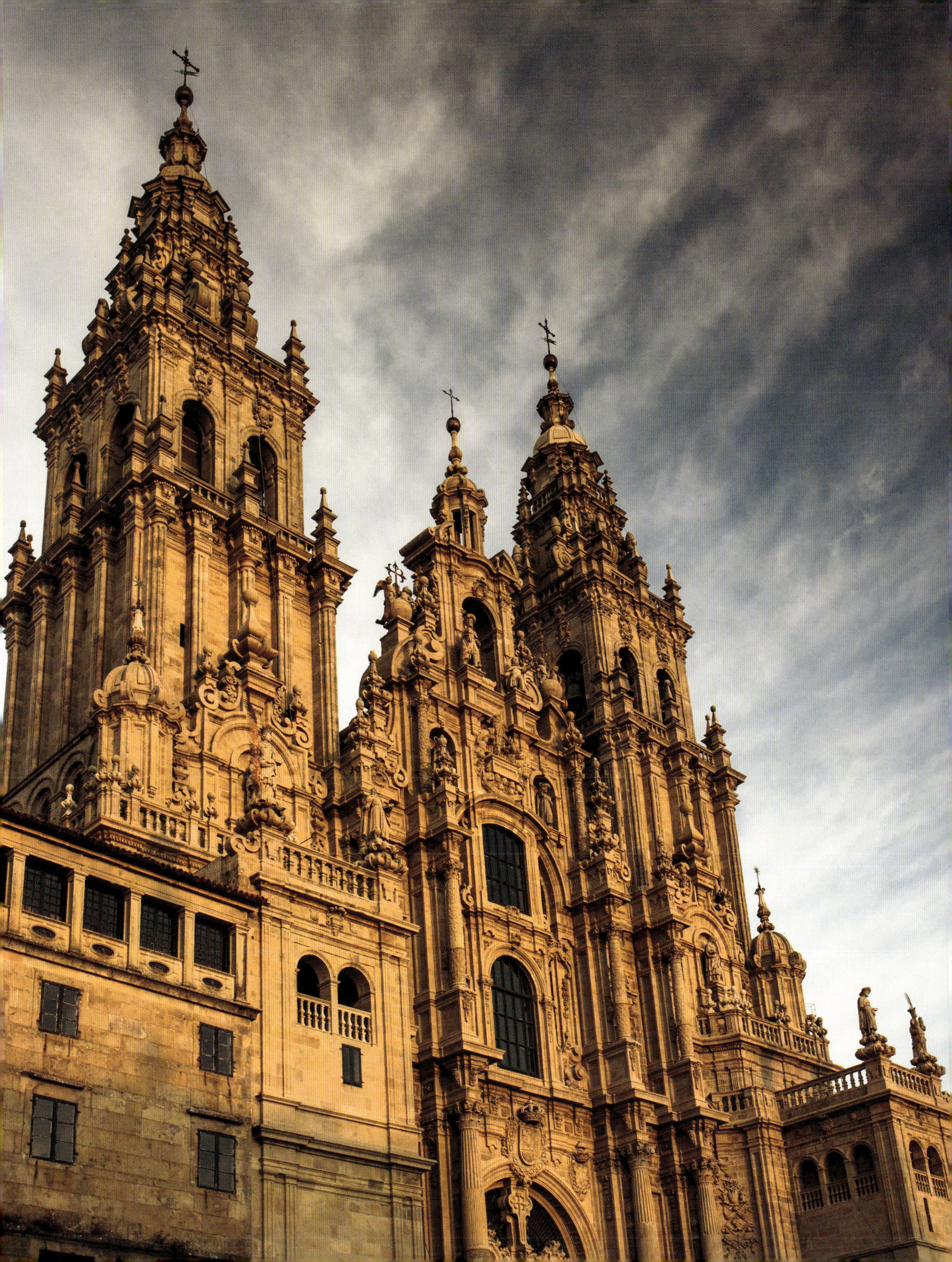

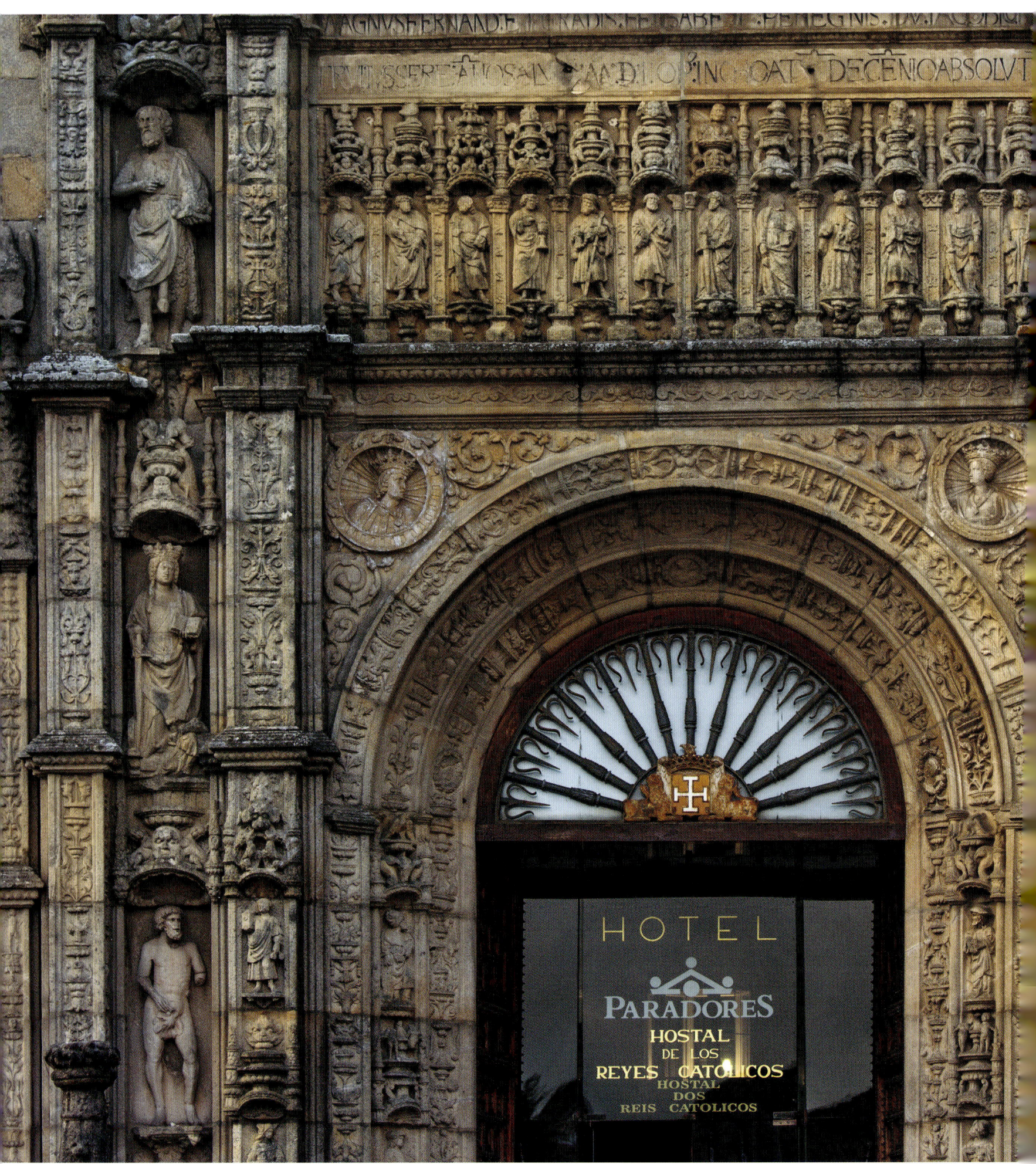

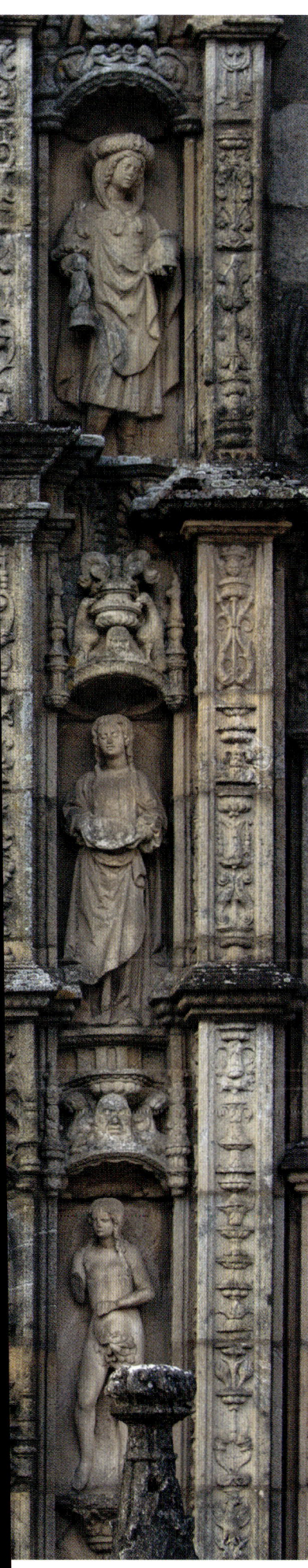

The Hostal de Los Reyes Catolicos now bears the distinctive logo of the nationwide Parador Hotels. The hotel may be more expensive than during its days as a charitable pilgrim hospice, but it nevertheless continues to honour the part of its original charter stipulating that pilgrims must be offered food and accommodation for up to three days. Beds are no longer possible, but the first ten pilgrims to present their accreditation each day qualify for three meals, albeit not in the 'silver service' restaurant.

Towards the end of that century, Alfonso III the Great, King of Asturias, built a larger church to cater for the increasing numbers of pilgrims drawn by rumours of miracles happening at St James's tomb. However, almost a century later, a Moorish incursion in 997 razed the church to the ground and all but destroyed the city. Fortunately, advance warning had allowed the apostle's reliquary to be taken away to safety. When the cathedral is reopened after the current restoration, the tall and sombre Romanesque nave and wide aisles will be physically unchanged and the awesome Baroque gold and silver altar will still gleam like a distant beacon, drawing pilgrims in towards the thirteenth-century statue of a seated St James, which is the centerpiece of the retable.

Undertaking a pilgrimage to Santiago de Compostela was, and still is, a deeply personal journey made for a variety of reasons. For the masses of largely illiterate medieval pilgrims, motivation was often based around the dire warnings of the consequences of sin conveyed in stained glass or sculpted visions. However, regardless of the reason why pilgrims over the centuries have taken to the road, they have all been dependent on the ethos of hospitable charity. From the early days of monastic hospices to the current hostels administered by confraternities, pilgrims have been helped along their way by the provision of low cost accommodation.

Standing adjacent to the cathedral in the Plaza del Obradoiro is the pilgrim's hospice, funded and built by order of the Catholic monarchs Ferdinand and Isabella following their visit to the shrine in 1486. Their actions were in direct response to complaints about the lamentable state of the existing hospice, but that description could never be applied to the magnificent Parador Hotel now occupying the same building.

Any time spent amid the labyrinth of narrow medieval streets surrounding the cathedral and other historical buildings is special (apart from having to dodge the Disney-type 'road trains' now used by tourists), and just to be an observer in the cathedral square as groups of arriving pilgrims collapse to the ground in varying states of exhaustion, euphoria or disbelief is a very moving experience.

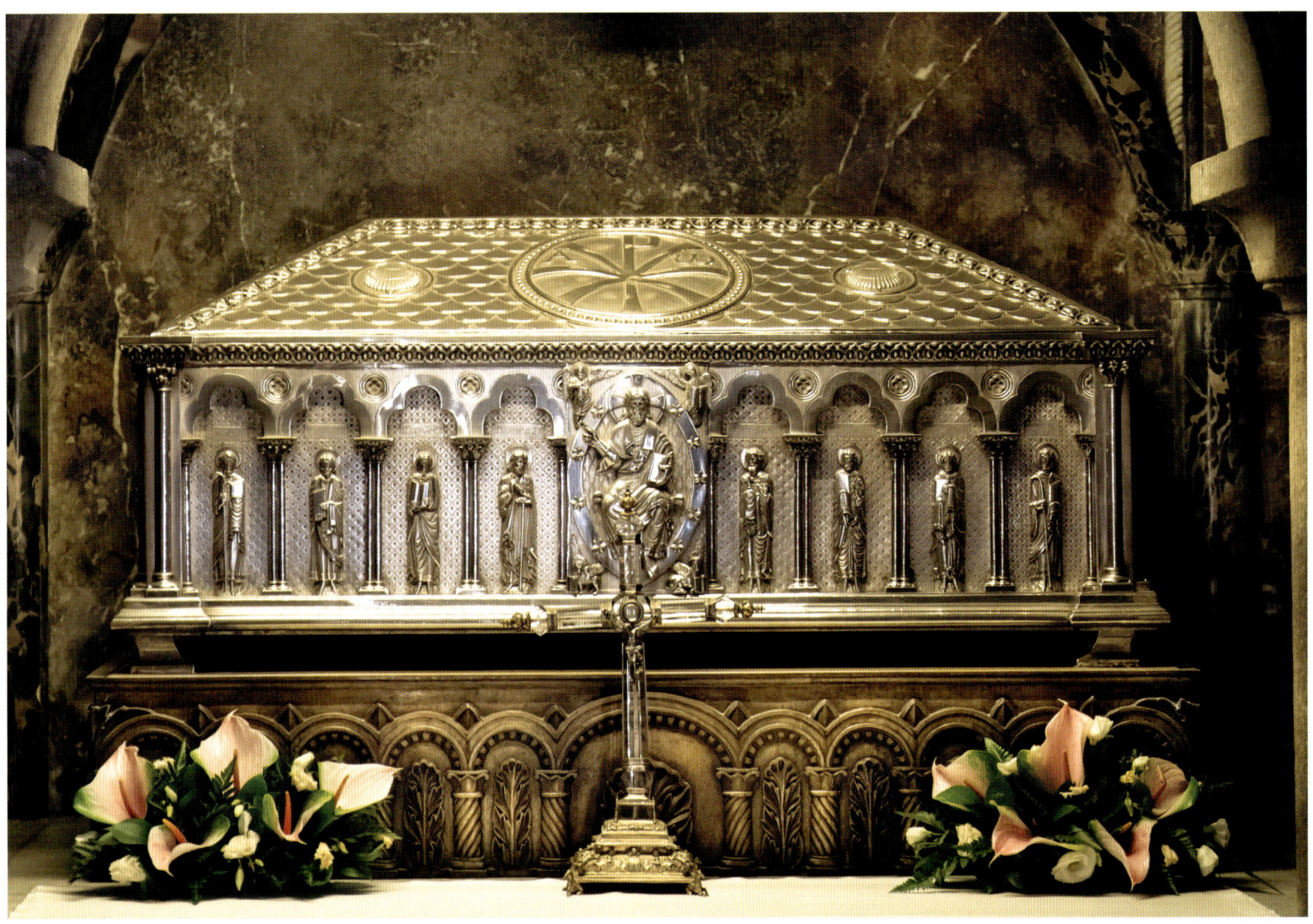

(*above*) The silver reliquary bearing the remains of St James lies in the cathedral's crypt and it is one of the two objects of interest for a newly arrived pilgrim. The other is the statue of St James accessed *via* steps leading up behind the altar.

(*right*) In the context of the Reconquest, St James the Apostle had the alternative identity of Matamoros (Moor slayer). This graphic sculpture sits on the pediment of the Town Hall opposite the cathedral and celebrates a Christian victory at the Battle of Clavijo in 844.

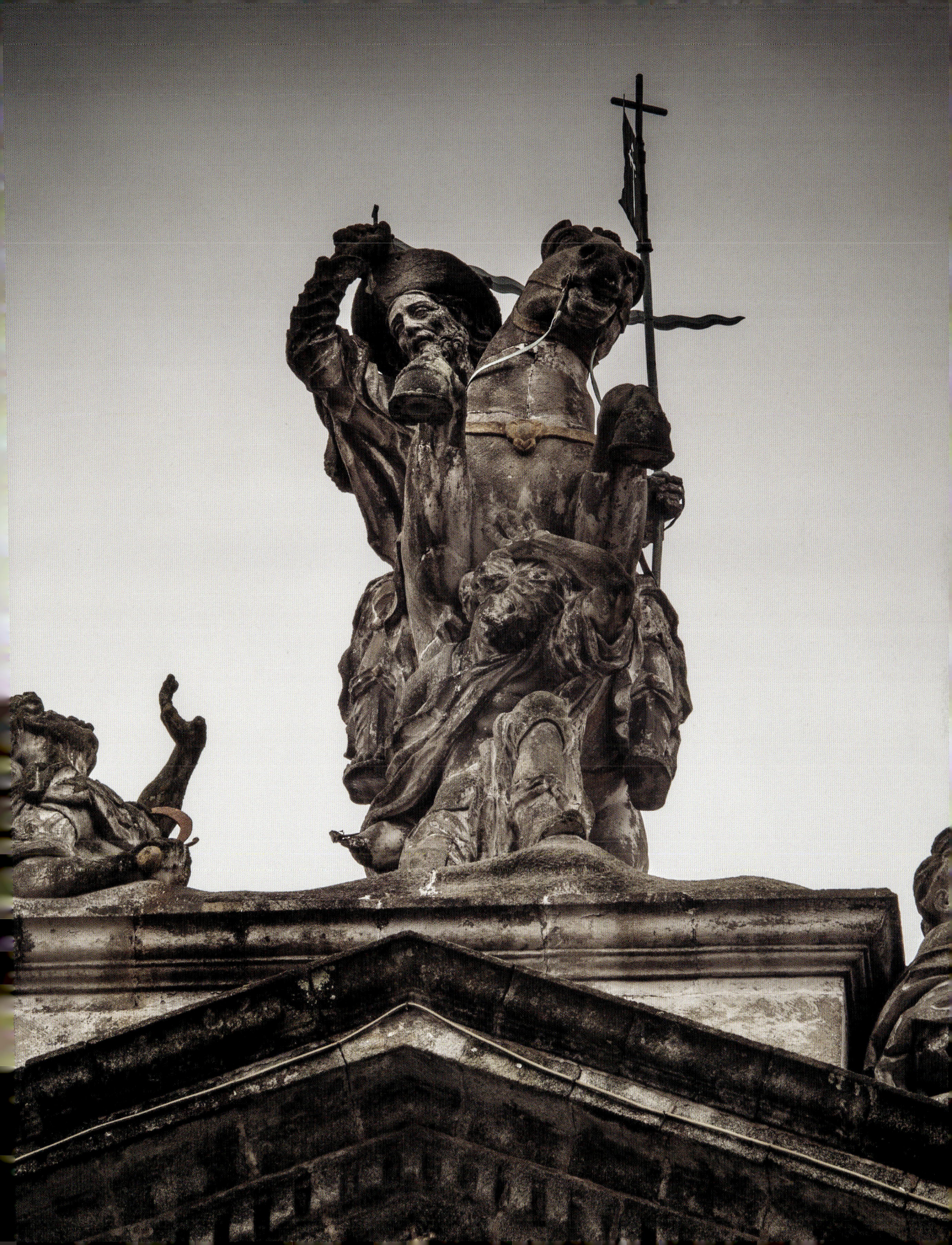

SPAIN
OUR LADY OF COVADONGA
Covadonga, Asturias

The remote sanctuary of Covadonga is an important Marian shrine on the western fringes of the Picos de Europa National Park. The Picos is a mountain range in the northern Spanish province of Asturias, comprising three separate massifs of spectacular jagged limestone peaks rising to more than 2,500 metres/8,200 feet. Steep-sided valleys linked by ancient tracks once used by traders and herdsmen are now popular hiking trails, and although this idyllic setting is ideal for today's tourists and outdoor enthusiasts, the very nature of the landscape was also perfect for guerilla warfare. Invariably, pre-tenth-century history can be vague about precise dates and the order in which notable events happened, but in terms of Spanish history, the eighth-century legend of the Battle of Covadonga was deemed to have been a catalyst for the Christian Reconquest to free Spain from the yoke of Moorish occupation.

Our Lady of Covadonga is the patron saint of Asturias and she is affectionately referred to as La Santina (Little Saint). It was the Virgin Mary's spiritual support that enabled a significantly outnumbered Christian force to defeat a Moorish army amid the wild, rocky valley of Covadonga. The locals used their intimate knowledge of the terrain (and its caves) to gradually overcome their enemy and any surviving Moorish fighters fled in panic across unfamiliar territory to either perish in the hostile terrain or be ruthlessly put to the sword.

The Asturian fighters were led by Pelayo, a Visigoth nobleman proclaimed King of Asturias in 718. The legend of the Virgin's statue invariably acquired several versions over time, but suffice to say that at some point prior to or possibly during the battle, Pelayo found himself in the cave with a statue of the Virgin. Therefore, the Christian victory at the Battle of Covadonga in 722 was attributed to Her influence.

The first shrine at Covadonga comprised a wooden chapel and altar to the Madonna and, despite the remoteness of its location, the cave became a significant place of pilgrimage. Unfortunately, a disastrous fire gutted the cave's interior in 1777, including the precious statue of the Virgin. A sixteenth-century replacement was donated by the Chapter of Oviedo Cathedral in 1778

The cave of Covadonga and diminutive chapel are one of the more unusual Marian shrines of Europe. Despite being significantly different to most of its peers, it nevertheless relies on the legend of the chance discovery of a Virgin statue for its existence.

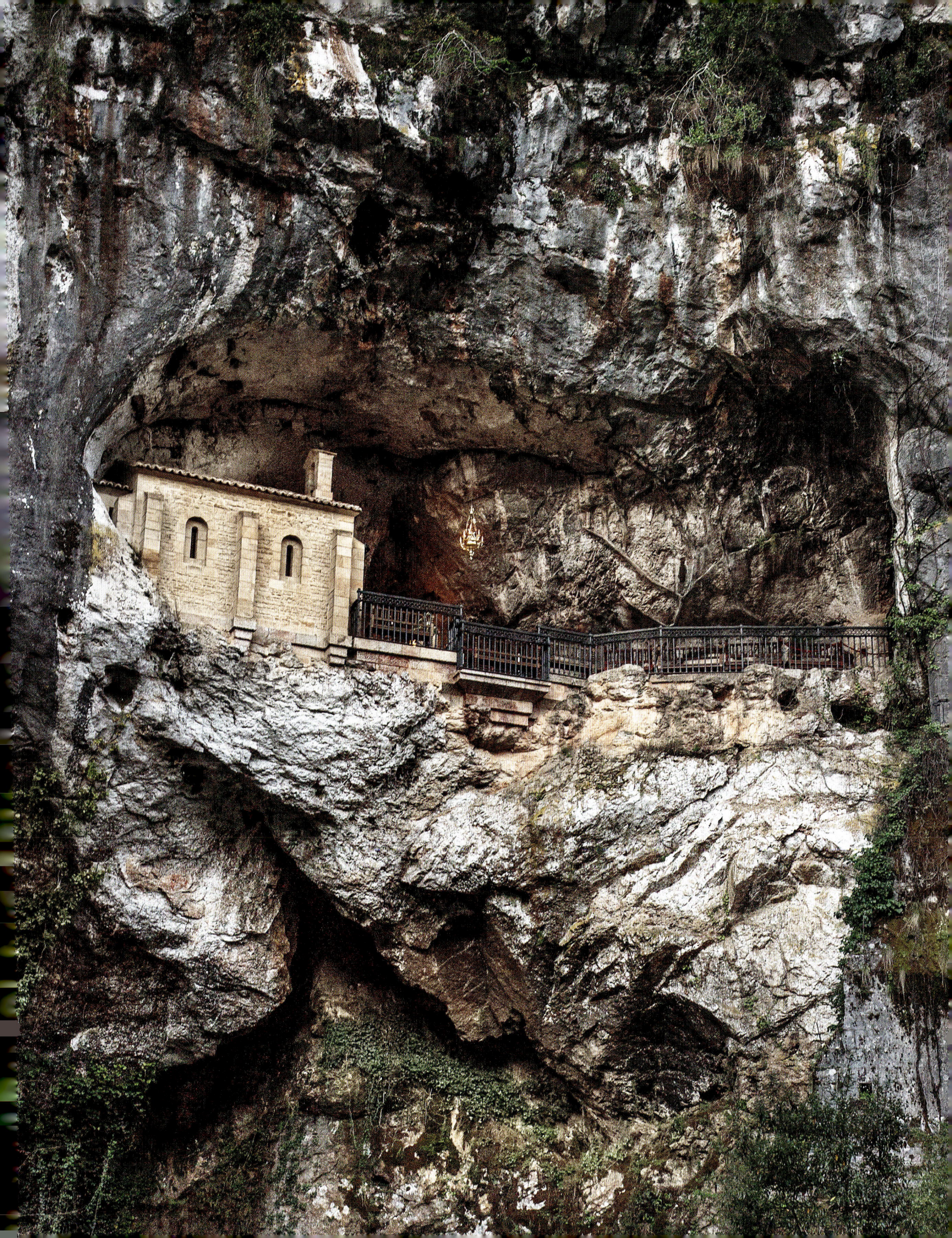

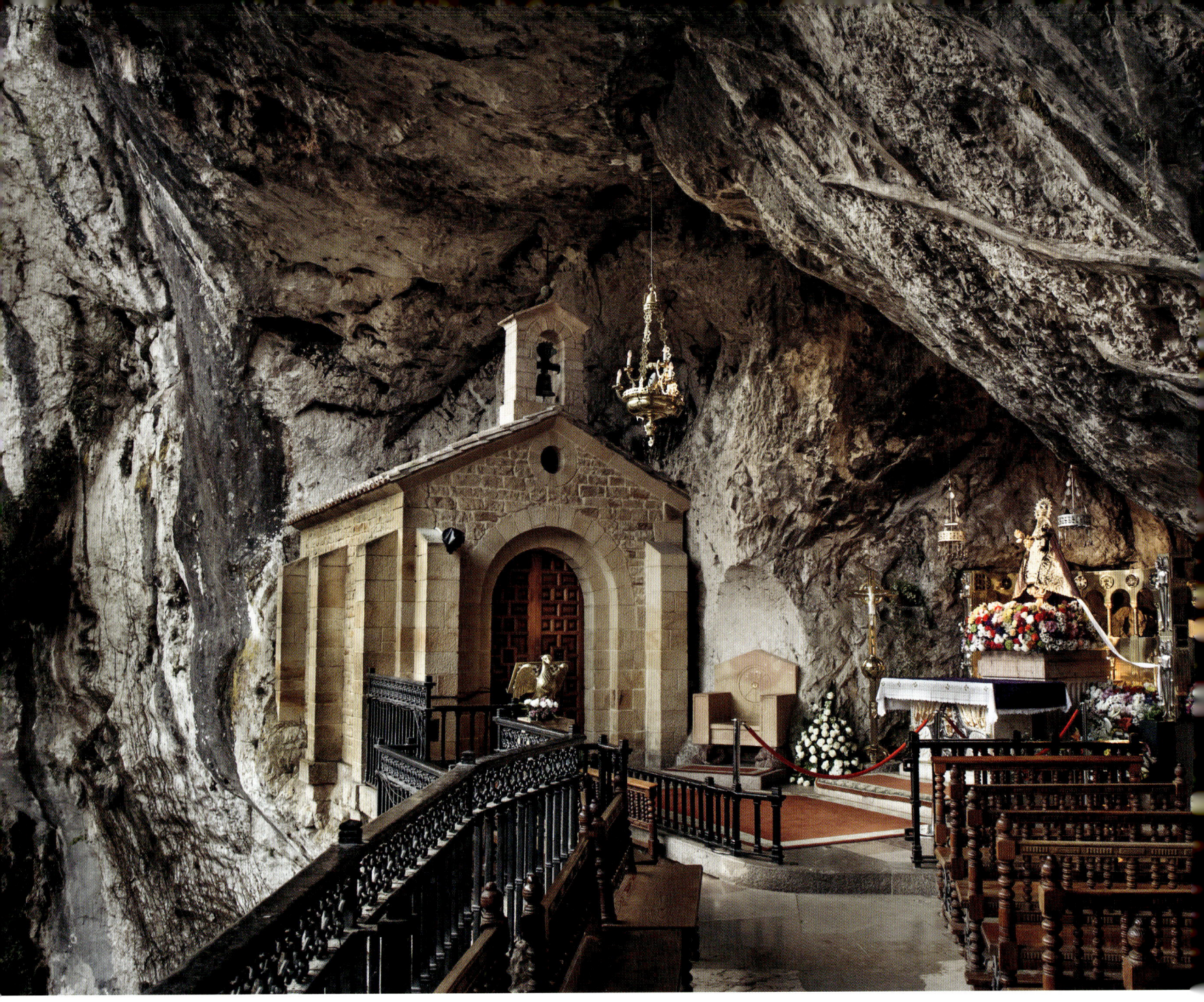

and so there was a huge incentive to rebuild as soon as possible and create a new shrine. However, attempts were spasmodic and the restorations never reached absolute fulfilment, although the adjacent basilica fared better, having been started in 1877. It was completed just twenty-four years later in 1901.

Unfortunately, all was still not well with the state of the cave shrine as the twentieth century progressed, not least when serious damage was inflicted during the Spanish Civil War (1936–9). Salvation finally, and somewhat belatedly, arrived when the renowned architect Luis Menéndez Pidal was commissioned to accomplish what so many before had failed to achieve: a worthy shrine for La Santina.

The cave is accessed either by a long flight of steps or through a tunnel hewn out of the solid mountain cliff. The lighting is just perfect because it creates atmosphere but ensures safety, and the chapel within the cave becomes more clearly visible with every step. The simple stone building was cleverly constructed in the distinctive Asturian pre-Romanesque style, and as pilgrims

The cave's interior is not over-endowed with space for pilgrims, worshippers and tourists, but a roped entry and exit system copes most of the time. The steep steps leading up from the roadside below were frequently climbed on hands and knees by pilgrims.

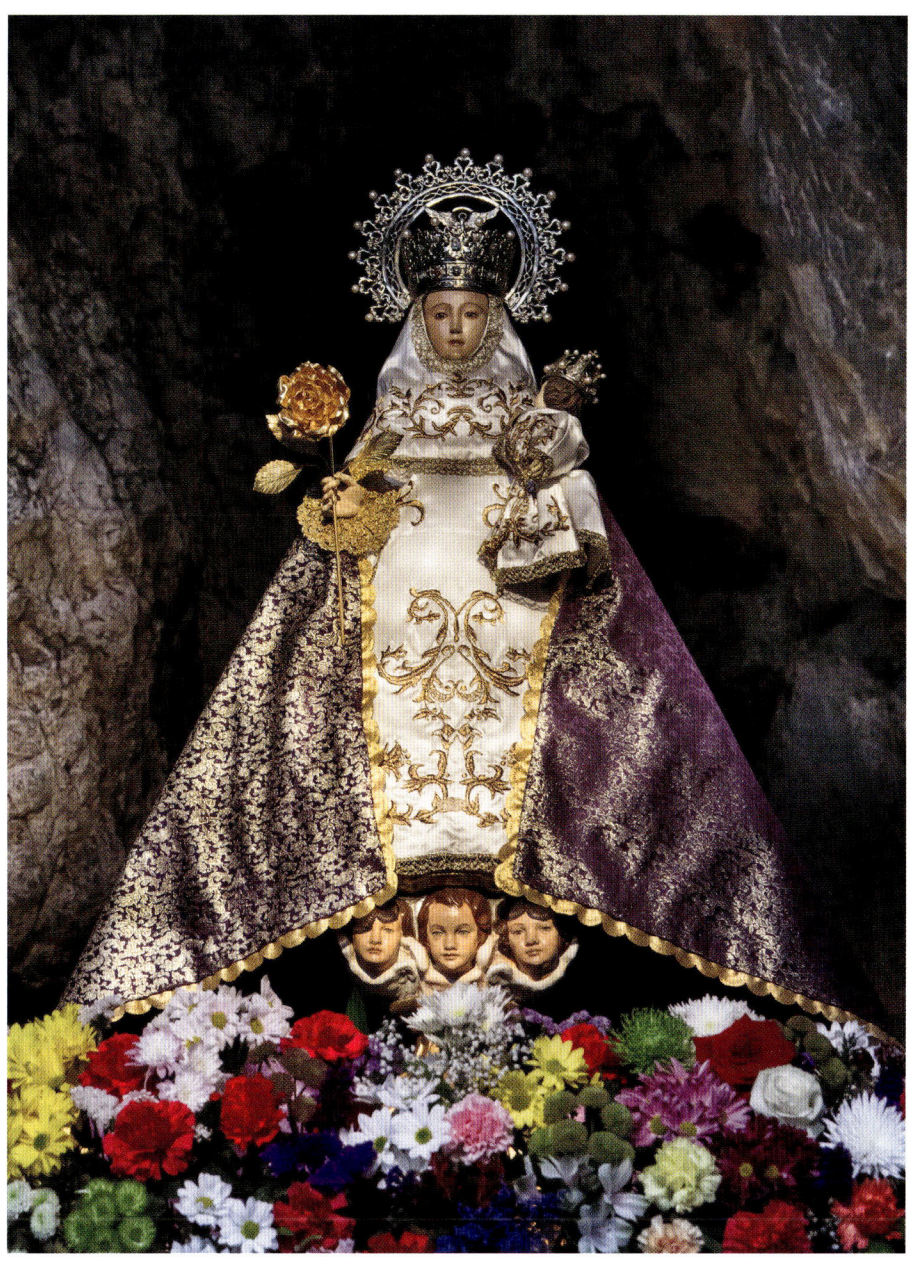

The Virgin and Child statue is the reason that many people visit to the shrine, but it can be frustrating for pilgrims wanting to engage in quiet contemplation and prayer while tourists simply want souvenir photographs.

(*overleaf*) The mighty basilica of Covadonga photographed at dusk.

enter the shrine by climbing a few final steps, they pass by the tombs of Pelayo, his wife and his daughter, all lodged inside a rock niche. Just below the cave, several individual spouts of water perpetually gush out from the rock face into a pool set immediately below. It goes without saying that as the pool stands right next to the basilica's access road, its rocky bottom glitters with coins.

The year 2018 was a significant and memorable one for Covadonga with many anniversaries to celebrate, not least the first centenary of the Virgin statue's canonical coronation by Pope Benedict XV in 1918, attended by the reigning monarch Alfonso XIII. That year also marked the one hundredth anniversary of the National Park's creation, and the access road up into the mountains now winds past Covadonga towards two spectacularly sited lakes, where tarmac peters out into stony paths. The monastic community at Covadonga has successfully evolved into being a dual-purpose destination: while still fulfilling its historical role as a much-revered Marian shrine, it now also caters for day-trippers heading up into the hills.

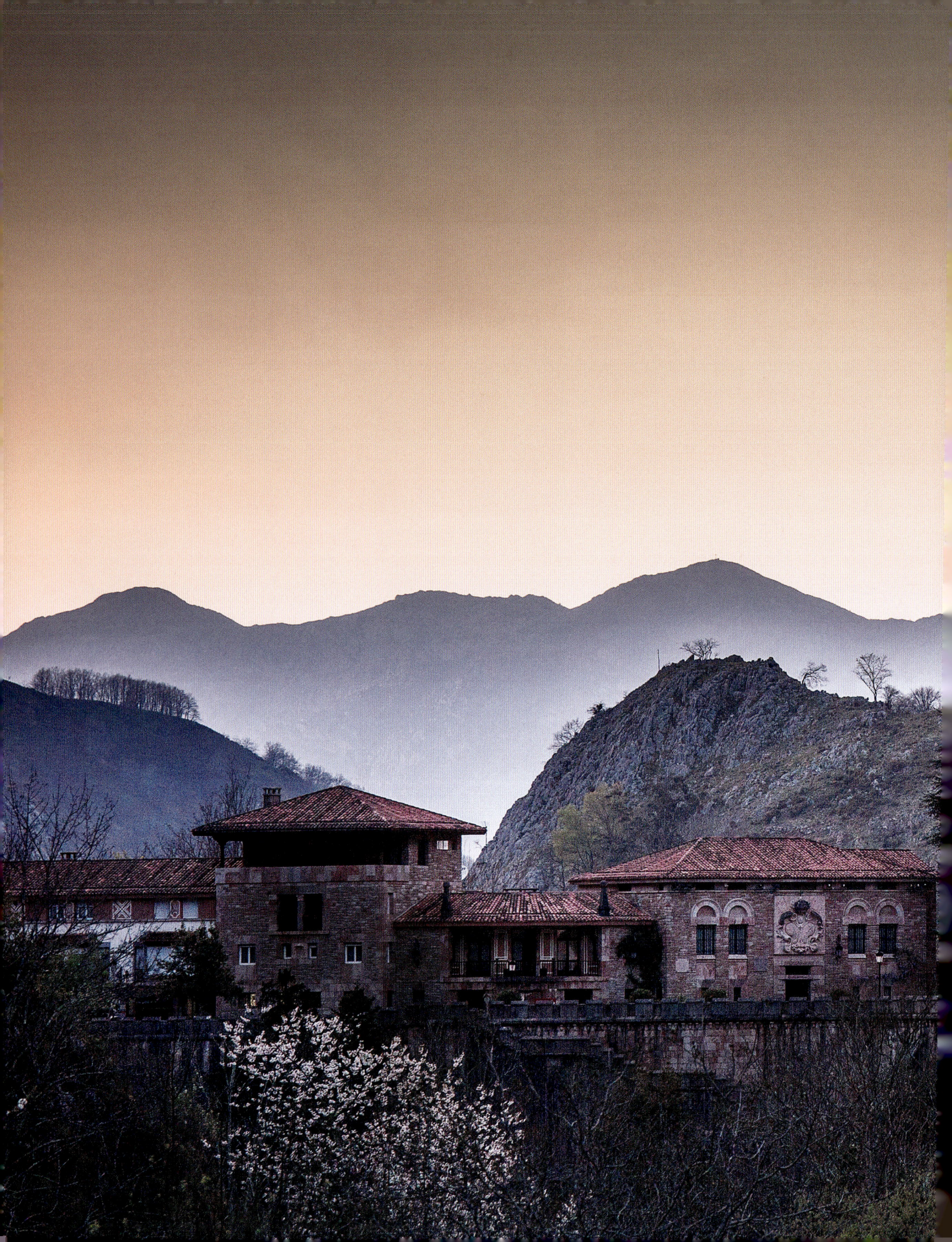

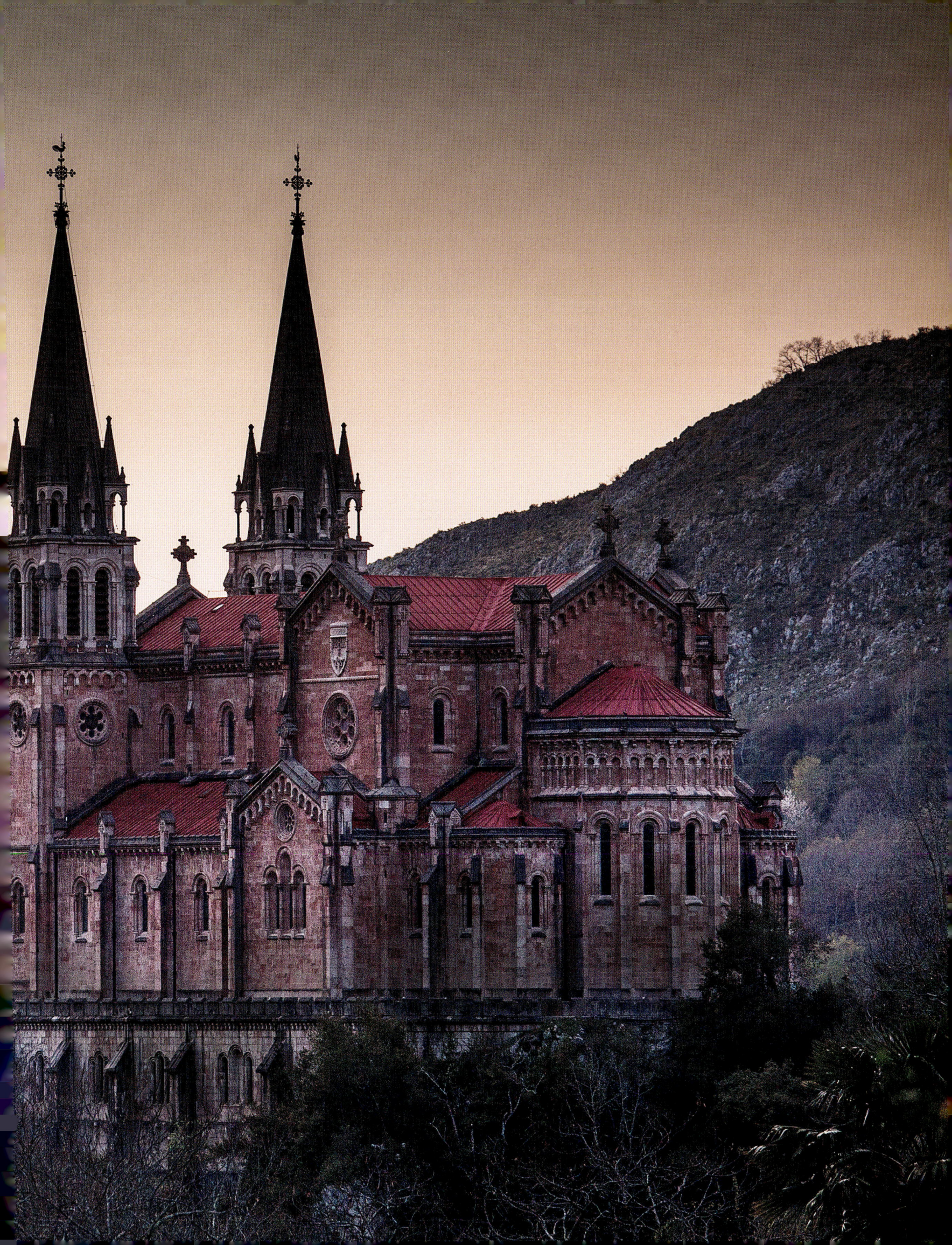

SPAIN
OUR LADY OF THE PILLAR
Zaragoza, Aragon

Much of what we hear about St James the Apostle relates more to the legend surrounding the miraculous discovery of his remains at the beginning of the ninth century than to his time in Spain as an Evangelist. Although doubts invariably exist about the validity of his actual travels, historians have traced confirmatory references in some seventh- and eighth-century manuscripts relating specifically to James and a small band of Christians preaching the Gospels. According to legends referring to the origins of the Holy Pillar, James was deep in prayer by the banks of the Ebro, seeking divine guidance, when he received a spiritual visitation from the Virgin Mary. He was instructed to build a church in Her name on the exact location of the encounter. Two variations exist around the 'pillar' element of the story. One tells of the vision of the Virgin standing on a pillar surrounded by angels; the other says that when the manifestation of the vision faded, a statue of the Virgin and Child mounted upon a marble pillar appeared in the ground as a physical token. Either way, the apostle complied with the Virgin's request by ensuring that a small chapel was erected on the exact site, and he then travelled back to the Holy Land and was subsequently martyred at the hands of Herod Agrippa I in AD 44.

Although the legend of the Virgin and the Pillar is dismissed by sceptics as pure fantasy, this becomes immaterial when one considers the significant contribution such stories have made to many aspects of religious, social and cultural history in both Zaragoza and the rest of Spain. The unfaltering devout veneration of the Virgin Mary as the Mother of God cannot be underestimated, and Our Lady of the Pillar is one of Europe's most influential Marian shrines. This deep affection is readily apparent in the huge numbers of women from Spanish-speaking nations who have been christened 'Pilar' in honour of the Virgin. Pope John Paul II made two pilgrimages to Zaragoza during the 1980s and affirmed Our Lady of the Pillar's role as 'Mother of the Hispanic peoples'.

Although the basilica is impressive in close-up from the adjoining plaza, from a more distant view one is able to better appreciate the complex ensemble of towers, domes and cupolas, whose mini-domes are symmetrically finished with visually arresting polychrome tiles.

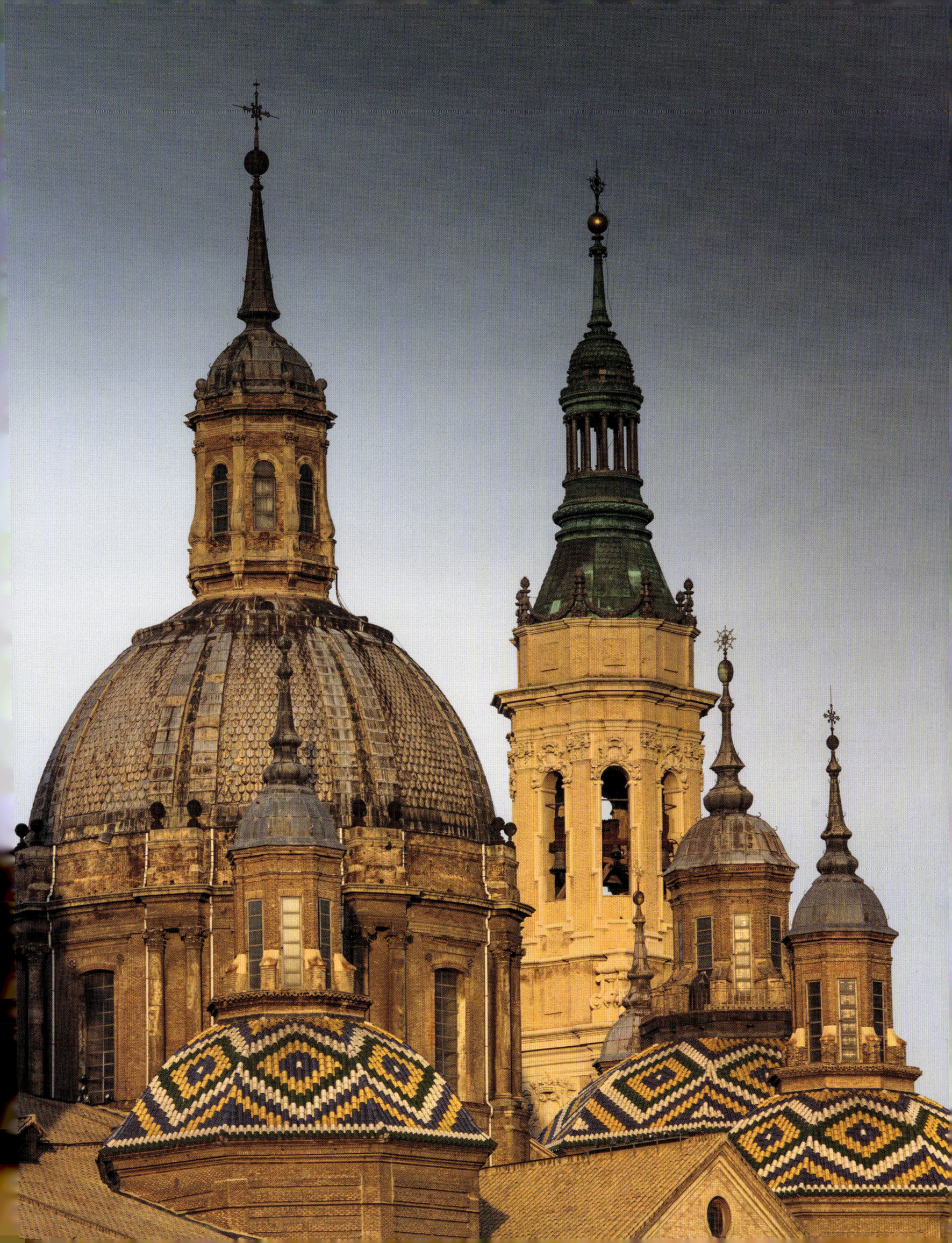

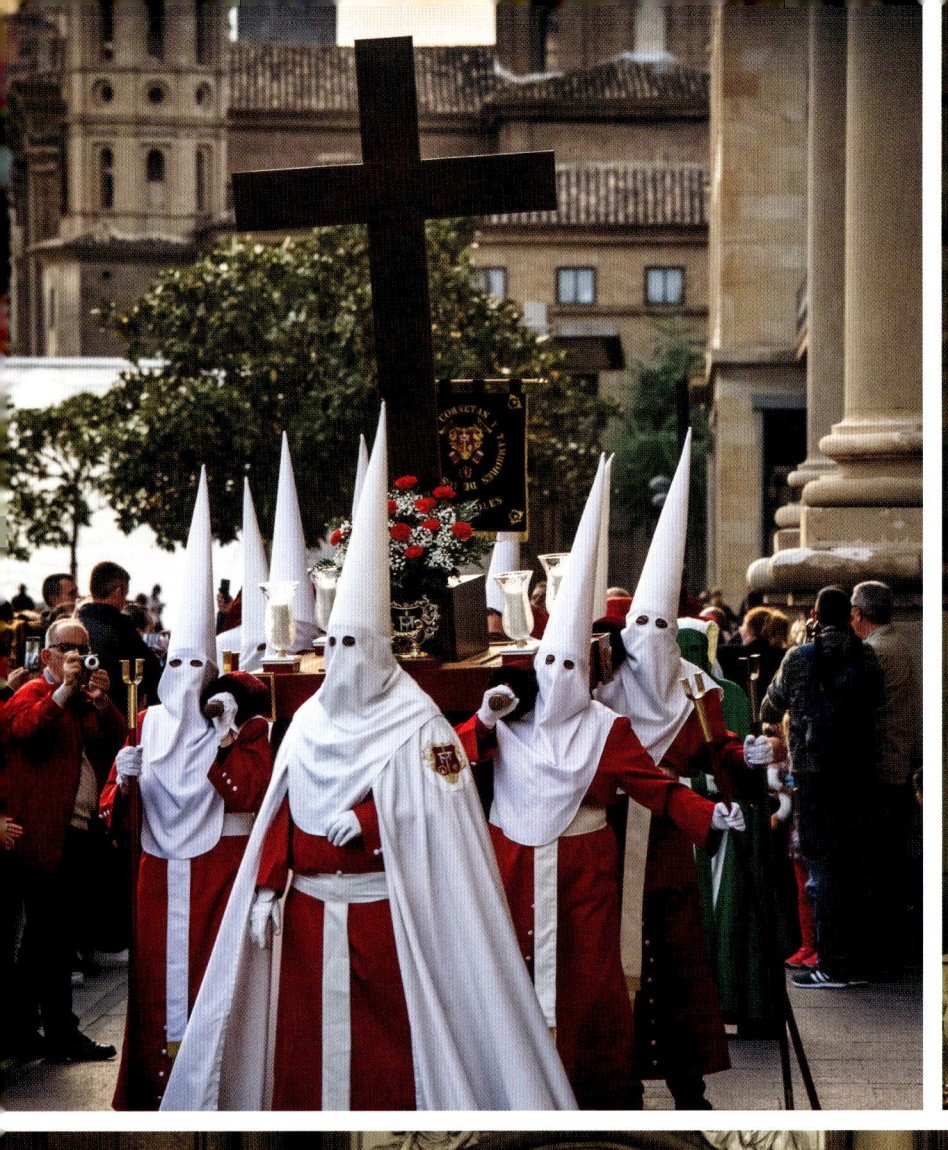
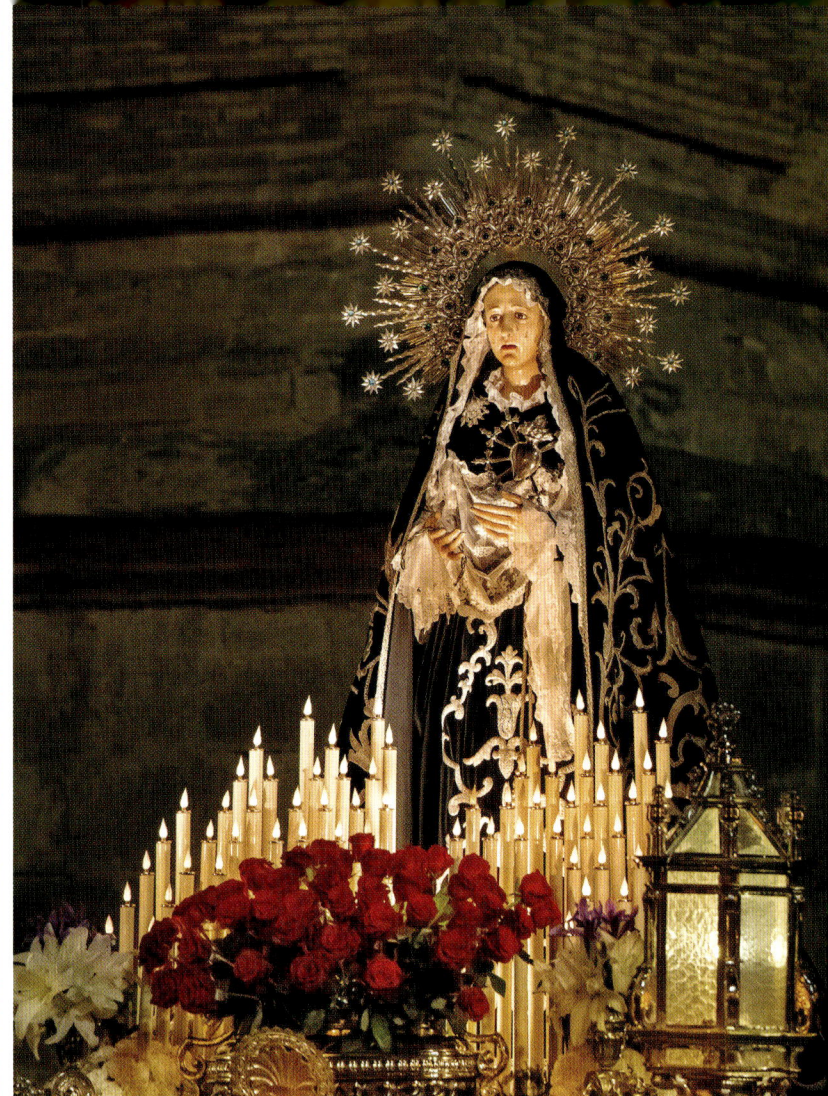

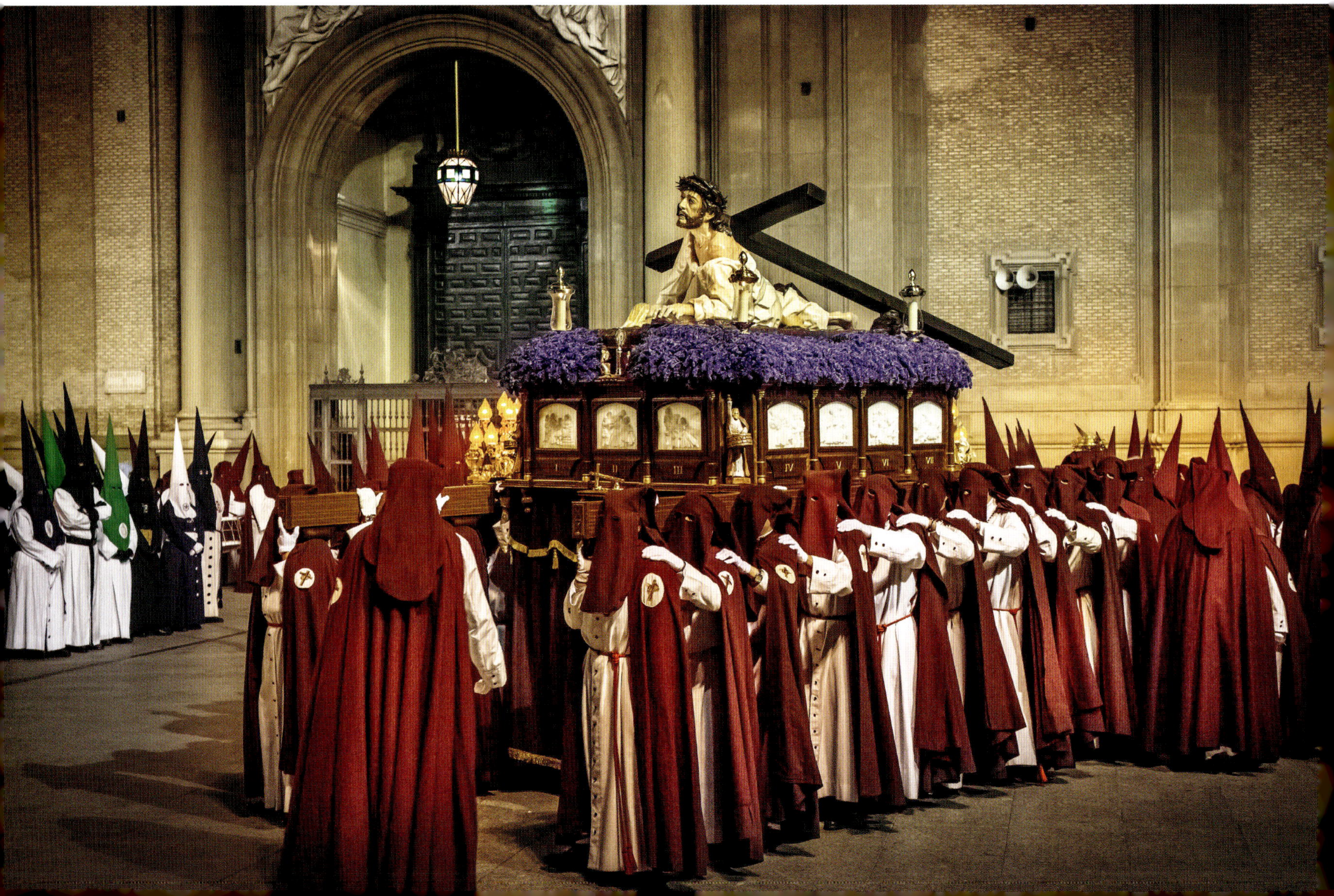

Holy Week is a significant event in Spain and Zaragoza's processions in the week leading up to Easter are particular moving. The robed figures (*nazarenos*) wear pointed hoods with eyeholes (*capirotes*) designed to enable the faithful to repent anonymously without being recognized as self-confessed sinners (*top left*). Each brotherhood presents a float bearing either an image of Christ Crucified (*bottom*) or another biblical scene and then a statue of the Virgin, usually portrayed as a mother weeping for her dead son (*top right*).

The eighth-century Moorish invasion of Spain left Zaragoza under Islamic rule until the Reconquest, when it was taken back into Spanish hands by the king of Aragon and Navarre, Alfonso I (the Battler) in 1118. There had, of course, been desecration of many Christian shrines during that period, but the people of Zaragoza ensured that the marble pillar was protected. A twelfth-century Romanesque church subsequently replaced the humble chapel and it is perhaps surprising that a small tympanum from that original building is featured on the current façade, given how the appearance, layout and alignment of the basilica have changed over time. The current church was instigated by Charles II in 1681, and regardless of how the successive architects and designers were commissioned to update and restyle the basilica – one immovable feature was the pillar bearing the Virgin and Child. The original had sadly been destroyed by fire in 1434, but its wooden successor was created by the Aragonese sculptor Juan de la Huerta shortly thereafter.

The Chapel of the Pillar was the work of architect Ventura Rodríguez, and although he was responsible for rebuilding substantial parts of the basilica in Classical style, he elected to use a Baroque treatment for the actual chapel. It is a magnificent oval structure entered through a curved line of huge columns, leading into the heart of the chapel where worshippers and pilgrims sit before three adjacent altars. The right-hand one hosts the statue of the Virgin; the left features a portrayal of St James and his first converts, and the central altar is dominated by a truly magnificent eighteenth-century interpretation of the Assumption.

The rest of the basilica is an imposing and impressive space, lined with many side chapels adorned with significant works of art in their own right, including frescoes and paintings by Goya and Velázquez. Aside from the intense atmosphere and artistry within the Chapel of the Pillar, the sheer majesty and riverside setting of the basilica must surely place Zaragoza near the top of any list of Europe's most impressively sited churches.

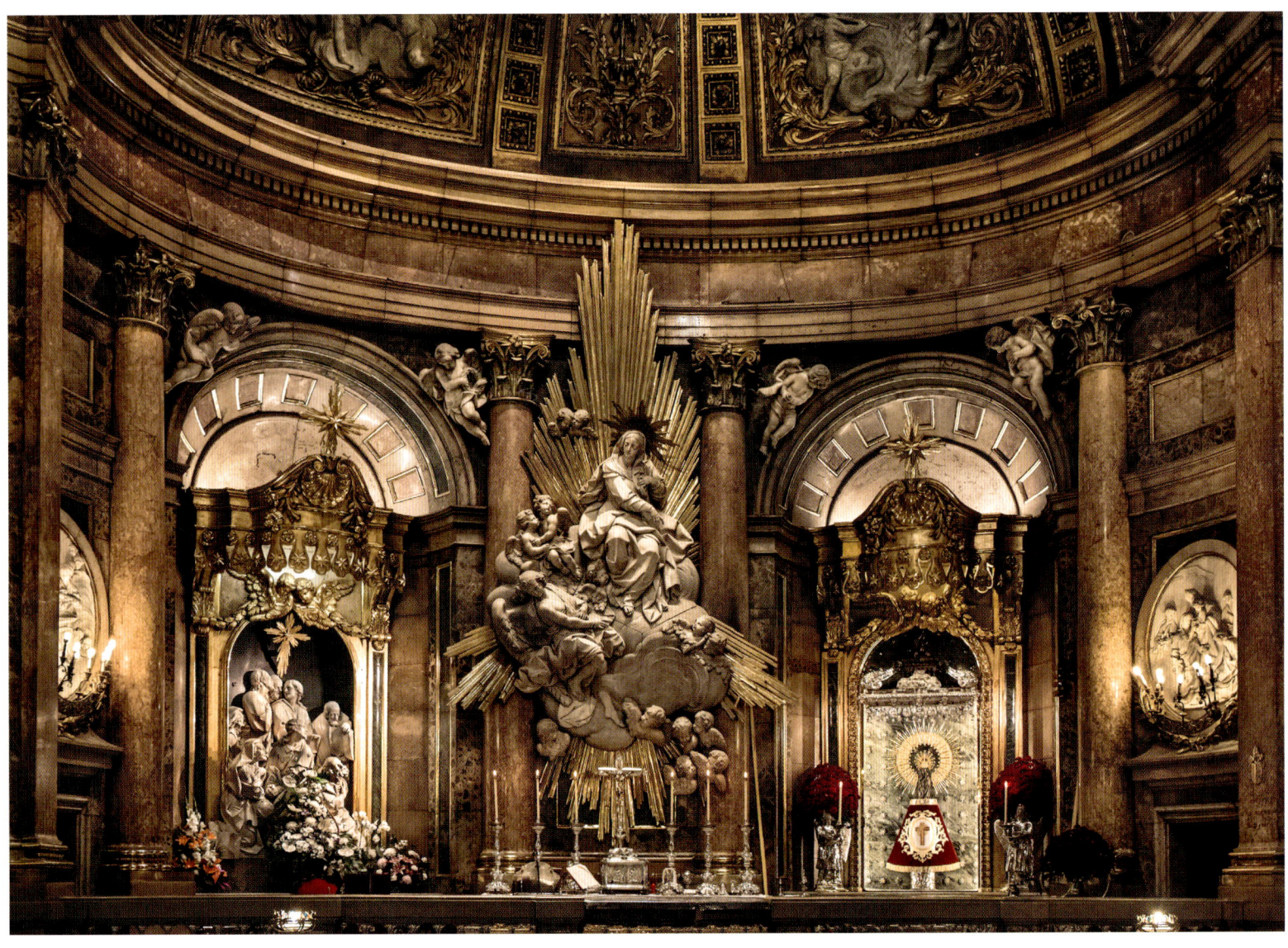

(*above*) The Chapel of the Pillar is almost a church within a church. The seating area for those seeking private prayer and devotion may be comparatively small, but a larger congregation gathered outside the perimeter of the columns, cleverly designed to embrace the chapel, can feel equally included during mass. The three altars (*from left to right*) feature a dramatically sculpted portrayal of St James and his first seven converts, the magnificent Assumption of the Virgin and the contrastingly diminutive statue of the Virgin set upon the pillar.

(*right*) Because the statue is only 38 centimetres/ 15 inches tall, the traditional elaborately decorated vestment customarily used to dress the Virgin in Marian shrines is instead placed over the upper section of the pillar.

(*overleaf*) The view looking directly upwards into the magnificent dome of the nave.

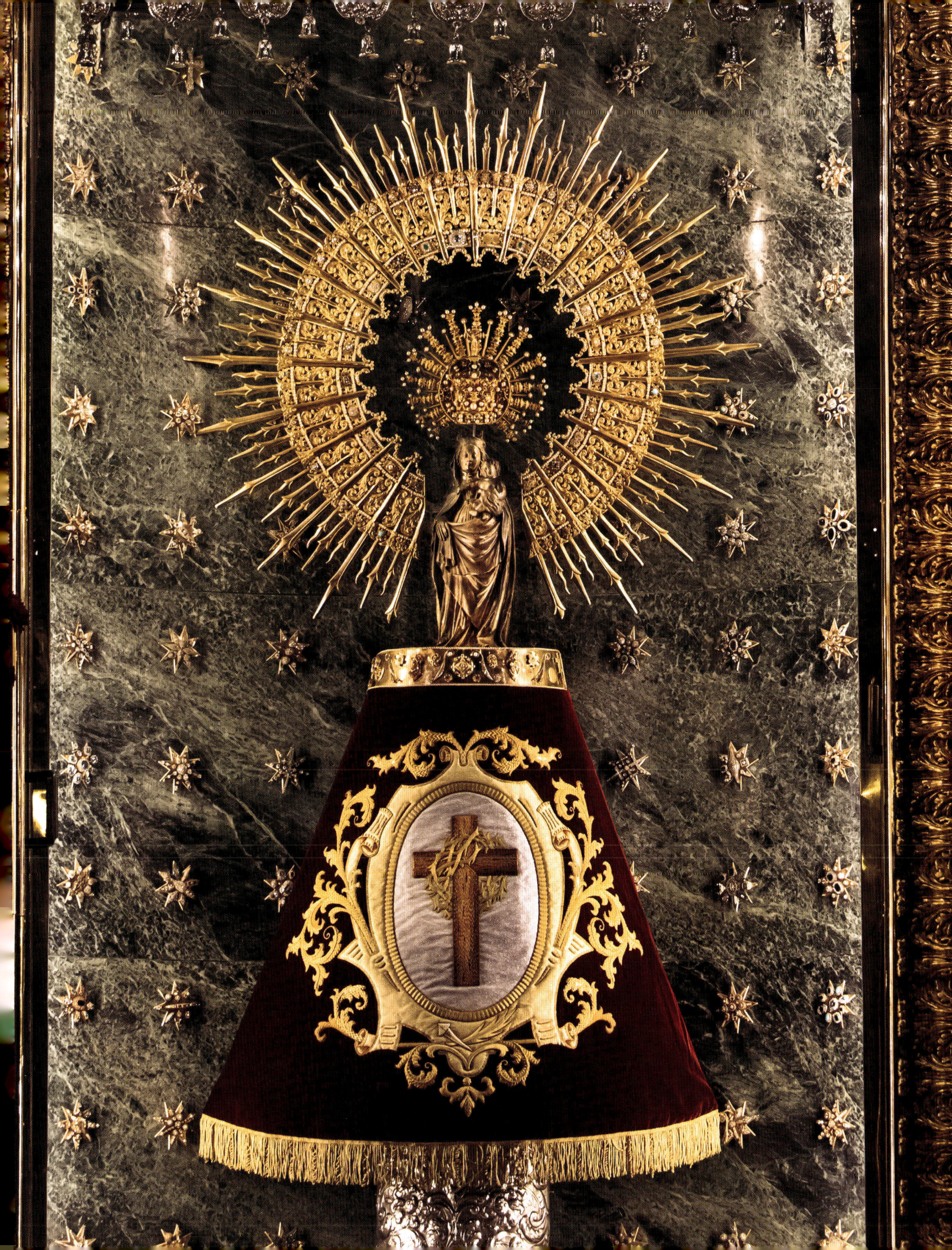

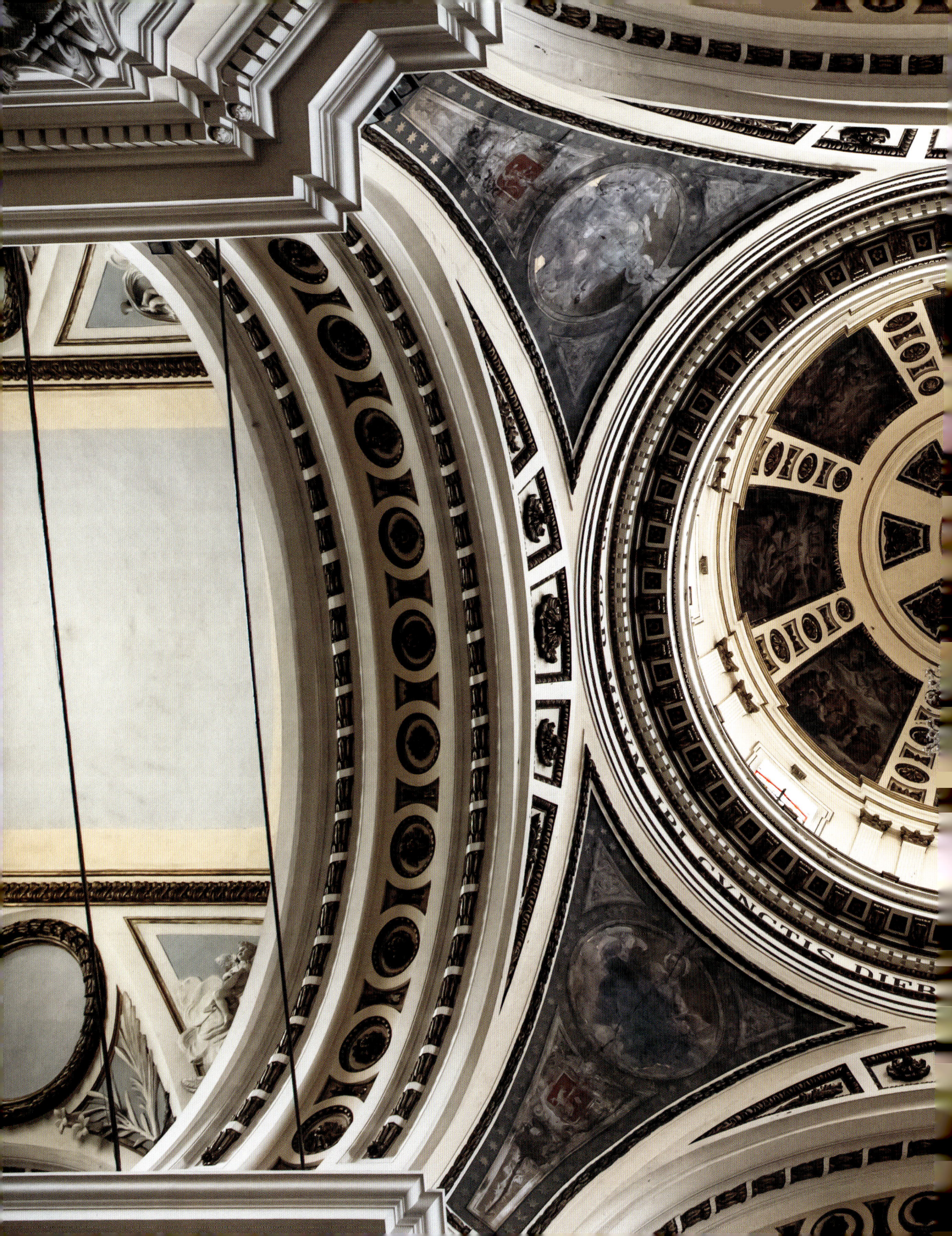

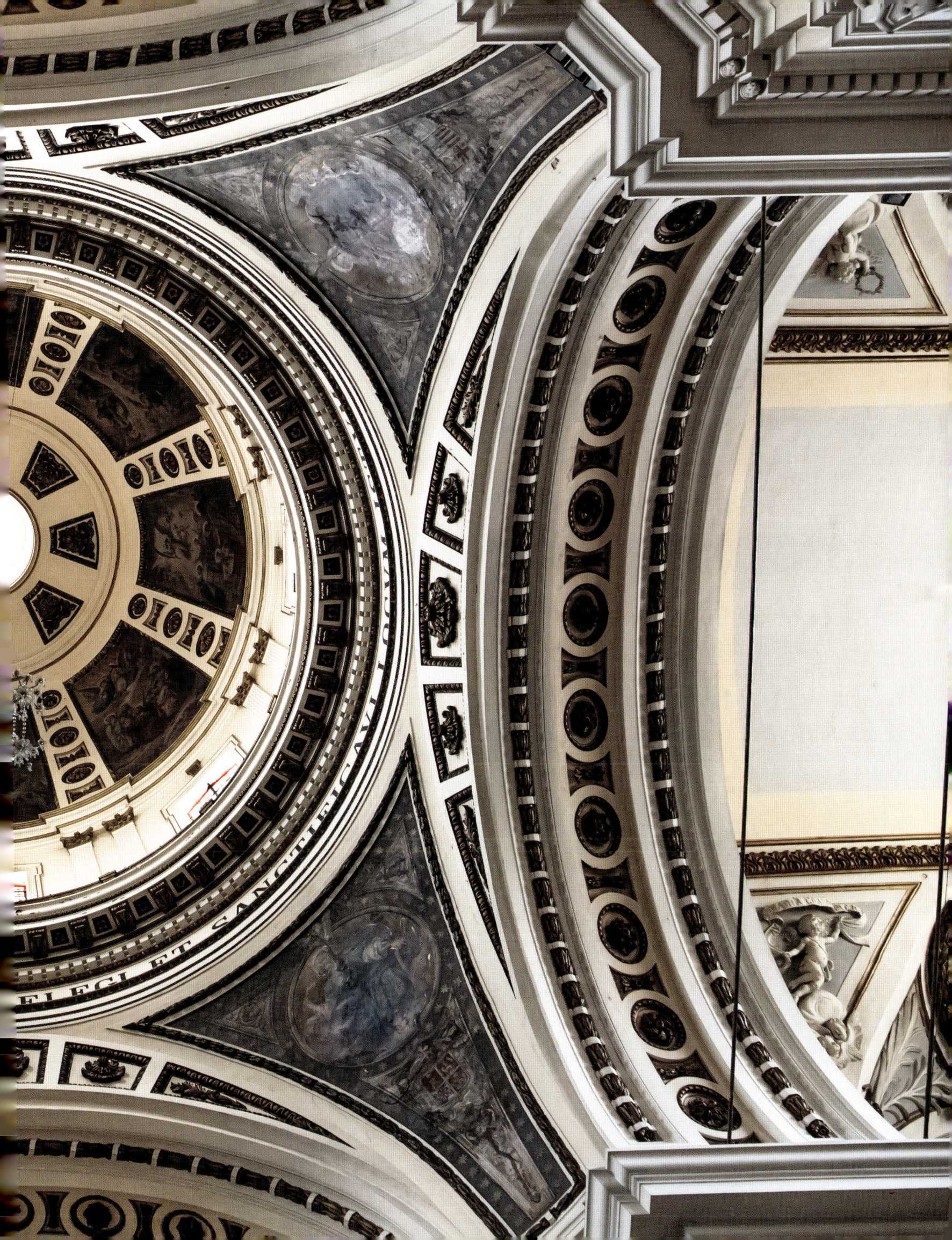

SPAIN
ABBEY OF MONTSERRAT
Montserrat, Catalonia

La Moreneta (the Dark One) is a dramatic polychrome statue of the Virgin located in the Benedictine monastery of Montserrat, some 30 kilometers/19 miles west of Barcelona. Pope Leo XIII officially proclaimed the statue of the Madonna as patron saint of Catalonia in 1881, but it had already been worshipped and revered for many years prior to receiving the papal accolade. The mountain landscape around the monastery has long been associated with remote hermitages and devout monasticism, but those small isolated outposts only began to flourish again once the area was released from Muslim occupation in 875. Four slightly larger hermitages with individual chapels were subsequently founded, and the one dedicated to Santa María (St Mary) was converted and expanded into a monastery by Oliva, Bishop of Vic and Abbot of Ripoll, who consequently became Montserrat's first abbot towards the end of the eleventh century. The actual origins of the monastic foundation date back to 880 and the alleged discovery of the Virgin statue by a group of young shepherd boys in the Santa Cova (Holy Cave). They alerted their parents and the local priest to the fact that they had been led to the cave and its precious contents after having repeatedly experienced a combination of bright shining lights and strange music wafting through the air. However, although it was an especially romantic account of the iconic discovery, there remains no tangible evidence that an ancient statue from that exact period existed. La Moreneta was actually sculpted during the late twelfth century and it is widely regarded as a jewel of Catalan Romanesque art.

Most Catholic pilgrimage shrines are endowed with a traditional Stations of the Cross route, providing the opportunity for prayer and contemplation before each of the fourteen sculpted tableaux. The length and complexity of the route depends on whether the shrine is in an urban or rural location. Given the spectacular setting of Montserrat, it comes as no surprise to discover that the Way of the Cross weaves through extended tranquil surroundings until it reaches a small chapel marking the Santa Cova grotto.

A small segment of the monastery's original fifteenth-century cloister serves as a poignant reminder of past architectural elegance, prior to the desecration and destruction inflicted during the early nineteenth century. A completely new cloister, with a garden and central fountain, was added in 1929.

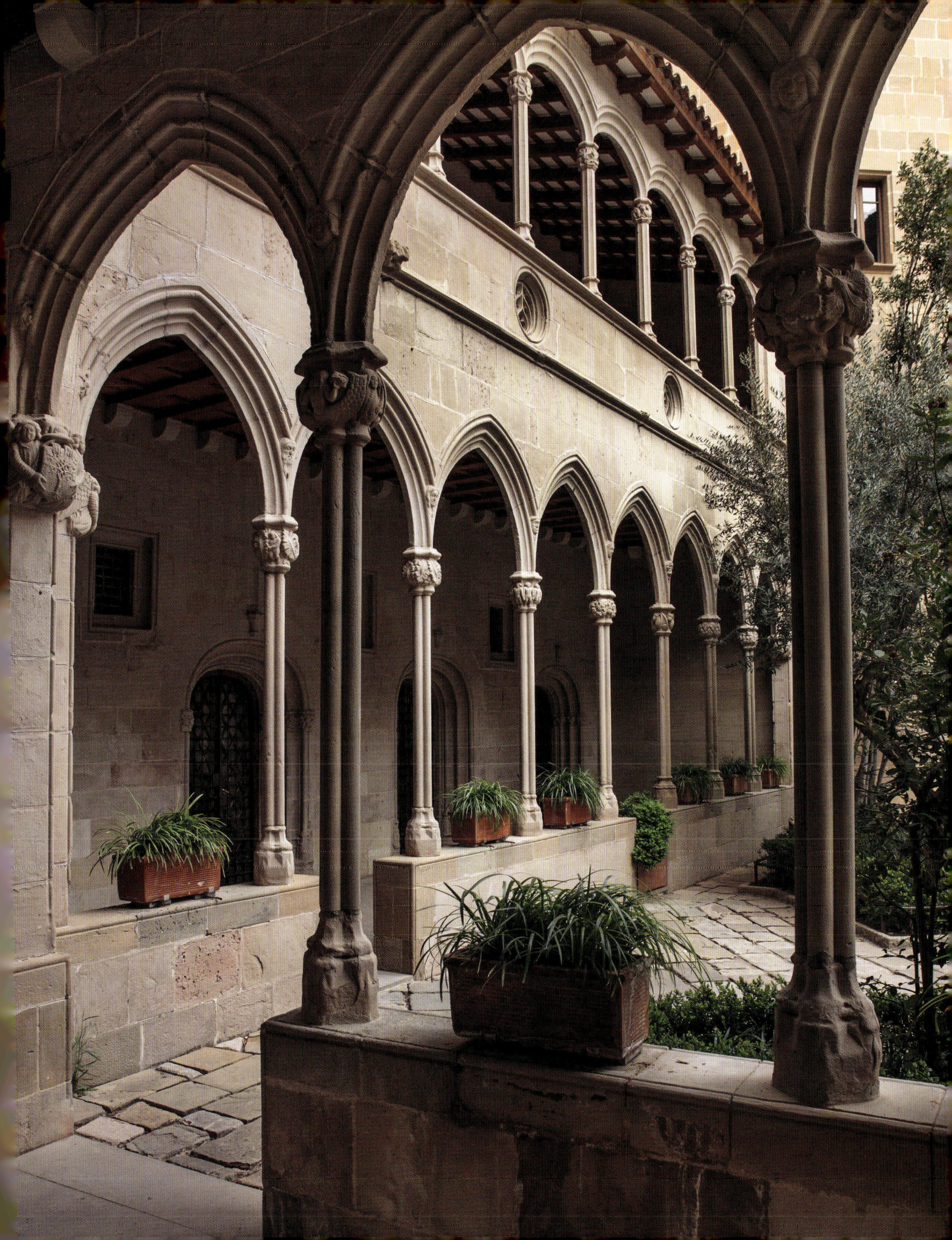

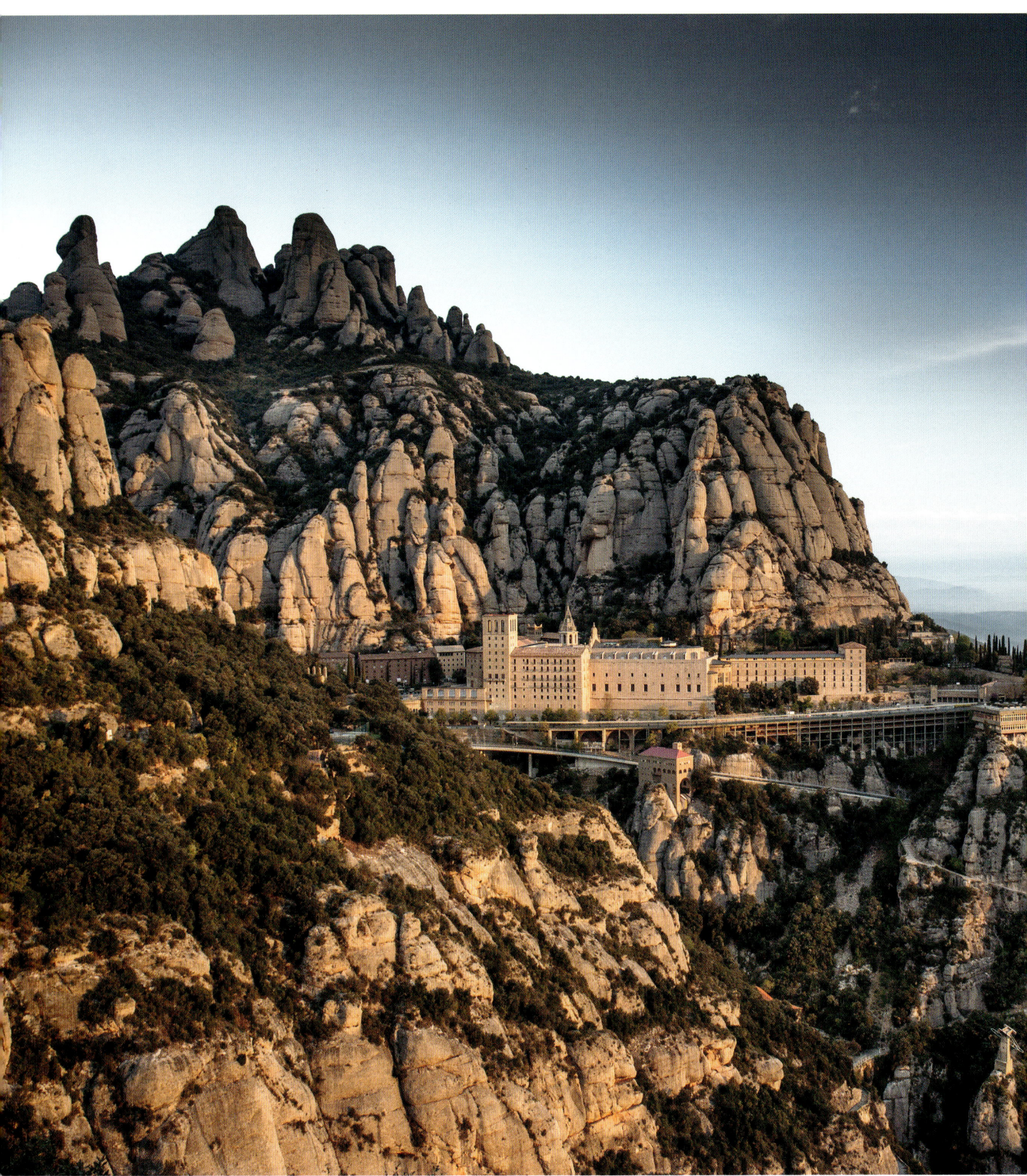

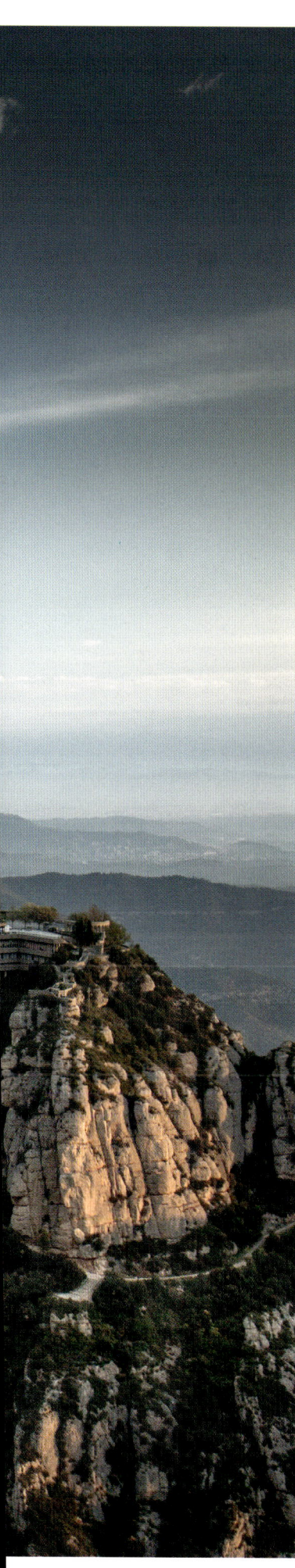

A distant view of the monastery at sunrise reveals its isolated setting beneath the saw-tooth mountain ridge from which Montserrat derives its name (serrated mountain). It also highlights the logistical problems faced by those who undertook its original construction centuries before the mountain railway existed.

The Gothic-style interior of the basilica is more than worthy of its role in the religious history of Montserrat, but it is sad that such a significant shrine should have suffered cataclysmic damage when most of the monastery buildings and basilica were looted and destroyed by Napoleon's army during the Peninsula Wars (1811–12). The process of reconstruction progressed through the nineteenth century and into the next, until the monastery was temporarily abandoned during the Spanish Civil War. The final stages of regeneration began with the laying of the first stone of the elaborate new façade in 1942, followed five years later by an important ceremony marking the enthronement of the image of the Mother of God. That formal reintroduction of La Moreneta was seen as a significant moment of faith and hope to aid the process of civic reconciliation during the post Civil War era.

Montserrat is a fully functioning Benedictine monastery with up to one hundred monks in residence, and it is renowned for its choir school, one of the oldest in Europe; its existence can be traced back to the fourteenth century. In common with many similar establishments, the school provides a balanced academic and musical education and the choir sing almost every day in the monastery's basilica. The Benedictine monks also run a successful independent publishing business, producing both religion-based and secular titles, many of which are printed in Catalan.

It is perhaps unfortunate for pilgrims and those seeking peace and solitude that Montserrat's relatively close proximity to Barcelona makes it day-trip perfection for tour operators. However, there is a hotel and other pilgrim accommodations attached to the monastery, and it is one of those magical dusk and dawn locations worthy of an overnight stay. Being able to savour the timeless atmosphere of Montserrat is made even easier by the fact that most independent travellers use the 5-kilometre-/3-mile-long rack railway that climbs smoothly up the mountain from the village of Monistrol below. Trains do not run very late into the evening or start particularly early in the morning and so a tranquil landscape, empty footpaths, an atmospheric cloister and silent basilica are all there to enjoy at one's leisure – until the coaches arrive.

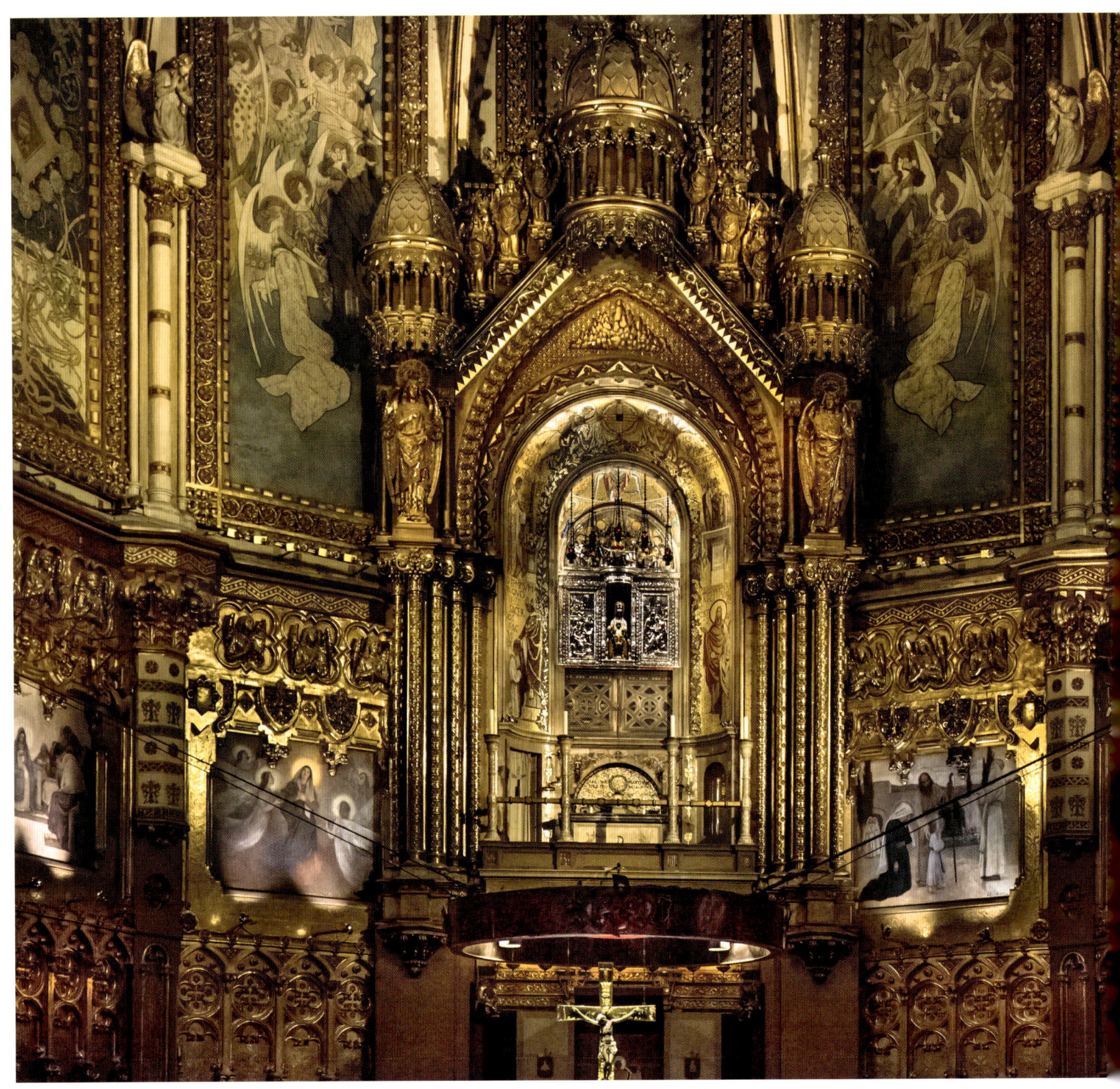

(*above*) The church's twentieth-century reconstruction largely respects its fifteenth-century predecessor in both layout and decoration. The 68m/223ft-long nave is supported on central columns bearing representations of Old Testament prophets, culminating in the high altar and apse hosting the shrine of La Moreneta.

(*opposite*) La Moreneta, the Black Virgin of Montserrat, is set in an elaborately engraved silver altar below a niche of glittering mosaics, protected by a curved glass screen. However, the Virgin's outstretched hand holding a golden orb remains exposed for personal devotional contact.

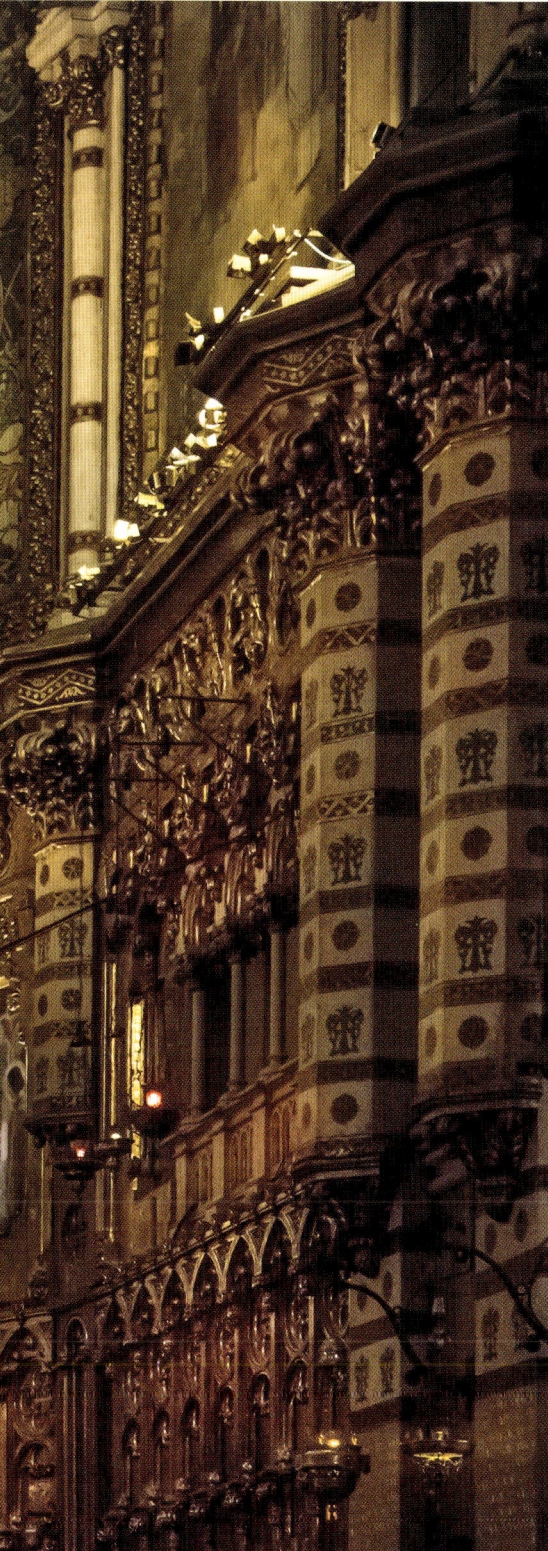

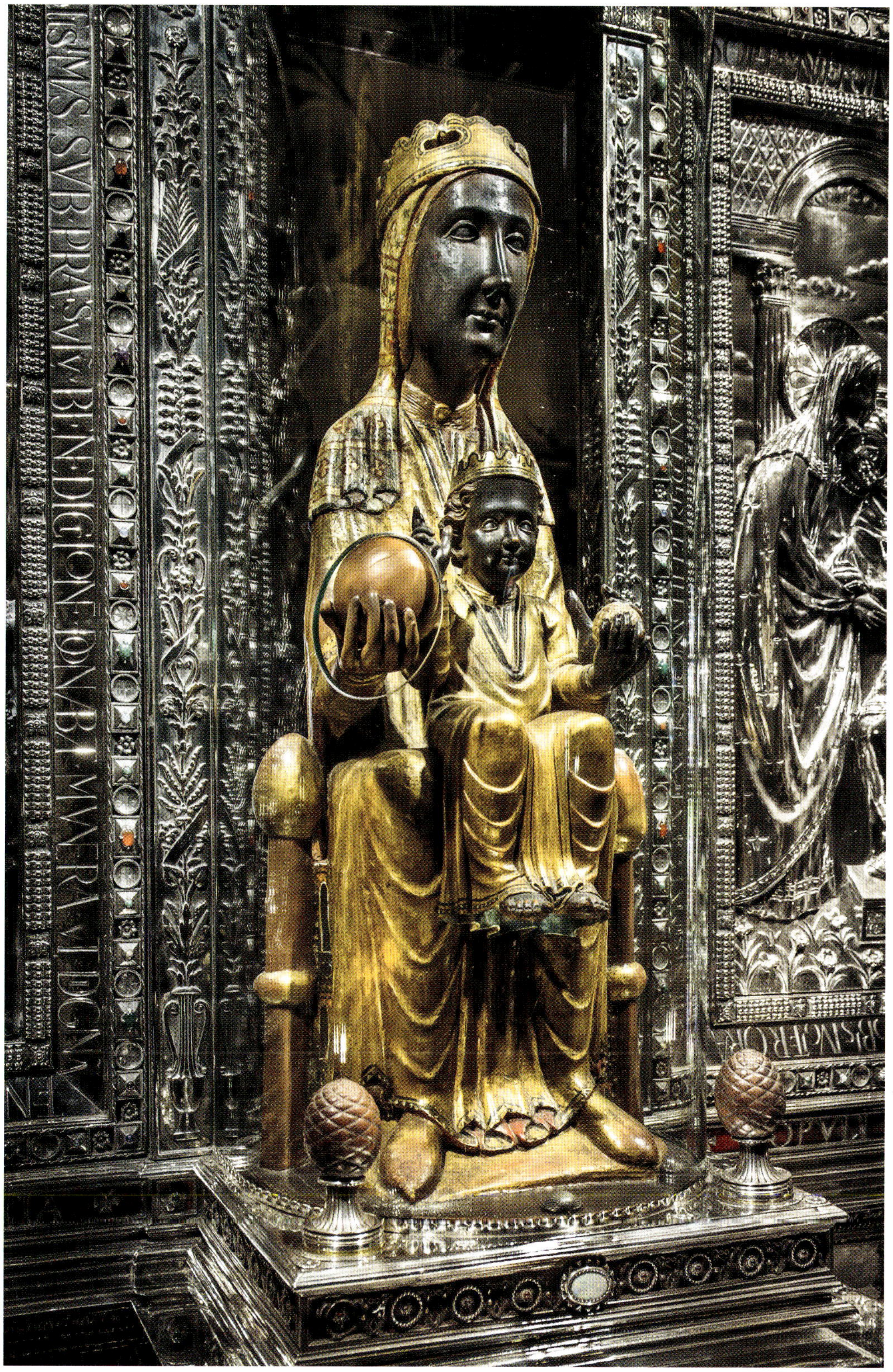

SPAIN

SANCTUARY OF OUR LADY OF EL ROCIO
El Rocio, Huelva

El Rocio's pilgrimage-related history can be traced back to the thirteenth century, and the discovery of the Virgin's statue by a local hunter. The icon was hidden in a tree trunk and a small chapel was soon erected to preserve the image. Although awareness was initially contained to a local level, rumours of miracles pertaining to both physical and mental well-being began spreading farther afield. By the seventeenth century, church brotherhoods from nearby towns began making the journey to El Rocio, and thereafter its popularity and reputation gradually spread outwards into the wider reaches of Andalucía. Some two centuries later, it was well established as an essential spiritual and social pilgrimage lasting up to two weeks.

Unlike many other feast days celebrated within the Catholic Church on fixed dates, the pilgrimage of El Rocio happens at Whitsun (Pentecost) and consequently fluctuates between May and June because Whitsun falls on the seventh Sunday after Easter, which itself is a movable feast. Anyone visiting El Rocio on a normal day and unfamiliar with the village's history might be nonplussed by the sight of empty streets of deep golden sand, rather than tarmac, flanked by deserted buildings, stables and chapels. At first glance, it feels like a Wild West film set, but travel to El Rocio on the big pilgrimage weekend and horses really will be everywhere. Most pilgrims still traditionally arrive from all over Andalucía on foot, on horseback, in ox carts or in horse-drawn wagons. The once-empty houses become full of people, with large tables on the verandas laid out with copious quantities of food and drink. These are the temporary residences of the church brotherhoods. Each group will have ceremonially gathered before their own parish church, or cathedral (in the case of those from Seville), and then travelled for up to four days to reach El Rocio. Although the destination is of huge significance, for most pilgrims it is the physical act of committing to an exhausting and difficult journey and the reaffirmation of community spirit that matter.

The procession of the many brotherhoods is conducted in respectful silence, but the return is accompanied by drums, whistles and joyous celebration. Men wear short-cut grey riding jackets, ladies favour traditional flamenco-style dresses and children emulate their parents with miniature versions.

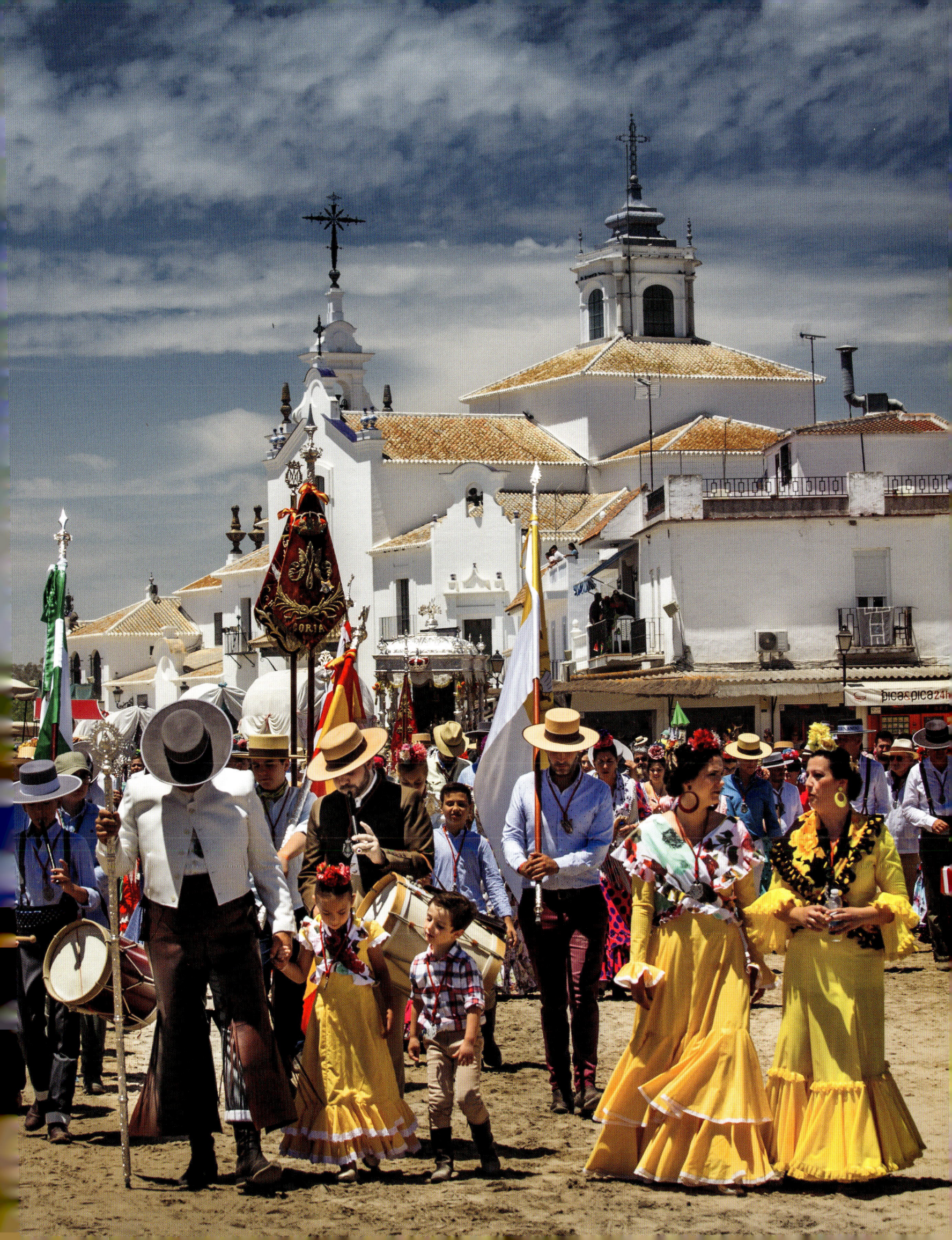

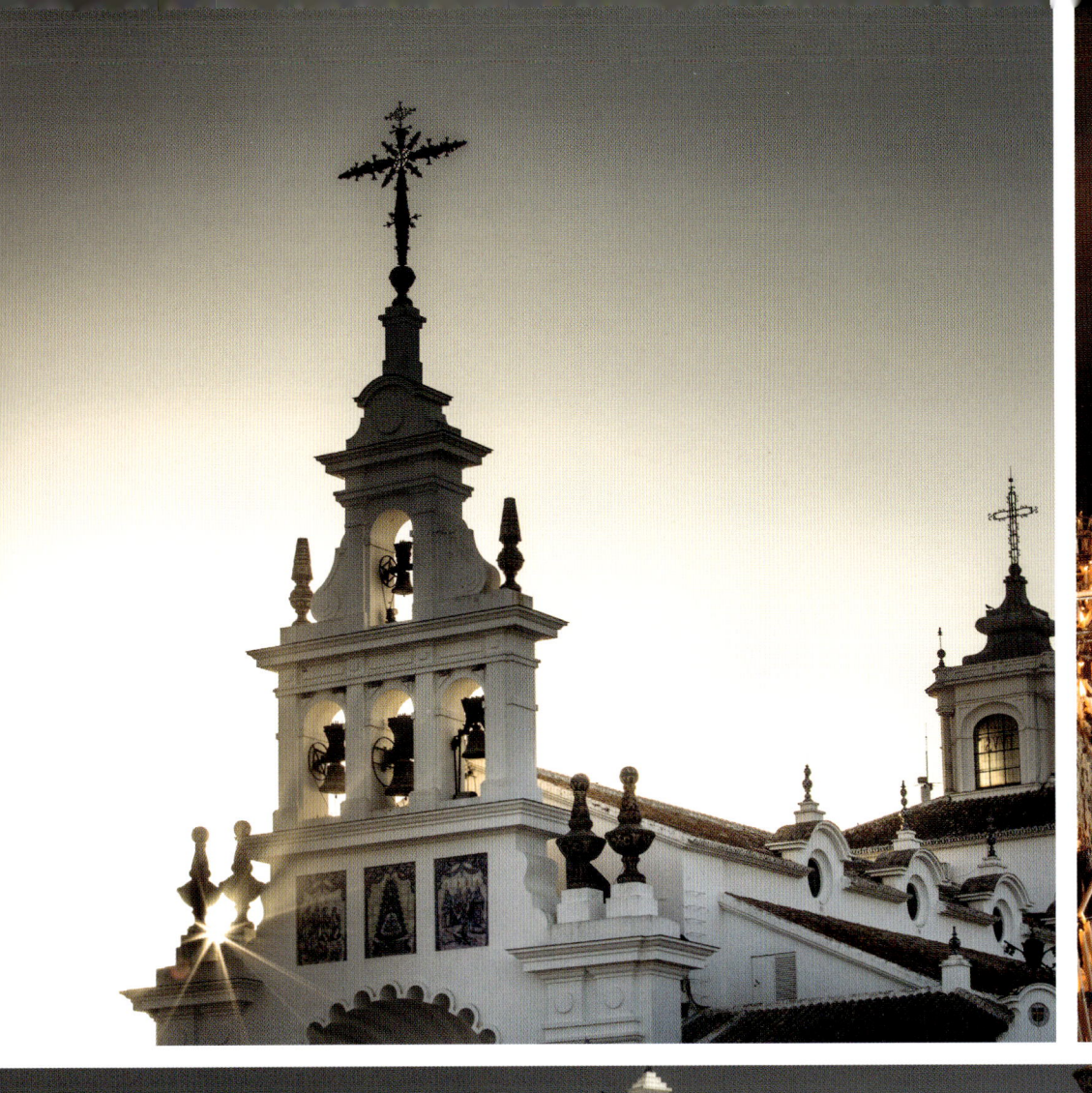
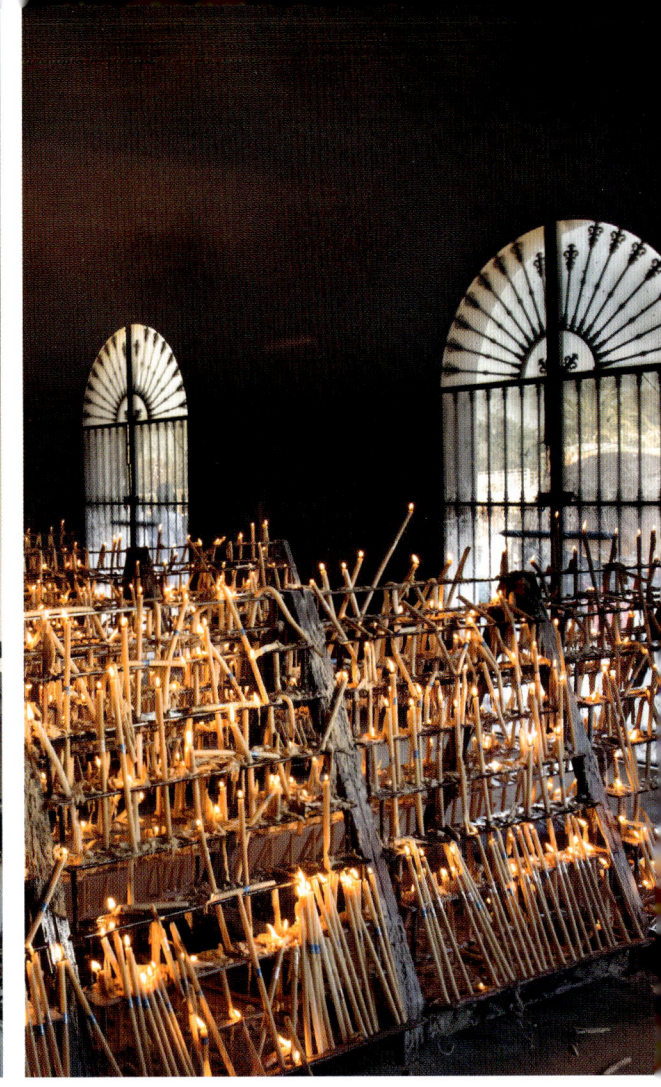

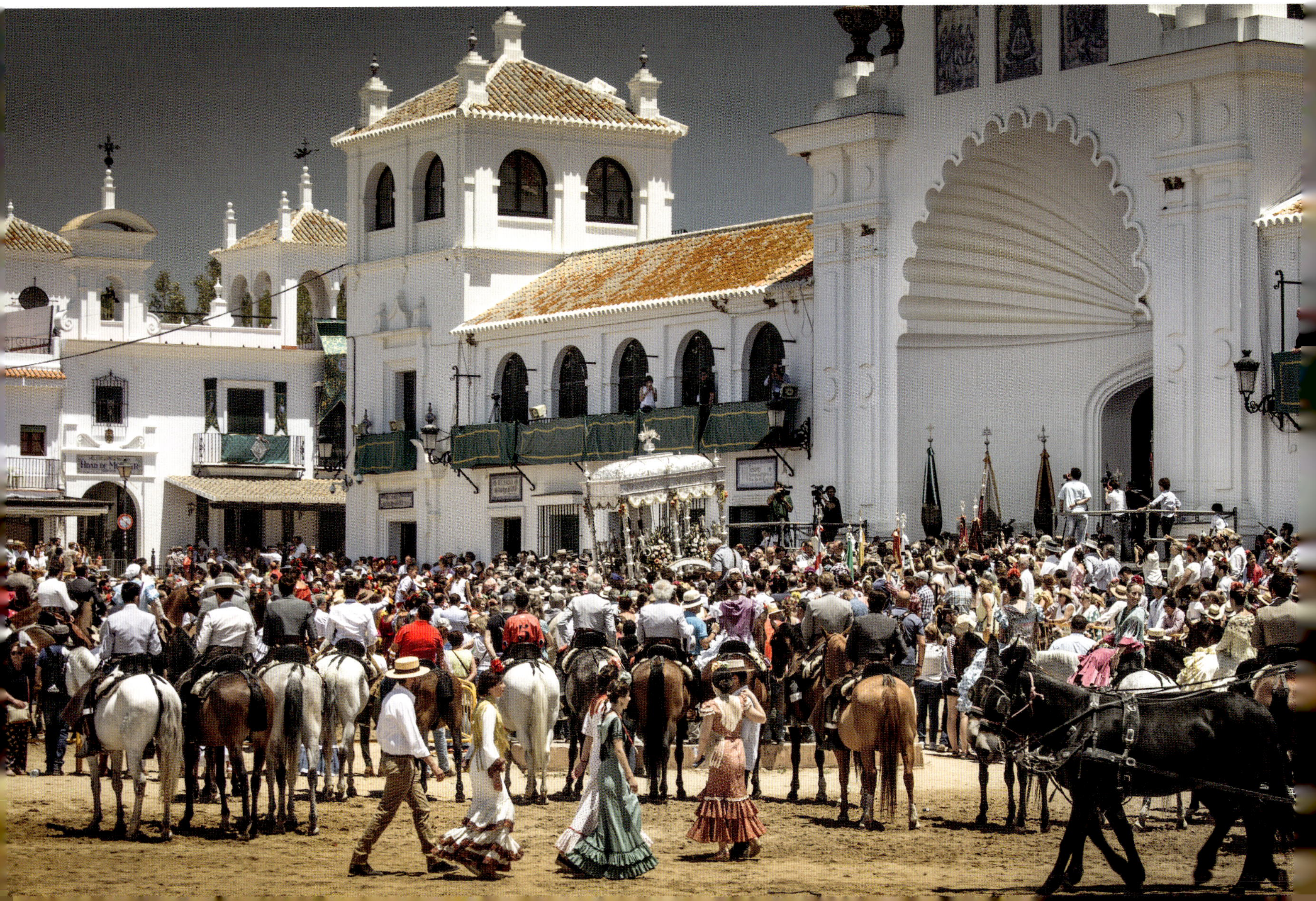

(*top left*) El Rocio's bell tower at sunrise. Although the church and shrine share an ancient legacy, the current building is comparatively new because its predecessor was badly damaged in the Lisbon earthquake of 1755, which wrought architectural chaos across vast swathes of the Iberian peninsula. (*top right*) The votive chapel adjacent to the church is constantly illuminated by many racks of flickering candles. (*bottom*) The Whitsunday Rosary procession into the church is attended by crowds of respectfully silent pilgrims, as each brotherhood pays homage before the shrine of the Virgin.

The ritual commences at noon on the Saturday, when each brotherhood in turn proudly processes to the church from their enclaves within the village. The custom is to walk behind a lavishly decorated carriage or ox-drawn cart, bearing a gold and silver replica of the El Rocio Virgin, a large embroidered emblem of the Virgin and the brotherhood's own parish insignia. Having formally presented themselves at the Virgin's sanctuary, the return to their houses is a joyous procession accompanied by drum beats and stirring flute melodies. There are more than ninety brotherhoods and the processions continue into the night, culminating in a ceremony at which the oldest from Almonte, established in 1640, formally presents its emblem before the altar.

As Saturday night rolls over into Sunday morning, the raucous sound of flamenco guitars and singing accompanied by percussive hand clapping shows no sign of abating. For many participants, the outdoor High Mass at 10 am on Whit Sunday arrives all too soon. More religious ceremony follows later on Sunday evening, when the brotherhoods all pray the Rosary by candlelight. After that, it is time for the event for which El Rocio is most famous, which is eagerly anticipated by all those viewing the live television broadcast throughout the region. Men from the Almonte brotherhood jump over the shrine's railing and tussle with each other to see who will be first to carry the statue of Our Lady of El Rocio out into the assembled crowds. She is then borne out of the church into the crowds who are excitedly awaiting the statue's appearance, all pushing and shoving in order to get close enough to touch the treasured icon.

It is a genuine miracle that the statue carried around El Rocio on a float has survived so long, because the chaos continues through the remaining hours of darkness and well into the harsh light of day. The procession visits every chapel in the village, with the passion unabated, until the moment Our Lady is returned to the tranquillity of the sanctuary. After such a protracted period of deep spiritual engagement, frenetic activity and joyous celebration, the return leg of the pilgrimage might seem to take a little bit longer to accomplish than the outbound journey.

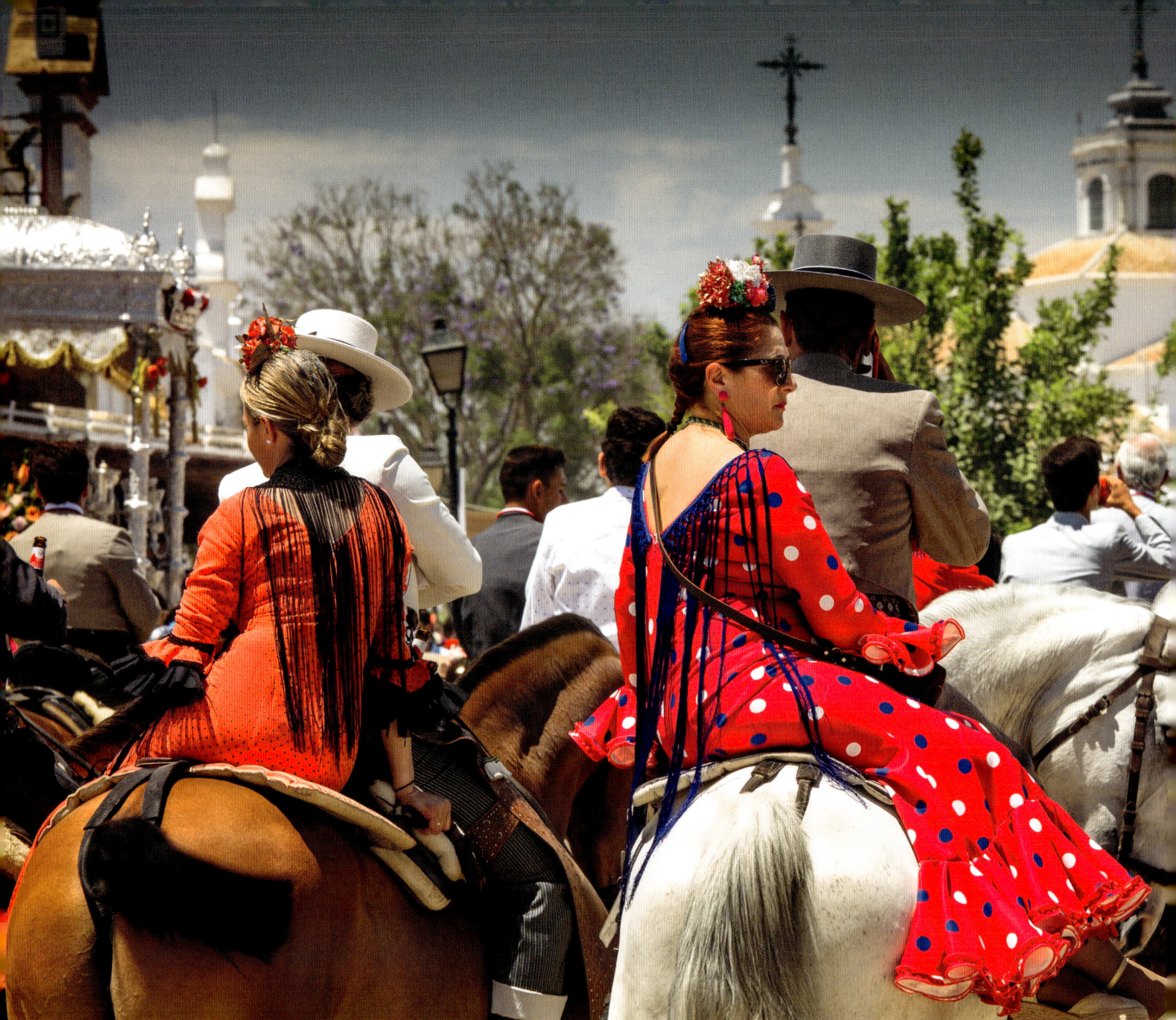

The sight of horses and riders in traditional dress is commonplace at major festivals in Andalucía. Although the gentlemen riders wear specialist clothes and boots, their female partners riding side-saddle cannot nimbly leap up on to the horse's back. The fact that the clothes are colourful and decorative might be deemed somehow disrespectful by visitors from more 'catholic' religious backgrounds, but nothing could be further from the truth. All members of the church communities who undertake the pilgrimage do so with the deepest humility and respect.

SPAIN AND PORTUGAL 247

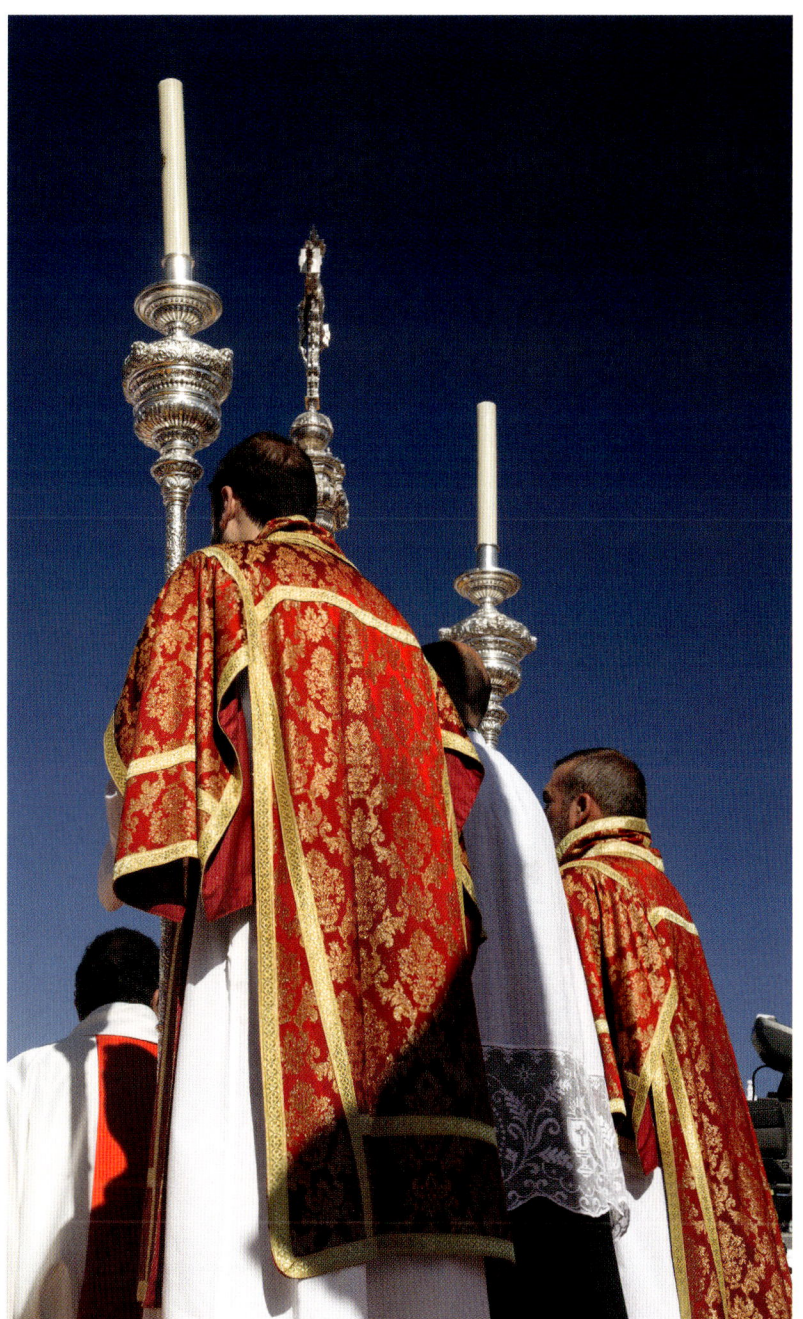

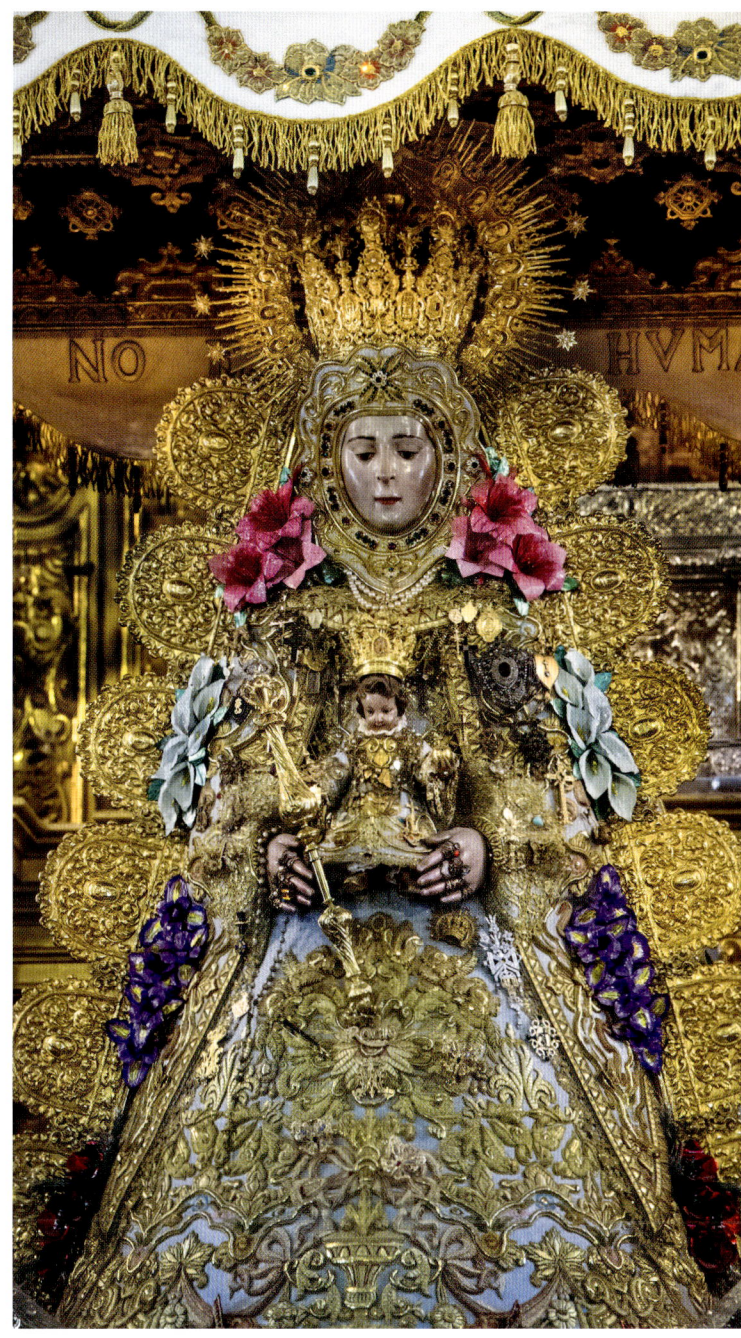

Priests with candles flank the high altar at the outdoor mass held on Sunday morning. The venue is a large square next to the church, with scaffolding platforms erected to create a raised altar with space for musicians, clergy and television cameras.

The statue of the Virgin is worshipped and revered, not only by the pilgrims attending the celebrations at El Rocio but also by countless numbers from Andalucía and farther afield. The event is thought to attract up to a million visitors each year.

PORTUGAL

THE SANCTUARY OF OUR LADY OF FÁTIMA
Fátima

At first glance, Fátima is seemingly just a small town set amid the pleasantly undulating countryside of central Portugal, but it also happens to be one of the world's most significant shrines of Marian visitation. As such, Fátima has to cater for and accommodate in excess of 5 million pilgrims each year. The shrine is breathtakingly beautiful and every single aspect of its architectural design and layout has been practically thought through and executed with aesthetic perfection.

Three young shepherd children (all aged under ten), Lúcia Santos and her cousins Jacinta and Francisco Marto, were born in the hamlet of Aljustrel close to Fátima and helped out their families by tending the sheep in adjacent fields. On three separate dazzling and extremely startling occasions during 1916, they received visitations from the Angel of Peace, who instructed them how to pray correctly, detailing the exact form of prayer they should use and the significance of sacrifice and offerings. This was actually just a prelude to prepare them for the monumental events that would take place during the following year, because on 13 May 1917, the children experienced the first of several encounters with the Virgin Mary. On that particular day, they had driven the sheep to a nearby natural hollow in Fátima named the Cova da Iria. Today, the field that was once grazed by sheep is covered by the vast colonnaded amphitheatre and basilicas comprising the Sanctuary of Our Lady of Fátima.

Lúcia described the Virgin Mary's first appearance as being 'brighter than the sun' and the sun also played a significant role in the sixth apparition several months later. Although the children tried to explain their encounters with the Mother of God to their parents, there was anxiety and disquiet about contacting anyone in higher authority due to the fact that Portugal was just a few years into its secular First Revolution. In fact, after the news that further visitations had taken place, the children were apparently arrested and taken into custody for questioning. They were detained in the ludicrous belief that the rumours of visitations, spiritual messages and secrets being delivered to the children were part of a subversive plot to undermine the new regime.

For many pilgrims, daybreak on the 13 October feast day begins with private prayers and contemplation in the Chapel of the Apparitions, before the crowds start to arrive. There is also a priest-led walk along the traditional fourteen Stations of the Cross.

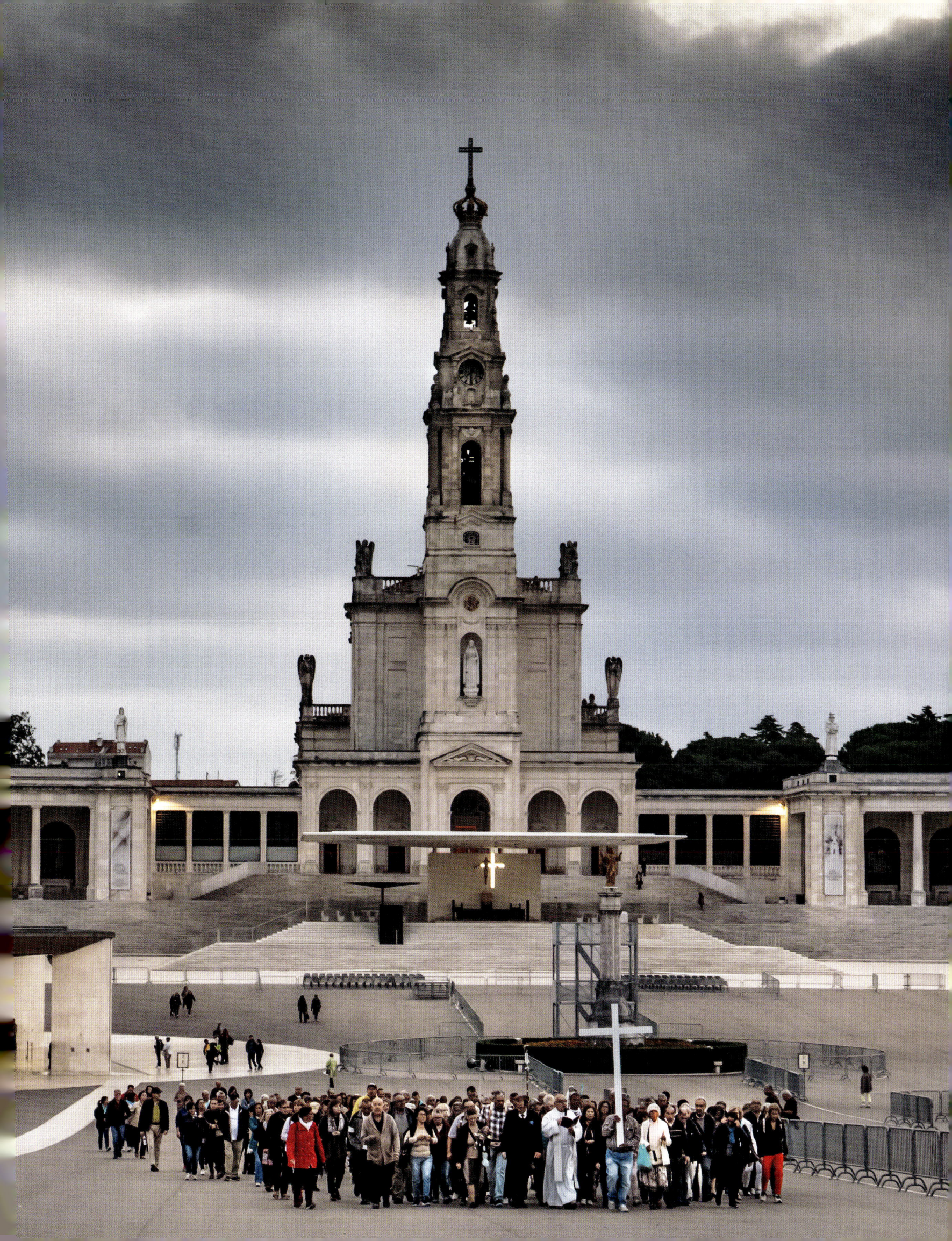

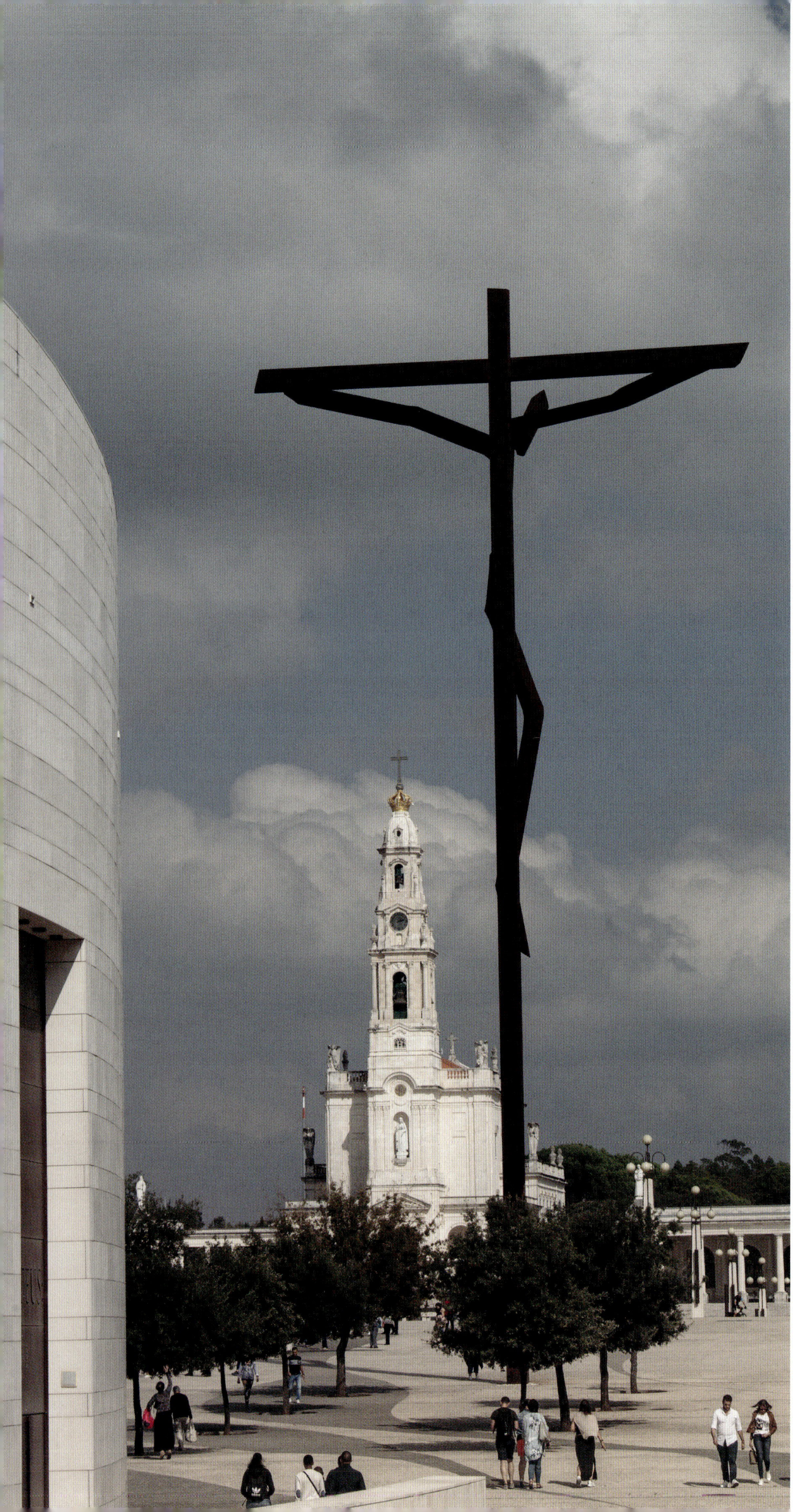

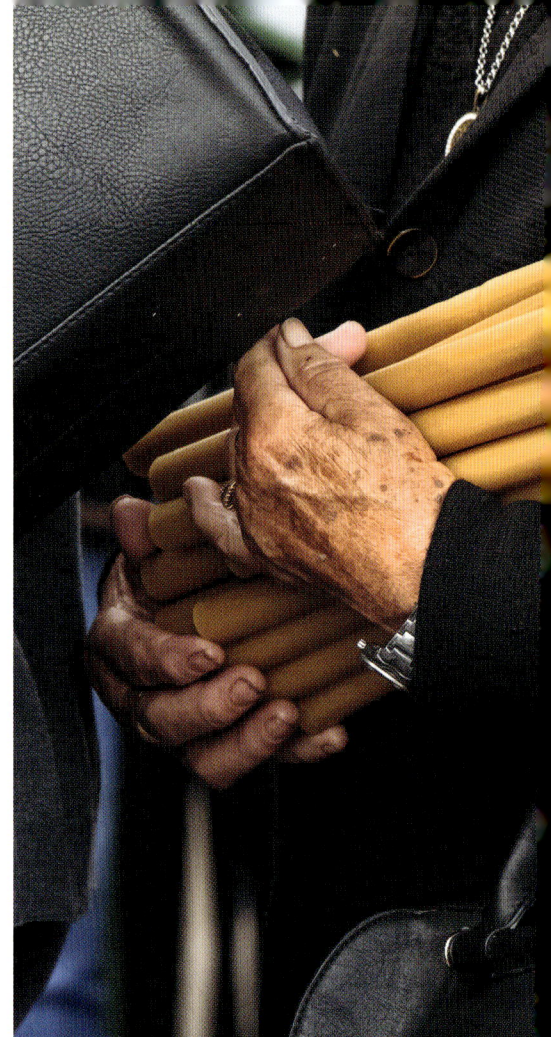

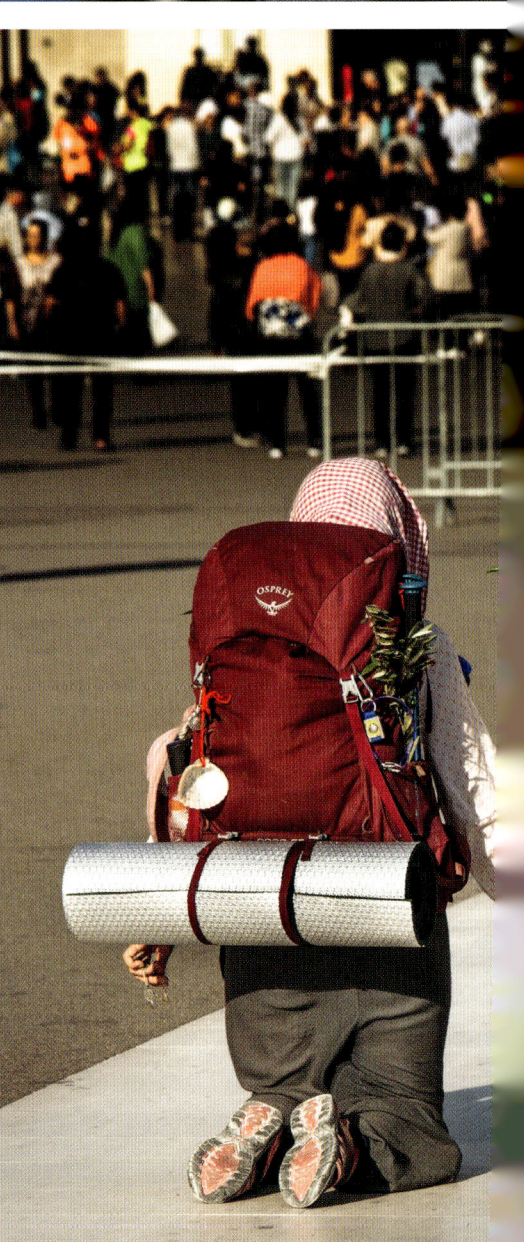

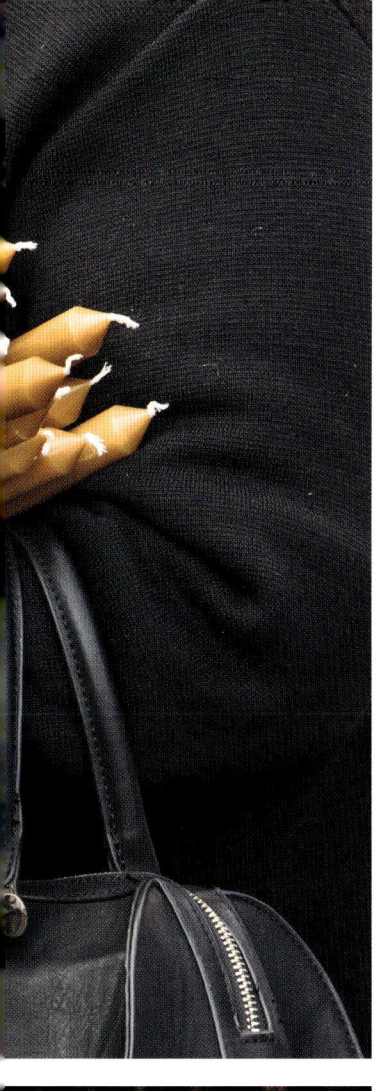
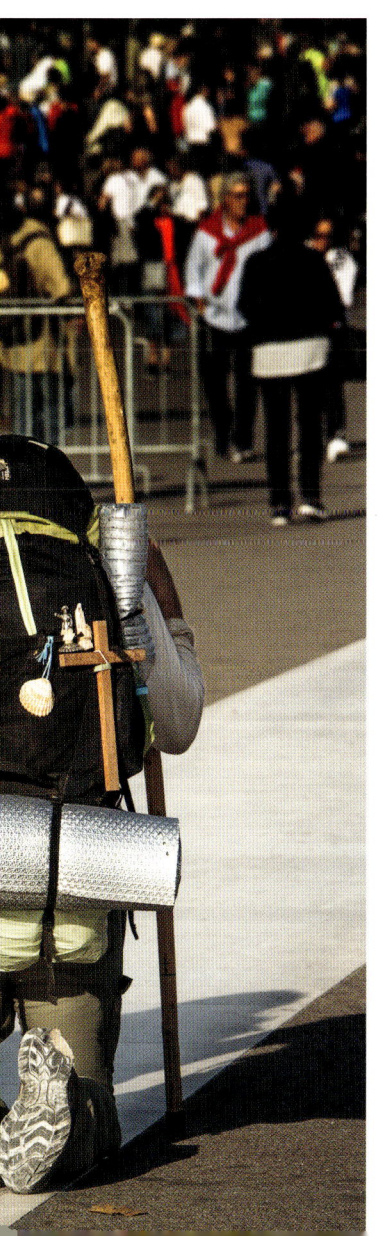

(*top left*) The grouping of the basilica of the Holy Trinity, a dramatically sculpted Crucifixion and the Basilica of Our Lady of the Rosary combine to convey the majesty of Fátima. (*top right*) Although there are a number of metal stands where votive candles may be individually placed and lit by pilgrims, there are also several flaming troughs at which people choose to bypass the normal procedure and throw their candles, either singly or by the armful into the fiery wax furnace. (*bottom*) Many pilgrims complete their journey to the Chapel of the Apparitions on a marble pathway on their hands and knees.

(*overleaf*) The finale of the ceremonial procession, in which the image of the Virgin is carried around the amphitheatre prior to the main liturgical celebration.

However, as the summer progressed, the visitations had become common knowledge and people were making their own pilgrimages to the site in the hope that they too might be blessed. The final and widely publicized event on 13 October was witnessed by 60,000 people, who gathered at the Cova da Iria. Contemporary newspaper photographs show densely packed crowds staring expectantly at the heavens and there was talk of dazzling lights, a dancing sun and other strange phenomena, although some people professed to seeing nothing out of the ordinary. Scientific experts suggested that anyone standing with a craned neck looking up into a bright sky or staring at the sun for protracted periods might well experience hallucinatory visions.

It took several decades for the Catholic Church to investigate and validate the children's stories and it was not until 13 May 1946 that Pope Pius XII granted a canonical coronation to the statue of the Virgin already enshrined within the sanctuary's Chapel of the Apparitions. The basilica of Our Lady of the Rosary of Fátima was begun in 1928 and was dedicated in 1954. It contains the tombs of Francisco and Jacinta, who both succumbed to the flu epidemic of 1918. Lúcia lived as a Carmelite nun for many decades until her death in 2005 aged ninety-seven. Although the basilica had held masses for many years, it was acknowledged that it did not have sufficient capacity, and so a modern alternative was designed and built during the first decade of the twenty-first century. The circular basilica of the Most Holy Trinity is cleverly sited at the southern end of the vast outdoor prayer area and it is large enough to seat more than 8,000 people. Celebrating the anniversary of 13 October remains one of the most significant events in the Fátima calendar. On the night before, the sheltered colonnades are filled with the prostrate forms of pilgrims in sleeping bags, the special car park for camper vans is completely full and just about every hotel bed in town is taken. Fátima is indeed a very special place and, regardless of one's religious beliefs, it is well worth a visit on one of the major feast days simply to savour the atmosphere and glorious architecture.

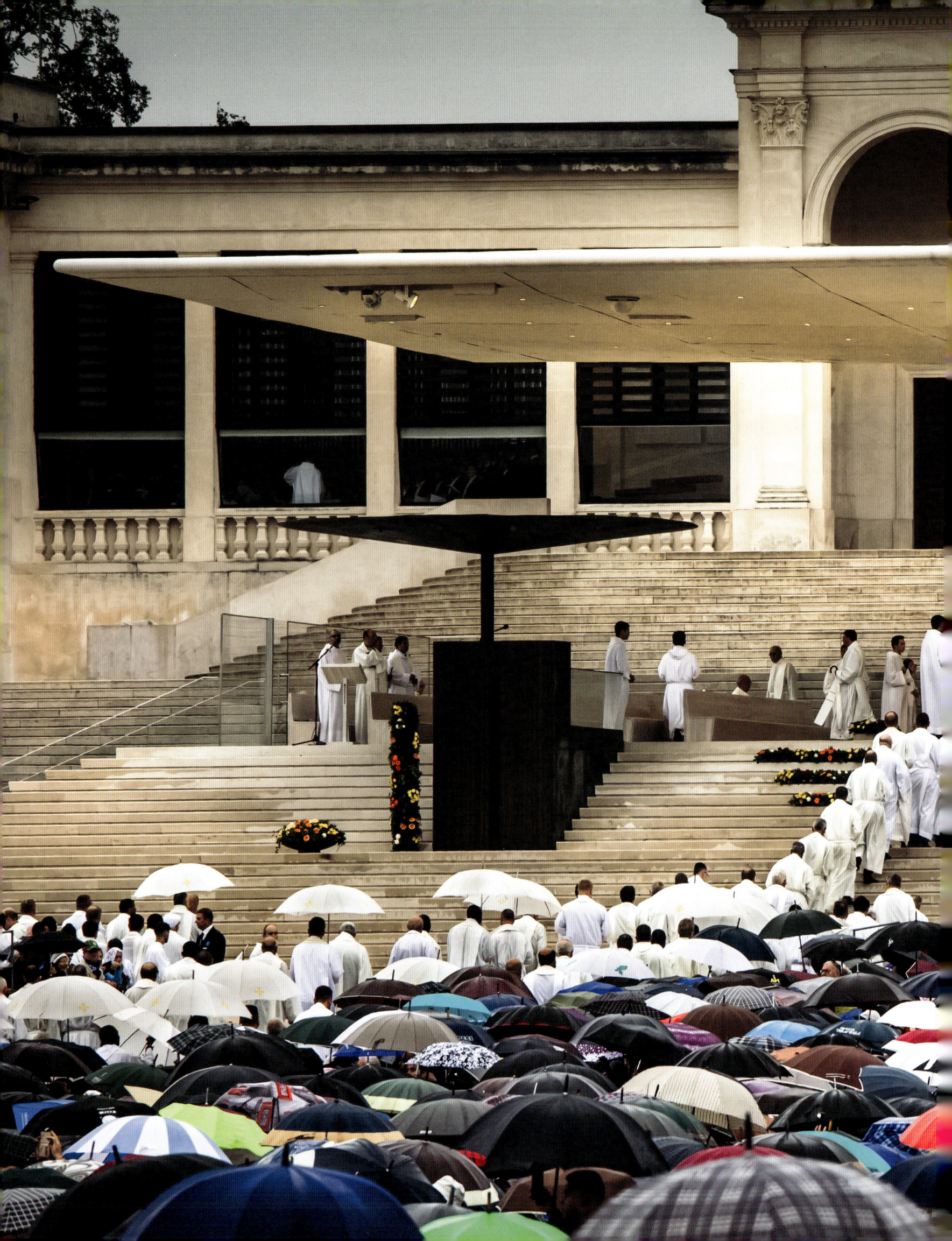

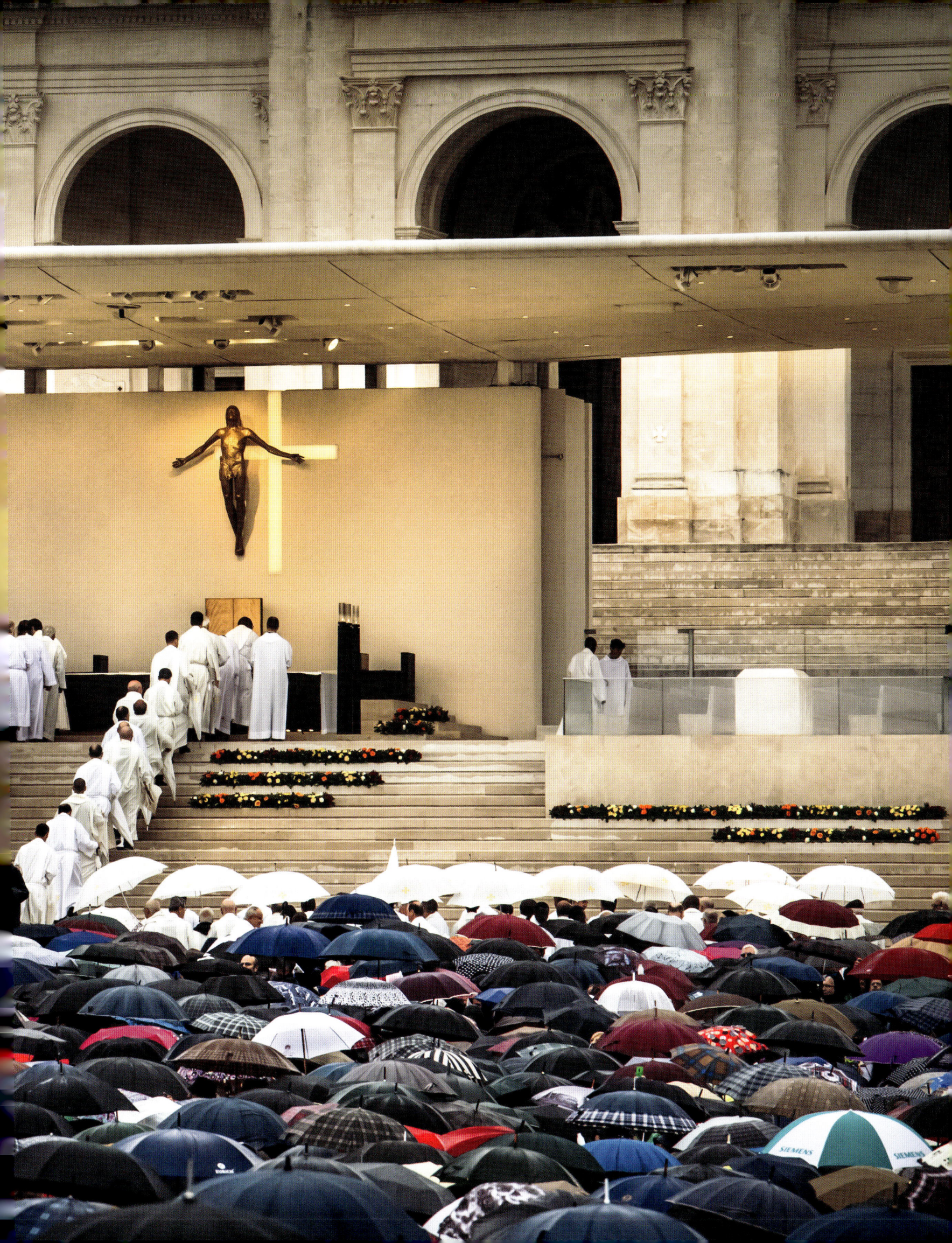

INDEX

Page numbers in *italics* refer to captions

A
Aachen Cathedral, Germany 8, 144–51
Abbey Church of Vadstena, Sweden 108–13
Abbey of Montserrat, Spain 236–41
Abraham 193
Aidan, St 14, *17*
Alan of Walsingham 23
Alexander III, Pope 99, 216
Alfonso I (the Battler) 231
Alfonso III the Great 219
Alfonso XIII 225
Andersen, Hans Christian 81
Anna, King 20
Ansgar, St 78
Anthony of Padua, St 172–9
Arcadius, Emperor 201
Archbasilica of St John Lateran, Italy *6*, 196–9
Asam, Cosmas and Egid *167*
Augustine, St 32
Austria 158–63

B
Bakičová, Angelika 130
Basilica of the Holy House, Italy 206–13
Basilica of Our Lady of Licheń, Poland *8*, *116*, 124–9
Basilica of Our Lady of Seven Sorrows, Slovakia 130–5
Basilica of St Anthony of Padua, Italy 172–9
Basilica of St Francis of Assisi, Italy *4*, 180–5
Basilica of St Paul Outside the Walls, Italy 200–5
Basilica of St Thérèse, France 40–3
Becket, Thomas 32, 35, 36, *36*
Benedict, St 164, 167, *167*
Benedict XV, Pope 225
Benedict XVI, Pope 155
Berg, Claus 87
Bernini, Gian Lorenzo 186, 189, *189*
Béthaire, St 44
Blanche, Queen 108
Boniface IX, Pope 111
Boulanger, Flaminio *197*
Bramante, Donato 189, 208, *208*
Bridan, Charles-Antoine *51*
Bridget, St 108, *108*, 111, *111*
Bruillard, Philibert de 62, 65

C
Callixtus II, Pope 216
Calvat, Mélanie 58, 62, 65
Canterbury Cathedral, England 32–7
Canute I 96
Canute IV 84–9
Carloman 152
Casas Novoa, Fernando de 216
Cathedral of Our Lady of Le Puy, France *40*, 52–7
Catherine of Alexandria, St *29*
Chapel of Grace, Germany 152–7
Charlemagne 8, 144, *144*, 147, *148*, *150*
Charles II the Bald 44
Charles II of Spain 231
Charles III John 99
Charles IV, Holy Roman Emperor *157*
Chaucer, Geoffrey 32, 36
Christian IV *93*
Christina, Queen 87
Christopher I 81
Clare of Assisi, St 180
Cologne Cathedral, Germany 8, 138–43
Constantine, Emperor 186, 189, 201, 202
Cuthbert, St 14, 17
Czobor, Count Imrich 130

D
da Forlì, Melozzo *211*
Denis, St *99*
Denmark 78–95
Diocletian, Emperor *83*
Donatello 175

E
Eadfrith, Bishop 14
Edgar, King 20
Edward, Prince of Wales *35*
Edward III, King 35, *35*
Einsiedeln Abbey, Switzerland *4*, *136*, 164–9
Elmelunde, Denmark 90–5
Elmelunde Master 93, *93*
Ely Cathedral, England *14*, 20–5
England 12–37
Eric I 84
Erlendsson, Archbishop Eysteinn 99
Etheldreda 20, 23

F
Fanefjord, Denmark 90–5
Ferdinand, King 219
France 38–75
Francis I, Emperor *161*
Francis of Assisi, St 172, *177*, 180–5
Frederick I 138, 144
Frederick II 147

G
Gaudin, Pierre *43*
George, St *83*, *94*
Germany 138–57
Gero, Archbishop *142*
Giotto 175, 182, *182*
Giovanni (Roman Patrician) 193
Giraud, Maximin 58, 62, 65
Gisico of Odense, Bishop 84
Giusto de' Menabuoi *177*
Godescalc, Bishop 52
Goya, Francisco 231
Gregory I, Pope 32
Gregory IX, Pope 175

H
Håkon Håkonsson 105
Henry II 32, *36*
Henry III 31
Henry VIII 8, 17, 23, 31, *36*
Herod Agrippa I 228
Hochstaden, Archbishop Konrad von 138
Honorius, Pope *202*
Huerta, Juan de la 231

I
Innocent III, Pope 180, *182*
Innocent XI, Pope *190*
Isabella, Queen 219
Isaiah, Prophet *47*
Italy 170–213

J
Jacob 193
James, St 6, 52, 108, 111, 167, 216, 219, *220*, 228, 231, *232*
Jasna Góra 9, 116–23
Jeremiah *47*
Jesus Christ 71, *157*
  Aachen Cathedral 147, *147*, 148
  Archbasilica of St John Lateran *6*, *197*
  Basilica of the Holy House 206, *208*
  Basilica of Our Lady of Seven Sorrows *133*
  Basilica of St Anthony of Padua 175, *177*
  Basilica of St Francis of Assisi 182
  Chapel of Grace 152, *152*, 155
  Cologne Cathedral 141, *142*
  Einsiedeln Abbey 164
  Ely Cathedral 23
  Nidaros Cathedral 96, 99
  Our Lady of Chartres Cathedral *47*, *48*, *51*
  Our Lady of Covadonga *225*
  Ribe Cathedral *83*
  Ringebu Stave Church *107*
  San Paolo Fuori le Mura *201*
  Santa Maria Maggiore 193, *193*, *194*
Johan III *111*
John VIII, Pope 202
John XV, Pope 186
John the Baptist, St *47*, 111, 147, *197*
John the Evangelist, St *197*
John Paul II, Pope 40, 108, 119, 127, 155, *190*, 228
Joseph, St 206
Joseph Ratzinger, Cardinal 155
Joshua 193
Julius II, Pope 189, 208

K
Kłossowski, Tomasz 124
Konstanz, Bishop of 164

L
Lanfranc, Archbishop of Canterbury 32
Le Strange, Henry L'Estrange Styleman 23, *23*

Leo III, Pope 144, *150*
Leo IX, Pope 71
Leo VIII, Pope 164
Leo XII, Pope *202*
Leo XIII, Pope 236
Leofdag, Bishop 78
Liberius, Pope 193
Lindisfarne Priory, England 14–21
Loreto, Marche 206–13
Louis, St 55
Louis I *158*, 161
Louis IX 55
Luke the Evangelist, St 116, 193

M
Magnus Eriksson, King 108
Makulski, Reverend Eugeniusz 127
Margaret, Queen *87*
María, Santa 236
Mariazell Basilica, Austria 158–63
Martin, Thérèse 40
Marto, Jacinta and Francisco 248, 251
Mateo, Master 216
Maximilian III Joseph *157*
Meinrad 164
Michael, St 6, *51*, *147*
Michel d'Aiguilhe, St 52
Michelangelo 189, *190*
Møn, Denmark 90–5
Morlhon, Archbishop Auguste de *57*
Moses 193

N
Napoleon I 58, 124, 239
Napoleon III *57*
Nero, Emperor 201
Nicholas V 189
Nicholas of Verdun 138
Nidaros Cathedral, Norway 96–101, 102, 105, 108
Norway 96–107

O
Obici, Giuseppe *201*
Odense, Funen 84–9
Olaf, St 96, *96*, 102, 105, 108, *108*
Olaf I 84
Olaf II Haraldsson 96
Oliva, Bishop of Vic 236
Oswald, King 14

Otto I, Holy Roman Emperor *150*, 164
Our Lady of Chartres Cathedral, France 44–51
Our Lady of Covadonga, Spain 222–7
Our Lady of the Pillar, Spain *216*, 228–35

P
Parry, Thomas Gambier *23*
Paschal II, Pope 84
Paul, St 6, 200–5
Paul III, Pope 189
Paul V, Pope *194*
Paul VI, Pope 133
Pauline brothers 116
Pedersen, Carl-Henning 81, *81*
Pelayo 222, 225
Peter, St 6, *47*, 127, 186, *186*, *187*, 189, 201, *201*
Peyremale, Father 71
Philip the Apostle 152
Pidal, Luis Menéndez 224
Pius IV, Pope *202*
Pius IX, Pope 133, 202, *202*
Pius VI, Pope 164
Pius XI, Pope 40, *40*
Pius XII, Pope 251
Poland 116–29
Poletti, Luigi 202
Portugal 248–53

R
Rainald, Archbishop 138
Ribe Cathedral, Denmark 76–83
Richard II 35
Richeldis de Faverches *29*, 31
Ringebu Stave Church, Norway 102–7
Rodríguez, Ventura 231
Rome 186–205
Rupert, Bishop of Salzburg 152

S
St Canute's Cathedral, Denmark 84–9
St Peter's Basilica, Vatican City *172*, 186, *186*, 189, *189*, 197
San Paolo Fuori le Mura, Italy 200–5

Sanctuary of Our Lady of El Rocio, Spain 242–7
Sanctuary of Our Lady of Fátima, Spain 248–53
Sanctuary of Our Lady of La Salette, France *4*, 58–67
Sanctuary of Our Lady of Lourdes, France 40, 68–75
Santa Maria Maggiore 116, 192–5
Santiago de Compostela, Spain 8, 52, 108, 167, 216–21
Santos, Lúcia 248, 251
Sciassia, Domenico 161
Sermei, Cesare *183*
Shrine of our Lady of Częstochowa, Poland 9, 116–23
Shrines of Our Lady of Walsingham, England 26–31
Sigeric, Archbishop of Canterbury 186
Simeon 20, *47*
Siricius, Pope 201
Slovakia 130–5
Solomon, King *150*
Soubirous, Bernadette 68, 71, *72*
Spain 216–47
Sweden 108–13
Sweyn II 84
Switzerland 164–9
Sylvester I, Pope 189, 201

T
Theodore, Duke of Bavaria 152
Theodosius I, Emperor 201
Thérèse of Lisieux, St 40–3
Torriti, Jacopo 194
Turpin, Archbishop *150*

U
Ulf 108
Urban V, Pope 108
Urban VIII, Pope 189

V
Valentinian II, Emperor 201
Vassalletto family *202*
Vatican City 186–91
Velázquez, Diego 231
Virgin Mary
  Aachen Cathedral 144, 147, *147*, *148*
  Abbey Church of Vadstena 111
  Abbey of Montserrat 236, *240*
  Archbasilica of St John Lateran *197*
  Basilica of the Holy House 206, 208
  Basilica of Our Lady of Licheń 124, 127
  Basilica of Our Lady of Seven Sorrows 130, *130*, *133*
  Basilica of St Anthony of Padua 175, *177*
  Cathedral of Our Lady of Le Puy 55
  Chapel of Grace 152, *152*, 155, *157*
  Cologne Cathedral 141
  Einsiedeln Abbey 164
  Ely Cathedral 23
  Mariazell Basilica *158*, *158*, 161
  Our Lady of Chartres Cathedral 44, 47, *47*, *48*
  Our Lady of Covadonga 222, *222*, 225, *225*
  Our Lady of the Pillar 228, 231, *231*, *232*
  Ribe Cathedral 78, *83*
  St Peter's Basilica *190*
  Sanctuary of Our Lady of El Rocio 245, *245*, *247*
  Sanctuary of Our Lady of Fátima 248, 251, *251*
  Sanctuary of Our Lady of La Salette 58, 62
  Sanctuary of Our Lady of Lourdes 68, 71, *72*
  Santa Maria Maggiore 193, *193*, *194*
  Shrine of our Lady of Częstochowa 116, 119
  Shrines of Our Lady of Walsingham 26, *29*, 31
Vladislaus II of Opole 116
Vladislaus Henry, Margrave *158*, 161

W
William I 20, 32

Y
Yevele, Henry 35, *35*

ACKNOWLEDGEMENTS

My grateful thanks to Arianna Osti for the wonderful layout design enriched by such an aesthetically perfect picture selection. Expanding the book's geographical horizons resulted in shorter individual chapters and so editing the photographs to fully convey the atmosphere, art and architectural splendour of each location presented a significant challenge.

Sincere thanks also to my publisher, Philip Cooper and editor, Michael Brunström from the Frances Lincoln imprint of Quarto Publishing. As we head further into the digitally dominated twenty-first century it is so reassuring to know that bookshelves will remain an integral item of household furniture and that publishers are still striving to ensure they are well stocked!

Most of the major pilgrimage destinations featured in this book have their own multi-lingual websites but listed below are a couple of interesting & helpful sites: Shrines of Europe (www.shrines-of-europe.com) represents the main Marian shrines of Europe and details each shrine's history, pilgrim routes and accommodation. The Holy See also has a fascinating website (www.vatican.va) with information about the workings of the Vatican, biographies of past popes and virtual tours of the main papal basilicas and chapels.

Great Pilgrimage Sites of Europe
First published in 2020 by Frances Lincoln,
an imprint of The Quarto Group.
The Old Brewery, 6 Blundell Street
London, N7 9BH, United Kingdom
T (0)20 7700 6700 F (0)20 7700 8066
www.QuartoKnows.com

Text and photographs © 2020 Derry Brabbs

All rights reserved. No part of this book may be reproduced or utilized in any form or by any means, electronic or mechanical, including photocopying, recording or by any information storage and retrieval system, without permission in writing from Frances Lincoln.

A catalogue record for this book is available from the British Library.

ISBN 978-0-7112-4508-2

10 9 8 7 6 5 4 3 2 1

Typeset in Warnock Pro and Scala Sans
Design by Arianna Osti

Printed in China

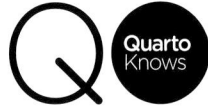

Brimming with creative inspiration, how-to projects and useful information to enrich your everyday life, Quarto Knows is a favourite destination for those pursuing their interests and passions. Visit our site and dig deeper with our books into your area of interest: Quarto Creates, Quarto Cooks, Quarto Homes, Quarto Lives, Quarto Drives, Quarto Explores, Quarto Gifts, or Quarto Kids.

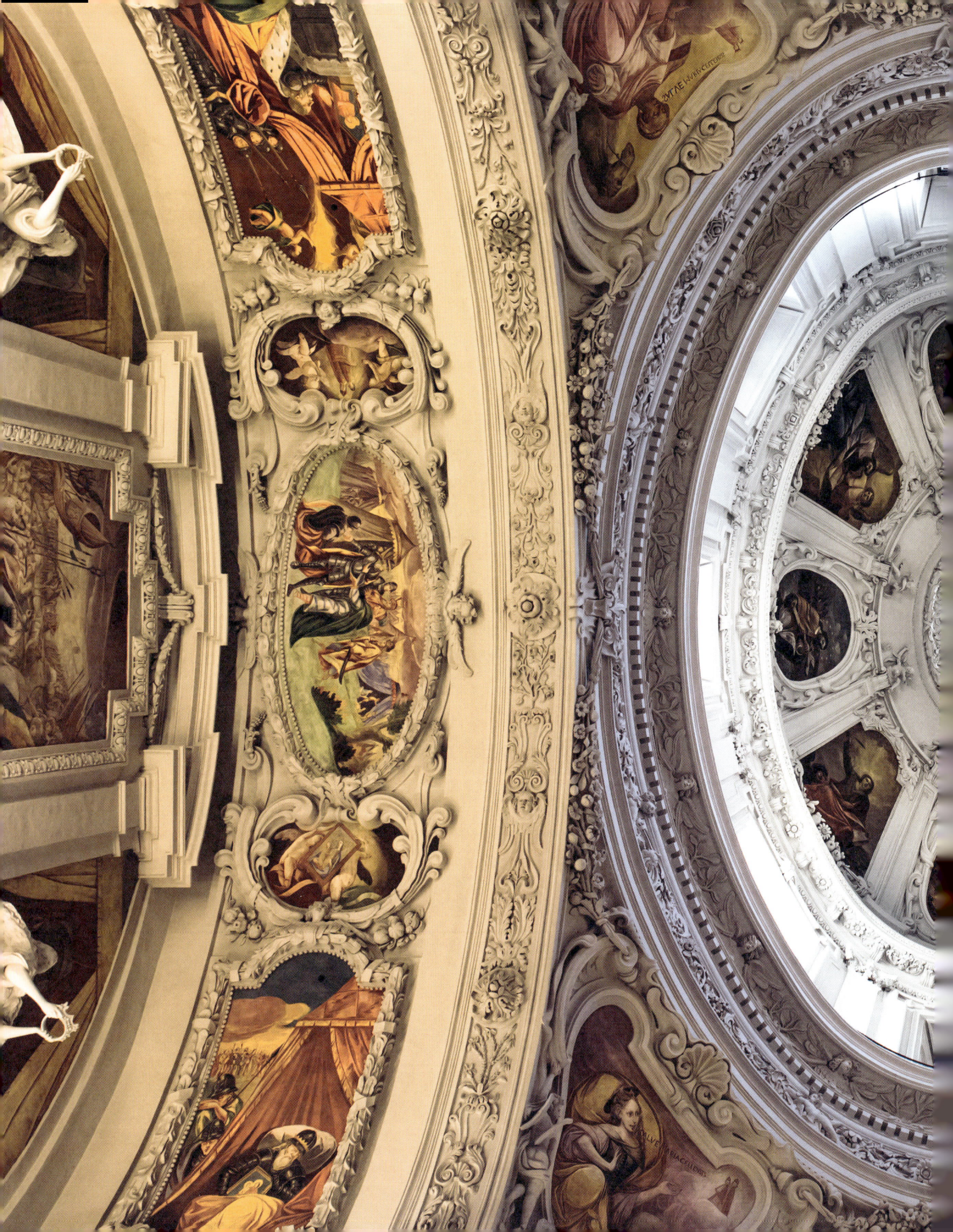